Special Edition
Using
Crystal
Enterprise™ 8.5

Steve Lucas
Roger Sanborn
Mitchell Chou
James Church
Evan Davies
Grant Eaton
Joe Estes
Neil FitzGerald
Justin Frank
Henry Kam
Ben Lockett
Stephen Mak
Quasar Business Solutions, Inc.
Cynthia Shelley
Tim Weir

201 W. 103rd Street
Indianapolis, Indiana 46290

CONTENTS AT A G...

SPECIAL EDITION USING CRYSTAL ENTERPRISE 8.5

International Standard Book Number: 0-7897-2616-5

Library of Congress Catalog Card Number: 2002102859

Printed in the United States of America

First Printing: June 2002

05 04 03 02   4 3 2 1

Trademarks

Warning and Disclaimer

Publisher
David Culverwell

Executive Editor
Candy Hall

Acquisitions Editor
Michelle Newcomb

Development Editor
Howard Jones

Managing Editor
Thomas F. Hayes

Project Editor
Tonya Simpson

Copy Editor
Kate Givens

Indexer
Kelly Castell

Proofreader
Plan-It Publishing

Technical Editors
Joe Estes
Aaron Graber
John Gusner
Ryan Marples
Tim Weir

Team Coordinator
Cindy Teeters

Interior Designer
Ruth Harvey

Cover Designer
Dan Armstrong

Page Layout
D&G Limited, LLC

CONTENTS

V Customizing Crystal Enterprise

13 Extending Crystal Enterprise   451

14 Integrating Crystal Enterprise with Your Corporate Intranet   491

FOREWORD

Imagine the following two scenarios:

Scenario One:

Having left work on a Friday, a group of friends gathers for drinks at a local bar. On the spur of the moment one of them suggests going to see a movie and pulls out her PDA; its "always-on" Internet technology allows her to go straight to her favorite entertainment Web site, where she searches for last-minute seats in local cinemas.

After some heated discussion, the friends choose from the five shows that have seats available. Unfortunately, the link to the cinema seat layout shows all remaining seats have restricted views. They agree on a second choice (which is the subject of more debate) and this time find that there are four prime seats left, so they click to reserve them. Behind the scenes, the PDA manages the transfer of payment from the bank account to the cinema box office. Upon arriving at the theatre they use the PDA infrared connection to beam confirmation to a machine at the box office, and they get their tickets and go into the film. After the film they decide they want to eat, so they search for Italian restaurants within three miles of the theatre that have an average price of less than $25 per head and a table for four free in 15 minutes. Soon they are discussing the film over pasta and salad.

Scenario Two:

A sales rep from a large manufacturing supply company is in a meeting to close a large repeat order. Midmeeting, the customer raises an issue with the level of support they have been receiving from the supplier. The account manager for the supplier is pretty sure that this is a negotiation ploy and asks if the PC in the corner has an Internet connection. It does, and so he logs on to his company's secure information portal over the Internet and looks up the customer's information on his corporate "all around customer view" system.

The account rep sees that in the past six months there have been 75 contacts for this customer, but by selecting Support Calls from the drop-down list he sees that there have been 45 support incidents with an average resolution time of five days. The customer is about to say that a five-day response is unacceptable when the account manager narrows the report to just Severity 1 incidents, which are the ones that stop a critical business activity. There have been three Severity 1 incidents and for each incident the initial response has always been within 10 minutes; furthermore, all have been resolved within two hours. Suddenly the focus has moved from the deal at hand (which now seems a formality) to questions about how the client could put such a system in place.

Far from being science fiction, these scenarios are a glimpse into the near future. The information revolution sparked by the growth of the Internet has only just begun, and far from being a spent force, it will change our everyday lives more in the next five years than it has in the past five years.

In five years, always-on high-speed Internet connections to both handheld devices and domestic computers will be as commonplace as telephones are today. Using this connectivity to form robust *information relationships* (like those in the preceding scenarios) is something that will make or break not just some organizations or most organizations, but *all* organizations. The impact of the Internet on how information is shared means that it will be the norm to have a unified information infrastructure that can individually identify every employee, customer, supplier, and partner and provide them with a level of information and analysis that is uniquely appropriate to them.

Three main layers of technology are required to build a unified information infrastructure:

- A relational database underlying every type of application. We are long past the point where there is universal agreement that applications of any significant size (Web or otherwise) need relational storage for their data.

- A Web infrastructure layer comprising a Web server and an Application layer sitting atop the relational data store. (Incidentally, the two dominating Web application layer standards are J2EE engine and Microsoft's .NET platform.)

- The third layer, provided by Crystal Enterprise, is an *information infrastructure*. This scalable layer will securely manage the flow of information from any database platform over a Web infrastructure application and present it in a usable form to any end user or customer.

Although this third layer is not yet as universally accepted as a "required" enterprise technology, more and more companies are starting to realize that just as they would never dream of building their own database infrastructure or their Web infrastructure layer, they do not want to build their own information infrastructure, either. The ironic part is that portions of an information infrastructure are built every day in different organizational initiatives through various Web and Windows business applications. It seems that, regardless of the application, one consistent requirement is reading a database and providing useful information to an application end user based on that data.

One of the biggest mistakes organizations will make in the next few years when undertaking information delivery and reporting projects is underestimating the complexities in this third information management layer. One of the biggest reasons for making this mistake is convincing themselves that delivering information is easy; after all, the Web is all about open technology standards. How difficult can it be to use ASP and ADO or JSP and JDBC to build such a solution for yourself?

The answer is that initially, for a few simple requirements for a few users, building your own information delivery mechanism probably is not that difficult. However, the challenge of sharing information on a large scale is similar to an iceberg, where the challenges that loom beneath the water's edge are much more ominous than the visible portion.

In a similar context, the information delivery portion of a project has many issues that initially either appear small or don't get taken into account at all. Just like the iceberg, however much you prepare yourself to expect more hidden issues than you can currently think of, you can be overwhelmed at the number of issues that come across from initial development right through to ongoing system maintenance.

The following is a brief synopsis of some challenges many organizations face today when developing applications that do not leverage a reliable information infrastructure:

- How do we keep the information in our application available all day, every day (fault tolerance)?
- How will the application cope with more and more users over time (scalability through clustering)?
- As we add more and more information, how will users still get their information in an acceptable time (report streaming)?
- How will we provide secure information through our firewall and our customers' firewalls (thin client HTTP-only delivery)?
- What about the different security and skill levels of our application users (feature-based security levering open standards like LDAP and Kerberos)?
- How do we allow nondevelopers to add information to the reporting system (separation of design and development)?
- How do we give some users more analytic capabilities above basic reporting (adding OLAP analysis)?
- What about the fact that some information needs to be up-to-the-second while other information needs to be prepared monthly (managing on-demand and prescheduled access)?

Crystal Enterprise is built on the same underlying Web technology standards you would use if you were tempted to build your own information platform, but it provides prebuilt answers to all the problems listed here and many more. Your organization can roll out these types of Internet survival systems many times faster and be assured that they can scale into the mission-critical systems they need to be.

This book provides a great insight into what should be expected of an information infrastructure, Crystal Enterprise, and the possibilities it can open up for your organization. Building highly available, multiuser information systems is never straightforward, but the Crystal family of products will provide you with a solid foundation and massive improvements in productivity. By reading this book (and implementing Crystal Enterprise), you will have taken another step into the new information age and begun a positive journey both for your career and your organization. Good luck!

ABOUT THE AUTHORS

Steve Lucas has been in the information technology industry for more than 10 years. He currently manages the Strategic Pre-Sales Team for North America at Crystal Decisions, working with some of Crystal's largest customers worldwide. Steve regularly speaks on current and future Crystal technology at significant events such as COMDEX. Prior to Crystal, Steve focused on Microsoft technology and consulting for the better part of his career. He is currently based in Denver.

Roger Sanborn is the Senior Program Manager for Crystal Enterprise at Crystal Decisions. He has been a key contributor to the direction and success of Crystal Enterprise and has been instrumental in successfully guiding the direction and delivery of Crystal Enterprise since its inception three years ago. Roger has been working in the software industry for the past eight years and has been focused on information delivery systems for the majority of that time. Over time, Roger has developed expertise in several enterprise technology areas, including Web development, application integration, security, and networking.

Mitchell Chou graduated with a degree in Computing Science from Simon Fraser University in Burnaby, British Columbia, Canada in 1998. He has been working as a technical consultant with Crystal Decisions since April 1999.

James Church is director of Crystal Analysis at Crystal Decisions, Inc. with responsibility for the technical direction and leadership of Crystal Analysis Professional and Crystal Holos. He joined Crystal Decisions (then Holistic Systems) in 1993 as a Holos consultant and has been involved in a range of analytical application implementations ranging from analytical reporting to financial modeling.

James earned a graduate diploma in Computer Science from North Staffordshire Polytechnic in 1987. He lives in Vancouver, British Columbia with his wife and two children.

Evan Davies was brought up in South Wales and educated at London University and the Hatfield Polytechnic, where he gained his Masters in Computer Science. Evan has spent close to 20 years in the IT industry and has had significant (and painful) experiences ranging from mainframe through client/server to the current Web-based n-tier architectures. His roles have encompassed development, consultancy, teaching, database design and implementation, to his current sales role within Crystal Decisions. He currently serves as a presales engineer responsible for the western states of Arizona, Utah, and Nevada and lives with his wife Nadine and the Zigmeister in Scottsdale, Arizona.

Grant Eaton is a senior consultant for Crystal Decisions in Seattle, Washington. He has used Crystal software extensively for six years, starting in 1996 with the development of a sales revenue reporting system for Walt Disney World. Prior to Disney, he worked as a sales-force automation consultant, database administrator, technical writer, and professional trainer. Some of his recent customers include Pfizer, 3M, Discover Card, Siemens, Microsoft, and the Bank of Canada. Grant enjoys international travel and one-of-a-kind adventures, such as whitewater rafting, parasailing, and skydiving. He may be contacted at mail@granteaton.com.

Joe Estes has more than eight years of experience in the information technology industry. He has been involved with the data reporting and analytical aspects of data warehousing and business intelligence initiatives almost exclusively over the past six years. Throughout his career, Joe has held positions varying from system analyst and developer at a Big 5 consultancy to project manager and system engineer at business intelligence software companies. Currently, he is the manager of the Midwest Systems Engineer team at Crystal Decisions in Chicago, Illinois. Working in a consultative role with some of the largest companies in the world, he has helped design and deploy enterprise-level business intelligence solutions that focus on increasing an organization's efficiency and competitiveness in the market. Joe is an avid enthusiast of running, snowboarding, in-line skating, and squash.

Neil FitzGerald has more than seven years experience working with information delivery, business intelligence, and enterprise reporting tools. He has combined this experience with his Bachelor of Computer Science degree from Queens University in Kingston, Canada and his MBA from the Ivey School of Business at the University of Western Ontario, London, Canada to help provide information solutions to an array of Fortune 500 companies throughout New York City and the northeastern United States. Neil currently is managing a top-shelf group of technical consultants in the New York/New England region for Crystal Decisions.

Justin Frank is a certified Crystal trainer and consultant for Crystal Decisions.

Henry Kam is a senior consultant who has more than six years of IT industry experience. He earned his Bachelor of Science degree in Computing Science from Simon Fraser University in Burnaby, British Columbia. He has consulted for more than 30 North American companies. Currently, Henry specializes in the design and implementation of enterprise reporting systems for Fortune 500 companies.

Ben Lockett has worked in the consulting industry for seven years. His main focus has been on project management relating to the delivery of enterprise software to Fortune 500 customers based in America, Canada, and Europe. Ben currently works for Crystal Decisions as the Western Regional Consulting Manager and is based in Denver.

Stephen Mak has been with Crystal Decisions since 1999. As a program manager with Crystal, he is responsible for the SDK and application development in the Crystal Enterprise product. When he's not working, Stephen enjoys spending time with his wife and their dog, Eddie.

Quasar Business Solutions, Inc. is based out of Vancouver, BC (Canada) as well as Palmyra, Virginia (USA). They focus on the growth markets of business intelligence and data access across all markets and specialize in the areas of business intelligence, 3-tier client/server applications, and intranet/Internet application development and training and consulting. They offer solutions to the Crystal BI product family as well as provide add-on products, complementing Crystal Decisions' information suite.

Cynthia Shelley Version 3.0 is an MCP with experience in designing and developing multitier applications, system analysis, and administration, as well as designing and delivering end-user and developer training. Cynthia currently is a training consultant at Crystal Decisions, where she is designing training for developers in C# and Visual Basic .NET on Crystal Reports for Visual Studio .NET. Cynthia also is a Crystal Certified Trainer and Consultant on Crystal Reports and Crystal Enterprise.

Cynthia studied Greek and Roman Classics and Microbiology in university but has since expanded her language vocabulary from Ancient Greek, Latin, VBScript and JScript to VB, VB .NET, and C#. Any time she can find an excuse to "waste" is dedicated to advancing her RPG characters in PC, Console, and board gaming.—"The last minute still has sixty seconds..."

Tim Weir has been with Crystal Decisions for more than three years and brings technical and business experience to the sales process. He resides in the Philadelphia area and provides support for the entire country. Prior to Crystal Decisions he spent several years with CSC (Computer Sciences Corporation) and Andersen Consulting (now Accenture).

DEDICATIONS

*To my best friend and wife, Shelley. If I have accomplished anything of import in this life, it has been with you by my side.—**Steve Lucas***

*To the three most important people in my life: my wife Christine and my two sons, Joshua and Jacob.—**Roger Sanborn***

ACKNOWLEDGMENTS

Steve Lucas: First and foremost, I want to thank my wife, Shelley, for all her support and encouragement throughout the writing of this book. I also want to thank Judy, who taught me how one act of kindness can enable someone to succeed. Thanks to my father and mother for teaching me the value of good, honest, hard work.

Roger, thanks for being there when it counted.

Thank you, Michelle Newcomb, for being there every step of the way. Howard and Tonya, thank you for providing great feedback and guidance. Thank you, Que Publishing for letting me be part of this wonderful family of technology references.

I also want to thank each and every contributing author and technical editor because this book couldn't have been written without your help. To Paul Bicknell, thank you for being my friend. Finally, thank you Crystal Decisions for creating exciting products, hiring inspiring people, and being a flexible organization by allowing me to write this book.

Roger Sanborn: There are many people I would like to acknowledge. First, I want to thank my wife, Christine, and my two sons, Joshua and Jacob, for the support you gave me and your patience throughout the process of writing this book. Getting the book done without you would have been quite difficult. Steve, what can I say? You were the one who got this started and were the driving force behind its completion. Great job! I want to thank Michelle Newcomb and everyone at Que Publishing for giving us the opportunity to write a book as good as the product it describes. I want to thank all the contributing authors and editors who helped put this book together. It's your knowledge and experiences with Crystal Enterprise that help make this book a valuable resource. Last but not least, I want to give a big thank you to the entire Crystal Enterprise research and development team for making an incredible product. Without you, none of this would be possible. I am very proud of your work.

Mitchell Chou: I'd like to thank Que Publishing and everyone at Crystal Decisions in making my chapter a reality. Completion of this book is like winning an Oscar: so many people to thank, yet so little space to write about...

I'd also like to give a big thanks to my mom and dad. Without their support and financial aid during my school years, I never would have made it this far. I'd also like to give a big thanks to my wife, Diana, who has lit up my life every day for the past eight years.

Evan Davies: I would like to thank Nadine and all my family and friends for trying to keep me partially sane. I also would like to give a tip of the hat to Kate, James, and Russell for hiring me into the company that's "going to change the world" (thanks Donald!!).

Joe Estes: Special thanks to my colleagues at Crystal Decisions, who are as enthusiastic and excited as myself when it comes to providing world-class solutions. To my beautiful wife, Aimee; you are my daily inspiration and the foundation of all I do.

Justin Frank: I would like to express my thanks to Steve Lucas for asking me to join this project and for his time in helping develop my chapter. I also would like to thank my wife for the many hours she gave up to let me accomplish this writing. Jeannette, you are the most amazing and wonderful woman! I love you very much!

Henry Kam: I would really like to thank my dearest Patty for her love and support.

Tim Weir: I would like to sincerely thank David Brown, Todd Eror, Michael Voloshko, and Kuhan Milroy. Their knowledge and expertise proved essential during the writing of my chapter.

WE WANT TO HEAR FROM YOU!

As the reader of this book, *you* are our most important critic and commentator. We value your opinion and want to know what we're doing right, what we could do better, what areas you'd like to see us publish in, and any other words of wisdom you're willing to pass our way.

As a publisher for Que, I welcome your comments. You can email or write me directly to let me know what you did or didn't like about this book—as well as what we can do to make our books better.

Please note that I cannot help you with technical problems related to the *topic* of this book. We do have a User Services group, however, where I will forward specific technical questions related to the book.

When you write, please be sure to include this book's title and author as well as your name, email address, and phone number. I will carefully review your comments and share them with the author and editors who worked on the book.

Email: feedback@quepublishing.com

Mail: David Culverwell
           Que Corporation
           201 West 103rd Street
           Indianapolis, IN 46290 USA

For more information about this book or another Que title, visit our Web site at www.quepublishing.com. Type the ISBN (excluding hyphens) or the title of a book in the Search field to find the page you're looking for.

INTRODUCTION

In this introduction

Today's organizations are swimming in data but thirsty for knowledge. The need to access data, effectively manage information, increase knowledge, and gain a competitive advantage from that information is an increasingly complex problem that organizations across the world contend with on a daily basis. Information management problems can range from simple questions, such as how to publish an employee list on a corporate intranet, to complex issues, such as how to gather relevant information from disparate data systems and present it over the Web in a meaningful, secure way.

Special Edition Using Crystal Enterprise was written to help you take on the challenge of deploying Crystal Enterprise as a solution to your organization's information delivery and reporting challenges. This book will help you understand where and how Crystal Enterprise can be applied to solve business problems. We've written the book to guide you through planning, deploying, administering, and managing an enterprise reporting system based on Crystal Enterprise. Some of the issues solved with this book include the following:

- Understanding the business problems associated with reporting tools and systems
- How to address common needs of business users, such as reporting, ad-hoc query, and data analysis
- The architecture of Crystal Enterprise and what technologies it employs within your network to deliver information
- Installation, configuration, and administration of the Crystal Enterprise system
- How to integrate Crystal Enterprise with your existing intranet or Internet site or application to deliver reports and information over the Web
- Leveraging your existing investment in Crystal Reports
- Using the new versions of Crystal Reports and Crystal Analysis Professional to design content for Crystal Enterprise
- Managing Crystal Enterprise in complex network environments

This book also provides real-world examples of how Crystal Enterprise has been deployed in complex network environments to solve some of the toughest reporting and information delivery challenges.

Special Edition Using Crystal Enterprise focuses on the entire solution that Crystal Enterprise and its supporting suite of report design tools (Crystal Reports and Crystal Analysis Professional) can deliver. Many books on the market today focus on only one tool provided by Crystal Decisions, such as Crystal Reports. This book completes the story, because reading a Crystal Reports book only provides a solution for creating interactive report content, not necessarily delivering it. That's where Crystal Enterprise steps in, and this book is your guide.

WHAT'S IN THIS BOOK

We've broken up the book into some logical parts because Crystal Enterprise has many facets that require different levels of expertise—system administrators and developers alike will find value in reading it. The first two parts are intended to help you get started with Crystal Enterprise as quickly as possible.

PART I: "CRYSTAL ENTERPRISE OVERVIEW AND ITS IMPACT"

Reading Part I (Chapters 1 through 3) helps you understand the potential of Crystal Enterprise and how to get an initial system up and running that can be quickly integrated with a local intranet site.

- **Chapter 1, "Introducing Crystal Enterprise"**—It's always challenging for some people to understand the impact that Crystal Enterprise can have on a business. This chapter introduces you to what Crystal Enterprise is, what business problems it can solve, and some broad technologies, such as DHTML, that are incorporated within the system architecture. You will begin to understand how Crystal Enterprise delivers Crystal Reports to users through a Web browser. Some concepts, such as enterprise reporting, information infrastructures, and business intelligence, are introduced because Crystal Enterprise encompasses all these buzzwords.

- **Chapter 2, "Discovering the Crystal Enterprise Utilities"**—When you install Crystal Enterprise, several utilities are installed along with it to help you administer the system, publish reports, and develop sample applications using the Crystal Enterprise SDK. This chapter explains what each utility is and where you can find more information in the book about its use.

- **Chapter 3, "Exploring the System Architecture"**—This chapter is critical to your understanding of exactly how Crystal Enterprise works. Crystal Enterprise is an n-tier solution that has many different components. Each server component can run on separate physical servers. This chapter helps you understand the role that each Crystal Enterprise server plays and how they interact with one another to deliver reports over an intranet application or the Web. You'll also learn ways to maximize the effectiveness of the different Crystal Enterprise server components.

PART II: "GETTING STARTED WITH CRYSTAL ENTERPRISE"

Part II explains how to install Crystal Enterprise, as well as how to use some of the "out of the box" functionality. This includes an overview of the Crystal Enterprise client application, ePortfolio. Part II also discusses how to customize ePortfolio for quick integration with a corporate intranet.

- **Chapter 4, "Installing Crystal Enterprise 8.5"**—This chapter contains the guide to installing Crystal Enterprise on a Windows 2000 Server. We chose to use Windows 2000 as the example because it is the most common implementation for customers. We also cover some of the operating system configurations settings you should take into account before installing Crystal Enterprise.

- **Chapter 5, "Using the Crystal Enterprise Launchpad"**—The Crystal Enterprise Launchpad is the link to most of the Crystal Enterprise "out of the box" functionality. This chapter reviews the different Web application links and samples found on the

Crystal Enterprise Launchpad, including the flagship Crystal Enterprise end-user client ePortfolio, as well as the system administration tool, the Crystal Management Console. You also will find a brief overview of how to use each of these applications and components. If you decide to deploy ePortfolio as your Web client to Crystal Enterprise, end users will undoubtedly have questions about how it works. This chapter provides a general overview of ePortfolio from an end user perspective so you will be prepared to answer those questions.

- **Chapter 6, "Customizing ePortfolio for Rapid Information Delivery"**—Chapter 6 covers how the look and feel of the Crystal Enterprise client application ePortfolio can be easily customized *without* programming. A few programmatic customization examples are provided as well, because ePortfolio does require the Crystal Enterprise system administrator to set parameters in cascading stylesheets (.css). An additional component in this chapter explains how ePortfolio works and what pages within the ePortfolio application provide specific functionality. This will be valuable later in the book when we discuss interfacing with Crystal Enterprise using the SDK.

PART III: "CREATING CONTENT FOR CRYSTAL ENTERPRISE"

Part III (Chapters 7 through 9) deals directly with content creation for Crystal Enterprise using a tool you might be very familiar with: Crystal Reports and a new productivity tool, Crystal Analysis Professional. This section should help you understand how to use these tools to create actionable, reusable report content for Crystal Enterprise. You also will find an extensive chapter, the first third-party publication in fact, covering Crystal Analysis Professional, a sister product to Crystal Reports for Analytic applications using OLAP data sources.

- **Chapter 7, "Publishing Content with Crystal Enterprise"**—Crystal Enterprise is really nothing without meaningful content such as Crystal Reports for users to interact with. This chapter covers what types of content can be created with the supporting tools for Crystal Enterprise, namely Crystal Reports and Crystal Analysis Professional. You will also be introduced to the Crystal Publishing Wizards, which help publish a large number of reports to Crystal Enterprise at once. If you already have a number of Crystal Reports that you want to publish quickly to Crystal Enterprise, this chapter will guide you through that process.

- **Chapter 8, "Creating Content with Crystal Reports"**—Crystal Reports is a content design tool for Crystal Enterprise. The chapter title makes sense only if Crystal Reports is used to create reports that are published to Crystal Enterprise.

  Based on its popularity, Crystal Reports is the most common reporting tool used with Crystal Enterprise. This chapter covers the latest version of Crystal Reports and some of its critical integration points with Crystal Enterprise. The chapter isn't intended to be an exhaustive review of Crystal Reports (that's a book in and of itself!), but an introduction to Crystal Reports and a review of some of the more recent feature additions, which you will find useful.

- **Chapter 9, "Creating Content with Crystal Analysis Professional"**—Crystal Analysis Professional is a new analytic application writer and reporting tool from Crystal Decisions. Much like Crystal Reports, Crystal Analysis Professional also integrates with Crystal Enterprise as a reporting tool for analytic OLAP data. This chapter provides an introduction to the tool and how to leverage its capability to create interactive analytic applications and reports for your Crystal Enterprise users. We take some time at the beginning of this chapter to introduce concepts such as OLAP to increase your understanding of the power of this tool.

PART IV: "ADMINISTERING AND DEPLOYING CRYSTAL ENTERPRISE IN COMPLEX NETWORK ENVIRONMENTS"

Part IV (Chapters 10 through 12) tackles more advanced administration concepts for Crystal Enterprise in complex network environments such as multiple firewall setups. It also discusses special deployment strategies that help you plan your implementation.

- **Chapter 10, "Administering and Configuring Crystal Enterprise"**—Crystal Enterprise has a significant number of functional areas and objects that must be managed, from servers to users, groups and reports. This chapter covers the management and administration tools for Crystal Enterprise, the Crystal Management console, and Crystal Configuration manager in detail and how those tools assist you in properly administering a large deployment of Crystal Enterprise.

- **Chapter 11, "Planning Considerations when Deploying Crystal Enterprise"**—No Crystal Enterprise deployment is ever successful without taking into consideration many factors that can affect the performance of the overall system and, ultimately, the satisfaction of your end users or customers. This chapter covers a broad range of considerations, both technical and nontechnical.

- **Chapter 12, "Deploying Crystal Enterprise in a Complex Network Environment"**—Crystal Enterprise is seldom deployed in a network without the need for secure reporting and information delivery. This includes dealing with firewalls and multiple networks. This chapter explains the ins and outs of each of these concepts and the best practices for creating a secure reporting environment.

PART V: "CUSTOMIZING CRYSTAL ENTERPRISE"

Part V (Chapters 13 through 15) is oriented toward the administrator or developer who intends to programmatically customize the look, feel, or function of Crystal Enterprise to suit specific organizational needs. You'll also find some information on the integration of Crystal Enterprise with some popular third-party portal tools.

- **Chapter 13, "Extending Crystal Enterprise"**—The power of Crystal Enterprise lies in the capability to customize every aspect of its look, feel, and function. Crystal Enterprise provides a COM-based SDK to allow developers to accomplish an array of tasks, such as modifying the behavior of ePortfolio or integrating Crystal Enterprise within a Web portal application. This chapter reviews the Crystal Enterprise object model, the associated SDK, and how to leverage and extend it with scripting languages such as VBScript or JavaScript.

■ **Chapter 14, "Integrating Crystal Enterprise with Your Corporate Intranet"**— This chapter extends the topics in the previous chapter by using examples of integrating Crystal Enterprise with a corporate intranet site. We use HTML, JavaScript, and VBScript for the Web examples in this chapter. This helps you understand how Crystal Enterprise can be rapidly integrated with a Web page so that an end user is aware of its presence but can enjoy all the functionality Crystal Enterprise provides. An example of how an organization would use the Crystal Enterprise Admin SDK to create a custom administration console is explored as well.

■ **Chapter 15, "Integrating Crystal Enterprise with Third-Party Portals"**—A growing demand for Crystal Enterprise is to integrate its capability with some popular third-party portal products. We review a few of the most widely used portal products in the market and various approaches to integrating Crystal Enterprise with those products. We also point you to several resource locations where existing Crystal Enterprise portal components can be found.

PART VI: "CRYSTAL ENTERPRISE SUPPLEMENTAL MATERIAL"

Part VI (Appendixes A and B) covers some relatively new topics for Crystal Enterprise: The Unix-based Sun Solaris installation of Crystal Enterprise and an add-in to Crystal Enterprise called the Report Application Server (SmartReporting, as Crystal Decisions calls it). The Report Application Server and associated SDK extend Crystal Enterprise to allow end users to customize and create reports and ad-hoc queries right over the Web, in the Crystal Enterprise DHTML environment.

■ **Appendix A, "Running Crystal Enterprise on Sun Solaris"**—A recent addition to Crystal Enterprise is support for Sun Solaris. This chapter covers the installation of Crystal Enterprise on Sun Solaris and some caveats of Crystal Enterprise functionality running on Sun Solaris. We don't directly address the process of administration of Crystal Enterprise from a user/group/object standpoint because the administration console and procedures are essentially the same as they are with the NT version. We do cover the exceptions to this.

■ **Appendix B, "Using the Report Application Server"**—A powerful server snap-in to Crystal Enterprise that provides report creation and customization over the Web, called Smart Reporting, was released in 2001. Although it is not shipped with Crystal Enterprise (there's an additional fee to install and use this with your Crystal Enterprise user base) it is a key part of any solution where users require ad-hoc report creation or modification over the Web. SmartReporting extends the Crystal Enterprise SDK as well, so we cover a host of additional programmatic capability added to Crystal Enterprise by the Report Application Server.

WEB RESOURCES

We've provided all the source code for the examples in the book at an easy to find Web site. Just go to www.quepublishing.com. You'll find easy to download application samples and code for you to leverage in your deployment and development efforts with Crystal Enterprise.

INTENDED AUDIENCE

We wrote this book to appeal to a wide audience of technical users. Crystal Enterprise is deployed differently in every organization, by users of varying skill sets. This book needed to reflect that. For Parts I and II of the book, you should be somewhat familiar with database, intranet, and Internet concepts to understand some of the examples used to explain Crystal Enterprise. These include the following:

- Database systems such as Microsoft SQL Server, Oracle, Sybase, and Informix
- Operating systems such as Microsoft Windows NT and 2000
- Web servers such as Microsoft Internet Information Server, Netscape iPlanet, and Apache
- Internet/intranet-based concepts such as HTML, DHTML, ActiveX, and Java

For Part III, you might already understand Crystal Reports, which places you that much further ahead. You should be familiar with common database concepts such as database schemas, tables, and records for this part of the book.

The concepts that apply to Parts I and II are applicable to Part III. To fully leverage the latter chapters in this part, an understanding of LAN/WAN setup and design is beneficial, as is a good understanding of firewalls.

Part IV requires some level of understanding of markup languages such as HTML, DHTML, and XML as well as scripting languages such as VBScript and JavaScript.

Appendix A requires knowledge of the Sun Solaris operating system and basic Unix commands.

Appendix B is of value to both administrators and developers because it covers both out-of-the-box functionality for Web-based ad-hoc query and report customization as well as the extension of this technology through the Report Application Server SDK. The skills required in Part IV are applicable to this appendix.

EQUIPMENT USED FOR THIS BOOK

For this book, we assume you have access to a computer that has at least a Pentium II or equivalent processor, 128MB of RAM, and Windows NT Workstation, 2000 Professional, Advanced Server, or Windows XP Professional with Microsoft Internet Information Server version 5.0 or higher installed.

All code samples in the book are based on Microsoft Internet Information Server as the Web server, although we discuss concepts related to other Web servers, languages, and technologies. Because Crystal Enterprise does support such a wide array of Web servers and operating systems, we couldn't possibly cover them all in this book. Crystal Decisions provides a supported platforms documents on its web site.

You also need to install Crystal Enterprise. And depending on your needs, optionally install

- Crystal Reports
- Crystal Analysis Professional
- Crystal SmartReporting with the Report Application Server

CONVENTIONS USED IN THIS BOOK

Several conventions are used within this book to help you get more out of the text. Look for special fonts or text styles and icons that emphasize special information.

- Code examples appear in mono, and can be found on the Que Web site as well.
- Code normally appears on separate lines from the rest of the text. However, there are special situations where small amounts of code appear directly in the paragraph for explanation purposes. This code appears in a special font like this: `Some Special Code`.
- Some issues might arise with the Web server you are attempting to use with Crystal Enterprise. We can't possibly address every issue that might arise with your Web server, so it's best to rely on the Crystal Enterprise product documentation, online knowledge base, or Crystal Decisions technical support for any specific issues you may encounter.
- In some cases, we may refer to your Web server as `<Machine Name>` because we don't know what your computer name is.
- You'll always be able to recognize menu selections and command sequences because they're implemented like this: Use the File, Open command.
- URLs for Web sites are presented like this: `http://www.microsoft.com`.

Note

Notes help you understand principles or provide amplifying information. In many cases, a note emphasizes some piece of critical information that you need.

Tip

All of us like to know special bits of information that make our job easier, more fun, or faster to perform. Tips help you get the job done faster and more safely. In many cases, the information found in a Tip is drawn from experience rather than through experimentation or the documentation.

CRYSTAL ENTERPRISE OVERVIEW AND ITS IMPACT

CHAPTER 1

INTRODUCING CRYSTAL ENTERPRISE

In this chapter

If nothing else, this book offers one guarantee: The amount of information that organizations capture and deliver will continue to grow. Not only will the amount of information that organizations manage continue to grow, but also it will grow at a faster pace over the next 3 to 5 years than a combination of the previous 20 years. Another safe assumption is that the number of devices and platforms from which data is received and to which information is sent will continue to expand as well.

Undoubtedly, the most successful organizations will implement a more efficient process of delivering information in any format, to any device.

This efficient process of delivering information begins with Crystal Enterprise, a scalable, extensible information infrastructure.

CRYSTAL ENTERPRISE 8.5 OVERVIEW

Crystal Enterprise provides organizations with one single system to address any reporting, ad-hoc query, or interactive data analysis requirements. Furthermore, any capability of Crystal Enterprise is fully extensible through a robust SDK.

Crystal Enterprise evolved over several years based on the needs of millions of developers and thousands of large organizations worldwide to quickly and reliably deliver their existing Crystal Reports over the Web. Crystal Enterprise provides these requirements with a collection of scalable servers to manage, process, and deliver Crystal Reports over the Web.

Fortunately, Crystal Enterprise is much more than a set of report processing and delivery servers that complement Crystal Reports.

As a system, Crystal Enterprise is intended to consolidate, accelerate, and enhance many of the information delivery projects that might be underway in your organization, each project tying into a variety of disparate data systems and tools intended to provide reporting and analysis or simple data retrieval from those data systems.

To understand the full value of Crystal Enterprise, consider the following scenario: Suppose a given organization, XYZ Corporation, decides that its internal sales force needs some reporting. To make it easy, let's say the requirement is just for sales commission statements. The sales group at XYZ Corporation, after an undoubtedly exhaustive evaluation process, decides to develop a custom reporting solution on its own using some standard development tools. It plans to design some simple commission statement reports and then send those reports out to all the sales reps.

During the process of developing its own solution, XYZ Corporation discovers that this simple request to view commission statement reports presents several challenges, such as preventing sales reps from viewing other sales rep's commission statements. This is just one of hundreds of considerations to be made, even when delivering a single, common report to many people.

Assume for now that XYZ Corporation gets all the issues for this commission reporting system ironed out. After the successful deployment of their new reporting technology, the sales reps are very happy with their newfound access to information, especially their commission statements. As time goes on, someone asks if he can specify some parameters on the report so that he can view specific commissions for one particular account at a time.

Is this starting to sound familiar?

Now that XYZ Corporation undertakes another project to implement parameterized reports, some sales managers start to notice the newfound happiness of their sales reps and ask for access to account activity data and regional commission attainment reports. It seems like a trivial extension of the existing application.

Then someone else asks if she can view reports as a Microsoft Excel spreadsheet (.xls) or an Adobe Acrobat file (.pdf). After that, someone else asks for the capability to schedule reports and e-mail them automatically. Next, they ask for access to the same information through a Web browser, and then on PDAs and cell phones.

After all this, the sales managers aren't happy because a new report request takes too long to fulfill, so they start asking for direct access to the data to do their own ad-hoc queries.

Then to top it all off, the XYZ corporate executives step in and decide they want to analyze the sales commission data across the entire organization.

Unbeknownst to the XYZ Corporate executives, the same scenario is taking place in dozens of other departments within the organization. None of the departments are leveraging off the work of another. Some departments, such as the sales group, have developed a custom solution. Other departments decide to purchase an off-the-shelf reporting solution. One must eventually ask the question: How much is it costing XYZ Corporation to maintain dozens of systems that perform similar functions, just with different data?

There seems to be an obvious conclusion here: Provide a reporting, query, and analysis solution that meets the common needs of multiple departments yet is flexible enough to integrate with the multiple types of existing data systems that different departments will need to do their jobs effectively. The immediate benefits of implementing such a solution would be a reduction in cost and an increase in organizational productivity through better access to information.

This scenario, played out in thousands of real organizations every day, is where Crystal Enterprise, an information infrastructure, provides a solution.

By implementing Crystal Enterprise, XYZ Corporation would immediately have access to a Web-based, common report management and delivery environment. Reports could be centrally secured and managed, scheduled or run as needed and made available in the file format users might request. In addition to preformatted reporting, users could perform ad-hoc queries or interactive data analysis when needed.

As a solution, XYZ corporation might opt to leverage the scheduling capability of Crystal Enterprise to run appropriate sales reports overnight, pushing resource-intensive database queries to off-peak hours. When the reports are complete, Crystal Enterprise caches and stores information relevant to the reports on the server. Whenever the managers and sales reps need to view the data, they encounter a lightning-fast environment to explore and analyze the information they need. Then the right decisions can be made based on accurate, consistent data delivered by Crystal Enterprise.

Based on the previously mentioned business scenario, Crystal Enterprise would appeal to a wide variety of users within XYZ Corporation: the administrator, who needs a secure, "out-of-the-box" solution with a rich Web application server environment to deliver reports over a Web browser; developers, who want to build a Web site or application but still want to minimize the amount of development needed to deliver information to users or customers; end users, such as managers and sales reps, who are looking for easy, consistent access to corporate reports or analytic information. All in all, Crystal Enterprise provides reliable access to corporate data and enhances everyday tasks such as report viewing and ad-hoc query as well as establishes a scalable Web infrastructure, shown in Figure 1.1, for information delivery.

Figure 1.1
Crystal Enterprise offers a more efficient multitier report processing and delivery architecture.

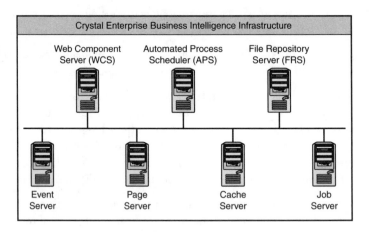

THE CRYSTAL ENTERPRISE SOLUTION

From a technical standpoint, Crystal Enterprise has a number of features to offer, from report management, scheduling, and processing, to DHTML delivery of report data through a Web browser. Reports can be highly interactive, with drill-down on data and charts to automated delivery of data-driven alerting to any third-party application or device.

Whether organizational requirements call for parameterized reporting or interactive data analysis, Crystal Enterprise is up to the challenge.

All these features, and many more discussed throughout this book, are wrapped inside the integrated, extensible security model Crystal Enterprise offers as part of the system.

Consider for a moment the raw number of installations of Crystal Reports in use today. All that Crystal Reports has to offer is integrated with Crystal Enterprise. Any existing Crystal

Reports that an organization might be using today are immediately compatible with Crystal Enterprise.

There are two versions of Crystal Enterprise, Standard and Professional, and it's important to determine which one you plan to use because certain features are available only in the Professional edition of Crystal Enterprise.

The Standard version of Crystal Enterprise is available in version 8.0 only, so although most of the topics in this book and many of the features apply, some do not. Check with Crystal Decisions for more information on the advantages of Crystal Enterprise Professional 8.5 over Crystal Enterprise Standard 8.0.

Crystal Enterprise Standard 8.0 has some of the same features of Crystal Enterprise Professional 8.5 but can be installed on only one physical server and has a very limited security model. Several features have been added with the release of Crystal Enterprise Professional 8.5, such as advanced scheduling options. A single server deployment is fine for small organizations but becomes impractical when the needs of more than a limited number of users must be met. This book focuses on Crystal Enterprise Professional Version 8.5.

Note

Upgrade information for Crystal Enterprise Standard can be obtained at `http://www.crystaldecisions.com`.

CRYSTAL ENTERPRISE AND CRYSTAL REPORTS INTEGRATION

The universal question that everyone seems to ask is, "How does a report designed in the Windows-based Crystal Reports designer on someone's desktop PC become an interactive Web report?" At the simplest level, a Crystal Reports writer or developer can install Crystal Enterprise on a workstation or server (with the proper Web server software—see Chapter 3, "Exploring the System Architecture," and Chapter 4, "Installing Crystal Enterprise 8.5") and publish new or existing Crystal Reports to Crystal Enterprise. Users can log in to Crystal Enterprise through several out-of-the-box sample Web applications to gain access to certain reports to which they have been granted permission (see Figure 1.2). The benefits of enabling multiple users to access a report centrally include the following:

- Reduced processing load on critical corporate databases through report scheduling
- Stored historical instances of data for later access
- Centralized security
- No ODBC or data connectivity software on the client PC or device

Publishing a Crystal Report to Crystal Enterprise for Web reporting is a relatively simple procedure, but hardly leverages the full potential of Crystal Enterprise. To maximize the technology investment made in Crystal Enterprise, it's important to understand the technical composition of the system and its architecture. A detailed exploration of the system architecture can be found in Chapter 3.

Figure 1.2
Crystal Reports are published to Crystal Enterprise and then delivered to end users' Web sites in the form of DHTML.

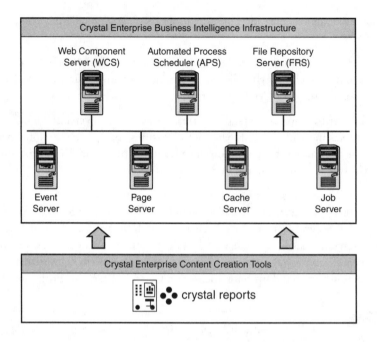

From a technical standpoint, Crystal Enterprise can be thought of as a Web-based, n-tier, scalable information management and delivery solution based on an open, extensible architecture. The open architecture is accessible from a variety of existing and emerging standards, including Visual Basic, C++, VBScript, JavaScript, HTTP, XML, SOAP and, shortly after this book is released, Java.

Note

SOAP (Simple Object Access Protocol) is an emerging Internet standard for accessing objects from disparate systems and sharing information across foreign platforms championed by several very large development companies such as Microsoft and IBM.

At the heart of this distributed component, open architecture is the Crystal eBusiness Framework. The Crystal eBusiness Framework manages communication and interaction between all client and server components installed in the Crystal Enterprise system.

Sitting atop the Crystal eBusiness framework, these server components can run on the same or physically separate servers. Crystal Enterprise servers are logically separated into the common processes that take place in a Web-based reporting, analysis, and information delivery solution. For example, report processing, query processing, security, scheduling, file storage, external event integration, and caching of information are all logically separated into specialized services provided by server components.

All Crystal Enterprise 8.5 server components are supported on Microsoft Windows NT, Windows 2000, and Sun Solaris 2.7 and 2.8. The architecture fully exploits multiple processor server systems. Chapters 3 and 4 explain the server architecture and function in more detail.

CRYSTAL ENTERPRISE IS "BUSINESS INTELLIGENCE"

Many common reporting and analysis functions, along with other ways to analyze data such as multidimensional OLAP information analysis, can be aggregated into an industry term commonly referred to as *business intelligence*. Business intelligence software provides a way for organizations to enhance their processes and interact with key customers and partners in a more intelligent fashion.

Crystal Enterprise is commonly referred to as a business intelligence platform.

Note

OLAP (On-Line Analytic Processing) is another way to manage or stage data in an efficient form for rapid response to analytic queries.

Scalability is a big challenge with common business intelligence solutions. Providing point solution applications for a small set of users with "thick" applications and tools is a very common offering from many BI vendors, a practice that can be entirely avoided with Crystal Enterprise.

One immediate advantage of using Crystal Enterprise, if not apparent at this point, is Web-based, central report viewing. You do not need to provide any installed components for report viewing in a browser. Crystal Enterprise delivers reports through a "zero client" interface within a Web browser using DHTML (Dynamic HTML).

As discussed earlier in this chapter, delivery of reports is a small part of the services provided by Crystal Enterprise; however, the benefits of central report delivery are pervasive throughout the system. Crystal Enterprise provides more efficient use of network resources through technologies such as Page-On-Demand, where users are sent only one page of a report at a time. This comes in handy for large reports that need to be sent to users over the Internet. Crystal Enterprise can even cache previously viewed report pages in case a user requests it again.

One major leap in report delivery is a technology called *report streaming*, where the delivery of information contained within a report is broken into smaller, manageable pieces that can be quickly streamed to a browser, creating a responsive, "Web speed" experience for the user.

KEY FEATURES OF CRYSTAL ENTERPRISE

While previous sections of this chapter have exposed some of the following points of value for Crystal Enterprise, it's worth exploring them in more detail. Those value points include

- Content management
- Content delivery
- Open interface

It's important to remember that the content creation portion of the solution is accomplished through integrated reporting products such as Crystal Reports, while Crystal Enterprise itself provides the server-based content management and delivery of actual reports. The value of the solution is that Crystal Reports and Crystal Enterprise are fully integrated to provide a seamless information delivery solution.

CONTENT MANAGEMENT

Corralling reports into a central location can be a daunting task. As organizations that undertake this effort quickly discover, the actual number of existing reports they have in use is significantly more than they might have estimated. Consider that Crystal Reports is bundled in almost every major application any large organization already has in-house, including major ERP and CRM solutions. These systems provide hundreds and, in some cases, thousands of prebuilt Crystal Reports that might be in use in your organization today.

Content management implies that Crystal Enterprise acts as an object store or repository for reports. This repository, referred to as the *InfoStore*, is the object storage and retrieval portion of the Crystal Enterprise object model. Crystal Enterprise provides out-of-the-box object management via the InfoStore for all report types created by Crystal Decisions reporting products. This is a very powerful component of the Crystal Enterprise solution, as organizations seek out ways to consolidate the number of reports that must be managed and delivered for users to make informed business decisions.

After a report is published to the Crystal Enterprise and held in the InfoStore, it is assigned both unique and generic meta properties that can be programmatically addressed for extension of the system. A unique property would be something like the report ID, which could easily be queried for in a Web application to call the report for viewing. A generic property of the report could be the report type, as there are multiple Crystal design tools that integrate with Crystal Enterprise. All the meta properties of a report, once stored in Crystal Enterprise, can be leveraged to help determine what to deliver to a user in a browser-based application.

CONTENT DELIVERY

After reports are stored in the managed environment of Crystal Enterprise, the next step is to deliver them to a group of intended users or customers in the form and fashion they've requested.

Content delivery is the first critical factor in the design of an integrated information delivery system. When populated with report objects, Crystal Enterprise is ready to feed an array of Web pages, sites, applications, and portals your organization might have within your organization. To put it in one sentence, Crystal Enterprise takes a Crystal Report and automatically turns it into an interactive Web page. Think of this as an "object transformation" service.

The information delivery concept of Crystal Enterprise can easily be taken beyond delivery of reports using DHTML, because Crystal Enterprise can export reports and the data contained within the report to XML. This enables Crystal Enterprise to instantly integrate with and feed external applications such as wireless portals or eCommerce systems.

After a report is requested from Crystal Enterprise, the first page of a report is delivered to the end user browser along with a viewer, which is a report control wrapper that provides a toolbar with controls such as a refresh button, export link, and page browsing (all optional controls, of course). Other report viewers are also provided with Crystal Enterprise besides DHTML, including the following:

- ActiveX Viewer
- Java Viewer
- Java Plug-in Viewer
- HTML Page Viewer
- Navigator Plug-in Viewer

These viewers essentially provide the same functionality, with subtle differences in terms of look and feel. Unfortunately, neither all Web browsers nor the people who use them are created equal. The viewers are provided for browser compatibility and personal preference reasons.

From an end-user standpoint, these report viewers enable interaction with a report. In the case of the DHTML viewer, the base rollout effort consists of installing Crystal Enterprise on a server or workstation, publishing any existing reports to Crystal Enterprise, and providing users with a URL to connect to a Web application where the report can be viewed. Obviously, this excludes any customization or integration with an existing Web site to work with Crystal Enterprise, which itself is very easy to do. More in-depth coverage of how Crystal Enterprise delivers reports and fulfills user requests can be found in Chapter 3.

The report viewers further empower the user by enabling the export of any Crystal Report delivered by Crystal Enterprise into a number of formats, including Microsoft Word, Excel, and Adobe Acrobat (PDF). The DHTML viewer, the most commonly implemented viewer, can be seen in Figure 1.3.

The DHTML viewer is the most easily integrated viewer for Web applications because it can be hosted in any portal without a plug-in and can be called from any development language.

Figure 1.4 shows a similar report, seen through the ActiveX viewer.

Figure 1.3
Crystal Enterprise can deliver reports to a Web browser through a variety of report viewers including DHTML, ActiveX, and Java. The DHTML viewer is shown here.

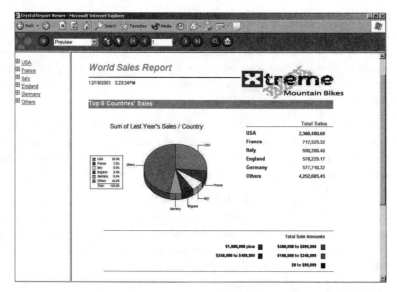

Figure 1.4
Crystal Enterprise can deliver reports to a Web browser through a variety of report viewers including DHTML, ActiveX, and Java. The ActiveX Viewer is shown here.

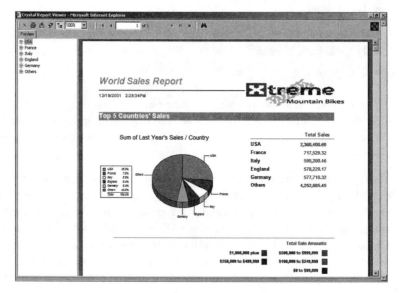

Figure 1.5 shows the Java Viewer, another popular option for viewing reports.

THE CRYSTAL ENTERPRISE OPEN INTERFACE

As stated earlier in the chapter, Crystal Enterprise has an extensible interface, commonly referred to as the *Software Developers Kit* or *SDK*. The Crystal Enterprise SDK provides a toolkit for building scalable Web applications that leverage every feature Crystal Enterprise has to offer and supports report viewing, exporting, and delivery across an organization's intranet or over the Internet via a COM-based object model. It supports major technologies and standards, including JavaScript and VBScript, enabling developers to rapidly build tailored Web applications. Emerging standards, such as Java and SOAP, will be supported soon.

Figure 1.5
Crystal Enterprise can deliver reports to a Web browser through a variety of report viewers including DHTML, ActiveX, and Java. The Java Viewer is shown here.

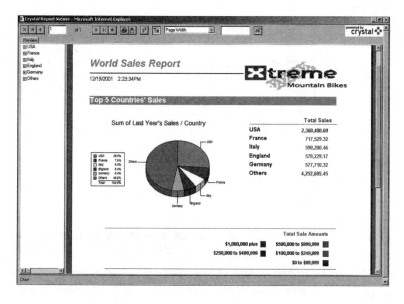

Note

At the time of writing, the Java SDK for Crystal Enterprise was in a beta stage. Check with Crystal Decisions for release status on the Java SDK.

For good examples of how the SDK can be leveraged, look at the sample Web sites and intranet-style applications that are provided with Crystal Enterprise, all of which are open source and written in either JavaScript or VBScript. When reviewing the open-source code on any of these Crystal Enterprise samples, it's apparent that the script is intended to be both functional and educational. Figure 1.6 shows an example of an open-source code sample client application shipped with Crystal Enterprise.

The extensibility of Crystal Enterprise enables integration with third-party portal applications, such as Microsoft Digital Dashboard, shown in Figure 1.7.

The advantage of building interactive Web pages and applications that are tied into Crystal Enterprise is the flexibility of the SDK. The SDK consists of a group of objects that handle all user, server, and object functionality contained within the Crystal Enterprise system, as well as a variety of plug-ins that control the functionality and behavior of the objects themselves. How the Crystal Enterprise SDK is used has implications for both the client side, or how users actually interact with Crystal Enterprise, as well as back-end processes, such as importing users and permission settings from a foreign security entitlement database.

Figure 1.6
Crystal Enterprise provides an array of open-source sample Web sites and applications for you to use, learn from, and customize.

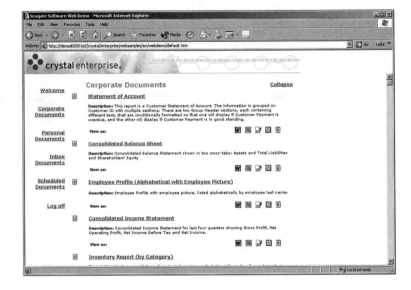

Figure 1.7
Crystal Enterprise can be integrated with any existing Web portal application, such as Microsoft Digital Dashboard.

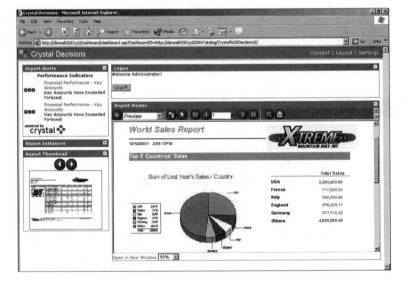

CUSTOMIZING CRYSTAL ENTERPRISE

After working with some of the developer sample Web sites and applications included with Crystal Enterprise for the first time, questions often arise; for example, "What if I want to use the sample Web site Crystal Decisions has developed but I don't want to show that option?" "What if I want to dynamically filter row-level data within a report depending on the users' ID?" All of this is possible through standard Web pages and scripting to the Crystal Enterprise SDK. If an organization wants to restrict a user from choosing an option or calling a function, it's simple; just delete it from the script or extend the script to show only the option based on the user ID. More information can be found on the Crystal Enterprise SDK in Chapters 13 and 14.

Note

> Dozens of third-party developers, such as Quasar Business Solutions, provide value-added custom application development services for Crystal Enterprise.

DETERMINING HOW USERS WILL GET THEIR INFORMATION

One of the most challenging stages when deploying Crystal Enterprise is determining how your user will interact with the system and what features to deliver. This shouldn't sound intimidating; in fact, it should be empowering. Many organizations find that they prefer one of the sample Web applications provided with Crystal Enterprise (that's why they're there), apply their own corporate logo, and roll it out as an instant intranet reporting application. The samples were written for Crystal Enterprise based on the most common applications and interfaces that customers of Crystal Decisions have deployed over the years.

This doesn't imply that there are just a bunch of sample client applications provided with Crystal Enterprise. There is a very robust default client tool for end users called ePortfolio. Several chapters of this book are dedicated to ePortfolio.

For B2C or business-to-consumer types of applications, most people are surprised when they discover that some of their favorite Web sites that they visit every day are using Crystal Enterprise to deliver information to customers. Organizations are using Crystal Enterprise for solutions beyond common reporting. These solutions include delivering external stock portfolios, bank statements, and cell phone bills over the Web. The list goes on and on.

More experienced organizations use the same Crystal Enterprise system to deliver B2B (business-to-business) application data. They might use the capability of Crystal Enterprise to export Crystal Reports to XML and then send the data to an external business partner.

CRYSTAL ENTERPRISE: AN INFORMATION INFRASTRUCTURE

Much has been said in this chapter about Crystal Enterprise as an information infrastructure. It is necessary to further define this because it will be referred to often throughout this book. An information infrastructure is actually a combination of two concepts already discussed in this chapter:

- The process of delivering enterprise information in a consistent manner.
- Delivering information through a common infrastructure.

To better understand what enterprise information delivery is, we need look no further than a standard corporate intranet. An intranet is a perfect example of applying Internet technology within an organization to deliver information to users. It's up to that organization to leverage the capability of an intranet by providing engaging, meaningful applications that deliver specific information that those customers and partners want and need.

What isn't typically practiced with a typical corporate intranet is the second and arguably the most crucial portion of an information infrastructure: the infrastructure itself.

The same holds true for Internet applications. Let's take the example of an online bookseller. To become an online bookseller, you need a few basic things: the perfect domain name (Crystal Enterprise can't help there) and a database that contains information such as the book title, stock status, ISBN number, title, description, price, and so on. When the database is in place, the online bookseller will need a Web application that allows a potential customer to browse for information about the books. When the customer has selected the book desired, the customer also needs a receipt.

Crystal Enterprise could be leveraged at several points within the transaction between the online bookseller and the recently acquired customer to help complete the sale. Every piece of information provided to the prospective online buyer about the book could be placed into a Crystal Report, without any coding efforts, and automatically delivered to the customer by Crystal Enterprise. Perhaps delivery of a receipt of the transaction, with additional summary information of all recent purchases made through the online bookseller, could be a report delivered by Crystal Enterprise. Armed with that information, a customer could understand his purchase history without having to call a customer service rep.

This online bookseller will undoubtedly benefit by delivering interactive Crystal Reports to users through Web sites, portals, e-mail, wireless devices, or any other device or application connected to the Internet or an intranet. This means that, by using Crystal Enterprise, your organization can standardize on a common information infrastructure product that can be easily integrated into any Web site.

The out-of-the-box functionality of Crystal Enterprise provides several different ways for the online bookseller to quickly provide secure reporting using code from various sample applications that are prebuilt and loaded, such as the ePortfolio application. ePortfolio is the flagship sample Web application that showcases many of the features and functions of Crystal Enterprise. More information on ePortfolio and other sample applications for Crystal Enterprise can be found in Chapters 5 and 6. These samples, as yours might be, are designed to be data-driven, allowing you to connect to databases, apply business logic to the data, and then control how the resulting information is displayed. They all support report viewing through standard browsers using ActiveX, Java, or DHTML.

Ultimately, the online bookseller must choose between buying an "off the shelf," extensible solution such as Crystal Enterprise or develop the reporting and data delivery functions it needs in house. The second alternative typically ends up being the more costly of the two and only solves one specific need for the bookseller.

BUILDING AN INFORMATION INFRASTRUCTURE WITH CRYSTAL ENTERPRISE

Enterprise information delivery isn't just about reporting and analysis, it's also about packaging and delivering information in the most effective fashion possible. While enhancing and adding value to information is what Crystal Enterprise and its complement of report design tools does well, delivering reports over the Web is just the tip of the iceberg, easily accomplished with Crystal Decisions' technologies.

Most organizations have too many tools in use across multiple departments to solve common problems. The return on investment with Crystal Enterprise begins by consolidating these tools through a single implementation of Crystal Enterprise. The bottom line: A standard Crystal Enterprise information infrastructure will help control organization development costs.

Standalone reporting tools are too narrow in scope to address the broad needs of a large organization. Even "broad-scope" business intelligence products that profess to meet the information needs of large enterprise organizations, as often painfully discovered, can be too complex and costly to maintain and still don't enable easy relational reporting and query capability. Dozens of point solutions that include some not-so-well-known tools and development objects across an organization all add up in terms of total cost of ownership.

When the Crystal Enterprise infrastructure is in place, organizations can develop entirely new revenue streams from existing customers by rapidly delivering information via Crystal Enterprise to Web sites, even in localized languages, from a single system with minimal additional effort. Figure 1.8 shows the application integration potential of Crystal Enterprise.

Figure 1.8
A single Crystal Enterprise system can provide information delivery services such as scheduled reporting to a variety of portals, Web sites, and mobile devices.

Realistically, any company like XYZ Corporation could take a development tool and some data connectivity objects and write a Web-based application that provides information to a user over the Web. The caveat to this is that the application typically ends up being somewhat anemic, with very little functionality other than a limited information supply from a database right onto a Web page—all that after a multimonth development effort with a team of multiple people gathering all the requirements, figuring out how to plan, write, test, and deploy a single-point solution for one specific reporting or analysis need.

Why use Crystal Enterprise to do this? It aggregates many of the complex tasks and development efforts associated with information delivery, reporting, and analysis and automates them to the point where a developer is focused on how to solve a business problem, not just how a piece of code is going to work. When it comes to delivering reporting and analysis information in Web-based applications, your organization will realize a massive productivity increase by adopting a Crystal Enterprise solution.

Organizations that fully leverage Crystal Enterprise view it as a solution that *enhances* any existing application where users want to view data.

When any of the following scenarios arise, some of which this chapter has discussed, Crystal Enterprise should be the solution:

- A sales manager sees sales figures
- A warehouse manager sees stock figures
- A call center manager sees rep productivity
- A banker sees a customer profitability listing
- A supplier sees a delivery history
- A consumer sees a portfolio or a phone bill

The real benefit to an organization is that end users don't have to know that a particular Web page, chart, alert, or report is coming from Crystal Enterprise. One good example is a company that delivers reports from Crystal Enterprise into a custom Web portal. None of the portal users know that any of the information they are looking at or the charts they click are actually Crystal Reports delivered into the portal from Crystal Enterprise. All that matters is that they are presented with a consistent environment and experience and that they have access to the critical data they need for better decision-making.

Organizations can find further leverage by using a single Crystal Enterprise system to touch and benefit every development underway. Let's analyze the XYZ Corporation custom development project in more detail. There were several groups of consumers that must have their needs met. End users, the sales reps, or customers of the intended application are the ones who will specify what information they need in the end result, or the application will see little to no use and of course, no ROI.

The developers must decide what data is to be delivered to users, how to deliver the information, and with what tools to develop the solution (Java, VB, ColdFusion, and so on). As in most Web development projects, the developers are also designated report designers and have to determine what the information will look like, how it will be laid out, and what level of interaction it will have.

Administrators must oversee the system, control security, and hope that the code that the developers wrote doesn't crash, or the end users won't be too happy. Last but not least, the managers of the project must approve all the above and fund the project. Naturally, they want to control costs and use existing technology and resources whenever possible. An entire ecosystem of stakeholders is in the project, all with their own wants and needs.

An information delivery infrastructure like Crystal Enterprise can address the needs of each of these constituents, not just on one particular project, but with almost every IT project within an organization:

- The end users benefit with a consistent function, look, and feel when interacting with data, even if the portal or "wrapper application" they are using is completely different.
- The developer's ability to interface with Crystal Enterprise through scripting languages such as VB Script, JavaScript, or Perl, thanks to the COM interface provided by Crystal Enterprise.
- The system administrators benefit from the flexible architecture of Crystal Enterprise that can be scaled up or out depending on needs and demand. Another big benefit for the administrators is the integrated security model that allows central control over what objects and information and functions a user or group of users has permission to access.
- Managers benefit through reduced project development time and cost containment.

THE REAL VALUE OF CRYSTAL ENTERPRISE: CONTENT

Within most organizations, there is a broad need for reporting, querying, and analyzing all types of data. The array of tools that are integrated with Crystal Enterprise enable the creation of the right type of content to meet those diverse needs. Crystal Enterprise would be of little benefit without engaging content for users to consume.

RICH CONTENT CREATION TOOLS: THE KEYS TO SUCCESS

Most people familiar with Crystal Reports have come to expect content (reports) developed using the tool to have interactive content—for example, the capability to click on a slice of a pie chart to drill down into the next layer of detail associated with that portion of the data. The key to success with Crystal Enterprise is combining the content creation and design capability of tools such as Crystal Reports with the management and delivery capabilities of Crystal Enterprise. Even simple requirements, such as parameters within a Crystal Report, can be automatically delivered through Crystal Enterprise. Each tool available to create content for Crystal Enterprise is targeted to leverage specific technologies to optimize the user experience when viewing and interacting with the report over the Web. The word "tools" is used because Crystal Reports is not the only integrated content-creation report designer available for Crystal Enterprise.

Currently, two available content-creation tools are integrated with Crystal Enterprise: Crystal Reports and Crystal Analysis Professional.

CRYSTAL REPORTS

The first content-creation tool that most organizations will readily use with Crystal Enterprise is Crystal Reports. With more than seven million licenses shipped, Crystal Reports is considered by most in the reporting industry to be the world standard for report design. Crystal Reports enables rapid creation of a wide variety of interactive report types, including conditional, summary, cross-tab, drill down, OLAP, Top N, multiple details, and mailing labels, as shown in Figure 1.9. Crystal Reports can connect to dozens of different types of OLAP, SQL, and PC databases using supported native, ODBC, and OLE DB connectivity. Reporting power can be extended by using subreports, which allows any report to be embedded within another report.

Figure 1.9
Columnar, Cross-Tab, and Summary reports are just a few of the ways Crystal Reports can enhance your information.

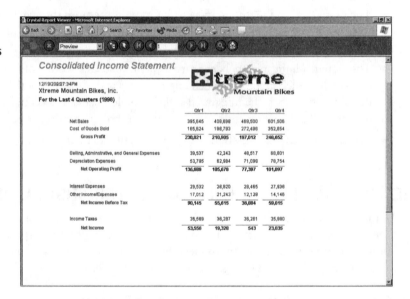

The power of Crystal Reports is not only in its scope of report creation capability, but the speed at which reports can be produced. Fast and easy report creation has been a selling point for Crystal Reports since it was first introduced. The report creation wizards and built-in functionality help novice and expert users quickly assemble interactive, engaging reports. An extensive formula language gives developers full control over report formatting, complex business logic, and data selection.

This robust report creation environment is the building block for success for Crystal Enterprise.

Crystal Reports also provides charts, drill-down, alerting, parameter prompts, hyperlinks, geographic mapping, field highlighting, running totals, Top N, Bottom N, and sorting to turn reports into compelling, interactive content. Reports can be exported to a variety of formats, including PDF, DHTML, RTF, Word, Excel, text, e-mail, and Version 7 Crystal Reports format. Crystal Reports version 8.5 is the latest release, providing full integration with Crystal Enterprise. This includes the capability to save reports directly to a Crystal Enterprise system. As previously mentioned, Crystal Enterprise is also tied directly into the technology built into Crystal Reports 8.5, namely XML support, report alerts, and PDF export. It's not necessary to use Crystal Reports version 8.5 to develop reports that will be published into Crystal Enterprise, but it's certainly recommended. Crystal Enterprise actually supports prior versions of Crystal Reports as well. Some other exciting new features in Crystal Reports version 8.5 include the capability to report off XML data or export an existing Crystal Report to XML, reviewed in Chapter 8, "Creating Content for Crystal Reports."

If the features in Crystal Reports sound redundant with what Crystal Enterprise offers, it should. Any feature available in Crystal Reports is fully supported by Crystal Enterprise, without any special coding efforts needed to publish the report to the Web. For a comprehensive review of report creation and publishing to Crystal Enterprise, refer to Chapters 7 and 8.

LEVERAGING EXISTING CRYSTAL REPORTS

Since 1993, Crystal Reports has been bundled or shipped with applications from companies such as Microsoft and PeopleSoft. Through these relationships, Crystal Reports has become a "ubiquitous technology" that can be found in most applications within your organization. If your organization has purchased anything from a database server to a robust ERP system, there is a high likelihood that a large set of prebuilt Crystal Reports are installed with the system as well. Those prebuilt Crystal Reports, even previous to version 7, can be imported into the Crystal Enterprise environment for instant delivery and interaction over the Web.

There isn't a formal import mechanism provided with Crystal Enterprise to bring in older versions of Crystal Reports. Most customers find the process relatively easy, because a report designed in Crystal Reports version 7.0 or higher can typically be published directly to Crystal Enterprise without any additional effort by opening them in Crystal Reports version 8.5 and then saving the report to the Crystal Enterprise system.

CRYSTAL ANALYSIS PROFESSIONAL

Although Crystal Reports provides a broad reporting capability, it doesn't fill the need for more interactive reporting applications that might require "what-if" analysis, calculative requirements, and dynamic interaction with data that power users need. Crystal Analysis Professional, also seamlessly integrated with Crystal Enterprise, is a sister reporting tool to Crystal Reports that provides powerful report creation for Multidimensional OLAP data sources. It's often referred to as Crystal Reports for OLAP. Crystal Analysis Professional enables the interactive data analysis for Crystal Enterprise mentioned earlier in this chapter.

Crystal Analysis Professional makes complex data analysis simple by allowing dynamic reports and views of OLAP cube data to be linked automatically and dynamically, all contained within a single briefing book. The user is presented with an interactive, engaging environment for data analysis, trending, dynamic cross-tab reporting, and charting as well as general data exploration. A Crystal Analysis Professional application, published via Crystal Enterprise, can be seen in Figure 1.10.

Figure 1.10
Crystal Analysis Professional applications are highly interactive, providing out-of-the-box capability such as drill-down on OLAP data and on-the-fly calculations.

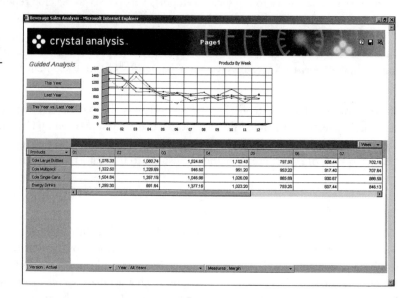

The Crystal Analysis Professional application designer is composed of an open workspace with drag and drop, prebuilt report parts, such as a worksheet object and a chart object, which allow rapid creation of multipage reports and applications (see Figure 1.11).

As with Crystal Reports, Crystal Analysis Professional is fully integrated with Crystal Enterprise. Any report created with Crystal Analysis Professional can be published through the same "Save to Crystal Enterprise" process as a Crystal Report. A full review of how to use Crystal Analysis Professional and publish applications to Crystal Enterprise can be found in Chapter 9.

CONTENT BEYOND REPORTS

Although Crystal Enterprise is optimized to handle content created through the default integrated report design tools mentioned in this chapter, the scope of what information or objects that can be delivered via Crystal Enterprise can be extended through the Crystal Enterprise SDK.

For example, many organizations are looking for ways to provide a common repository for Microsoft Word documents and Excel spreadsheets. More than just storing the documents in a central location, they need to deliver those documents over the Web.

Figure 1.11
Crystal Analysis Professional combines the flexibility of Web page design and the efficiency of a report writer into one application.

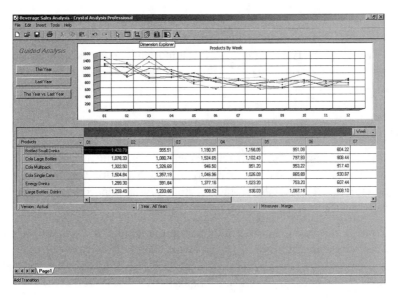

Rather than writing a complex process that applies capabilities such as security to individual objects, many organizations will opt for extending to Crystal Enterprise via the SDK that enables it to store third-party objects. It is important to note that in order for Crystal Enterprise to manage a third-party object, such as a Microsoft Word document, an *object extension* must be written so that Crystal Enterprise will understand what to do with the documents.

Once that extension is written, objects such as Microsoft Excel spreadsheets are handled within Crystal Enterprise similar to any other object like a Crystal Report. This means, for example, that the existing security model within Crystal Enterprise and any existing security configurations implemented within Crystal Enterprise can now be applied to the Excel spreadsheet once placed into the Crystal Enterprise framework. Refer to the Crystal Enterprise SDK documentation for more information on storing and managing third-party objects in Crystal Enterprise.

ADDING AD-HOC QUERY CAPABILITY TO CRYSTAL ENTERPRISE

Crystal Decisions has taken steps to deliver on the promise of the open architecture of Crystal Enterprise by developing a powerful server add-in called the Report Application Server.

Referred to as "Smart Reporting," the Report Application Server plugs into an existing Crystal Enterprise deployment and provides a series of prebuilt, open-source code report modification and creation wizards for users to modify existing reports or complete ad-hoc data queries over the Web.

Because SmartReporting must be purchased in addition to Crystal Enterprise to enable ad-hoc query, it is not included in the main body of this book. Because SmartReporting is regularly used with Crystal Enterprise, it is important enough to spend some time on it. More information can be found on the Report Application Server in Appendix B, "Using the Report Application Server."

SUMMARY

Crystal Enterprise is an extensible content management and delivery platform designed to deliver information to any user, anywhere, on any device. One major benefit of Crystal Enterprise is the capability to plug existing Crystal Reports into the system and deliver those reports over the Web through DHTML.

Crystal Enterprise is an n-tier information infrastructure for enterprise information delivery. Crystal Enterprise provides a robust object management store called the InfoStore that can be extended using the Crystal Enterprise SDK, which is accessible through a variety of Internet standards, protocols, and languages.

Crystal Enterprise can enhance Web sites, portals, and applications through standard Web technologies. Crystal Enterprise integrates with world-class reporting and analysis technology found in Crystal Reports and Crystal Analysis Professional. For virtually any data source or application, Crystal Enterprise offers a customizable, Web-based solution for providing secure access to interactive, actionable information for employees, customers, and suppliers.

Crystal Enterprise delivers reports created from a suite of content-creation tools, including Crystal Reports and Crystal Analysis Professional. These content-creation tools can connect to virtually any data source and are completely integrated with Crystal Enterprise. They all support instant publishing of reports and information to Crystal Enterprise. When information is published into Crystal Enterprise, any existing Web sites or applications that are tied into Crystal Enterprise will be automatically updated with the newly published content for users to consume.

Crystal Enterprise provides a scalable infrastructure to meet the needs of large organizations with tens of thousands of users. Requirements for standard reporting, ad-hoc query, and OLAP analysis are often referred to as *business intelligence*. Crystal Enterprise is a business intelligence infrastructure for enterprise information delivery.

CHAPTER 2

DISCOVERING THE CRYSTAL ENTERPRISE UTILITIES

In this chapter

Chapter 1, "Introducing Crystal Enterprise," provided an introduction to Crystal Enterprise and its supporting role of content-creation tools, including Crystal Reports and Crystal Analysis Professional. Now that some general concepts related to Crystal Enterprise have been explained, a brief overview of the Crystal Enterprise end user and administrative utilities is needed before the actual installation should begin.

Upon installing Crystal Enterprise, several useful applications and administrative tools are provided for both end users and system administrators, some of which are essential to running the Crystal system. Certain utilities are available only through a Web browser, such as the administrative console for Crystal Enterprise, referred to as the Crystal Management Console.

WEB-BASED UTILITIES

The primary Crystal Enterprise Web-based utilities are

- ePortfolio, the default client application for Crystal Enterprise
- Crystal Management Console, the default administrative tool for Crystal Enterprise
- Web-based documentation and help

Additional materials are accessible from the Crystal Launchpad, which will be reviewed later in the chapter.

THE CRYSTAL LAUNCHPAD

After installing Crystal Enterprise, the first and, arguably, most important resource to launch is the Crystal Launchpad. The Crystal Launchpad is essentially a Web page that provides links and information to Crystal Enterprise end-user and administrative sample applications, documentation, system update information, help files, the Web developer guide, and administrative tools. The Crystal Enterprise Launchpad appears in Figure 2.1.

The Crystal Launchpad provides similar functionality to the Launchpad in version 8 of Crystal Enterprise; however, it has received some aesthetic changes. Additional developer samples for Crystal Enterprise 8.5 are linked from the Crystal Launchpad, including samples developed with new portions of the Crystal Enterprise SDK.

To start the Crystal Launchpad, from the Windows Start menu, choose Start, Programs, Crystal Enterprise, Crystal Launchpad.

Refer to Chapter 5, "Using the Crystal Enterprise Launchpad," for a detailed overview of the sample applications included with Crystal Enterprise, including ePortfolio and the Crystal Management Console. The rest of this section provides a high-level overview of ePortfolio and some of the administrative functions accessible from the Crystal Launchpad.

Figure 2.1
The Crystal Enterprise Launchpad, the central location for Crystal Enterprise applications.

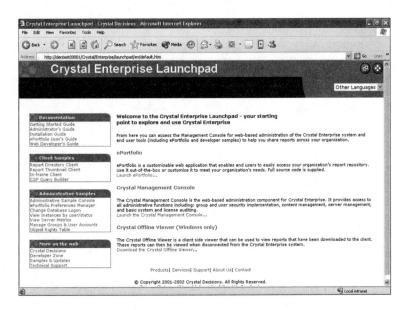

UNDERSTANDING EPORTFOLIO

Although ePortfolio isn't technically a "utility," it is the most functional Crystal Enterprise end-user client application that is widely used as the default Crystal Enterprise interface. ePortfolio is a fully functional, open-source code example of what report delivery and analysis capability can be deployed over the Web using Crystal Enterprise. Figure 2.2 displays the out-of-the-box look of ePortfolio.

ePortfolio received a face lift for version 8.5 of Crystal Enterprise, as well as additional functionality that exploits some of the new, rich features of Crystal Enterprise 8.5.

Note

For users familiar with the predecessor to Crystal Enterprise, Seagate Info, ePortfolio is essentially the replacement for the Info Desktop.

ePortfolio, written in JavaScript, provides a DHTML-based user interface that supports secure report viewing and scheduling. Crystal Decisions, as well as many third-party partner organizations, provide applications that add extended functionality to ePortfolio. Refer to the partner section of the Crystal Decisions Web site to find which consulting organizations develop extensions to Crystal Enterprise and ePortfolio.

Figure 2.2
ePortfolio is the
default end-user
client interface for
Crystal Enterprise.

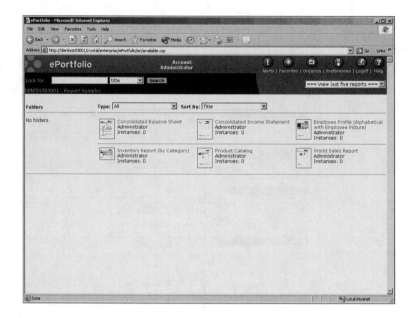

> **Note**
>
> A great example of extending ePortfolio is a Web-based report modification and cre-
> ation server add-in for Crystal Enterprise called SmartReporting, from Crystal
> Decisions, that extends and enhances the functionality of ePortfolio. Organizations that
> require ad-hoc report creation capability typically use the SmartReporting add-in for
> Crystal Enterprise.

Many organizations in the initial stages of evaluating or deploying Crystal Enterprise will
adopt ePortfolio or a customized version thereof as the reporting portal of choice due to the
extensive functionality integrated within the application.

A more detailed overview of ePortfolio can be found in Chapter 5. Chapter 6, "Customizing
ePortfolio for Rapid Information Delivery," provides details on how to customize the look
and feel of ePortfolio to integrate with a corporate intranet's look, feel, and function.

THE CRYSTAL MANAGEMENT CONSOLE

The formal administrative program for Crystal Enterprise is called the Crystal Management
Console. The general administrative features and functions within Crystal Enterprise are
accessed through a DHTML interface. This includes control of users, groups, report
objects, and the Crystal Enterprise servers themselves. Security settings for all Crystal
Enterprise objects are configured here as well. System usage statistics, such as the number of
users logged in to Crystal Enterprise and current scheduled report jobs, are also found here.
Figure 2.3 shows the Crystal Management Console.

Figure 2.3
The Crystal Management Console provides Web-based system administration and user management for Crystal Enterprise.

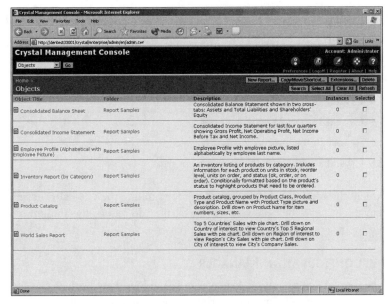

The Crystal Management Console also has an updated user interface from version 8, as well as a host of new functions that exploits new technology in Crystal Enterprise 8.5.

The main benefit of providing a DHTML-based administrative console in Crystal Enterprise is accessibility. System administration can be performed from any computer within an organization, as long as a Web browser that supports DHTML is installed. This makes remote management of Crystal Enterprise an effortless process.

The Crystal Management Console sometimes is confused with the Crystal Configuration Manager; a Windows-based application, which provides some of the same functions as the Crystal Management Console, as well as additional server management capabilities. There's a reason why Crystal Decisions provides a Windows-based server manager tool to compliment the Crystal Management Console rather than relying solely on the Web console itself. Crystal Enterprise depends on a Web server, such as Microsoft IIS, to provide access to the Crystal Management Console through a Web browser. If the Web server becomes unavailable or isn't functioning properly, the system administrator will have no way of configuring any of the Crystal Enterprise servers, users, or objects.

More information about the Crystal Management console can be found in Chapter 5, but Chapter 10, "Administering and Configuring Crystal Enterprise," is dedicated to the topic of administration of Crystal Enterprise.

WINDOWS-BASED CRYSTAL ENTERPRISE UTILITIES

Although Crystal Enterprise is primarily a Web-based reporting solution, it is necessary to provide certain system functions and other utilities as Windows applications. The following are the main Windows-based Crystal Enterprise utilities:

- Crystal Configuration Manager
- Crystal Import Wizard
- Report Publishing Wizard
- Crystal Web Wizard

Not all the utilities listed are necessary for running the Crystal Enterprise system; in fact, they might never be necessary. However, they do reduce the amount of effort required for certain processes related to Crystal Enterprise.

CRYSTAL CONFIGURATION MANAGER

The Crystal Configuration Manager is a Windows-based server management tool for Crystal Enterprise. This tool is primarily an administrative tool for Crystal Enterprise that comes in handy when there are problems accessing the Crystal Management Console over the Web. Figure 2.4 shows the Crystal Configuration Manager, which displays all active Crystal Enterprise server processes.

> **Note**
>
> Although there is some overlap in functionality between the Crystal Configuration Manager and the Crystal Management Console, the Crystal Configuration Manager does not provide any end-user or object administration, only server configuration.

Figure 2.4
The Crystal Configuration Manager is a server-management tool used for advanced Crystal Enterprise system configuration.

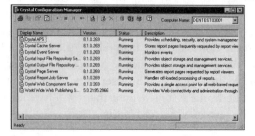

Recovering Crystal Enterprise servers when issues arise with the Crystal Configuration Manager isn't the only reason why the Configuration Manager is provided. The Crystal Configuration Manager provides administration over extended server and component properties, such as port configuration settings when using Crystal Enterprise in an environment with firewalls. A component discussed later in Chapter 3, "Exploring the System Architecture," called the Web Connector—which is useful in network environments with firewalls—can be configured using the Crystal Configuration Manager. Further use of the Crystal Configuration Manager is discussed in Chapter 10.

CRYSTAL IMPORT WIZARD

If a previous version of Crystal Enterprise or Seagate Info (the predecessor to Crystal Enterprise) isn't installed, skip this section.

The Crystal Import Wizard provides an efficient means of importing users, groups, folders, and reports from previous versions of Crystal Enterprise 8 and Seagate Info into the Crystal Enterprise 8.5 environment. Figure 2.5 shows the Import Wizard.

PART
I
CH
2

Figure 2.5
The Crystal Import Wizard provides a way for Crystal Enterprise and Seagate Info system administrators to import existing users, groups, reports, and folders into Crystal Enterprise 8.5.

> **Note**
>
> Be sure to back up the APS system database for Seagate Info or Crystal Enterprise before using the Import Wizard. More information can be found describing the APS system database in Chapters 3 and 10.

The Import Wizard in Crystal Enterprise 8.5 imports objects and folders, as well as related permissions for users and groups.

THE CRYSTAL PUBLISHING WIZARD

The Crystal Publishing Wizard is an extremely useful utility provided with Crystal Enterprise. It allows an administrator or user with the proper permissions to publish multiple reports into Crystal Enterprise. Figure 2.6 shows the Crystal Import Wizard, which walks a system administrator through the report publishing process.

The multiple report-publishing feature proves to be the most useful of this application, because the Crystal Management Console allows for only one report to be published at a time to Crystal Enterprise. This is impractical when dealing with large numbers of reports.

Figure 2.6
The Crystal Publishing Wizard allows multiple reports to be published at once to the Crystal Enterprise system.

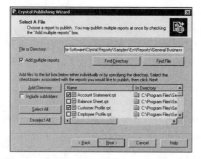

THE CRYSTAL WEB WIZARD

Chapter 1 mentioned that a custom interface to Crystal Enterprise could be built using standard scripting languages such as JavaScript or VBScript. The challenge in building a custom interface for Crystal Enterprise is getting started. Figure 2.7 shows the Crystal Enterprise Web Wizard, which creates a sample Crystal Enterprise application based on the answers to a few questions.

Figure 2.7
The Crystal Enterprise Web Wizard creates open-source applications for Crystal Enterprise based on responses to application look, feel, and function questions.

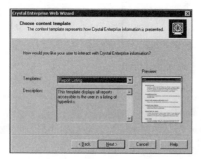

By answering this set of questions on how a sample Crystal Enterprise application should look, feel, and function, the Crystal Web Wizard will build a functional Crystal Enterprise application with no coding effort on part of the Crystal Enterprise administrator or developer. The application is open source, ready for customization, and automatically published to a Web directory if Microsoft Internet Information Server is being used along with Crystal Enterprise.

Some options include authentication types that the sample application should use, color schemes, and interface styles. The utility is self-explanatory, so this is the only section of the book that covers it.

SUMMARY

Crystal Enterprise is a Web-based reporting infrastructure. This is true even in the case of system administration. Crystal Enterprise includes a DHTML-based administrative application called the Crystal Management Console. The Crystal Management Console can be found in the central point for Crystal Enterprise applications, the Crystal Launchpad. The Crystal Launchpad can be found in the Crystal Enterprise program group.

Although it is advantageous to have administrative functions available in a browser, this is not entirely practical. Crystal Enterprise depends on a Web server such as Microsoft Internet Information Server (IIS) to provide the Crystal Management Console. If Microsoft IIS is not functioning properly, system administration will be impossible. Server administration in this situation could be done through the Crystal Configuration Manager, a 32-bit Crystal Enterprise administrative utility.

The Crystal Configuration Manager is one of several useful Crystal Enterprise utilities that aid in the process of administration, report publishing, and client interface creation. The utilities include the following:

- Crystal Configuration Manager
- Crystal Import Wizard
- Report Publishing Wizard
- Crystal Web Wizard

Not all the utilities are necessary for running the Crystal Enterprise system; in fact you might never use some of them.

The Crystal Enterprise utilities are provided to enrich the Crystal Enterprise experience. It is always important to back up any key components of Crystal Enterprise, such as the APS System Database, that might be affected by using one of these utilities.

PART

I

CH

2

CHAPTER 3

EXPLORING THE SYSTEM ARCHITECTURE

In this chapter

This chapter introduces the Crystal Enterprise Framework and the components that make up its architecture. It describes how each of the services that are part of the Crystal Enterprise Framework operate and what role they have in a universal information infrastructure. The chapter also discusses the benefits of having a distributed architecture that allows an enterprise reporting system to not only scale up on a single physical server but also provides the flexibility to scale out across multiple machines.

CRYSTAL ENTERPRISE ARCHITECTURE OVERVIEW

The architecture of Crystal Enterprise is designed to provide organizations with a massively scalable information infrastructure that can be deployed and configured in ways that meet any business need. Although it is a multitier architecture that provides the services necessary to ensure that the system is scalable, it also can be configured in ways that make the most efficient use of physical machines and network resources.

The tiers within the Crystal Enterprise architecture, shown in Figure 3.1, are the client, management, processing, and data tiers:

- The client tier consists of tools such as the Crystal Publishing Wizard for adding content to Crystal Enterprise, end-user Web applications such as ePortfolio (explained in Chapter 2, "Discovering the Crystal Enterprise Utilities") and administration applications such as the Crystal Management Console. Crystal Reports and Crystal Analysis Professional also belong to this tier. These rich reporting and analysis tools can easily publish their content to Crystal Enterprise from the client tier.

- The management tier consists of services provided by servers registered with the Crystal Enterprise Framework to apply security to report objects as well as to manage, categorize, and store these objects. It also provides services that allow an organization to quickly and easily customize Crystal Enterprise to fit into its portals or custom Web applications. Web applications, such as ePortfolio, use the services of this tier.

- The processing tier makes it possible for the reporting and analysis objects (Crystal Reports and Crystal Analysis Professional reports) within Crystal Enterprise to connect to a datasource available in the data tier and retrieve the appropriate information from a database, data warehouse, or multidimensional OLAP source required to create reports for users of the system.

Note

> The processing tier is used for both on-demand querying of information and for scheduled requests for information.

When organizations try to cross the business intelligence hurdle discussed in Chapter 1, "Introducing Crystal Enterprise," it's important to consider how that information is going to be managed, secured, and distributed. Crystal Enterprise was designed from its inception to solve the challenge of bringing together an organization's two most important assets—people and information—to make better, faster, more strategic decisions. To do this, it has been structured to discover properties of the reports that have been published to the system. By publishing reports to Crystal Enterprise, they are formal report objects, where each property of the report is held in a system database. The properties of the objects will be queried and evaluated more than any other effort within Crystal Enterprise. More will be reviewed on this topic later.

Figure 3.1
The Crystal Enterprise architecture consists of three major tiers of functionality.

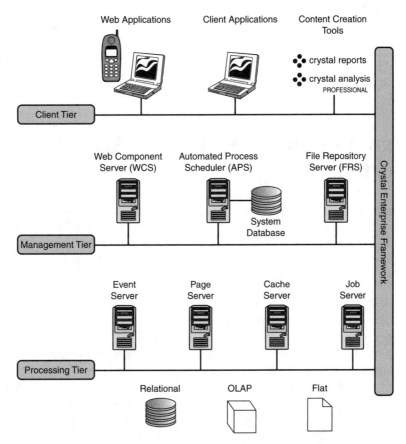

A key part of the Crystal Enterprise architecture is its modularity. Crystal Enterprise provides a series of objects that can be used to organize and manage the content, to secure it, and to manage servers used in an enterprise-reporting system deployment. Each object is represented by a component used by the Crystal Enterprise Framework to understand what type of object it is and what actions can be carried out when interacting with that object. The following section on the Crystal Enterprise Framework describes these components in more detail. This modularity allows Crystal Enterprise to be extended with new functionality, such as new content types or new security mechanisms, without the need for the system administrator to redeploy the system. By providing a modular architecture, Crystal Enterprise can be easily expanded for future reporting and information delivery applications.

Chapter 1 mentioned that Crystal Enterprise can play an important role in an organization's information delivery needs. One of the most important things that an organization must consider is how an information delivery system fits into its existing infrastructure. Crystal Enterprise was architected with application integration as a key design principle at all levels. This means that existing infrastructures, such as Web servers or database servers, already in use in a given organization can be fully leveraged by Crystal Enterprise. Crystal Enterprise can be seamlessly integrated into existing Web applications and portals that might be in use. (This is covered in later chapters.)

The remainder of this chapter provides details on the Crystal Enterprise architecture, what role each of the Crystal Enterprise servers performs, and the framework that makes it all possible.

INTRODUCTION TO THE CRYSTAL ENTERPRISE FRAMEWORK

The Crystal Enterprise Framework, the heart of Crystal Enterprise, provides a distributed mechanism that manages the interaction and communication of the Crystal Enterprise servers. Each Crystal Enterprise server uses the framework to describe the services it offers and to discover other servers that are registered with the framework. The framework treats each of the registered servers as equals, which makes it possible for one server to use the service of another Crystal Enterprise server directly.

As mentioned previously, the Crystal Enterprise Framework uses components known as plug-ins to represent each object type within Crystal Enterprise. These plug-ins contain all the relevant "knowledge" needed to handle an object within Crystal Enterprise, such as a Crystal Report or a user account, and determine how Crystal Enterprise should interact with it. When developing a custom application using Crystal Enterprise, it is the plug-ins that the SDK uses to call the services of Crystal Enterprise, not the servers themselves. Figure 3.2 demonstrates how the plug-in is used. The figure shows how a service, such as the customization capabilities provided by the Web Component Server, uses a plug-in such as the report plug-in to query for the report's properties. Notice that the service is able to communicate with the plug-in through the Crystal Enterprise SDK. In order for any service made available by the servers to be registered with the Crystal Enterprise Framework, they must use the SDK to retrieve the plug-in's properties. The Web Component Server section of this chapter introduces the customization services.

The object types that are part of the Crystal Enterprise Framework can be classified in the following groups:

- Administration
- Authentication

- Content
- Distribution

Figure 3.2
A plug-in is the way Crystal Enterprise exposes the services of a server on the framework.

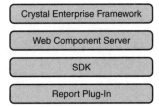

ADMINISTRATION PLUG-INS

Administration plug-ins provide a way to manage the Crystal Enterprise servers. Each plug-in exposes control and configuration properties of a server within the Crystal Enterprise system so that an administrator can configure the behavior of each Crystal Enterprise server. These plug-ins also provide activity metrics for each server.

PART
I
CH
3

AUTHENTICATION PLUG-INS

Authentication plug-ins provide a mechanism for Crystal Enterprise to interact with external security systems and treat these systems as native authentication sources. The authentication plug-ins provided with Crystal Enterprise are

- Crystal Enterprise
- Windows NT
- LDAP

These authentication types are discussed in more detail in the servers section of this chapter.

CONTENT PLUG-INS

Content plug-ins describe the types of objects that end users (report viewers) would typically interact with, such as, but not limited to, a Crystal Report. The content types that are provided as part of Crystal Enterprise are

- Folder
- User Folder
- Shortcuts
- Crystal Reports
- Crystal Analysis Professional
- Microsoft Word
- Microsoft Excel

- Rich Text Format
- Adobe Acrobat
- Text
- Users
- User Groups
- Servers
- Server Groups
- Events
- Connections
- Licenses

Distribution Plug-Ins

A distribution plug-in allows anyone who is scheduling an object such as a Crystal Report to be able to send that report outside the Crystal Enterprise environment. Hence the ability of ePortfolio (see Chapter 5, "Using the Crystal Enterprise Launchpad") to schedule reports to destinations such as e-mail. Distribution plug-ins that are provided with Crystal Enterprise are

- Disk location
- FTP Server
- Email-SMTP

Note

Crystal Enterprise also provides the capability for a Crystal Report to be scheduled to a printer. The printer object is not exposed as a distribution object, but rather as a function of the Crystal Report content plug-in.

These plug-ins play a fundamental role in the Crystal Enterprise Framework by encapsulating and exposing the knowledge of the object type that they represent. The remainder of this chapter discusses how these plug-ins are used by the Crystal Enterprise servers within the Crystal Enterprise Framework. Chapter 13, "Extending Crystal Enterprise," reviews how an application developer can create objects in Crystal Enterprise using the application programming interfaces (the Crystal Enterprise SDK) exposed by these plug-ins.

Overview of the Crystal Enterprise Servers

Now that it's clear that the functionality of individual Crystal Enterprise servers is exposed through plug-ins, it's important to understand exactly what that functionality is. The Crystal Enterprise servers are designed to register themselves with the Crystal Enterprise Framework and provide one or more services that can be consumed by other servers or by the plug-ins described in the last section. The services offered by each of the servers is dependent on the type of task that the server is expected to perform. Each server operates as an NT service or as a daemon when on Unix.

Note

An overview of Crystal Enterprise on Solaris is provided in Appendix A, "Running Crystal Enterprise on Sun Solaris."

The following list shows the servers that are delivered with Crystal Enterprise. These servers can be thought of as "core servers." Crystal Enterprise also supports add-on servers such as the Report Application Server, which is introduced in this chapter and explained in more detail in Appendix B, "Using the Report Application Server." These additional servers do not ship as part of the default Crystal Enterprise but can be added to a deployment if an organization chooses to use the additional functionality they provide. The "core" servers available with Crystal Enterprise are

- Automated Process Scheduler
- Web Component Server
- Cache Server
- Page Server
- Job Server
- Event Server
- File Repository Server

These servers can be seen in the architecture diagram in Figure 3.3.

PART

I

CH

3

Figure 3.3
The core server architecture for Crystal Enterprise.

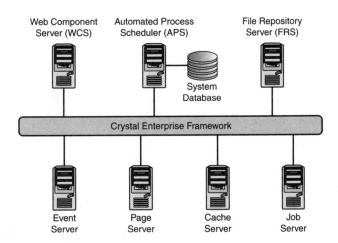

With these servers in place, Crystal Enterprise can manage any reporting content, such as Crystal Reports or Crystal Analysis Professional, as well as offer rich customization services allowing organizations to deeply embed and integrate Crystal Enterprise into their already established applications or Web services.

It's important to note that multiple instances of the same server operating in the Crystal Enterprise Framework at the same time is fully supported. By doing this, Crystal Enterprise provides a scalable, reliable, and fault-tolerant system.

CRYSTAL AUTOMATED PROCESS SCHEDULER

The Crystal Automated Process Scheduler (APS) is the server that provides some of the core services that the Crystal Enterprise framework uses, such as allowing other servers to register with the framework, users to be authenticated with the system, and the storage mechanism for persisting the metadata about each object. The services provided by the APS could be categorized into three main categories, which are

- Controlling access to system content
- Managing content
- Managing servers that have the capability to process content

The services provided by the APS are

- System security
- Object metadata storage
- Nameserver
- Object management
- Object scheduling
- Event handling
- Server clustering
- License management

SYSTEM SECURITY

The security service breaks security down into three main elements:

- Authentication
- Aggregation
- Authorization

Crystal Enterprise provides mechanisms to allow for third-party authentication services to be used as the basis of user and group/role definition. The APS interacts with these third-party authentication mechanisms by using the following authentication plug-ins, described earlier in the chapter:

- Crystal Enterprise security plug-in
- Windows NT security plug-in
- LDAP security plug-in

The enterprise security plug-in enables organizations to define users and groups directly within Crystal Enterprise and restrict use of an external source for those users. This is useful if an organization has chosen not to use an external security source or has not yet defined one. All authentication information is stored in Crystal Enterprise and does not rely on an outside source to determine whether a user is valid.

The NT security plug-in allows a customer to map any number of users and groups into Crystal Enterprise. An administrator is required to go into the Crystal Management Console (see Chapters 5 and 10) or use an application written using the SDK and define the default NT domain as well as any NT groups that might need to be mapped to Crystal Enterprise. After this initial mapping is complete, Crystal Enterprise will dynamically query for users within that group and establish those users as Crystal Enterprise users. When a user logs on for the first time, the security service using the NT security plug-in will ask the NT security database if this is a valid NT user and whether the user belongs in any of the mapped groups. If the user is indeed a valid user, he will be granted access to Crystal Enterprise. If at any time in the future that user is removed from that NT group, he will not be granted access to Crystal Enterprise (and, hence, reports within the system) because the security service would be told that this user is no longer a valid NT user. There's no requirement for the administrator to manually inform Crystal Enterprise that the user is no longer a valid NT user.

The LDAP security plug-in operates in a similar manner to the NT security plug-in; however, instead of talking to the operating system for a list of valid users or groups, this security plug-in communicates with a directory server using the LDAP protocol. Crystal Enterprise does not require the LDAP schema in the directory server to be modified in any way for use with Crystal Enterprise. This security plug-in provides default mappings for several directory servers, including

- iPlanet Directory Server
- Lotus Domino
- IBM Secureway
- Novell Directory Services
- Custom

PART

I

CH

3

Note

Crystal Decisions might provide support for additional directory servers, so it's helpful to check its Web site for updates.

Users and groups are queried by leveraging attributes within the LDAP schema, such as InetOrgPerson, which is an attribute used by iPlanet Directory Server. If the directory server that's planned to be used with Crystal Enterprise is not in the preceding list, it's also possible to create a custom mapping of LDAP attributes. The attributes that are used to define a group or user must be mapped to the LDAP security plug-in for these attributes to be used when querying for a user or a group.

Crystal Enterprise can aggregate or group users in two ways, as Chapter 10, "Administering and Configuring Crystal Enterprise," reviews in some detail. A group can be created directly in Crystal Enterprise or it can be mapped from one of the external authentication sources. The grouping within Crystal Enterprise is quite powerful because native and mapped groups can be used at the same time. If this method of user aggregation is taken, a native group could contain a mapped group. The use of mapped groups is important because as users are added or removed from groups in the external systems, the changes in group membership will be reflected in Crystal Enterprise. It's also possible to create a hierarchy of groups to better organize the end users of the system.

After configuring Crystal Enterprise with external users and groups is complete, it's necessary to determine which objects within the system an end user has the authority to see. After all, that's the whole point in deploying Crystal Enterprise, providing a central mechanism to control who has access to certain reports. Setting up authorization rules or access control is straightforward once users and reports have been added to the system. Chapter 10 reviews how to apply access control on objects in the system.

Note

Authorization within Crystal Enterprise is enforced through a strong inheritance model throughout the system. This enables an administrator to set desired access levels at a root folder for a large group and have that setting be respected, regardless of how many new subfolders are created or objects are added to those folders (as well as any new users added to groups or subgroups).

OBJECT METADATA STORAGE

One of the tasks that the APS performs is storing in a repository information about each object. After this information is stored, it becomes available to other objects or servers within the system. This persistent information is what is used to describe an object (such as a Crystal Report) and makes it possible to dynamically query the system and discover the properties of an object.

If the information was not stored in a repository, the system would not scale because it would be dependent on the information being stored in memory on one physical server. The APS stores this information by writing it to a relational database. The storage service is able to access these databases by using ODBC or by a direct interface to the database. The following shows databases supported by the APS and how they are accessed by Crystal Enterprise 8.5 when the APS is operating on Windows NT:

Databases Supported By Using ODBC

- Microsoft Data Engine—MSDE
- Microsoft SQL Server 2000 SP1
- Microsoft SQL Server 7 SP3
- Sybase Adaptive Server 12.5
- Informix Dynamic Server 2000 v 9.21

Databases Supported via a Direct Interface

- Oracle 8i (8.1.7)
- Oracle 8.0.6
- DB2 UDB 7.2

The databases that the APS can access on Unix are a subset of what's available on NT. If the APS is operating on Unix, it's able to use the following databases. All database connections for the APS repository are done by a direct interface.

- Oracle 9i
- Oracle 8i (8.1.7)
- Oracle 8.0.6

The default database that the APS will use if one is not provided is the MSDE. Because performance of the APS database can dramatically affect system performance, MSDE is used to provide an organization a useful out-of-the-box experience. The repository is set up and configured without the need for interaction with a database administrator. If Crystal Enterprise is initially configured to use the default repository database and the need arises to move the repository to a different database server, Crystal Enterprise provides tools (the Crystal Configuration Manager) to easily migrate the data from one server to another.

NAMESERVER

The Nameserver is a service of the APS that allows all other Crystal Enterprise servers to register with the Crystal Enterprise Framework. After the server has registered through the Nameserver, it is able to discover the other servers active within the framework and use any services it needs from those servers.

OBJECT MANAGEMENT

One of the key benefits of Crystal Enterprise is how it manages objects. After an object (such as a Crystal Reports) is published to Crystal Enterprise, the properties of that object are read and added to the repository. The object is then represented by metadata in the repository, which makes it possible for other services to interact with the object, and the object is formally considered a "managed object" by the system.

The concept of managed objects is a critical benefit because it facilitates the manageability of Crystal Enterprise. After an object is managed by the system, the actual location of the object becomes unimportant (that is, it doesn't have to be on a network share). If a server needs access to the object, it asks the APS for an ID to the object. If a client Web application wants to display the object, it doesn't need to know where the object lives and whether it has the appropriate machine-level mappings, such as network shares, available to it. This also makes it possible for Web applications displaying content from Crystal Enterprise to become much more dynamic.

In typical Web applications, a developer will provide access to an object through a hyperlink, which is pointing to a document on disk. Such is the case with a Crystal Report, where a hyperlink on an ASP page can call a standalone RPT file using a URL line, similar to `http://servername/reportname.rpt?init=dhtml`.

By having objects managed, a Web application developer can simply ask Crystal Enterprise for a listing of objects. Rather than having to know the filename or network share location, the developer can ask for all objects in a certain folder or of a certain type. Each time a user accesses the Web application, the content might be different, depending on the actual reports (objects) published into Crystal Enterprise.

Managed objects can be categorized into folders, which themselves are managed objects. This categorization adds to the manageability of Crystal Enterprise because content can be easily organized into something that is meaningful to application end users through the Crystal Management Console.

It's much easier for users to find the report content important to them if it is organized. Otherwise, users would end up spending their time looking for the content that contains the information rather than leveraging the information within these reports or objects to make decisions that affect their business.

Although navigating categories of information can be time-consuming, Crystal Enterprise offers the capability for users to subscribe to objects and place them in a home folder. This "home folder" also happens to be managed and stored by Crystal Enterprise. When users are added to the system (see Chapters 5 and 10), a home folder is created for them. When users find some content—a report for example—that they would like to access on a frequent basis, they can easily add it to their home folder by either copying it or creating a shortcut to it. When copying it, a new object is added to the system. The user then is able to make any changes to the object that she desires without affecting what other users might see. If the user creates a shortcut, it points to the actual object and inherits any changes made to the original object. ePortfolio, the out-of-the-box Crystal Enterprise end-user application, demonstrates all this capability.

For objects that can be scheduled, such as Crystal Reports, object management is extremely important to ensure that the system remains organized and performs at peak efficiency at all times. When objects are scheduled, they produce a new version of the object known as an instance. If the object is scheduled many times, it might become necessary to clean up older, unused instances. Rather than having an administrator manually clean up these instances, the system can be configured to automatically do this by setting object quotas in the Crystal Management Console.

Quotas can determine how often instances are removed from the system. Instances can be removed based on their age or how many instances exist per object. These quotas can be configured at three different levels:

- The global level affects all objects within the system.
- The folder level enables an administrator to set different quotas for each folder or subfolder.
- The third level is at the object itself. This setting allows the administrator to set quotas that are unique to each individual object within Crystal Enterprise.

At each level, the administrator can configure different quotas for different groups or users within the system. See Chapter 10 for details on object instance quotas or limits.

OBJECT SCHEDULING

The scheduling service of the APS makes it possible for objects such as Crystal Reports to be processed at a particular time or on a recurring basis. This service determines when an object gets processed using the Job Server. When a schedule occurs, the two main servers that interact with the object are the Job Server and the Event Server.

When scheduling a job, the scheduling service gathers information from various objects before being ready to run. It needs information from the report object regarding how to connect to the database, the desired format to output the report to, where it might be delivered (such as an e-mail address) and which server is going to process it (if there are multiple Job Servers). An object can be scheduled to be run at a particular date/time or on a recurring basis. This information is then stored in the system as a scheduled instance of the object. This is known as a `ProcessingInfo` object.

The `ProcessingInfo` object contains all the properties set on the report object when it was scheduled. It knows when the job will run, all the data-connection information, as well as formatting and distribution settings. Although it knows whether a specified Job Server is required, if that Job Server is not available, the schedule can be configured to retry the job.

A scheduled object can be dependent on an event to occur within the Crystal Enterprise system before the schedule can run. By using events with schedules, it's possible to control the necessity for a schedule to be run. If an object is due to run every day but the databases that it queries are updated sporadically, an event can be used to initiate the running of the scheduled job.

In a typical Crystal Enterprise system, it's important to have a small group of people schedule an object and then have the object owned by particular users. The scheduling service makes this possible by allowing a job to be scheduled on behalf of another user. This is useful when an organization wants to configure their system to only show instances of objects to a user if he or she "owns" that instance. Without the capability to schedule on behalf of another user, an organization would need to give each Crystal Enterprise user formal scheduling rights.

EVENT HANDLING

Crystal Enterprise supports three types of events. Events make it possible for users to ensure that scheduled jobs are processing only when external systems, say a database, are ready to be accessed. All events interface with the APS Event service when an event has been triggered.

The first event type is a *scheduled event*. The scheduled event allows an organization to create dependency chains when scheduling reports. This enables the user to determine whether a report should run depending on whether the preceding report was successfully completed or if it failed. An end user could easily configure a schedule event condition such that if report 1 is successful, run report 2. If report 1 is not successful, then run report 3. This can continue so that a process flow is established.

The next event type is a *custom event*. The custom event is sometimes also called a *generic event* in the predecessor to Crystal Enterprise, known as Seagate Info. This event requires application developer interaction to trigger the event by using the `Trigger()` method via the Crystal Enterprise SDK. This event type gives an organization a great deal of flexibility. Having an event that can be triggered by code makes it possible to have an external system determine when the event is triggered and the scheduled jobs that are dependent on it to run. A good example of this would be a database update trigger user event for Crystal Enterprise. Another might be an action performed by a user trigger event.

The third type is a *file-based event*. These events are managed by the Event Server and are discussed later in the chapter.

SERVER CLUSTERING

As a Crystal Enterprise system grows and access to information that it contains becomes more mission critical to an organization, it's important that the system be fault-tolerant, ensuring that end users are always able to access their information.

The APS can be clustered to provide load balancing and fault tolerance for the services that it provides. When two or more APSs are clustered, they perform as an active-active collection of servers. By being active-active, they are sharing the workload, which translates into increased scalability and performance.

LICENSE MANAGEMENT

Crystal Enterprise can be licensed to operate in three configurations: Named User, Concurrent Access, or Processor. The APS manages access to the system based on the type of license key provided. Although a brief overview is provided here, Chapter 10 reviews this in detail.

A Named User license enables an organization to assign licenses to specific users. Using this license method ensures that these users always have access to the system. It requires that the organization obtain a license for the number of users required to access the system.

A Concurrent Access license is more flexible for organizations that might not know exactly how many users need access to Crystal Enterprise. By using the Concurrent Access license model, an organization can add as many users to the system as it likes, but Crystal Enterprise will only allow users to access the system concurrently up to the actual number of licenses. For example, if 100 concurrent access licenses (CAL) are available and there are already 100 active users in Crystal Enterprise, the 101st user would be denied access until one of the first 100 logged out or a session expired.

Crystal Enterprise can easily be configured to use both Named User and Concurrent Access license models at the same time. This gives an organization the best of both worlds. As many users as necessary can be defined in the system, and then Crystal Enterprise can determine, based on the licenses available to the system, which users are treated as concurrent access users or as named users. Following the scenario used previously with the 100 CAL licenses, if this same system also had 10 Named User licenses the administrator could define up to 10 users as a named user. When the system has 100 active users, the 10 users configured as named users are still able to log on to Crystal Enterprise because they are not counted in the concurrent access number. A typical deployment of Crystal Enterprise has higher-level organizational executives as named users.

The Processor license allows an organization the greatest degree of flexibility in regards to the number of users that can be active in the system at any one time. The level of activity is based on the hardware given to Crystal Enterprise. With the license tied to the number of processors being used by Crystal Enterprise, an organization should determine the expected user load on the system to ensure that sufficient resources are available. If hardware resources become strained as load increases and the processor license model is being used, additional licenses will need to be obtained. A Processor license model cannot be mixed with a Named User or Concurrent Access license.

Each license model is useful depending on the requirements of the system. An organization should determine how the system is expected to be used and any anticipated growth plans should be considered before choosing the model best suited for the system. The following section on scaling the system describes scenarios when one license is used over another.

Note   Crystal Decisions updates the licensing model occasionally, so refer to its Web site for updated information.

WEB COMPONENT SERVER

The Web Component Server is an *application server* provided by Crystal Enterprise that delivers seamless integration of Crystal Enterprise content into any Web application. This integration can be hosted on a variety of Web servers and provides a robust scripting inter-face known as Crystal Server Pages that enables the creation of rich server-side Web appli-cations. For more information on Crystal Server Pages, refer to Chapters 6 and 13.

WEB CONNECTORS

The Web Component Server interacts with Web servers through a component known as the Web connector. The Web connector typically operates as an in-process extension of the Web server. The only exception to this rule is the CGI engine.

Crystal empress provides Web connectors for

- Microsoft Internet Information Server
- iPlanet Enterprise server
- Domino Web server
- Apache
- CGI

The purpose of the Web connector is to redirect certain Web requests from a Web server to the Web Component Server. By having the Web connector reside on the Web server and communicate with the Web Component Server, possibly on another physical server, it allows the deployment of the Web Component Servers in a way that will facilitate "scaling out," or adding additional physical servers to the Crystal Enterprise architecture.

The Web connector is listening for several potential requests, including Crystal server pages and Accessing objects.

CRYSTAL SERVER PAGES

The first of these requests is for a Crystal server page (CSP). The Crystal server page is analogous to an active server page but runs on the Web Component Server rather than directly on the Web server and provides the customization services for the Crystal Enterprise Framework. The benefit of using Crystal server pages is that they give the capability to author server-side business logic, have a process on one platform and enable the integration with a Web server of choice. The use of Crystal server pages does not tie one to a particular Web server. By using Crystal server pages, it is quite simple for a Web application developer to quickly author a dynamic Web application populated with Crystal Enterprise content (such as a corporate portal, which can have many different types of content, one portion being Crystal Enterprise content). CSP provides a way of direct interaction with the Crystal Enterprise application programming interface. An example of an application written using Crystal server pages is ePortfolio, an application delivered with Crystal Enterprise. Chapter 13 provides details on how CSP pages can be used.

ACCESSING CSP APPLICATIONS

Because of the distributed nature of Crystal Enterprise, it's likely that the Web Component Server is not on the same physical server as the Web server. If this is the case, it becomes necessary to provide two copies of the application: one on the Web server to handle any requests for HTML pages and images, and the other on the Web Component Server to handle requests for CSP pages. It's much more efficient on a corporate network to do this because it avoids files being transferred between the Web server and Web Component Server. It's necessary to map the location of the CSP pages located on the Web Component Server to a virtual folder located on the Web server. This virtual path mapping makes it possible for a Web server's virtual folder to be translated into the path on the Web Component Server where the CSP pages exist and enable the Web Component Server to properly run the CSP.

ACCESSING OBJECTS

Another request that the Web connector will send to a Component Server is known as a Crystal Web request, or CWR. A CWR is a server-side object that exists on the Web Component Server and provides access to managed objects contained within the Crystal Enterprise repository.

As mentioned earlier, managed objects are a way for Crystal Enterprise to understand and interact with a given object. However, Crystal Enterprise can also interact with unmanaged objects, although they do not have access to the same services that managed objects do, such as scheduling. An unmanaged object is one that exists outside of Crystal Enterprise and is referenced directly by a URL to the report object. Chapter 7, "Publishing Content with Crystal Enterprise," provides a good example of using an unmanaged object.

Unmanaged object interaction is a mechanism that an organization can use to leave their reports outside the system and access these reports through a URL. This is most useful for organizations using Crystal Reports that have created an application before investing in Crystal Enterprise. Interacting with objects in an unmanaged way allows the customer to keep their existing application working without interruption, while at the same time giving them the capability to move those reports to the Web in a seamless way.

To use a report in an unmanaged way the reports must be accessible from a virtual directory on a Web server and a URL needs to be constructed. This URL references the report directly and can contain several URL querystring parameters.

In order for an application to use unmanaged reports, the system first must have a valid license. When the report is requested, the Web Component Server will ask for a license from the license service.

JOB SERVER

The Job Server is responsible for processing jobs that have been scheduled in the system. It provides services to the framework that allow objects being scheduled to access the necessary datasource required, be analyzed for proper access control to that data by providing row-level data security services, and then distribute the content to a location set by the user. Job Servers are informed about the content that they process by loading a Job Server plug-in. This plug-in, like all other Crystal Enterprise plug-ins, describes what capabilities it exposes to the service using it. In Crystal Enterprise 8.5 the only Job Server plug-in is for Crystal Reports.

Essentially, the Job Server provides three main services to Crystal Enterprise:

- Database access
- Distribution of objects
- E-mail

DATABASE ACCESS

When a scheduled job is about to be processed by the Job Server, it gathers the appropriate information from the ProcessingInfo object mentioned earlier. This information includes database connection information and any filters or parameters required that determine what the final query is. After it has this, it opens the object and queries the database for the appropriate information. The data is retrieved and stored back into the system as an instance.

DISTRIBUTION OF OBJECTS

It's the Job Server's responsibility to distribute the object to the destination set by the user scheduling the job. To do this, the distribution service interacts with the distribution plug-ins mentioned earlier. This service receives the necessary information that was set at sched-ule time to perform its tasks. For example, if a user scheduled a job to be delivered by e-mail, the distribution service would get the To:, Cc:, subject, and body properties as well as the SMTP server that is configured for use with Crystal Enterprise. Chapter 10 shows how to configure the distribution service.

This service enables a user to send a report outside the Crystal Enterprise environment and deliver it to one of four destinations using the distribution plug-ins mentioned earlier.

E-MAIL AS A DESTINATION

Crystal Enterprise uses SMTP as its e-mail distribution mechanism. SMTP is a protocol that all mail servers support, so it's easy for an organization to integrate Crystal Enterprise into its mail system, regardless of platform. By supporting standards such as SMTP, organi-zations are not restricted in the e-mail server types that can be used with Crystal Enterprise.

FTP SERVER AS A DESTINATION

The FTP Server capabilities of the distribution service allow organizations to send objects directly to an FTP server location so that it's available for other users or applications. This is useful for getting information that can be used offline by customers, partners, or suppliers. A report can also be scheduled to update information at an FTP location on a regular basis that is needed to drive another application or business process. For example, a report could be designed to provide a product pricing list, including dynamic calculations of discounts that vary by customer, and then deliver it automatically to an FTP folder on a customer's Web server. Another example might be a scheduled Crystal Report that is output to an XML document sent via FTP to an external server for a business partner's application to pick up.

UNMANAGED DISK AS A DESTINATION

The unmanaged disk distribution service is used in the same fashion as the FTP server except that this service is distributing the scheduled report to a disk location that's available on an organization's internal network. Building on the preceding example, an organization could have Crystal Enterprise distribute a general pricing list to a location on disk and have this information populated on a purchase form or as a way of populating values into a Web service.

PRINTER AS A DESTINATION

Distributing reports to a printer available on the network is as simple as deciding what printer is to be used when the report is processed. Printing reports often is necessary when the information on the report needs to be shared with people who don't have access to a computer during analysis of that information. Situations such as team or board meetings often require that each member have a printed copy of the information to be covered.

INTERACTING WITH EXTERNAL SYSTEMS

Sometimes, it's necessary for a job to be intercepted before being run. Typically, organizations choose to do this so that information from an external entitlement database can be queried, and they can determine what data the user is allowed to view and modify the filter to reflect their restrictions. This is done in Crystal Enterprise using a component called a *processing extension*. The processing extension is loaded by the Job Server during a schedule or by the Page Server if being viewed. This extension allows for row-level security. Row-level security makes it possible for organizations to have content, such as a Crystal Report, shared by many users but the actual data that they see is targeted to them. It's also important to note that defining row-level security does not affect the content template but rather filters the view that the user sees based on the data that user has the right to see. There is no need to go into Crystal Reports and modify the report to affect which pages a user can see.

Processing extensions are just that, an extension of Crystal Enterprise. Some examples of processing extensions are available for Crystal Enterprise with the product.

PAGE SERVER

The Page Server is responsible for delivering three services to the framework. The primary service is to generate pages for viewing reports. This capability is important to performance and scalability of viewing reports because it only ever sends a single page of the report to the viewers rather than the entire report. It does this by using a service known as Page on

Demand. Other services performed by the Page Server are refreshing a report's data using a service know as on-demand viewing as well as the capability to download a report in another format.

PAGE ON DEMAND

The Page on Demand service, (also mentioned in Chapter 1) receives a request to view a certain page of a report and then generates just enough information to have the report viewers display the page. As described previously, it's much more efficient in a multiuser environment to have pages of a report, rather than the entire report sent to the viewer. This service not only ensures a positive user experience by getting them the view of the report they're after, it also is important to administrators.

Page on Demand minimizes demand on network bandwidth. Each page of the report generated by the Page Server is approximately 2KB in size. A report is usually much larger than this, especially if it's many thousands of pages containing thousands, if not millions, of rows of data. It should now be apparent why Page on Demand is a useful service. This service goes one step further by ensuring a positive user experience through a technology known as *report streaming*.

Report streaming builds on Page on Demand by determining which objects in the page might take longer to calculate than others and then deliver them to the viewer slightly behind objects that can be generated quickly. For example, the report might contain summaries or charts that require additional calculations to be performed before rendering for the end user who is viewing the report. Report streaming will ensure that the rest of the information, such as the details making up the chart or summaries, is sent to the user right away. The remaining portions of a report are sent as soon as they are calculated on the server. Report streaming is similar to the placeholder technologies that browsers use when loading images.

ON-DEMAND VIEWING

The Page Server allows a user to refresh the view of the report dynamically instead of scheduling the report. To take advantage of this service, users first must be granted the proper access level for the object that needs to be updated.

If a user has this access level, he has the capability to force the report to connect to the database upon their request. When the user refreshes the report, he will be prompted to enter any relevant information the report requires, such as database connection information or parameter values. Before enabling on-demand viewing for all users, the use of the system and size of reports must be taken into consideration. If many users are querying the database at the same time, are they asking for similar information? If so, the report could be run once and then shared among many users. What amount of data is expected to be returned or how long is the report expected to run? Often, a report might be too complex to enable all users in an organization to run it themselves. Based on the amount of time spent in the database, on the network, and in the report engine, a report can take several seconds, or even minutes, to complete. If this situation occurs, it makes sense to schedule any complex reports that spend a lot of time processing and allow that report to be shared among the users.

Exporting to Other Formats

The Page Server makes it possible for users to request to have the report presented to them in a format other than Crystal Reports. These formats are Microsoft Word, Microsoft Excel, Adobe Acrobat, rich text format, text, or XML. The user can request these formats by either using the querystring described previously or by selecting the Export button in the report viewers. The text and XML formats are not available when using the export feature of the viewers. Using the Crystal Enterprise SDK, there are a number of ways to export a report into any format supported by Crystal Enterprise, including XML.

Row-Level Security

In the same manner as the Job Server, the Page Server is able to restrict information presented to users based on a row restriction set by a processing extension. The main difference here is the Page Server is providing this capability at view time rather than at schedule time. Each method has its benefits. If a report has a row restriction applied to it during scheduling, the amount of data being returned to the report is filtered during the query. This means that the report instance only contains data that is relevant to the user who scheduled it. Another method is to apply the row restriction at view time.

If restrictions are applied at view time, the report instance contains the data necessary for the report, regardless of who is viewing it. When a user requests the report, the Page Server communicates with the processing extension to determine the row restriction to be applied for the user viewing the report. The data is then dynamically filtered so that the user is seeing only the data that he is able to see.

Cache Server

The Cache Server is an integral component to the overall scalability of Crystal Enterprise. It establishes a cache of report pages generated by the Page Server and promotes the sharing of this information. This is an important facet of the Crystal Enterprise Framework because, instead of having the report page regenerated for each user who requests it, the Cache Server determines whether the page can be shared among users. If it can, it will return the cached page. The Cache Server receives these requests from the Web Component Server and when the request is received, it checks to see whether the page requested is available in cache. If it is, the page is returned to the Web Component Server to complete the request. If it is not, the request is sent to the Page Server to have it generated.

Cache Management

The Cache Server is responsible for maintaining a cache of report pages generated by the Page Server on disk. When a request for a page is received, the Cache Server checks to see whether the page is available in its cache and whether it can be shared. If it is a sharable page, the server will return the page to the user. If the page cannot be shared, the request is sent to the Page Server to generate a new page.

CONSTRAINTS

Sometimes, pages are not sharable. The Cache Server determines that a report page is not sharable if it meets one of these conditions:

- **Row-level security is being enforced**—If row-level security is being used, the page of information is valid only for the user who requested it; therefore, the Cache Server is unable to pass this page onto another user.

- **The query within the report has changed**—The query for the report can change if a user chooses to view a report and change the filter already previously defined or change a parameter value. When this occurs, the cached page is invalidated and must be regenerated.

EVENT SERVER

As you learned earlier in the chapter, events are actually managed by a formal server in Crystal Enterprise. The Event Server provides a way for Crystal Enterprise to monitor events that are occurring outside its environment. It enables an organization to trigger the running of scheduled jobs that are dependent on a certain event in their environment to occur.

The main service that the Event Server provides is the capability to monitor the outside system for the existence or modification of a file. Using a file to trigger an event is a useful way of determining when the event is triggered because the generation of a file is a common thing for a lot of systems to do. For example, an organization might perform a nightly data warehouse update.

An organization would want the reports to wait until this load is complete because if they run when the data warehouse is offline, all the scheduled jobs would fail and the users would be upset when they went to view their reports. To ensure that reports don't run until the load is complete, they configure the Event Server to monitor the file system for a log of the completed update to be created. When this file is created, an event in Crystal Enterprise is triggered and the Event Server notifies the APS. Any reports that are dependent on this event are initiated and sent to the Job Server for processing.

FILE REPOSITORY SERVER

The File Repository Server provides the Crystal Enterprise Framework with two core services. The first is the capability to provide a centralized content storage facility, and the other is the capability to abstract the location of these objects from other services within the framework.

CENTRALIZED STORAGE OF CONTENT

Crystal Enterprise provides two File Repository Servers. An input FRS is used to store any content that has been published to Crystal Enterprise by the Publishing Wizard or from the design tool. When content is published to Crystal Enterprise, the object is copied from the client to a location on the FRS. This location is set by the installation of Crystal Enterprise but can be controlled by the administrator by modifying the root directory of the FRS. The objects are placed into unique folders on the server and are given unique names to ensure that there will not be any conflicts with other objects.

An output FRS is used to store the content generated by a scheduled job. The output server operates in the same manner as the input server by generating a unique name and location for each object.

ABSTRACTION OF CONTENT LOCATION

Now that the content is centrally stored and managed, the FRS provides a powerful way of abstracting the actual location of the objects from the other framework services. This abstraction is delivered by using Uniform Resource Identifiers, or URIs. The FRS uses the URIs as a way of providing a virtual location to the content. This makes it easy for services to request an object from the FRS without the need to ensure that it has access to the actual physical disk location. From a deployment and administration perspective, the job is much easier if objects are referred by URI. There is no need for complex network configurations, such as setting each service to run as a user account so they can access network shares.

REPORT APPLICATION SERVER

The Report Application Server is a powerful add-on server to the Crystal Enterprise Framework. It enables organizations to take their Web reporting a step or two further than viewing content over the Web. The Report Application Server provides three new components for the framework: a new viewer that can be embedded more directly into Web applications, a full object model for creating and modifying a Crystal Report, and a dedicated server for handling the creation and modification requests. The Report Application Server is discussed in detail in Appendix B.

Note

Based on the current licensing model for Crystal Enterprise, the SmartReporting (Report Application Server) add-in must be purchased in addition to Crystal Enterprise. Refer to Crystal Decisions for updates to their licensing models.

AD HOC QUERY CONCEPTS

One of the main benefits of adding the Report Application Server to the Crystal Enterprise Framework is that organizations can quickly and easily add ad hoc query capabilities to their Web applications. The Report Application Server makes it possible to connect to a server-side datasource, query for information, and then display that information, all with a zero client viewer in a Web browser. By using any of the built-in clients that are delivered with the Report Application Server or using the object model to create a custom user interface, it's possible to take ad hoc querying to the next step by formatting the data into a presentable report.

WEB REPORT DESIGN

The Report Application Server can take the data returned as part of the previously mentioned ad hoc query issued by an application user and allow them to begin to format the report. The user is able to modify the query in many ways to format it into a quality report. End users can sort data, group it, and create calculated fields to manipulate data into a view that is suitable for them. After retrieving the data from a database, additional visual components can be applied to the report. The user can modify font information on the report for a more visually appealing look.

A report style can be applied to quickly update the entire report view to a preformatted style. Many times a report requires visual elements, such as charts, to be added for users of the report to quickly understand the data within the report. The Report Application Server also provides end users with the capability to embed a chart. The charts can be any type supported in Crystal Reports. The major benefit is that none of this detracts from Crystal Enterprise's major appeal: a zero-client environment. The embedded ePortfolio sample for Report Application Server is entirely DHTML.

INTEGRATED, EMBEDDED VIEWING

When it comes to viewing the results of a recently created report or query, organizations have the flexibility to deeply embed the Crystal Enterprise report viewer into their Web applications. There is no need to use frames and dedicate one of the frames to the report viewer application. There is no need to have the report loaded into a new window. The report viewer that is delivered with the Report Application Server has the capability to be embedded into a <DIV> statement. This makes it possible for a Web application developer to place the viewer exactly where he wants it to appear. Another benefit of this viewer is that it provides an object model that enables it to be manipulated on the server. The application developer has the capability to modify the viewer with properties that allow the toolbars and navigation trees to be turned off.

The viewer supports an event model that provides application developers with the information selected by the user in the viewer. This makes it easy for organizations using the Report Application Server to make closed loop systems.

This means that when the event model is used, a report can become much more interactive and drive more business value. For example, a retail organization is using Crystal Enterprise to present their product catalog to their users. The reports are very useful and allow users to browse the catalog, drill in for more details on items, and so on. If the user wants to order something, he needs to navigate to another form to enter his order and he has to keep looking back to the catalog report to remember the part number he wants to order.

Using the event model of the Report Application Server this organization can, without changing their catalog report, enable the user to click on the item he wants right within the view of the catalog. This event captures the data that the user clicked on and will allow the Web developer to populate the order screen with this information with no user interaction. If the report also displayed inventory counts, the report could be updated as soon as the user finished their transaction.

RICH OBJECT MODEL

The Report Application Server provides a powerful object model that allows an organization to control any aspect of how a user performs an ad hoc query or formats it. In typical ad hoc tools the users are given the same tool and the organization deploying the tool has no say in how the user is able to perform their tasks.

With the Report Application Server and its object model, an organization can determine the best way to present ad hoc reporting capabilities to their user base. For example, an organization might decide to deploy an ad hoc tool that allows end users to determine what data elements they need to see but there is no facility to apply a filter. This is because the administrator of this organization established a filter for the users and has stored this in a hidden database. The application developer takes this value and applies it to the user's query programmatically, all without the user knowing that this is occurring.

THE CRYSTAL ENTERPRISE ARCHITECTURE IN ACTION

This section takes a look at how all the Crystal Enterprise services come together and which of the services are used when a user requests objects. Each scenario is based on the following situation: Over a corporate intranet site, a user is browsing a CSP page that connects him to a Crystal Enterprise system. The user has provided proper login credentials and is logged into Crystal Enterprise. He has been presented with a list of report objects that he has rights to access.

For this scenario to occur, a browser has connected to a Web server, and in turn the Web server passes the .CSP request to the Crystal Web connector. The Web connector then passes this request to the Web Component Server for processing. The .CSP is processed and in this scenario, the page asks the user for logon credentials and is returned to the user to complete. The credentials are submitted and passed to the Web Component Server. The Web Component Server now takes this information and attempts to log on to the APS using the security service. After the user is logged on to Crystal Enterprise, the APS is queried to present a list of folders and reports to the user. (The query is generated within the CSP page as well.) This scenario diagram can be seen in Figure 3.4.

PART

I

CH

3

Note

The numbered flow in Figures 3.4, 3.5, 3.6, and 3.7 represent the flow of information and requests to get a report processed and delivered to the end user. Dashed lines in the figures represent optional steps.

Figure 3.4
The login process for
a user validated by
Crystal Enterprise.

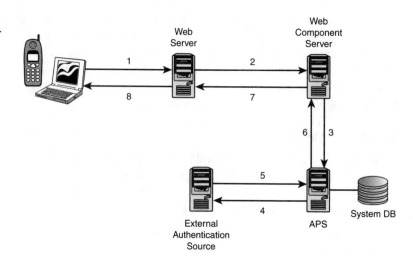

REQUESTING A CRYSTAL REPORT

The user in the preceding scenario has two methods of viewing a report.

The first method is to view an instance of a previously scheduled job. If an instance is chosen, the report contains cached data from when the job was run. When the request to view the report is received, the Web Component Server asks the Cache Server if the first page of this report is available in cache. If the first page is available, the Cache Server returns the page to the Web Component Server so it can be delivered to the report viewer. The report viewer then displays the report for the user. If the page is not in the cache, the request is forwarded onto the Page Server to generate the page.

As Figure 3.5 shows, when the Page Server receives the request, it loads the report from the output File Repository Server. After the report is loaded by the Page Server, it generates the page that has been requested and then passes it back to the Cache Server. The Cache Server sends the page onto the Web Component Server to be given to the report viewer.

The second method for viewing a report is to view the report itself, which is also known as on-demand viewing. If a user selects the report itself, she must first have the "view on demand" access level. When the report is requested it goes through the same process as shown in Figure 3.5; however, because the report does not have any cached data within the report like the instance has, the Cache Server passes the request directly onto the Page Server.

Figure 3.6 shows the extra steps required for on-demand viewing. The Page Server queries the input File Repository Server for the report and loads it. After it has the report loaded, the user will be asked to enter the database logon information and any parameters for the report to run. The Page Server then passes this information to the Crystal Reports engine through the report plug-in. The Crystal Reports engine connects to the database and queries for the necessary data. After the data has been returned to the report engine, the report is recalculated and page information is determined. The Page Server now generates the first page of this report and sends it to the Cache Server, which in turn passes it to the Web Component Server and then to the report viewers.

Figure 3.5
The report-loading process in Crystal Enterprise.

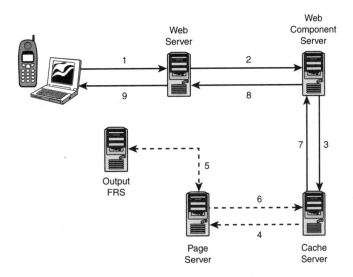

Figure 3.6
The report loading process for on-demand viewing.

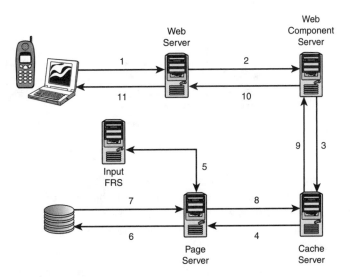

In both scenarios of viewing a Crystal Report, if a processing extension is being used with this report, the cache is then not sharable. The Cache Server will pass the request directly to the Page Server. The Page Server will load the report from the File Repository Server. During the time that the report is being loaded, the processing extension is engaged to determine the proper row-level restrictions that need to be applied to the cached data within the report. The cached data is then filtered and the page is generated with information that is viewable by that user only.

SCHEDULING A CRYSTAL REPORT

When a report is scheduled, Crystal Enterprise requires the appropriate information so that the scheduling service knows what tasks are to be performed. Figure 3.7 depicts a typical scenario where an end user schedules a report with the appropriate criteria set. This information is passed to the Web Component Server, which in turn forwards the information to be stored in the APS. The schedule is set to run at a particular point in the future. When the schedule time occurs, the APS loads the information from the repository and submits the request to a Job Server. The Job Server asks the input File Repository Server for the report and then loads it into the report Job Server plug-in.

Figure 3.7
The process for scheduling reports.

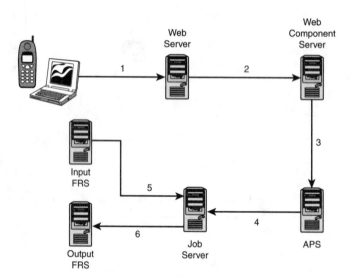

With the report loaded, the Job Server applies any of the parameters set when the user scheduled the report earlier. These parameters might be filters that affect the overall data query. If a processing extension is in use, the report would be further manipulated. After the processing extension is finished with the report, the Job Server connects to the database and completes the processing of the report.

When the job has completed, the Job Server checks two remaining pieces of information the user would have set when scheduling the report; the format in which the report is to be delivered and where it will be delivered. At this stage, the Job Server would output the report into a supported Crystal Enterprise format, including Crystal Reports, Microsoft Word, Excel, Adobe Acrobat, rich text format, or text.

> **Note**   The default output format for all Crystal Enterprise servers is Crystal Reports.

Next, the Job Server needs to distribute the report to the desired location. As previously mentioned, these locations can be a location on disk, an FTP server, or an e-mail address, or remain in the managed Crystal Enterprise environment by distributing it to the output File Repository Server as a report instance object. Regardless of where the user decides to distribute the object, a copy is always stored in the output File Repository Server so that it can be shared between users.

REQUESTING A CRYSTAL ANALYSIS PROFESSIONAL REPORT

If an organization is using Crystal Analysis Professional, it's important to note that report viewing is handled differently from a Crystal Report. Requesting a Crystal Analysis Professional report starts by the user clicking on a link to the report in a Web browser.

The request is delivered to the Web Component Server, and it asks the APS for the object that was asked for. The object is returned to the Web Component Server and then is loaded by the Crystal Analysis Professional engine. The reports created in Crystal Analysis Professional are dynamic queries to a multidimensional cube of data—the CA engine must connect to the cube referenced in the report.

After a connection to the cube is made, data is retrieved and populated into the .CAR file, which is an XML document. This XML document is transformed through a style sheet into DHTML and delivered as the first view of the report. This information is sent from the Web Component Server to the Web browser along with the Crystal Analysis Professional DHTML viewer. The viewer will make additional requests for data from the cube via the Web Component Server as it is needed to populate the view of the report.

PART

I

CH

3

TAKING ADVANTAGE OF THE CRYSTAL ENTERPRISE DISTRIBUTED ARCHITECTURE

This section of the chapter discusses how the Crystal Enterprise Framework and all the services that it provides are most effectively deployed. As mentioned earlier, Crystal Enterprise is designed as an n-tier distributed system for information delivery. This distributed nature gives an organization a great deal of flexibility in how it might want to deploy Crystal Enterprise in its environments. How Crystal Enterprise is deployed will depend on the way in which the system is expected to be used, how many users are expected to be active in the system at any given time, and how many objects are expected to be processed at any given time.

SCALING UP

The term *scaling up* means that a software product is able to take full advantage of the physical hardware resources it has access to and ultimately increase in scalability as the hardware increases. Crystal Enterprise was designed from its inception to effectively scale up.

All the Crystal Enterprise 8.5 servers are multithreaded components that are able to scale based on physical hardware resources. They have been designed to operate on multiprocessor machines efficiently. When a system is under high load, even being multithreaded isn't enough. If the load on the servers is high enough, I/O might start to become the limiting factor. Crystal Enterprise deals with this by allowing an organization to configure multiple instances of a server on the same physical piece of hardware. This makes it possible for additional servers to share in the load and remove any I/O bottlenecks. A benefit in doing this is that automatic load balancing kicks in, making the system that much more efficient.

SCALING OUT

Building on the scalability in Crystal Enterprise for scaling up, the capability to distribute report processing loads to multiple physical machines is also available. This is beneficial in many ways.

As an example, an organization can scale its systems to very large levels by adding physical servers to the environment when needed. In the license management service portion of this chapter, it was described how the license chosen would be a determining factor when deploying Crystal Enterprise. If an organization chooses to license Crystal Enterprise using named or concurrent access licenses, additional hardware resources can be added to the environment as needed without purchasing additional Crystal Enterprise user licenses. If processor licenses are initially purchased, new processor licenses must be purchased when the additional hardware is added. This is why it's important to understand the expected usage of the system as well as project the future growth of the system so that the appropriate license model is chosen.

The second benefit is the capability to assign tasks to certain computers. For example, the Job Server, Page Server, and File Repository Server could be grouped together on the same physical computer. The Page Server and Job Server both connect to databases and both communicate with the File Repository Server. Locating them on the same computer makes sense in many situations.

The next benefit of scaling out with Crystal Enterprise is fault-tolerance. Crystal Enterprise provides the capability not only to have multiple instances of the same service running on the same computer, but also allows for those servers to be spread across multiple machines. Crystal Enterprise has automatic fail over support in each of its servers to complement the automatic load-balancing capabilities. This means that if a server goes offline for any reason, other servers registered to the Crystal Enterprise Framework will automatically pick up the workload without user interruption.

SCALING ACROSS PLATFORM BOUNDARIES

Some deployments of Crystal Enterprise might require a distributed system on different operating systems. Crystal Enterprise makes it possible for an organization to deploy Crystal Enterprise across any of its supported operating system platforms. This provides a way for organizations to decide what deployment scenario best fits their needs, given the hardware available to them. A key benefit to being able to do this is that organizations might want to seamlessly mix functionality available from different operating systems. For example, an organization might require that reports process on Unix but still have the users authenticated using Windows NT accounts.

There might be situations in which it's necessary to have certain servers running on one operating system and the rest of the system running on another. For example, an organization might have the majority of Crystal Enterprise operating on Unix, but want to seamlessly integrate the SQL Server Analysis cubes being used in the Crystal Analysis Professional reports created by the finance department. These reports can easily be added to the Crystal Enterprise system running on Unix, as long as a Web Component Server is running on Windows so that the Crystal Analysis Professional reports have access to SQL Server Analysis Services.

EXTENDING CRYSTAL ENTERPRISE

An important aspect of information delivery is how the information is presented to the user community. Crystal Enterprise enables organizations to easily customize how information is presented to end users by providing a rich object model for Web application developers to tightly integrate Crystal Enterprise into their Web applications. Developers can present content to end users, as well as provide Web-based administration applications to their organization, using the Crystal Enterprise SDK. Future chapters, such as Chapter 13 and Chapter 15, "Integrating Crystal Enterprise with Third-Party Portals," detail the flexibility of Crystal Enterprise and how easily it can be integrated into any environment.

SUMMARY

This chapter provided an overview of how the Crystal Enterprise Framework and all the servers that register to it work. It provides a solid foundation for the chapters that follow. Understanding the modular nature of Crystal Enterprise is important for any aspect of using the system. By knowing the services that each server provides, designing the system for deployment is straightforward. The administrator can make wise decisions on where to place servers in the overall organization's IT infrastructure. The administrator can see how Crystal Enterprise can easily leverage existing components in the organization, such as operating system platforms like Windows NT/2000 or Solaris, database management systems such as SQL Server, Oracle, or DB2 as well as authentication systems like OS authentication or LDAP servers.

Understanding the architecture is also important to the Web application developer. Knowing how the SDK interacts with each of the plug-ins makes it easy for the developer to modularize his code because he can interact with each type of object in a distinct manner.

Each of the chapters that follow go into a great deal of detail on their topic but also require you to understand the architecture. By finishing this chapter, the architecture of Crystal Enterprise should be clear and make it much easier to understand the concepts introduced in later chapters.

GETTING STARTED WITH CRYSTAL ENTERPRISE

CHAPTER 4

INSTALLING CRYSTAL ENTERPRISE 8.5

In this chapter

Building on the comprehensive overview of the Crystal Enterprise system architecture in Chapter 3, "Exploring the System Architecture," this chapter describes how to install Crystal Enterprise 8.5 on Windows NT/2000.

Topics covered in this chapter include installation system requirements and supported platforms, preinstallation configuration activities, procedures concerning various installation scenarios, using the Crystal Configuration Manager to manage Crystal Enterprise servers/services, and expanding or scaling an installation.

Available configuration tools and scaling your installation are discussed as well, along with an overview of the upgrade process from Crystal Enterprise 8 to 8.5 and troubleshooting tips to get you on your way.

Please see Appendix A, "Running Crystal Enterprise on Sun Solaris," for information on installing Crystal Enterprise 8.5 for Sun Solaris.

PREPARING A WINDOWS NT/2000 SERVER FOR INSTALLING CRYSTAL ENTERPRISE

Taking time to ensure proper configuration of a Windows 2000 server before Crystal Enterprise is installed will go a long way toward ensuring proper function and expected behavior. The following list introduces items to inspect and prepare before installation:

- Preparing a server to host the APS system database
- Confirm availability of a Web server
- Using Windows administrator privileges
- Configuring the Windows Temp directory
- Installation path considerations
- Understanding network protocol requirements
- Client connectivity
- ODBC configuration/database client software
- Virtual memory

Following this section on your system preparation check, you will learn how to perform different types of Crystal Enterprise installations.

Note

The term *Server* can also be used in this text to denote a Windows Service. A Crystal Enterprise Server is installed as a Windows Service, and the terms may be used interchangeably: Job Server or Job Server Service.

PREPARING A SERVER TO HOST THE APS DATABASE

As discussed in Chapter 3, the Automated Process Scheduler, or APS, requires its own relational database to store object and user metadata. Also recall from Chapter 3 that the APS System Database can be hosted in several database platforms; however, the connection to the system database from Crystal Enterprise is always through ODBC.

Microsoft SQL Server 7.0 is the default database choice for the installation. If Microsoft SQL Server 6.5 is installed on the intended APS server, it is recommended that SQL Server 6.5 be upgraded to SQL 7 or 2000. This can be migrated to another supported database server.

CONFIRM WEB SERVER AVAILABILITY

A Crystal Enterprise–compatible Web server must be installed on the planned Crystal Enterprise server or be available to the Crystal Enterprise server on the local area network before beginning the Crystal Enterprise installation.

> **Note**
>
> Installing Crystal Enterprise 8.5 within a firewall environment is covered later in the chapter in the section titled "Installing Crystal Enterprise Components in a Multiple Firewall Configuration." Also refer to Chapter 12, "Deploying Crystal Enterprise in a Complex Network Environment," for an in-depth review of Crystal Enterprise and firewalls.

PART

II

CH

4

USING WINDOWS ADMINISTRATOR PRIVILEGES

To install Crystal Enterprise 8.5, log on to the Windows 2000 Server as a local administrator or an account that belongs to the local administrator's group for the server; otherwise, the installation will not proceed.

CONFIGURING THE WINDOWS TEMP DIRECTORY

The TEMP system environment variable is a key part to the installation of Crystal Enterprise—or to the installation of any application, for that matter. When an installation package is opened, the files contained within that compressed package are expanded into the TEMP directory on the local server. If a TEMP system environmental variable is defined incorrectly, the installation can fail.

There are two ways to ensure that the TEMP directory is set up correctly:

- Go to the Control Panel, System Control Panel, and choose the Environment tab. Scroll down in the System Variables section and look for TEMP and TMP. They should both be defined and point to a valid directory. (In Windows 2000, in the System Control Panel, go to the Advanced Tab and click the Environment Variables button in the center section.)

- Go to a command prompt, type **SET**, and then press Enter. TEMP and TMP should appear in the display. Ensure that they are pointing to a valid directory.

If a variable is changed, the System Control Panel must be used. After changing it, a reboot is necessary. This TEMP directory process is a critical step not only for installation, but also for proper operation of the Windows server(s).

INSTALLATION PATH CONSIDERATIONS

The directories and files under the system drive C:\Program Files\Seagate Software or C:\Program Files\Crystal Decisions are shared components for all Crystal Decisions products. It's not possible to specify where the shared components will be placed. They will always be installed on the system drive (which is usually the C partition).

> **Note**
>
> Because the company name was changed from Seagate Software to Crystal Decisions, Crystal Enterprise 8.5 is installed under the Crystal Decisions folder in Program Files. Prior versions of software from Crystal Decisions, such as Crystal Enterprise 8.0 and Crystal Reports 8.5, were installed in the Seagate Software subdirectory in the Program Files folder. Because Crystal Reports 8.5 is the most current release of Crystal Reports at the time of publishing this book, Crystal components will obviously be found in two places under the Program Files folder: Seagate Software and Crystal Decisions.

It is suggested that at least 200MB of free disk space on the system drive be available after the installation of Crystal Enterprise, but more is highly recommended.

UNDERSTANDING NETWORK PROTOCOL REQUIREMENTS

To communicate using the Crystal eBusiness Framework, TCP/IP must be installed. Because TCP/IP Name Resolution is required to use a server as a Web server, problems with TCP/IP are usually found when installing and troubleshooting the Web server. The following is a pair of tests to conduct:

- Launch a Web browser and type the URL **http://yourservername**—the default Web page should appear.
- Go to a command prompt and ping the server name: **ping yourservername**.

CLIENT CONNECTIVITY

All Web desktop clients must be able to access the corporate Web servers used with Crystal Enterprise. Crystal Enterprise does not replace a Web server, such as Microsoft Internet Information Server, but rather compliments it. As long as users can access the Web servers linked to Crystal Enterprise, accessing reports and information from within Crystal Enterprise shouldn't be an issue.

ODBC CONFIGURATION/DATABASE CLIENT SOFTWARE

Ensure the ODBC configuration or database client software for all reports within Crystal Enterprise is properly installed on the physical server that is the destination for the Page and Job Servers. For further reference on how to set up ODBC, refer to Chapter 8, "Creating Content with Crystal Reports."

VIRTUAL MEMORY

The recommended virtual memory size for Windows is equivalent to 1.5 times the amount of physical memory or RAM installed on the system. Increasing the amount of RAM will assist with reduced use of paging files. For mission-critical servers, a paging file no smaller than the RAM size should be placed on the same partition as the operating system.

UNDERSTANDING CRYSTAL ENTERPRISE SYSTEM REQUIREMENTS

The following list represents the baseline system requirements for Crystal Enterprise. Note that Crystal Decisions provides updates to its technology on a regular basis, so this list might have changed. Refer to the Crystal Decisions Web site for a definitive list of support Crystal Enterprise–related technologies.

- Internet Explorer or Netscape Navigator
- 256MB RAM or greater
- 700MB free disk space
- Minimum of one network interface card and one or more IP address
- Supported Web server software available

PART

II

CH

4

WINDOWS OPERATING SYSTEMS SUPPORTED BY CRYSTAL ENTERPRISE

The following list represents the supported Windows technologies for Crystal Enterprise.

Crystal Enterprise Server Components

- Windows 2000 Server SP2
- Windows NT4 Server SP6a

Crystal Enterprise Client Components

- Windows 2000 Server SP2
- Windows 2000 Workstation SP2
- Windows NT4 Server SP6a
- Windows NT4 Workstation SP6a
- Windows 98 SE
- Windows ME

WEB BROWSERS SUPPORTED BY CRYSTAL ENTERPRISE

Crystal Enterprise supports primarily Microsoft Internet Explorer and Netscape, based on market adoption of these technologies.

- Internet Explorer 5.01 SP2 to 6
- Netscape 4.78 to 6.1

Note

When using Crystal Analysis Pro with Crystal Enterprise, refer to the release notes for specific browser version support.

WEB SERVERS SUPPORTED BY CRYSTAL ENTERPRISE

The following is a list of supported Web servers:

- Microsoft IIS 5.0 and 5.0 (ISAPI and CGI on Windows)
- iPlanet Web Server Enterprise Edition 6.0 (NSAPI and CGI, on Windows)
- iPlanet Web Server Enterprise Edition 4.1 SP8 (NSAPI and CGI, on Windows)

APS DATABASE PLATFORMS SUPPORTED BY CRYSTAL ENTERPRISE

The APS database is not restricted to a Windows-based RDBMS. It can reside in almost any supported database software for either Windows or Unix platforms.

Supported Windows-Based Databases for the APS

- Microsoft SQL Server 2000 SP1 (ODBC)
- Microsoft SQL Server 7 SP3 (ODBC)
- Microsoft MSDE (ODBC)
- Oracle 8i (8.1.7) (native)
- Oracle 8.0.6 (native)
- DB2 UDB 7.2 (native)
- Sybase Adaptive Server 12.5 (ODBC)
- Informix Dynamic Server 2000 v 9.21 (ODBC)

SUPPORTED LDAP SERVERS FOR CRYSTAL ENTERPRISE

It's important to note that these are the "out-of-the-box" LDAP directory servers that Crystal Enterprise supports. Other directory servers can be connected to via LDAP and custom mapped into Crystal Enterprise.

- iPlanet Directory Server 5.0
- iPlanet Directory Server 4.13
- Novell NDS eDirectory 8.5.1
- Lotus Domino 5.0.8
- IBM SecureWay Directory 3.2.1

Supported Firewalls for Crystal Enterprise

The following are the firewalls that Crystal Enterprise supports to protect your environment:

- Checkpoint Firewall-1 4.1
- Microsoft ISA Server
- NEC eBorder 1.2

Types of Crystal Enterprise Installations

As with many other types of software applications, either all or some components of the software can be installed at any given time. For a fully functioning Crystal Enterprise system, almost all server components must be installed, but there is substantial flexibility in the configuration of each component. The word "almost" is used here, because components such as the Events Server don't necessarily need to be installed or active unless external events are going to be used with Crystal Enterprise.

This section reviews how to perform the following:

- **A standalone Crystal Enterprise installation**—All Crystal Enterprise Servers and Client Components are installed on one Web server.
- **A custom Crystal Enterprise installation**—The installation process for installing individual components of the application on a machine.
- **Expanding or scaling your installation**—How to scale an existing Crystal Enterprise installation to support greater system usability requirements.

As a review of Crystal Enterprise utilities from Chapter 2 and the architecture from Chapter 3, a brief description of each of the Crystal Enterprise servers (installed as Windows services) and client utilities are provided in Tables 4.1 and 4.2.

Part
II

Ch
4

TABLE 4.1   SERVER COMPONENTS

Server Components (Installed as Windows Services)	Description	Service Dependencies
Crystal APS	Provides scheduling, security, and system management services.	Event Log MSSQL Server NT LM Security Support Provider Remote Procedure Call (RPC)

TABLE 4.1   CONTINUED

Server Components (Installed as Windows Services)	Description	Service Dependencies
Crystal Cache Server	Stores report pages frequently requested by report viewers.	Event Log NT LM Security Support Provider Remote Procedure Call (RPC)
Crystal Event Server	Monitors file, schedule, and custom events.	Event Log NT LM Security Support Provider Remote Procedure Call (RPC)
Crystal Input File Repository Server	Provides object storage and management services for report objects added to Crystal Enterprise (reports with no saved data).	Event Log NT LM Security Support Provider Remote Procedure Call (RPC)
Crystal Output File Repository Server	Provides object storage and management services for report objects added to Crystal Enterprise (reports with saved data such as report instances).	Event Log NT LM Security Support Provider Remote Procedure Call (RPC)
Crystal Page Server	Generates report pages requested by report viewers.	Event Log NT LM Security Support Provider Remote Procedure Call (RPC)
Crystal Report Job Server	Handles off-loaded (scheduled) processing of reports.	Event Log NT LM Security Support Provider Remote Procedure Call (RPC)

TABLE 4.1   CONTINUED

Server Components (Installed as Windows Services)	Description	Service Dependencies
Crystal Web Component Server (WCS)	Provides a single access point for all Web-based requests to the Crystal eBusiness Framework.	Event Log NT LM Security Support Provider Remote Procedure Call (RPC)
Web connector	Installed on Web Server and connects to WCSs installed.	Not installed as a service

TABLE 4.2   CLIENT COMPONENTS

Client Components	Description
Crystal Configuration Manager	A server-management tool that enables you to configure each of your Crystal Enterprise server components.
Crystal Publishing Wizard	A locally installed Windows application that enables both administrators and end users to add reports to Crystal Enterprise.
Crystal Import Wizard	A locally installed Windows application that guides administrators through the process of importing users, groups, reports, and folders from an existing Seagate Info or Crystal Enterprise implementation to Crystal Enterprise.
Crystal Web Wizard	Creates the structure and key components of a Crystal Enterprise Web-based application.

PART

II

CH

4

STANDALONE/SINGLE SERVER INSTALLATION

This section explains how to perform an installation where all Crystal Enterprise server and client components are installed on one server. Before you begin, a brief explanation of the APS and its database is provided.

During the installation, if Microsoft SQL Server 7 or 2000 is installed, Crystal Enterprise will attempt to log on to the SQL Server using the username sa and a blank password. If the installation is unable to log on using this logon combination, a dialog box will appear prompting the user to enter another logon username and password combination.

If no SQL Server or MSDE database is found, Microsoft's MSDE will be installed—a five-user license of SQL Server. This is what Crystal Enterprise will use for the APS system database, which is why the DSN will use the SQL Server driver.

Sometimes, Access becomes the system database. For example, if SQL Server 6.5 is installed, the Crystal Enterprise installation won't upgrade that server to MSDE, the equivalent of SQL Server 7. Instead, it will create the system database as an Access database. The installation version checks the SQL Server that is installed and knows whether or not to install MSDE and which database type (SQL or Access) is needed for the system database.

To continue with a description of the setup, the installation of Crystal Enterprise is very simple and straightforward. The installation options are minimized to a few questions and use the Windows Installer interface, which is common to several software applications, not just Crystal Decisions products.

For most standalone installations of Crystal Enterprise, the default setup options can successfully be left as-is.

DEFAULT STANDALONE CRYSTAL ENTERPRISE INSTALLATIONS

The following installation will use all the default options. Please follow the numbered list in sequence to complete the steps for the installation procedure.

1. Unless Autoplay is enabled for the server CD-ROM drive, run setup.exe from the win32 directory of the product distribution CD.

Note

When beginning the installation, the Microsoft Windows Installer might need to be installed or upgraded on the local server. If so, the Installation Wizard performs the necessary modifications and notifies you when finished.

If this is necessary, click Yes to restart the server and resume the installation automatically.

2. Proceed through the Setup program dialog boxes and follow the instructions until you reach the Installation Type dialog box.
3. Enter the appropriate Name, Organization, and the Product ID code, as shown in Figure 4.1.
4. Click Next to proceed to the installation type screen shown in Figure 4.2.
5. Select New, and then click Next to proceed to Figure 4.3.
6. In the Start Installation dialog box, click Next. The installation of files begins immediately.

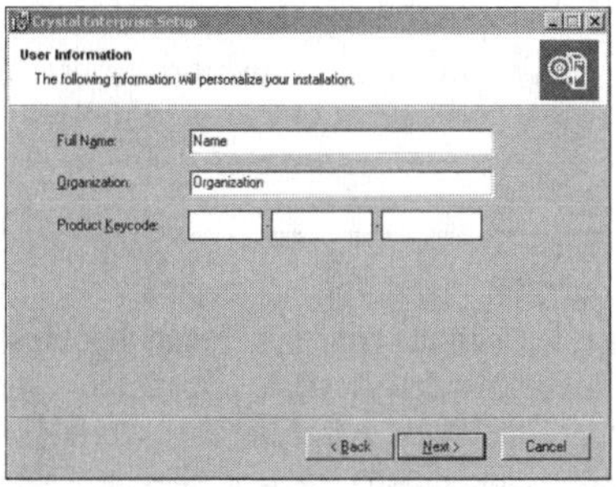

Figure 4.1
Crystal Enterprise
Setup User
Information screen.

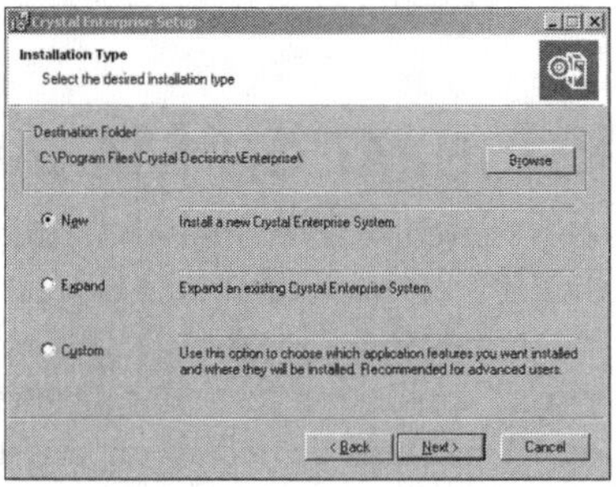

Figure 4.2
Crystal Enterprise
Installation Type
screen.

Figure 4.3
Crystal Enterprise
Start Installation
screen.

Note

Each of the servers will install as services and log on to Windows using a local system account by default. These settings can be changed later using either Windows Services or the Crystal Configuration Manager covered later in this chapter, or in more detail in Chapter 10, "Administering and Configuring Crystal Enterprise."

7. Click Next. The installation scans to see whether there are any programs running that might interfere with the installation. Some applications might need to be shut down during installation of Crystal Enterprise.

8. After clearing this hurdle, a dialog box appears that displays information about the installation progress. The lower-left corner contains the option to Launch Crystal Publishing Wizard. Uncheck this check box, and then click Finish.

The Crystal Publishing Wizard can be launched from the Crystal Enterprise program group at a later time and is covered further in Chapter 7, "Publishing Content with Crystal Enterprise."

Note

Intermittently, the Windows Installer dialog box might appear during installation of Crystal Enterprise. This is because the WISE application that Crystal Decisions uses for installation makes calls to the Windows Installer program to register which files are being installed and where. The Windows Installer keeps track of all installed programs and ensures that one application doesn't overwrite files installed by another application.

USING THE CRYSTAL CONFIGURATION MANAGER

The Crystal Configuration Manager is reviewed at several points in this book. This is a brief preview of the functionality of the Crystal Configuration Manager to provide a minimal understanding of how its functions are necessary for some server installation tasks. The Crystal Configuration Manager is a Win32 application that allows viewing and modification of server settings in Crystal Enterprise. It's installed by default on any server where any Crystal Enterprise server is installed.

Windows Services can be used to manage some of the configuration options for each Crystal Enterprise server; however, more detailed options are available only within the Configuration Manager, such as migrating the APS system database to a new RDBMS. Additionally, the Web Connector is configurable only through the Crystal Configuration Manager.

The Crystal Configuration Manager allows you to start, stop, configure, restart services, component options, as well as add and manage other servers in a Crystal Enterprise deployment.

If a Crystal Enterprise server is running, a green arrow icon next to the server name is always displayed. Stopped server services have a red arrow.

To start and stop Crystal Enterprise servers using the CCM (see Figure 4.4), implement the following steps:

1. Choose Start, Programs, Crystal Enterprise, Crystal Configuration Manager.
2. Using the VCR-style controls in the button bar, click the Stop button to stop the server.
3. Click the Start button to start the server.
4. Within a moment, the CCM will refresh its server listing to show the updated server list status.

Figure 4.4
Crystal Configuration
Manager.

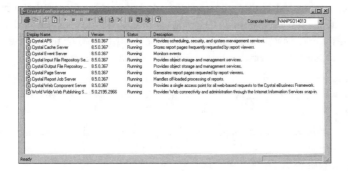

Most importantly, the CCM also allows configuration of Crystal Enterprise remotely through a corporate network. By entering or choosing another server from the top-right drop-down list where the server name appears, the CCM can connect to other Crystal Enterprise servers and control services.

For further information on other functionality using the CCM to manage servers, refer to Chapters 5 and 10.

CUSTOM CRYSTAL ENTERPRISE 8.5 INSTALLATION

As with a new installation of Crystal Enterprise, the same basic hardware and platform requirements apply. Please refer to the "Understanding Crystal Enterprise System Requirements" section in this chapter for further information on these topics.

To perform a Custom installation of Crystal Enterprise, the beginning screen dialogues, such as the license agreement and entering the user's full name, are the same.

Follow these steps to complete the procedure:

1. When the Installation Type Screen appears, choose Custom.

2. Select Custom and click Next, as shown in Figure 4.5.

Figure 4.5
Crystal Enterprise
Select Features
screen.

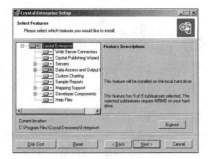

PART

II

CH

4

3. By default, several of these boxes are shaded gray. This means that a portion of the product will not be installed. Clicking on one of the boxes yields a dialog box that enables you to install the feature on the local hard drive or install the entire feature on the local hard drive, or the entire feature will be unavailable.

4. For the purpose of this chapter's instruction, ensure that all the options are installed by choosing Entire Feature Will Be Installed on Local Hard Drive for all options on all servers.

5. The next dialog box asks whether APS clustering should be enabled. For the purpose of this exercise, choose No. These settings can be adjusted later using the Crystal Configuration Manager.

Note

Refer to Chapter 3 for information on the benefits of APS clustering. Chapter 10 covers the process of enabling APS clustering.

6. Click Next.

7. A dialog will appear asking permission to proceed with the installation. Click Next.

8. If the Crystal Enterprise installation is repeated, which includes the APS, and a previous APS database is detected, the screen in Figure 4.6 will appear.

Figure 4.6
Current SQL
/Microsoft Windows
configuration.

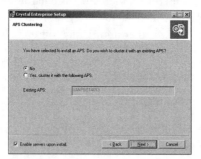

9. The APS database can be overwritten with a new, empty database, or the installation can be aborted. Click Next to begin the custom installation.

10. The remaining dialog boxes and screens notifying of successful installation completion will appear.

As with the standard installation covered earlier in this chapter from this final screen, uncheck the Launch Crystal Publishing Wizard option to prevent this program from running following completion of the installation. This application can be run at a later time.

EXPANDING AN EXISTING CRYSTAL ENTERPRISE INSTALLATION

This section describes planning and scaling an existing Crystal Enterprise installation using various scenarios where some server components are installed on different physical servers or the same type of server component is installed more than once on the same server. This and other scaling strategies are discussed later in this section.

Before looking at scaling your deployment, an introduction to using the Crystal Configuration Manager to add and remove server services is provided.

Note

Each machine where Crystal Enterprise components are installed must meet the basic hardware requirements as in a full standalone installation.

To add new Crystal Enterprise server components on the same or other physical servers (which also increases the hardware available to Crystal Enterprise), relaunch the Setup program select the Expand option in the Installation Type screen. You also can add new Crystal Enterprise server components by using the Add/Remove Server option in the Crystal Configuration Manager.

PART

II

CH

4

Note

When installing Crystal Enterprise components on multiple physical servers, ensure that each target server is able to communicate over TCP/IP with the server that's running as the Crystal Enterprise APS. Additionally, the Web Server, such as Microsoft IIS, must be able to communicate with the physical server that's running the Crystal Enterprise Web Component Server (WCS) service. This communication is enabled via the Crystal Enterprise Web connector, which must be installed directly on the Web server.

Note

If Crystal Analysis Professional is being used, the Crystal Analysis Professional Server plug-in must be installed on the Web server where the Crystal Enterprise Web connector resides.

BASIC SCALING CONSIDERATIONS FOR CRYSTAL ENTERPRISE

A few considerations should be taken into account before adding new servers, physical or logical, to a Crystal Enterprise deployment.

THE APS AND SYSTEM PERFORMANCE

Adding Page or Job Servers to Crystal Enterprise will certainly increase the system processing horsepower and improve performance. Adding report processing servers alone is not necessarily the only system component to be considered when scaling up or out.

As each report or object is added to Crystal Enterprise, this requires a record to be kept of its status and location, thus placing additional load on the APS. Performance of Crystal Enterprise can be improved by scaling the APS through native APS clustering with Crystal Enterprise.

Besides simply maintaining a shared record of each object, the APS also replies to requests to log on to Crystal Enterprise, maintaining a list of available servers and scheduling objects. Adding other APS servers on dedicated physical servers will efficiently share the tasks and maintenance of the Crystal Enterprise system.

GENERAL REPORTING CONSIDERATIONS

When considering whether to allow Crystal Enterprise users to view reports either On-Demand or as scheduled Report Instances, bandwidth traffic and hardware resources are of primary concern, as well as a number of other areas.

The following topics will help you better understand and optimize your Crystal Enterprise deployment for its best performance.

ON-DEMAND REPORTS

Allowing users to view On-Demand reports invokes a chain of events, starting with the user's request to view a report. Following this request, the APS may query several servers, including the Input File Repository Server (to access the report template), the Page Server (to connect to the corporate database and produce each page of the report), the Cache Server (to hold viewed report pages), and so on. Each On-Demand report is run as if every user were refreshing the report from within Crystal Enterprise. The result can be increased processing efforts by the corporate database and the Crystal Enterprise servers, as well as increased bandwidth traffic.

If the deployment plans for Crystal Enterprise call for allowing a large number of users to view On-Demand reports, consider adding multiple instances of Page Servers on the same physical server or other physical servers. As with other servers, such as the Job Server (for processing scheduled reports, explained in the following section), ensure that adequate network bandwidth is available to allow the server to connect to the corporate database to retrieve the data for the report. What is "adequate" bandwidth is challenging to define; it's really only determined through rigorous testing of report processing times in Crystal Enterprise. As well, it is suggested that the Page and Job Servers be installed on a separate physical server from the corporate database. It really doesn't make sense to have the Page and Job Servers contending for CPU cycles with the very database they are querying.

Report Instances

Recall from earlier chapters that report instances are Crystal Report files, stored in Crystal Enterprise with saved data, that have been scheduled by a user. Allowing users to view only report instances (reports with saved data) will minimize processing time, hardware, and bandwidth requirements. Scheduling a report either once or on a recurring basis by invoking the Job Server will create a report instance. From that point forward, users viewing an instance will not invoke Crystal Enterprise to repeatedly connect to the corporate database to retrieve new data.

In addition to the benefit of preserving system resources, more restrictive security permissions may be given to the users or groups viewing the reports when you use report instances.

➔ **See** Chapter 10 for more information on security settings related to report objects.

Besides adding Job Servers, the Event Server can be used to create dependencies, for example, creating an event dependency to test for a database update or replication or to notify one report that the next report is ready for processing. Chapter 3 reviews the Event Server in detail.

Optimizing Crystal Reports for Web Delivery

There are many considerations in creating a Crystal Report for deployment on the Web in Crystal Enterprise. For more information on creating reports and design considerations for Crystal Enterprise, see Chapter 8.

Web Server Considerations

Because Crystal Enterprise is a Web-based application, high priority must be given to monitoring and improving HTTP response speeds to serve the application and its users.

Some recommended considerations are increasing available network bandwidth between the Crystal Enterprise WCS and the Web server, improving Web server hardware, or creating a *Web farm* of multiple Web servers. Each of these Web servers can be made available to Crystal Enterprise by installing a Web connector on each of the Web servers that will be used by the application. As well, two or more Web Component Servers can take advantage of the dynamic load balancing built into the Web Connector, which is installed on a Web server to link it to Crystal Enterprise. As an added benefit, the Web Connector will distribute requests evenly for load balancing among multiple Web Component Servers.

Overall System Maintenance and Monitoring for Scaling

This section provides areas to monitor on your physical servers using Windows Performance Monitor and some examples of the impact on Crystal Enterprise server configuration and performance.

Although the Crystal Management Console can be used to monitor some system statistics related to Crystal Enterprise performance, this section concentrates on the operating system for this purpose.

This section also gives several Crystal Enterprise server configuration scenarios. The following sections provide instructions on adding and deleting servers.

PHYSICAL SERVERS

As with any other service or component in Windows, monitoring system resources is recommended on all machines where Crystal Enterprise Servers are installed.

Some things to look for include the following:

- **Processor(s)**—The % Processor Time counter indicating high processor time can signal that the server is handling heavy workloads or working hard to keep up with demands. In other words, threads of a process require more processor cycles than are available. The Processor Queue Length counter can also be used to count the number of applications queued for that processor. To assist this situation, consider a few options:
  - Add further processors.
  - If you already have multiple processors, you may use the Set Affinity option to assign an application to a processor.

Crystal Enterprise scales effectively over multiple processors, consistently increasing throughput as processors are added to the system. As an example of when to look at processors, you may calculate the maximum number of processors needed for either the Job Server or Page Server functions and allocate that number of processors for report processing.

Installing a second instance of a Page or Job Server on the same machine, each with its own processor, will more effectively utilize processor usage.

Also consider increasing processors and splitting the Crystal Enterprise Servers over physical servers to maintain exclusive access to its own processor, memory, and so on.

- **Memory**—Easily the most serious of all potential deficiencies, a limited amount of memory can cause excessive paging using the hard disks. Monitoring both Physical Disk\Avg. Disk sec/Transfer and Memory\Pages/sec counters together will indicate whether paging is taking place with values exceeding 0. To increase the amount of memory, consider the following:
  - Add more memory
  - Create and/or increase the size of the paging file(s) on other fast hard disks

Although the APS is not typically a memory-intensive server, the increased process of scheduling your reports and the maintenance of reports, users, folders, and so on will use memory for each object loaded or unloaded from memory.

Because they are more memory-intensive servers, the Page and Job Servers also should be monitored when looking at increasing memory.

■ **Disk Space**—Monitoring disk space and activity is of critical importance to the overall health of your server and the optimal functioning of your applications. At a minimum, the following disk counters should be used on all physical servers:

- Disk Reads/sec and Disk Writes/sec
- Current DiskQueue Length
- % Disk Time
- Logical Disk\% Free Space

If any of these counters indicate that your disks are busy or lack sufficient space, consider doing the following:

- Upgrade the size or quantity of your disks
- Implement fault-tolerant strategies and create striped volumes over disks

Within Crystal Enterprise, more intensive disk use occurs when report files are expanded or compressed by the Page and Job Servers for processing. Also, the Input and Output File Repository Servers store all reports in Crystal Enterprise. By maintaining disk health and redundancy you are assured of keeping your reports safe.

Note

> Regarding the database in which you maintain the APS database, engage best practices in your maintenance and backup strategies as supplied by your database manufacturer.

■ **Network**—Network monitoring typically consists of measuring overall network traffic by capturing and measuring packets from the LAN and observing server resource use. Monitor the following network settings to ensure Crystal Enterprise has sufficient resources for network operations:

- Where it can be controlled, provide sufficient bandwidth to allow for optimal communication across the network.
- Monitor throughput at all Network layers to indicate performance.
- Enable maximize throughput for network applications in your LAN connections.

The maintenance and improvement of available bandwidth will improve the performance of this type of client/server or distributed application. Because the servers require bandwidth to communicate for each request, improving throughput will improve response and machine utilization times throughout your network.

CRYSTAL ENTERPRISE SERVERS

Besides physical server considerations, the number of Crystal Enterprise servers combined with the number of users and servers in your deployment provide the groundwork to plan the scale of your installation. Measure your peak and idle utilization hours, your user base, and both physical and Crystal Enterprise servers to calculate the best scaling scenario for your deployment.

Note

For more information about Crystal Enterprise sizing and scaling best practices and metrics, please contact Crystal Services at `http://www.crystaldecisions.com/services`.

The following list is a brief description of each of Crystal Enterprise's server components as they relate to system performance:

- **Page and Cache Servers**—Depending on your concurrent user base, because the Page and Cache Servers will work in tandem to service requests to view and temporarily store report pages, consider adding multiple Page and Cache Servers either on one or separate physical servers. Match the Maximum Simultaneous Processing Threads to the same values for both servers. At a minimum, there should be one Page Server per processor.

- **Job Server**—The Job Server runs as a process instead of as a thread. It is designed for "heavy lifting," or larger report jobs as opposed to speedy jobs, such as the Page Server. By default, the Job Server will process a maximum of five jobs. If your user base is most often going to run scheduled reports, it is advantageous to calculate your potential use and add multiple Job Servers or Job Servers that are scheduled to come online during times of heavy scheduled report processing. When calculating, take into account the length of time to process the report.

- **Web Component Server (WCS)**—The WCS is essentially an application server by both handling available threads for each user and each user request, as well as sessions for each concurrent user. As your user request base scales consider adding one Web Component Server per processor to your deployment. This is recommended because the Web Connectors allow the WCSs to load-balance if the WCSs are distributed in a Crystal Enterprise deployment.

- **Automated Scheduling Processor (APS)**—The APS has four primary duties:
  - Managing objects and security (reports, folders, instances, and so on)
  - Managing users and groups
  - Managing Crystal Enterprise servers
  - Managing scheduling (keeps a record in the APS database)

The addition of one APS per processor on physical servers is advised. Take advantage of clustering APSs for redundancy and to increase the number of concurrent users your deployment will support.

The ideal number of APSs for clustering in your deployment will be determined by several measurements, including number of concurrent users, scheduled jobs, user requests, and so on. Typically, it is recommended to have at least one extra APS in your deployment, in addition to a back-up that is installed and can be brought online if one member of the cluster drops to pick up the slack, Jack.

It's also recommended not to install the APS database on the same physical server as the APS server. The APSs in a cluster institute load-balancing, and the utilization of the database will interfere with measurements.

■ **Input and Output File Repository Servers (FRS)**—As mentioned earlier, both File Repository Servers are used to store reports, either as a template (Input FRS) or as a Report Instance (Output FRS). Because their primary duty is storage, they are akin to File Servers. It's beneficial to enable their physical servers to Maximize Throughput for File Sharing in their network settings.

Covered earlier in this section on Disk Space, the File Repository Server's main requirement is sufficient disk space to both exist and grow. Having at least one processor per File Repository Server and a suitable quantity of disk space is recommended. As when maintaining files on regular file servers, a disaster and recovery strategy is highly recommended to ensure that backups are performed often.

For a Crystal Decisions document on Disaster Recovery Planning for Crystal Enterprise, go to `http://support.crystaldecisions.com`.

■ **Event Server**—The Event Server polls for three different types of events before scheduling reports. These types include file, schedule, and custom-based events. Out of the three event types, the file event is the most intensive because it polls the server for the existence of a file over several seconds that can be specified. As the number of seconds lowers, the server will require more processing power and memory resources.

ADDING AND DELETING CRYSTAL ENTERPRISE SERVERS

Assuming that the end-user community that works with Crystal Enterprise increases in size, so too will the Crystal Enterprise system itself and the load placed upon it. This will undoubtedly require the addition of processors to existing Page or Job Servers (not something this book covers; that's a hardware issue) or the addition of a physical Page or Job Server.

The Crystal Enterprise system is designed to be fluid. As an example, an existing Crystal Enterprise implementation might have multiple physical single processor Page or Job Servers that could be migrated by a system administrator to a single, faster server with multiple processors.

Earlier, this chapter described how to use the Crystal Configuration Manager to start and stop Crystal Servers. This section shows how to add and delete servers from a Crystal Enterprise system.

ADDING A CRYSTAL ENTERPRISE SERVER

If a physical server has been added to the Crystal Enterprise architecture, or a second logical instance of a Crystal Enterprise server process needs to be added to a single physical server, the Crystal Configuration Manager must be used.

> **Note**
>
> Although the reason for adding a *physical* server to the Crystal Enterprise architecture provides obvious benefits, such as increased scalability and some level of redundancy, adding a second *logical* instance of a Crystal Enterprise service on the same physical server isn't as apparent. The reason is scalability. Adding multiple instances of a Crystal Enterprise service to the same physical server increases the scale-up potential of that physical server in terms of Crystal Enterprise jobs and tasks.

The Crystal Management Console, the Web-based administrative interface for Crystal Enterprise, only allows for enabling and disabling existing servers.

> **Note**
>
> To complete this procedure, log in as an Administrator of the local Windows NT/2000 server.

1. Start the Crystal Configuration Manager on the Crystal Enterprise server on which you want to install a new server.
2. On the toolbar, click the Add Server button. The Add Crystal Server Wizard displays its Welcome dialog box.
3. Click Next. The Server Type and Display Name Configuration dialog box appears, as shown in Figure 4.7.

Figure 4.7
Server Type and Display Name configuration.

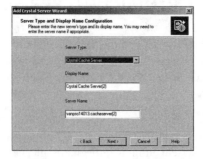

4. Click the Server Type list and select the kind of server you want to add. The drop-down list includes the following servers:
   - APS
   - Cache Server

- Input File Repository Server
- Output File Repository Server
- Page Server
- Report Job Server
- Web Component Server
- Event Server

5. Change the default Display Name field if you want a different name to appear in the list of servers in the CCM.

Note

The display name for each Crystal Enterprise server on the local physical Windows server must be unique.

6. Change the default Server Name field if required.

Note

This topic is important enough for a little reinforcement: Each server on the Crystal Enterprise system must have a unique name. The default naming convention for Crystal Enterprise servers is *HOSTNAME.servertype* (a number is appended if more than one server of the same type is on the same host server). This server name is displayed when managing Crystal Enterprise servers over the Web in the Crystal Management Console (CMC).

7. Click Next. The Set Configuration for This Server dialog box appears, as shown in Figure 4.8. The contents of this dialog box vary slightly, depending on the type of server that's being installed.

Figure 4.8
Set Configuration for
This Server.

PART

II

CH

4

> **Note**
> If port number options are displayed in this dialog box, do not modify them. Instead, change ports through each server's command-line controls. Chapters 10 and 12 discuss port configurations in some detail.

8. Type the name of the APS with which you want the server to communicate.

9. Click Next to accept any other default values, or modify them to suit your environment.

10. Confirm the summary information is correct; then click Finish. The new server appears in the list, but it's neither started nor enabled automatically.

11. Use the CCM (or the CMC) to start and then enable the new server when you want it to begin responding to Crystal Enterprise requests.

DELETING A CRYSTAL ENTERPRISE SERVER

If a server needs to be deleted, you can either use the Crystal Management Console or the Crystal Configuration Manager to accomplish this task. The following procedure uses the Crystal Configuration Manager to delete a server:

1. Start the Crystal Configuration Manager on the Crystal Enterprise server on which you want to delete a server.

2. On the toolbar, click the Delete button.

The server will disappear from the server list after the CCM has refreshed its server listing.

INSTALLING CRYSTAL ENTERPRISE COMPONENTS IN A MULTIPLE-FIREWALL CONFIGURATION

Crystal Enterprise can be configured to work with different types of firewalls that support packet filtering or Network Address Translation (NAT).

This section describes how to configure the Web connector in a multiple firewall environment, often referred to as a *Demilitarized Zone* (DMZ). This section assumes that the Web connector and the Web Component Server (WCS) reside on separate computers. If they reside on the same computer, their communication is uninterrupted by firewalls, and no additional configuration is required.

→ **See** Chapter 12 for an extensive review of Crystal Enterprise and firewalls.

In most cases, end users access information through a Web server running in a DMZ. Typically, the DMZ is set up between two firewalls; an outer firewall and an inner firewall.

The only Crystal Enterprise component required to provide direct service to external clients is the Web connector, which must be installed on a Web server, such as Netscape, Apache, or Microsoft Internet Information Server.

When a client makes a request to the Web connector, the Web connector makes a TCP/IP request to the WCS on a specific port (the default port is 6401). The most logical and secure way to position the Web server and the Web connector is to place them in the DMZ. All the other Crystal Enterprise components can then be placed on the internal network.

CONFIGURING THE WEB CONNECTOR

The following procedure explains how to configure the Web connector to send and receive on specific ports:

1. Start the Crystal Configuration Manager.

2. Stop the World Wide Web Publishing Service.

3. On the toolbar, click the Configure Web Connector button; the Web Connector Configuration screen appears similar to Figure 4.9.

Figure 4.9
Set configuration for the Web Connector.

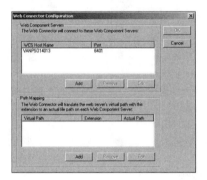

4. In the WCS Host Name field, type one of the following:

   • The name of the server that's running the WCS. This server must be routable from the Web server that's running the Web connector.

   • The external translated IP address of the server that's running the WCS. This IP address must be fixed; that is, the firewall must use static IP translation to grant the WCS server a fixed IP address.

   • If the WCS has been customized so that it listens on a port other than the default, type the new port number in the Port field. Otherwise, ensure that the default port number (6401) appears.

5. Click OK twice to return to the CCM.

6. Start the World Wide Web Publishing Service.

CONFIRMING A SUCCESSFUL CRYSTAL ENTERPRISE INSTALLATION

Although the Crystal Enterprise installation can be launched from the Add/Remove Programs control panel, it isn't necessary to do it this way. The setup executable will make the Windows Installer aware of what is being done and it will inform the Add/Remove Programs control panel. Figure 4.10 shows the Add/Remove programs group in the Windows control panel after Crystal Enterprise has been installed.

Figure 4.10
The Add/Remove Programs window.

In addition to ensuring system integrity when installing, the Windows Installer works in conjunction with the Add/Remove Programs control panel to display statistics of how many resources each program is using and how often they are used, and launches the install application to repair, change, or remove an application. Clicking either the Change or Remove buttons will launch Setup.exe again, which is a simple interface for modifying or removing Crystal Enterprise.

When checking the Crystal Enterprise application listing in the Add/Remove Programs window, the Crystal Enterprise application, along with the installed plug-ins, should be listed.

If a default installation of Crystal Enterprise has been completed, the menu options in Figure 4.11 will be available from the Crystal Enterprise program group after the installation is complete.

TESTING THE INSTALLATION

After a successful installation, test the applications to confirm they launch. The Crystal Enterprise system components should have all been installed and started as Windows services.

Figure 4.11
The Crystal Enterprise program group.

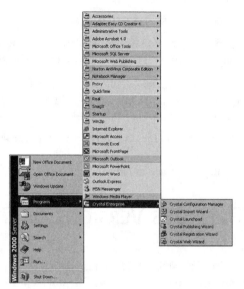

The server components installed with Crystal Enterprise each run as a service. If the installation was successful, the services will exist. The easiest place to see this is in the Crystal Configuration Manager.

Each of the servers listed within the Crystal Configuration Manager has an icon beside the name. If a server is running, the arrow in the middle of the icon will be green. Red arrows in the icons indicate a stopped server.

CHECKING THE APS SYSTEM DATABASE

The Crystal APS has a system database where all the security and scheduling information is stored. The APS communicates to this DSN through ODBC. If the APS was installed correctly, there will be an ODBC DSN for the System Database. To check to see whether it exists, look to the ODBC Data Source Administrator.

If this is a new installation the DSN will say CE 85. If it is an upgrade from Crystal Enterprise 8, you will see two DSNs with one that says CE 8 and a second that says CE85. The following list refers to checking for a new installation's DSN:

- In Windows NT, navigate to the Control Panel, and then choose the ODBC Control Panel. On the System DSN tab there should be a DSN named CE85 using the SQL Server or other database driver.

- In Windows 2000, go to Start, Programs, Administrative Tools and choose Data Sources. On the System DSN tab, there should be a DSN named CE-85 using the SQL Server or other database driver.

PART

II

CH

4

CONFIRMING THE CRYSTAL LAUNCHPAD IS FUNCTIONING

Finally, and most importantly, the real proof that the installation was successful is to go to the front page and see the product in action. There are two ways to get there:

- In the Program Group for Crystal Enterprise, choose the icon for Crystal Launch Pad. This will load a Web browser that contains links to the different samples and user interfaces. The ePortfolio is the Web desktop that ships with Crystal Enterprise.

- Open a Web browser and type `http://localserver/crystal/enterprise`.

Formal troubleshooting information is provided later in the chapter.

UPGRADING FROM PREVIOUS VERSIONS OF CRYSTAL ENTERPRISE

When upgrading from Crystal Enterprise 8 to 8.5, the installation program will also migrate any custom settings made during the Crystal Enterprise 8 deployment forward. This includes custom settings made when using the Report Application Server and Crystal Analysis Professional. It's important to confirm the custom settings after the install has completed to ensure that everything has been retained.

UPGRADE IMPACTS TO THE APS DATABASE

When upgrading Crystal Enterprise version 8 to 8.5, the installer will not create a new APS database automatically if the original system has the MS SQL Server 2000 client (but not the server) installed on the server. In this scenario, administrators will need to create a database and ensure that the target APS database is specified correctly in the Migration Wizard when performing the APS database migration.

If an appropriate SQL Server version has been used for the previous Crystal Enterprise installation, a new database named CE85 will be created with a corresponding DSN.

UPGRADING FROM SEAGATE INFO TO CRYSTAL ENTERPRISE

With this release of Crystal Enterprise, even more functionality has been made available from Seagate Info in CE 8.5, such as scheduling to destination, events, Seagate Analysis reports server (OLAP reporting tool) now in the form of Crystal Analysis Professional, and more.

When upgrading Seagate Info to Crystal Enterprise, an application called the Crystal Import Wizard (part of the Crystal Enterprise program group) can be used. This application allows administrators to migrate items to Crystal Enterprise.

Users and groups in their hierarchical structure will migrate. The Info Security settings for folders and report objects will not migrate. Also, report scheduling information, instances, passwords, and password restrictions will not be migrated from Info; however, the reports and their hierarchical structure can be successfully migrated.

Please contact Crystal Services via http://www.crystaldecisions.com/services to plan and execute your upgrade path from Seagate Info to Crystal Enterprise.

TROUBLESHOOTING

The following section explores common troubleshooting tasks and options to ensure successful Crystal Enterprise installation and functioning.

HARDWARE AND SOFTWARE REQUIREMENTS

Ensure that client and server servers are running supported operating systems, database servers, database clients, and appropriate server software. For more information, see the platforms.txt file, included with your product distribution.

Verify that the problem is reproducible, and note the exact steps that cause the problem to recur.

CRYSTAL ENTERPRISE SERVER/SERVICE DEPENDENCIES

When installed on Windows, each server in Crystal Enterprise is dependent on at least three services: the Event Log, NT LM Security Support Provider, and Remote Procedure Call (RPC) services. If difficulties persist with a Crystal Enterprise server, check to ensure that all three services appear on the server's Dependency tab.

If individual Crystal Enterprise server components are configured differently, consider setting up alternative service dependencies. To add and remove server dependencies using the Crystal Configuration Manager, implement the following steps:

1. Use the CCM to stop the server whose dependencies you want to modify.
2. With the server selected, click Properties on the toolbar.
3. Click the Dependency tab.
4. To add a dependency to the list, click Add.
5. The Add Dependency dialog box provides you with a list of all available dependencies. Select the dependency or dependencies, as required, and then click Add.
6. To remove a dependency from the list, select it and click Remove.
7. Click OK.
8. Restart the server.

SERVER PRIVILEGES

In some cases, the logon account from the default (System Account) used by Crystal Enterprise servers, such as Job Servers, Page Servers, and Web Component Servers, must be changed to another network user or service account. These cases arise either because the server needs additional network permissions to access the database or printer, or because the database client software is configured for a particular Windows user account.

Another good example arises when using Crystal Analysis Professional reports in Crystal Enterprise. Crystal Analysis Professional installs a server add-in to the Web Component Server that, unless specified otherwise in the Crystal Management Console, uses the Web Component Server service account to traverse a corporate network and connect to the intended OLAP server.

CHANGING A CRYSTAL ENTERPRISE SERVER'S ACCOUNT

In some cases, instead of using a system account, a user account might provide more appropriate permissions for a server's operation. The following procedure explains how to change a server's account:

1. Use the Crystal Configuration Manager to stop the server whose logon account is to be modified.
2. With the server selected, click Properties on the dialog box shown in Figure 4.12.

Figure 4.12
Server Properties screen.

3. In the Properties tab, clear the System Account check box.
4. Enter the Windows NT/2000 username and password information. When started, the server process will log on to the local server with this user account. In addition, all reports processed by this server will be formatted using the printer settings associated with the user account supplied.
5. Click Apply, and then click OK.
6. Start the server.

CRYSTAL REPORTS 8.5 NECESSARY UPDATES

Because Crystal Reports 8.5 was released prior to Crystal Enterprise 8.5, one important update needs to be loaded on report designer workstations where Crystal Reports is installed to allow Crystal Reports to function properly with Crystal Enterprise 8.5.

Please refer to Chapter 8 for more information on the program to install the update required for Crystal Reports 8.5.

TROUBLESHOOTING PUBLISHED CRYSTAL REPORTS

For troubleshooting other Crystal Report problems that might occur with Crystal Enterprise, an installation of Crystal Reports 8.5 (with patches) on each of the Crystal Enterprise Page and Job Servers is recommended. Inappropriate DSNs and connectivity issues sometimes cause these potential problems. Testing the Crystal Report by refreshing it from the Page and Job Server will help diagnose the problem; that is, if the report cannot successfully connect to the database from Crystal Reports, the Page or Job Server will share the same problem.

TROUBLESHOOTING USING MULTIPLE VERSIONS OF THE SAME CRYSTAL ENTERPRISE SERVER

Determine whether the problem is isolated to one Crystal Enterprise server or is occurring on multiple servers. For example, if a report fails to run on one processing server (Job Server or Page Server), see whether it runs on another processing server.

If the problem is isolated to one server, pay close attention to any configuration differences in the two servers, including operating system versions, patch levels, and general network integration.

If the problem relates to connectivity or functionality over the Web, check that Crystal Enterprise is integrated properly with your Web environment. For more information, see "Troubleshooting Path Mappings" in the Crystal Enterprise Administration Guide found in the Doc folder on the installation CD.

TROUBLESHOOTING WCS COMMUNICATION ERRORS WHEN ACCESSING THE CMC

If a user receives the following communication error message in their browser, the WCS is either not running or is incorrectly referenced in the Web Connector configuration:

> Communication failed with all configured Web Component Servers because they are disabled or not currently running. If this problem continues, please contact the system administrator.

Use the CCM to start the WCS, and then enable it. (If the WCS was already started and enabled, use the CCM to restart it.)

If restarting the WCS does not correct the situation, check the mappings between the Web Server, the Web Connector, and the WCS.

TROUBLESHOOTING APS CONNECTION ERRORS WHEN LOGGING ON TO THE CMC

If the following error message appears after you attempt to log on to the CMC, the APS is not running:

> Unable to connect to APS (*<servername>*) to retrieve cluster members. Logon cannot continue.

Use the Crystal Configuration Manager to restart the APS.

FINDING OTHER HELP

Look for solutions in the documentation included with your product, such as in the Doc folder on the installation CD.

Check out the Crystal Care technical support Web site for white papers, files, and updates, user forums, and Knowledge Base articles: `http://support.crystaldecisions.com`.

SUMMARY

This chapter explored Crystal Enterprise system configuration options, walked through various installation scenarios, delivered advice on system and server settings, and provided troubleshooting techniques for potential Crystal Enterprise installation issues.

In addition to its ease of installation, Crystal Enterprise provides powerful options in scaling, configuring, and monitoring its own resources. This chapter has mainly explored the installation of Crystal Enterprise, but read on to discover how powerful and flexible our system is to supply your organization, from small to global with the information you need to make smart decisions right now.

CHAPTER 5

USING THE CRYSTAL ENTERPRISE LAUNCHPAD

In this chapter

WHERE TO START

After installing Crystal Enterprise, several default system interfaces are created that provide useful insight into the capabilities and potential use of Crystal Enterprise. These sample applications can be used in the actual deployment of Crystal Enterprise, or they can be easily customized to meet more specific system requirements. This section provides an introduction to these sample applications and what can be expected after installing Crystal Enterprise.

OVERVIEW OF CRYSTAL ENTERPRISE LAUNCHPAD NAVIGATION

The Crystal Enterprise Launchpad is the Web-based starting point to explore and use the Crystal Enterprise system. The Launchpad provides quick access to all the primary sample applications. These sample applications include end-user tools, such as ePortfolio and the client samples, as well as the Crystal Management Console and the administrative samples. System documentation and links to online resources can also be found in the Launchpad.

WHERE TO LOCATE THE CRYSTAL ENTERPRISE LAUNCHPAD

The Crystal Enterprise Launchpad is accessed through a Web browser, such as Microsoft's Internet Explorer or Netscape Navigator.

Note

The minimum Web Browser requirements for Crystal Enterprise in a full standalone installation (all components on one physical server) are as follows: Microsoft Internet Explorer 5.5 SP2 or Netscape 4.78.

To start the Crystal Enterprise Launchpad, select Programs and then go to the Crystal Enterprise program listing, where there will be a shortcut to the Crystal Launchpad. To access the Launchpad from a PC other than the server, open a browser window and navigate to the following URL, assuming that the PC has appropriate network access to the Crystal Enterprise server:

```
http://physicalservername/crystal/enterprise/launchpad/en/default.htm
```

Note

In this URL, *physicalservername* should be replaced by the unique name or IP address of the server where Crystal Enterprise is installed.

COMPONENTS OF THE CRYSTAL ENTERPRISE LAUNCHPAD

This section introduces each of the primary Web samples and intranet applications, as well as system documentation, as they are installed with the "out-of-the-box" Crystal Enterprise system. These applications found in the Launchpad provide a combined focus on simplified administration and system maintenance, as well as providing for an intuitive end-user experience. Each of the following components can be located from the Crystal Enterprise Launchpad (see Figure 5.1):

- ePortfolio
- Client Samples
- Crystal Management Console
- Administrative Samples
- Crystal Online Documentation
- Crystal Offline Viewer

Figure 5.1
The Crystal Enterprise Launchpad offers quick access to the primary interfaces, sample applications, and documentation of the Crystal Enterprise system.

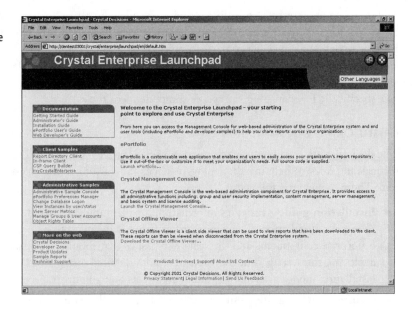

PART
II

CH
5

EPORTFOLIO

Out of all the Web-based applications and samples provided with Crystal Enterprise, ePortfolio is the most functional and feature-rich out-of-the-box end-user Web application for Crystal Enterprise. ePortfolio provides extensive functionality, such as on-demand report viewing, historical report viewing (based on archived report instances), and scheduling.

CLIENT SAMPLES

Additional end-user application samples provide a better understanding of how to power a variety of Web applications with Crystal Enterprise. Each of these samples offers a unique style and appearance. These samples demonstrate various uses and applications of Crystal Enterprise within intranet and Internet sites. One particular sample, the In-Frame Client, demonstrates how reports can be viewed "in context" in a multiframed Web environment— the DHTML report viewer is launched in the application's center frame of an existing frameset, while the organizational structure of this sample remains in the left-most navigation frame.

CRYSTAL MANAGEMENT CONSOLE

The Crystal Management Console (CMC) is the primary Web-based administration interface for Crystal Enterprise. It provides access to all administrative functions, including Crystal Enterprise security settings, report and object content management, server management, and basic system and license auditing.

ADMINISTRATIVE SAMPLES

Additional administrative application samples provide a better understanding of how to delegate and decentralize the various administrative tasks associated with managing a Crystal Enterprise deployment. Each of these samples offers a unique administrative task and appearance. For example, IT help desk personnel might require an interface to simply reset and manage user passwords, while the Architecture & Engineering group requires an interface specifically for managing the server components of the system.

CRYSTAL ONLINE DOCUMENTATION

The documentation and online help section provides access to standard Crystal Enterprise manuals intended to help install, deploy, manage, and customize the Crystal Enterprise system. These include the following:

- **Installation guide**—Provides information for planning and executing a Crystal Enterprise installation. Conceptual information is included to help explain the Crystal Enterprise components and the scalability issues that should be considered before deploying the system. The guide also includes detailed instructions for the different installation modes available to system architects and administrators.

- **Getting Started guide**—An introduction to the basic features of Crystal Enterprise, this guide is a useful document for both administrators and end users. It includes a step-by-step approach to everything from logging in to the Crystal Management Console to explaining how to export reports over the Web. It describes how to create and manage user accounts, view and schedule reports, and access Crystal ePortfolio and the various Crystal Report Viewers. In addition, the Getting Started guide includes an overview of all the components that make up Crystal Enterprise and how they interact with an existing infrastructure to deliver reports over the Web.

- **Administration guide**—Describes how to manage all aspects of a Crystal Enterprise implementation, with a focus on four areas: system architecture, account administration, server management, and report publishing. Also included in the Administration guide is information specific to working in a Windows NT environment and troubleshooting details. This manual is intended for system administrators.

- **ePortfolio user's guide**—An introduction to the Crystal ePortfolio Web application, the primary out-of-the-box application that enables users to access reports over the Web. This guide outlines how to view, schedule, print, and export reports without installing Crystal Reports on the local workstation. It also discusses how to take advantage of the system's personalization features to create a personalized view of the public desktop, save favorite reports, organize a user's Favorites folder (such as the subscription folder), and use the various report viewers.

- **Web Developer's guide**—Provides information about the tools and components that are needed to create a customized Crystal Enterprise Web application. It is intended for developers who are familiar with Active Server Page (ASP) technology, and who want to use the Crystal Enterprise SDK to build or customize a client desktop (that is, an ePortfolio) with report viewing, scheduling, exporting, and advanced capabilities. As well as presenting an overview of the Crystal Enterprise architecture and object model, this guide offers a comprehensive tutorial and programming reference that will guide developers through the Web development process.

OFFLINE CONTENT AND THE CRYSTAL OFFLINE VIEWER

The Crystal Offline Viewer is a client-side report viewer installed locally on a user's desktop. This viewer can be used to look at Crystal Report files downloaded to an end-user's desktop without being connected to ePortfolio or the Crystal Enterprise system. The offline viewer is essentially a robust offline client that allows users to continue interacting with reports when disconnected from the Crystal Enterprise system. The Offline Viewer offers the additional flexibility for Crystal Enterprise users to open and view report files with the .RPT file extension at their leisure, whether sitting in a corporate office or on an airplane.

When using report content with Crystal Enterprise there are two options. First, the report can be exported to any of the non-Crystal formats (Excel, Word, PDF, and so on) and interact with the content within the confines and limitations inherent with the corresponding application. This option limits the amount of interaction available with the report content because it's a static file. Second, the report could be exported from the Crystal Enterprise system in the native Crystal Report format (the .rpt file type) and use the Crystal Offline Viewer, preserving the capability to navigate and interact with the report content in a more dynamic and actionable manner.

The Crystal Offline Viewer provides the capability to print or export reports, select specific data to view, drill down for more detail in the report, sort data, and view multiple reports. The Crystal Offline Viewer also supports tasks such as defining record selections, sorting records, graphing, and defining Top N values.

The Crystal Offline Viewer extends the use and productivity of a corporate workforce beyond the inherent limitations of an online system. For example, business travelers can download and save their reports locally to use them while traveling, or any place where they might be removed from the networked environment. Although the Offline Viewer is not an independent product offering available for purchase without Crystal Enterprise, the capability it provides to extend the reach of reporting beyond the online system is valuable. The Crystal Offline Viewer could very easily be located on a shared network location and made available through a hyperlink from any Crystal Enterprise application for users to download.

Note

Only licensed users of the Crystal Enterprise system can use the Crystal Offline Viewer. The deployment of the Crystal Offline Viewer requires specific licensing consideration, and usage guidelines should be obtained directly from Crystal Decisions at www.CrystalDecisions.com.

Note

Although the term *interface* is used in a generic manner to describe any system application (whether Web- or Windows-based) that manages the interaction with any of the system components, the terms *Web Desktop* and *Web Application* specifically refer to the Web-based interfaces of the Crystal Enterprise system. These include ePortfolio and the Client Samples as end-user Web applications, and the Crystal Management Console and the Administrative Samples as system administration Web applications.

CRYSTAL ENTERPRISE WEB APPLICATIONS FOR END USERS

The out-of-the-box Web samples and applications play an important role not only by offering an intuitive and meaningful experience for an end-user's interaction with the system, but also by providing robust functional applications that can be quickly deployed to a large group of Crystal Enterprise users.

ePORTFOLIO WEB APPLICATION

As stated earlier, ePortfolio provides the most extensive functionality of any of the Crystal Enterprise sample applications and can be easily and quickly deployed as a central information-delivery interface for enterprise reporting initiatives. Like all the Crystal Enterprise Web-based interfaces, ePortfolio is a completely customizable application that enables end users to easily access an organization's report repository (see Figure 5.2).

The ePortfolio Web application is written using the HTML, JavaScript, and VBScript programming languages. Each of these languages is commonly known, and virtually every company in today's marketplace has experienced professionals familiar with each of them. Considering the availability and proliferation of skills surrounding these languages, it is quite reasonable to expect that Crystal Enterprise applications can be quickly and easily designed, created, and delivered to very large user communities.

ePortfolio, much like the Client Sample applications, offers access to system reports organized in a folder hierarchy structure. Folders, like the default Report Samples folder set up during the installation of Crystal Enterprise, then can contain any number of subfolders and/or report objects—this is often referred to as a parent-child hierarchical relationship of objects. Each folder object can be a parent to, or child of, another folder object and can contain reports that are relevant to the logical organizational structure that the object hierarchy is created to represent.

Figure 5.2
The ePortfolio application provides extensive functionality and incorporates many of the commonly desired Enterprise Reporting features.

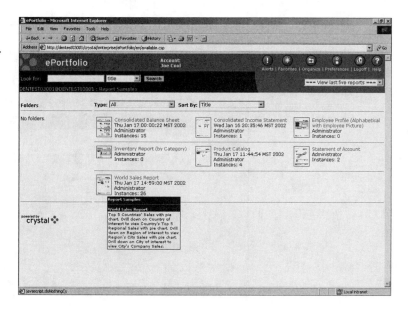

To view reports, select a report by clicking on its name, or small thumbnail icon if available. Then, select View from the fly-out list that is dynamically presented. The fly-out list presented also contains the option to View Last Instance of a report as long as a previously run instance of the report is available.

The ePortfolio application also allows end users to schedule reports based on the desired day and time the users would like the reports to run, while specifying parameter values, database logon credentials, filter criteria, report destination, and report format if applicable. In addition to scheduling, users can quickly view a history listing of previously executed reports, allowing for fast access to historical report instances. Historical report instances offer users the capability to view the data as it existed at an earlier point in time.

As a user of the system, both the Schedule and History windows can be accessed from the fly-out list presented when you select the report name or thumbnail icon. Each report instance has a number of properties that are displayed here, such as Schedule Time, Run By, Parameters, Format Type, and Status. From the History window, selections can be made on any of the available instances. The various actions include Delete, Pause, Resume, Clear All, and Select All (see Figures 5.3 and 5.4).

USER ACCESS LEVELS

There are six default user access levels in Crystal Enterprise. These include:

- **No Access**—The user or group is not able to access the object or folder. ePortfolio, the Crystal Publishing Wizard, and the Crystal Management Console enforce this right by ensuring that the object is not visible to the user.

PART

II

CH

5

Figure 5.3
The ePortfolio Schedule window offers users with the appropriate system privileges to define unique schedules for reports to be run.

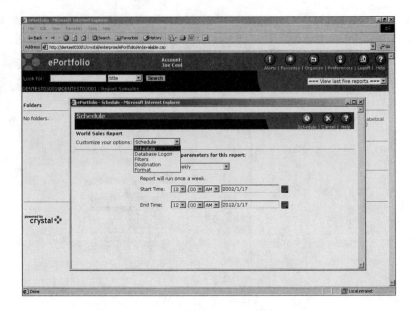

Figure 5.4
The ePortfolio History window enables users with the appropriate system privileges to quickly view historical report instances, reflective of the data as it existed at an earlier point in time.

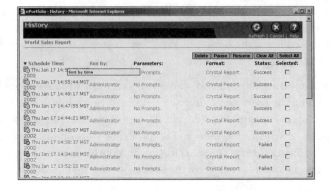

- **View**—If this access level is set at the folder level, the user or group is able to view the folder, the objects contained within the folder, and all generated instances of each object. If this access level is set at the object level, the user can view the object, the history of the object, and all generated instances of the object. The user cannot, however, schedule the object or refresh it against its data source.

- **Schedule**—The user or group is able to view the object or folder and its contents, and to generate instances by scheduling the object to run against the specified data source once or on a recurring basis. The user or group can view, delete, and pause the scheduling of instances that they own. They also can schedule to different formats and destinations, set parameters, specify database logon information, pick servers to process jobs, add contents to the folder, and copy the object or folder.

- **View on Demand**—In addition to the rights provided by the Schedule access level, the user gains the right to refresh data *on demand* against the data source.

- **Full Control**—This access level grants all the available advanced rights. It is the only access level that allows users to delete objects (folders, objects, and instances) and to modify all the object's properties. This access level is designed to provide a user or group with administrative control over one or more folders or objects. Users with Full Control rights also can log on to the Crystal Management Console and add, edit, and delete content as required, without being members of the actual Administrators group.

- **Advanced**—This access level does not include a predefined set of object rights. Instead, it allows customization of user or group access to an object by selecting from the complete range of available object rights.

The View option requires that the user have View On Demand access to the object, while the View Last Instance and History options only require that the system user have View privileges. The Schedule option requires that a user has Schedule, View On Demand, or Full Control access privileges for the applicable report object. Access privileges are specified and managed within the Crystal Management Console (CMC) application by system administrators, and can be assigned on either a User Group basis or User basis per report or folder object within the system.

VIEWING REPORTS IN ePORTFOLIO—CRYSTAL VIEWERS

When viewing reports from any of the Crystal Enterprise Web applications, the default format in which the reports are presented is the native Crystal Reports format. Designated with an .rpt file extension, Crystal Report files are presented through a Web browser window via one of the Crystal Viewers. Using the Crystal Reports format is advantageous for several significant reasons. The Crystal Reports viewers in Crystal Enterprise allow viewing reports created with Crystal Reports, navigation through multiple pages, refreshing data, drilling down to see details behind charts and summarized data values, parameters selection, and so on. The Crystal Viewers also have powerful printing and exporting capabilities.

More specifically, each of these Crystal Viewers is capable of supporting Crystal's "page-on-demand" technology, which facilitates fast delivery of report files to the client browser without requiring the entire report file to be rendered and downloaded before viewing the report content. By viewing reports in the Crystal Reports format, drill-down on the report contents, such as chart objects and summary values to quickly access the underlying details within the report, is enabled. This drilling down to details is based on the grouping structure and organization of the report at design time, and it does not require any additional programming or development skills to create. Figure 5.5 shows the ActiveX report viewer, just one of many available viewer options.

Figure 5.5

The ActiveX report viewer offers a clean and highly functional interface, enabling a user to print the report, export the report to various formats, refresh the report, navigate to any report page, and search the report contents.

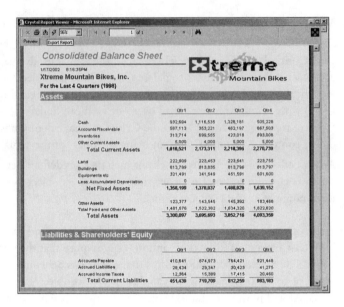

The online Crystal Report Viewers support ActiveX, Java, and HTML. In general, a Crystal Enterprise administrator selects the viewer type best suited to an organization's needs so that the desired default viewer is launched each time a report is viewed. Six specific viewers are available for viewing Crystal Reports files within Crystal Enterprise:

- ActiveX Viewer
- DHTML Viewer
- HTML Page Viewer
- Java Viewer
- Java Plug-in Viewer
- Navigator Plug-in Viewer

These options are designed to accommodate varying corporate standards and feature richness requirements.

In addition to the functions provided on the Web browser's Standard toolbar, the Crystal Viewers encompass the following additional functions on their respective custom toolbar (varying slightly depending on which of the six viewers is used):

- Close current view
- Print report
- Export report
- Refresh
- Toggle group tree

- Zoom
- Go to first page
- Go to previous page
- Page number
- Go to next page
- Go to last page
- Stop loading

Finished reports can be exported to several reporting formats, as well as to popular word processor and spreadsheet formats. This makes the distribution of information easier. Crystal Enterprise provides six different export format types, including the following:

- Crystal Reports 8
- Crystal Reports 7
- Microsoft Excel (.xls)
- Microsoft Word (.doc)
- Adobe Acrobat (.pdf)
- Rich Text Format (.rtf)

Note

When exporting a report to a file format other than Crystal Reports format (.rpt), some of the formatting that appears in a report might be lost. The Crystal Offline Viewer also provides other formats for exporting.

In addition to viewing reports in the previously mentioned formats, the Crystal Report Application Server (RAS) can also be used to provide for dynamic ad-hoc report modification purposes via a browser-based DHTML interface (pure zero-client application). The Report Application Server allows authorized users to modify the contents, structure, layout, and presentation of a report file, with the added option of saving the modified report to any authorized folder within Crystal Enterprise.

PERSONALIZATION FEATURES IN ePORTFOLIO

The ePortfolio Web application offers an end user the capability to set several personal preferences associated with a desired application layout and presentation-specific requirements. After logging on to ePortfolio, select the Preferences option from the upper-right window area. This presents a new application page to control user preferences that can then be stored in the Crystal Enterprise repository. Regardless of what physical computer ePortfolio is accessed from, the application preferences will always be presented as specified within the Crystal Enterprise system.

These preferences include items such as initial folder view location, show/hide top-level folder bar, presentation views, maximum number of reports to display per page, report properties to display (author, description, date, instance count, and thumbnail), desired Crystal Viewer for all .rpt formatted reports, and application color scheme. Because this page is also customizable by system administrators, users might be provided with the capability to control any combination of these setting options (see Figure 5.6).

Figure 5.6
The ePortfolio user preferences window provides the capability to set several personal preferences associated with a desired application layout.

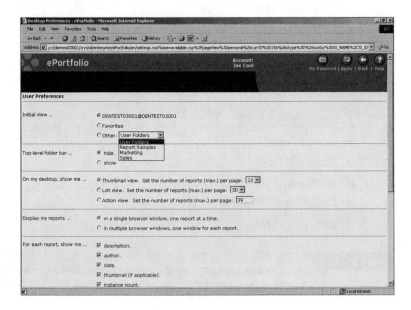

ePortfolio also provides a Favorites folder for each individual system user. The Favorites folder can be organized to include either copies of existing reports that are accessible or links to the folder locations of other reports within the Crystal Enterprise system.

ePortfolio can be used as it exists out-of-the-box or customized to meet specific organizational requirements. Chapter 6, "Customizing ePortfolio for Rapid Information Delivery," provides additional details on customizing the ePortfolio application.

Chapters 13 and 14 also provide more detailed coverage of how to customize the Crystal Enterprise system.

CLIENT SAMPLE APPLICATIONS

The Client Samples (with a hyperlink located on the left side of the Crystal Launchpad screen) available within Crystal Enterprise provide additional end-user interfaces that offer a better understanding of how to power a wide variety of Web applications with Crystal Enterprise. The Client Samples provide basic demonstrations and full source code that highlight how various reporting functionality can be integrated into Web applications through the use of the Crystal Enterprise SDK. The samples include the following Web site example applications:

- Report thumbnail client
- Report directory client
- In-frame client
- CSP Query Builder
- MyCrystalEnterprise

As with the ePortfolio Web application, each of the Developer Samples is also created using the HTML, JavaScript, and VBScript programming languages.

REPORT THUMBNAIL SAMPLE APPLICATION

This sample demonstrates how to use familiar graphical metaphors to navigate and organize reports. It displays thumbnails of each report and allows scheduling and viewing of reports by clicking on the thumbnail images. Although it is a very simple sample with no scheduling or historical report instance viewing, it illustrates how an Enterprise Reporting application can be visually integrated into any existing or planned Web interfaces (see Figure 5.7). The Report Thumbnail sample can be accessed at the following URL:

```
http://severname/crystal/enterprise/websamples/en/thumbnails/available.csp
```

Figure 5.7
The Report Thumbnail sample demonstrates how to use familiar graphical metaphors to navigate and organize reports.

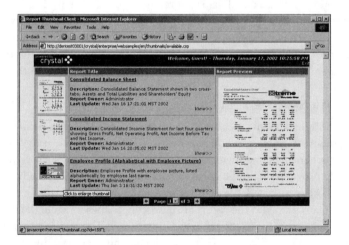

PART

II

CH

5

REPORT DIRECTORY SAMPLE APPLICATION

The Report Directory sample application uses the structure and organizational scheme common with various Web directory sites, such as Yahoo! and Excite, to enable access to system reports. As such, it offers a more intuitive search capability within the application's presentation. The entire Crystal Enterprise system can be searched for specific words or string values present within report titles, report descriptions, or all report property fields, quickly and with minimal effort. It is primarily text-based, and the structure is built dynamically based on the folder and file layout in the system report repository (see Figure 5.8).

Figure 5.8
The Report Directory sample uses the structure and organizational scheme common with various Web directory sites to provide access to system reports.

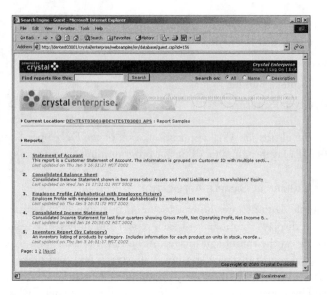

Unlike the report thumbnail sample, the Report Directory application incorporates authentication for a secured and managed reporting environment. Log on to the application by clicking on the Logon link in the upper-right of the application window and identifying yourself in the following Logon page. The report directory sample also includes access to a Favorites folder for each individual system user, although this folder is managed by the system administrator rather than by each individual user as it is in the ePortfolio application.

IN-FRAME SAMPLE APPLICATION

This sample demonstrates how reports can be viewed "in context" in a multiframed Web environment. Similar to how the Report Directory sample uses a structure and organizational scheme common with various Web directory sites, such as Yahoo! and Excite, this sample provides more of a personalized directory structure much like myYahoo, myExcite, or mySAP.com. The Crystal Enterprise DHTML report viewer is launched in the application's main frame (to the right) of an existing frameset, while the organizational structure of this sample remains in the left navigation frame. The application organizes reports into four distinct and logical groups: corporate documents, personal documents, inbox documents, and scheduled documents.

The Corporate Documents area is where users can easily view all documents that exist within the system. When connecting to the system, it will automatically redirect the end user to the Corporate Documents listing. The Personal Documents area will display all documents that have been posted to the system by the currently logged-in user. The Inbox Documents area displays all objects that are gathered from other areas of the system and to which the currently logged-in user is subscribed. The Scheduled Documents area will display all documents that have been successfully scheduled.

After selecting one of these groups, a report listing is then presented in the main frame of the application window (see Figure 5.9). When you click Expand in the upper-right of this report listing frame, the report description and small icons representing various file formats are displayed under each listed report. Any of the file format icons, such as Microsoft Word, Microsoft Excel, or Adobe Acrobat (.pdf), can be selected to view any of the listed report items in the desired format.

Figure 5.9
The In-Frame sample shows how reports can be viewed in context and incorporates meaningful icons that allows you to view reports in a variety of file formats.

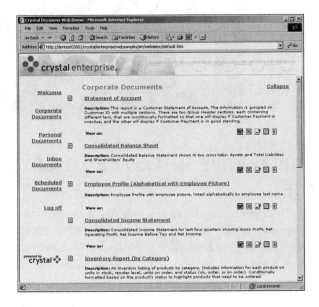

XTREME CORPORATE WEB SITE SAMPLE APPLICATION

This sample demonstrates a tight level of integration between Crystal Enterprise and a fictitious corporate Web site, the Xtreme Mountain Bike Company (see Figure 5.10). The application shows how simple hyperlinks can provide easy, one-click access to reports. The fictitious corporate Web site is divided into logical areas—Products, Suppliers, Investor Relations, and Press Releases—each containing a number of relevant reports. When you click on one of the report thumbnail images, the respective report is opened in the main frame of the application window using the HTML online viewer. The Xtreme Corporate Web Site sample can be accessed at the following URL:

```
http://servername/crystal/enterprise/websamples/en/xtreme/frames.html
```

The organizational structure and content for each of the sample applications is presented dynamically based on the Crystal Enterprise system's report repository (that is, Crystal Enterprise APS), such that the folders and report files presented within each of the applications is being read dynamically from the repository. This illustrates the power and potential use for customized interfaces of the Crystal Enterprise system—multiple interfaces (applications) can be supported from a common repository.

Figure 5.10
The Xtreme
Corporate Web site
sample shows how
simple hyperlinks can
provide easy, one-
click access to
reports.

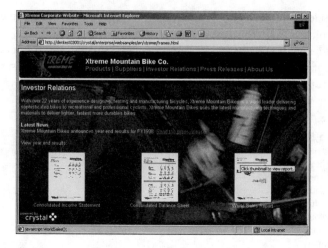

THE ADMINISTRATIVE INTERFACE TO CRYSTAL ENTERPRISE

Similar to the user interfaces, the administrative interfaces provide for a simple way to administer and manage the entire Crystal Enterprise environment. The primary administrative interface to the Crystal Enterprise system is a Web-based application called the Crystal Management Console, or CMC.

This section introduces the main administrative interfaces to Crystal Enterprise and provides a brief overview of each respective component. For additional details, see Chapter 10, "Administering and Configuring Crystal Enterprise," which provides a more comprehensive review on administrating the Crystal Enterprise system.

INTRODUCTION TO THE CRYSTAL MANAGEMENT CONSOLE (CMC)

The Crystal Management Console (CMC) is the Web-based administrative application designed to facilitate the administration and maintenance of the Crystal Enterprise system. The CMC is used to perform tasks related to user accounts, user group/subgroup management, folder/subfolder management, report publishing, content management, server settings, system metrics, and license keys. Using a Web browser, system administrators can access the CMC from anywhere within the network.

The CMC offers a DHTML "zero-client" interface for remote administration of the Crystal Enterprise system (see Figure 5.11). As long as system administrators have access to the local intranet where Crystal Enterprise is installed and accessible, administration and management can be completed from a Web browser (such as Internet Explorer or Netscape Navigator) from virtually anywhere in the world.

Figure 5.11
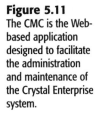
The CMC is the Web-based application designed to facilitate the administration and maintenance of the Crystal Enterprise system.

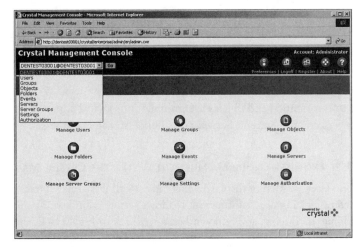

ACCESSING THE CRYSTAL MANAGEMENT CONSOLE

There are two methods to access the Crystal Management Console: Select Crystal Launchpad from the program group or enter the URL path of the Crystal Enterprise server directly into the browser.

To access the Crystal Management Console from the Start menu program group (this option is available only on servers that have Crystal Enterprise components installed):

1. From the Crystal Enterprise program group, click Crystal Launchpad. The Crystal Enterprise Launchpad appears.

2. Click the Crystal Management Console link. The Crystal Management Console Log On page appears.

To access the Crystal Management Console from a URL line:

1. Launch a Web browser.

2. Enter the following URL: `http://servername/crystal/enterprise/admin/`

   The Crystal Management Console Log On page appears.

To log off from the Crystal Management Console, select the log off link located in the upper-right corner of the CMC application interface.

NAVIGATING THE CRYSTAL MANAGEMENT CONSOLE

Because the Crystal Management Console is a Web-based application, it allows for simplified navigation through the use of standard hyperlinks to system resources. The application itself provides several useful features to make administration of Crystal Enterprise easier:

■ An application "breadcrumb trail" of object hierarchy locations for easy navigation, such as Home, Content Management, Folders, Parent Folder, Child Folder, Sub-Child

PART

II

CH

5

Folder, and so on. Above the title of each page, a navigation path indicates the location within the CMC. Select these options to quickly return to previously visited areas of the application or jump to different parts of the CMC application.

- Navigation buttons in the browser that provides the capability to move through various object property pages.

- Information and objects are grouped into logical administrative system functions: Account, Content, Server, and Global Management areas.

USER AND USER GROUP MANAGEMENT WITHIN THE CRYSTAL MANAGEMENT CONSOLE

The Users section of the CMC encompasses all tasks related to creating, importing, changing, and organizing user information. It allows system administrators to perform tasks specific to adding, modifying, and removing user accounts within Crystal Enterprise (see Figure 5.12).

Figure 5.12
The CMC's User Management section provides access to all the tasks related to creating, importing, changing, and organizing user information.

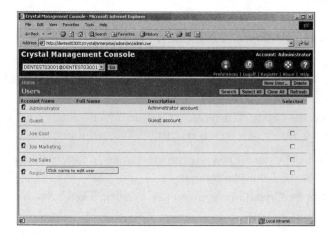

Before creating accounts, it is useful to plan the hierarchy of user groups and the level of access various users will require to the organizational folders and reports within Crystal Enterprise.

Upon installation, three default groups are created within Crystal Enterprise: Administrators, Everyone, and New Sign-Up Accounts. Not only do group specifications allow for organizing users and simplifying administration, groups provide system administrators with the capability to determine the functionality that system users need and can access:

- **Administrators**—Users who belong to the Administrators group are able to perform all tasks in all the Crystal Enterprise applications (Crystal Management Console, Crystal Configuration Manager, Crystal Publishing Wizard, ePortfolio, and Developer Samples).

- **Everyone**—By default, each user is a member of the Everyone group. Users are able to access all the Crystal Enterprise applications. This group allows access to all the reports added to the default Report Samples folder.
- **New Sign-Up Accounts**—Users who belong to the New Sign-up Accounts group have created their own accounts through the sign-up feature in the ePortfolio application. By default, members of this group are able to view reports specified by the administrator and perform applicable report and folder tasks.

In addition to the default groups, administrators can also create custom groups. These groups can include a collection of users who belong to the same department, perform similar job functions, or work in the same region. Custom groups enable administrators to provide for and restrict access to reports for a large number of users at one time.

> **Note**
>
> Crystal Enterprise Standard edition includes only the Administrators and Guest users, and does not allow for the creation of custom groups.

OBJECT AND FOLDER MANAGEMENT WITHIN THE CRYSTAL MANAGEMENT CONSOLE

The Object and Folder areas of the CMC are focused primarily on managing report and folder objects within the system, including the process of publishing reports.

As with file system management, folders provide for the capability to organize and simplify report administration, as well as system use (see Figure 5.13). They are useful for creating an organizational structure based on the need to offer logical categories for users to access the various system reports. Folder structures can be created based on corporate departments, divisions, or other functional groups that facilitate the capability for users to quickly and effectively navigate the system. Specifying this type of structure is extremely beneficial as the volume of reports increases and as additional users need access to the application.

The Folder Management section contains information about how to perform folder tasks, such as creating folders and subfolders, copying and moving folders within the defined structure, and removing folders and subfolders from the system.

Within the Object Management section, administrators can complete the report publishing process. This is the process of adding new or existing reports to the Crystal Enterprise environment and making them available in the Web desktop of authorized users. Administrators, or anyone with applicable privileges, can publish reports using the Crystal Publishing Wizard or the Crystal Management Console. With both of these methods, publishers are able to determine which reports are added, where they should be located, who should be able to access them, and how often the data should be updated.

Figure 5.13
The CMC's Folder Management section is focused on managing folder objects within the system.

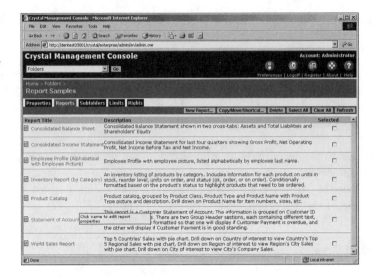

The third option of publishing reports into the Crystal Enterprise system is using the Crystal Reports design client. Within the Crystal Reports application, the designer can select the Save As option from the File menu item, and then identify the desired Crystal Enterprise APS location to save the report.

> **Note**
>
> The Crystal Publishing Wizard is a locally installed, 32-bit Windows application. The wizard is made up of a series of 12 screens. Only the screens applicable to the published reports or folders are shown. After the report has been generated, it will appear in the specified folder location in ePortfolio (or other Web Desktop) and in the Objects area of the Crystal Management Console. See Chapters 2 and 7 for an overview of the Crystal Publishing Wizard.

As an alternative to adding reports individually to the system, several reports can also be published simultaneously (known as publishing report directories). Publishing a directory enables the addition of a group of reports without having to specify each report separately.

After adding reports to Crystal Enterprise, some changes to the report location, schedule, and/or access privileges might be required. The Object Management area of the CMC allows administrators to specify the following:

- Copy or move a report within the Crystal Enterprise folder structure
- Update report schedules (recurrence) information
- Modify report access privileges
- Modify database, parameter, and selection details
- Remove reports from the system

The Object and Folder Management sections of the CMC also include the capability for administrators to specify object rights—user and/or group privileges based on the unique report and/or folder objects within the system. For each report and folder in the Crystal Enterprise system, administrators can specify explicit access privileges that each user and/or group have in relation to the respective object. There are six levels of objects rights: No Access, View, Schedule, View On Demand, Full Control, and Advanced.

MANAGING CONTENT CREATED FROM PREVIOUS VERSIONS OF CRYSTAL REPORTS With few exceptions, Crystal Enterprise supports reports created in versions 6 through 8 of Crystal Reports. Once published to the Crystal Enterprise system, all reports will appear in version 8 format when they are launched from ePortfolio (or other Web Desktop). Thus, it may be beneficial to first open and run reports that have been created in an older version, such as version 6 or 7 of Crystal Reports, to verify that the formatting and feature implementation (such as formulas, calculations, and so on) are optimized for the version 8 formatting. For the most part, Crystal Reports 8 simply expands on the feature options and adds enhancements to report formatting when compared to the earlier versions. These advancements offer additional capabilities that can be easily implemented by updating older report files in a newer version of the content design product.

EVENT MANAGEMENT WITHIN THE CRYSTAL MANAGEMENT CONSOLE

Event-based scheduling provides for additional control over scheduling reports. Events can be set up so that reports are processed only after a specified event occurs. Working with events consists of two steps: creating the event and scheduling a report with events. When an event has been created, it can be selected as a dependency when a report is scheduled. The scheduled job is then processed only when the event occurs.

- **File events**—When a file-based event is defined, a filename for which the Event Server should monitor the presence of is specified. When the file appears, the Event Server triggers the event.

- **Schedule events**—When a schedule-based event is defined, a report is selected whose existing recurrence schedule will serve as the trigger for the event. In this way, schedule-based events allow for the establishment of contingencies or conditions between scheduled reports. For example, it might be beneficial for certain large reports to run sequentially, or for a particular sales summary report to run only when a detailed sales report is run successfully.

- **Custom events**—When a custom event is defined, a shortcut is created for triggering an event manually. The custom event occurs only when an administrator clicks the corresponding Trigger This Event button in the CMC, or when another application is programmed to initiate this trigger by design.

It is important to remember that an object's recurrence schedule still determines how frequently the report will run. For example, a weekly report that is dependent upon a file-based event will run, at most, once a week (as long as the file specified in the event appears in the

PART

II

CH

5

appropriate location every week). The event also must occur within the timeframe established when the event-based report is actually scheduled.

SERVER AND SERVER GROUP MANAGEMENT WITHIN THE CRYSTAL MANAGEMENT CONSOLE

This section focuses on a few of the functions available within the CMC to manage the Crystal Enterprise servers. More formal discussions on Crystal Enterprise administration can be found in Chapter 10. The Crystal Enterprise system is comprised of different servers that process and manage report requests, and depending on the Crystal Enterprise implementation, all of these servers may be located on one physical server or spread across many:

- Crystal APS (Automated Process Scheduler)
- Crystal Web Component Server
- Crystal Cache Server
- Crystal Event Server
- Crystal Job Server
- Crystal Page Server
- Crystal Input File Repository Server
- Crystal Output File Repository Server

The Server Management section provides access to a range of server tasks, from simple tasks such as starting and stopping the various servers, to more complex ones dealing with server configuration (see Figure 5.14). The following scenarios using the CMC can be accomplished:

- Modify server status
- Modify properties and settings for the respective servers
- Access server metrics
- Specify and manage server groups

Figure 5.14
The CMC's Server Management section provides access to a range of server-related tasks.

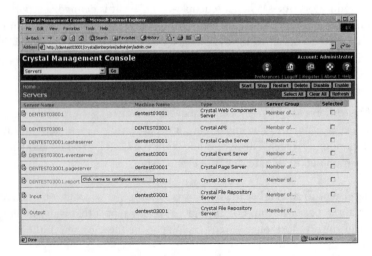

For example, follow these simple steps to stop and restart a server process.

To stop a server for system maintenance purposes:

1. In the Server Management area, click Servers.
2. Select the check box associated with the required Crystal Enterprise server.
3. Click Stop.

To start a stopped server:

1. In the Server Management area, click Servers.
2. Select the check box associated with required Crystal Enterprise server.
3. Click Start.

> **Note**
>
> Crystal Enterprise users will lose the respective services from each system server component during a restart of that specific server. As an alternative to performing this two-step operation of stopping and starting a server, there is also the option to restart any server component as a single click of the mouse. Restarting a server process stops the server and returns it to its previous state.

GLOBAL MANAGEMENT WITHIN THE CRYSTAL MANAGEMENT CONSOLE

The Global Management area (including the Settings and Authorization sections of the CMC) allows administrators to quickly access vital information as it pertains to the Crystal Enterprise system, such as system activity use and licensing information. The Settings section of the Global Management area offers information on the current Crystal Enterprise system database, current version of the Crystal Enterprise system in use, APS cluster name and designated members, account activity as it pertains to existing user accounts established within the system, currently active accounts, and overall purchased Crystal Enterprise licenses. It also shows details on the current running report jobs (running, pending, and waiting status values) and total processed report jobs (both successful and failed) for the Crystal Enterprise system.

Crystal Enterprise administrators can specify report instance controls within the Limits tab of the Settings section. As an authorized administrator, excess instances on a global level can be deleted based on any combination of three settings:

- Delete excess instances when there are more than N instances of an object
- Delete excess instances for the following users/groups
- Delete instances after N days for the following users/groups

The Authorization section offers information on managing system licensing, passwords, and external authentication integration specifications (such as LDAP and NT authentication). The Licensing tab focuses on the current license keys in use and the corresponding named and/or concurrent user licenses each provides, as well as processor-based licenses if applicable. This is where restrictions can be set for password enforcement and how they should be applied to the system's users, as well as system Logon restrictions (see Figure 5.15). Additional tabs within the Authorization section include Enterprise (native Crystal Enterprise security module), NT, and LDAP listings. These tabs allow administrators to enable and map to external authentication sources and to create or assign alias accounts appropriately within the Crystal Enterprise system.

Figure 5.15
The CMC's Authorization Management area allows administrators to manage vital aspects of the Crystal Enterprise system, such as user authentication restrictions, external security system integration, and licensing information.

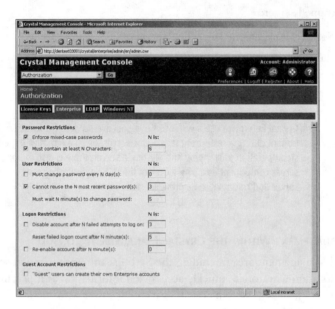

SYSTEM USAGE AND METRICS

The first, and perhaps quickest, means to view system usage information is through the Crystal Management Console (CMC). System usage and licensing information about the Crystal Enterprise system can be obtained by accessing the Global Management area within the CMC.

As mentioned earlier in the chapter, the Global Management area is divided into the Settings and Authorization sections. System information is divided into Properties and Metrics, each with its respective tab under the Settings section. The Properties tab contains the product build date, build number, version number, data source, and database details, while the Metrics tab contains account activity and job information (see Figure 5.16).

The Web Component Server also manages a log file that can be created and used for administrative purposes (see Figure 5.17). The settings for this server log file are specified within the CMC application, within the Logging area of the Properties tab under Server Management, Servers, *Servername* Web Component Server. The amount of detail and location of the log file can be set in this area. By default, the log file is stored in the C:\Program

Files\Seagate Software\WCS\logging location within the physical file directory of the server. The types of information that can be written to this log file include the following:

- Date
- Time
- Duration
- Bytes transferred
- Used cache
- Method
- URI
- URI-stem
- URI-query
- IP address and port
- Status
- Location of audit log files

Figure 5.16
The CMC's Metrics tab under the Settings section displays a variety of current account activity and report job information.

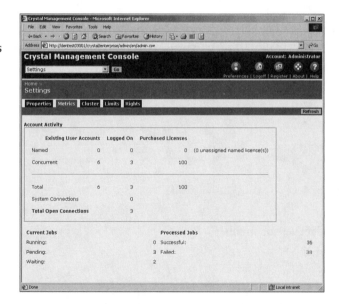

Note

The IIS/Proxy Driver for Crystal Reports can be used as a report datasource. Default reports based on these log files are not included with Crystal Enterprise because the log schema can vary depending on what details each customer chooses to include in the log within the CMC application (as mentioned previously).

Figure 5.17
The WCS server properties page allows administrators to specify a variety of logging and report viewing criteria for the Crystal Enterprise system.

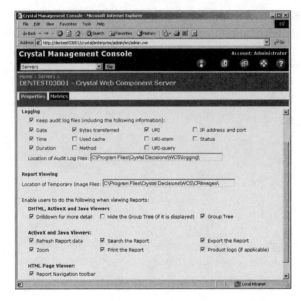

The Metrics tab, found by choosing Server Management, Servers, *Servername* Web Component Server, also displays a variety of server and product details. These include the following:

- Operating system
- Number of CPUs
- Local time
- Start time
- Disk space
- Used disk space
- RAM
- WCS product version number
- Total requests
- Current requests
- Total bytes sent
- Average bytes per request
- Total time taken (seconds)
- Average time taken per request (seconds)

Reports showing activity and use patterns can be created against system log files that then can provide a high-level view of the entire system.

Note

Because all the Crystal Enterprise Web applications include the source code for each of these user interfaces, companies can add custom auditing capabilities to any of these applications as required. Details on how to create and customize these applications can be found in Chapters 13 and 14.

SUMMARY

Upon first installing Crystal Enterprise several default sample applications and system interfaces are created, each made available through the Crystal Enterprise Launchpad. This chapter has explained how to begin using the out-of-the-box interfaces of Crystal Enterprise, and has provided an introduction to the standard functionality associated with each application. These samples and interfaces provide for a quick and useful insight into the capabilities and potential use of the system.

The Crystal Enterprise Launchpad is designed to be used as the primary starting point for newly established systems. The Launchpad also serves as an on-going source for reference materials, such as system documentation, client and administrative samples, product updates, and technical support contacts. Regardless of whether the default out-of-the-box user applications with Crystal Enterprise are used or an organization develops its own custom application, the Launchpad can still serve an important role in providing quick and easy Web-based access to information regarding the Crystal Enterprise system.

Although any of the sample user applications can be used in the actual deployment of the system, or perhaps customized to meet more specific system requirements, the ePortfolio application is designed to provide the most robust and feature-rich user interface. The ePortfolio application offers a full range of functionality that is often required to deliver a secure, managed, and distributed enterprise reporting architecture. It has been fully designed and tested to support high-volume scaled deployments that could include tens of thousands of users.

Deciding which Crystal Enterprise application is right for your organization will likely include an evaluation of key functional and technical system requirements, with consideration also being given to the various needs of your organization's end-user communities. Often, multiple user applications are developed with Crystal Enterprise to meet the demands of differing organizational user communities, whether internal or external. This scenario might include an intranet application for employees to access commonly requested reports (such as training schedules and company documentation) and an extranet application for customers that offers quick and easy access to invoices or account information. Regardless of the scenario, the Crystal Enterprise system can support these varying needs and provides you with the flexibility to deliver the appropriate solution for any enterprise reporting projects.

PART

II

CH

5

CHAPTER 6

CUSTOMIZING ePORTFOLIO FOR RAPID INFORMATION DELIVERY

In this chapter

Although ePortfolio is intended to be an out-of-the-box, highly interactive client interface for Crystal Enterprise, it is by no means a static application. It can be easily customized to meet more of the look, feel, and function that an organization requires.

Essentially, ePortfolio is a Portal application written for Crystal Enterprise consisting of

- Crystal Server Pages (CSP) pages
- Cascading Style Sheets (CSS)
- Graphic images (gif files)

All these opensource components comprising ePortfolio can be easily manipulated to an organization's preference.

Any organization wanting to modify ePortfolio, either from an aesthetic perspective or programmatically, will need to modify all or part of these components.

Note

CSP Pages are essentially the equivalent of Active Server Pages (ASP) with a few minor differences. This means if a developer has ASP development skills, she will be able to write CSP pages. They are just Crystal Enterprise's way of knowing what pages have to do with its system. Refer to Chapters 13 and 14 for more details on customizing CSP pages. CSP pages are covered in minor detail in this chapter.

→ For a detailed overview of the features and default functions of ePortfolio, **see** Chapter 5, "Using the Crystal Enterprise Launchpad."

The reason ePortfolio was created in such a modular manner, for example using CSS documents to drive the appearance, was to facilitate quick customizations. Although an end user, by default, can set his own preferences for ePortfolio, an organization can choose to limit this. Another organization might want to set a default corporate color scheme and not allow the user to change this, which would necessitate applying a different style sheet to ePortfolio.

It's important to note that while many organizations will find their information delivery requirements fully met with a combination of vanilla ePortfolio and a well-thought-out Crystal Enterprise security implementation (see Chapter 10, "Administering and Configuring Crystal Enterprise"), others will want to take advantage of the opensource nature and customizability of ePortfolio.

This chapter reviews some common customizations that organizations can easily and quickly implement for ePortfolio. The simplicity of making changes to some of the ePortfolio CSP pages is what enables a Crystal Enterprise administrator or developer to quickly and easily affect the functionality of ePortfolio available to a single user or group of users.

Before actual customizations are made to ePortfolio, a quick review of how ePortfolio interacts with Crystal Enterprise will help you understand which customizations to make to affect certain portions of the application.

UNDERSTANDING EPORTFOLIO'S INTERACTION WITH CRYSTAL ENTERPRISE

To emphasize a point, the ePortfolio interface is just one of an infinite number of front-end interfaces to the functionality provided by Crystal Enterprise. The differentiating factor for ePortfolio is that Crystal Decisions treats ePortfolio as the default Crystal Enterprise client tool.

Regardless of interface to Crystal Enterprise, ePortfolio included, each one interacts with Crystal Enterprise through an underlying object model that can be driven through a COM-enabled scripting language such as JavaScript (see Figure 6.1 for a schematic). ePortfolio is such an application. The CSS files are an added benefit because they enable quick modification of color schemes to match an intranet site.

Figure 6.1
A simple diagram highlighting the flow of ePortfolio interaction with Crystal Enterprise.

The ePortfolio CSP pages and CSS documents can be found in the ePortfolio folder. For reference, the location is Install Drive\Program Files\Crystal Decisions\Web Content\Enterprise\eportfolio\en.

Later chapters discuss the object model and advanced customization in great detail, but it's helpful to initiate the discussion of customization by developing a preliminary understanding of both CSS documents and CSP pages. A savvy ASP developer will be able to skip the next few sections and get right into the customization portions.

UNDERSTANDING CASCADING STYLE SHEETS

Cascading Style Sheets (CSS) are rules that dictate how to display different HTML tags to a Web browser. These rules can specify several different display style properties (such as text color and font size) and can generally be stored in three different locations:

- Inline styles that apply to a single HTML tag
- Document-level styles that apply to a complete HTML document
- External style sheets (CSS files) that can be applied across multiple HTML documents

PART

II

CH

6

The out-of-the-box ePortfolio interface uses external style sheets to set styles across all its involved pages.

Listing 6.1 highlights a sample rule from the default ePortfolio CSS file, default.css. This rule specifies both color and font attributes for all the HTML tags that use the class of "header" (see Listing 6.2) within Crystal Enterprise.

LISTING 6.1 SAMPLE CASCADING STYLE SHEET RULE

```
.header {
    background-color: Blue;
    color: white;
    font-family: verdana;
    font-size: 9pt;
}
```

LISTING 6.2 SAMPLE OF AN HTML TAG USING THE CLASS HEADER

```
<td class="header" valign='middle' colspan='3'>
```

Note

For advanced information on cascading style sheets, please see a reference on HTML and/or Cascading style sheets.

As stated previously, modifying the external style sheets used by ePortfolio enables customization of the basic look and feel of the Crystal Enterprise interface to best integrate into a specific corporate standard look and feel.

An administrator or developer will be able to access and edit these pages and styles from a simple text editor or through a more functional tool such as Visual Studio, FrontPage, or TopStyle. Although style sheets are an important part of ePortfolio, they only drive the appearance of the client tool, not the function. Many organizations require the capability to remove certain portions of ePortfolio functionality because it might exceed the scope of their deployment. Modification of ePortfolio functionality is accomplished by editing the CSP pages that comprise the interface.

UNDERSTANDING CRYSTAL SERVER PAGES

Crystal Server Pages (CSP) are files that contain a mixture of HTML and scripting code such as VBScript or JavaScript, very much like Active Server Pages. Please refer to Chapters 3 and 13 for a more exhaustive explanation of CSP pages. The pages that comprise ePortfolio are designed to provide an end user with his own unique zero-client DHTML interface to Crystal Enterprise. These end-user interfaces are delivered to the end user through a combination of static HTML and dynamically run server-side scripts that access the Crystal Enterprise SDK functionality.

The actual CSP pages that make up ePortfolio are found in Install Path\Program Files\Crystal Decisions\Web Content\Enterprise\ePortfolio\en. Each of these files has a .csp extension and can be edited with a simple text editor such as Notepad or an application such as FrontPage or Visual InterDev. Examples in this chapter demonstrate how to make simple functional modifications to these CSP pages that will ultimately affect the Crystal Enterprise end user's experience when retrieving reports.

To further clarify how a CSP page is processed, refer to Chapter 3, "Exploring the System Architecture." To review, a CSP page contains HTML and some relevant script such as JavaScript. When a Web server such as Microsoft Internet Information Server encounters a CSP page, it knows to forward the entire CSP page to the Crystal Enterprise Web Component Server for processing of the page.

The Web Component Server (WCS) contains a processing engine that will execute the script. This script usually contains information such as a Crystal Enterprise username and password, as well as some description of the desired actions the user is trying to complete, typically viewing a report.

In the case of a report-viewing request, Crystal Enterprise would process the report and ultimately return a DHTML page to the Web server, which in turn is sent to the end user's Web browser.

There is actually much more to the process than detailed previously, so please refer to Chapter 3 for more detail.

It's important to note that an end user is never exposed to any part of the CSP pages or what they actually do. The end user is completely isolated from the business logic encapsulated in the CSP pages and only receives the produced HTML output.

The CSP pages are evaluated by the WCS (see Chapter 3 for a review), and only HTML or client-side functions are sent back to the user's browser. Additionally, no scripts are ever executed on the Web server itself (a key differentiator from ASP, which processes scripts on the Web server). The exception to this would be if the Crystal Enterprise Web Component Server were installed on the same physical machine as the Web server.

→ For an in-depth look at CSP pages, **see** Chapter 15.

UNDERSTANDING EPORTFOLIO'S STRUCTURE

The central hub for ePortfolio interface is the available.csp page. It includes numerous server-side CSP pages and client-side JavaScript files, and provides links to the remaining default ePortfolio pages. This page is responsible for implementing the desktop user's interface and supporting its main reporting functions. With its default settings, the ePortfolio should resemble Figure 6.2.

Figure 6.3 highlights how available.csp interacts with the remaining provided ePortfolio CSP pages and what JavaScript libraries it uses. All the introductory functionality configurations/customizations covered in this chapter focus on editing this central csp hub.

Figure 6.2
Default V8.5
ePortfolio interface.

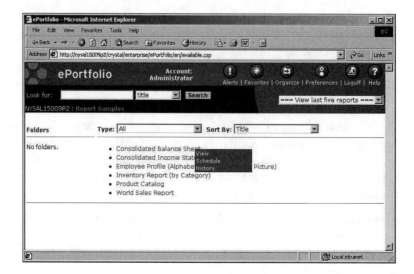

Note

To find additional supporting infomation on the ePortfolio CSP pages, please reference the online Web Developer's Guide accessed from the Crystal Launchpad.

CUSTOMIZING EPORTFOLIO FOR AN INTRANET DEPLOYMENT—THE MAPLE LEAF EQUIPMENT SCENARIO

The rest of this chapter reviews an ePortfolio customization scenario that will enable a hypothetical company—Maple Leaf Equipment (MLE)—to customize the Crystal Enterprise ePortfolio interface to suit its particular corporate look, feel, and business requirements.

MLE is a sporting equipment corporation that has decided to implement an enterprise reporting system. The IT/IS and e-business groups wanting to realize the benefits of Crystal Enterprise immediately have decided to implement ePortfolio with some simple configurations as their initial interface.

To summarize, MLE's high-level information delivery requirements include the following:

- A quick deployment of enterprise reporting functionality
- An MLE corporate look and feel to include its corporate logo
- A consistent MLE color scheme within its enterprise reporting system
- A restriction on its end user's capability to edit the corporate color scheme
- The application of an MLE-specific naming convention across the Crystal Enterprise interface

Figure 6.3
ePortfolio CSP page
schematic.

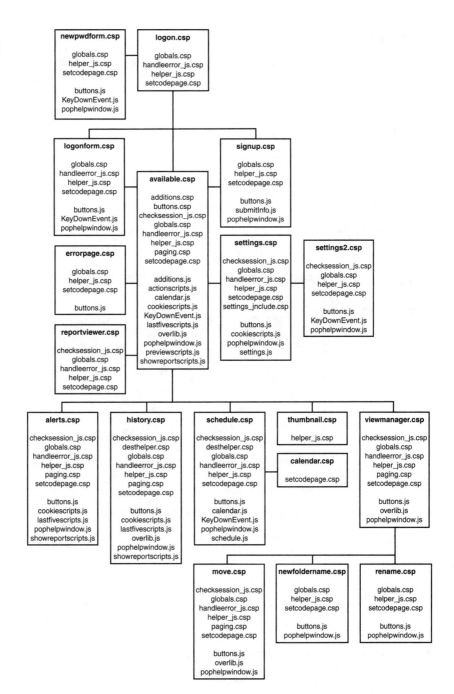

Note

Before changing any of the CSS or CSP files in ePortfolio, make a backup of the en directory (or appropriate localized language) in case a file needs to be restored. This method also provides some level of version control for ePortfolio customization.

LOCATING ePORTFOLIO COMPONENTS

One of the initial implementation requirements of the e-business team at MLE is that all internal and external Web interfaces of the company maintain a consistent look and feel. The e-business leaders at MLE understand that they will be able to edit the default styles for ePortfolio by editing the provided CSS files.

Compare the MLE home page in Figure 6.4 to the default ePortfolio page in Figure 6.2. From this home page MLE employees will link to their enterprise reporting system.

Figure 6.4
Maple Leaf
Equipment home
page.

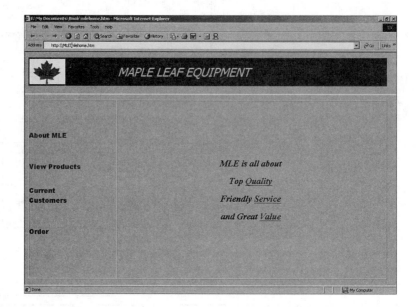

The default ePortfolio CSS files are located in Install Path:\Program Files\Crystal Decisions\Web Content\Enterprise\ePortfolio\en\css. These files should be edited to reflect the desired style changes to mimic the MLE standard look and feel.

CUSTOMIZING ePORTFOLIO THROUGH STYLE SHEETS

Although CSS files can be edited with as little as a text editor and an HTML/CSS reference book, to facilitate a quick and easy configuration, the e-business team from MLE uses the style sheet editor distributed on the Crystal Enterprise CD—TopStyle Lite. This can be installed from the CE CD or downloaded from Bradsoft's Web site at http://www.bradsoft.com/topstyle/.

Using TopStyle, the e-business developer from MLE opens up default.css from the css sub-folder in the ePortfolio directory. In TopStyle, the CSS customization interface is displayed in Figure 6.5. For contrast, a simple text interface appears in Figure 6.6. The GUI-based interfaces are recommended because of their ease of use and productivity benefits (such as when selecting accurate colors and ensuring browser compatibility).

Figure 6.5
TopStyle Lite's easy-to-use CSS editing interface.

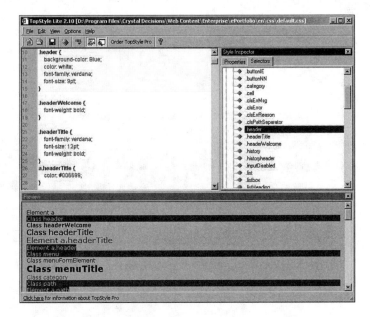

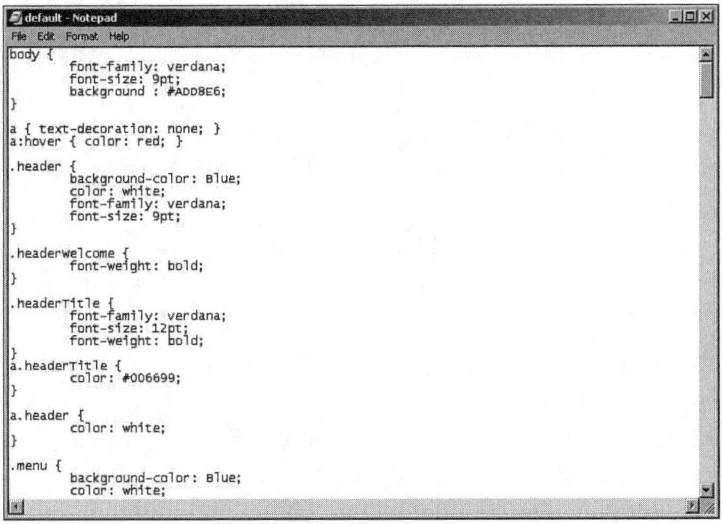

Figure 6.6
Default.css opened in a text editor.

The MLE developer experiments with different color and font combinations by selecting specific classes (such as header or menu) and changing the default selections to best match their standard look and feel. After some quick color and font edits in the default ePortfolio style sheet, MLE settles on the results shown in Figure 6.7.

Note

When trying to view changes to the CSS files for ePortfolio in a Web browser, the cached versions of the old CSS files might need to be deleted by clearing the Web browser's cached files. In Internet Explorer, select Tools, Options, and select Delete Temporary Internet Files.

Figure 6.7
ePortfolio with the MLE color scheme.

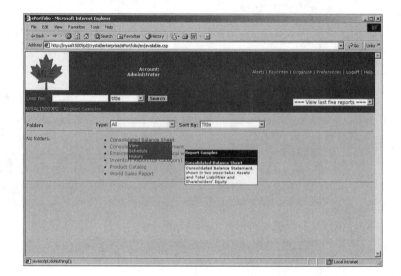

It's worth noting that this seemingly drastic change to the ePortfolio look and feel was accomplished by editing only six different CSS classes, replacing only two graphic images, and changing only one of the default user preferences.

These six affected classes clearly provide the users of Crystal Enterprise with a quick path to a custom and integrated user interface. These classes follow with a quick description of their effects on ePortfolio:

- **.Header**—This class is used to affect the top section or band of the ePortfolio interface, where the MLE logo sits.
- **.Menu**—The second band in the ePortfolio header (where Search is located).
- **.Category**—The third area of the ePortfolio header (where the top-level folders are displayed).
- **.Path**—The fourth band in the ePortfolio header.

- **.List**—This class is used to affect the main listing area of ePortfolio where the reports and folders are displayed.
- **.Body**—This class affects the entire area on which the rest of the ePortfolio interface sits (such as the background of surrounding Web page).

Experimentation with the look and feel of the ePortfolio interface is accomplished by changing the settings on the variety of other classes highlighted in the CSS files. As a matter of good practice it's recommended that a copy of the en folder in the ePortfolio directory be made as a backup to refer to the original ePortfolio. Now take a quick look at some additional changes (two images and one user preference setting) made to create this custom MLE interface.

CUSTOMIZING EPORTFOLIO THROUGH PREFERENCES

You might have noticed that the custom MLE interface has different graphical icons than were present in the default ePortfolio interface (see the upper-right sections of Figures 6.5 and 6.8). The default ePortfolio icons were removed by MLE because their colored background did not match MLE's standard look and feel. These icons were set to not display by simply changing one of the default ePortfolio preferences found under the Settings hyperlink. Although Chapter 5 reviews this in more detail, a user can set some ePortfolio preferences through the preferences screen displayed in Figure 6.8.

Figure 6.8
The User Preferences screen.

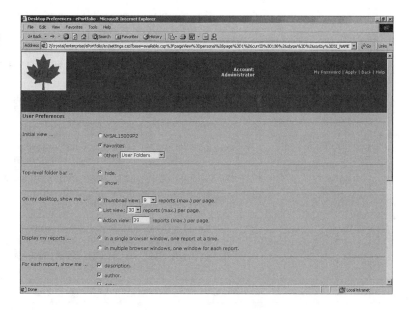

PART

II

CH

6

The User Preferences screen is accessed from the default ePortfolio page. It enables end users to customize the individual look and feel of their personal ePortfolio interfaces. One of the configurable settings found here is the format of the menu display.

MLE decided to only show text and not the provided graphical buttons as options for selection. An alternative solution they could have considered would have been to edit the actual graphics images (GIFs) in a graphics editing package such as JASC PaintShop or CorelDRAW. The next section covers this customization process, but it's important to note the different types of customizations available by default under the preferences.csp page. They are listed in Table 6.1.

TABLE 6.1 AVAILABLE USER PREFERENCE SETTINGS IN PREFERENCES.CSP

Setting	Effect
Initial View	Users can have their initial folder view set to be any of the folders to which they have access. This can include their personal favorites folder, any public folder to which they have secured access, or the highest-level root folder.
Top Level Folder Bar	Determines whether the list of folders available is displayed in the header section of ePortfolio.
Desktop Display Options	Enables the selection of three different types of report listings: *Thumbnails* display where each report is represented graphically by a thumbnail representing the first page of the report. *Listing* displays a simple listing of the accessible reports. *Action* displays all accessible reports and all accessible actions on the individual reports.
Browser Window Setting	Enables reports to either be successively displayed in a single browser window or in multiple browser windows.
Report Metadata Options	Enables the selection of specific report metadata to be displayed to the end users. The available metadata includes report description, report author, report date, thumbnail (if applicable), and instance count.
Menu Options	Enables the selection of the menu display settings to incorporate either text, graphical buttons, or both.
Color Scheme	Enables the selection of different default color schemes for ePortfolio. Five different default settings come out-of-the-box.
Report Viewer	Enables the selection of the report viewer to be used when viewing any Crystal Report. The six viewer options include ActiveX, DHTML, HTML Page, Java, Java plug-in, and Navigator plug-in.
Time Zone	Enables the selection of the time zone.

CUSTOMIZING EPORTFOLIO IMAGES

Although it's beyond the scope of this chapter and book to discuss the capabilities that exist around customizing images for Web page deployment, it's important to highlight the location of the default ePortfolio images and highlight two that will regularly be updated or replaced through even simple customization.

All the images for ePortfolio are located on the Crystal Enterprise installation drive in the following path:

\Program Files\Crystal Decisions\Web Content\Enterprise\ePortfolio\en\images

Two images that many organizations will likely replace are the ePortfolio graphic pictured in Figure 6.9 and another circular graphic that is subtly placed in the default ePortfolio interface.

Figure 6.9
The default ePortfolio graphic/icon.

In the MLE example, the MLE Web developer replaced the ePortfolio graphic, called eportfolio_default.gif, with its own corporate logo.

A more subtle customization is the replacement of this second image when organizations do not want to use the circular theme implied by this small graphics file. With the MLE example, this file was replaced with a solid colored graphic. For reference, this file is called menu_dot_bg_default.gif and has a corresponding smaller relative file called small_dot_default.gif that will also likely need to be edited in many implementations.

A Web developer or Crystal Enterprise administrator should review the images that are provided with ePortfolio and edit them as required to meet specific user interface requirements.

CUSTOMIZING EPORTFOLIO FUNCTIONALITY THROUGH CSP PAGES

Having successfully captured the standard MLE look and feel in the ePortfolio interface, the e-business team at MLE now wants to focus attention on modifying the default ePortfolio functionality to best meet its specific end user and system requirements. Because the central page of ePortfolio is the available.csp page, the team begins its functionality changes by opening this page with a selected development environment such as Microsoft Visual Studio (see Figure 6.10). Other editors such as FrontPage or even a text editor can be used as well.

Figure 6.10
The available.csp page being edited in Visual Studio.

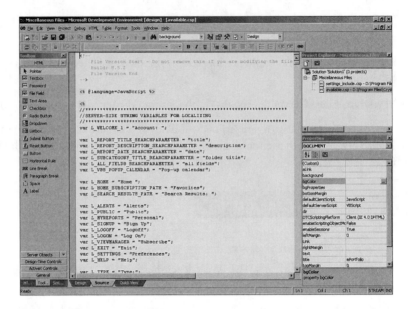

CHANGING ePORTFOLIO USER PERSONALIZATION AND SUBSCRIPTION OPTIONS

As part of its implementation, the MLE team chose to have end users start their navigation within the Crystal Enterprise system at the highest level common folder. However, the team did want to enable end users to take advantage of Crystal Enterprise's personalization functionality and quickly navigate to their preselected set of favorite reports.

Although the ePortfolio interface provided personalization (favorites) and subscription (organize) capabilities out-of-the-box that met many of the business requirements, the MLE team wanted to customize the names in the default interface to Persona and Subscribe. To accomplish this, the team searched the available.csp page for the following two server-side string variables:

```
    var L_MYREPORTS = "Favorites";
var L_VIEWMANAGER = "Organize";
```

and replaced them with

```
    var L_MYREPORTS = "Personal";
var L_VIEWMANAGER = "Subscribe";
```

These settings, along with several others defined at the beginning of each .csp page including available.csp, can quickly be edited and even localized to specific regions or countries.

MLE was satisfied with these small name changes; however, other organizations might want to explore other areas of personalization and subscription customization by editing their default ePortfolio interface. A few areas of interest are highlighted in the following sections, along with some suggestions about the types of simple customizations possible.

CHANGING EPORTFOLIO ORGANIZE AND FAVORITES OPTIONS

If MLE had decided to further edit or eliminate some or all of the personalization and subscription functionality held within the default ePortfolio interface, the best starting point would be in accessing the appropriate functions and the associated function calls in available.csp (see Listing 6.3).

LISTING 6.3   AVAILABLE.CSP CODE SNIPPET

```
// LAUNCH THE ORGANIZER DIALOG WINDOW
function ViewManager() {

    //CENTER WINDOW ON SCREEN
    LeftPosition = (screen.width) ? (screen.width-700)/2 : 0;
    TopPosition = (screen.height) ? (screen.height-325)/2 : 0;

<%
    Response.Write("    winProps =
'width=700,height=350,location=no,status=yes,scrollbars=yes,
➥menubars=no,toolbars=no,
    resizable=yes,top='+TopPosition+',left='+LeftPosition;" + vbCRLF);
    Response.Write("    reportWindow = window.open('viewmanager.csp?currSID=
    " + currentID + "', 'u', winProps);" + vbCRLF);
%>
}
.
.
.
function changeFolder(id, pageView)
{
    document.obtypeform.currID.value = id;
    if(pageView)
        document.obtypeform.pageView.value = pageView;
    document.obtypeform.searchString.value = "";
    document.obtypeform.searchParameter.value = "";
    document.obtypeform.page.value = 1;
    document.obtypeform.submit();
}
```

Additionally, the calls made to ViewManager and Changefolder functions are in the code shown in Listing 6.4.

PART
II

CH
6

LISTING 6.4   AVAILABLE.CSP CODE SNIPPET

```
buttonLinks += "<td align=middle><a class='header'
➥href='javascript:ViewManager()
'" + GenerateButtonEvents("Organize", strStyleSheetName) + "><img name=
'Organize' src='" + GetLinkPath() + "images/organize_up_" +
strStyleSheetName + ".gif' alt='"+L_VIEWMANAGER+"' valign='bottom' border=
'0'></a></td>";

simpleLinks += "<td align=middle><a class='menuItem' href=
'javascript:ViewManager()'>" + L_VIEWMANAGER + "</a></td>";
        .
        .
        .
buttonLinks += "<td align=middle><a class='header'
➥href='javascript:changeFolder
(0, \"" + menuLink + "\");'" + GenerateButtonEvents(imgName, strStyleSheetName)
 + "><img name='"+imgName+"' src='" + GetLinkPath() + menuImg + "' alt=
'"+menuName+"' valign='bottom' border='0'></td>";

simpleLinks += "<td align=middle><a class='menuItem' href=
'javascript:changeFolder(0, \"" + menuLink + "\");'>" + menuName + "</a></td>";
```

As highlighted in the code, the ViewManager function is responsible for presenting a pop-up window (see Figure 6.11) that enables the end user to copy, move, delete, rename, or create shortcuts to report objects in folders to which they have been granted access.

Figure 6.11
The View Manager pop-up window.

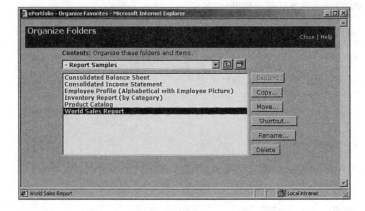

The location of the window, its viewing properties, and its display location can be modified through the provided JavaScript. More advanced customization can be achieved by editing the ViewManager.csp file and modifying as required. The following are two configuration scenarios that organizations regularly consider at this point:

■ Elimination of some of the available actions from the organize/subscribe window.

■ Narrowing the focus of the destination folder to be only the current user's personal folder.

MLE technical specifications called for a "subscribe" feature in its Crystal Enterprise solution that would enable users to create shortcuts to reports within their personal Favorites folder; however, the team did not want to provide all the default folder and report organization capabilities out-of-the-box.

To accomplish the required customization, MLE removed the capability of its end user to move, copy, rename, or delete any report objects. Additionally, MLE limited the destination folder for these shortcuts to be only the specified user's favorites folder.

A Crystal Enterprise developer or administrator should familiarize himself with the available.csp and ViewManager.csp pages for this type of customization. Remember, it's always good practice to maintain copies of the original source CSS and CSP files for backup.

Changing ePortfolio End-User Preferences and Defaults

The previous section outlined a myriad of end user configurable options in ePortfolio. Although impressed with the personalization capabilities of the product, the MLE development team decided that it in fact wanted to limit the interface options that can be configured by end users. Specifically, users should maintain the corporate color scheme the MLE team applied for all users. This means not allowing end users to select different color schemes in ePortfolio. Additionally, the MLE staff decided to use the term User Settings instead of the default ePortfolio term Preferences.

To accomplish the new naming convention, the available.csp page was searched for the following server-side string variable:

```
var L_SETTINGS = "Preferences";
```

and replaced the variable with

```
var L_SETTINGS = "User Settings";
```

To eliminate the capability for end users to edit the selected corporate color scheme from the User Preferences screen, the MLE staff made some changes to the settings_include.csp page called from the settings.csp page. The relevant component of the original settings.csp screen appears in Listing 6.5.

LISTING 6.5   SETTINGS.CSP CODE SNIPPET BEFORE MLE EDITS

```
    // LAUNCH THE SETTINGS DIALOG WINDOW
function LaunchSettings() {
<%
if( !bSearch )
    Response.Write("    var baseRef = 'available.csp?pageView=" + pageView +
     "&page=" + StartPage + "&currID=" + currentID + "&otype=" + strType +
     "&sortby=" + sortby + "'" + vbCRLF);
else
    Response.Write("    var baseRef = 'available.csp?pageView=" + pageView +
     "&otype=" + strType + "&sortby=" + sortby + "'" + vbCRLF);
%>
    document.location = "settings.csp?base=" + escape(baseRef);
}
```

The call to this page is made from available.csp in Listing 6.6.

LISTING 6.6 AVAILABLE.CSP CODE SNIPPET

```
    buttonLinks += "<td align=middle><a class='header' href=
'javascript:LaunchSettings();'" + GenerateButtonEvents("Settings",
strStyleSheetName) + "><img name='Settings' src='" + GetLinkPath() +
 "images/preferences_up_" + strStyleSheetName + ".gif' alt='"+L_SETTINGS+
"' valign='bottom' border='0'></a></td>";

simpleLinks += "<td align=middle><a class='menuItem' href='javascript:
LaunchSettings();'>" + L_SETTINGS + "</a></td>";
```

The settings.csp page references the relevant csp page, (settings_include.csp) that will need editing in Listing 6.7.

LISTING 6.7 SETTINGS.CSP INCLUDE CODE REFERENCE

```
<!--#include file="settings_include.csp"-->
```

The settings_include.csp page enumerates through all the different configurable user settings. To eliminate one or more of these settings, MLE simply needs to delete the appropriate, well-documented section. The color scheme configuration setting is called by the code in Listing 6.8 and, when this is deleted (or commented out) the desired result is achieved.

LISTING 6.8 COLOR SCHEME USER CONFIGURATION CSP/HTML

```
    <tr>
    <td class="main" width="20%" valign="top">
        ➥Display my desktop with this color scheme
        ➥</td>
    <td>
    <table width="100%" border="1" cellspacing="1" cellpadding="0">
    <tr>
     <td class="main" align="center" style="background:#006699;"> </td>
     <td class="main" align="center" style="background:#990000"> </td>
     <td class="main" align="center" style="background:#009966"> </td>
     <td class="main" align="center" style="background:#333399"> </td>
     <td class="main" align="center" style="background:#CC9900"> </td>
    </tr>
    <tr>
     <td width="16%" class="main" align="center" style="background:black;
     color:white;"><span style="font-weight:bold"> </span><br></td>
     <td width="16%" class="main" align="center" style="background:black;
     color:white;"><span style="font-weight:bold"> </span><br></td>
     <td width="16%" class="main" align="center" style="background:black;
     color:white;"><span style="font-weight:bold"> </span><br></td>
     <td width="16%" class="main" align="center" style="background:black;
     color:white;"><span style="font-weight:bold"> </span><br></td>
     <td width="16%" class="main" align="center" style="background:black;
     color:white;"><span style="font-weight:bold"> </span><br></td>
    </tr>
    <tr>
```

LISTING 6.8   CONTINUED

```
<%
strChk = new Array(6)
for(i = 0; i < 6; ++i)
{
    strChk[i] = "";
}
strChk[csn] = " checked";

Response.Write("<td class='main' style='color:#006699;'
➥align='center'><INPUT type=
    'radio' name='csn' value='0'" + strChk[0] + ">" + L_DEFAULT + "</td>"
    ➥+ vbCRLF);
Response.Write("<td class='main' style='color:#990000;' align='center'>
➥<INPUT type=
    'radio' name='csn' value='1'" + strChk[1] + ">" + L_RED + "</td>" +
    ➥vbCRLF);
Response.Write("<td class='main' style='color:#009966;' align='center'>
➥<INPUT type=
    'radio' name='csn' value='2'" + strChk[2] + ">" + L_GREEN + "</td>" +
    ➥vbCRLF);
Response.Write("<td class='main' style='color:#333399;' align='center'>
➥<INPUT type=
    'radio' name='csn' value='3'" + strChk[3] + ">" + L_PURPLE + "</td>" +
    ➥vbCRLF);
Response.Write("<td class='main' style='color:#CC9900;' align='center'>
➥<INPUT type=
    'radio' name='csn' value='4'" + strChk[4] + ">" + L_GOLD + "</td>" + vbCRLF);
%>
    </tr>
    </table>
    </td>
</tr>
```

Figures 6.12 and 6.13 highlight the changed end-user interface and the removal of the user preference option to edit the ePortfolio color scheme.

As with the color scheme user configuration, organizations might want to disable any of the end-user settings by simply editing the settings_include.csp code. Some fairly common settings for which organizations set universal standards are Viewer Type (such as Zero-Client DHTML Viewer) or Report Format (such as Crystal Reports).

CHANGING EPORTFOLIO ALERTING

The MLE team needed to customize the Alert name in the default interface to Notifications. To accomplish this, the team searched the available.csp page for the following server-side string variable:

```
var L_ALERTS = "Alerts";
```

and replaced it with

```
var L_ALERTS = "Notifications";
```

The Alerts function and the associated call to it from within available.csp are highlighted in Listing 6.9.

PART

II

CH

6

Figure 6.12
The Settings screen highlighting color settings before edits.

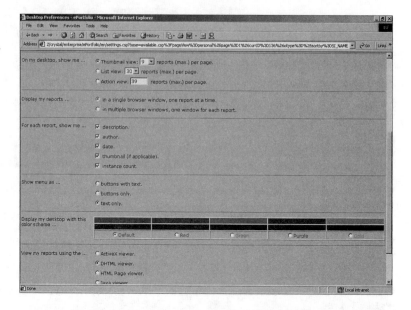

Figure 6.13
The Customized Settings screen after edits.

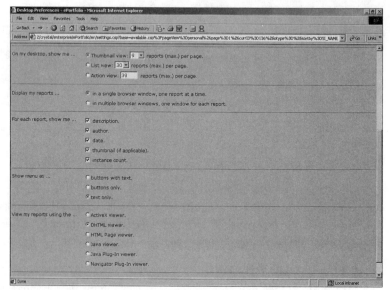

LISTING 6.9   ALERTS FUNCTION IN AVAILABLE.CSP

```
    // LAUNCH ALERTS DIALOG WINDOW
function Alerts() {
    //CENTER WINDOW ON SCREEN
    LeftPosition = (screen.width) ? (screen.width-800)/2 : 0;
    TopPosition = (screen.height) ? (screen.height-430)/2 : 0;
    winProps = "width=800,height=430,location=no,scrollbars=yes,
        ➥...menubars=no,toolbars=no,resizable=y
    es,top="+TopPosition+",left="+LeftPosition;
```

Listing 6.9   Continued

```
    UtilWindow = window.open("alerts.csp?id="+currentID,"u", winProps);
}


if(currentID != 0)
    {
     buttonLinks += "<td align=middle><a class='header' href=
     'javascript:Alerts();'" + GenerateButtonEvents("Alerts",
     ➥strStyleSheetName) +
     "><img name='Alerts' src='" + GetLinkPath() + "images/alerts_up_" +
     strStyleSheetName + ".gif' alt='"+L_ALERTS+"' valign='bottom' border=
     '0'></a></td>";
     simpleLinks += "<td align=middle><a class='menuItem' href=
     'javascript:Alerts();'>" + L_ALERTS + "</a></td>";
    }
    else
    {
        buttonLinks += "<td align=middle><img name='Alerts' src='" +
    GetLinkPath() + "images/alerts_up_" + strStyleSheetName + ".gif' alt='"+
    L_ALERTS+"' valign='bottom' border='0'></td>";
        simpleLinks += "<td align=middle><span class=
    'listUnavailable'>" + L_ALERTS + "</span></td>"
    }
```

If an organization such as MLE requires customization to the data displayed in the Alerts window, it should refer to the alerts.csp page and complete any necessary changes. A common customization for alerts is to change the report metadata that is reported back to the user in the Alerts window (including report description). The standard alerting window is easy to customize, and any number of small customizations can be performed on that interface.

Changing ePortfolio Help Options

If the MLE team had a requirement to customize the Help name in the default interface to something like "MLE Help," it would need to search the available.csp page for the following server-side string variable:

```
var L_HELP = "Help";
```

and replaced it with

```
var L_HELP = "MLE Help";
```

The Help function is called from Listing 6.10 in available.csp.

Listing 6.10   Calls to Help in available.csp

```
    buttonLinks += "<td align=middle><a class='header' href=
'javascript:popHelpWindow();'" + GenerateButtonEvents("Help",
strStyleSheetName) + "><img name='Help' src='" + GetLinkPath() +
"images/help_up_" + strStyleSheetName + ".gif' alt='"+L_HELP+"' valign=
'bottom' border='0'></a></td>";
simpleLinks += "<td align=middle><a class='menuItem' href=
'javascript:popHelpWindow();'>" + L_HELP + "</a></td>";
```

The JavaScript function that is called from available.csp is actually sourced from a JavaScript file—dPopHelpWindow.js—that is included in help.csp with the code in Listing 6.11.

```
Response.Write("<script language='javascript' src='" + GetLinkPath() +
  "pophelpwindow.js'></script>" + vbCRLF);
```

LISTING 6.11 POPHELPWINDOW FUNCTION

```
function popHelpWindow() {

    var sw = 800;  //SCREEN WIDTH VARIABLE
    var sh = 600;  //SCREEN HEIGHT VARIABLE

    //CENTER WINDOW ON SCREEN
    LeftPosition = (screen.width) ? (screen.width-sw)/2 : 0;
    TopPosition = (screen.height) ? (screen.height-sh)/2 : 0;

    winProps = "width="+sw+",height="+sh+",location=no,
          ➡...scrollbars=yes,menubar=no,toolbar=no,
    resizable=yes,top="+TopPosition+",left="+LeftPosition;
    helpWindow = window.open("help.csp", "helpWin", winProps);
}
```

The location of the Help window, its viewing properties, and its display location can be modified through the provided JavaScript code. More advanced customization can be achieved by editing Help.csp and modifying as deemed necessary. Alternatively, if an organization like MLE wanted to provide its own custom version of help, it could simply replace the reference to help.csp with a reference to its own custom application help.

CHANGING ePORTFOLIO SCHEDULING OPTIONS

One last area in which MLE required customizations was the scheduling interface. In addition to using the security model to grant and deny scheduling rights to its systems covered in the administration chapter, MLE required a change to the scheduling options made available to end users through some quick customization work on the scheduling interface (see Figure 6.14).

Figure 6.14
The default scheduling interface.

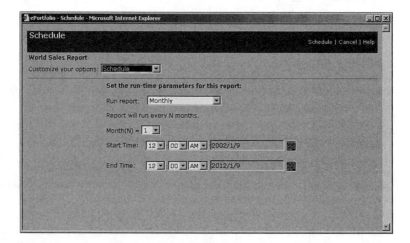

The scheduling function, `schedule()`, is accessed from available.csp through the inclusion of the actionscripts.js JavaScript file, as shown in Listing 6.12.

LISTING 6.12   SCHEDULE FUNCTION

```
    //FUNCTION WHICH OPENS THE SCHEDULE DIALOG WINDOW
function Schedule() {
    if ( PreviewLaunch != 0 ) {
        //CENTER WINDOW ON SCREEN
        LeftPosition = (screen.width) ? (screen.width-800)/2 : 0;
        TopPosition = (screen.height) ? (screen.height-430)/2 : 0;

        winProps =
        ➥"width=800,height=430,location=no,scrollbars=yes,
        ➥menubars=no,toolbars=no,...resizable=yes,top="+
        ➥TopPosition+",left="+LeftPosition;
        UtilWindow = window.open("schedule.csp?id="+PreviewLaunch, "u",
        ➥winProps);
    }
}
```

The location of the scheduling window and its viewing properties and display location can be modified through the provided JavaScript code in Listing 16.12. Advanced customization can be achieved by editing the Schedule.csp file and modifying as required.

Some potential scheduling customizations may include the exclusion of a subset of the default scheduling options in the interface, such as filters, destination, formats, and so on. By excluding one of these interfaces or even limiting the options available within one of the options, organizations can enforce corporate standards or restrict certain end-user behaviors. One common restriction imposed is the disabling of e-mail as a report destination to limit network traffic and potential communication of sensitive corporate information.

TROUBLESHOOTING

When making customizations to any of the provided CSS or CSP pages, it's good practice and extremely productive to keep backups of all changed files. By performing this safety step, organizations will always be able to restore previously saved pages and move back to a previous state of customization.

SUMMARY

This chapter provided a summary of some of the more common customizations that organizations implement with ePortfolio, the default Crystal Enterprise end-user client application.

ePortfolio is composed of primarily three opensource components:

- CSP pages written in JavaScript
- Cascading Style Sheets (CSS files)
- .gif images

Manipulating these files, either exclusively or all together, enables an organization change the look, feel, and function of ePortfolio to meet their specific needs.

Additionally, some JavaScript (.js) files support some ePortfolio functionality. It is not recommended that these files be modified.

A fictitious organization, MLE, completed customizations to ePortfolio to meet its specific business and end-user interface requirements for ePortfolio. This enabled the organization to rapidly deploy Crystal Enterprise.

It's important to note that the possible configurations and customizations highlighted in this chapter barely scratch the surface of the flexibility with which the information delivery functionality of Crystal Enterprise can be delivered to users and applications through a Web browser.

PART III

CREATING CONTENT FOR CRYSTAL ENTERPRISE

CHAPTER 7

PUBLISHING CONTENT WITH CRYSTAL ENTERPRISE

In this chapter

Most organizations adopting Crystal Enterprise have an existing investment in Crystal Reports and have many prebuilt reports to publish and test. Although content management incorporates the management of many objects, such as folders, within Crystal Enterprise, this chapter focuses exclusively on publishing content into Crystal Enterprise.

The following two chapters actually discuss more about the content creation/report design tools for Crystal Enterprise, but this chapter precedes them because many readers are familiar with the primary reporting tool for Crystal Enterprise, Crystal Reports, and are eager to begin publishing reports.

CONSIDERATIONS BEFORE PUBLISHING CONTENT

As mentioned in Chapter 1, "Introducing Crystal Enterprise," two report types, by default, are managed by Crystal Enterprise:

- Crystal Reports
- Crystal Analysis Professional Applications

As Chapters 8 and 9 point out, each of these report types is linked to a specific datasource, held as a value within the report file itself. For example, the Inventory.rpt sample Crystal Report has an ODBC connection (System DSN) called Xtreme Sample Database, pointing to the Xtreme.mdb sample database as its datasource. A Crystal Analysis Professional report can be linked to a dynamic OLAP server datasource or an offline files-based cube source.

Note

Xtreme.mdb is a database installed by both Crystal Enterprise and Crystal Reports as a sample datasource.

Having two content-creation technologies for Crystal Enterprise, Crystal Reports and Crystal Analysis Professional, presents some significant advantages, namely that the individual design tools focus heavily on exploiting the features and functions of the specific datasources to which they connect. Crystal Analysis Professional, for example, provides support for almost every feature of each OLAP datasource to which it connects.

A few challenges are associated with multiple content-creation tools as well, primarily, multiple object or file types. The main difference between a Crystal Report and a Crystal Analysis Professional report object is which Crystal Enterprise server actually processes the report after it has been published and requested for viewing by an end user.

CONSIDERATIONS BEFORE PUBLISHING CRYSTAL REPORTS

Whatever the datasource might be—relational, flat file, and so on—the Crystal Reports designer application must have access to a given datasource to build the .rpt (Crystal Report).

After the Crystal Report has been published into Crystal Enterprise, an identical datasource name must be present on the Crystal Enterprise Page and Job Servers. This can become tricky to manage, especially if an organization has a Crystal Enterprise architecture with dedicated Page and Job Servers on separate physical servers. Chapter 3, "Exploring the System Architecture," points out that Page and Job Servers process on-demand and scheduled reports, respectively. So if there isn't a need for scheduled reports, the Job Server wouldn't need ODBC configured for a given report.

If a Crystal Enterprise architecture scenario were in place where a Page Server and Job Server were installed on physically separate servers, the datasource for each and every Crystal Report within Crystal Enterprise must be configured on both the Page Server and the Job Server.

For ODBC datasources, this implies that a proper System DSN name must be configured on the Page and Job Servers. For a native database connection, the native database client software must be installed and configured on the Page and Job Servers. Chapter 8, "Creating Content for Crystal Reports," discusses native database connections in some detail. If the datasource for a Crystal Report is a flat file on a network drive, the Page and Job Server service accounts should have access to that shared network resource.

Considerations Before Publishing Crystal Analysis Professional Reports

In addition to the obvious differences to Crystal Reports, such as a separate application designer, Crystal Analysis Professional reports work in a different manner than Crystal Reports after it's published to Crystal Enterprise. First of all, they aren't executed on either the Page or Job Server. A dedicated Crystal Analysis Professional processing plug-in is installed on the Web Component Server that directly connects to an OLAP datasource. This is an optional install available with Crystal Analysis Professional.

This means that all processing of analytic reports created by Crystal Analysis Professional is done on the Web Component Server. The implications of this are significant. After a Crystal Analysis Professional report is published into Crystal Enterprise, there are several options for configuring an account to authenticate against the OLAP server to which the report is intended to connect. The default option is to use the Web Component Server (Web Component Server) service account under which the Web Component Server runs. If this option is used, the Web Component Server service account must have domain privileges to connect to the specific OLAP server.

To learn more about the Web Component Server add-in for Crystal Analysis Professional, see Chapter 9, "Creating Content with Crystal Analysis Professional."

Understanding Unmanaged and Managed Report Content Before Publishing to Crystal Enterprise

Crystal Enterprise provides the capability to deliver both unmanaged and managed content, or reports. Managed content is the primary emphasis with Crystal Enterprise; however,

PART

III

CH

7

many organizations leverage unmanaged content delivery capabilities within Crystal Enterprise as well, so an explanation of managed and unmanaged content is warranted.

Users of Crystal Reports and the Crystal Reports Web Component Server will be familiar with the concept of unmanaged content. Previous versions of Crystal Reports included a scaled down report sharing server, also referred to as the Web Component Server, that would read .rpt files from a directory and produce output to a Web browser in a variety of formats, much like Crystal Enterprise. The Web Component Server available in previous versions of Crystal Reports is not to be confused with the Crystal Enterprise Web Component Server; however, for compatibility purposes, the Crystal Enterprise Web Component Server provides the same functions.

The Crystal Enterprise version of the Web Component Server is much more scalable than the similarly named Web Component Server available with versions of Crystal Reports prior to 8.0. Additionally, the Crystal Enterprise Web Component Server is one of several services available in the Crystal Enterprise framework.

The word "delivering" is used to describe unmanaged content, as a report really isn't "published" to Crystal Enterprise. Publishing a report implies a number of things, to be discussed in the "Managed Report Content Overview" section of the chapter.

UNMANAGED REPORT CONTENT

Unmanaged content means that Crystal Enterprise can be used to publish a Crystal Report object to a browser, but remain "unaware" of the presence of the report in question. In other words, the report is never stored in Crystal Enterprise, the APS is unaware of its presence, and no record of it is kept in the File Repository Server.

The Web Component Server, which is the server that provides output of reports to the Web from the Crystal Enterprise framework, can be "controlled" via a URL line for publishing unmanaged reports. In other words, a Crystal Report can be stored in a given Microsoft Internet Information Server virtual directory and viewed by a Web browser without being managed or published within the Crystal Enterprise framework.

When Crystal Enterprise is installed, requests to view an .rpt extension on Microsoft IIS (Internet Information Server) via a URL line are forwarded to the Web Component Server. The Web Component Server, in turn, processes the report on demand, connects to the intended database (assuming the Page Server has the proper datasource or OBDC connection configured), and returns the report result in a specified report viewer. If a viewer type is not specified, ActiveX is chosen as the default.

DELIVERING UNMANAGED REPORT CONTENT WITH CRYSTAL ENTERPRISE

To demonstrate this unmanaged Crystal Report publishing capability, the Inventory Report (Inventory.rpt) sample Crystal Report that is installed with Crystal Enterprise is sufficient. This assumes you have Microsoft Internet Information Server installed and running. To confirm Microsoft Internet Information Server is installed and running, open the Windows Control Panel, select Administrative Tools, and click the Services option. Scroll to the bottom of the list and verify that the service titled World Wide Web Publishing is installed and running. If not, this service can be added in the Add or Remove Programs section of the Windows Control Panel.

To find Inventory.rpt, browse the drive that has Crystal Enterprise installed to the Drive:\Program Files\Crystal Decisions\Enterprise\Samples\En\Reports folder (see Figure 7.1). Typically the C drive is the preferred installed location, so start looking there.

Figure 7.1
The Inventory.rpt sample can be found under the Install Drive:\Program Files\Crystal Decisions\Enterprise\Samples\En\Reports folder.

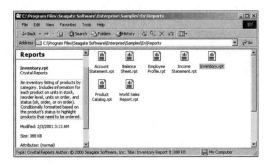

After Inventory.rpt has been located, it needs to be copied into the C:\Inetpub\wwwroot directory, as shown in Figure 7.2. This is the default Web-publishing directory for Microsoft Internet Information Server.

Figure 7.2
Place the Inventory.rpt file in the Inetpub\WWWroot directory where Microsoft Internet Information Server is installed.

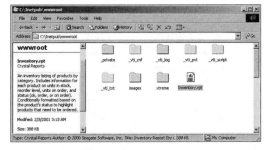

Any virtual directory could also be used for the same process. The URL line to call the report should reference the virtual directory where the report is stored.

After the report is placed in the directory, it can be called from within a browser through a URL line (see Figure 7.3). To call the report, launch Internet Explorer and enter the following in the URL line:

```
http://yourIISservername/Inventory.rpt
```

This type of publishing can be incredibly useful, but has its drawbacks:

PART

III

CH

7

Figure 7.3
After the request for the report is made using the URL line, the Web Component Server returns the resulting processed report content through the ActiveX viewer in the browser.

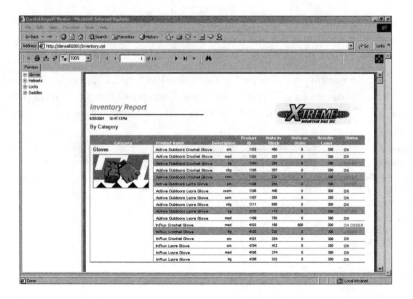

- No Crystal Enterprise security is involved in the view request.
- No scheduling is possible.
- No use of the overall Crystal Enterprise framework.
- This unmanaged report delivery process does not work for Crystal Analysis Professional Reports (see Chapter 9), only Crystal Reports.
- File management and version control problems can result with a large number of unmanaged reports sitting in a directory. There is no real means for tracking what each report does, what datasource it connects to, and so on.

Regardless of these issues, there are times when delivering unmanaged content is more than appropriate. The good news is that there is a set of URL commands to control the output of this unmanaged report from the Web Component Server. For example, if the desired report viewer were the DHTML viewer rather than ActiveX, the URL line for the same report would appear similar to Figure 7.4:

`http://yourIISservername/Inventory.rpt?init=dhtml`

If Java were the preferred viewer type, the following URL command could be issued to the Web Component Server with a result similar to Figure 7.5:

`http://yourIISservername/Inventory.rpt?init=Java`

Clearly, several different viewers can be called from the URL line. These same viewers are available for managed Crystal Reports as well. This method of calling and running Crystal Reports from a URL line seems like something of a black box function of the Web Component Server, and it is. If an administrator or developer wishes to properly interface with the Web Component Server and request reports for viewing, it should be done through the managed report approach discussed shortly.

Figure 7.4
DHTML output of the unmanaged inventory report.

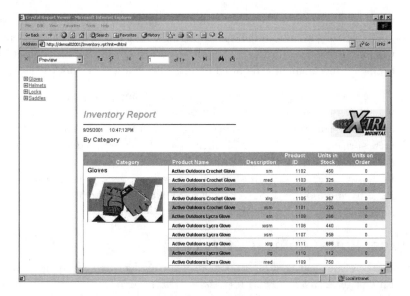

Figure 7.5
Java output of the unmanaged inventory report.

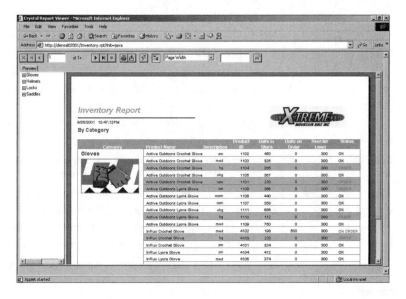

Report parameters, selection formulas, and other options also can be passed through the URL line. This actually comes in handy for both unmanaged and managed reports.

If the Inventory.rpt were a parameterized report, the URL line might look like the following:

```
http://yourIISservername/Inventory.rpt?prompt0=Gloves
```

Bear in mind that the Inventory report isn't configured with a parameter, so the URL line specifying the parameter values of gloves won't work unless a parameter is set on a product within the report. If a report has parameters but those parameters are not specified in the URL line and passed into the .rpt through the view request, the Web Component Server will prompt the user for them when the report is refreshed. This is significant because no coding or development is required to pick a list that will prompt the user for a value.

There is a significant amount of potential for passing parameters to reports over a URL line. One useful implementation of passing parameters to a report would be to create hyperlinks off of data values within one Crystal Report to another unmanaged or managed parameter-driven Crystal Report. Chapter 8 provides an example of leveraging hyperlinking to drive parameter-driven reports. Another example might be to link a Crystal Analysis Professional report through Microsoft Analysis Services Actions to an unmanaged report. Refer to Microsoft SQL Server Analysis Services documentation for more information on Actions.

MANAGED REPORT CONTENT OVERVIEW

Working with managed report content is the fundamental advantage to using Crystal Enterprise. A *managed report* (or *managed content*) implies that Crystal Enterprise is aware of the report.

Crystal Enterprise can work with two types of managed reports out of the box: Crystal Reports (.rpt) and Crystal Analysis Professional Applications (.car). The term "out of the box" is used because Crystal Enterprise will undoubtedly mature and enable all kinds of content to be published and managed by the Crystal Enterprise framework (data files, documents, and so on). As a brief overview, Crystal Reports typically contain data from relational databases or flat files (however, they can contain data from other datasource types as well), whereas Crystal Analysis Professional Applications contain analytic data from OLAP datasources.

→ *OLAP* stands for *On-Line Analytical Processing.* For more information about Crystal Analysis Professional and OLAP, **see** Chapter 9, "Creating Content with Crystal Analysis Professional."

After a report has been published by one of three mechanisms into Crystal Enterprise, a Crystal Enterprise object has been created to represent the report within the framework. Each of those object properties, the object metadata stored in the APS system database, can be called and controlled to integrate the report within a given Web application.

→ For examples of how to work with a report object's properties within Crystal Enterprise, **see** Chapter 13, "Extending Crystal Enterprise," and Chapter 14, "Integrating Crystal Enterprise with Your Corporate Intranet."

PUBLISHING MANAGED REPORT CONTENT

The three mechanisms for publishing content into Crystal Enterprise are as follows:

- The Crystal Publishing Wizard
- The Crystal Management Console
- Using the Save As function with a report designer application

This chapter covers the first two mechanisms. The third option, using the Save As function with a report designer application, is discussed in Chapters 8 and 9.

Note

Technically, there is a fourth way to publish content into Crystal Enterprise. The administrative portion of the Crystal Enterprise SDK can be leveraged to build a custom application that accomplishes the same tasks as the Crystal Management Console. After all, each mechanism that publishes a report object into Crystal Enterprise is actually using a function of the SDK.

PUBLISHING MANAGED REPORT CONTENT WITH THE CRYSTAL PUBLISHING WIZARD

As mentioned in Chapter 2, "Discovering the Crystal Enterprise Utilities," the Publishing Wizard is a Windows-based application that is installed with Crystal Enterprise. The Publishing Wizard is the only out-of-the-box mechanism within Crystal Enterprise that allows multiple reports to be published at one point in time. It becomes very useful when trying to publish hundreds of existing reports all at once.

Any additional Crystal Enterprise security that is required for reports must be accomplished using the Crystal Management Console, post publishing of the reports.

It's important to note that there are actually two publishing wizards. One publishing wizard is installed with Crystal Enterprise and only supports the publishing of Crystal Reports into Crystal Enterprise. The other publishing wizard is installed only if Crystal Analysis Professional is used.

Note

The Crystal Reports Publishing Wizard will publish reports to both Windows NT/2000 and Sun Solaris installations of Crystal Enterprise.

The two publishing wizards are fundamentally the same, so there isn't a need to provide information about how to publish Crystal Analysis Professional reports because the process is identical to that of Crystal Reports.

To find the Crystal Analysis Professional Publishing Wizard, from the Windows taskbar:

1. Click Start.
2. Select Programs.
3. Select Crystal Analysis Professional.
4. Click Crystal Publishing Wizard.

To launch the default Crystal Publishing Wizard found in the Crystal Enterprise directory, from the Windows taskbar:

PART

III

CH

7

1. Click Start.

2. Click Programs.

3. Select Crystal Enterprise.

4. Select Crystal Publishing Wizard.

Figure 7.6 shows the Crystal Publishing Wizard.

Figure 7.6
The default Crystal Publishing Wizard.

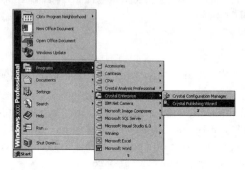

To confirm that the Publishing Wizard for Crystal Reports is being launched, the executable can be found in the Crystal Enterprise Install Path under Program Files\Crystal Decisions\Enterprise\win32_x86\RptPubWiz.exe.

After the Publishing Wizard is launched, a welcome screen describes some of the capabilities of the wizard (see Figure 7.7). Another easy way to tell whether the Publishing Wizard works with Crystal Reports is that the welcome screen mentions scheduling reports, something you cannot currently do with Crystal Analysis Professional reports and applications.

Figure 7.7
The Crystal Publishing Wizard welcome screen.

Proceed to the next dialog box by clicking Next. The default option for the Publishing Wizard is to publish a single report (see Figure 7.8).

Figure 7.8
The default option of publishing a single Crystal Reports enables a user to browse for a single .rpt file from any network-accessible or local file location.

When using the Publishing Wizard, most situations necessitate publishing multiple reports, especially if several reports are published from a test environment to a production Crystal Enterprise environment at one time. Select the Add Multiple Reports check box, and additional dialog boxes will prompt to enable the selection of multiple reports from a single list.

For this exercise, select the Add Multiple Reports check box. Select the Find Directory button and add the following directory shown in Figure 7.9 to the selection in the Crystal Enterprise install path: \Program Files\Crystal Decisions\Enterprise\Samples\En\Reports.

Figure 7.9
In the Browse for Folder dialog box, select the samples folder in the Crystal Enterprise directory.

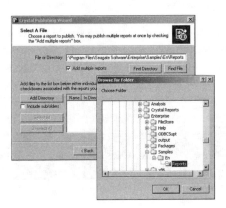

Click the Add Directory button. After the directory has been added, a list of reports with check boxes becomes available for selection, as seen in Figure 7.10.

Select the Inventory.rpt and World Sales Report.rpt files. Click the Next button to proceed.

Before the reports can be submitted and formally published into Crystal Enterprise, the publisher must provide valid authentication credentials, the target APS server name, and an authentication type to proceed (see Figure 7.11). Publishing reports to public folders is a default right for members of the Everyone group within Crystal Enterprise.

PART

III

CH

7

Figure 7.10
Select reports to publish into the Crystal Enterprise system.

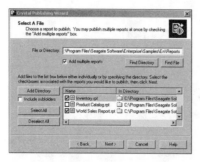

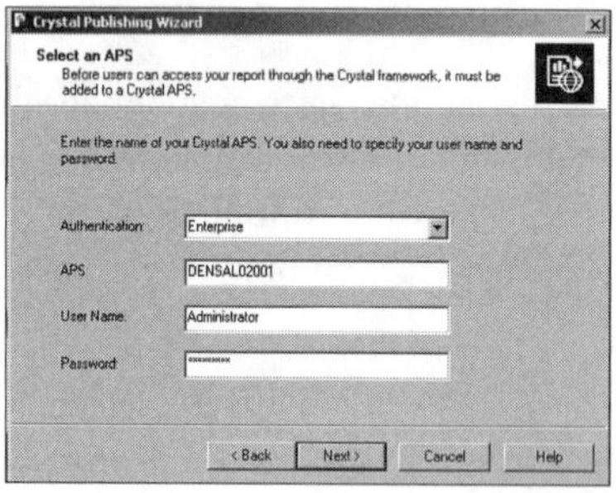

Figure 7.11
Select the proper authentication type and specific APS server to publish reports into.

A permission of Add Objects to the Folder within the Crystal Management Console can be changed on a particular folder under the Advanced Rights of a Crystal Enterprise group (see Figure 7.12). This provides more granular control over publishing rights.

Figure 7.12
The Add Objects to the Folder option can be specified in the Crystal Management Console. Refer to Chapter 10 for more details on using the Crystal Management Console.

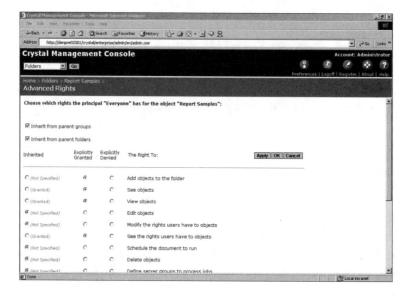

Crystal Enterprise administrators should limit the access to most publicly available Crystal Enterprise folders.

→ For more information about specifying the credentials required to publish reports, **see** Chapter 10, "Administering and Configuring Crystal Enterprise."

Enter the username and password that has permission to publish reports to Crystal Enterprise, and click Next. If Crystal Enterprise has recently been installed, the default Administrator password is blank.

Select a folder into which to publish the Inventory.rpt and World Sales Report.rpt. To create a new top-level folder, select the APS name at the top of the folder tree and click the new folder by selecting the New Folder icon above the folder tree, as shown in Figure 7.13. Enter a name for the new folder. Leave the folder highlighted and click Next.

Figure 7.13
The Report Publishing Wizard allows the selection of existing folders and the creation of new folders as well.

The Inventory.rpt and World Sales Report.rpt are displayed under the previously selected folder. Reports can also be dragged and dropped onto other folders within the tree (see Figure 7.14). When the reports are in a satisfactory folder, click Next.

Figure 7.14
Reports can be dragged to different folders at this point in the Publishing Wizard.

Select an option for scheduling reports and click Next. If Let Users Update the Object is selected, report-processing schedules can be set at a later date, as shown in Figure 7.15.

PART

III

CH

7

Figure 7.15
If Run on a Recurring
Schedule is selected,
the report processing
recurrence schedule
can be configured at
the same time.

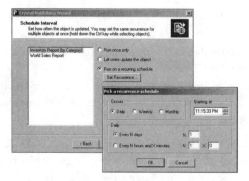

Select Review or Modify Report Properties and click Next. If this option is not selected, the Publishing Wizard will proceed to the confirmation screen where the reports are committed to Crystal Enterprise (see Figure 7.16).

Figure 7.16
A report's title and
description can be
changed while using
the Publishing
Wizard.

The Publishing Wizard reads the properties of each report being published and builds a tree from which you can navigate each report and change the title and description and choose whether Crystal Enterprise should generate a thumbnail image.

Accept the default options and titles and select Next.

Note

A *thumbnail image* is a JPEG (.jpg) image of page 1 of the report. This image can be called from Crystal Enterprise to give an end user a sense of the layout of the report before its execution. ePortfolio uses report thumbnails as a way of displaying report icons.

Note

The option to generate a thumbnail isn't available unless the option has been set from within the Crystal Reports designer.

The Publishing Wizard allows the database connection information to be changed. This includes location, username, and password.

Expand the properties list for the Inventory.rpt by clicking the + (see Figure 7.17).

Figure 7.17
Expand the data properties for the report object by selecting the +.

If the datasource for the Inventory.rpt report is selected, the database location, logon username, and password can be modified (see Figure 7.18). The username and password are the user account you want Crystal Enterprise to use when connecting to the datasource when a report is processed.

Figure 7.18
Select the datasource under the Inventory.rpt report to configure the data-source location as well as a logon username and password.

These fields are not required, because Crystal Enterprise can prompt a user for their own username and password at the view or schedule time of a given report.

After the proper datasource settings have been configured for each report, click Next.

The next screen is a confirmation dialog box. Click Next. The objects are committed to the APS and a summary screen details all reports successfully committed to the Crystal Enterprise system (see Figure 7.19).

PART

III

CH

7

Figure 7.19
The Inventory.rpt and
World Sales
Report.rpt have been
committed to the
Crystal Enterprise
system.

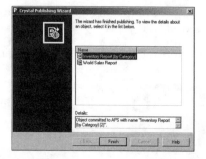

PUBLISHING CONTENT WITH THE CRYSTAL MANAGEMENT CONSOLE

Another option for publishing reports is using the Crystal Management Console. The
Crystal Management Console, as explained in earlier chapters, is the Web browser–based
administrative interface to Crystal Enterprise. Few system administrators feel comfortable
giving most users or power users access to the Crystal Management Console, so the reasonable option is the Crystal Publishing Wizard.

To open the Crystal Management Console, open the Crystal Launchpad by clicking Start,
Programs, Crystal Enterprise, Crystal Launchpad (see Figure 7.20).

Figure 7.20
The Crystal Enterprise
Launchpad is the
starting point to find
default applications
such as the Crystal
Management Console
and ePortfolio.

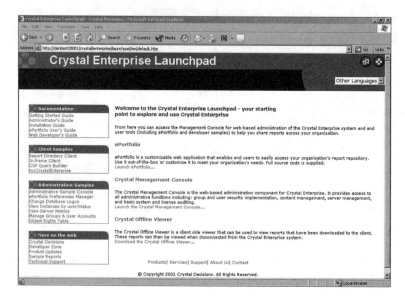

From the Crystal Launchpad, select the Crystal Management Console hyperlink. The
Crystal Management Console, as explained in Chapter 10, is a collection of .csp pages that
interface with the Crystal Enterprise administrative SDK.

Although this section explains how to publish reports using the Crystal Management Console, technically an application could be created using the administrative SDK with Crystal Enterprise to publish reports. Refer to Chapter 13 for more information on the administrative portion of the SDK.

Enter the administrator username and password and click Log On, as shown in Figure 7.21.

Figure 7.21
The Crystal Management Console requires a user with administrative privileges to log in before reports can be published.

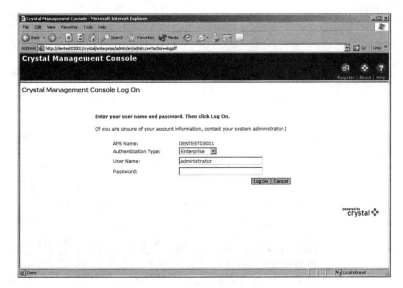

The Crystal Management Console is reviewed in detail in Chapter 10, so this section focuses solely on publishing a report into an existing Crystal Enterprise folder (see Figure 7.22).

From the Crystal Management Console, select the Manage Objects icon. The objects page can also be accessed by clicking on the drop-down pick list in the upper-left corner of the Crystal Management Console and selecting Objects.

After the Manage Objects icon has been selected, select the New Report Hyperlink near the top of the page, shown in Figure 7.22. The New Report dialog box is opened, as shown in Figure 7.23.

A convenient function of the Crystal Management Console is a single process or interface for Crystal Reports and Crystal Analysis Professional applications or reports. It's also important to note that only one report can be published at a time, which makes the Publishing Wizard the ideal tool when multiple reports must be published.

PART

III

CH

7

Figure 7.22
The Crystal Management Console's opening interface provides easy access to a host of administrative features, including report publishing.

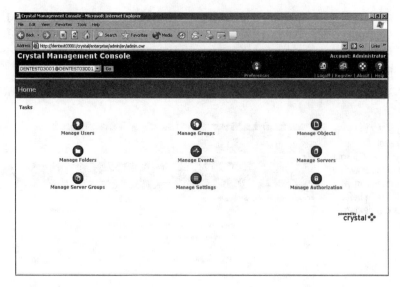

Figure 7.23
The New Report hyperlink begins the report publishing process.

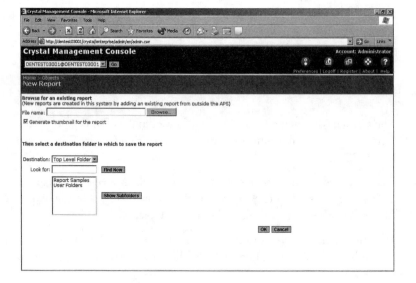

The New Report page (shown in Figure 7.24) requires the physical file location of the report object, whether it's a Crystal Report or a Crystal Analysis Professional report. A destination folder location within Crystal Enterprise should be selected. Note that the report will inherit whatever security its soon-to-be parent folder has established. This is the case unless the Crystal Enterprise system administrator configures object-level security on the report itself.

Figure 7.24
The New Report page offers all the settings necessary to publish a report into Crystal Enterprise.

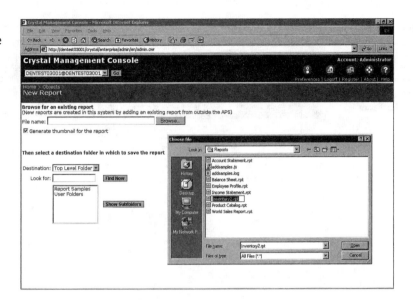

In the Choose File dialog box, select the Browse button and browse to the Inventory.rpt report from the following location: Crystal Enterprise Install Path\Program Files\Crystal Decisions\Enterprise\Samples\En\Reports.

In the Destination dialog box, select a folder into which to publish the report. For this example, choose User Folders and select the Show Subfolders button. Then select the Administrator folder. This tells Crystal Enterprise that the Administrators private folder is the destination for the report. The Destination dialog box allows the navigation of all folders in Crystal Enterprise, including user folders.

After selecting the Administrator user folder or another suitable destination within Crystal Enterprise, click OK. Note that the Report Samples folder already has the Inventory Report published, so trying to publish an identical report to this folder will result in an error.

The Crystal Management Console automatically links the view to the Administrator user folder and opens the Properties view for the report that has just been published, as shown in Figure 7.25. Here the Report Title and Description can be modified, along with the option to publish a preview thumbnail. Several other options, such as Database login settings, Parameter options, Filters, Schedules, Destinations, Formats, Limits, and Rights can be configured as well.

→ To learn more about the various options for a report object, **see** Chapter 10.

Note

If end users must be prompted to set parameters for a report when viewing on-demand, this must be specified for each parameter. Click the Parameter tab, and click an individual parameter to specify this option.

PART

III

CH

7

Figure 7.25
The Properties page for the report is loaded. Each tab allows granular control of report properties and behavior.

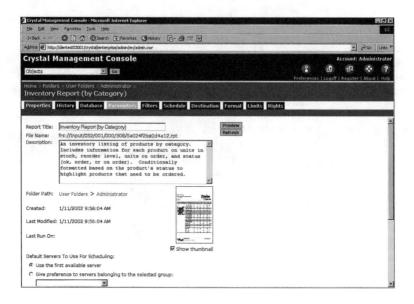

THE ROLE OF THE FILE REPOSITORY SERVER

Recall from earlier chapters that after a report object is published into the Crystal Enterprise system, the physical file is actually stored in the File Repository Server (FRS). The FRS, as explained in Chapter 3, consists of two directories, Input and Output, which hold published report templates (Input) and, in the case of Crystal Reports, report instances with historical data (Output).

Several things happen before the report is stored in the FRS when publishing from the Crystal Management Console:

- The Web Component Server reads the necessary information about the reports' properties and then passes this information to the APS so that it can be stored in the APS System Database.

- The APS System Database, as explained in Chapter 3, is a relational database where metadata about a report object and its properties are stored.

- By default, the report is published to Crystal Enterprise without saved data within the report template, even if the individual report is configured with saved data to optimize information being stored in the APS database. You can override this setting by using a VBS or JS script to add a property called SI_USESAVEDDATA for each report being added to Crystal Enterprise. Set its value to true. Refer to Chapters 13 or 14 of this book for more details on creating such scripts with the Crystal Enterprise SDK.

- If the thumbnail image is available and the publisher specified its inclusion with the report, it too is copied and passed on.

- The actual Report file is stored in the Input directory of the FRS.

Note

When publishing using the Crystal Publishing Wizard, the Web Component Server is not involved. The Publishing Wizard transfers the report file from the Windows desktop directly to the FRS and passes the meta properties to the APS.

Upon completion of publishing the report, it is now recognized as a formal object, which can be called and controlled through the Crystal Enterprise SDK. Report objects in the APS system database correspond directly to a physical file stored in the FRS Input directory.

To view the report files stored in the FRS directories, browse to the install drive where the FRS resides, and then go to Program Files\Crystal Decisions\Enterprise\FileStore (see Figure 7.26).

Note

Crystal Enterprise server components can be installed on multiple physical server systems. See Chapters 3 and 4 for more details. The FRS can be installed on a completely separate physical server from all other Crystal Enterprise server components.

Figure 7.26
The Input and Output directories of the FRS should be secured so that common network users cannot access them.

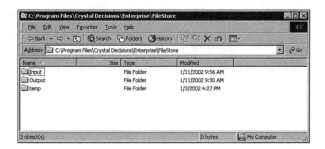

Inside the FRS output directory are folders created and managed by Crystal Enterprise to store the various report instances that users create when reports are scheduled. To locate a report's location within the File Repository Server's directories, refer to the report's Properties tab in the Crystal Management Console.

To check the location of the Inventory.rpt published earlier in the chapter, launch the Crystal Management Console from the Crystal Launchpad. For more information on finding the Crystal Management Console or finding a report's properties page, refer to the earlier section of this chapter, "Publishing Content with the Crystal Management Console."

After the Inventory.rpt report has been located in the Crystal Management Console, select the Properties tab. Note that directly under the Report Title dialog box is a reference to the storage location of the report object in the FRS directory. The reference should look similar to frs://Input/53/153/3e4228d737998c.rpt.

Every time a report is added to the system, a directory is created using the report or CI_ID of the object as the directory name. If a thumbnail exists for the report object, it is written to the same directory as a .jpg image.

Use of the Output directory applies only to Crystal Reports. Crystal Analysis Professional reports cannot currently be scheduled and hence do not create report instances or require the use of the Output directory.

PART

III

CH

7

VIEWING PUBLISHED CONTENT

There are several ways to view published content such as Crystal Reports after they have been successfully committed to the Crystal Enterprise system. The Crystal Management Console provides a Preview button, selected and shown in Figure 7.27, under the Properties tab of the report object.

Figure 7.27
Successfully viewing a report from the Crystal Management Console confirms that the report is functioning properly in the Crystal Enterprise environment, and the database connection is properly configured.

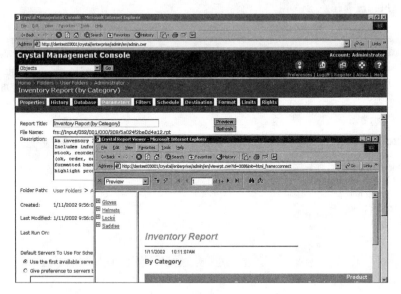

Viewing the report from the Management Console provides a good troubleshooting mechanism for reports as well. If an organization has developed a custom Crystal Enterprise application and report viewing isn't working, you can determine whether the issue lies with the Crystal Enterprise client application or with the report itself.

To confirm that the published report works from a Crystal Enterprise client application, refer to the Crystal Launchpad, click the ePortfolio hyperlink, and log in as Administrator. Notice that the Inventory Report is available in the private folder, to which ePortfolio takes users upon initial login. Click the Inventory.rpt hyperlink and select View from the options list.

→ For more information on using ePortfolio, **see** Chapter 5, "Using the Crystal Enterprise Launchpad."

TROUBLESHOOTING

When publishing reports to Crystal Enterprise, the most common issues that arise include the following:

- The user publishing reports doesn't have the proper permissions to a specific Crystal Enterprise folder.
- The APS server isn't available or there might be problems with the APS system database.

These types of issues result in a user not being able to find the proper folder to publish a report into or a rejected logon request to Crystal Enterprise from either the Publishing Wizard or the report designer.

To confirm the user has the proper permissions to publish a report to a specific folder, open the Crystal Management Console and confirm the user has at least View rights. Refer to Chapter 10.

If Advanced permissions are configured in Crystal Enterprise, the user might have the right to add objects to the folder set to Explicitly Denied. Refer to Chapter 1 for more detail on report object permissions.

To confirm the APS is available, check under the Crystal Configuration Manager, covered in Chapters 5 and 10, to verify that the APS service is started and enabled.

Once reports are actually published to Crystal Enterprise, the most common issue if the report does not run (retrieve data) properly is a missing or incorrectly configured datasource name or client.

A common message received (which actually indicates an error) when this is occurring for on-demand reports (reports run on the Page Server) is a continual prompt for a database username and password. Although this could simply be a case of an improper username and password, more often this looping prompt is an indication of an improper datasource connection configuration or lack of one altogether.

A common error message received when attempting to schedule a report in ePortfolio when the ODBC datasource isn't properly configured on the Job Server is

```
Error: Cannot open SQL Server.
```

To correct this problem, in the Windows Control Panel, check the name of the ODBC datasource used to design the Crystal Report, and configure an ODBC System DSN with an identical name on the Crystal Enterprise Job and Page Servers. If the Job and Page Server services reside on the same physical server, this needs to be done only once. For organizations with large, complex Crystal Enterprise configurations and multiple Job and Page Servers, this will need to be configured for each server.

These procedures are applicable for Crystal Reports that use native database connection software as well. Crystal Reports actually "piggybacks" on database-native client software to establish a native connection, which usually is more efficient and executes queries faster than an ODBC connection.

For example, if a Crystal Report has been designed using a Microsoft SQL Server database via a native SQL Server connection, the Microsoft SQL Server client software must be installed and properly configured on the Page and Job Servers for proper execution of the Crystal Report.

For Crystal Analysis Professional reports, the most common errors when attempting to view a recently published report are related to the windows user account.

Whatever specific service account is configured for the Web Component Server, this is the default account used to traverse a Windows NT/2000 network environment and attempt to log on to the Analysis Services Server when a view request is made by an end user in a Web application for a Crystal Analysis Professional report.

The best option is to open the Crystal Management Console, select the Crystal Analysis Professional report in question, select the Datasource Logon tab, and choose Logon Using Specific Credentials or Secondary Logon for Each Application.

Logon Using Specific Credentials passes a generic username and password to the Microsoft Analysis Services Server regardless of the user whom is actually logged into Crystal Enterprise. This option prompts a user each time a view request is made for a Crystal Analysis Professional report.

SUMMARY

There are two primary means by which content can be published into Crystal Enterprise:

- The Crystal Publishing Wizard
- The Crystal Management Console

There are additional ways to publish reports into Crystal Enterprise, including saving reports directly from Crystal Reports or Crystal Analysis Professional, as well as using the Crystal Enterprise SDK to programmatically add a report.

The Crystal Publishing Wizard has the advantage of publishing multiple reports at a single pass but does not offer the capability to configure report security. Report security must be configured within the Crystal Management Console.

The Crystal Management Console provides easy report publishing from a single interface, for both Crystal Reports and Crystal Analysis Professional reports.

CHAPTER 8

CREATING CONTENT WITH CRYSTAL REPORTS

In this chapter

As stated in Chapter 1, "Introducing Crystal Enterprise," Crystal Reports is the most popular reporting tool in the world, in use by millions of report designers. Because Crystal Reports is fully integrated with Crystal Enterprise, this combination represents the most cohesive match of content creation and Web delivery technology available in the business intelligence market place.

New features in version 8.5, such as Report Alerts, as well as dramatically increased report processing speed, have increased the scope and role of Crystal Reports within most global organizations. As with any software tool that evolves with the needs of its customers, Crystal Reports continues to provide new and innovative solutions for data delivery with cutting-edge support for technologies such as XML document and COM object connectivity.

Crystal Reports is a graphical report design tool installed locally on a report designer workstation intended for creating reports for other end users to consume. Publishing Crystal Reports to Crystal Enterprise directly from the Crystal Reports designer is as simple as choosing Save As, as you'll learn later in this chapter. Refer to Chapter 7, "Publishing Content with Crystal Enterprise," for more details on publishing content to Crystal Enterprise.

This chapter reviews using Crystal Reports to create content for Crystal Enterprise through rapid report design using the standard Reporting Wizard. This chapter also explains some fundamental concepts, such as adding parameters and using formulas.

In addition, this chapter covers some relatively advanced concepts, including using Crystal Reports to access a COM Provider (.dll) to read dynamic ADO recordsets, as well as using Crystal Reports to access XML documents.

Note

The best results will be gained when following along in Crystal Reports 8.5.

INSTALLATION AND CONFIGURATION OF CRYSTAL REPORTS

Because using Crystal Reports involves accessing potentially dozens of datasources during report design, proper installation of the software is of the utmost importance.

PREPARING THE OPERATING SYSTEM FOR INSTALLATION

As with any software, certain operating system settings should be checked and properly configured before installation. The following items should be verified on the local workstation where Crystal Reports will be installed:

- Ensure at least 64MB of RAM and 300MB of hard disk space are available on the system.

- Verify that the Temp variable and directory is set up on the Microsoft Windows operating system. The Temp variable can be configured in the System Properties dialog box under the Advanced tab, shown in Figure 8.1. (Read on for more information on this.)

Figure 8.1
Windows 2000
system settings.

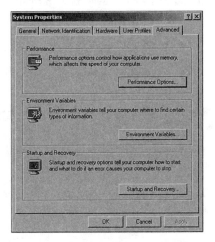

- Check the virtual memory settings on the Windows system. Choose Start, Settings, Control Panel. Then, open the SYSTEM icon; from this location there will be options for the local system settings.
- The Advanced tab contains a button for Performance Options. This page file setting indicates the size of the virtual memory for the operating system, which should be at least the physical amount of RAM plus 10% that is available on the system.

- Be sure the ODBC configuration is properly installed. For further reference on how to set up ODBC refer to the "Troubleshooting" section later in this chapter.

Note

The recommended size for the virtual memory is the amount of physical RAM on the machine plus 11MB.

Note

It's important to remember that Crystal Reports uses local operating system resources. There should be enough virtual memory available to handle reports that are processed locally on the report designer's workstation.

Crystal Reports provides an array of connectivity options to most relational, flat-file, and OLAP datasources. One of those forms, and quite possibly the most common, is ODBC (Open Database Connectivity). This is an extremely important connectivity layer that must be properly configured for optimal reporting performance. Each Crystal Report has this connectivity option at the start of a report design, and choosing the one that best fits the business and technical requirements for the reports can make all the difference.

→ For a further discussion on the benefits of each database connection type, **see** "Preparing to Access Corporate Data," **p. 193**. This section will help define the benefits of each connection type and where it's best suited.

Additional information for configuring the connection type can be found in the "Troubleshooting" section. However, if this is already functioning properly or there is no need for additional information, proceed to the next step in the installation process.

Note

If other installed applications on the intended installation PC workstation use ODBC, ensure they are able to run on ODBC 3.51 or higher because this is installed with Crystal Reports 8.5.

Now that the preparatory steps to installing Crystal Reports have been covered, the software can be installed on the workstation.

INSTALLING CRYSTAL REPORTS

When the CD auto load starts, the installer application launches. In the top-right corner of the splash screen, choose the Install Crystal Reports option. This starts the installation process shown in Figure 8.2. Optionally open the product CD and double-click setup.exe to begin the same process.

Note

For additional information on the Crystal Reports application architecture and framework, refer to computer-based training files on the Crystal Reports CD.

Figure 8.2
Starting the Crystal Reports installation screen.

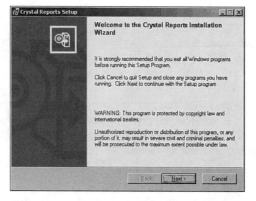

For most installations of Crystal Reports, the default setup process is appropriate. For this example, use the standard or complete installation options. After accepting the license agreement, enter the supplied license key, which can be found on the back of the Crystal Decisions disc jacket. After choosing Next, select the preferred installation directory.

Tip

It's a good idea to install Crystal Reports on the physical Crystal Enterprise Job and Page Servers because this will allow for troubleshooting report data connectivity issues if the need should arise. As this chapter will explain, Crystal Reports requires a data-source name and link. When a report is designed and subsequently published to Crystal Enterprise, that datasource name and link must exist on the Page and Job Servers and be identical to the name and link specified in Crystal Reports.

Note

It's good practice to leave the installation path at its default location on the local system drive (C:\Program Files\Seagate Software\Crystal Reports). If this path is changed, approximately 70MB worth of files are still installed on the local root drive, regardless of preference, mostly comprised of critical .DLL files.

From the Custom Install dialog box, there are several options to determine which components of Crystal Reports should run locally on the report designer workstation versus running off the CD. Select the desired options and choose Next. (It's recommended to use the default values, unless certain custom drivers or features of Crystal Reports, such as Geographic Mapping, are deemed unnecessary.) Selecting Next begins the actual installation for the Crystal Reports files on the local workstation.

Note

One option in the installation process that's not added by default is *custom charting*. Although older versions of Crystal Reports provided this option as part of the default installation process, it must be explicitly specified.

Note

After installing Crystal Reports, apply the update patch for Crystal Reports on the Crystal Enterprise 8.5 disk. This enables proper integration and provides updated components for Crystal Reports, such as the COM driver.

PREPARING TO ACCESS CORPORATE DATA

Now that Crystal Reports is installed, accessing actual data is the next step. One of the challenges that most organizations face when accessing corporate data in a variety of disparate datasources is determining the best mechanism by which to connect to and retrieve data from a given datasource. The good news is that Crystal Reports provides a multitude of data connectivity options, to be discussed shortly.

One of the major decisions you must make is what will be the most efficient way to access specific datasources and how many sources will be used in any given report. Determining a connectivity strategy can drastically affect the performance of the reports, as will be evident later in this section.

To ensure that potential pains of data access are avoided, there are some initial checkpoints to go through that will ensure success. All of these suggested routes for connecting to corporate datasources will vary, report by report.

This section contains an in-depth look at each type of data connection type. If you already know this, it might be appropriate to skip to the section titled "Creating Reports."

The Data Access layer is the key component to Crystal Reports because all communication between the designer and the datasource location happens at this layer. Crystal Reports provides the following options for connecting to various relational, flat-file, and OLAP datasources that might be found in a typical organization:

- ODBC (Open Database Connectivity)
- Native data connection
- Local query file or metadata
- PC database connection
- OLAP (OLE DB, Microsoft, DB2, and so on)

Each of these choices has its own unique advantages. For example, using an ODBC driver to access an Oracle database might not be as fast in data retrieval as using the Oracle native driver for Crystal Reports. To help determine the best connectivity strategies, it's important to weigh the performance factors of each connectivity method against the flexibility needed within the report.

Even if the performance difference between two connection methods such as ODBC and native driver might be nominal, consider that difference across potentially hundreds or thousands of reports that might be run within Crystal Enterprise by a large number of end users. Of course, speed must always be balanced with flexibility, as discussed in the connection type overviews.

ODBC (OPEN DATABASE CONNECTIVITY)

The first benefit to using ODBC is its universal connectivity capability. It's safe to say that any common datasource such as Oracle, Microsoft SQL Server, IBM DB2, Sybase, or Informix has an ODBC connection available, whether written by the specific vendor or by a third-party company. Another major advantage of using ODBC to connect to a datasource is that it allows Crystal Reports to connect to more than one database within a single report. In other words, Crystal Reports allows multiple ODBC connections within a single report to multiple, disparate datasources.

When a report is processed using the ODBC connectivity option, Crystal Reports sends SQL query statements generated by the ODBC driver to the intended database system.

If an organization plans to use ODBC to connect to a datasource, an ODBC DSN (datasource name) must be created. A DSN is an ODBC configuration file that contains all the necessary datasource location and configuration information needed for an application such as Crystal Reports to connect to and retrieve data from a given source.

To create a new DSN, from the Windows Start button go to Start, Settings, Control Panel and from this window open the Administrative Tools icon. Now open the Data Source (ODBC) Administrator, shown in Figure 8.3.

Figure 8.3
The Microsoft
Windows ODBC
Administrator
console.

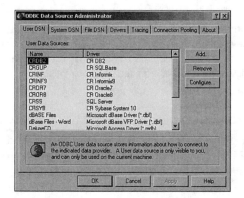

From the ODBC Administrator window several options are available for various ODBC configuration options. The second tab is the System DSN tab. From this location, data-sources can be created and used for Crystal Reports as well Crystal Enterprise Page and Job Servers if configuring ODBC on a server.

When choosing DSN names, try to keep a consistent datasource name for all workstations or servers that will have Crystal Reports or Crystal Enterprise installed. The reason for this is Crystal Reports only encodes the DSN name for each report. If the DSN name is consistent then using the report on different physical workstations will be easy.

These ODBC datasources contain connection information and the authentication types for database servers. For example, consider an example where a connection has been created to a Microsoft Access database called Xtreme Sample Data. The actual name and physical location of the Access database is inconsequential to Crystal Reports, because Crystal Reports will refer to the source by its ODBC DSN name in Figure 8.4, if this is the intended connectivity option.

Figure 8.4
Xtreme Sample Data
access database.

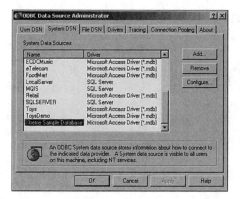

The System DSN tab contains a list of available ODBC drivers that have been configured on the local workstation. When a new ODBC connection is necessary, it's recommended to use the Crystal-specific drivers provided in the Add list.

> **Note**
>
> Any driver in the list that starts with "CR" is a Crystal-specific driver. These are recommended because they were designed by Crystal Decisions and as such, Crystal Decisions can modify the driver as the database manufacturer changes its underlying system database architecture and connectivity requirements.

> **Note**
>
> A connection to Microsoft SQL Server is an exception to the practice of using Crystal-provided ODBC drivers. In the case of Microsoft SQL Server, the driver provided for the ODBC connection to SQL Server is recommended.

After you select the appropriate driver, the next dialog box requires the DSN name and appropriate server name. As for the actual DSN name, no specific standard is set as to what the name should be; it's a user preference. However, as Chapter 7 highlights, the data-source's name used on Crystal Reports "designer" machines should be duplicated on the Crystal Enterprise Page and Job Servers. Getting into the practice of replicating datasource names on the designer desktops and Crystal Enterprise servers provides easy transition of Crystal Reports from a development environment to a production environment such as Crystal Enterprise.

ADDING A NEW ODBC CONNECTION

To add a new ODBC connection, implement the following steps:

1. Specify an ODBC driver. To add a new ODBC datasource to the local workstation for Crystal Reports to access, select an appropriate driver, such as the Microsoft Access Driver from the ODBC administrator, System DSN tab dialog box in Figure 8.5, and click Finish.

Figure 8.5
Selecting an ODBC driver.

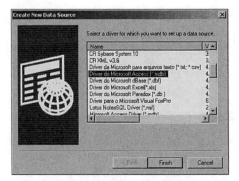

2. Specify the datasource location. For this example, the ODBC DSN is going to reference a Microsoft Access database file, so you must supply the directory path to the .MDB file. Click the Select button and browse to the installation directory of Crystal Reports. Select the Xtreme.MDB database.

Note

Crystal Reports and Crystal Enterprise both install a copy of Xtreme.MDB. Try to use the copy found in `C:\Program Files\CrystalDecisions\Enterprise\Samples\En`.

Note

As a side note, for ODBC connections to datasources such as Microsoft SQL Server, a dialog box will prompt for a username and password necessary to log on to the database if attempting to configure ODBC. This username and password will persist with the report, even in Crystal Enterprise, unless the report designer specifically changes it using the Crystal Management Console. Refer to Chapter 10, "Administering and Configuring Crystal Enterprise," for more information on this topic.

To understand what type of additional options should be used in a specific database connection, consult a network or database administrator. Most organizations have some ODBC connectivity and communication guidelines for proper communication across the network with the least impact to a given database.

After adding any additional settings specific to a given datasource, select the OK button shown in Figure 8.6. The connection to the database will be added to the DSN list. Additional options will be available for different datasources.

Figure 8.6
Adding a Microsoft Access database as a new ODBC System DSN.

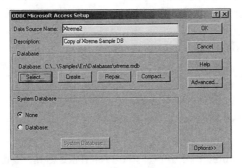

The new ODBC datasource is ready to be accessed by Crystal Reports.

Tip

It's important to note that although ODBC is perceived as a simple data access layer, it actually has many layers. Common data access problems with ODBC can be attributed to multiple instances of ODBC access files existing on one workstation.

NATIVE DATABASE CONNECTIVITY

Another efficient way to connect to a datasource is by using a native connection. Essentially, Crystal Reports "piggybacks" onto datasource client connectivity software provided by a given vendor to submit SQL statements and receive data returns from the datasource. This connection method often is the preferred method of connecting to a datasource for a number of reasons:

- A native connection provides faster delivery of the SQL statement generated by Crystal Reports to the database. The reason for this is there is no translation of the request sent to the database, unlike ODBC connections that were referred to earlier. Native connections send native SQL syntax specific to the appropriate database.

- A native connection is far less likely to fail than any other connection type. An ODBC connection is substantially more complicated. Fewer layers of components are involved in a native connection to a datasource, thus reducing the risk of configuration and version issues.

Although this connection type is a preferred method of connecting to a datasource, some drawbacks are critical when selecting a connection type before designing a Crystal Report:

- Using the connection type currently only allows for one database type to be connected to one report (that is, SQL, Oracle, or Sybase at one time).

- Fewer native connections than ODBC connection types are supported by Crystal Reports.

LOCAL QUERY FILES

Although the two preceding data access types, OBDC and Native, are extremely flexible, there are some needs that aren't addressed by either one. Two additional datasource types, Query and Metadata Files, provide added flexibility when designing Crystal Reports.

UNDERSTANDING CRYSTAL .QRY FILES

A Query file essentially is a subset of data extracted from a datasource such as Microsoft SQL Server that is held in a separate file location and typically stored on a secure shared location. .QRY files are created using the Crystal SQL Designer, which can be found by selecting Start, Programs, Crystal Reports Tools, and then selecting the Crystal SQL Designer icon.

The SQL designer is a very simple tool to use, so no reference example is provided to use the tool in this chapter.

Using .QRY files can be an extremely efficient way to access a given set of data. A good example of how organizations leverage the Crystal SQL Designer is with a data staging process whereby the SQL Designer executes a query, retrieves data, and stores it in a .QRY file. Crystal Reports then connects directly to the .QRY file and reads the relevant data in the file. Crystal Reports does not actually connect to the underlying database in this situation.

When query files like the one in Figure 8.7 are populated, they are similar to a table within a database.

Figure 8.7
A sample Crystal
Query file.

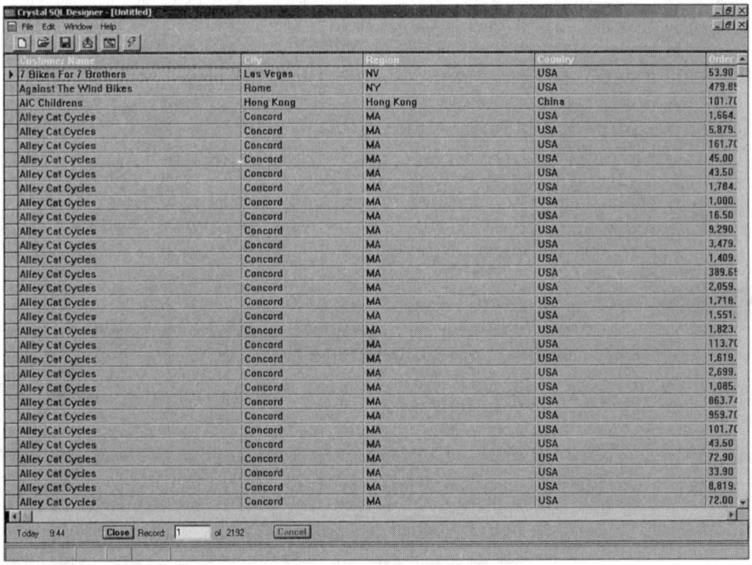

USING METADATA FILES

The second area gaining popularity in the Crystal Reports content creation arena is a Metadata layer or Metadata file. Metadata files are simply data about data. In most cases they are used to explain what users can see from a column and row level.

Using a Metadata file can provide simplified report creation because the complex names and relationships typically found within a database can be masked by a Crystal dictionary.

Many forms of these layers can be used to explain how data can be accessed. Using these files will help protect sensitive data from users who are not supposed to see it.

Crystal has several types of metadata, including Crystal Reports themselves. One particular meta capability available for Crystal Reports is Crystal Dictionaries. The major benefit of Crystal Dictionaries is that they contain no data, so they are very small files to store on the server. There is also no need to update them. Crystal Dictionaries allows all the joining of tables and renaming of complex field names to be completed before less "database-savvy" report designers try to build a report.

To create a new Crystal Dictionary choose Start, Programs, Crystal Reports Tools, and then select the Crystal Dictionaries tool.

To create a new dictionary, complete the following steps:

1. Select New. Several options are available to create the dictionary file. The first step in creating a dictionary is to connect to the appropriate datasource and add specific tables, as shown in Figure 8.8. As within a Crystal Report using ODBC, multiple databases can be accessed.

Note

The more database connections that are used in a dictionary, the longer it will take to process a report based on that dictionary.

Figure 8.8
Adding tables to a Crystal Dictionary.

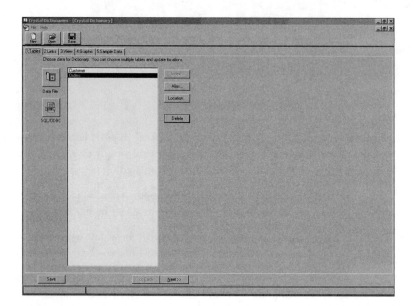

2. The next step is to link all the tables included in the dictionary, shown in Figure 8.9. An advantage to prelinking tables is taking this activity out of the hands of less technical report developers. Any time this can be done, it's recommended because it ensures the proper table linking is done.

3. One of the last steps is to define the fields that will be used in the dictionary. Figure 8.10 shows this. Adding fields to a dictionary removes this task from most report developers, increasing productivity.

Figure 8.9
Linking tables in a
Crystal dictionary.

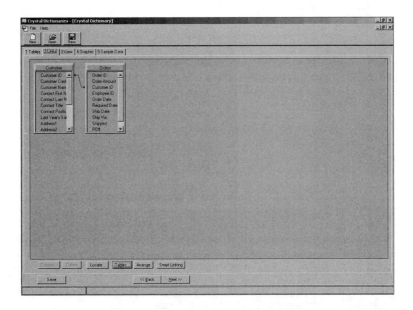

Figure 8.10
Adding database
fields to the Crystal
Dictionary.

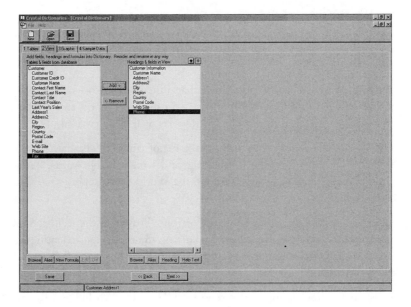

4. Save the dictionary. At this point the dictionary is finished. Click Save and select a file
   share location for use by Crystal Report designers. Crystal Dictionaries can be used for
   a report published to Crystal Enterprise.

PC DATABASE CONNECTION

Another type of datasource connection is a PC Database connection. Within many organizations, a number of "grass-roots" data sources can sprout up without warning, such as Microsoft Access (.mdb) files and Excel (.xls) spreadsheets. These datasources can contain valuable data, but a significant challenge that remains is there is no effective way to share what is contained within them. One way to connect to these data files through Crystal Reports is using the direct data file access.

The real challenge with accessing smaller data files is linking multiple instances together in a single report.

CREATING REPORTS

After the appropriate connectivity method is chosen and properly configured, it's time to start creating reports. As with all reports that are created, a significant amount of planning and requirements gathering should be done before creating the report. This will minimize the number of revisions necessary to complete the report. You might want to ask the following questions of the persons who need the report:

- Why is this report being created?
- Who is the intended audience?
- What are the basic functions this report should deliver?

Building a basic Crystal Report is not that difficult of a process. For this section, a sample report included with Crystal Enterprise 8.5 called the World Sales Report, which demonstrates a variety of features in Crystal Reports, will be re-created.

The World Sales Report has many of the major components that Crystal Reports provides, including charting, formulas, formatting, and some valuable extras. Before going any further it might make sense to browse through the World Sales Report to get an idea of what's being created.

Refer to Crystal Enterprise, launch ePortfolio, browse to the Report Samples folder, and launch the World Sales Report by clicking on the report and selecting the View option. Refer to Chapter 5, "Using the Crystal Enterprise Launchpad," for more information on using ePortfolio.

To begin building a sample sales report similar to the World Sales Report, launch Crystal Reports. Launching Crystal Reports opens the designer options for a new report. There are three options:

- Use the New Report Expert
- Create a Blank Report
- Open an Existing Report

The easiest way to create a report is by using the Report Expert. This expert is a step-by-step process of creating a complete report with all the Crystal Reports/Crystal Enterprise–specific functionality.

USING THE REPORT DESIGN WIZARD

Click the radio button that indicates the Report Expert, and then click OK. With the Report Expert, a host of available design templates, shown in Figure 8.11, can be used in creating a report. For each template, there is a preview of the format on the right side of the dialog box. As with most reports that are created, the Standard template is used in the World Sales Report example that follows.

> **Note**
>
> In the list of available wizards, the Standard Wizard is the base option. All the others are specialized formatting options for the Standard Wizard.

Figure 8.11
The Standard Report Wizard opening dialog box allows the selection of several design templates.

1. Select the Standard Report template, shown in Figure 8.11, and click OK. The Report Wizard for a standard report consists of eight tabs that guide the designer through the basics of building a report (see Figure 8.12). An additional tab appears if table linking is required for data within a report. This is a dynamic tab that will appear only if two or more tables are selected.

2. Select the Database button to specify where the data for the report is stored. This is the reason why the earlier sections of this chapter reviewed the different types of data access for Crystal Reports. The Report Wizard presents three options for this specification. For the purpose of this example, the Database button in Figure 8.12 shows the available sources necessary to complete the example. Click the Database button to continue.

Figure 8.12
The Report Wizard
Data tab allows easy
access to various data
types for creating
Crystal Reports.

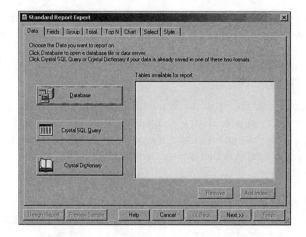

3. Select Xtreme Sample Database from ODBC datasources. All connection types, such as ODBC, native drivers, and direct file access, are available in the Data Explorer shown in Figure 8.13, which is launched after clicking on the Database button. To create the sample sales report, use the Xtreme Sample Database, which contains all the information necessary to create the report. The Xtreme sample database actually is an Access database installed with Crystal Reports.

Expand the ODBC listing in the Data Explorer by clicking on the + beside the name, and then expand the Xtreme Sample Database. The Data Explorer provides a view of all tables available to the report designer in this view. If a logon is required for a particular datasource, Crystal Reports will prompt for it at this time.

Figure 8.13
Using the Data
Explorer in Crystal
Reports allows for
easy table selection.

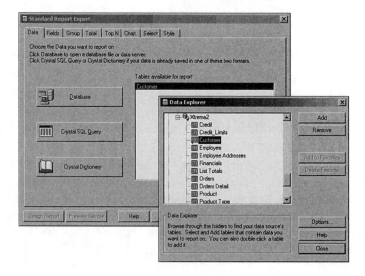

Note

The datasources used with ODBC connections must exist on all physical servers in the Crystal Enterprise architecture that process reports. This includes report design workstations and the Page and Job Servers for Crystal Enterprise delivery.

An advantage of using an ODBC connection to a database, at least with Crystal Reports, is that other tables can be added from different datasources to build this report. As each table is added to the report a green check mark will be placed on the top-left corner of the table icon.

4. Select the Customer table from the Xtreme Sample Database. For this example, the Xtreme connection is all that is required. From the list of available tables in the Xtreme Sample Database, select the Customer table by highlighting the table and clicking the Add button, as shown in Figure 8.13. After selecting the table, click the Close button to close the Data Explorer dialog box.

After closing the Data Explorer dialog box, the report designer is returned to the Standard Report Expert. Again, if multiple tables have been selected, the report designer will display a Linking tab, which provides manual and SmartLinking capability for multiple tables. Manual linking allows the report designer to define joins such as Inner, Outer, and Equal joins. SmartLinking links tables based on several criteria, including common field name, data type, and length. Because only one table was selected, the first tab available for interaction is the Fields tab. Be sure to click Next to move to the Fields tab.

→ For more information about linking in the expert, **see** the "Troubleshooting" section, **p. 260**.

5. Select fields for the report. For this report, only two initial fields will be selected:

   • Customer name

   • Last year's sales

To specify that a given field should be included in a report as shown in Figure 8.14, expand the Customer table in the Available field window, highlight Customer Name, and either drag it over to the Fields To Display window or click Add. Repeat this for the Last Year's Sales field.

Technically, there will be more fields in this report than just Customer Name and Last Year's Sales, as some fields will be added to aid in grouping the data in the report. These fields will be specified in the Groups tab later on in the example.

At any point in time, you can click the Finish button on the Report Wizard to process the report as is. Click Finish to see a columnar view of the two fields, Customer Name and Last Year's Sales, in the report. After doing so, return to the Report Wizard by clicking the Report menu item from the Crystal Reports menu and choosing Report Expert. Click Yes to acknowledge that changes to the report might be lost by doing this.

Figure 8.14
The Fields tab of the Report Expert enables a report designer to easily specify which fields should be included in a report.

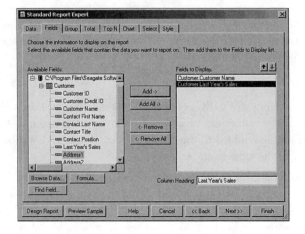

Note

If you're unfamiliar with a particular database field, click the Browse button on each page of the Report Wizard. This will display the first 100 records of field data from the table as well as data type and length.

CREATING A FORMULA FIELD

You also can create Formula fields by clicking the Formulas button in the Report Wizard. A Formula field is a field that isn't available from a datasource itself, such as a variance between two time periods.

Formulas are used to manipulate, modify, calculate, and change data coming from the database. When the Formula button is selected, the Crystal Reports formula editor will launch. The initial dialog box prompts for a name of the formula by which Crystal Reports can refer to it. It's good practice to have a standard formula naming convention that will assist with report clarity.

Although this report doesn't require a formula per se, it's worth exploring for a moment. Click the Formula button in the wizard. Supply a formula name, such as TestFormula, and then click OK. The formula editor in Figure 8.15 launches, which provides access to four cells used to create formulas.

The main area at the bottom is the actual formula editor window. The top-left window is where all the report and database fields are selected. Available functions included in the formula editor can be found in the middle pane. The window on the right side lists available operators. For a complete list of options on how to use different operators and functions, refer to the Help file included in Crystal Reports.

After you create a formula, you can click the X+2 button at the top of the screen to call the script check procedure. This should be used to check all formulas created in the report. Although this button does not inform the designer if the actual formula is written to return proper data, it will ensure that the syntax necessary to execute the formula is entered correctly. One of the biggest challenges in the formula editor is determining what the proper formula syntax should be.

Figure 8.15
The Crystal Reports formula editor allows for formulas to be written in Crystal Syntax or VB syntax.

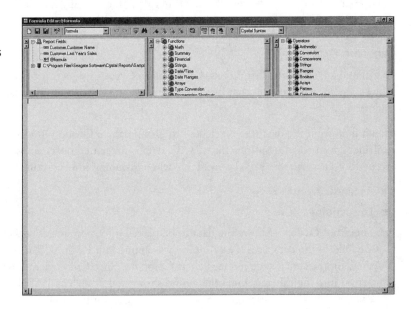

You can create formula fields that simply equal the value of a database field. In the formula editor, expand the list of available fields and double-click on a given field, such as last year's sales. There isn't a need to create any logic, such as "formula = XYZ" in the code pane, because the formula editor assumes that any syntax or code comprises what the formula equates to. Although this won't be used in the World Sales Report example, it demonstrates how simple formulas can be created (see Figure 8.16).

Figure 8.16
The formula editor in Crystal Reports allows creation of simple or complex calculations as well as operations such as date conversions and so on.

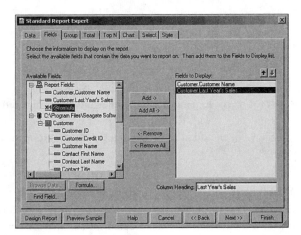

The script check button will always place the cursor in the general area where a formula problem might be. After the syntax is checked, the formula can be saved and the editor window closed. This will return the report designer to the Fields tab in the Report Wizard. The newly created formula is treated like any other database field in Crystal Reports. Be sure to click the Next button to move on to the Group tab.

GROUPING DATA

To group data, select the Group tab. Grouping in Crystal Reports provides a way to logically group any information that has a similar context, such as grouping sales data by city or country.

After a field from the database is selected to group data, a Group Options dialog box is available. This provides options for how the data is presented onscreen when the report is executed. Four sort types are also available when grouping information:

- **Ascending**—A to Z
- **Descending**—Z to A
- **Specified Order**—Allows the data to be placed into "containers" other than how they are held in the database. If a grouping was applied on Regions, for example, instead of showing the actual state name such as Colorado, Specified Order allows the data to be placed into logical containers that could show a value such as West Region. This feature enables data to be presented in several ways, based on the preference of business users, not necessarily database administrators.
- **Original Sort Order Type**—Using this option posts the report data the way it's organized in the database itself.

For the sales report example there will be four groups. Add the following fields to the Group By selection:

- Country
- Region
- City
- Customer name

Each group is based off a field from the Customer table, as shown in Figure 8.17. Select the Group tab in the Report Wizard. Expand the Customer table and highlight each of the four fields for the grouping and select Add. Refer to the Fields tab and notice that Country, Region, and Customer have been added as fields selected for this report.

CREATING TOTALS

After clicking the Next button, select the Total tab to add any field totals required for this report. The Total tab appears in Figure 8.18. Any fields that were added in the Fields tab that are of numeric type will automatically be selected for summarization. Subtotals of these numeric fields at each group level will automatically be created as well. Note that each group in the report (Country, Region, City, and Customer Name) will each have a subtab under the Total tab. Each of these tabs allows for control of the summary data at each group level.

Figure 8.17
Report data can be organized by grouping fields into common groups, such as City or Country.

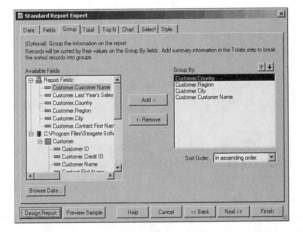

Figure 8.18
The totaling expert provides an easy way to create summary values within a report.

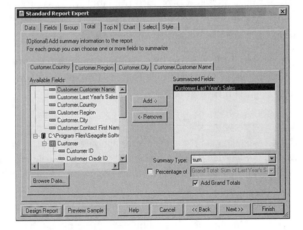

By default, all the subtotals will use a Sum function and a Grand Total will also be added to the report. If an additional numeric field is added to any group to provide an extra total, a few additional options can be set.

The first option is a drop-down list that allows the choice of operators used to total the data. A number of choices, from Sum to Median totals, can be specified here. Yet another option is to add a Grand Total using a check box. Explore these options in detail to understand all the totaling available in Crystal Reports.

For the sales report example, be sure the Last Year's Sales field is totaled at all group levels.

ADDING A TOP N SELECTION TO A REPORT

The Top N in the Report Wizard provides the capability to set Top N selections on data. The Top N expert allows for selecting or limiting data shown on the report. A good example would be to specify that the report should only show the Top 10 countries based on last year's sales, which can be a typical management request. For Top N or Bottom N reporting, a Top N selection is a conditional setting applied after the data is retrieved from the database. This is due to the fact that the Top N functionality is specific to Crystal Reports and a request cannot be sent to the database for this using a SQL query. This means that *all* data is retrieved from the database for *all* customers, and *then* a Top N selection is applied. In other words, the Top N Wizard is changing the SQL that Crystal Reports is generating in the background. This is a consideration for report design with large amounts of data.

Note

The Top N setting is applied at a group level, which implies a group must be created in the report or this will be unavailable in the wizard.

In the Top N dialog box an option to change the grouping from sorting all records to using Top N or Bottom N filtering is provided. One of the possible settings here would be to include other groups not part of the Top N with the label XYZ, typically "Others." In almost all cases, this is a good option to select because the Grand Totals will still reflect all customer sales, even if they are not displayed on the report.

For the sales report example, only the top five regions and countries are to be shown based on requirements gathering from management. Both Country and Region group levels must have the Top N set to 5, shown in Figure 8.19.

Note

One consideration to keep in mind when applying Top N is that this option does not filter data downloaded from the database. It only displays data within the Top N; however, the Grand Total fields will reflect the total for *all* data retrieved from the database.

The sample sales report is almost complete. The next three tabs, Chart, Select, and Style, are all optional because they're not required for a report to function properly. However, they do enhance the report content, look, and feel.

ADDING CHARTS TO A REPORT

Select the Chart tab, as shown in Figure 8.20. Several options provide the capability to deliver high-quality charting within the report, requiring minimal customization.

Figure 8.19
The Top N dialog box allows for a dynamic selection of the Top N groups, even at multiple levels within a report.

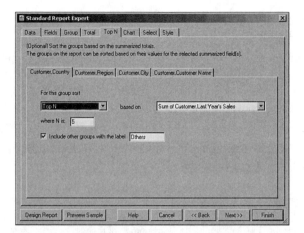

Figure 8.20
Crystal Reports provides a wide variety of charts for any report.

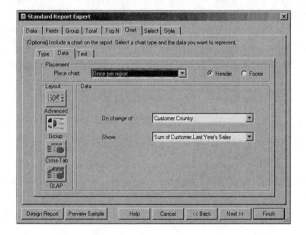

The first selection dialog box prompts for the type of chart to display. After a chart type is selected, options for the display type prompt the report designer. In other words, a 3D bar chart or a flat chart can be specified.

The second step for charting, the most critical, is to specify the data that will be used in the actual chart. The two main types of charts that can be assigned are

■ Group data

■ Advanced data set

Group data sets require that at least one group with a summary value exists within the report. This is the case with the sample sales report. The Advanced tab is extremely useful when plotting multiple data points on a chart.

The Text tab allows custom text to be applied to the chart. "Less is more" is a good practice when it comes to entering text on a chart.

It's extremely important to note that only one chart can be added to a report from the expert, but this is *not* the case outside the expert. When the Report Expert is finished, multiple charts can easily be added to the report by selecting Insert from the Crystal Reports menu. The sample sales report has a specification for three charts, so additional charts would need to be added after the report is finished in Report Expert.

Within the Report Wizard, the initial chart to be applied to the report will reside in the Report Header, based on Country totals.

Note

If, after clicking Finish in the Report Wizard a chart is not displayed, it's probably because the Data tab in the Chart portion of the wizard wasn't selected. Notice that the wizard takes a guess at the appropriate chart data. Even if the data selection isn't changed, it still won't display a chart unless the tab has been selected.

To move on, click the Next button or the Select tab. The Select tab allows for rich manipulation of the where clause in the SQL statement generated by Crystal Reports, which will ultimately query the database.

Highlighting a field and adding it to the Select Fields window allows the field to be set equal to a value, less than or greater than a value, between a value, and so on.

In any case, once the field is selected as a filter on the data, a drop-down list allows for different types of filters. For example, the choice of One Of allows the definition of multiple values, used to choose more than one row from the database field. (That is, for a field that contains State information, One Of would allow the choices of CA, CO, MI, MA, FL.)

Note

Selections can be made with any field from the database as long as it makes sense for the report. A good example might be a report that has a Top N of 5 applied, yet only one value for one field is selected in the Select tab. This would cause the chart to lose its meaning and impact.

The sample sales report should have a select statement that removes any values less than zero. Add the Last Year's Sales field to the Select window and choose the statement Is Greater Than and enter 0 as the value, as shown in Figure 8.21.

APPLYING A STYLE

Clicking the Next button opens the Style tab in the Report Wizard. The Style tab in Figure 8.22 allows for selection of predefined report styles and report names. The first text dialog box prompts for a report name, which will be placed on the top of the report.

Figure 8.21
Selection options in
Crystal Reports affect
the Where clause of a
SQL query in the
report.

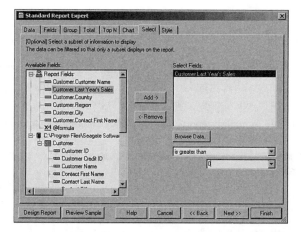

Figure 8.22
Style settings provide
an instant format on
a Crystal Report with-
out tedious effort on
the part of the
designer.

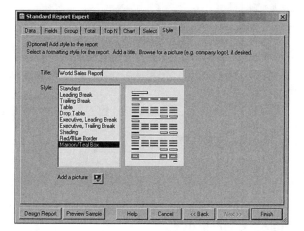

The second option is for the type of report style that will be applied to the report. By default, a standard report style will be applied to the report for the formatting of objects such as fields and text. For the most part these report styles are a useful point to gain ideas on how to format a presentation-quality report.

An additional option on the Style tab is to add a logo to the report. Crystal Reports supports several picture formats, including BMP and JPEG.

In the case of the sample sales report, most of these styles will not work if the goal was to create an exact replica of the World Sales Report found in Crystal Enterprise. For the purposes of this example however, the Maroon/Teal boxes formatting will suffice.

VIEWING THE REPORT

After selecting the Maroon/Teal style, click the Finish button on the Report Wizard. This will launch the report and send the SQL query created by the Report Wizard to the database. The database server processes the SQL query and returns the result to the Crystal Reports application. Crystal Reports then applies formulas, formatting, and so on to the report and displays the finished results, as shown in Figure 8.23.

→ For a review of how to add or publish reports into the Crystal Enterprise system, **see** Chapter 7.

Figure 8.23
The sample World Sales Report, complete with a chart and formatting.

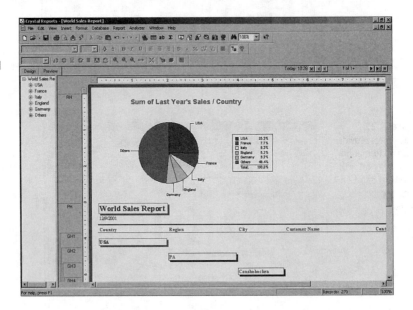

USING THE CRYSTAL REPORTS DESIGNER

After the report in the preceding section is complete, click on the Design tab found on the left side of the Crystal Reports designer.

Before proceeding any further, it's important to understand how a Crystal Report is structured. A Crystal Report is organized into logical sections. Each section will print data on the report based on the section type. For example, anything in the Report Header section, such as an image, will print only once per report. Move that same image to the Page Header section, and the image will print once per page, at the top of the page.

The same holds true for data fields. A data field in the details section of a report will print once per row of data. Hiding the details section alone creates more of a summary report, where double-clicking on the group summary values when viewing the report will open up the details section. This is reviewed later in the chapter.

Manipulating various sections adds power and value to a Crystal Report. This manipulation of sections may include things like dynamic hiding or suppression of a section.

ADDING CHARTS TO AN EXISTING REPORT

To get closer to the preceding section's goal of replicating the World Sales Report, additional charts must be added. For this section, continue to use the report created in the preceding section, or choose another one from the Report Samples folder. To add a chart, click on the Insert menu item in Crystal Reports and select Chart.

The same options are available for building the chart as shown in the Report Expert. For the sales report sample, an additional chart is needed to finish the report. The second chart will be based on regional data found in the group footer 2 section under the Design tab. For the object placement, choose for every country to show the region's last year's sales.

Figure 8.24 shows the report with multiple charts.

Figure 8.24
Additional charts
added to the sample
sales report.

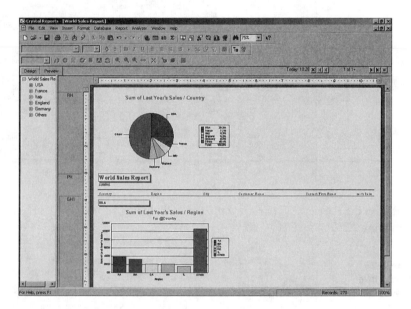

HIDING REPORT SECTIONS

Another key element of the report that was not completed in the Report Expert was hiding certain sections. This can be done in the Design mode. Design mode is the open access panel to the raw report design.

In Crystal Reports, click on the Design tab. Each section of the report is exposed. Right-clicking on each section of the report and selecting Hide allows for information in the report to be drilled into by an end user but hidden upon initial view, thus creating a management summary-level view of the data, rather than listing all the detail level records initially. When referring to "drilling into" an item in a Crystal Report, this typically implies viewing a lower level of detail data.

The Hide option allows users to drill down to the next level of data, whereas the Suppress option will not allow any exploration of lower levels of data (see Figure 8.25).

Note

When a section is hidden or suppressed it will have gray slash marks through it indicating that it is not shown on initial print.

Figure 8.25
Hiding report sections allows data to be explored but hidden upon initial view of the report.

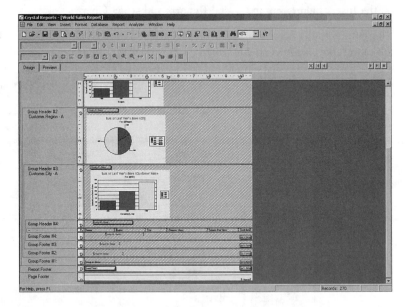

Select the Preview tab to review the results of hiding sections of the report (see Figure 2.26).

Figure 8.26
Initial print from preview.

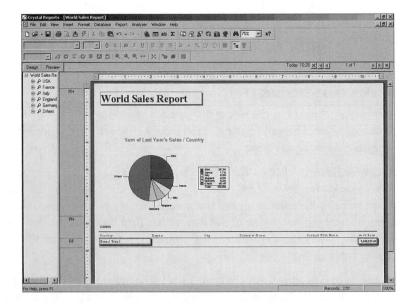

The new World Sales Report is now ready to publish to Crystal Enterprise. Before publishing, take a few minutes and explore the data and charts.

USING COMMON FORMULAS IN CRYSTAL REPORTS

As described earlier in this chapter, the formula editor allows for advanced formula creation of values not necessarily found in the database itself. This next section provides a review of the different types of formulas that can enhance a report or manipulate data from a database.

➔ For further discussion on how to resolve errors or syntax issues with formulas, **see** the "Troubleshooting" section, **p. 260**.

Formulas can be used to manipulate data because this is a necessary component with most reports in production environments. Within the Crystal formula editor are more than 450 different functions that can be used to accomplish formula-related tasks.

Another key feature of the formula editor is the capability to switch between syntax types. A drop-down list allows a report designer to choose between Crystal or Basic Syntax (these options can also be set by choosing File, Options, Reporting tab, as a default for all reports).

Crystal Syntax is typically used for most common formulas. It works best when Crystal is being leveraged in a standalone environment or along with Crystal Enterprise solutions. Crystal Syntax is processed locally where the report designer is installed, or on the Page a nd Job Server for Crystal Enterprise. Crystal Reports formulas are processed after data is retrieved from the database; they do not affect the SQL statement Crystal Reports generates.

When using the formula editor the most noticeable point is that Crystal Syntax is slightly different than other development languages. For example, there is no ending of control structures, such as an If-Then-Else statement, which does not employ an End If.

Because of these subtle differences in the formula editor, it's always good practice to use the Check Script button in Figure 8.27 to verify proper syntax.

UNDERSTANDING COMMON FORMULA OPERATORS AND FUNCTIONS

The first step in any formula creation is to know when to use operators. Certain operators, such as addition and subtraction, should be relatively easy to understand, so they aren't covered here. Other, more complex operators such as a Control Structure (found in the formula editor) help to extract or evaluate data that has been populated in an uncommon manner. For example, the phone number field in a database that has been formatted with dashes can present challenges when reading.

Create a simple columnar report using Xtreme Sample Data with no groups that contains two fields, Customer and Phone. In this scenario, using a loop will allow Crystal to pass across the data as many times as necessary to evaluate the field and correct potential problems with the data.

Figure 8.27
The Check Script button in the formula editor verifies proper formula syntax.

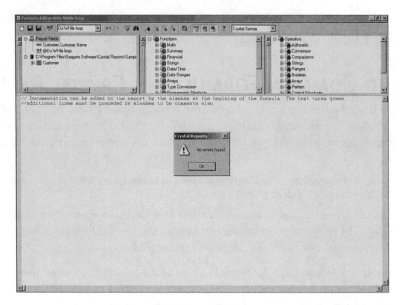

Two types of loops, the Do-While type and the For type, are common in Crystal Reports.

THE Do-While OPERATOR

The first option is a Do-While loop shown in Figure 8.28. This allows Crystal to pass across the data an indefinite amount of times to extract or process the information.

Figure 8.28
The formula editor control structure list contains the Do-While loop.

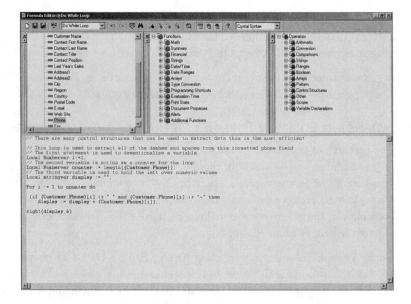

The example in Figure 8.28 shows how a loop can handle difficult data. For example, a formatted phone field has spaces and parentheses. The formula in Listing 8.1 extracts these pieces of data so the numeric values can be used to present an account number for the customer.

In Listing 8.1 there is an easy extraction of data through the process of a Do-While loop.

LISTING 8.1 THIS FORMULA EXTRACTS CHARACTERS FROM THE DATABASE FIELD AND DISPLAYS THE LAST SIX NUMBERS

```
//this loop is being used to extract the right six characters
//of the customer phone field. Spaces and dashes need to be removed.

//a few variable need to be created. The first is a counter:
Local Numbervar i := 1;

//the next variable is created to discover the length of the field
local numbervar Counter := length({Customer.Phone});

//create a variable as a container for the result set
local stringvar PhoneVar;

While i <= Counter do
(If {Customer.Phone}[i] <> "-" and
{Customer.Phone}[i] <> " " then
PhoneVar := PhoneVar + {Customer.Phone}[i];
i := i+1);
right(PhoneVar,6)
```

Notice in Figure 8.29 that the different items in the control structure, such as comments, are shaded differently.

Note

It's good practice to add comments to any formulas created with the Crystal Reports formula editor.

THE For OPERATOR

An operation similar to the one in Figure 8.30 can be easily accomplished by using a For loop. This loop works in a similar manner to the Do-While; the major difference is a For loop only passes across the data a specific number of times.

In the case of the example in Figure 8.30 the formula is specifying the number of times it will take to extract the data properly. This example tells Crystal it will take X amount of times to extract the appropriate data.

Notice the end result of the For loop and the Do-While from the previous section displayed in Figure 8.31. Both the Do-While and For loops return the same result of the new account number from the phone field.

Figure 8.29
A Do-While loop in Crystal Reports allows the report to evaluate a data field until a certain condition is met.

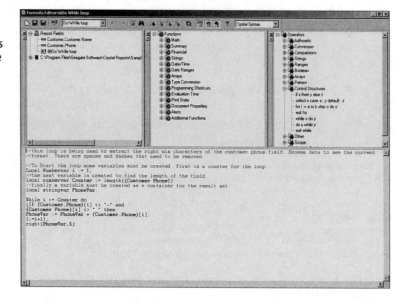

Figure 8.30
A For loop control structure allows browsing data.

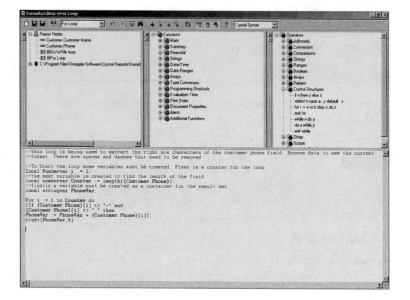

USING THE ToText FUNCTION

Another type of formula function that is extremely useful is the ToText function. This is a Conversion Type function, which as the name implies, coverts fields like date values to text. Often, it's necessary to convert values such as dates into string values to calculate items such as the difference between two dates.

Figure 8.31
A sample report using different loop operators to create a formula field that shows the last six digits of a phone number.

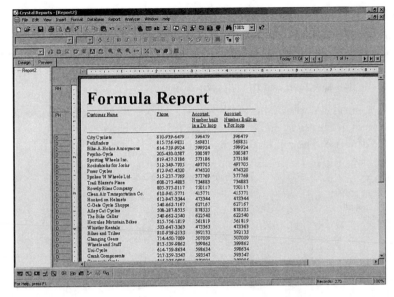

If, for example, the Orders table in Xtreme Sample Database were added to a report, two fields such as Ship Date and Order Date might be included. Converting both fields to text using the `ToText` function allows a formula such as

```
totext ({Orders.Ship Date} - {Orders.Order Date},0,"") + "Days"
```

Figure 8.32 shows an example of converting a date into a string.

Figure 8.32
Using Conversion Type functions on a data field can resolve type mismatches in formulas.

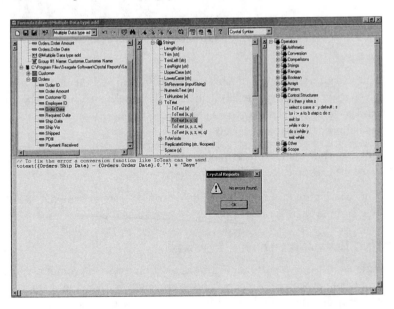

OTHER USES FOR FORMULAS

Another useful role of formulas in Crystal Reports is to create multiple groups off of a single data field. In Crystal Reports, a database field can be used natively only one time to create a group. As stated, with formulas, this can be overcome if a formula is used to hold the value of the database field and then "grouped" on.

A practical example of this can be seen in Figure 8.33. Notice the group tree that has been created in the report and contains a nested group based off the Customer name field from the database. The top-level group in the report is based off a formula.

Figure 8.33
Using multiple groups in a report built off formula fields.

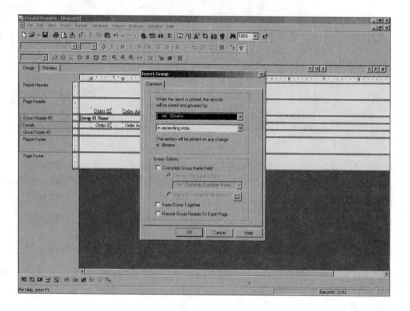

The actual formula only contains the database field and the first character displayed. {Customer.Customer name} [1] is the actual formula entry, where the numerical value in the brackets [1] is called *subscripting*. This is used to select a certain number of characters from the leftmost character in a given field.

Note the end result of this grouping off the database field Customer Name and a formula based off Customer Name in Figure 8.33.

Notice in Figure 8.34 how a few simple formulas can increase the ease of using a report. The group tree for a report is easier to navigate and provides a more fluid experience.

CREATING PARAMETER-DRIVEN REPORTS

Parameter-driven reports allow for Crystal Enterprise to prompt users for specific information before processing a report. This is extremely powerful in that Crystal Enterprise automatically prompts a user for parameters if the Crystal Enterprise system administrator specifies so. Parameters are user-defined data requests that can be used to affect

- SQL statements
- Conditional suppression of columns and sections
- Manipulation of formula fields

Figure 8.34
A finished report with formulas and grouping improves end-user interaction.

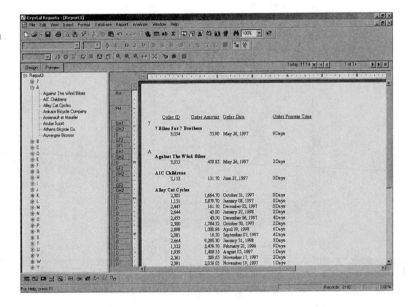

ACCESSING AN EXISTING REPORT

Parameters are created in the Field Explorer. The example in this section uses the World Sales Report. Start Crystal Reports and open the World Sales Report from Crystal Enterprise by selecting the Enterprise button, logging into Crystal Enterprise, browsing to the Report Samples folder, and selecting the report. A text parameter that affects the region shown in the World Sales Report will be added.

ADDING A PARAMETER

To add a parameter to a report, select Insert, Field Object from within Crystal Reports to launch the Field Explorer dialog box. Under this dialog box is a Parameter Field section, shown in Figure 8.35. To create a new parameter, right-click the Parameter Field listing in the Field Explorer and select New.

When the Parameter dialog box launches, some basic information for the parameter is required. This includes the name of the parameter. As with all fields created in the designer there must be a unique name that identifies the field. Parameter names are appended by a question mark. Enter the text **Region** for the name of this parameter.

Figure 8.35
The Field Explorer provides access to edit and create parameter fields.

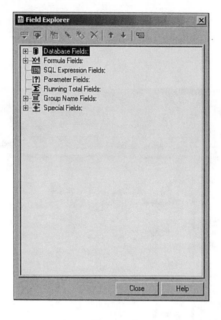

Whatever name is given to the Parameter field will also be the default column heading used in the design of the report.

Another option is Prompting Text. Up to 270 characters can be used to create statements that will display to an end user when the report is processed in Crystal Enterprise. Enter **What Regions would you like to see?** for the prompting text (see Figure 8.36).

Figure 8.36
Parameter fields can prompt the user for data entry before a report is processed.

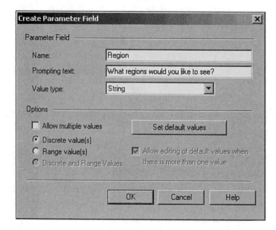

An additional selection for a parameter is the value type for the parameter. Enter a value of String for this because the field for this selection is also a type of String. Before creating the parameter it is always a good idea to refer to the Field Explorer, expand the list of available fields in the report, right-click on the field on which the parameter is going to be based, and select Browse Data to confirm the Data type (see Figure 8.37).

Figure 8.37
Browsing data in the Field Explorer to confirm data types.

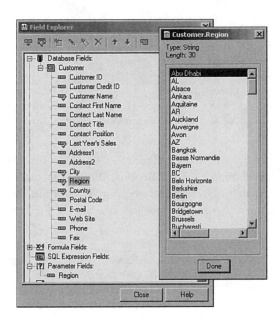

CREATING DEFAULT VALUES FOR A PARAMETER

At this point, a basic parameter has been created. However, if the parameter is going to be used to affect specific data such as a field from the database, default selections—basically a pick list—must be created.

To do this, click on the Set Default Values button in the Create Parameter Field dialog box. This will invoke the dialog box to specify on which table and fields a parameter should be based, shown in Figure 8.38.

As shown in Figure 8.38 there are several selections available from this dialog box. Two selection boxes at the top of the screen, Browse Table and Browse Field, allow the assignment of the parameter to a specific table and field in the database. For this example, select Customer for the table and Region for the field.

From these dialog boxes, the first 100 records from the database table are returned for a specific field. These records can be used to create default values presented to the user to choose from when the report is processed in either Crystal Reports or Crystal Enterprise. Each of these items can be highlighted and moved to the available default values one at a time, or as multiple selections. Click on the double arrow >> button to move all region values over to the Default Values pick-list section.

Figure 8.38
Setting Parameter
default values is a
simple process from
the Set Default Values
dialog box.

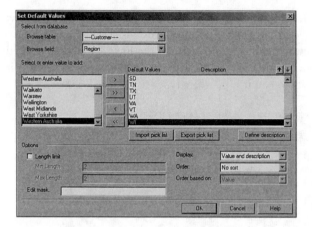

Another useful option is to specify an external pick list. A pick list can be created from a static text file that is maintained outside Crystal Reports. When using external pick lists, be aware that the report maintains a UNC path connection to a text file. Every time the pick list needs to be updated, the report must be opened and the pick list reimported.

> **Note**
>
> Crystal Enterprise allows dynamic selections from a pick list to be passed to a Crystal Report. Several methods can be used to enable dynamic pick lists with Crystal Enterprise, from ADO database connections on a simple .ASP page to the SmartReporting technology available through Report Application Server, which is an add-on to Crystal Enterprise.

With the pick list linked to a text file, this implies the text file must be created from the same database. Usually this means creating a second report from the database to generate the specified text file being used. This second report would do nothing other than process inside Crystal Enterprise and then output as a .txt file to a file share location. This can be accomplished by leveraging the schedule and output of reports to a file location capability of Crystal Enterprise. The "main" Crystal Report, the one using the test file to populate the pick list, will always read off this pick list file, in effect creating a "dynamic" pick list. Because of these issues, most Crystal Reports do not employ pick lists.

> **Note**
>
> Static pick lists should be used when based on rarely changing data, such as dates or organizational names.

This section does not review actually using an external text file to populate a pick list. The existing records moved over to the Default Values windows will be used. After these default values are set, click OK.

SPECIFY ENTRY CRITERIA FOR THE PARAMETER

After selecting OK, the main parameter dialog screen is displayed again. There are two final selections for consideration related to parameters:

- **Allow editing of default values when there is more than one value**—This selection can be used, if unchecked, to force the user to only select from the default values supplied.

- **Allow multiple vales**—This setting will affect how the parameter can be used in relation to the SQL statement. For example, when using a record selection as in the following example, caution should be exercised regarding the value type selected. Discreet values are selected values that can be set to any Record Selection criteria. However, the ranged and multiple values are limited to only a few selections.

Save the World Sales Report to a local file location on the Crystal Reports workstation. Use the name World Sales Report2. Although the parameter is properly configured, Crystal Reports is still unaware that it should apply a selection based on this parameter to the SQL statement in the report.

APPLYING THE PARAMETER TO A REPORT SELECTION

To apply a user-supplied parameter to a Crystal Report, the Select Expert must be used.

The Select Expert changes the Where clause in the SQL query submitted to the database when a Crystal Report is processed. As a good exercise, view the SQL statement before and after applying this selection. To view the SQL query for a report, click the Database menu item and click Show SQL Query.

To apply the parameter, from Crystal Reports, select the Report menu item, and then choose Select Expert. The first dialog box shown in Figure 8.39 prompts to which field the Select Expert will apply a selection formula. Choose Region because this was the field specified in the parameter name Region created in the preceding section. Click OK. The Select Expert allows for selections to be applied to data within a report based on certain operators such as "is equal to," "is between," "is greater than," and so on.

Figure 8.39
The Select Expert dialog box allows for advanced selection criteria based on parameters.

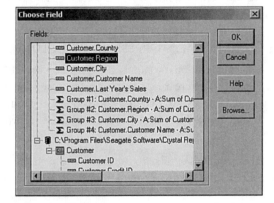

Note

Remember, the options used in the Select Expert will be applied to the Where clause in the SQL statement.

The Select Expert dialog box appears in Figure 8.40.

Figure 8.40
The Select Expert can apply user-entered parameter data to the Where clause of the report's SQL statement.

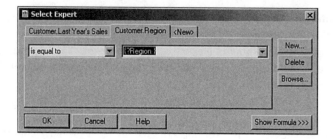

The first tab available in the Select Expert is the Customer Region tab because this was previously specified in the Select Field dialog box. From the operator drop-down list, which currently displays Is Any Value by default, select Is One Of, which will allow for multiple values to be selected. Two additional boxes will populate the Select Expert dialog box. One is a drop-down list of the options available in the pick list created for the Region parameter. Notice the selection option at the top of the pick list is {?Region}, which represents the region parameter created in step 2.

By selecting {?Region}, the report designer is telling Crystal Reports that the selection criteria, which should be inserted into the Where clause of the SQL statement, is going to be provided through user input before the report is processed. After selecting {?Region}, click OK. Notice that the report will now prompt for a user-entered parameter value. The report will prompt for this any time the Refresh report button is selected.

If this report were published to Crystal Enterprise, the parameter would not prompt the user by default. This should be specified in the Crystal Management console by selecting the report, selecting the Parameters tab, clicking on the actual parameter, in this case Region, and checking the Prompt User box.

USING PARAMETERS FOR CONDITIONAL SUPPRESSION OF COLUMNS AND SECTIONS

Parameters can also be used to conditionally suppress any section or field in a report. This feature can be extremely useful when creating a single report to support hundreds or thousands of users. A Crystal Enterprise user ID could be forced into a parameter that inserts the user ID into the SQL statement. This would enforce database security based on user IDs.

Parameter creation for this example is similar to the preceding section, with the exception of specifying a data table and field within the parameter, which is not done in this instance.

Open the World Sales Report in Crystal Reports. Create a parameter called Conditional and supply two static values, Manager and Sales Representative into the Data Values section of Set Default Values dialog box (see Figure 8.41).

Figure 8.41
Conditional parameters allow suppression of report sections and columns.

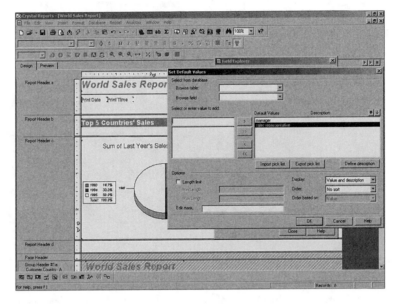

After the Conditional parameter is created, it can be used for a variety of purposes.

In the World Sales Report, select the Design tab and right-click on the Report Header section, and then click on Format Section. The Section Expert lists options for actions such as suppressing sections of a report. Be sure the Report Header section is selected and click the X+2 button by the Suppress (No Drill Down) option. By selecting the formula option for suppression, this tells Crystal Reports to suppress the section based on the result of a formula. The formula, in this case, will be to evaluate the value of the Conditional parameter.

After selecting the X+2 button by the Suppress option, the Format Formula dialog box launches. Enter the following formula, similar to Figure 8.42, in the formula dialog window:

```
{?Conditional} = "Manager"
```

This will force suppression of the Report Header section if the parameter is set to Manager.

Close the Formula window by selecting the Save and Close option. Refresh the report data by selecting the Refresh button and entering the value of Manager for the parameter prompt.

The real advantage gained through using conditional suppression based on parameters is that any given user can customize the look and feel of a report. A manager might prefer viewing a report with just summary data, whereas a project manager might need to see specific levels of detail. Consider using this feature for suppressing irrelevant sections when viewing reports in Crystal Enterprise.

Figure 8.42
The section expert allows for sections to be suppressed, either manually or conditionally, based on a formula.

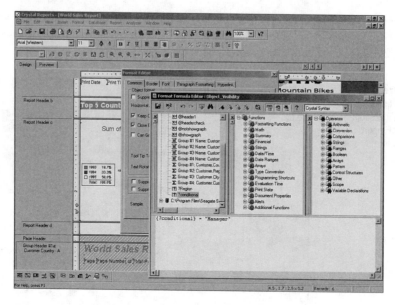

USING ALERTS IN CRYSTAL REPORTS

The Alerts feature was added in version 8.5 to enable Crystal Reports and Crystal Enterprise to highlight subsets of data within a Crystal Report based on certain triggers. Instead of searching through an entire report for specific information, an alert can identify a point of information based on specific criteria or threshold values being met and subsequently launch a text notification. Refer to Chapter 5 for more information on using alerts in Crystal Enterprise.

The potential for alerts goes way beyond what Crystal Enterprise provides out-of-the-box. If an alert was triggered in a scheduled report in Crystal Enterprise, through minor customization of ePortfolio, the text notification and location of the report in Crystal Enterprise could be e-mailed to an end user, sent to a discussion forum, or kick off a database process.

Alerts can be set using the formula editor, so anything the formula language in Crystal Reports can evaluate can trigger an alert.

In the following example, an alert is added to the World Sales Report. Open the World Sales Report, select the Report menu item, and then click Create Alert. The Create Alerts dialog box is initialized, as shown in Figure 8.43.

Select New, which launches the New Alert dialog box. Supply a name and alert message. For this example, use Alert for the name and "Sales are below forecast" for the message seen in Figure 8.44.

Figure 8.43
The Create Alerts dialog box allows for alerts to be created and managed within a given report.

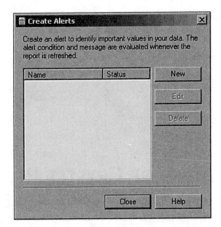

Figure 8.44
Alerts can be created with alert text to notify users of certain data conditions.

To set a trigger for the alert, click on the Condition button. This launches the formula editor. Enter the following formula:

```
{Customer.Last Year's Sales} < 1000
```

Click the Save and Close button in the formula editor. Click OK to accept the settings for the alert in the Create Alert dialog box. Be sure the status of the alert is Enabled. If it's not, edit the alert and check the Enabled option. Close the Create Alert dialog box.

Now that the alert is completed, it can be tested. Select the Refresh Report button. The report will connect to the database and load new data, which will trigger the condition. The Report Alerts dialog box will pop up, indicating which alerts have been triggered (see Figure 8.45). Crystal Reports even allows you to view the report with a record selection based on data that applies only to the trigger by selecting the View Records button.

If this report were published back to Crystal Enterprise and then scheduled, the alert would be triggered and populate the Alerts dialog windows in ePortfolio. Refer to Chapter 7 for more information on publishing reports to Crystal Enterprise and Chapter 5 for information on how to view an alert in ePortfolio.

Figure 8.45
The Report Alerts dialog box indicates which alerts have been triggered.

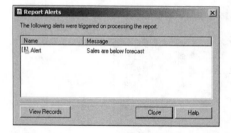

USING ADVANCED FEATURES OF CRYSTAL REPORTS

Up until this point, this chapter has provided a review of fundamental report design concepts and techniques. This next section explores some of the advanced features of Crystal Reports that can be leveraged by Crystal Enterprise. These include

- Using hyperlinks
- Building a report from a COM Provider datasource (.dll)
- Building a report from an XML datasource
- Publishing a Crystal Report as an XML document

USING HYPERLINKS IN CRYSTAL REPORTS

The hyperlinking feature in Crystal Reports is exactly what a report designer would expect: the ability to create hyperlinks on text and images, as well as dynamic hyperlinks driven by data values or formulas. To see this functionality, select a text object or data field within a Crystal Report, right-click the object, select Format Object, and select the Hyperlink tab.

Hyperlinks in Crystal Reports also can be leveraged to link multiple Crystal Reports together. This provides an endless number of business application possibilities because a Crystal Report can accept parameters through a URL line. This means that a user can click on a data value in one Crystal Report and, through a hyperlink, have that particular value passed automatically over a URL line to another Crystal Report that accepts parameters.

In Crystal Reports, open the World Sales Report from the Crystal Enterprise Report Samples folder. A company logo is present in the report. From the logo, a hyperlink can easily be attached to link directly to the corporate Web site. To do this, right-click on the logo and select Format Field. From the Format Editor dialog box, select the Hyperlinks tab (see Figure 8.46).

From the Hyperlinks tab, select A Web Site on the Internet radio button in Figure 8.47 and enter a hyperlink. Click OK to close the dialog box. The Hyperlink tab can be found on the Format dialog box for most objects in Crystal Reports.

Figure 8.46
The Hyperlink tab in the Format Editor dialog box has several options for linking Crystal Reports data to other Crystal Reports, Web sites, files, and a host of other options.

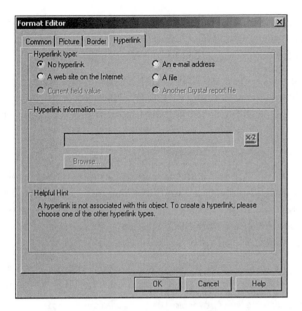

Figure 8.47
Selecting a Web site on the Internet allows for any URL to be entered.

The Web Site on the Internet option is of significance in that the URL could actually be a formula, as indicated by the X+2 button. This is directly related to the example mentioned previously, where two or more Crystal Reports could be linked via a parameter over a URL line. Refer to Chapter 7, which explains how to "drive" an unmanaged report via a URL line. This is also mentioned in Chapter 1. A report can be placed in a virtual directory on an IIS Web server. The report would have some parameters configured, much like the example where a parameter for region was added to the World Sales Report.

As an exercise, take the World Sales Report with the parameter Region and copy it to the Rootdrive\Inetpub\wwwroot directory of a Microsoft Internet Information Server. Rename the report to ws.rpt. This will make calling the report from a URL line easier. Now launch a Web browser. Enter the following:

```
HTTP://YouIISserverNAme/ws.rpt?prompt0=Paris
```

This URL line will tell the Crystal Enterprise Web Component Server that an unmanaged report has been requested for viewing with the parameter value of Paris. Additional prompts, as well as specifications to the type of report viewer to deliver the report (ActiveX, DHTML, Java), could be specified in the URL line.

Creating a hyperlink as a formula by selecting the X+2 button when entering a Web site hyperlink launches the formula editor. Assuming ws.rpt is still present, a hyperlink formula could be entered to make the prompt value passed over the URL line dynamic:

```
"http://YourIISserverName/ws.rpt?prompt0=" + {Customer.Region}
```

The Current Field Value option in Figure 8.48 could leverage a data field that has a Web site or e-mail address. This would launch an e-mail application or Web browser and direct the application to the supplied address in the actual data field. The only down side to this is when this type of hyperlink is selected, the field value does not turn blue or underlined as would be expected from typical Web page behavior.

Figure 8.48
Actual field values are useful when e-mail or Web site field data is stored in a database and presented on a report.

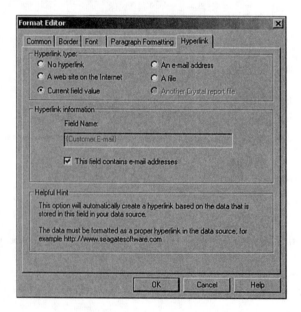

Two additional hyperlink options, e-mail and file, are straightforward and don't require explanation.

The last hyperlink type, to another Crystal Reports file, can be extremely useful. Linking to other Crystal Reports using this method provides another way to link reports without using the subreport approach.

BUILDING A REPORT FROM A COM PROVIDER DATASOURCE

Although Crystal Reports provides connectivity to most datasources within a given organization, such as flat files, relational datasources, and OLAP cubes, this connectivity does not satisfy everyone's data connectivity needs.

With the proliferation of Internet technology into almost every business application available today, advanced data concepts, such as streaming data objects, are extremely popular methods of connectivity for these applications. One very good example is a COM Provider, which connects to a data source and then writes retrieved data to a recordset.

UNDERSTANDING WHAT A COM PROVIDER DOES

A COM Provider is essentially a Windows .dll which contains some code within it that, upon request, connects to a datasource and returns a recordset result. COM Providers can come in many forms and can do just about anything, so the previous example might be a bit oversimplified, but it serves to explain the concept.

There are several obvious benefits to developing a COM Provider that connects to a source and streams out a consistent recordset or data return.

One obvious benefit is that the object can serve many business applications. Another benefit is that the object is just that, an object. A developer can make anything happen within that object (data transformation, calculations, and so on). All a consumer application, in this case Crystal Reports and Crystal Enterprise, would need to know about is the returned recordset.

THE CRYSTAL DECISIONS COM DRIVER

Crystal Decisions has developed a COM Driver that allows Crystal Reports, and ultimately Crystal Enterprise, to create the same interactive reports it is known for off of COM Providers that return an *ADO* recordset.

> **Note**
>
> ADO stands for ActiveX Data Objects. The reference library is created by Microsoft. Visit the Microsoft Web site for regular updates to this library.

> **Note**
>
> The COM Provider to be used for Crystal Reports must return an ADO recordset using the Microsoft ADO library. Contact Crystal Decisions for information about potential future enhancements to its COM Driver.

Using a COM Provider with the Crystal Decisions COM Driver solution for reporting couldn't make the process of report creation any easier. The ADO recordset, when viewed by Crystal Reports, looks like nothing more than a database table, with all the data needed right at the report designer's fingertips. The challenge is actually developing an appropriate COM Provider that will meet the needs of an organization's reporting requirements.

The significance of having such a driver is the key point of this section. Often, report designers will ask, "What can I do in the COM Provider?" The answer is the best part: Anything you want. Organizations are using the COM Driver to report off of COM Providers that do everything from accept incoming parameters, such as a user ID and password before the ADO recordset is actually generated, to connecting to an OLAP source via ADO MD and flattening OLAP data for easier analytic reporting. The possibilities are limited only by an organization's willingness to build a COM Provider.

The beauty of the COM Provider is that many organizations already have very useful COM Providers (.DLLs) that serve a number of existing applications, such as Internet or intranet ASP applications. These could be leveraged with Crystal Enterprise and the COM Driver.

The company maintains that this is an update to Crystal Reports 8.5, which can be installed from the Crystal Enterprise 8.5 CD. The update found on the CD adds the COM Driver to Crystal Reports, which is actually an updated version of P2SMON.DLL and can be found in the WINNT\SYSTEM32 folder of the system where Crystal Reports or Crystal Enterprise is installed.

The rest of this section focuses on how to actually build a COM Provider and use it to create a simple columnar report in Crystal Reports.

CREATING A COM PROVIDER (.DLL)

In order for Crystal Reports to report off of a COM Provider, it's helpful to actually have one. This section of the chapter explains how write a simple COM Provider using Microsoft Visual Basic.

Note

A COM Provider destined for use by Crystal Reports or Crystal Enterprise shouldn't have any user interface as part of the file, or Crystal Enterprise will hang when trying to process the report.

Note

Be sure a copy of Microsoft Visual Basic 6.0 is installed and available because this is the application used to develop this sample COM .dll. A recent version of Microsoft's ADO reference library should also be installed on the local workstation. This example uses ADO Version 2.6. The version number of the ADO reference library currently available can be verified under the Projects menu in Visual Basic. Select the References option and scroll down to items that start with Microsoft ActiveX Data Objects.

The COM Provider created in this section will use Microsoft's ADO library to connect to Xtreme Sample Database via ODBC and, using a SQL query, retrieve three fields:

- City
- Region
- Customer

Xtreme.mdb is installed with Crystal Reports or Crystal Enterprise, and the ODBC connection is automatically configured as well. To confirm this is installed, go to Control Panel, Administrative Tools, Data Sources and check for the System DSN titled "Xtreme Sample Database."

These three fields from Xtreme will be returned as an ADO recordset that Crystal Reports will bring into a report.

OPEN MICROSOFT VISUAL BASIC

To begin creation of the COM Provider, launch Microsoft Visual Basic and select New Project. Under the New Project dialog box, select ActiveX DLL, as shown in Figure 8.49.

Figure 8.49
Start a new ActiveX DLL project from the New Projects menu in Visual Basic.

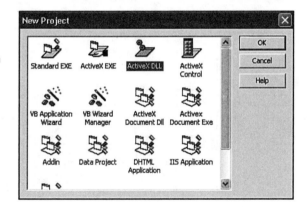

CONFIRM ADO 2.6 OR HIGHER IS REFERENCED

A few housekeeping items are in order to ensure the proper ADO library is referenced. In Visual Basic, select the Project Menu and choose References. Several reference libraries are listed. Scroll down to find the Microsoft ActiveX Data Objects 2.6 Library seen in Figure 8.50.

CHANGE THE PROJECT AND CLASS NAMES

Now that the references are done, it's time to change the name of the project. In the Project window, highlight the top-level object in the hierarchy currently titled Project1. In the Properties pane, rename the project to COMprovider as shown in Figure 8.51.

Figure 8.50
Be sure the Microsoft ADO Library is added to the references for this Visual Basic project.

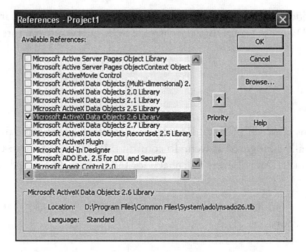

Figure 8.51
The Project window now indicates the project name is COMprovider.

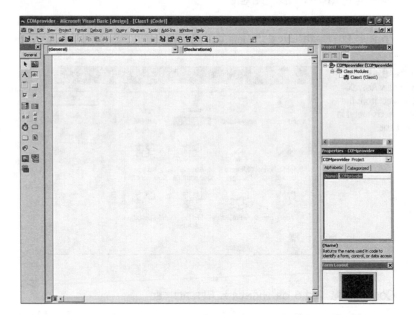

In the Project window, if it isn't already expanded, expand the Class Modules folder to expose the only class listed for the COMprovider project, Class1. Select Class1 in the Project window, and then rename Class1 to COMproviderClass in the Properties window seen in Figure 8.52.

Note

Please note that these names for both the project and class are not required to make the COM Driver functionality work. These are names to help keep track of what portion of the .dll is providing certain functionality.

Figure 8.52
The default class in
the project, Class1,
has been renamed to
COMproviderClass.

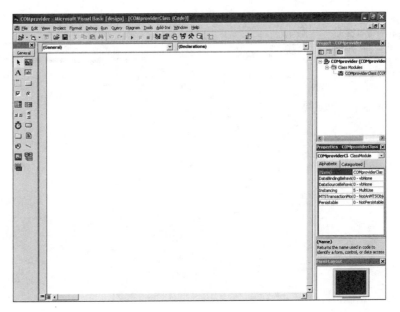

INITIALIZE THE ADO CONNECTION

Now it's time to actually enter some code. The first step will be to set two variables as an
ADO connection and recordset, respectively. Enter the following code into the General section of the code page:

```
Option Explicit
    Private demoConnection As ADODB.Connection
    Private demoRecordset As ADODB.Recordset
```

demoConnection will act as the handle to the ADO connection that must be initiated, and
demoRecordset will collect the data returned from the query.

Before the actual code is entered to create the query, it's necessary to do some "good housekeeping" code up front. Any time a COM Provider executes and returns data, it is initiating
connections and gathering data that uses up memory. If these connections and recordsets
aren't released, this could cause serious performance issues on the Crystal Enterprise server,
if this driver was to be deployed there.

Select the Code drop-down combo box and choose Class. Then select Terminate from the
second combo box to indicate this code will be executed upon termination of the class. Feel
free to delete the extra code listed here for the Initialize procedure because it's unnecessary
for this project.

```
Delete this code:
Private Sub Class_Initialize()
End Sub
```

The main body of the code for the COM Provider is ready to be entered. The project at
this point should look similar to Figure 8.53.

Figure 8.53
Code may now be entered for the actual class in the Visual Basic project.

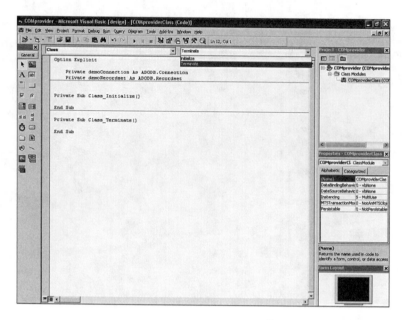

Now enter the code shown in Listing 8.2 to provide clean-up upon termination of the COM Provider.

LISTING 8.2   CLEAN-UP CODE FOR THE ADO RECORDSET

```
Private Sub Class_Terminate()
    If TypeName(demoRecordset) = "Recordset" Then
        If demoRecordset.State = adStateOpen Then
            demoRecordset.Close
        End If
    End If
    If TypeName(demoConnection) = "Connection" Then
        If demoConnection.State = adStateOpen Then
            demoConnection.Close
        End If
    End If
    Set demoRecordset = Nothing
    Set demoConnection = Nothing
End Sub
```

Each For loop tests for the connection state of both demoConnection and demoRecordset. If it's determined that they are open, they are closed and their values are set to Nothing; thus any occupied memory is freed up for other applications.

Now that proper clean-up of the code and connections is assured, it's necessary to actually connect to the datasource and retrieve the data.

A Public function must be created to initiate the ADO connection, connect to the database, and execute the query. This Public function will be called retrieveDATA. The name of the

Public function isn't a requirement of the COM Driver and doesn't need to be a predetermined string. Because this chapter isn't supposed to be a tutorial on using Visual Basic, it's sufficient to just enter the following code, which will complete the COM Provider, right after the End Sub portion of the clean-up code (see Listing 8.3).

LISTING 8.3 THE CODE THAT QUERIES THE DATASOURCE

```
Public Function retrieveDATA() As ADODB.Recordset
    Dim demoQuery As String
    demoQuery = "SELECT City, Region, Country FROM CUSTOMER"
    Set demoConnection = New ADODB.Connection
    Set demoRecordset = New ADODB.Recordset
    If LCase(TypeName(demoConnection)) = "connection" Then
        demoConnection.Mode = adModeRead
        demoConnection.Open "DSN=Xtreme Sample Database"
        If demoConnection.State = 1 Then
            demoRecordset.Open demoQuery, demoConnection, adOpenForwardOnly
            Set retrieveDATA = demoRecordset
        End If
    End If
End Function
```

This code declares demoQuery as a string to hold the actual SQL that will be passed to the database. demoQuery is then set to

```
SELECT City, Region, Country FROM CUSTOMER
```

This was cut and pasted from the SQL query window in Crystal Reports. Both demoConnection and demoRecordset are set and then initialized:

```
Set demoConnection = New ADODB.Connection
Set demoRecordset = New ADODB.Recordset
```

demoConnection is set to read mode and the connection string is passed into the connection, as shown in Listing 8.4.

LISTING 8.4 PASSING IN A CONNECTION STRING

```
Option Explicit

    Private demoConnection As ADODB.Connection
Private demoRecordset As ADODB.Recordset

Private Sub Class_Terminate()

    If TypeName(demoRecordset) = "Recordset" Then
        If demoRecordset.State = adStateOpen Then
            demoRecordset.Close
        End If
    End If

    If TypeName(demoConnection) = "Connection" Then
        If demoConnection.State = adStateOpen Then
```

LISTING 8.4   CONTINUED

```
                demoConnection.Close
        End If
    End If

    Set demoRecordset = Nothing
    Set demoConnection = Nothing

End Sub
```

It's critical to be sure the DSN name refers to the same name on the workstation where this is being developed. The same will hold true when it comes time to publish this report to Crystal Enterprise and the Job or Page Server needs to process the report.

Note

Crystal Reports is a read-only environment, so the Transaction feature of ADO with the COM Provider should not be used at any time. It will cause problems for the COM Driver.

The final code populates the recordset and sets the Public function retrieveDATA to the data return.

```
demoRecordset.Open demoQuery, demoConnection, adOpenForwardOnly
Set retrieveDATA = demoRecordset
```

Listing 8.5 shows the entire code set for the project.

LISTING 8.5   THE ENTIRE CODE SOLUTION FOR THE COM PROVIDER.DLL PROJECT

```
Option Explicit

    Private demoConnection As ADODB.Connection
Private demoRecordset As ADODB.Recordset

Private Sub Class_Terminate()

    If TypeName(demoRecordset) = "Recordset" Then
        If demoRecordset.State = adStateOpen Then
            demoRecordset.Close
        End If
    End If

    If TypeName(demoConnection) = "Connection" Then
        If demoConnection.State = adStateOpen Then
            demoConnection.Close
        End If
    End If

    Set demoRecordset = Nothing
    Set demoConnection = Nothing

End Sub
```

It might seem daunting at first, but actually creating a COM Provider can be a very simple process. However, the process to enable Crystal Reports to access this newly created COM Provider isn't quite complete.

TEST THE COM PROVIDER CODE

It's necessary to test the code to be sure it works. To do that, click the Start Code button (which looks like a VCR control for Play) to be sure there aren't any errors in syntax. It's anticlimactic at best to watch this code execute because nothing actually happens (it's not supposed to). The rest is up to Crystal Reports.

After the code is entered correctly and no bugs are present, it's necessary to compile this code as a .dll for Crystal Reports to access. To do this, select File, Make COMprovider .dll. Visual Basic changes the menu to refer to the project, COMprovider, by name as a matter of convenience. Figure 8.54 shows how to compile the code to a .dll.

Figure 8.54
The File menu provides an option to compile the code as a .dll for Crystal Reports to access.

For this example, choose to save the new .dll in a folder on the root of the C drive in a folder called comprovider. If the folder doesn't exist, create it, and then return to Visual Basic and finish the compile process.

Note

A COM .dll can be saved anywhere on a Windows workstation or server. A specific location on the workstation isn't necessary because the .dll must be registered with Windows. It is the registration of the .dll that enables Crystal Reports to locate and call it.

After COMprovider.dll has been saved to the C:\comprovider folder, it's necessary to register the .dll. This is required because Crystal Reports must be able to call the .dll for report processing.

REGISTER THE NEW .DLL ON THE WORKSTATION OR SERVER

To register the newly created .dll, from the Windows Start button, select Run. In the Run dialog box, use Regsvr32 to register the .dll as follows:

```
regsvr32 "D:\comprovider\comprovider.dll"
```

Click OK. Upon successful registration of COMprovider.dll, the message shown in Figure 8.55 appears.

Figure 8.55
This dialog box indicates successful registration of the COMprovider.dll.

Now that the .dll is registered, Crystal Reports is ready to access and leverage the COM Provider for reporting.

BUILDING A CRYSTAL REPORT OFF A COM PROVIDER (.DLL)

In the previous section, a COM .dll called COMprovider.dll was created to allow access to three fields in Xtreme Sample Data through an ADO recordset. To access this COM .dll, Crystal Reports needs to know the progID of the .dll. This is actually easy to figure out.

The progID for COMprovider.dll is the .dll name and then the class name that will be read by Crystal Reports. This means that COMprovider.dll has a progID of COMprovider.COMproviderClass. You should recall that COMproviderClass was the class name provided in the development sample.

Note

A great utility for detecting the progID of every .dll installed on a workstation is RegCtrls.exe from SoftCircuits.

1. Launch the Standard Report Wizard. After launching Crystal Reports, select the Standard Report Wizard and click OK, as seen in Figure 8.56.

2. Select the COM Data access method as seen in Figure 8.57, click on the Database button, expand the Active Data tree, and select COM Data.

Figure 8.56
The Crystal Reports
Stand Report Wizard.

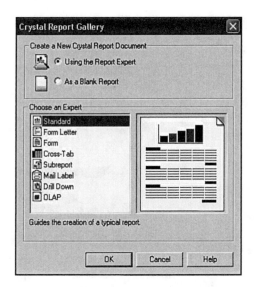

Figure 8.57
The updated COM
Driver enables the
COM area of the
database connections
for active data.

3. Enter the ProgID for the COMProvider .dll. This will prompt for the progID of the intended COM Provider. If following along with the example in this chapter, enter the following:

    `COMprovider.COMproviderClass`

    `COMprovider` is the .dll name and `COMproviderClass` is the class name within the .dll. If another .dll is being used, enter the appropriate ProgID for that .dll. Figure 8.58 demonstrates this.

4. Select the recordset "table." Select the retrieveDATA table shown in Figure 8.59 (actually the Public Function created in the .dll code). Click Close.

Figure 8.58
Enter the progID of
COMprovider.dll.

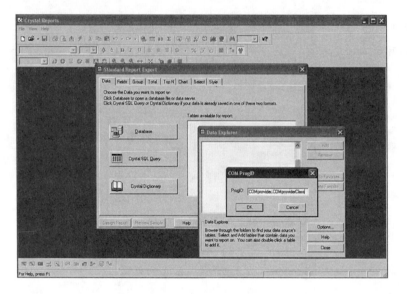

Figure 8.59
Crystal Reports views
the Public function
retrieveDATA as a
table.

5. Select fields from the recordset. In the Standard Report Wizard, select the Field tab to view the available fields provided by COMprovider. As shown in Figure 8.60, City, Region, and Country are now available as fields for report creation.

As for the rest of the report, it's exactly the same as creating any other report. There is no need to walk through the rest of the Report Creation Wizard.

PUBLISHING A REPORT USING THE COM DRIVER TO CRYSTAL ENTERPRISE

Undoubtedly, after a COM Provider (.dll) has been written and reports have been created off of this powerful datasource, the next requirement will be to publish this report to Crystal Enterprise. Doing so requires two things for proper processing of the report:

Figure 8.60
The COMprovider .dll
now returns three
fields for Crystal
Reports to access.

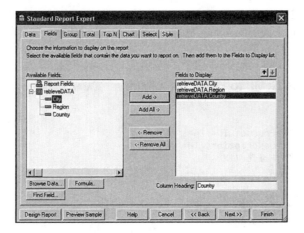

- The COM Provider must be registered on each physical Page or Job Server.
- All physical Page and Job Servers must have the COM Driver update (updated P2SMON.DLL) installed.

If an organization has just one physical Crystal Enterprise Page/Job Server, this task will be relatively easy. It can, however, be challenging to keep track of this, so it's important to have excellent process management and version control in place when undertaking this type of reporting project.

BUILDING A REPORT FROM AN XML DATASOURCE

Before a report can be built from an XML datasource, it's necessary to understand a little about what XML is, how it's structured, and why it's so popular. This chapter doesn't provide an exhaustive review of XML, but enough to review the relevant topics.

UNDERSTANDING XML

Extensible Markup Language (XML) is the universal format for sharing data on the Web. XML gives developers a markup language that allows them to easily describe, deliver, or share structured, meaningful data from any application in a consistent fashion.

XML is not a replacement for HTML; however, it does provide an incredible complement to HTML. XML and HTML actually descend from the same standard SGML.

Note

SGML became a standard for the International Organization for Standardization in 1986.

To compare HTML and XML, take the example of a business that wants to share product information over the Internet. Using HTML, the product information would look similar to Listing 8.6.

LISTING 8.6 USING HTML TO REPRESENT A PRODUCT CATALOG ENTRY

```
<TABLE BORDER=1>
        <TR>
                <TH>Product ID</TH>
                <TH>Description</TH>
                <TH>Price</TH>
        </TR>
        <TR>
                <TD>A123459-B</TD>
                <TD>Desktop Computer</TD>
                <TD>$599.00</TD>
        </TR>
</TABLE>
```

Although the data contained in the HTML in Listing 8.6 would display properly in a Web browser, there are still several limitations that would prevent effective sharing of this data with other applications.

For example, how would an application know to associate the text Product ID in the first column of the table with the value A123456-B? The problem might not be so challenging, if an application or end user wanted to get data from just one source. What if an application or query needed to gather information from several different sites or sources at once? Each HTML page might have a different way of expressing Product ID, for example.

Because the data is contained within the HTML itself, it also presents challenges when trying to deliver this information to different types of Internet devices, such as handheld PDAs. XML provides the benefit of removing the actual data from the presentation layer.

Another significant benefit of XML is tagged markup, or elements, as shown in Listing 8.7.

LISTING 8.7 USING XML TO REPRESENT A PRODUCT CATALOG LISTING

```
<product>
        <id>A123456-B</id>
        <description>Desktop Computer</description>
        <price>$599.00</price>
</product>
```

It's easy to see from this simple XML data example the hierarchical structure and self-describing nature of XML, as well as how a given application would easily read this data if it were an XML document.

The elements in this XML document include Product, ID, Description, and Price. The elements ID, Description, and Price are children of the element Product.

XML has become so pervasive, it can be found in almost any Web application. The most familiar form that XML takes is an XML *document*, which is a structured metadata document that adheres to a rigid, predictable hierarchy.

Some emerging uses of XML include using Web service objects such as COM Providers or Java components to deliver streaming XML to applications. Other applications include using XML inside Web-based protocols themselves, as is the case with SOAP (Simple Object Access Protocol).

Many related XML technologies, such as XLink and XPath, fall outside the scope of what Crystal Reports can currently work with, so there is no reason to review those in this chapter.

This section focuses on the current Crystal Reports support for XML, which is direct access to XML documents.

CRYSTAL REPORTS AND XML DOCUMENTS

Crystal Reports version 8.5 has the capability to connect to and report off of XML documents. There are three specific types of XML documents that Crystal Reports can access:

- **Raw**—No specific schema defined
- **IE data island**—Data schema held in a separate file
- **ADO**—Contains data structures and the data

From a high level, the different types of XML documents listed here essentially provide the capability to define the data type of elements in the documents, as is the case with IE data islands and ADO. Raw XML documents do not contain a specified data schema, nor do they allow for data types to be defined.

A document available on the Crystal Decisions Web site titled "Using XML with Crystal Reports" details the different data types that can be defined within XML documents and how Crystal Reports interprets these.

Note	Cr_xml_data_sources.pdf can be found on the Crystal Decisions documents library under the support section.

The types of XML documents that Crystal Reports can access are due to the connectivity method Crystal Reports (and Crystal Enterprise) employs. Crystal Reports uses the Merant ODBC driver, which is a third-party ODBC driver bundled in the product. This means that as long as Crystal Reports uses the Merant ODBC driver for XML, connectivity will be limited to what the driver can support. The actual .dll providing this driver capability is CRXML15.dll.

This doesn't mean that accessing objects such as COM .dlls that stream XML to data applications are out of reach for Crystal Reports. The COM Driver would be applicable in that situation. See the earlier sections of this chapter on using a COM Provider for details on that approach.

The XML document this chapter uses to create a report is a simple example of an XML document, a contact list. Listing 8.8 shows the actual document. The ContactInfo.XML file for the Crystal Reports example is available on the Que Publishing Web site.

LISTING 8.8 AN XML DOCUMENT CONTAINING A CONTACT LISTING

```
<?xml version="1.0" encoding="UTF-8"?>
<Contact_Info>
    <Name>
            <FirstName>David</FirstName>
            <LastNAme>Johnson</LastNAme>
    </Name>
    <PhoneNumber>
            <Home>555-555-1212</Home>
            <Work>555-555-1213</Work>
    </PhoneNumber>
</Contact_Info>
```

This XML document has a root node of <Contact Info> and child elements of <Name> and <PhoneNumber>. Although this might seem simplistic, the exercise could be extended to a much larger, more complex XML document.

An XML file similar to ContactInfo should be created and saved to a folder on the workstation disk. This can be done by creating a text file in Notepad and saving it as ContactInfo.XML.

Before actually accessing the XML document using Crystal Reports, the Merant ODBC driver must be configured.

CONFIGURING THE XML ODBC DRIVER

The driver can be found in the ODBC datasource's Administrator by choosing Windows Control Panel, Administrative Tools. After launching the ODBC Administrator, select the System DSN Tab and choose Add. Then, highlight the CRXML v3.6 driver from the list and click the Finish button. The driver must be configured to access the appropriate XML document; in this case, ContactInfo.xml.

The ODBC XML Driver Setup dialog box includes Data Source Name, Description, and Location parameters on the General tab. Figure 8.61 shows accessing an XML document from a URL source.

Figure 8.61
XML documents can be accessed through a file location or URL.

Accessing XML documents through a URL can be especially useful if, for example, a business publishes an XML datasource over the Internet for its business partners to consume using Crystal Reports.

For this example, the ContactInfo.xml document provided earlier in the chapter should reside in a folder on the root of the C: drive, called XML. Crystal Reports will access this document through the file system rather than through a URL, which brings up an important consideration when using file-system access to XML documents: file system permissions. The Crystal Enterprise Page and Job Servers must have permissions to the file store where XML documents reside, if this is the approach to be used.

In the ODBC XML Driver Setup dialog box, enter the following parameters:

- Data Source Name: ContactInfo
- Description: Crystal Reports XML Data Source
- Location: C:\XML

Note

The datasource location can be any file location. A specific file or folder name isn't required.

After the required parameters have been entered, click Test Connect to verify connectivity to the XML documents. If prompted for a username and password, select the Advanced tab and remove the Require User ID/Password check box.

Selecting the Advanced tab allows for entry of Table and Row hints. These might be required because of a current limitation in the Merant ODBC XML driver. Only one level within an XML document hierarchy can be accessed for reporting. This means that for the ContactInfo.xml sample, the Table hint would be /Contact_Info, but it's easier to address everything by leaving the Table Hint blank and just filling in the row hint by entering /Contact_Info/Name. The Row Hint would imply that <Contact_Info> is the table and any element under Name is a row, as shown in Figure 8.62.

Figure 8.62
The supplied Row Hint of /Contact_Info/ Name implies that any child elements of <Name> will be treated as rows by Crystal Reports.

Note

Allowing access to just one level of a hierarchy within an XML document poses some challenges for fully leveraging the power of XML. This can be minimized by using multiple ODBC sources from one single XML document or multiple XML documents. Crystal Decisions has plans to improve this in future versions of Crystal Reports with enhanced XML drivers.

After the table and row hints have been entered, click OK. All other options on the Advanced tab are explained in detail in the online documentation provided by Crystal Decisions.

CREATING A CRYSTAL REPORT FROM AN XML DOCUMENT

Now that the Merant ODBC driver is configured, launch Crystal Reports, and choose to use the Report Expert to create a standard report.

Select the Database button, expand the ODBC sources in the datasource hierarchy, and expand the ContactInfo source to expose the XML.ContactInfo table.

Select the XML.ContactInfo table and choose Add. A green check mark will appear on the table to indicate it is included in the report.

Click Close on the Data Explorer window. The Report Wizard will walk through the rest of the reporting steps. Because there is only one table in this report, there won't be a Tables tab. Select the Fields tab and add FirstName and LastName to the Report as shown in Figure 8.63.

Figure 8.63

FirstName and LastName are available as fields for selection out of the XML document.

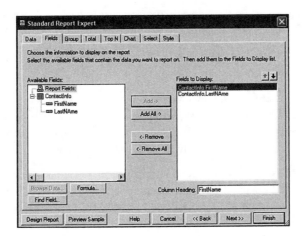

Now click the Finish button to quickly run the Crystal Report and view the information accessed from the XML document. Now the report is finished and any additional capabilities Crystal Reports has to offer from highlighting to formulas and filtering could be applied to this report.

The point of this exercise is that Crystal Reports enables reporting off of XML datasources, without any coding efforts. If a report writer can access a "traditional" datasource, the same skill set can be applied to XML data.

PUBLISHING AN XML DATASOURCE REPORT TO CRYSTAL ENTERPRISE

The only two considerations to take into account when publishing a Crystal Report to Crystal Enterprise that uses the ODBC XML driver are

- Confirm that the Page and Job Servers in the Crystal Enterprise architecture have the Merant ODBC Driver for XML installed and properly configured
- Confirm the Job and Page Servers have physical access to the XML document

With these considerations accounted for, the report should run properly in Crystal Enterprise as any other report connected to any traditional datasource would.

USING CRYSTAL REPORTS FOR XML DOCUMENT CREATION

One of the most valuable features of Crystal Reports related to XML is its capability to export to XML. Crystal Enterprise, by default, inherits this capability. This means that *any* Crystal Report that lives within Crystal Enterprise could be exported as an XML document, even verified against an external XML schema or DTD document.

Note

> An XML *schema* is an actual document written in XML with the sole purpose of verifying the hierarchy and structure of a given XML document. A DTD is an older standard with a similar function that is not used widely because it does not use the XML syntax.

Consider a scenario where two supply chain partner organizations want to share information with each other. Organization A requests that its supplier system be updated with order data from Organization B. Organization B has a set of order reports written in Crystal Reports that it currently shares internally using Crystal Enterprise.

Organization B decides to schedule a set of Crystal Reports via Crystal Enterprise to export to an FTP site as XML documents. These documents, upon export, adhere to the schema both organizations agreed upon, which will make it easy for Organization A's supplier system to programmatically access and incorporate the data contained within these XML documents.

Organization B enabled this transaction with no programming efforts. It simply leveraged the capability of Crystal Reports to design a report with the proper XML hierarchy to adhere to the schema, and use Crystal Enterprise's scheduling and export capability to enable the process.

This is an incredibly powerful and mutually beneficial undertaking by both organizations, with minimal cost due to the capability provided by Crystal Reports and Crystal Enterprise.

EXPORTING A CRYSTAL REPORT TO XML

Exporting a report to XML is a relatively straightforward process. There are a few decisions that need to be made up front, but the actual export is easy.

The choice to be made before exporting a Crystal Report to XML is the schema that a report designer intends the report to adhere to. If a report is exported to XML without a specified schema, the CrystalML (Crystal Markup Language) schema will be used.

Note

> The CrystalML schema is a publicly available schema definition created by Crystal Decisions for this exact purpose, exporting data to XML. Two given organizations could adopt the CrystalML schema as a mutually agreed upon schema for exchanging data.

The other alternative is to suppress certain sections of the XML export (not sections of the report) to adhere to an existing XML schema (.xsd).

To examine this further, take the example of exporting a simple customer list report. To create a customer list report for this exercise, launch Crystal Reports, select the Report Wizard, choose standard Report, and then click OK.

Select the Database button in the Report Wizard, expand the ODBC datasources, and expand Xtreme Sample Database.

Select the Customer table and choose Add. A small green check mark will appear on the customer table, indicating it has been added to the report. Click the Close button. Select the Fields tab and add Customer Name, Country, and Web Site to the report, seen in Figure 8.64. Click Finish.

Figure 8.64
Add Customer Name, Country, and Web Site to the report.

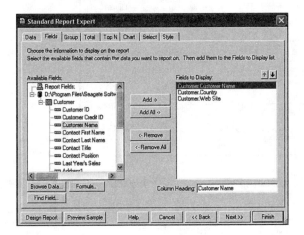

In the Crystal Reports designer, click on the Insert menu, choose Group, and select Customer.Country from the pick list. Click OK. This will group all data on the report by country.

To export the report using the CrystalML schema, click on the Export button in the Crystal Reports designer, choose XML, and click OK as shown in Figure 8.65.

The XML Export dialog box will prompt for a file location for the XML file, shown in Figure 8.66. Choose a folder on the root of the C: drive for easy access, preferably a folder called XML so as to follow along with the example.

To view the exported Crystal Report XML document, open the Customer_List_Report.xml in an XML editor, as shown in Figure 8.67. This chapter uses XML Spy 4.0 to view the XML file, but if no formal XML editing software is installed, Internet Explorer can be used to view the XML file. Open the Customer_List_Report.xml in the C:\XML folder to view the results of the export.

Figure 8.65
The Export button in Crystal Reports provides easy access to exporting a report to XML.

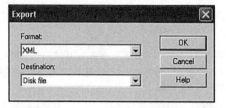

Figure 8.66
Export the Customer List report with the filename Customer_List_Report.xml. Crystal Reports creates a subfolder by default in the target export directory and assigns the folder the name entered into the XML Export dialog box.

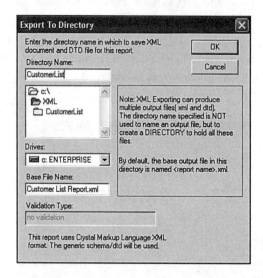

Figure 8.67
The exported data from the Customer List report in XML.

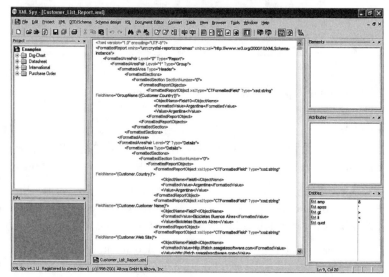

Note

Crystal Reports creates a subfolder by default in the target export directory and assigns the folder the name entered into the XML Export dialog box.

It's obvious by the hierarchy and structure of the XML document that the CrystalML schema is thorough in exporting data and can be rather complex to read.

Some organizations might determine that hierarchy used in the CrystalML schema is too complex for their needs and will resort to a custom schema. To create a customer schema for the report, select the Format menu in the Crystal Reports designer and choose XML Format. This launches the XML Format dialog box seen in Figure 8.68.

Figure 8.68
The Crystal Reports XML Format dialog box.

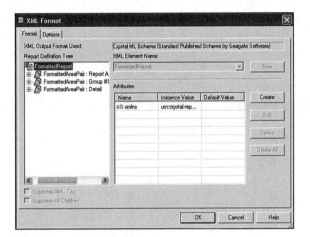

Before any customizations to the format can begin, select the Options tab and select the radio button Custom Format. This allows for the schema to be modified. Now check the Create External Validation box and leave the default of .XSD selected. This will automatically generate an XML schema file (.xsd) for the XML documents created in this example. This is an incredibly valuable feature in that there is no effort for an organization to write a validation schema that could be shared with other business units or organizations for data exchange (see Figure 8.69).

Figure 8.69
The Options tab of the XML Format dialog box allows for custom formats to be created and XML schemas to be specified or created as well.

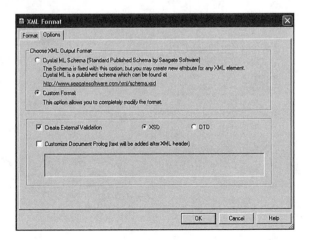

Note

Tag attributes can be created and applied to XML tags by selecting the Create button on the XML Format dialog box. For developers familiar with XML attributes, this is a powerful way to apply data field values to individual tags.

Now select the Format tab to begin customizing the XML hierarchy. Each section of the report can be suppressed upon XML export. This is different than suppressing the section of the report in the actual design. Suppression here affects only the XML export. The hierarchy of the XML elements can be expanded. Suppress the sections of the report in Table 8.1 by highlighting the section in the Report Definition Tree and then checking the Suppress XML Tag box.

TABLE 8.1 AREAS TO SUPPRESS IN THE CRYSTAL REPORT FOR EXPORT TO XML

XML Tag	Action
Report Area	Suppress XML Tag
Report Header	Suppress XML Tag and Suppress All Children
Report Footer	Suppress XML Tag and Suppress All Children
Group 1 Top Level	No Action—Do Not Suppress
Group Header	Suppress XML Tag and Suppress All Children
Group Footer	Suppress XML Tag and Suppress All Children
Details	Suppress XML Tags for All Levels of Detail Except the Actual Fields: Customer Name, Country, and Web Site

The Report Definition Tree should look like the one in Figure 8.70.

Figure 8.70
Suppress all report sections except the lowest-level details and the top-level group in the Report Definition Tree.

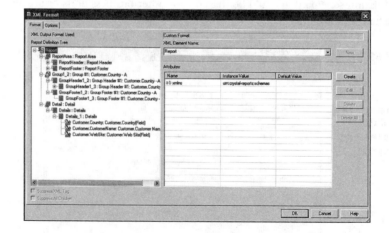

Select OK in the XML Format dialog box to accept the changes. From Crystal Reports, export the report to XML and call the file CustomerList2. Figure 8.71 highlights the difference in the newly exported XML document.

Figure 8.71
The Customer List report with a customized XML schema.

Notice that in the subfolder created by Crystal Reports upon export, the file Customer_List_Report.xsd has also been created. This is the XML schema definition file that Crystal Reports automatically generates, based on the selection in the Options tab of the XML Format dialog box. This can be seen in Figure 8.72.

Figure 8.72
The Customer List custom XML schema automatically generated by Crystal Reports.

It's important to note that the design of the report, grouping, and so on affects what is available in the XML Format dialog box. So a blend of creative Crystal Reports design coupled with proper hierarchy design allows for effective XML documents creation without coding.

USING CRYSTAL ENTERPRISE TO EXPORT A CRYSTAL REPORT TO XML

Although exporting a report from Crystal Reports to XML can be useful, many organizations will want to couple XML export capability with the scheduling power and destination capability of Crystal Enterprise 8.5. To do this, all that needs to be in place is a call to U2FXML.dll from a Crystal Enterprise application.

Just as Crystal Enterprise exports to MS Word, Excel, and so on, the process is the same for XML. In fact, a useful exercise would be to take one of the sample Crystal Enterprise applications in the Developer Samples section of the Crystal Launchpad and customize the script such that U2FXML.dll is called in place of something like rich text, to get a feel for how this could work.

SAVING GENERAL REPORT CONTENT TO CRYSTAL ENTERPRISE

After any given Crystal Report is complete, it can be published to Crystal Enterprise for on-demand viewing or scheduled processing. Open the Sales With Geographic Map.rpt found in the Crystal Reports samples directory. For reference, this file is located in \Program Files\Seagate Software\Crystal Reports\Samples\En\Reports\General Business.

In Crystal Reports, select the File menu and click Save As.

The last location option on the left side of the dialog box is Crystal Enterprise. Selecting this option will prompt the report designer for login credentials to Crystal Enterprise. Enter the appropriate system login credentials. Only folders for which the report publisher has access in Crystal Enterprise will be displayed.

The next window lists the available folders in Crystal Enterprise. Select a folder by highlighting the object, and then enter a report name by which Crystal Enterprise will refer to the report.

Select Save. The report is now committed to the Crystal Enterprise system. For more information on publishing reports to Crystal Enterprise, refer to Chapter 7.

TROUBLESHOOTING

This section provides some technical tips on the following subjects:

- ODBC data access
- Formulas
- Re-creating the schedule process
- Necessary patches

DATA ACCESS

Many implementations of Crystal Reports and Crystal Enterprise use ODBC data connectivity as the connection of choice because of its inherent flexibility. Along with ODBC comes some issues that are bound to arise when connecting datasources through Crystal Reports.

Because ODBC is used by just about any application that requires data connectivity, Crystal Reports included, there is potential for overlap of different versions of ODBC layers. An ODBC layer refers to the number of files involved in establishing an ODBC connection to a given datasource.

Some care is required to ensure that an ODBC layer is solid on a given workstation and that the proper version (ODBC 3.51 or higher) is installed before Crystal Reports or Crystal Enterprise is used. Some tips for consideration are

- Search all local drives on both the Crystal Reports workstation and Crystal Enterprise servers to ensure that only one version of ODBC exists. Search for ODBC*.*.

- The ODBC layer installed on a Windows operating system consists of 13 files. When designing Crystal Reports, all 13 files within this layer are in use when accessing a given database. These files are usually installed in the \winnt\system32 directory.

- If additional locations and files are found, these files should be renamed with the extension .old to remove them from the workstations reference ODBC layer.

For native connections, a database client such as Microsoft SQL server client used to connect to a database should also be verified for proper standalone function; that is, the client can connect to a database without Crystal Reports installed on the workstation.

FORMULAS

Formulas are one of the most troublesome areas for most report designers. The reason for this is the syntax is just a little different than any other application that has been used. Take a moment, though, to review the following information to see some ways to ensure formulas are set up correctly.

The first thing to use is the Check Script button (this is the X+2 icon). The Check Script button will not look at the efficiency of a particular statement, it will look for the syntax and how it's set up.

The error messages received in the editor are not the most descriptive definitions. One of the key ways to identify where the error is occurring is to look at where the cursor lands in the editor. Usually it's to the left of where the error is found. Most of the time, the problem ends up being a syntax error.

There is very solid documentation about most of the functions and operators and their uses in the help guide inside the design tool.

Note

From the menu bar select Help, and then select Crystal Reports Help.

This dialog box is where most of the sample code and suggested uses of formulas can be found. As with most functions that are included in the formula editor there are suggested uses for each one.

Crystal Reports has always included a tool called SmartLinking that tries to automatically link the tables that have been added into the report. The way this works is SmartLinking looks for three basic components:

- **Field name**—The reason that this is looked for first is there could potentially be hundreds of fields between two tables. Searching for matching records would be impractical; therefore, SmartLinking looks for field name matches. If there are no matching field names, no links are established.

- **Data type**—There must exist the same type of data to link. For example, if there were a date-time field then there would have to be another date-time field in the alternate table to attach to.

- **Data length**—This is not as important as the other settings. However, if the fields are not the same length, SmartLinking will not automatically link the two fields.

Note

If SmartLinking does not link in a proper manner—in other words one solid, valid link per set of tables—turn SmartLinking off by choosing File, Options, and then selecting the Database tab. The Database tab contains a selection for auto-smart linking.

Note

To better understand what links and join types should be used, refer to the database administrator. Usually that person can explain what settings should be used. Also, another great resource is a database map that could be made available from the database administrator.

From the Linking tab there is a visual representation of all the tables on the screen. For each set of tables shown there will be a link that shows on the screen. By default, all links that are established, either by SmartLinking or manual link, will be equal joins. There are many join types that are possible with a database; Crystal Reports supports these numerous join types.

The down side to the fact that these are supported is it can take real effort to figure out which is the best choice to extract the data. For the best reference of this information, refer to the database administrator. If the report designer is the DBA, the most important thing to keep in mind when figuring this setting out is *know the data*. Every link that is established can be individually selected. If selected, a Link Options tab to the side of this dialog box is available. When this Options tab is selected, certain SQL options will be presented. From this location any standard SQL join types can be set.

RE-CREATING THE SCHEDULE PROCESS

Any time a Crystal Report is published to Crystal Enterprise, it's good practice to schedule a report for testing purposes. The situation might arise where a report will publish successfully to Crystal Enterprise, and then fail when scheduled by a user.

When these cases arise it's necessary to go to the Job or Page Server and walk through the following steps:

1. Log on to the local Windows server as the account under which services run. In most cases the local administrator account is sufficient, unless another account was specified.

2. Open the report in Design mode in Crystal Reports.

3. Go to Database, Set Location. From this location it's important to verify table by table the connection is set up appropriately.

4. Go to Database, Verify Database. This checks that the table structure and fields exist on the database.

5. Refresh the report to collect the data and run any local Crystal functionality.

6. Go to the last page of the report to mimic the page creation process.

7. Save the report to the location of the input file repository server. This ensures that the user has access to the directories.

8. Export the report to the cache location in any format that is available. This is mimicking the creation of EPF viewing file creation. Because there is no export to EPF, just send it in any format that is available to check for directory access.

This process is worthwhile walking though on any physical server or workstation that is added to the Crystal Enterprise system (Crystal Report designers, Page Servers, Job Servers). In most cases this procedure will tell exactly where the problem is in running the report.

NECESSARY PATCHES

Because Crystal Reports 8.5 was released before Crystal Enterprise 8.5 a product update needs to be loaded on report designer machines. The update is the Crystal Reports patch for Crystal Enterprise 8.5. This enables the functionality to interface with the APS for accessing and saving Crystal Reports. It's important to apply this update to ensure a successful user experience with Crystal Enterprise 8.5.

In any case where a Crystal Reports designer is loaded this patch will be necessary. Be sure this update is applied from the Crystal Enterprise 8.5 CD.

For more troubleshooting tips, techniques, and suggestions visit support.crystaldecsions.com and community.crystaldecisions.com. Each site has an abundance of technical references that can be used in all report solutions.

SUMMARY

Crystal Reports, the world's most popular report creation software, is seamlessly integrated with Crystal Enterprise. All Crystal Reports features are supported by Crystal Enterprise, which means any report-specific feature, whether it be parameters, alerts, or special connectivity to COM Providers or XML datasources, are available to an organization's end users through a zero client DHTML Web interface.

With increased speed, power, and tools, Crystal Reports continues to mature as the world standard for interactive report writing. Some new features of Crystal Reports combined with Crystal Enterprise include

- XML export and reporting
- Report alerts
- Increased report processing speed
- Accessing ADO recordset data via a COM Driver

Crystal Reports can be instantly published to Crystal Enterprise, using the Save As option found under the File menu.

CHAPTER 9

CREATING CONTENT WITH CRYSTAL ANALYSIS PROFESSIONAL

In this chapter

The key challenge facing today's organizations is getting the right information in front of a line of business managers, enabling them to make the correct decisions in a timely manner based on concrete data. This is highlighted by something Bill Gates said: "Managers…in every company need precise, actionable information because they're the ones who need to act. They need an immediate, constant flow and rich views of the right information."[1]

As a follow-up to this quote, Bill Gates suggests that the middle managers in an organization "should be seeing their sales numbers, expense breakdowns, vendor and contractor costs…online, in a form that invites analysis."

This chapter shows how Crystal Analysis Professional can be used to deliver compelling analytical reports to end users, empowering them to make the decisions that power business.

OVERVIEW OF CRYSTAL ANALYSIS PROFESSIONAL

Crystal Analysis Professional is a new kind of reporting tool that enables organizations to deliver action-based analysis to end users. It unlocks greater value for more people from multidimensional OLAP data, and enables better insights to help decision-makers affect business performance.

Power users can create analytical reports, based on OLAP data, using a powerful designer. Reports can contain many pages, each presenting a different predefined view of the OLAP cube. Data can be presented in tables or visualized through a wide range of charts, as shown in Figure 9.1.

Figure 9.1
Designing an analytical report with Crystal Analysis Professional.

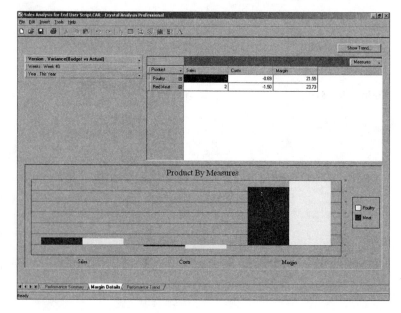

Guided analysis through exception highlighting, sorting and filtering, and analysis buttons makes analysis accessible to less sophisticated users. Business managers can use the resulting analytical reports to drive the business decisions they need to make every day.

Analytical reports can be delivered to users through a Web browser using Crystal Enterprise. The reports are viewed using Dynamic HTML (DHTML), meaning that no Java applets or ActiveX controls need to be downloaded (see Figure 9.2). The DHTML viewer is fully functioning with all of the analytical capabilities of the desktop tool available in the browser.

Figure 9.2
An analytical report deployed using DHTML.

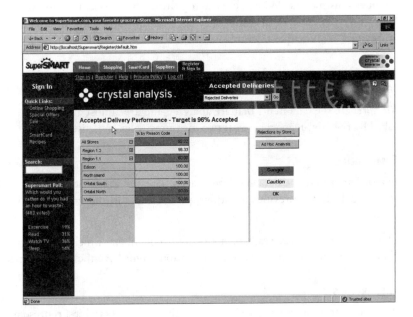

Crystal Analysis Professional is suitable for a wide range of business requirements, including sales and marketing, financial reporting, key performance indicator reporting, supplier performance and billing analysis, and clickstream analysis. Because it's a pure Web solution, Crystal Analysis Professional is suitable for delivering analytical reports inside an organization as well as to customers, suppliers, and business partners outside the company.

Note

Before using Crystal Analysis Professional it's necessary to have cubes defined in Microsoft SQL Server Analysis Services.

THE VALUE OF MULTIDIMENSIONAL OLAP DATA

Relational data is well understood, and very much taken for granted. It's difficult to imagine an organization of any size that doesn't have a relational database of some kind.

OLAP databases are far less widespread but their adoption rate is increasing rapidly. In this type of database, the data is exposed multidimensionally. This offers some unique advantages and is a prerequisite for using Crystal Analysis Professional.

WHAT IS OLAP?

The term *OLAP*, or *Online Analytical Processing*, was invented in the late 1980s to describe systems that enabled the analysis of huge volumes of data in real time.

Business analysis problems are inherently multidimensional. A regional sales manager might ask questions such as "What were the top five selling products in my region this month?" or "How do costs this month compare to last month?" and "How do my sales compare to similar regions"? These questions reveal two fundamental OLAP concepts: *measures* and *dimensions*.

MEASURES

Measures are the data items that are analyzed and are almost always numeric. The questions asked by the sales manager reveal two measures: sales and costs.

DIMENSIONS

Dimensions classify the data and often can be equated to entities in traditional entity relationship models. In the previous questions, product, region and time can be identified as dimensions.

Dimensions are themselves broken down into members, which are the individual classifications within the dimension. A time dimension might have the weeks as members.

HIERARCHIES

The members of a dimension can be organized into hierarchies, representing relationships between them. The time dimension might roll up the weeks into periods, quarters, and an annual total. An example of this type of hierarchy appears in Figure 9.3.

Hierarchies may have clearly defined levels that group together members at the same depth in the hierarchy. Our time dimension has the following levels:

Year

    Quarter

        Period
        Week

CUBES

After the measures and dimensions have been identified, they can be brought together to form a cube (see Figure 9.4). The sales manager's requirements can be represented as a three-dimensional cube with two measures: sales and costs.

Figure 9.3
Dimensions comprise
several members that
can be organized into
hierarchies.

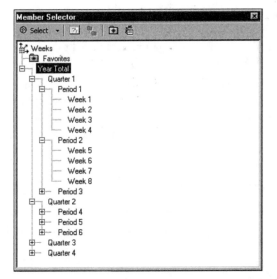

Figure 9.4
Dimensions are col-
lected together to
form cubes of data.

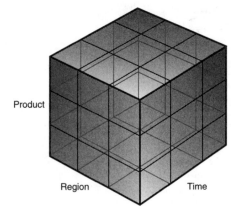

THE BENEFITS OF OLAP

An OLAP server is not a replacement for a relational database—for example, an OLAP
server is unsuitable for storing detailed transactional data—but it offers many advantages
when performing analytical reporting. Most enterprise reporting applications would benefit
from a combination of relational and OLAP data.

The main benefits of using OLAP are

- **Organization**—After data has been organized into dimensions it becomes easy for business users to find the data they need.

- **Predictable, uniform query performance**—An OLAP database stores data in a way
  that is specifically designed to be queried by any dimension, so query performance is

consistent regardless of which queries the user performs. Furthermore, the OLAP server will efficiently handle aggregated data. Again, query performance will be close to uniform regardless of how much aggregation is required to satisfy it. By providing fast access to the data, OLAP enables Speed of Thought exploration of the data.

- **Rich analytical capabilities**—The OLAP server will offer a rich range of analytical calculations, including sophisticated sorting and filtering. A major benefit is the capability to calculate along any dimension, making it easy to perform calculations such as period to date, which can be challenging with traditional SQL queries.

BENEFITS OF USING CRYSTAL ANALYSIS PROFESSIONAL

The combination of sophisticated report design, guided analysis, and secure distribution provides significant benefits for the IT department, power users, and business users. These benefits are summarized in Table 9.1.

TABLE 9.1   SUMMARY OF BENEFITS OF CRYSTAL ANALYSIS PROFESSIONAL

IT Department	Power User	Business User
Leverage existing investment OLAP is being used increasingly in data warehouses. However, the challenge is not in getting data into cubes, but in how best to use it when it's there. Crystal Analysis Professional fully leverages the capabilities of OLAP for maximum benefit.	**Utilize business knowledge** Using Crystal Analysis Professional, power users can quickly create analytical reports that enable users to manipulate and analyze the data they show to give the answers to their business problems. This removes the need to pass all reporting requirements through the IT department.	**Easy access to actionable information** Using Crystal Analysis Professional, users can quickly create analytical reports that allow them to manipulate and analyze the data they show to give the answers to many business problems.
Self-service reporting Power users can perform sophisticated ad hoc analysis and create interactive analytical reports to share with other users. This frees IT from the need to create analytical reports in the majority of cases.	**Share analytic reports** Using Crystal Enterprise, the power user can publish analyses to be shared with other users.	**Simplification of OLAP** Multidimensional data often is difficult to understand. Most people can visualize a three-dimensional cube of data, but a typical OLAP cube might have seven or more dimensions. Thinking in seven-dimensional space is a challenge.

IT Department	Power User	Business User
		Crystal Analysis Professional makes it easy to navigate through multi-dimensional data, allowing all users to benefit from OLAP.
Crystal Enterprise Infrastructure The tight integration between Crystal Analysis Professional and Crystal Enterprise makes it easy to securely manage and share reports for intranet, extranet, or Internet deployments.		

TABLE 9.1   CONTINEUD

INSTALLING CRYSTAL ANALYSIS PROFESSIONAL

This section explores the different components of Crystal Analysis Professional and their relationships to Crystal Enterprise. The most common installation scenarios are explained with step-by-step instructions.

> **Note**
>
> More information about the installation options is available in the Crystal Analysis Professional installation guide.

MAJOR COMPONENTS

Crystal Analysis Professional is comprised of three major components:

- **Crystal Analysis Professional Designer**—A desktop design tool for creating analytical reports.
- **Crystal Enterprise Plug-ins**—Additions to Crystal Enterprise that enable Web viewing of analytical reports.
- **Web Server Files**—Scripts, HTML pages, and stylesheets that are installed into a virtual directory on the Web server.

Figure 9.5 shows the relationship of these components to Crystal Enterprise.

Figure 9.5
Crystal Enterprise
architecture showing
Crystal Analysis com-
ponents.

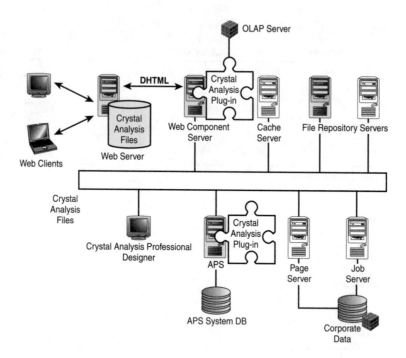

COMMON INSTALLATION SCENARIOS

The following are the three most common scenarios for installing Crystal Analysis
Professional:

- **All components installed on a single machine**—The Crystal Analysis Professional
  designer and Web distribution are installed on a single machine, most commonly used
  when evaluating software.

- **Installing the Crystal Analysis Professional Designer**—For users who just need to
  design Crystal Analysis Professional reports.

- **Installing Web Distribution for Crystal Analysis Professional**—Following this scenario will install the designer and allow reports to be published to Crystal Enterprise.

INSTALLING CRYSTAL ANALYSIS PROFESSIONAL

To install Crystal Analysis Professional, insert the CD. This will automatically display the
autorun screen. Click Install Crystal Analysis Professional, shown in Figure 9.6.

Tip

If the autorun menu is not displayed when you insert the CD, browse to the root directory of the Crystal Analysis Professional CD-ROM drive and double-click the start.exe
file.

Figure 9.6
Choosing to install Crystal Analysis Professional from the autorun menu.

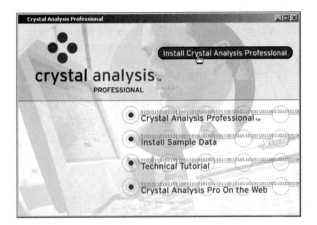

The first four screens of the installation wizard are common to all installation scenarios:

1. The first dialog box displays a welcome message that recommends that all other Windows programs be closed during the installation process. Click Next to continue.

2. The second dialog box displays the Crystal Analysis Professional license agreement, which must be accepted before continuing with the installation. Select I Accept the License Agreement, and click Next to continue.

3. The third dialog box asks for user information including the product ID, which can be found on the CD packaging. Enter the Product ID information and click Next to continue.

4. The final dialog box contains installation options, shown in Figure 9.7. The installation scenarios provide guidance on how to use these options.

Figure 9.7
The Installation Type dialog box screen.

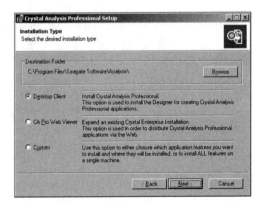

INSTALLING ALL COMPONENTS ON A SINGLE MACHINE

By default, a custom installation will install all parts of Crystal Analysis Professional, including Web distribution.

Caution

Crystal Enterprise must be installed before the Web distribution components of Crystal Analysis Professional. If Crystal Enterprise is not installed it will not be possible to view Crystal Analysis reports through the Web.

To complete the installation, follow these steps:

1. Change the install location, if required, using the Browse button.
2. Choose Custom from the installation options.
3. Click Next.
4. Leave the Custom install options set at their defaults.
5. Click Next.
6. Click Next again to confirm the selections and begin the installation process.

The installation will now proceed to completion without asking further questions.

INSTALLING THE CRYSTAL ANALYSIS PROFESSIONAL DESIGNER

This scenario is addressed by the Desktop Client installation option. To complete the installation, follow the same three initial steps as mentioned previously, and select the following options when the Installation Type dialog box is presented:

1. Change the install location, if required, using the Browse button.
2. Choose Desktop Client from the installation options.
3. Click Next.
4. Click Next again to confirm the selections and begin the installation process.

The installation will proceed to completion without asking further questions.

INSTALLING WEB DISTRIBUTION FOR CRYSTAL ANALYSIS PROFESSIONAL

This scenario is addressed by the CA Pro Web Viewer install option presented in the Installation Type dialog box (refer to Figure 9.7). This installation must be performed on *every* machine running Crystal Enterprise and all Web servers that will communicate with Crystal Enterprise.

To complete the installation, follow the same three initial steps as previously mentioned, and select the following options when the Installation Type dialog box is presented:

1. Change the install location, if required, using the Browse button.
2. Choose CA Pro Web Viewer from the installation options.
3. Click Next.
4. Click Next again to confirm the selections and begin the installation process.

The installation will proceed to completion without asking further questions.

PART

III

CH

9

Caution

This installation must be carried out on every server that is running Crystal Enterprise Web Connector and every Web server that will communicate with Crystal Enterprise. Failure to do this will result in the inability to view analytic reports created with Crystal Analysis Professional within the Crystal Enterprise system.

COMPLETING THE INSTALLATION

The final stage in the installation is to register Crystal Analysis. Registration enables enrollment in Crystal Decisions' online user community, with access to additional content through the Web. It also ensures notification of updates to the Crystal Analysis Professional product offering.

INSTALLING THE SAMPLE DATA

The Crystal Analysis Professional CD contains four sample OLAP cubes:

- Sales Reports
- KPI Reports
- Budget Reports
- Web Logs

These are installed separately from the main Crystal Analysis Professional installation using the Install Sample Data option in the autorun menu, shown in Figure 9.8.

The sample cubes can be installed to a SQL Server instance or locally as .cub files. The local .cub files can serve as offline OLAP sources for remote analysis when disconnected from a SQL Server instance.

Note

OLAP administrator privileges are required if the cubes are installed on a SQL Server. No special privileges are needed to install or access local .cub files

Figure 9.8
Installing sample
cubes for Crystal
Analysis Professional.

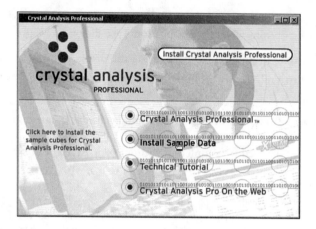

ACCESSING OLAP DATA WITH CRYSTAL ANALYSIS PROFESSIONAL

Before Crystal Analysis Professional can be used, it's necessary to have access to cubes in Microsoft SQL Server. Figure 9.9 shows the major components required for a Crystal Analysis client to access SQL Server cubes.

Figure 9.9
Major client compo-
nents.

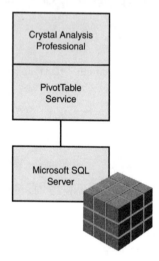

> **Note**
>
> The Microsoft SQL Server Client, or PivotTable Service (PTS), must be installed before any cubes can be accessed from the Crystal Analysis Professional designer. Installation kits for PTS can be found in the Tools directory of the Crystal Analysis Professional CD.

The cube is selected using the OLAP connection browser, shown in Figure 9.10.

Figure 9.10
Selecting which OLAP server and cube to connect to.

SQL Server organizes cubes into databases. Typically, related cubes will be grouped together into a single database, although this is decided by the OLAP administrator. Figure 9.11 shows the organization of cubes and databases in Microsoft's SQL Server Analysis Manager.

Figure 9.11
SQL Server Analysis Manager showing the relationship between cubes and databases.

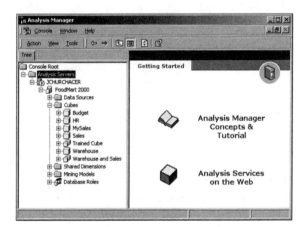

From the Crystal OLAP Connection Browser window, new OLAP servers can be added to the tree using the Add Server button. This will then display the New Server dialog box. There are several ways to connect to a SQL Server cube, all of which can be defined through this dialog box.

OLAP SERVER

After the Add Server button is selected, the New Server dialog box appears. The first option in this window is OLAP Server, which defines a regular client/server connection to the

OLAP Server. This is the most common type of connection when working on a corporate network. It's compatible with thin client delivery when Crystal Enterprise and the SQL Server are on the same side of the firewall.

Figure 9.12 shows this type of server being defined in the New Server dialog box. The server name is typed into the Server Name box, and the caption is automatically filled in. The caption can be changed to give the server a more descriptive name as required.

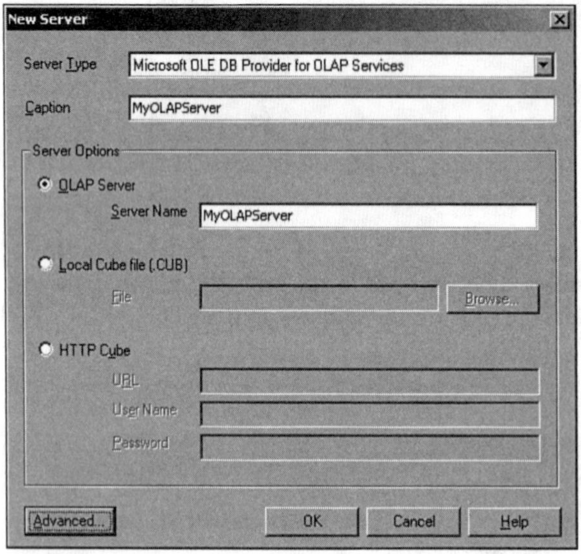

Figure 9.12
Adding a regular client server connection to the Crystal OLAP Connection Browser.

LOCAL CUBE (.CUB) FILES

SQL Server Analysis Services enables a user to create an offline cube file containing a subset of the data held in SQL Server. These cubes can be accessed using Crystal Analysis Professional when the user is away from the network—for example, when traveling with a laptop. Figure 9.13 shows a .cub file being defined in the New Server dialog box. The Browse button enables the user to navigate through their directories to locate the .cub file. A caption has been defined to make the entry in the OLAP Connection Browser more readable.

HTTP CUBES

The transport between PTS and SQL Server can be tunneled through HTTP, allowing connections through firewalls and proxy servers. Figure 9.14 shows an HTTP connection being defined in the New Server dialog box. A username and password can optionally be specified.

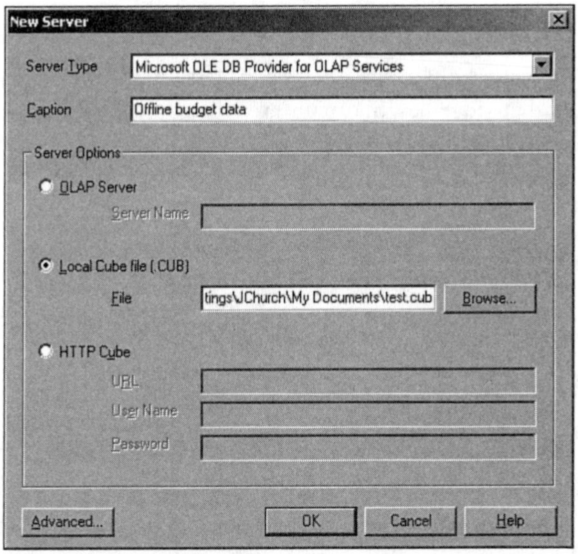

Figure 9.13
Adding a .cub file to the OLAP Connection Browser.

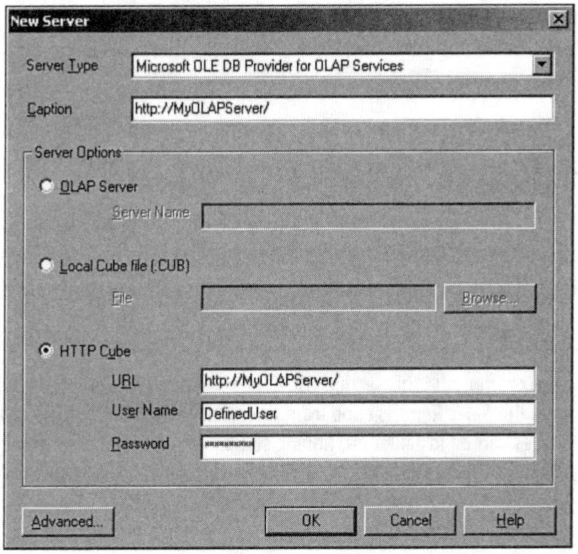

Figure 9.14
Adding an HTTP cube server to the OLAP Connection Browser.

Note

HTTP cubes were introduced in Microsoft's SQL Server 2000 and require Microsoft's Internet Information Server (IIS) to be used as the Web server. More information on configuring SQL Server for HTTP access can be found in the SQL Server 2000 documentation.

FAVORITE CUBES

Favorite cubes are a feature of Crystal Analysis Professional that enable users to create shortcuts to frequently used cubes. Shortcuts are created by simply dragging a cube into the Favorites folder from within the Crystal OLAP Connection Browser window (see Figure 9.15). Once defined, a shortcut can be renamed if required.

Figure 9.15
Creating a shortcut to a favorite cube.

BUILDING EFFECTIVE ANALYTIC REPORTS

This section describes how Crystal Analysis Professional can create compelling analytical reports, enabling users to understand their data. It shows how Guided Analysis techniques can be used to identify and prioritize problems, driving maximum value from OLAP data.

Note

The examples in this section use Crystal Analysis Professional 8 Maintenance Release 1 and the Sales Reports cube from the installed Crystal Samples collection. The sample cubes can be installed by running setup.exe in the Samples subdirectory on the Crystal Analysis Professional CD.

Tip

The technical tutorial on the Crystal Analysis Professional CD gives a very thorough introduction to building an analytical report. It can be accessed from the CD's autorun menu.

DESIGN ENVIRONMENT OVERVIEW

Crystal Analysis Professional provides a point-and-click, free-form designer for creating analytical reports. Figure 9.16 shows the major features of the Crystal Analysis Professional designer.

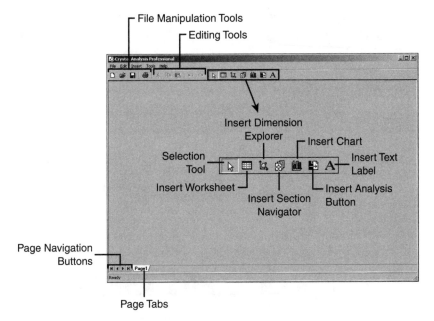

Figure 9.16
The Crystal Analysis
Professional designer.

At the top of the window is a toolbar divided into three sections:

- File manipulation tools including New, Open, Save, and Print
- Editing tools including Cut, Copy, Paste, Undo, and Redo
- Object manipulation tools including Selection tool, Worksheet, Chart, Dimension Explorer, Slice Navigator, Analysis Button, and Text Label

There is also a menu bar with many standard options, as well as others that are specific to Crystal Analysis Professional.

Tip

The lock option in the Tools menu, using an optional password, prevents other users from changing a report.

At the bottom of the window is a group of controls for managing the pages in the report.

GETTING STARTED

Crystal Analysis Professional provides a selection of experts and templates to speed up the creation of analytical reports. When the designer is started it displays a welcome dialog box, shown in Figure 9.17. From here there are three options:

- Use an expert to create a report or application
- Create a blank report
- Open a previously created report

Figure 9.17
The Crystal Analysis
Professional Welcome
dialog box.

> **Tip**
>
> If the Welcome dialog box is not displayed on startup, it can be reenabled from the Options item on the Tools menu.

USING EXPERTS

Experts allow for the rapid creation of common report layouts. The following experts are available:

- Financial Reporting
- KPI Reporting
- Sales Analysis
- Web Log Reporting

The expert is selected from the New Application dialog box, shown in Figure 9.18.

Figure 9.18
The Crystal Analysis
Professional applica-
tion expert options.

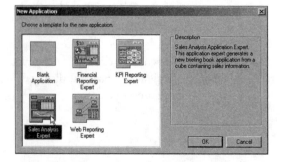

Each application expert steps the user through a wizard, prompting for a cube to connect to and then identifying key dimensions, such as time and product. Finally, the wizard generates a set of pages to report on the cube, shown in Figure 9.19.

Figure 9.19
Choosing which pages to generate in the Sales Analysis expert.

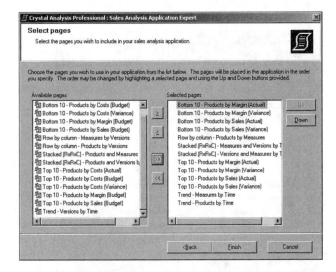

CONNECTING TO AN OLAP CUBE

Whether using an expert or creating a blank report, the first step is to connect to a cube. The cube is selected using the OLAP Connection Browser dialog box, shown in Figure 9.20.

Figure 9.20
Choosing which OLAP server and cube to connect to.

For more information on adding cube servers, see the preceding section, "Accessing OLAP Data with Crystal Analysis Professional."

ADDING PAGES

New pages are added to the report using the Insert, Page Menu option. A New Page template dialog box, shown in Figure 9.21, enables pages to be created quickly. If none of the page templates are suitable, a blank page can be inserted.

Figure 9.21
Using templates to create pages quickly.

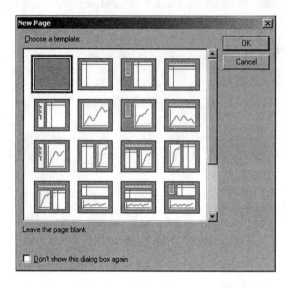

> **Tip**
>
> If the New Page template dialog box is not displayed when pages are inserted, it can be reenabled through the Tools, Options menu settings.

New pages are automatically inserted at the end of the report and named Page 1, Page 2, and so on. A page can be renamed by right-clicking on its tab and selecting Rename from the menu. The order of the pages can be changed by dragging the tabs or right-clicking and choosing Move or Copy. The creation of analytical reports with multiple pages closely resembles the power of a custom application, such that it provides varying perspectives of the cube and facilitates further exploration of the cube's data.

USING CRYSTAL ANALYSIS PROFESSIONAL OBJECTS

Individual objects, such as worksheets, charts, and text boxes, can also be added to a page, either through the Insert menu or using the toolbar icons.

While in Design mode, the currently selected object is indicated by a hatched border and object selection handles, as shown in Figure 9.22.

Figure 9.22
A hatched border shows which object is currently selected.

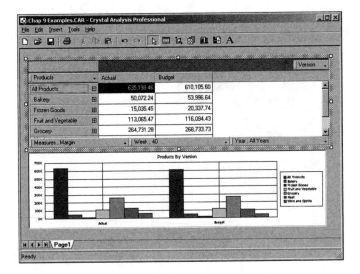

The currently selected object is live and will respond to mouse clicks; for example, a selected worksheet will enable drill-down operations.

> **Tip**
>
> The Lock option in the Tools menu prevents users from moving or adding report objects. This is useful for finished reports because all the objects become live, making the report much more intuitive to use. A locked report can optionally be protected with a password, which must be typed in before the application can be unlocked.

FORMATTING PAGES

After the basic objects have been placed on a page, Crystal Analysis Professional allows a significant amount of freedom in defining the appearance, placement, and formatting of the objects.

MOVING AND RESIZING OBJECTS

Objects can be moved within a page using the mouse to drag the hatched border. As the mouse is moved over the border the cursor indicates when dragging is possible, as shown in Figure 9.23.

> **Tip**
>
> When dragging objects, the designer snaps the objects to a grid for easier alignment. Using the cursor keys in conjunction with the Ctrl key enables finer adjustments to be made.

Figure 9.23
Moving a worksheet using the mouse.

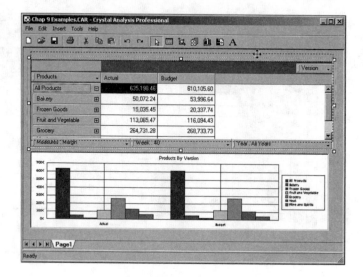

An object can be resized by dragging the select handles at each corner and on each side of its borders.

SETTING ROW AND COLUMN DIMENSIONS

When dimensions are displayed in a page, they fall into one of three categories: Rows, Columns, or Slices. This is illustrated using the worksheet in Figure 9.24.

Figure 9.24
Row, Column, and Slice dimensions in a worksheet.

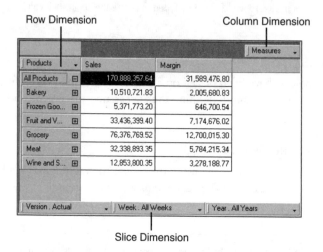

Worksheets can be pivoted using the mouse to drag dimensions between rows, columns, and slices. A chart on the same page as the worksheet will also pivot.

A worksheet can display several row and column dimensions, as shown in Figure 9.25. This technique is often referred to as the nesting of dimensions, permitting multiple dimensions to be displayed in the Row or Column positions.

PART

III

CH

9

Figure 9.25
A page showing two dimensions nested in the columns.

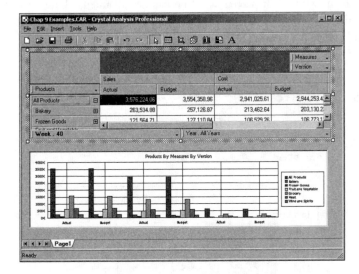

CHANGING THE PROPERTIES OF OBJECTS

The appearance of objects in Crystal Analysis Professional is changed through their properties. An object's properties are displayed by right-clicking on the hatched border and choosing Properties from the menu. In Figure 9.26, the worksheet properties have been changed to make it display as a simple table.

Figure 9.26
Setting the properties of a worksheet.

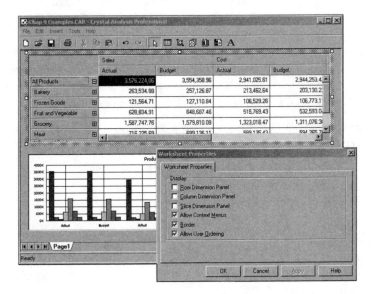

CHOOSING WHICH MEMBERS TO DISPLAY

Worksheet and chart objects both enable the user to navigate through dimensions by expanding (drilling down) or collapsing (drilling up) the hierarchies. In the worksheet, any member name with a + displayed next to it can be expanded, whereas those member names with a – displayed can be collapsed. In charts these are options in the shortcut menu for a member, as shown in Figure 9.27.

Figure 9.27
Drilling down in a worksheet and chart.

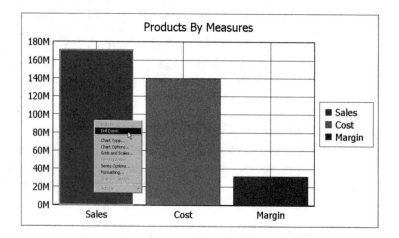

The member selector provides much greater flexibility in choosing the members to display. A member selector can be invoked for any dimension, as shown in Figure 9.28. Check boxes are presented next to each member, and changes happen in real time and are reflected in the page as soon as a member is selected or deselected.

Alternatively, the Select menu within the Member Selector dialog box enables more sophisticated operations to be performed (see Figure 9.29). This is also available as a shortcut menu from each member.

Figure 9.28
The member selector.

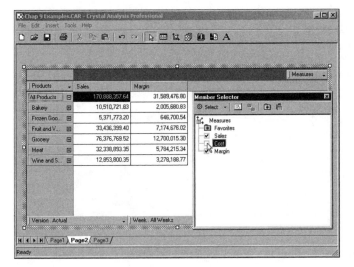

Figure 9.29
Adding the children
to the displayed
members through the
member selector.

> **Tip**
>
> If a dimension has multiple hierarchies, the Select Hierarchy button on the Member Selector toolbar is enabled. This allows the active hierarchy to be chosen.

CHANGING THE DISPLAY ORDER OF MEMBERS

By default, members are displayed in a worksheet in the natural dimension order, which is the order in which they are returned by the OLAP server. This might not always be what is required.

The shortcut menu for any row or column dimension member contains the option Reorder Dimension Members. Selecting this option displays the dialog box shown in Figure 9.30.

Figure 9.30
Changing the display
order for selected
dimension members.

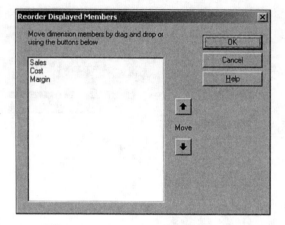

The order of the dimension members can be changed through drag-and-drop operations or using the up and down arrow buttons on the dialog box.

Note

The chosen order will be lost if a drill-down or drill-up operation is performed on the dimension. This feature is best suited to flat dimensions, such as measures, where the displayed order tends to be more critical.

NUMBER FORMATTING

Individual rows and columns can have number formatting applied. This is especially useful for calculated members, but it also can be used when the formatting applied by the OLAP server is not appropriate.

Formatting is added by choosing Format, Add from a dimension member's shortcut menu. This displays the Format dialog box, shown in Figure 9.31.

Once added, formats can be edited and removed through the shortcut menu.

CHANGING THE WIDTH OF COLUMNS

The width of the worksheet columns can be changed through drag and drop, as shown in Figure 9.32.

Note

All columns are displayed at the same width. The DHTML Web client in Crystal Analysis Professional 8 Maintenance Release 1 does not honor column widths.

Figure 9.31
Changing the display
format of data for a
selected member.

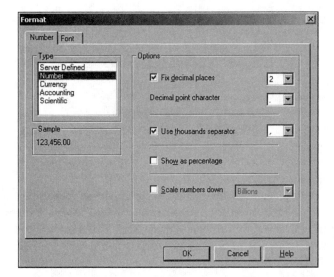

Figure 9.32
Changing the width of
worksheet columns.

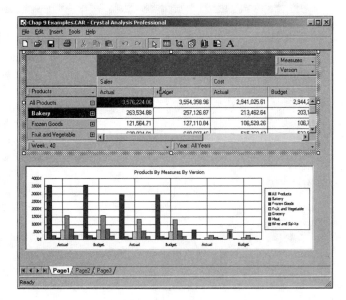

CHANGING THE DISPLAYED CAPTION FOR A MEMBER

By default, each member is displayed using the name defined for it on the OLAP server. In
some cases a different name might be required. Crystal Analysis Professional allows the caption to be changed by right-clicking on a member and choosing Change Caption from the
menu. The Change Caption dialog box appears in Figure 9.33.

Figure 9.33
Changing the caption of a dimension member.

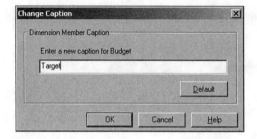

AUTOMATIC TOTALS

The worksheet can generate a sum calculation for either the rows, columns, or both directions simultaneously, and automatically update it as the worksheet changes. This is useful when an arbitrary selection of members is made, such as a group of products. Figure 9.34 shows the sum of a selection of products for each measure, with the calculation labeled Total on the worksheet.

Figure 9.34
Displaying automatic totals down the columns of a worksheet.

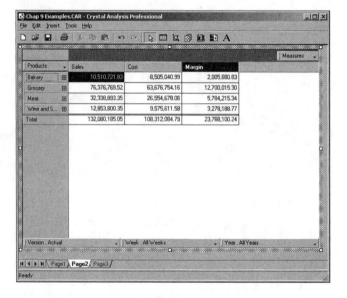

The shortcut menu of any row or column dimension member in the worksheet controls the automatic totals.

The behavior of the total calculations changes when a filter is added to the column dimension. In Figure 9.35 a Top 10 filter has been added to sales, so the worksheet is now showing just the top 10 products. The automatic totals now display the following:

- The sum of the displayed members
- The sum of the members that have been filtered out
- The total of all members considered by the filter

Figure 9.35
Automatic totals with a filter applied.

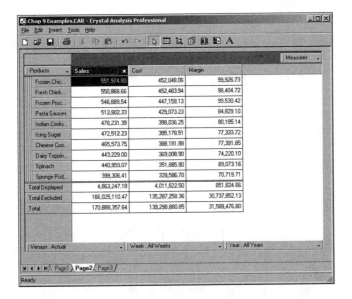

CHART OPTIONS

Crystal Analysis Professional uses the same charts as Crystal Reports and has the same level of flexibility when defining chart options. There is fine control over most aspects of the chart, including axis definitions, colors, chart types, and fonts. The chart options are accessed through the shortcut menu of any chart, shown in Figure 9.36, along with the Chart Type dialog box. This shows the enormous variety of built-in chart formats supplied.

Figure 9.36
The chart's shortcut menu and options dialog box.

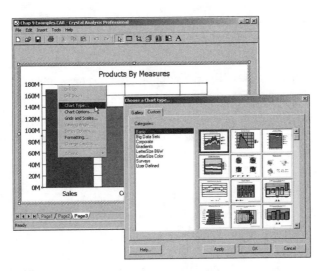

GUIDED ANALYSIS

The term *guided analysis* refers to the capability of Crystal Analysis Professional to help users identify significant points of interest within the data, and then take them through a series of steps, or actions, to analyze and classify any problems that might exist.

CALCULATIONS

Calculations add value to the data in a cube, providing the capability to generate data that's not included in the OLAP cube. Common examples include comparisons such as variance, ratio, and growth. To add a calculation in Crystal Analysis Professional, right-click on a member or a dimension name, and then choose the calculated member menu item. This is shown in Figure 9.37.

Figure 9.37
Adding a calculation through the worksheet.

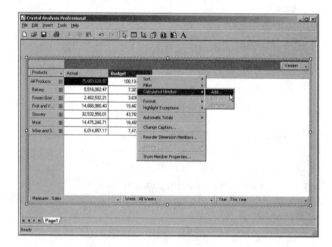

In an OLAP cube, it's common to have a dimension representing different versions of the data, usually actual and target. To draw attention to poor performance it's useful to calculate a variance between the two existing data elements.

To add a variance calculation, choose Variance in the Calculation Type list. Then, drag members from the member selector to the Compare and Target fields, as shown in Figure 9.38.

Note

Crystal Analysis Professional automatically chooses a name for the calculation. This can be overridden by typing the required name in the Calculation Name edit box.

The variance calculation is now displayed as a new column in the version dimension, and the result is shown in Figure 9.39.

Figure 9.38
Using the variance calculation expert.

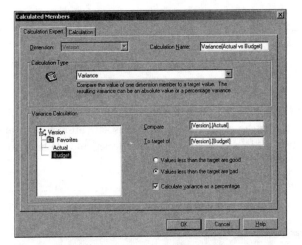

Figure 9.39
The results of the variance calculation.

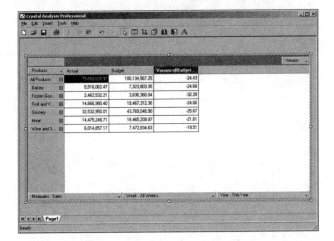

Other calculation experts provided by Crystal Analysis Professional are

- **Contribution**—Calculates how much each member of a hierarchical dimension contributes to its parent. For example, how much does each week, period, and quarter contribute to total sales?

- **Growth**—Calculates how much a value has changed from one period to the next. For example, what is the percentage growth in sales week on week, period on period, and quarter on quarter?

- **Ranking**—Calculates the rank of each member in a dimension, usually based on a measure. For example, rank each product based on sales.

> **Note**
>
> Further information on each of the calculation experts is available in the Crystal Analysis Professional documentation.

SORTING AND FILTERING

Both sorting and filtering can be used in reports to isolate important information. They answer questions such as "What are my top 5 variances?" and "Which products have the highest sales growth?"

Sorts can be applied to any row or column simply by right-clicking on its heading and using the Sort submenu items, shown in Figure 9.40.

Figure 9.40
The worksheet Sort menu.

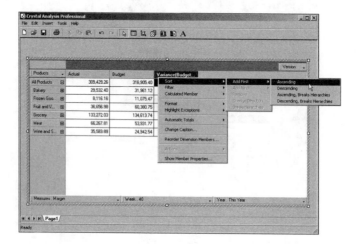

Adding an ascending sort to the variance column highlights the poorest performers by moving them to the top of the worksheet, as shown in Figure 9.41.

The sort is indicated by an arrow displayed next to the member name. The arrow points up to indicate an ascending sort and down to show a descending sort. Clicking on the arrow changes the direction of the sort.

By default, a sort will respect any dimension hierarchies; that is, the members will be sorted within their hierarchical groupings. This behavior is changed through the Sort menu and the result of changing the sort to a "breaks hierarchies" sort is shown in Figure 9.42. The hierarchical relationship between All Products and its children has been broken, and it now appears as the fourth row.

Figure 9.41
Sorting the variances in the worksheet.

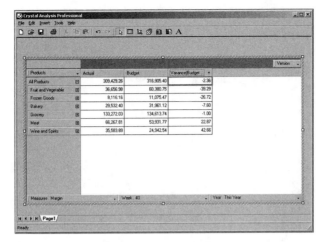

Figure 9.42
Using the Break Hierarchies option can change the order in which the sorted values are displayed.

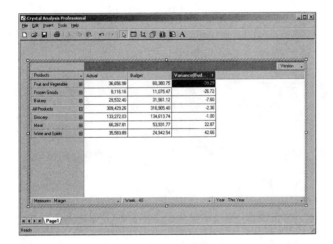

> **Note**
>
> Sorts can be nested up to three deep. To add further sorts use the Add Next option in the Sort menu. Nested sorts are indicated by a 1, 2, or 3 displayed next to the sort arrow.

Filters can be applied to any row or column, and also can be applied to the whole worksheet. Filtering the whole worksheet allows null rows and columns to be removed. This is accessed by right-clicking in the gray area at the top-left corner of the worksheet and selecting from the resulting menu list, as shown in Figure 9.43. This is a common requirement when using sparsely populated OLAP cubes.

Figure 9.43
Applying a filter to the whole worksheet, removing null rows and columns.

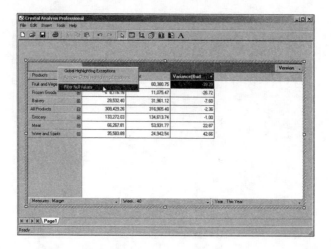

Filtering a specific row or column can be used to pick out the important information in a report. Figure 9.44 shows a filter being added to the variance column, with the aim of isolating product groups with adverse variances.

Figure 9.44
Applying a filter to a column in the worksheet.

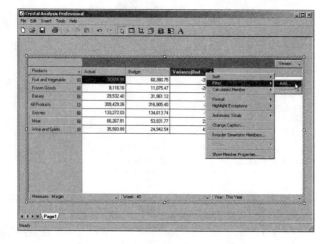

The Define Filter dialog box allows the type of filter to be set or changed. In this example the filter will display only variances that are less than zero. These settings appear in Figure 9.45, and the results can be seen in Figure 9.46.

Note

The presence of a filter is indicated by an x displayed in the Variance column heading. The filter can be edited by clicking on the x icon.

Figure 9.45
Applying a filter to
display variances less
than zero.

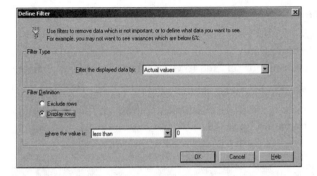

Figure 9.46
A filtered worksheet.

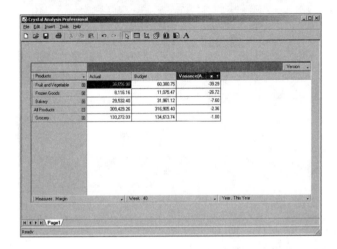

In this example the filter was applied based on the displayed data values. Other types of filters are available from this dialog box:

- **Top/Bottom n**—Used to highlight exceptionally good or bad performance; for example, the top or bottom 10 selling products.

- **Top/Bottom n%**—Used to answer questions such as "Which products contribute the top 5% of sales?" and "Which stores contribute the bottom 5% of Margin?"

Tip

A filter will consider only members that were displayed in the worksheet. To apply a filter that identifies the top five products, first select no members and then select base members in the Member Selector dialog box. As a result, the filter will consider only the base-level members.

EXCEPTION HIGHLIGHTING

Exception highlighting, also known as conditional formatting or traffic lighting, is a technique using color to draw attention to values that are out of the ordinary. It may be used on the entire worksheet or only for selected rows or columns of the worksheet.

Exception highlighting for the whole worksheet is accessed by right-clicking in the gray area at the top-left corner of the worksheet and selecting the Global Highlighting Exceptions option. This is shown in Figure 9.47.

Figure 9.47
Applying exception highlighting to the whole worksheet.

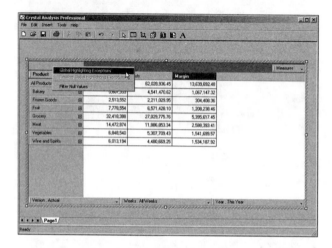

Highlighting exceptions can also be applied to a single row or column simply by clicking on its heading, as shown in Figure 9.48.

Figure 9.48
Applying exception highlighting to a column in the worksheet.

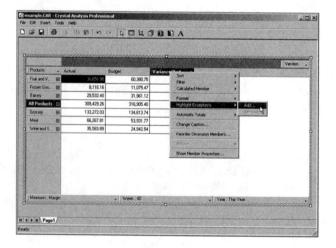

This displays the Highlight Exceptions dialog box (see Figure 9.49), which defines the upper and lower limits for highlighting and the formatting to be applied. Here, any values less than 0% are highlighted in red, while values over 5% are highlighted in green. Those values between 0% and 5% will be highlighted in yellow. The result appears in Figure 9.50.

Figure 9.49
Applying exception highlighting to a column in the worksheet.

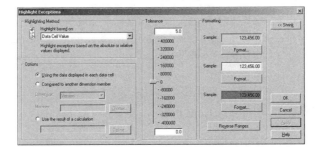

Figure 9.50
Exception highlighting, showing adverse variances in red.

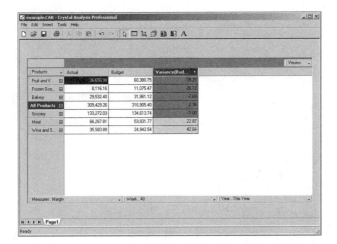

In this example, the exception highlighting is applied based on the displayed data values. This works well where the data value is a percentage but is problematic for absolute values, which change magnitude as the user drills down. To cater to these situations, other types of exception highlighting are available from this dialog box:

- **Compared to Another Member**—Highlights the displayed values according to their relationship to another member on the same dimension. For example, color-coding could be applied to Actual values based on their relationship to Budget. This comparison is valid at all levels of the hierarchy.

- **Based on an MDX Calculation**—Enables more sophisticated situations to be catered to, such as "bubble up" reporting, where the number of exceptions below a parent member is used to highlight members higher up the hierarchy. This method also works well when drilling down.

ACTIONS

Actions are a feature of Microsoft SQL Server Analysis Services. They enable a database administrator to predefine named operations for report users, related to the OLAP data within the database environment. Context from the OLAP cube, such as a selected dimension member, can be passed into the designated action.

As an example, an action called Customer Home Page could be created on a customer dimension to display the customer's Web site, or a product dimension may have an action called Display Product Information to display a report of relational data from the product master tables.

Actions are accessed in Crystal Analysis Professional by right-clicking any dimension member. If an action is available, the Actions menu option will be enabled; otherwise, it's disabled.

In the Crystal Analysis Professional designer each action appears in the Actions submenu. In the Web (DHTML) client the actions are displayed in a dialog box. Figure 9.51 shows an action being called in the designer, using the Employee dimension of the Foodmart 2000 HR cube.

Figure 9.51
Invoking an action from the worksheet.

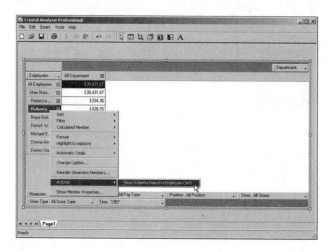

Tip

Because any Crystal Enterprise object can be referenced as a URL, it's possible to define an action that would call a Crystal Report. Report parameters can be coded into the URL, allowing context such as a selected product to be passed from the analytical report into the Crystal Report.

Note

Only the URL action type is available in the Crystal Analysis Professional Web (DHTML) client.

More information on actions can be found in the documentation for Microsoft SQL Server Analysis Services.

ANALYSIS BUTTONS

Analysis buttons are a powerful feature of Crystal Analysis, enabling users who are unfamiliar with OLAP to carry out complex exploration and analysis. They can be used within a page of a report, or to move between pages for faster train-of-thought analysis.

Consider a two-page analytical report designed to help a store manager understand product sales. The first page, shown in Figure 9.52, might contain a worksheet view of measures by product group, whereas the second, Figure 9.53, shows the trend data over time for a particular product or product group.

Figure 9.52
First page of an analytical report showing measures by products.

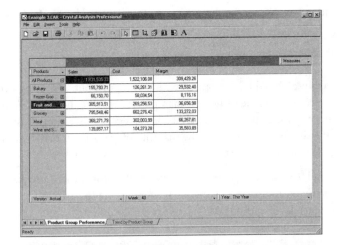

Figure 9.53
Second page of an analytical report showing the trend data for a particular product or product group.

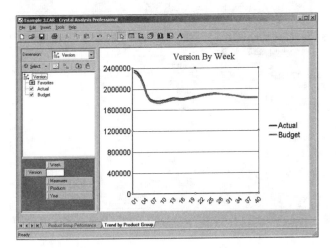

An end user could answer a number of questions with this report, such as

Q. What is the trend of sales for Fruit and Vegetables?

A. Go to the 2nd page.

   Using the combo box in the dimension explorer, select the product dimension.

   Find Fruit and Vegetables and select just that member.

Q. How does that trend compare with the Margin?

A. Using the combo box in the dimension explorer, select the measures dimension.

   Deselect Sales.

   Select Margin.

Q. How does Fruit and Vegetables compare to other product groups?

A. Using the combo box in the dimension explorer, select the product dimension.

   Deselect Fruit and Vegetables.

   Select another product group.

Many other analyses could be performed with this report, but answering even these basic questions requires knowledge of how to manipulate OLAP cubes. Although this knowledge is common among power users and analysts, it's less common among business managers. This means that it would be hard for the majority of users in an organization to gain the maximum value from this report.

Figures 9.54 and 9.55 show how analysis buttons allow these questions to be presented to the user explicitly on the page, making it easy for anyone to carry out the analysis, regardless of their experience level with OLAP.

Figure 9.54
Simplified exploration using analysis buttons.

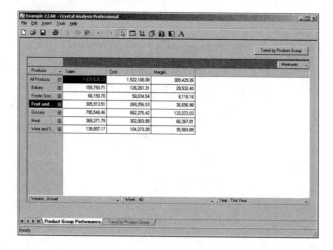

Figure 9.55
Simplified exploration, page two.

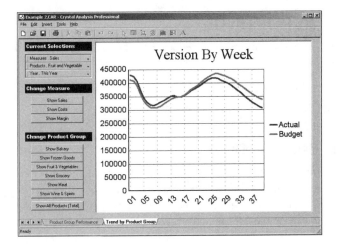

Q. What is the trend of sales for Fruit and Vegetables?

A. Click on Fruit and Vegetables.

Click the Trend by Product Group button. (This automatically moves to the trend page and slices on Fruit and Vegetables.)

Q. How does that trend compare with the Margin?

A. Click the Margin button on the second page.

Q. How does Fruit and Vegetables compare to other product groups?

A. Click one of the product group buttons to the left of the chart on the second page.

A full discussion of analysis buttons is beyond the scope of this chapter, but more information can be found in the Crystal Analysis Professional tutorials.

Now the same result is accomplished in four simple operations where the report without analysis buttons required nine relatively complex operations.

Tip

It's possible to use analysis buttons while keeping the full analytical capability of a worksheet, as illustrated in Figure 9.54. This enables ad hoc analysis and guided analysis in the same report, leading users to use the more advanced capabilities of Crystal Analysis Professional as their confidence increases.

PART

III

CH

9

ADVANCED REPORTING

This section covers some more advanced aspects of Crystal Analysis Professional reports. These are as follows:

- Use of favorite groups
- Using MDX for calculations and queries

USING FAVORITE GROUPS IN DIMENSIONS

Users can create groups of favorite dimension members in a member selector. This can be used to store commonly used members or to create ad-hoc totals for groups of members. As an example, a user might be interested in products that are currently on promotion. Figure 9.56 shows a dimension member being added to a favorite group in the member selector.

Figure 9.56
Adding Decaffeinated Coffee to a favorite group.

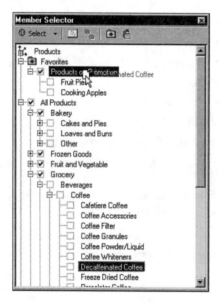

Now these products can be easily located to perform repeated analysis to understand how the promotion is progressing. Figure 9.57 shows the products and the group total displayed in the worksheet.

Note

Favorite groups defined in the designer cannot be seen when the report is viewed through Crystal Enterprise and the Web (DHTML) client. Favorites are not available in the thin client when logged on to the guest account.

Figure 9.57
Displaying members in the Products on Promotion favorite group.

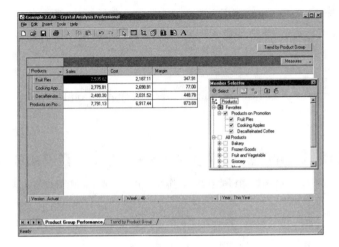

USING MDX WITH CRYSTAL ANALYSIS PROFESSIONAL

MDX (Multidimensional Expressions) is the query language of Microsoft SQL Server Analysis Services. Crystal Analysis Professional allows MDX to be used when defining calculated members and for retrieving entire queries.

The Calculation tab of the Calculated Members dialog box shows the MDX created by the built-in calculation experts, allowing it to be modified if required. The Custom Calculation expert goes straight to the MDX editor and is used for calculations that are not covered by the other experts.

To view or change the MDX query used to generate the current page, the MDX editor, shown in Figure 9.58, is available from the Edit MDX option in the Tools menu.

Figure 9.58
The Crystal Analysis MDX editor.

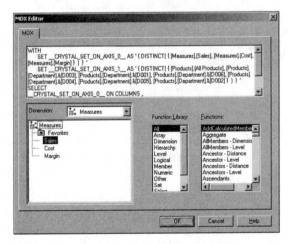

More information on using MDX can be found at the Crystal Decisions Developer Zone at `http://www.crystaldecisions.com/products/dev_zone`.

A full discussion on MDX can be found in the documentation for Microsoft SQL Server Analysis Services.

PUBLISHING CONTENT TO CRYSTAL ENTERPRISE

Before an analytical report can be viewed through Crystal Enterprise, it must be published to a Crystal Enterprise folder. There are two ways to achieve this:

- Saving directly to Crystal Enterprise from the Crystal Analysis Professional designer
- Using the Crystal Analysis Professional Publishing Wizard

SAVING TO CRYSTAL ENTERPRISE

To save an analytical report directly to Crystal Enterprise, choose Save As from the designer's File menu. This displays the Save As dialog box. Clicking the Enterprise icon will prompt for credentials to log in to the Crystal Enterprise system, as shown in Figure 9.59.

Figure 9.59
The Crystal Analysis Save As dialog box.

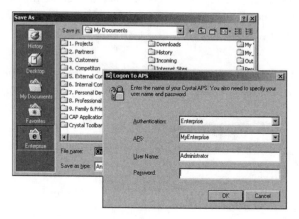

Having logged into Crystal Enterprise, it is then possible to browse through the system folders, saving the analytical report in the required location. This is shown in Figure 9.60.

USING THE PUBLISHING WIZARD

The Publishing Wizard offers an alternative method of making analytical reports available through Crystal Enterprise. It can be used to publish single reports but probably is more useful when several reports need to be published at once. The wizard is found in the Crystal Analysis Professional program group of the Start menu.

Figure 9.60
Saving the report to
an Enterprise folder.

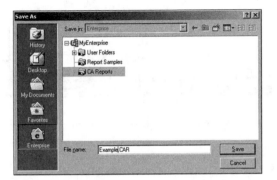

The Crystal Analysis Publishing Wizard is used similarly to the Crystal Reports Publishing Wizard; the main difference is there are no scheduling options for analytical reports. For full details, see Chapter 7.

UNDERSTANDING THIN CLIENT CAPABILITY WITHIN CRYSTAL ENTERPRISE

When published to Crystal Enterprise, analytical reports can be viewed through ePortfolio, the sample desktops, or a custom Web application. Management of the analytical reports is performed in the same place as Crystal Reports administration, the Crystal Management Console.

Reports are viewed using a sophisticated Dynamic HTML (DHTML) client. This ensures that no software needs to be downloaded to the client PC, but still offers almost 100% of the capabilities of the Crystal Analysis Professional designer.

THIN CLIENT USER INTERFACE

Figures 9.61 and 9.62 show the thin client user interface for Crystal Analysis reports, using the two-page report discussed previously. The user interface is similar to the designer. The objects on the report page behave in the same way as they do in the designer, with drag and drop to pivot the worksheet and a full set of shortcut menus. The dialog boxes for defining filters and calculated members are reproduced in full detail. The main difference is that a toolbar runs across the top of the report, replacing the toolbar and the page selection tabs in the designer.

The DHTML client enables Crystal Analysis reports to be deployed through a Web browser, with no software being installed on the user's computer, while retaining the full functionality of the Windows client. This enables analytical reports to be shared with business partners and customers through an extranet, in addition to east distribution through an intranet.

Figure 9.61
Viewing an analytical report in the thin client.

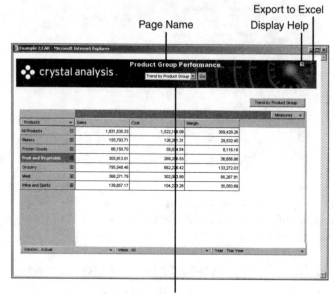

Export to Excel
Display Help
Page Name

Change Displayed Page

Figure 9.62
Viewing an analytical report in the thin client.

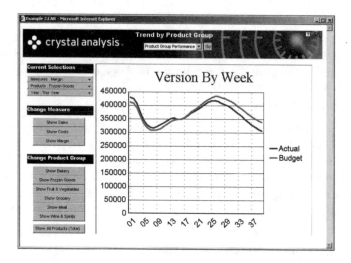

Tip

The background image for the toolbar is held in a file called analysisbanner.gif on the Web server. This image can be modified to incorporate company logos or other content.

ADMINISTRATION TOOLS

Analytical reports are managed in the Crystal Management Console (CMC). Most of the options are the same as for Crystal Reports. This section covers the CMC options that are specific to Crystal Analysis. Figure 9.63 shows the Data Source options. These can be changed to use a different cube to supply the data.

Figure 9.63
Data Source information in the CMC.

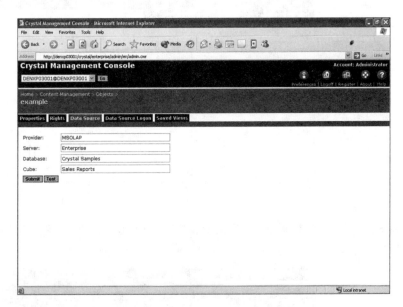

Figure 9.64 shows the Data Source Logon options. These settings control how users are authenticated against Microsoft SQL Server Analysis Services. There are three options:

- **Logon Using WCS Credentials**—All users are logged on to SQL Server using the same username that was used to start the Web Component Server. This is probably the least-used option.

- **Secondary Logon for each Application**—This option prompts for a username and password each time the analytical report is started.

- **Logon Using Specified Credentials**—In this case, the username and password entered in the dialog box will be used each time a user starts the report.

Crystal Analysis Professional enables users to save their preferred view of a report to Crystal Enterprise, subject to their Enterprise permissions. The Crystal Management Console provides a facility to manage these save views, shown in Figure 9.65.

Figure 9.64
Data Source Logon information in the CMC.

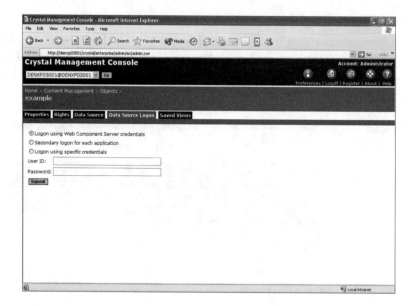

Figure 9.65
Managing saved views in the CMC.

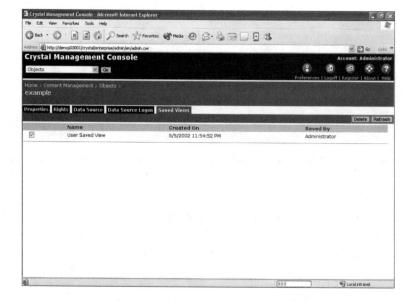

Tip

More information on saved views can be found in the Crystal Analysis Professional documentation.

MAIN DIFFERENCES BETWEEN THE DESIGNER AND THE DHTML CLIENT

The DHTML client is designed to mimic the designer as closely as possible, in terms of functionality and user interface. However, there are a small number of differences; the major examples follow:

- **MDX Editor**—The MDX editor is not available in the DHTML client.

> **Note**
>
> These differences are specific to Crystal Analysis Professional version 8 Maintenance Release 1, and might change with later releases of Crystal Analysis Professional.

- **Column Widths in the Worksheet**—It's not possible to change the width of columns in the DHTML worksheet. Column widths set in the designer are not reflected in the thin client.
- **Printing**—The DHTML client does not have any specific printing capability. Browser printing can be used, or a view can be exported to Microsoft Excel and printed from there.
- **Chart settings**—The DHTML client has a chart type dialog box, but with a reduced number of options compared to the designer.
- **Saved Views**—A user can save modifications made to a report through the thin client. To do this, the user needs sufficient privileges to create an object in the Enterprise folder containing the analytical report.

TROUBLESHOOTING

This section provides some guidance on resolving problems that might occur. The product documentation contains more information about the configuration of Crystal Analysis and Crystal Enterprise.

I cannot connect to Microsoft SQL Server Analysis Services from the designer...what's the problem?

Connecting to Microsoft SQL Server Analysis Services requires PivotTable Service (PTS) to be installed on the client PC. This usually is installed as part of the SQL Server client or later version of Microsoft Excel. PTS can be installed by running PTSFull.exe from the \tools\pts\en directory on the Crystal Analysis Professional CD.

I can view Crystal Reports from ePortfolio—why can't I view Crystal Analysis reports?

Before Crystal Analysis Professional reports can be viewed through Crystal Enterprise it's necessary to ensure that the Web viewing components have been installed on every Crystal Enterprise server and every Web server. This is covered in the installation section of this chapter.

SUMMARY

Crystal Analysis Professional is a tool for creating rich analytical reports using data stored in Microsoft SQL Server OLAP cubes. Analytical reports combine rich interactive views of the data, guiding users through the data to find exceptions, anomalies, and trends. Analysis buttons can be added to reports to make them even easier for novice users.

Tight integration with Crystal Enterprise ensures reliable, scalable delivery of reports to all users inside and outside the organization. This has advantages across the enterprise:

- Power users can create their own reports without needing to go through the IT department, using the Crystal Analysis designer.
- Business managers can use the reports each day in support of their core activities, with analysis buttons to mirror their business procedures.
- The IT department can manage analytical reports through exactly the same tools that it uses for Crystal Reports.

A sophisticated DHTML zero client is used to view the analytical reports through a Web browser, offering full functionality without the need for software to be downloaded. This will be increasingly important as organizations require analytic capabilities to be delivered to suppliers, customers, and business partners.

All the items discussed in this chapter help ensure that actionable information can be placed in the hands of those who need it, enabling business managers to make more effective decisions every day. This also empowers every business user in the organization to make more informed decisions, increasing the organization's competitiveness in the market.

ENDNOTES

1. Bill Gates, "Manage with the Force of Facts," in *Business @ the Speed of Thought* (Penguin Books, 1999).

PART IV

ADMINISTERING AND DEPLOYING CRYSTAL ENTERPRISE IN COMPLEX NETWORK ENVIRONMENTS

ADMINISTERING AND CONFIGURING CRYSTAL ENTERPRISE

In this chapter

This chapter reviews the administration tools for Crystal Enterprise, including best practices and other important information related to the management of the Crystal Enterprise system. Also covered are common system administration tasks, such as adding new users, groups, folders, and reports, as well as configuring various Crystal Enterprise server components. The primary application for managing the Crystal Enterprise objects and components is the Crystal Management Console. A supplement to the CMC is the Crystal Configuration Manager, a Windows-based application for managing certain server functions.

Note

> Recall from Chapter 2, "Discovering the Crystal Enterprise Utilities," that the reason the Crystal Configuration Manager is supplied is because, as discussed in the next section, the Crystal Management Console is a Web-based management application. If the primary Web server to which Crystal Enterprise is tied were to become unavailable, the Crystal Configuration Manager provides backup server management capabilities.

Also note that while this chapter deals with the out-of-the-box Crystal Enterprise administrative functions, the Crystal Enterprise SDK provides programmatic access to the capability provided through the CMC.

→ To see an example of using the SDK to develop a custom administrative console, **see** Chapter 14, "Integrating Crystal Enterprise with Your Corporate Intranet."

THE CRYSTAL MANAGEMENT CONSOLE

Holding true to the zero client model of Crystal Enterprise for end-user applications, the Crystal Management Console (CMC) is a DHTML-based tool for managing and configuring the Crystal Enterprise system. The CMC provides Crystal Enterprise administrators with an intuitive way to manage any type of system object, including users, groups, reports, and folders.

As discussed in Chapters 2 and 5, you can start the CMC by clicking the Crystal Management Console link in the Crystal Enterprise Launchpad. You initialize the Crystal Enterprise Launchpad by clicking Start, Programs, Crystal Enterprise, Crystal Launchpad. The Launchpad provides a link to the CMC. Visiting the URL directly can also start the CMC. The URL for the Crystal Management Console looks similar to `http://yourservername/crystal/enterprise/admin/en/admin.cwr`, seen in Figure 10.1.

Note

> The functionality found in the CMC is also accessible through the administrative portion of the Crystal Enterprise (Admin) SDK. Chapters 13 and 14 review the Admin SDK capability.

Figure 10.1
Only system administrators can log on to the Crystal Management Console.

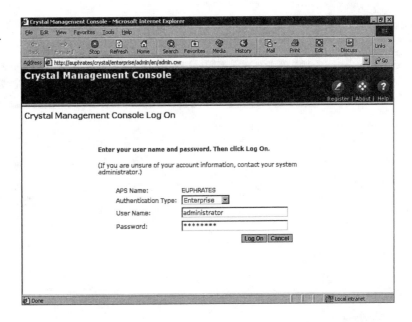

Note

> If this is the first login to Crystal Enterprise, the Administrator password is set to blank. It's advisable to change this as soon as possible.

After logging in to the CMC, the Crystal Enterprise administrator is presented with a desktop-style screen from which all CMC functions can be accessed. Icons linking to frequently accessed CMC functions are prominently displayed. They include

- Managing Users
- Managing Groups
- Managing Objects
- Managing Folders
- Managing Events
- Managing Servers
- Managing Server Groups
- Managing Settings
- Managing Authorization

These common procedures, in addition to several others, may also be accessed by clicking the CMC drop-down menu in the upper-left corner of the screen. The Crystal Enterprise administrator can return to the main CMC screen at any time by clicking the Home link at the top of every page (see Figure 10.2).

PART
IV

CH
10

Figure 10.2
All Crystal
Management Console
functions can be
accessed from the
main screen.

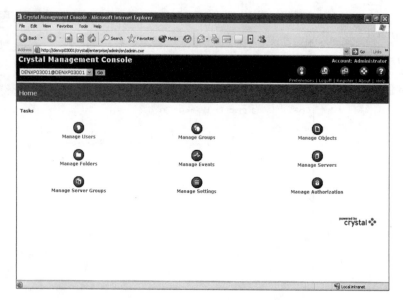

This chapter groups the previously listed common system functions into broader groups because tasks such as managing groups and users are intertwined. This first group of sections focuses squarely on the CMC, because a bulk of administration time will take place there.

The first section, "Managing Accounts," includes sections on managing users and groups. The second section, "Managing Content," covers objects and folders. The third section, "Managing Servers," reviews individual server configuration for all the Crystal Enterprise servers and server groups. The last section on the CMC, "Managing the System," covers management of system settings and authorization.

A subsequent section to these shifts gears to focus on the Crystal Management console.

MANAGING ACCOUNTS

The most common use of the CMC is to manage user accounts. Although this chapter provides a review of managing user accounts, this should always be combined with an effective user-management strategy appropriate for your organization. For example, managing users is best accomplished through an effective group inheritance model, where object restrictions are never assigned to individual users, but rather to groups. When users are placed as members within those groups, they will inherit the restrictions of the group.

Note

Restrictions are not assigned to users or groups, but to the objects within Crystal Enterprise themselves (Reports and Folders). This is explained later in the chapter.

In the Account Name field, enter a unique name that the user will type to log on to Crystal Enterprise. Generally, usernames are entered as a single word in lowercase (for example, geaton for Grant Eaton). If the Crystal Enterprise administrator prefers, the username can contain mixed-case letters as well as spaces. Crystal Enterprise is not case-sensitive to usernames.

Tip

If a single sign-on method isn't in use with Crystal Enterprise, the administrator can help users remember their logon names by maintaining consistency between Crystal Enterprise and network username naming conventions.

Next, enter the user's proper name in the Full Name field. The full name can contain mixed-case letters and spaces. A freeform text description can be included.

The Crystal Enterprise administrator may also specify a password in the Password Settings dialog box; however, it's not necessary because users can be forced to change their passwords the first time they log on. Checking Password Never Expires exempts the username from the Crystal Enterprise global password expiration rules (discussed later in this chapter). Selecting User Cannot Change Password prevents end users from changing their passwords in the future.

The Connection Type radio buttons enable the Crystal Enterprise administrator to indicate whether the username will capture a concurrent user license or a named user license when logged in to Crystal Enterprise. A concurrent user license is not absorbed unless the user is logged in to Crystal Enterprise.

Note

Recall from earlier chapters that a session within Crystal Enterprise is tracked from the moment a user logs in. This session is tracked using a token, usually issued in the form of a cookie, held on the client. This means that session state isn't held on a Web server, which is a big benefit when using Web farms. Refer to Chapter 11, "Planning Considerations when Deploying Crystal Enterprise," where control over session length is discussed.

After the user's session ends, a default of 20 minutes, the concurrent license is released. This means that another user within Crystal Enterprise can log in to Crystal Enterprise and use the concurrent license. A named license is relinquished only when the username is deleted or changed to use a concurrent license. An in-depth discussion of license keys is covered later in this chapter in the Authorization section of the CMC. More information on the Crystal Enterprise licensing models is provided later in the chapter.

After the required information for creating a new user is provided, click the OK button at the bottom of the screen. The new user is created. Refresh the User Properties screen.

This section reviews all the various components that factor into account management
includes users and groups.

MANAGING USERS

To access Crystal Enterprise resources, a physical end user must possess a username.
initial installation, by default, Crystal Enterprise creates the Administrator user and t
Guest user only.

The Guest account is a generic account meant for use in a scenario where certain gl
reports contain public information that could be accessed by anyone using Crystal
Enterprise. Without an assigned username, a user may log on only as an administrat
they know the password) or a guest (provided the Guest account remains enabled).

Note

The Administrator and Guest accounts are required for proper system functiona
The Guest account can be disabled by the system administrator; however, it sho
be deleted.

All Crystal Enterprise permissions ultimately originate from, or apply to, individua
accounts/user names. In light of this, one of the most important aspects of system a
tration is the creation of new user accounts. Whether adding one user or several hu
the Crystal Management Console makes this process fast and intuitive. To begin a
new users, click the New User icon displayed on the main CMC screen (see Figur

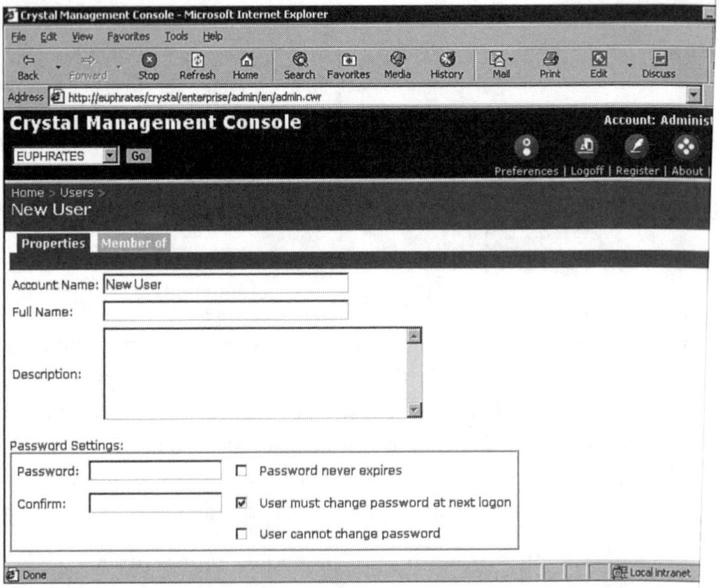

Figure 10.3
The initial CMC page
for adding a new
user.

Note that the User Properties screen reload is the only confirmation that the new user was successfully added to the system.

After the User Properties screen has been reloaded, two new options appear at the bottom of the page. The Authentication setting enables the administrator to specify whether the user's password validation will be processed by Crystal Enterprise, LDAP, or Windows NT. By default, Crystal Enterprise handles authentication. The Account Is Disabled option disables an account without deleting it. Although the account can always be enabled again in the future, this is useful for employees who might take a leave of absence from the company.

A list of all the users in the system, including the Crystal Enterprise administrator, can be accessed by selecting Users from the CMC drop-down menu (see Figure 10.4).

Figure 10.4
All user management functions are accessible from the Users screen.

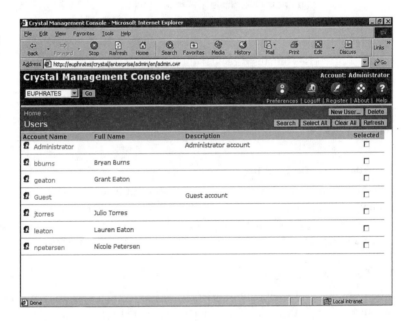

From the Users screen, the administrator can search for specific usernames, edit an existing username, add a new user, or delete an existing user. To delete a username, place a check mark in the corresponding box on the right side of the screen. The administrator may select more than one username. After a minimum of one username has been selected in this manner, click the Delete button at the top of the screen. The Crystal Management Console will then prompt to confirm deletion of the user account.

MANAGING GROUPS

A user *group* is a collection of Crystal Enterprise users with one or more logical characteristics in common. For example, the users in the Marketing department should be grouped together based on the fact that they all belong to the same business division. Because these users work together, they are more likely to share the same reports. Creating groups such as marketing enables the system administrator to globally assign permissions to a broader audience.

Groups are useful for classifying users according to their job function and report needs. In most cases, it's advisable to create a series of logical user groups to reduce the complexity of managing permissions in Crystal Enterprise.

> **Tip**
>
> Globally managing permissions for user groups is significantly less complex than trying to manage permissions for each individual user. However, there might be situations in which it's desirable to make an exception to a group's security policy for a minimum number of users within that group. Crystal Enterprise has the flexibility to make object restriction exceptions on a user-by-user basis.

Crystal Enterprise contains three default user groups:

- Administrators
- Everyone
- New Sign-Up Accounts

THE ADMINISTRATORS GROUP

The Administrators group is for system administrators only. Users who belong to this group have full, unrestricted access to Crystal Enterprise, including the capability to manage servers using the Crystal Management Console. Administrators can run any report and access any report folder. *Use discretion when adding users to this group.*

THE EVERYONE GROUP

The Everyone group contains all users by default. When new users are created, they are automatically enrolled in the Everyone group. The Everyone group is useful for globally setting permissions for all Crystal Enterprise users.

NEW SIGN-UP ACCOUNTS

New Sign-Up Accounts is a special group that contains users who have created their own new accounts through the Register option in ePortfolio (see Chapter 5, "Using the Crystal Enterprise Launchpad"). Note that this capability can be disabled.

CREATING NEW USER GROUPS

To create a new user group, click the New Group icon on the home CMC page (see Figure 10.5).

Figure 10.5

Creating new user groups is a fundamental system administration task. It's often helpful to seek input from business users when formulating user group names and hierarchies.

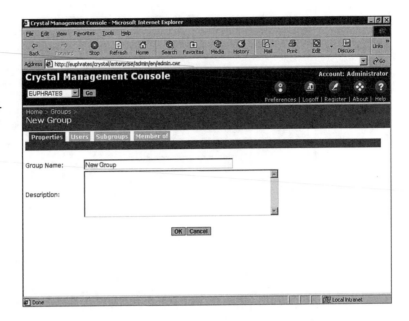

In the Group Name field, enter the group name exactly as it should appear in Crystal Enterprise. The group name field accepts upper- and lowercase, spaces, and punctuation. A freeform text description is optional. After the required information has been provided, click OK to create the group.

After clicking OK, the group creation screen should momentarily reload. This indicates that the group was created successfully. The Crystal Enterprise administrator now has access to three new tabs at the top of the screen: Users, Subgroups, and Member Of, seen in Figure 10.6.

ADDING USERS TO A GROUP Creating a group name is the first step in configuring a new group. By default, the new group will not contain any users. The administrator must click the Users tab to add users to the group (see Figure 10.7).

The Users tab will not contain any users initially. To add users to the new group, click the Add/Remove Users button at the top of the screen. A list of all Crystal Enterprise users appears on the left side of the screen, as seen in Figure 10.8. Highlight the users to add to the group. To select a range of users, click the top-most username in the desired range. Then, while holding down the Shift key, click the bottom username in the range. All users between the top and bottom names will be selected.

Figure 10.6
New group manage-
ment options are
made available after
the group has been
created.

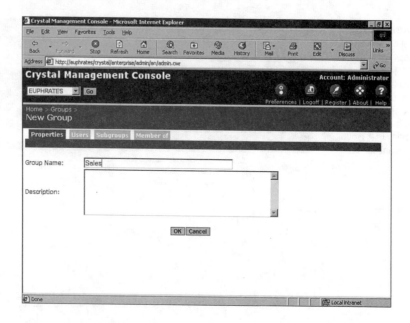

Figure 10.7
Initially, the Users tab
will be empty. New
users can be added
to the group by click-
ing on the Add/
Remove Users button.

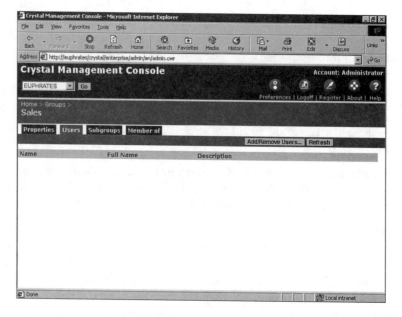

You can select several, noncontiguous names by holding down the Ctrl key when clicking.
After the desired usernames are highlighted, click the Add button to verify the selection.
Highlighted users will be moved from the Available list to the Users list. When satisfied
with the selections, click OK to commit, as seen in Figure 10.9.

Figure 10.8
All Crystal Enterprise users appear in the list box on the left.

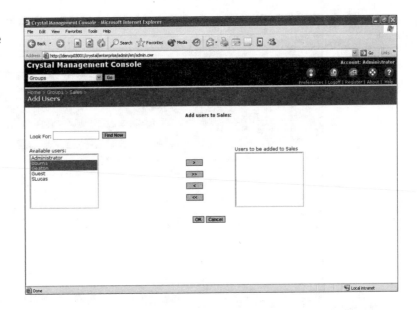

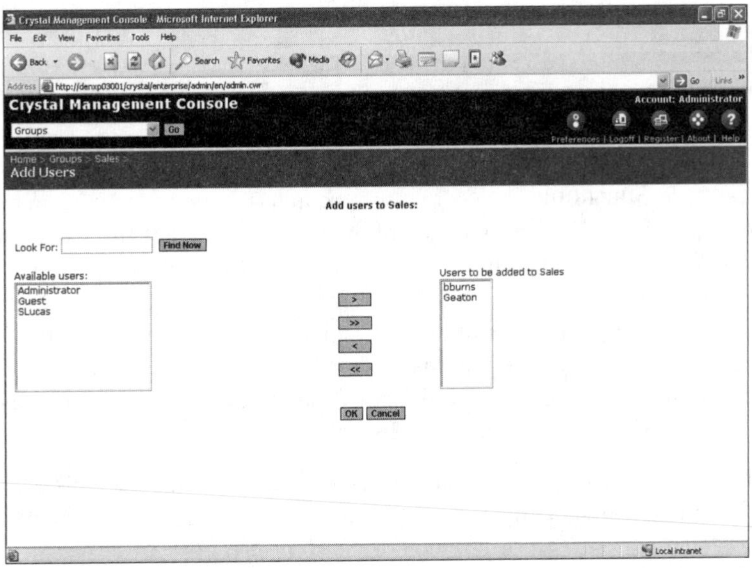

Figure 10.9
Any changes to the group membership will not be committed until the Crystal Enterprise administrator clicks OK.

The Crystal Management Console will return to the Users tab after the changes have been committed. The Users tab immediately reflects the membership of the group, as seen in Figure 10.10. Keep in mind that Crystal Enterprise allows a single user to be a member of multiple groups, so it's possible for users to belong to other groups, such as the Everyone group.

Figure 10.10
The new group now contains several users.

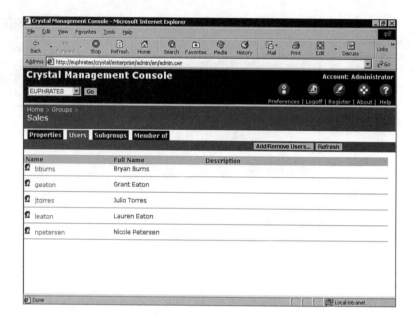

> **Tip**
>
> The Crystal Enterprise administrator can edit a user's settings by clicking on his name in the Users tab of the Group Configuration screen.

CREATING SUBGROUPS   Now that the group has users, subgroups can be created. As the name implies, a *subgroup* is a child of the parent group. Subgroups can be used to further define user roles and permissions at a more detailed level. A top-level group can contain several subgroups, and those subgroups can also contain subgroups, as Figure 10.11 shows. The benefit is that permissions need not be applied at a user level, even though they can be. Even if an individual user's needs might seem unique, there is always the distinct possibility that someone else could come along with similar requirements. Creating subgroups minimizes individual user permission/restriction management.

In a major business division such as Sales, subgroup functionality is especially useful for representing the granularity of different sales regions. For example, the parent group Sales can contain subgroups for each region of the company:

- Sales group
  - North America subgroup
    - Western Region subgroup
    - Central Region subgroup
    - Eastern Region subgroup

- South America subgroup
  - Peru subgroup
  - Argentina subgroup
- Europe subgroup
  - Belgium subgroup
  - Germany

Figure 10.11
The Subgroups tab identifies any child groups that belong to the current parent group.

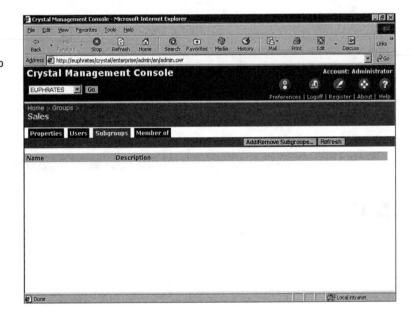

Click the Subgroups tab to add new subgroups.

Click the Add/Remove Subgroups button to create a new subgroup. The Add/Remove Subgroups page works just like the Add/Remove Users screen. All available groups are listed in the list box on the left.

To be clear, a subgroup is not a special kind of group, but rather an ordinary group that has a hierarchical relationship established with another group. Like parent or top-level groups, subgroups are created by using the New Group option on the main CMC screen.

If a subgroup needs to be created (that is, it doesn't exist yet), the administrator will need to create the new subgroup in the same manner as other groups would be created, from the New Groups screen. Figure 10.12 shows a list of groups where the intended Sales subgroups have already been defined.

Figure 10.12
The South America Sales and North America Sales groups are intended to become subgroups of the Sales group.

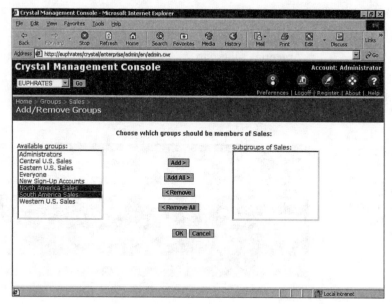

Any group can also be a subgroup. This can get a bit messy with respect to restrictions, because overlapping inherited security can be confusing.

Add the subgroups to the parent group and click OK to commit the change to the system database. The Crystal Management Console returns to the subgroup listing screen, which now reflects the new subgroups (see Figure 10.13).

This particular subgroup tree is only one level deep. It's possible to create subgroups of subgroups for more granular management of users. For example, a few regional subgroups (East, Central, and West) could be added to the North America Sales subgroup. To do this, the administrator needs only to click the name of the subgroup, and then repeat the preceding steps to add another subgroup.

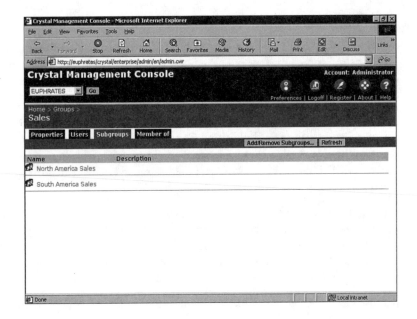

Figure 10.13
The North America Sales and South America Sales subgroups are now children of the parent group Sales.

MANAGING CONTENT

Managing content means managing all the various reports, both Crystal Reports and Crystal Analysis Professional reports that are published to Crystal Enterprise. As discussed in earlier chapters, all of these reports are referred to as *content*.

The management of content implies a host of tasks, from organizing reports into various container folders to applying restrictions to the actual objects. If not planned correctly, content management can be one of the most time-consuming tasks for a Crystal Enterprise administrator. Crystal Enterprise's flexible architecture will accommodate almost any content-management scheme. However, there are some general guidelines to follow when determining the best approach to content management. A content management scheme consists of a folder/subfolder tree that can be defined within Crystal Enterprise and the associated permissions on those folders.

An effective content-management scheme should have the following characteristics:

- Folder and report names that are both descriptive and easy to understand
- A standard report naming convention consistently applied throughout the system
- Strictly controlled report access that adheres to the organization's business rules
- A folder hierarchy that facilitates rapid end-user navigation to every report object
- Reliable reports with accurate database logon information

MANAGING OBJECTS

Objects in Crystal Enterprise are reports created by either Crystal Reports or by Crystal Analysis Professional that are published into the object store. Both types of report objects, when published into Crystal Enterprise, are managed through the Crystal Management Console. This chapter uses the terms *report* and *object* interchangeably.

This book has already provided some object publishing and management review, found in Chapter 5 and Chapter 7, "Publishing Content with Crystal Enterprise." Chapter 7 reviews the Publishing Wizard, a Windows-based application for publishing reports to Crystal Enterprise. This chapter reviews object publishing and management from the CMC perspective.

It's also important to note that the object type, Crystal Reports or Crystal Analysis Professional, determines the options and properties available to the Crystal Enterprise system administrator. Because Crystal Analysis Professional reports are not scheduled objects like Crystal Reports can be, no scheduling options are displayed when administering a Crystal Analysis Professional report.

Because Crystal Reports are the most widely used report type, this chapter focuses primarily on that report type.

PUBLISHING OBJECTS FROM THE CMC

→ For more information on objects in Crystal Enterprise, **see** Chapter 1, "Introducing Crystal Enterprise," and Chapter 3, "Exploring the System Architecture."

To add a new report to Crystal Enterprise, start the Crystal Management Console and, from the home page, select New Report as seen in Figure 10.14.

Figure 10.14
The New Report function enables the administrator to add a new Crystal Report or Crystal Analysis Professional report to Crystal Enterprise.

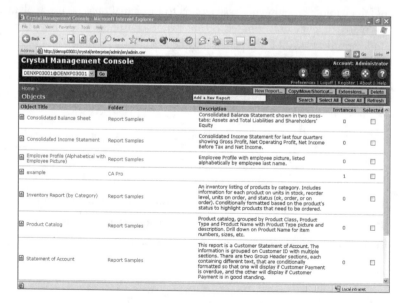

After selecting New Reports, the New Report dialog box launches, as seen in Figure 10.15. To add a report, type the path and filename of the report in the File Name box, or click the Browse button to locate the report file. Valid file extensions include .rpt (Crystal Reports) or .car (Crystal Analysis Report).

Figure 10.15
The New Report dialog box enables the administrator to add new Crystal Reports (.rpt) and new Crystal Analysis Professional Reports (.car) to Crystal Enterprise from an external directory location.

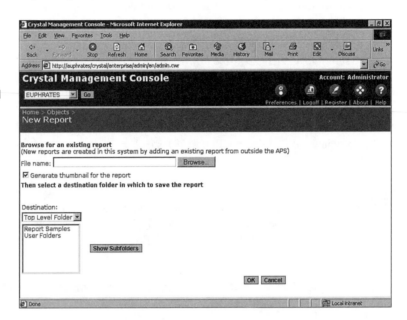

After selecting the report filename, indicate whether a thumbnail image of the report should be generated and displayed. A report *thumbnail* is a snapshot of page one of the report. This feature is currently available for Crystal Reports only. A thumbnail is merely a property of the report object, something that can be called programmatically or displayed only as an option. ePortfolio is a good example of an application that uses the report thumbnail.

The Generate Thumbnail for the Report option is useful for visually identifying reports, and it's recommended that the Crystal Enterprise administrator leave the setting enabled.

Because the Generate Thumbnail for the Report option only applies to Crystal Reports objects, the report must be saved with the Save Preview Picture option at design time. This must be enabled in the Crystal Reports application, by clicking File, Summary Info.

While enabling this option, it's highly recommended that the Title, Author, and Comments fields be filled in because this information will be available to users in Crystal Enterprise applications for report identification and searching. All these properties are stored in the Crystal Enterprise system database and can be leveraged for more specific report discovery.

The Summary Info dialog box must be completed during report creation for the thumbnail (or report description details) to be available inside Crystal Enterprise.

The final step to adding a new report to Crystal Enterprise is to select the desired enterprise folder that will contain the report. This is done using the Destination option at the bottom of the New Report screen. Simply highlight the folder that should house the new report and click OK. The Crystal Enterprise administrator can also navigate to subfolders by highlighting the parent folder and clicking the Show Subfolders button.

CONFIGURING REPORT PROPERTIES

The Crystal Management Console now displays a report Properties tab, seen in Figure 10.16. The Report Title is indicated at the top of the screen. This is the actual name that Crystal Enterprise displays when users browse for the report. The report name is actually taken from the report's Title field, which can be edited in the Summary Info dialog screen in Crystal Reports. The Crystal Enterprise administrator may override the default title by manually typing a different title. Report titles can contain upper- and lowercase characters, as well as spaces.

> **Note**
>
> Use a consistent naming convention for all reports, and make the report titles reasonably descriptive. This will reduce object management issues when dealing with hundreds or thousands of distinct reports.

Figure 10.16
The top half of the report Properties screen displays key information about a report and enables the Crystal Enterprise administrator to make changes to the report title, description, and other pertinent details.

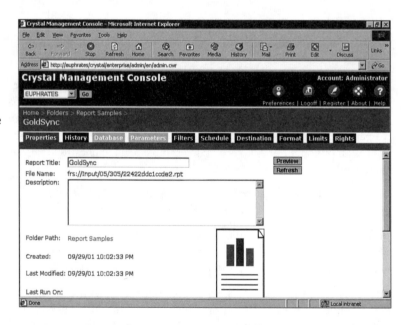

The File Name field indicates the true path and location of the actual report file (.rpt or .car) as it is managed by the File Repository Server (FRS). This information is controlled by Crystal Enterprise and *cannot* be edited. It's displayed as a reference for troubleshooting purposes.

The Description field can be used to add a detailed paragraph to note any special information about the report. The Description field is displayed in ePortfolio, and it also will be parsed by ePortfolio's report keyword search feature.

Note

> The Description property sometimes used by developers as a catch-all for keywords about the report that can be searched by a Crystal Enterprise application. Although this might be effective for a small number of reports, it can adversely affect system performance when you're dealing with large numbers of reports and is not recommended. Properties such as Description are not indexed, and when used for generic keywords, it causes all objects to be queried.

The Folder Path field is a system-maintained field that indicates the report's container folder. Clicking the folder name displays a listing of all reports within that folder.

PART

IV

CH

10

Note

> The value contained in the Folder Path field is supplied by Crystal Enterprise; to relocate the report, click the Objects option in the CMC drop-down menu. The Objects screen has a Copy/Move/Shortcut button for moving report objects between folders.

The upper-right corner of the report Properties tab contains a Preview button and a Refresh button. The Preview button runs the report immediately on the first available Page Server. This option is useful for verifying database connectivity for the report without opening ePortfolio. The Refresh button reloads the default report title and description information from the original .rpt (Crystal Report) or .car (Crystal Analysis Report) file.

The bottom of the report Properties tab, seen in Figure 10.17, allows the Crystal Enterprise administrator to enable the report thumbnail image using the Show Thumbnail check box. Be aware that the report must be designed with the Save Preview Picture option enabled for this setting to take effect, in addition to the settings required in Crystal Reports discussed earlier.

The Default Servers to Use for Scheduling dialog box controls which server group will execute the report. This is a powerful new feature of Crystal Enterprise 8.5.

Server groups are useful for categorizing servers by geographic region or processor speed. The server group options are useful for ensuring that reports are executed on a Crystal Enterprise Job Server that's in close physical proximity to the database server. For example, reports scheduled in Paris against the Paris sales database should be executed by a Job Server that's on the same network segment as the Paris database to maintain maximum report performance. Server groups can also be used to direct high-priority reports to servers with the most processing power.

For example, this option could be used to force the CFO's weekly financial reports to execute on the fastest server in the company. (A detailed discussion of server groups appears later in this chapter.)

Figure 10.17
Additional options in
the Report Properties
tab.

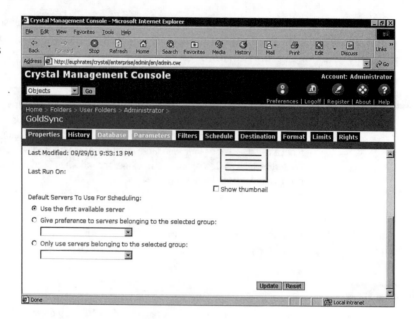

The Use the First Available Server option is enabled by default and should remain enabled in most cases. This allows the report to be processed by the first available Job Server. However, the Crystal Enterprise administrator can direct Crystal Enterprise to use a specific server group when possible by enabling the Give Preference to Servers Belonging to the Selected Group option. If this option is enabled, Crystal Enterprise forces the report to execute on the first available Job Server in the group. If no Job Server is available, the report will be executed by the first available Job Server outside the specified server group.

The option to Only Use Servers Belonging to the Selected Group causes the report to execute only on Job Servers within the specified group. Crystal Enterprise will queue the scheduled instances of the report for the first available Job Server in the specified group. If no server is available, the report will remain in the queue until one becomes available.

Note

Be aware that the option to Only Use Servers Belonging to the Selected Group restricts Crystal Enterprise's ability to intelligently designate a Job Server for the report, and may cause scheduled instances of the report to remain in the job queue longer than normal. Exercise caution when enabling this feature.

If any changes are made to the report Properties tab, the Crystal Enterprise administrator needs to click the Update button at the bottom of the screen to commit the modifications to the system. After clicking Update, the Properties tab will refresh; this indicates that the changes were successfully committed to the system database.

REVIEWING REPORT HISTORY

In addition to the report Properties tab, several other tabs pertain to the report. The first is the History tab. The History tab, seen in Figure 10.18, displays all instances of the report, including completed instances—successful or otherwise—pending (queued) instances, recurring instances, currently running instances, and paused instances. The Crystal Enterprise administrator may use this screen to manage all instances of this report.

Figure 10.18
The History tab lists all instances of the report.

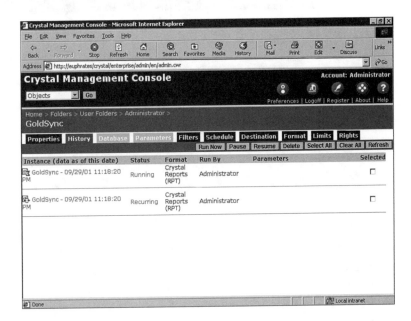

PART
IV

CH

10

Recall that a report instance is a version of the parent report that has been scheduled and run at a specific point in time. The instance might have certain parameters that were specified at the time of scheduling, so very few assumptions about the report instance can be made without verifying this information. Fortunately, Crystal Enterprise stores the schedule time, scheduling user, start time, end time, and so on, as properties of the instance.

Note

Although the number of report objects and instances stored and managed within Crystal Enterprise is, in theory, unlimited, the hardware dedicated to the APS and File Repository Server plays a major role in determining true system scalability.

To see the details of instances (including error messages for failed instances), click the instance date/time stamp, seen in Figure 10.19, or the instance status message.

Figure 10.19
The instance's condition can be reviewed in the CMC.

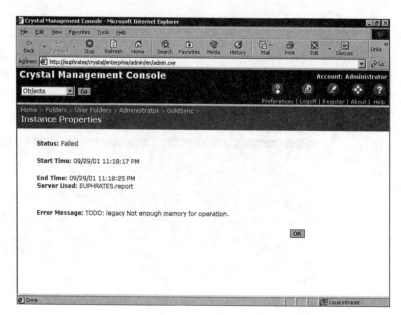

In the upper-right corner of the History tab is a row of action buttons:

- **Run Now**—Schedules a new instance of the report for immediate processing.
- **Pause**—Pauses, but does not cancel, processing of any selected pending or running instances.
- **Resume**—Releases any selected paused instances so the report can continue processing.
- **Delete**—Permanently removes selected instances from Crystal Enterprise.

CONFIGURING OBJECT DATABASE PROPERTIES

The Database tab contains database logon information for the report, seen in Figure 10.20. Although the database information, such as server name, is stored in Crystal Enterprise, by default, database logon information is not stored and can only be added on this tab by the system administrator.

When a user attempts to run a report that does not already have database logon information provided, Crystal Enterprise prompts the user to type the database username and password. Note, however, if the Crystal Enterprise administrator has already configured database logon information for the report, the user is not required to enter any additional passwords. This is the preferred method for running reports that do not rely on database-level security.

Figure 10.20
The Database tab allows for management of database logon information for the report object. Storing the logon information along with the report makes it possible for users to run the report without having to know a database username and password.

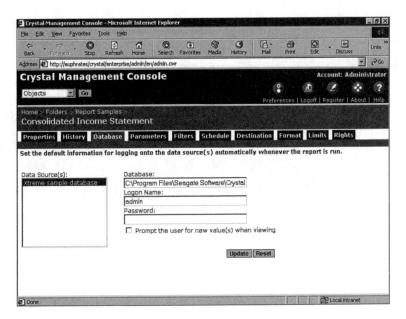

To configure database login information, click the Database tab and highlight the report data source to configure first. All report data sources appear in the Data Source(s) list box. Most reports only have one data source; however, reports that contain subreports or multiple databases might have more than one data source. Note that each data source must be configured independently.

To store database logon credentials with the report, highlight a data source and fill out the database, logon name, and password for the data source. Remember to click the Update button to confirm the changes. If the report has multiple data sources, the administrator is required to highlight each data source and provide the proper logon information. Database logon information is encrypted in the Crystal Enterprise system database, and it cannot be accessed by end users, even by querying the system database directly.

Enabling the Prompt the User for New Value(s) When Viewing option causes Crystal Enterprise to confirm the default database logon information each time the report is viewed.

MANAGING OBJECT PARAMETERS

The Parameters tab options, seen in Figure 10.21, can be used to provide default values for parameters in the report. Specifying default parameter values can reduce the number of steps required for a user to schedule a report. Of course, users can always override the default values if they want. To specify a default value for a parameter, click the parameter value listed in the Value column. Unspecified values are indicated as [EMPTY].

Figure 10.21
The Parameters tab can be used to store default values for report parameters. Users have the capability to override the default values with their own values.

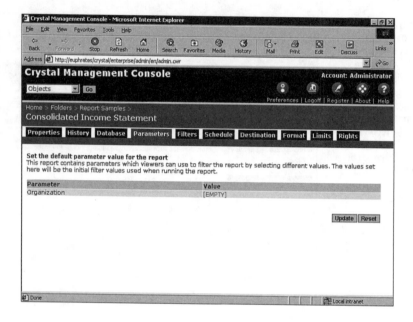

The Crystal Enterprise administrator may select a default value for a parameter from the drop-down list of default parameter values (see Figure 10.22). The values that appear in the drop-down list were provided at the time of report creation in Crystal Reports. If the desired values do not appear, the Crystal Enterprise administrator may type a new value by clicking the Edit button. Certain types of parameters, such as range parameters, can accept both a beginning and ending default value.

Figure 10.22
A default value for a parameter can be specified. Range parameters can have default values for both beginning and ending values.

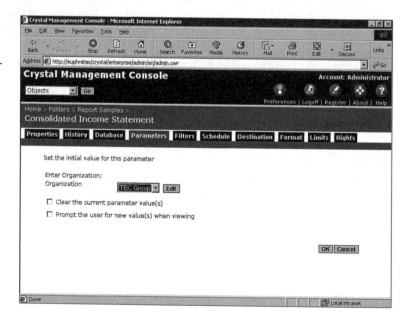

The Clear the Current Parameter Value(s) option erases the parameter's current default values, while the Prompt the User for New Value(s) when Viewing option ensures that users are reminded to confirm or modify the default parameter values each time the report is run. Any changes made to the Parameters tab must be confirmed by clicking the OK button.

The benefit of using parameters with reports in Crystal Enterprise is that the user will be prompted for value entry if the report is run or scheduled. No special programming is required, regardless of the report viewer in use.

→ For information on programmatically passing parameters to Crystal Enterprise, **see** Chapter 13, "Extending Crystal Enterprise."

> **Note**
>
> Parameters are resubmitted to Crystal Enterprise over the URL line by default. Some organizations limit what is displayed over the URL line by using Report Application Server.

CONFIGURING REPORT FILTERS

The Filters tab enables the system administrator to set the default record selection expression for the report, seen in Figure 10.23. The default record selection is normally adopted from the original report file. In most cases, the default selection expression should be left intact, but it can be useful to override this feature for specific purposes. With a proper understanding of Crystal syntax, the Crystal Enterprise administrator may modify the Record Selection Formula or Group Selection Formula manually.

Figure 10.23
The Filters tab can be used to override the report's preconstructed record selection expression. The Crystal Enterprise administrator will need to have a solid understanding of Crystal Reports record selection expression syntax to modify the default filter.

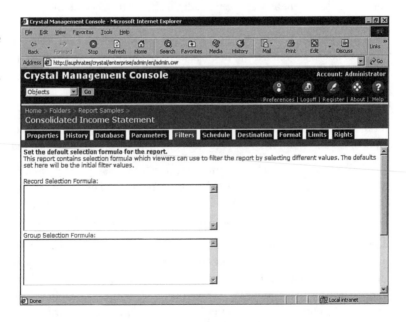

At the bottom of the Filters tab is a section for indicating which Processing Extensions the report will use. A Processing Extension, discussed in Chapter 3, is an optional programmatic library for controlling the display of report data. Processing extensions are new to Crystal Enterprise 8.5. For example, a Processing Extension can capture a report that's in the processing or viewing queue and manipulate properties of the report.

One good example of a Processing Extension is *view-time security* (VTS). This Processing Extension example, available from Crystal Decisions for Crystal Enterprise 8.5, enables the Crystal Enterprise administrator to schedule one master report instance that contains all data for all users. When users view this report instance, the Processing Extensions will enforce a custom record-selection expression to filter the report data.

To further clarify this point, instead of scheduling a separate report instance for each sales region, the Crystal Enterprise administrator could optionally schedule one master instance that contains the data for all regions. A Processing Extension could then restrict the data visible to each user (or user group) by applying a personalized record selection expression at report view-time.

Processing Extensions can be programmed to honor even the most complex business rules. As stated earlier, these business rules must be expressed in either C or C++, and must be compiled for the platform on which the Crystal Enterprise Job Server runs (for example, Sun Solaris, Microsoft Windows NT, and so on). Refer to the Crystal Enterprise documentation for more information about developing custom Processing Extensions the system administrator.

MANAGING OBJECT PROCESSING SCHEDULES

The Schedule tab enables the system administrator to schedule the report to run at selected times (see Figure 10.24). The Crystal Management Console provides this feature as a matter of convenience so the administrator doesn't have to refer to ePortfolio for scheduling. When scheduling a report, the number of retries allowed (and the retry interval in seconds) can be specified before the report instance is marked as failed.

MANAGING OBJECT DESTINATIONS

Another new feature to Crystal Enterprise 8.5 is object destinations. A destination, as implied, is a location for a report to be sent when processing is completed.

The Crystal Enterprise administrator may specify a default destination, seen in Figure 10.25, for the report output on the Destination tab. The default destination is the Crystal Enterprise File Repository Server. This is generally the preferred destination for all report instances because the report maintains its status as a managed object.

However, the administrator may configure Crystal Enterprise to output the report's instances to a network folder using the Unmanaged Disk option, for example. Crystal Enterprise also supports FTP (File Transfer Protocol), which is useful for transmitting the report instances to a remote Web server. Another option, Email (SMTP), is a popular solution for distributing reports as an e-mail attachment. The Printer destination configures the report to print immediately on the specified network printer.

Figure 10.24
The Schedule tab provides the same report scheduling functionality as ePortfolio.

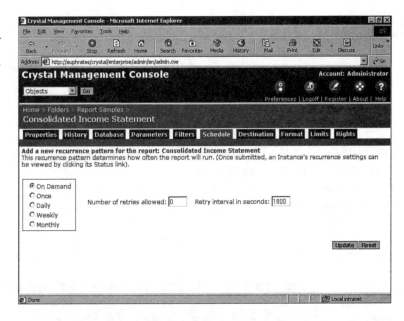

Figure 10.25
The Destination tab enables the Crystal Enterprise administrator to specify a default output location for all new scheduled instances of the report. Supported destinations include network shares, FTP, SMTP email, and direct-to-printer.

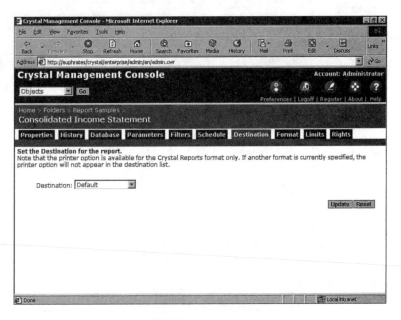

Note

The Crystal Enterprise Job Server must have a destination enabled for destination scheduling features to work. Job Server destinations are configured from the Servers section of the Crystal Management Console, covered later in this chapter.

Note

If Printer is selected as the default destination for the report, the Crystal Enterprise administrator should verify that the Crystal Enterprise Job Servers are configured with the correct printer driver. Without the appropriate printer driver, the Job Servers won't send the report instances to the printer.

DETERMINING OBJECT FILE FORMATS

Not to be confused with the format or look and feel of a report, object formats imply a file format. The Format tab, seen in Figure 10.26, enables the Crystal Enterprise administrator to specify a default output format for the report. Keep in mind that certain cosmetic report formatting features might not be supported by every export format. Also, proprietary Crystal Report features, such as drill-down and on-demand subreports, are supported only in the native Crystal Report format. These special features will be ignored when exporting a report to a non-Crystal format.

Figure 10.26
Use the Format tab to specify the default output format for the report. Popular output formats include Excel, Adobe Acrobat PDF, Word, and CSV (Character-Separated Values).

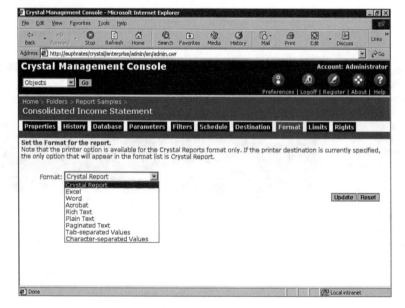

A large Crystal Enterprise deployment might generate thousands of report instances every day. Over time, the accumulation of old report instances will unnecessarily consume system resources. Crystal Enterprise has instance-limit controls for automatically managing the expiration (deletion) of old report instances. There is a global instance expiration setting in the Settings section of the Crystal Management Console (discussed later in this chapter). The global expiration limits apply to all report instances in Crystal Enterprise, unless the system administrator defines exceptions on a report-by-report basis.

If a report is scheduled and a format other than Crystal Reports is specified, it's still stored in the Crystal Enterprise system database as a report instance. This means that report instances could be Microsoft Excel spreadsheets, Word documents, and so on. Crystal Enterprise provides a series of server plug-ins that enable objects to be stored in the system database that are not of type Crystal Reports or Crystal Analysis Professional.

MANAGING OBJECT LIMITS

Exceptions to the global instance expiration limits are defined on the Limits tab for each report. The Limits tab, seen in Figure 10.27, enables the Crystal Enterprise administrator to override the global or folder instance expiration limits for the current report only. In the upper-left corner of the Limits tab is an option to Delete Excess Instances When There are More Than N Instances of an Object. The Crystal Enterprise administrator can use this option to trigger old report instances to be deleted when the specified threshold has been exceeded.

Figure 10.27
The Limits tab can be used to configure report instance expiration rules for the current report object. Object-level expiration limits take precedence over folder and global limits.

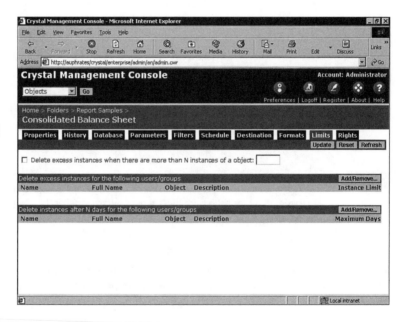

This setting applies to all users and user groups unless an exception is made in the Delete Excess Instances for the Following Users/Groups section of the Limits tab. The Crystal Enterprise administrator can click the Add/Remove button in this tab to add overriding expiration limits for specific users or user groups. The user/group expiration limits take precedence over any global or folder expiration limits.

MANAGING OBJECT RESTRICTIONS

The Rights tab, seen in Figure 10.28, is used to grant report access/restrictions to different users and user groups. By default, report objects inherit the same rights as their parent folder.

Figure 10.28
Report privileges are assigned on the Rights tab. The Crystal Enterprise administrator can use rights to define permissible actions for each user and user group.

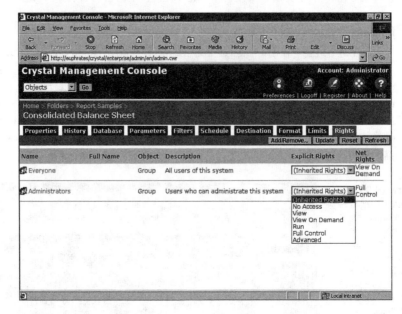

> **Tip**
>
> Much like managing groups is more effective than managing individual users, it's much easier to set restrictions for those groups by folder rather than by report objects themselves.

The Rights tab lists all the users and groups with permissions explicitly defined for the current report object. Note that if a group is not listed, permissions have not been defined for the group.

The Everyone group and the Administrators group are automatically attached to all new objects and folders in the system, and cannot be removed.

Each user or group can be assigned one of the following rights:

- **Inherited Rights**—The user or group inherits the parent folder's rights. This is the default setting for all new objects.
- **No Access**—The user or group is not aware of the object's existence.
- **View**—This setting enables the user or group to view instances scheduled by other users. On-demand viewing and scheduling is not available.

- **View on Demand**—The user or group has View rights in addition to the ability to run the report on demand.

- **Run**—The user or group will be able to schedule the report, run the report on demand, and view instances scheduled by other users.

- **Full Control**—The user or group is granted all privileges except the capability to delete, hold, and release their own instances.

- **Advanced**—This option enables the Crystal Enterprise administrator to set detailed, specific permissions for the user or group, and is generally reserved for only the most complex security models.

In most organizational security models, the Everyone group is assigned the No Access privilege, or the parent folder's permissions are set to No Access for the Everyone group. Doing so prevents users from accessing an object, unless access is specifically granted through another user group.

Permissions in Crystal Enterprise are cumulative. In other words, the net rights of a user are equal to the sum of the permissions granted to the user. To further clarify this point, consider the permissions scenario in Table 10.1.

TABLE 10.1   DERIVING NET SALES FOLDER PERMISSIONS FROM GROUP MEMBERSHIP

Group	Folder	Assigned Rights
Everyone	Sales	No Access
Sales	Sales	Run
Management	Sales	Full Control

Because permissions are cumulative, the net rights of each user are equal to the sum of the rights assigned to each group to which the user belongs, seen in Table 10.2.

A user's net permissions are determined by combining the rights they inherit from their group memberships. By combining permissions derived from group memberships, Crystal Enterprise enables a user to have access to the Sales folder as long as at least one of their group memberships permits it. Table 10.2 illustrates why the user Nicole is allowed Full Control of the Sales folder, even though the Everyone group is denied access as defined in Table 10.1.

TABLE 10.2   GROUP MEMBERSHIPS AND THEIR NET PERMISSIONS FOR THE SALES FOLDER

User	Everyone	Sales	Management	Net Permissions
Grant	X	X	X	Full Control
Lauren	X			No Access
Dennis	X	X		Run
Nicole	X		X	Full Control

MANAGING FOLDERS

Without exception, each report object in Crystal Enterprise must reside inside a folder. A folder in Crystal Enterprise is analogous to a folder on a Windows-based workstation or server. Many objects can populate a single folder, and folders can be nested inside other folders.

In general, the Crystal Enterprise folder hierarchy and report management behaves just like a standard network file system. The difference between the folder hierarchy in Crystal Enterprise and a standard network folder hierarchy is that any information about the folders is stored in the Crystal Enterprise system database and can be queried for, just as report objects themselves.

Folder management tasks can be accessed by selecting Folders from the Crystal Management Console's drop-down menu. The Folders screen in Figure 10.29 appears with a listing of all top-level folders in the folder hierarchy tree. The Crystal Enterprise administrator can click a folder name to see a list of all the reports the folder contains.

Figure 10.29
The Folders screen displays all top-level Crystal Enterprise folders. You can navigate to the entire folder hierarchy from here.

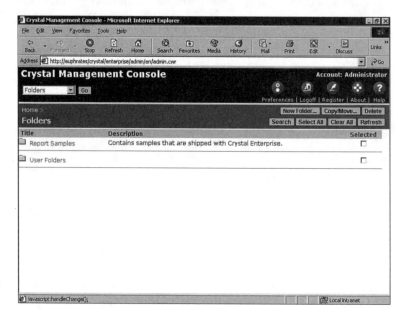

> **Note**
>
> The Users folder contains a private subfolder for each Crystal Enterprise user. These personal folders store users' favorite reports, if an application such as ePortfolio allows for it.

To add a new top-level folder, click the New Folder button. On the Properties tab, seen in Figure 10.30, type the folder name. The folder name can include spaces. The Crystal

Enterprise administrator may also type a freeform description. After entering a new folder name, click the OK button to commit the change to the system database. Four additional tabs for configuring the folder are now available.

Figure 10.30
From the New Folder screen the Crystal Enterprise administrator can create a new folder, add reports and subfolders, specify instance expiration limits, and set folder rights.

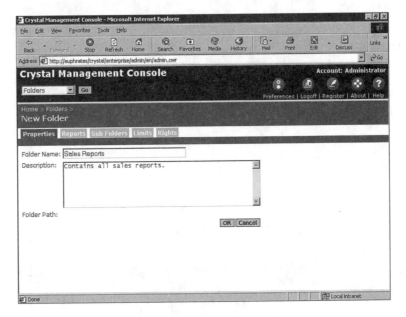

PART
IV

CH

10

ADDING REPORTS TO FOLDERS

The Reports tab, seen in Figure 10.31, can be used to add new reports to the folder or copy/move/shortcut/delete unwanted reports.

Note

The Copy function duplicates a report object and assigns the duplicate object a slightly different filename on the File Repository Server (FRS); the Shortcut function creates a duplicate report listing that points to the same filename on the FRS (similar to Windows file shortcuts). The Move function relocates the report to another folder.

The Sub Folders tab in Figure 10.32 enables the Crystal Enterprise administrator to create and manage subfolders of the current top-level folder. Subfolders are useful for subcategorizing reports. For example, an administrator could add subfolders for Executive Reports and Sales Rep Performance to the top-level Sales folder to organize reports and manage report security. Each subfolder can also have one or more child folders. Like a file system, the nesting of folders can traverse as many levels as necessary to convey the hierarchy of an organization.

Figure 10.31
The Reports tab is used to add new reports to a folder. The Crystal Enterprise administrator can also manage existing reports from this screen.

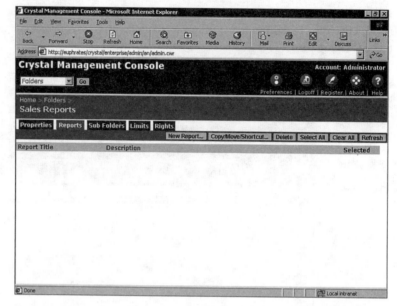

Figure 10.32
The Crystal Enterprise administrator can use the Sub Folders tab to add one or more sub-folders to a top-level folder. In turn, each subfolder can have one or more sub-folders (nested subfolders).

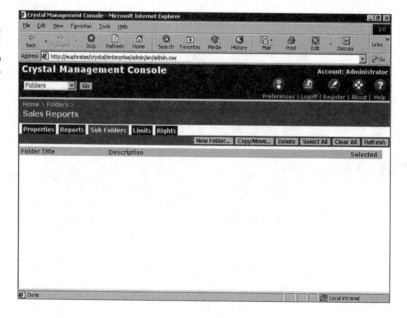

FOLDER LIMITS

The Limits tab, seen in Figure 10.33, controls instance expiration limits for reports contained within the folder. Note that report object limits (if specified) take precedence over folder limits. Folder limits only take precedence over global limits.

Figure 10.33
Like report objects, folders can be configured to override the global instance expiration limits.

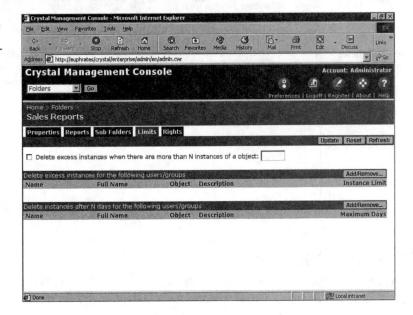

Note

Report object limits take precedence over folder limits, and folder limits take precedence over global limits.

The folder Rights tab, seen in Figure 10.34, is used to control access to report objects. The rights provided at the folder level are the same as those provided on the object level. (Refer to object rights for a definition of each option.) Instead of trying to manage rights for each individual report object, it's usually easier to secure reports by specifying rights at the folder level only. Report objects always inherit the rights of their parent folder, unless exceptions are configured at the object level.

Figure 10.34
Any rights specified on the folder Rights tab will be inherited by new report objects. Unless a report object has object-level rights specifically configured, it will inherit the rights of its parent folder.

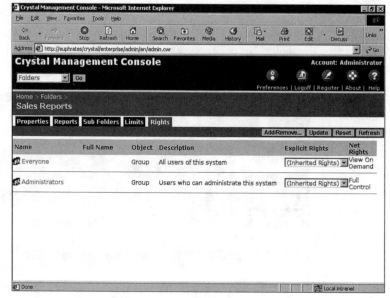

MANAGING SERVERS

As Chapter 3 discusses, Crystal Enterprise is built on the Crystal eBusiness framework. At a high level, the eBusiness framework provides Crystal Server Page (CSP) processing, file and security management, job processing, and interservice communication.

Each major function listed above, and many more, are provided by a Crystal Enterprise Server or *service*. Services are compartmentalized processes that perform a specific task. The use of individual services affords fault-tolerance (service redundancy), load-balancing, scalability, and greater system reliability.

Crystal Enterprise can run all services on one physical server or can run services on several different machines. Most large-scale Crystal Enterprise deployments incorporate more than one server for some level of redundancy or fault tolerance. In the context of Crystal Enterprise, a server does not necessarily denote a physical entity. Because services are often run on different machines, Crystal Decisions refers to them as *servers*. It's common for one physical server to have several Crystal Enterprise servers (services) running at any given time. Furthermore, multiple instances of the same service can run on one physical server at any given time, increasing system scalability.

CONFIGURING SERVERS

Managing Crystal Enterprise servers is straightforward with the Crystal Management Console. The Crystal Enterprise administrator can use the CMC to stop, start, and restart various services from almost any location on the network, as well as change service-specific settings.

To manage servers, select Servers from the Crystal Management Console drop-down menu. Figure 10.35 shows a standard list of Crystal Enterprise servers in the CMC. Buttons in the upper-right corner enable the administrator to start, stop, restart, delete, disable, or enable any server on the framework. Additionally, the Crystal Enterprise administrator can specify the order of the servers list by clicking on the column heading to specify a sort order. This feature is helpful for organizing the server list in deployments with several different server machines.

Figure 10.35
All configured servers (services) in Crystal Enterprise can be managed from the Crystal Management Console.

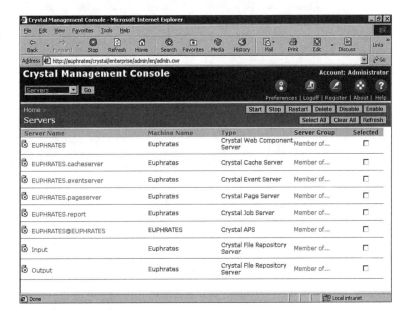

> **Note**
>
> A disabled server cannot be started until it is enabled, even if the machine is rebooted. Disabling a server can be useful for, among other things, temporarily interrupting the server's availability while maintenance tasks or hardware repairs are performed.

Before discussing the configuration of individual services, it's important to note that each service has a series of performance and resources measurements called *metrics*. To view the metrics for a specific server or service, simply click the Server Name and then select the Metrics tab. The Metrics tab, seen in Figure 10.36, displays a variety of data, such as the amount of available disk space, free RAM, and software revision number. In addition, each server type will have special metrics for gauging its performance.

Figure 10.36
Performance and server resource data is displayed on the Metrics tab for each Crystal Enterprise service. This information can be used to monitor the activity of each service.

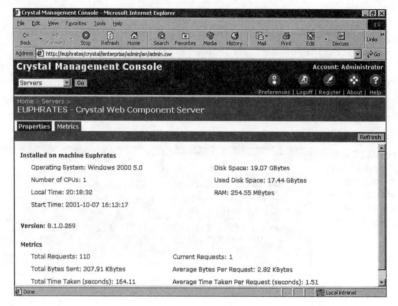

MANAGING THE WEB COMPONENT SERVER (WCS)

As discussed in Chapter 3, the Web Component Server (WCS) is responsible for server-side script processing for all .csp files. Note that the Web Connector and Web Component Server fulfill different roles. The Web Connector resides on a Web server, such as Microsoft Internet Information Server or Apache on Solaris, intercepting URL requests for .cwi, .cwr, and .csp pages and forwarding them to the Web Component Server. The Web Component Server then interprets the requests, processes scripts, and passes instructions to the appropriate Crystal Enterprise service. For more information on inter-server communication processes, refer to Chapter 10, "Administering and Configuring Crystal Enterprise."

Another major role the Web Component Server plays is in managing sessions. The Web Component Server, working in tandem with the APS, issues a token, often in the form of a cookie, to an end-user's browser. Although there are other ways to handle a session for an end user, the cookie method is ideal because session state is not held on the Web Server or the Web Component Server. This implies that if multiple physical Web servers (a Web farm) or Web Component Servers are in use (or both), the end user can make requests and receive report data without concern for which server is handling the request. Additionally, if a server in a Web farm fails, the end-user session is not terminated.

Unfortunately, the default session length is not configurable from the CMC. It is, however, configurable programmatically. Refer to the latest Crystal Enterprise SDK documentation for the session timeout capability.

The Web Component Server has several configuration options available from the Properties tab seen in Figure 10.37. To access this tab, click the Web Component Server name on the main Servers page.

Note

The NT Single Sign-On option enables Windows NT users to log on to Crystal Enterprise without entering their password because authentication is discreetly handled by Windows NT. Microsoft Internet Information Server (IIS) is the only Web server to support Windows NT Single Sign-On. Note that the users must also use Microsoft Internet Explorer to take advantage of this feature.

Figure 10.37
The Properties tab for the Crystal Web Component Server features several options for controlling logging and report viewer availability.

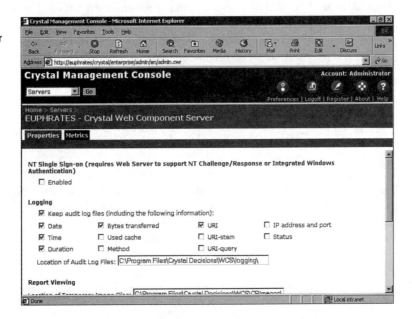

Various logging options for recording Web Component Server activity are also displayed. Generally these should be left unchanged except for specific troubleshooting purposes. Excessive logging consumes system resources unnecessarily.

Note

The Web Component Server logs can be an excellent source of data for system auditing, such as which users are viewing certain reports. Consider building a Crystal Report from the Web Component Server logs. Crystal Decisions provides some prebuilt Web Component Server log reports as well.

Options for managing report viewer availability and behavior are located at the bottom of the Web Component Server Properties page. These options enable a Crystal Enterprise administrator to specify which actions (drill-down, print, zoom, export, search, and so on) users can perform in the different report viewers.

Remember to click either Update or Apply to commit the changes. Changes to the WCS configuration will not take effect until the WCS service is restarted.

MANAGING THE CACHE SERVER

When a user views a report, Crystal Enterprise does not send the entire .rpt file to the user's machine. Report files with saved data can be substantial in size and slow to transfer. Furthermore, most users are only interested in looking at the first or last page of a report—not necessarily at every page in between.

To expedite report delivery, Crystal Enterprise features a technology called Page on Demand. Instead of sending a large .rpt file to the end user, Crystal Enterprise streams highly compressed, interactive snapshots of report pages as they are requested. This delivery method is fast and efficient, especially for dial-up users. This method also allows for page caching, where viewed pages of a report are cached for faster retrieval.

Cached report pages consume a fraction of the storage space of an actual .rpt file. The average cached page ranges from 10KB to 30KB in size, yet retains all the presentation quality of a true Crystal Report, including interactive drill-down, charts, and hyperlinks. The Crystal Cache Server is responsible for serving cached report pages to the users.

To adjust the settings for the Cache Server, click the Cache Server name from the main Servers screen. The Properties tab seen in Figure 10.38 will appear for the Cache Server. The Location of Cache Files field contains the path to the actual cached report files. This path is local to the Cache Server machine. The Maximum Cache Size Allowed field specifies the maximum size of the cache directory. When the threshold has been exceeded, Crystal Enterprise will delete the oldest, least-used cache files first. Preserving old cache files is not critical because missing cache files will be rebuilt on-the-fly, transparent to the user.

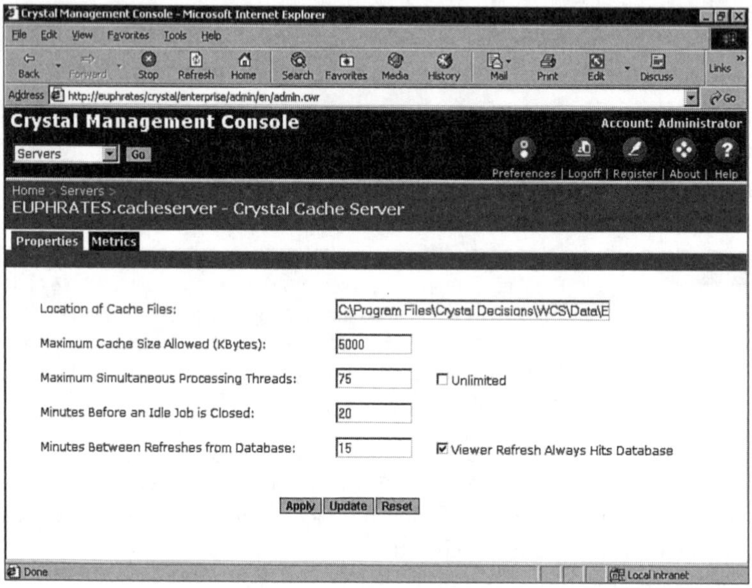

Figure 10.38
The Crystal Cache Server serves up pages for the report viewer. The Properties tab enables the Crystal Enterprise administrator to control the number of processing threads and the length of time that untouched cache pages will remain loaded in RAM.

The Maximum Simultaneous Processing Threads option restricts the number of application threads that can be spawned concurrently by the cache server. A processing thread is responsible for converting .rpt pages into cache pages. In most cases, it's not necessary to adjust the default setting of 75 threads. In the unlikely event that 75 users simultaneously request previously uncached pages, the cache server will queue the excess threads and process them as soon as possible. Queued threads are usually executed within a fraction of a second.

The Minutes Before an Idle Job is Closed option causes the cache server to release a stale cache page from RAM to make room for other cache pages. The cache page is still physically stored on the disk, but it's no longer kept in RAM. By default, cached pages that have not been requested for 20 minutes are released from RAM and will have to be reloaded from the disk if they are requested again.

Minutes Between Refreshes from Database controls the persistence of cached pages for on-demand reports. For example, assume that John requests an on-demand copy of the World Sales Report at 3:00 p.m. A few minutes later, at 3:04 p.m., Jane requests an on-demand copy of the World Sales Report with exactly the same parameters and record selection formula as John specified—an identical report in every way. Instead of spawning a resource-consuming database hit, Crystal Enterprise serves Jane the same cached pages that John loaded only moments before. This has the benefit of giving Jane the fastest possible response time while relieving the database and Page Server of additional processing work.

By default, on-demand cached pages will expire after 15 minutes. In the aforementioned example, if Jane requested the World Sales Report again at 3:16 p.m., the report would be rerun with fresh data from the database to ensure that it accurately reflected the condition of the data.

Keep in mind that users have the option to hit the database and rerun the report by clicking the Refresh button within the report viewer. The Viewer Refresh Always Hits Database option causes the report to be rerun against the database, not the cached data, if the user clicks the Refresh button within the report viewer. Normally, this option should remain enabled to give users the flexibility to "freshen" the report data at their convenience.

PART
IV
CH
10

Caution

Most transactional databases are frequently updated. In the case of OnLine Transaction Processing (OLTP) systems, thousands of records may be added every hour. The Minutes Between Refreshes from Database setting enables the Crystal Enterprise administrator to define the threshold between fast report delivery and up-to-date report data. By default, cached pages for on-demand reports expire after 15 minutes. In most cases, it's acceptable to use an on-demand report that's younger than 15 minutes. However, if the underlying data change frequently, consider lowering the 15-minute expiration window to be sure that on-demand reports always reflect the condition of the data.

MANAGING THE EVENT SERVER

The Event server, as explained in Chapter 3, is designed to allow Crystal Enterprise to interact with events external to the system. Events are conditions that trigger report processing to occur. For example, a Crystal Enterprise administrator could configure scheduled reports to run only after a nightly database load has completed. To do this, the administrator needs to configure the database load procedure to write an empty text file to a known location upon successful completion of the load. If an event has been configured, the Crystal Event Server would recognize the presence of this file as an indication that it should release certain reports for processing. The Crystal Event Server polls the system at set intervals to determine whether any configured events have been triggered. This is shown in Figure 10.39.

Figure 10.39
The Event Server periodically polls the system to check for triggered events. Setting a short poll interval value could negatively affect system performance.

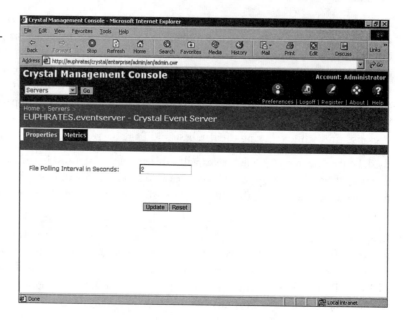

The File Polling Interval in Seconds option enables the Crystal Enterprise administrator to control the frequency of the Event Server's polling process. A lower value results in faster recognition of triggered events, but it also expends CPU cycles that might otherwise be devoted to more important tasks. A value of 10–60 seconds between system polls is generally acceptable. However, the Event Server is efficient in its use of system resources, and frequent polling probably will not cause an appreciable difference in report performance.

MANAGING THE PAGE SERVER

The Crystal Page Server handles all on-demand report requests. The Properties tab of the Page Server has several options for controlling Page Server performance, as seen in Figure 10.40. The Maximum Simultaneous Processing Threads setting controls the maximum number of concurrent application threads allowed. On-demand reports consume a minimum of one processing thread; if all available threads are busy, Crystal Enterprise will queue any excess threads for processing on a first-come, first-served basis.

Figure 10.40
The Crystal Page Server is responsible for processing on-demand report requests. The Page Server and Job Server often reside on the same physical server, although the components can run on separate servers to prevent scheduled jobs from impacting on-demand jobs, and vice-versa.

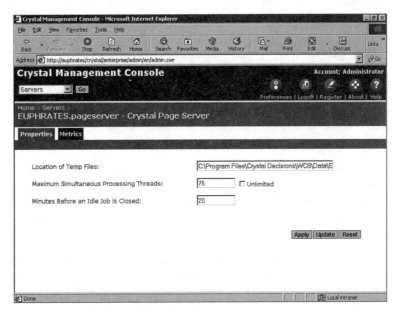

The Minutes Before an Idle Job Is Closed option affects the persistence of open Page Server jobs. For example, if a user starts to view an on-demand report and walks away from her desk without closing the report viewer, the job is left open until the specified period of inactivity has passed. If the user does not request any new pages within the default 20-minute window, the job is closed. New page or drill-down requests reset the 20-minute job expiration timer.

MANAGING THE JOB SERVER

The Job Server processes scheduled reports. Job Servers are capable of executing multiple report jobs in parallel, to increase report throughput. Each concurrent job consumes processing cycles, however, which results in slower completion of other concurrent jobs.

> **Tip**
>
> When issues arise with scheduled reports, there are a few places to check with the Job Server. Most issues involve network permissions for the Windows NT/2000 service account under which the Job Server is running. Just as a DBA must have network permissions to access databases, network file shares, and printers, so too must the Job Server service account. To access and change the service account that the job server uses, open the Crystal Configuration Manager and double-click on the Job Server.

For example, assume that the World Sales Report sample takes three minutes to run. If only one instance is scheduled, the report will be completed in three minutes. However, if *two* instances of the World Sales Report are scheduled simultaneously, both jobs will finish after approximately six minutes. If five jobs are executed simultaneously, it can take up to 15 minutes for all the jobs to finish running.

Simultaneous job processing has compelling advantages. For example, much of the time spent report processing is actually spent waiting for the database servers to return a resultset to the Job Server. If multiple jobs are executed, reports are processed more efficiently because the jobs are completed as the data is returned from the various database servers. In other words, a few very slow reports do not hold up the queue for faster reports because several reports can run concurrently. In a multiple-job environment, an extremely slow or stalled report will not hold up processing for other reports.

From a user's perspective, it's also desirable to execute several jobs at once. Because ePortfolio clearly reflects the processing stage of each scheduled report, users are more likely to become impatient with a queued report than with a currently processing report. A status of processing often gives the user the perception of faster report throughput, and in most cases, concurrent report throughput *is* faster.

The Maximum Jobs Allowed setting in Figure 10.41 affects the maximum number of reports that the Job Server can execute simultaneously. A setting of five concurrent report jobs is generally considered a harmonious balance between report throughput and server resources. Each concurrent report thread consumes significant system resources, not only in CPU cycles, but also in temporary disk space use, RAM overhead, and database resources. A robust multiprocessor machine with 2GB of RAM can comfortably process 10 jobs simultaneously. However, most servers run best with five or fewer concurrent jobs.

Figure 10.41
The Job Server processes scheduled reports only. The administrator can specify the number of jobs the Job Server can simultaneously process.

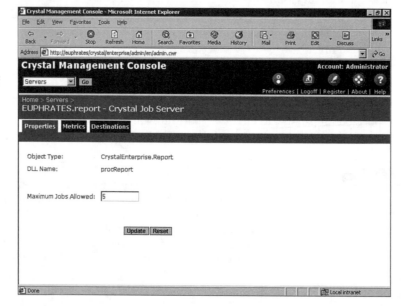

MANAGING THE APS

The APS, or Automated Process Scheduler, is responsible for object and user security as well as scheduling of jobs. The APS is the heart of Crystal Enterprise. Without the APS present, the entire system is useless. The name can be a bit misleading because it implies that the APS's main job is to schedule reports. The name is merely a carry over from older software from Crystal Decisions.

In addition to its role in enforcing object permissions, the APS monitors and records the processing status of every scheduled job. The Properties tab of the APS displays a listing of all currently connected users, as well as the number of sessions opened by each user ID (see Figure 10.42). Note that most of the time, a user ID will have only one session open. However, it's possible for two people to log in with the same user ID from different computers, in which case the user ID would reflect two concurrent sessions. Each session consumes a license until the user logs off, or the session is released after 20 minutes of inactivity.

Figure 10.42
The APS handles object and user security, as well as management of report instances.

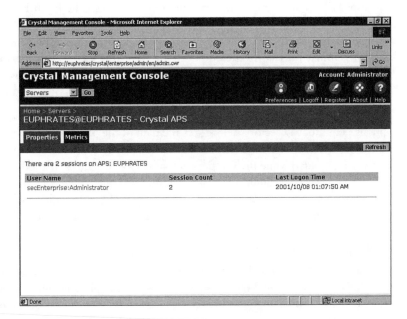

Possibly the most critical feature of the APS is clustering. Crystal Enterprise includes out-of-the-box clustering capability for the APS. This means that without any special hardware, two physical APS servers can be clustered together. If one becomes unavailable, the other APS will support authentication requests and scheduling tasks. APS clustering is reviewed in the "Managing Settings" section of this chapter.

MANAGING THE INPUT/OUTPUT FILE REPOSITORY SERVERS (FRS)

File Repository Servers are services that manage the storage and retrieval of report files from the file system. Crystal Enterprise contains an Input FRS and an Output FRS. Both FRS systems store report files using a somewhat mysterious naming convention. For example, the report template for the World Sales Report might be named 73422e16f293d0.rpt by the Input FRS. Any instances of the World Sales Report would be assigned a similarly cryptic name by the Output FRS. Both FRS servers store name translation information in the APS system database, enabling users to see the true English name of a report instead of the cryptic file system name.

> **Note**
>
> Crystal Enterprise 8.5 introduces the capability to name report instances or append certain values such as schedule date to the instance name.

The Input FRS and Output FRS serve different purposes. The Input FRS stores report templates and is responsible for locating and transmitting .rpt files to the Page/Job Server for processing. The Input FRS only stores .rpt files that do not contain saved data. By contrast, the Output FRS stores the output of the Page/Job Server as a report instance. A report instance is an .rpt file that contains saved data. The Output FRS is also responsible for passing report instances to the Cache Server for generation of cached pages.

The Properties tab in Figure 10.43 for the Input and Output FRS has two configuration options. The Root Directory field stores the path of the physical file repository on the server's file system. This path is local to the FRS server. The Input FRS stores .rpt templates in one folder, while the Output FRS stores .rpt instances in another folder. Both servers also have a Maximum Idle Time option that controls the amount of time that an idle .rpt file will remain cached in the FRS memory. When the idle time expires, the .rpt files are dropped from the memory cache and must be loaded from disk if required again.

MANAGING SERVER GROUPS

A large Crystal Enterprise deployment can have several physical Page and Job Servers spread over a wide area network. Some of the servers might have more processing power than others, and some might be located in specific regions such as San Francisco and New York. In multiple-server environments, it's often advantageous to categorize servers into specific groups. Server groups are helpful for managing servers that are located in different regions; they also can assist in organizing servers according to processing power.

After a server group has been created, the Crystal Enterprise administrator can configure reports to process on specific server groups. For example, the CEO's personal reports could be configured to execute on a server group that contains one or more high-powered Job/Page Servers. This would ensure that the CEO's reports always process on the most powerful servers available, and thereby finish running as quickly as possible. Without server groups, the CEO's reports might get routed to a slower Job/Page Server, and the CEO would end up spending more time than necessary waiting for critical information.

Figure 10.43
The Input and Output File Repository Servers have the same Properties tab settings. Note that a special tab called Active Files displays any .rpt files currently in the memory cache.

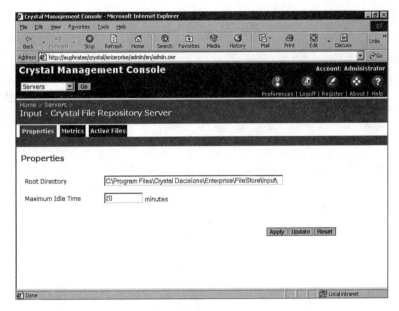

Server groups are also useful for forcing reports to execute on a Job/Page Server that's in close proximity to the report's database server. The Crystal Enterprise administrator could, for example, configure the Berlin sales reports to execute only on the Berlin server group, closest to the Berlin database server. This would ensure minimal transatlantic network traffic, and as a result, faster report processing. If the administrator did not employ server groups in this example, it's possible that the Berlin sales reports might be executed on a Job/Page Server in Los Angeles or New York.

To create a server group, select Server Groups from the drop-down menu in the Crystal Management Console. Click New Server Group, and then type the name of the server group in the Server Group Name field. An optional Description for the server group may also be entered. Click the OK button to add the new server group to Crystal Enterprise. Figure 10.44 shows a Server Group.

Server groups work just like user groups. Each server group can have one or more servers, and a server can reside in more than one group. Server groups also support subgroups. After the administrator has created a server group, a minimum of one server must be added to it. Click the Servers tab to add severs to the group. After servers have been added to the new server group, the Crystal Enterprise administrator can start, stop, delete, disable, and enable them by following the server control procedures used on the main Servers screen. If the administrator has many physical servers, it's usually easier to manage them from the Server Groups screen, where only a few logically grouped servers will be listed, instead of from the main Servers screen, which lists every server in the system.

PART

IV

CH

10

Figure 10.44
Server groups are configured like user groups. The Crystal Enterprise administrator can create groups and add servers to them. A server can reside in more than one group, and a group can also have several subgroups.

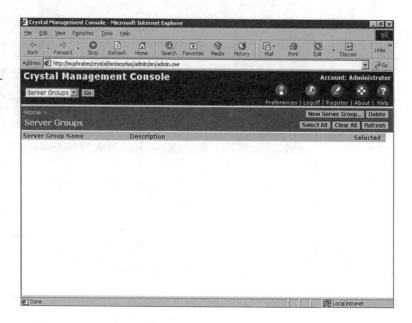

Subgroups can be added to the server group for more granular control. Server subgroups work on the same principle as user subgroups and are created in the same way. Refer to the "Managing Users" section on creating user subgroups for a detailed explanation of subgroups.

MANAGING THE SYSTEM

Managing the Crystal Enterprise system entails a number of systemwide settings that aren't specific to a particular server.

MANAGING SETTINGS

Crystal Enterprise has several systemwide settings that affect instance limits, user rights, and clustering. To configure system settings, select Settings from the Crystal drop-down menu in the Crystal Management Console.

SYSTEM PROPERTIES

The Properties tab in Figure 10.45 lists general information about Crystal Enterprise, including the Build Date, Build Number, and Product Version. Additional information about the APS system database is also displayed. The Data Source field displays the name of the ODBC Data Source Name (DSN) used to connect to the APS system database. The Database Name field indicates the name of the SQL Server in which the APS database resides, as well as other general information about the database back end. The Database User Name field contains the user ID that's used to connect to the APS database.

Figure 10.45
The information on the Properties tab is for display only and cannot be altered.

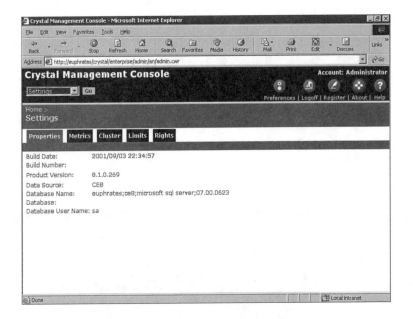

SYSTEM METRICS

The Metrics tab in Figure 10.46 contains several systemwide measurements for determining the number of access licenses in use. Other metrics include counts of the number of report jobs grouped by job status. The information on the Metrics tab can be used to monitor the number of concurrent user connections, as well as the number of failed report jobs.

Figure 10.46
The Metrics tab displays helpful system information such as the number of access licenses currently in use. Information presented on the Metrics tab is updated by the system and cannot be modified.

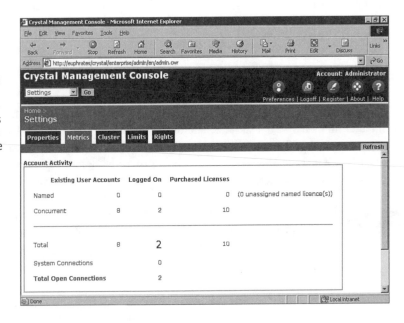

SYSTEM CLUSTERING

The Cluster tab displays information about the Crystal Enterprise cluster, if one has been configured. A cluster is a group of two or more APS machines working in tandem to provide fault tolerance and load balancing. If one machine in the cluster fails, the remaining machines will seamlessly recover activity of the inoperable APS. APS clustering is a common feature of large Crystal Enterprise deployments. The Cluster tab lists each APS participating in the cluster. Clustering is configured from the Crystal Configuration Manager.

SYSTEM LIMITS

The Limits tab in Figure 10.47 contains global settings for report instance expiration.

Figure 10.47
The Crystal Enterprise administrator can specify systemwide rules controlling the life span of report instances on the Limits tab. After the age limits for a report instance have been exceeded, the APS will automatically delete the instance from the system.

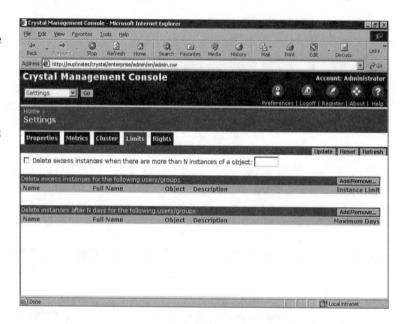

The instance limits specified on this tab apply to every report instance in the system, unless different limits have been specified at either the folder or report object level. In the upper-left corner of the Limits tab is an option to Delete Excess Instances when There Are More Than N Instances of an Object. The Crystal Enterprise administrator can use this option to cause old report instances to be deleted when the specified threshold has been exceeded.

Note

Remember that folder-level and object-level limits, if specified, take precedence over the global instance limits.

This setting applies to all users and user groups unless an exception is made in the Delete Excess Instances for the Following Users/Groups section of the Limits tab. The Crystal Enterprise administrator may click the Add/Remove button in the Limits tab to add over-riding expiration limits for specific users or user groups. The user/group expiration limits take precedence over the Delete Excess Instances when There Are More Than N Instances of an Object option.

SYSTEMWIDE RIGHTS

By default, new folders and objects in Crystal Enterprise inherit the rights of their parent folders. Top-level folders do not have a parent folder. Instead, top-level folders inherit their rights from the global Rights tab. Any user rights that have been assigned on the Rights tab are automatically inherited by top-level folders and their report objects, unless exceptions have been specified at the folder-level or object-level (see Figure 10.48).

PART

IV

CH

10

Figure 10.48
The Rights tab controls user rights at the top level of the Crystal Enterprise folder hierarchy. Any rights specified on this tab will be inherited by all folders and objects in the system, except where folder-level or object-level rights have been specified.

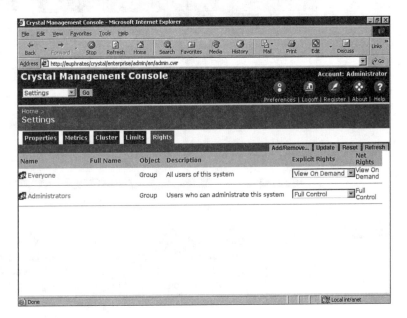

MANAGING AUTHORIZATION

There are two key components to managing Crystal Enterprise authorization:

- Licensing
- Authentication

The first one is a less technical topic but still important to understand. The second is discussed in subsequent sections.

MANAGING LICENSING

The License Keys tab displays important information about each license key (see Figure 10.49). Most Crystal Enterprise installations have only one key, but it's possible to have more than one key. Highlight a license key to display specific information about the key. Crystal Enterprise supports three types of licenses: named licenses, concurrent licenses, and processor licenses.

Figure 10.49
The License Keys tab provides information about each of the Crystal Enterprise license keys.

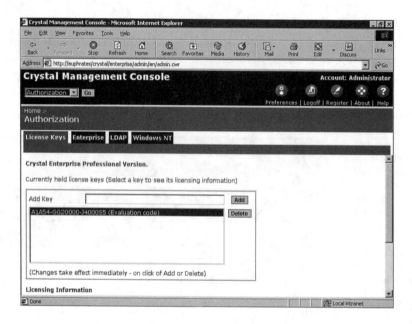

> **Note**
>
> The license certificate keys determine the number and type of licenses available (name user or concurrent access). During the initial install of Crystal Enterprise, a license key was entered. Additional licenses can be added to Crystal Enterprise from the License Keys tab on the Authentication section of the Crystal Management Console.

Crystal Enterprise provides an administrator the flexibility to mix and match license types. *Named licenses* are assigned to specific users. Any number of named licenses can be simultaneously logged in to the system.

Concurrent licenses permit an unlimited number of named users to be added to the Crystal Enterprise, but only a certain number of those users can access the system simultaneously.

Processor licenses allow an unlimited number of both named and concurrent users for a specific processor. Processor licenses are most efficient in high-powered server environments where the server CPU is robust enough to support a large number of concurrent users.

It's best to contact Crystal Decisions and discuss the optimum licensing strategy for your organization.

MANAGING AUTHENTICATION

Also found under the Authorization portion of the Crystal Management Console are the different types of authentication that can be leveraged with Crystal Enterprise.

Crystal Enterprise provides several authentication models for providing secure report access, including Native Crystal Enterprise authentication, Windows NT Authentication, and LDAP authentication. Crystal Enterprise supports single sign-on for both the Windows NT and LDAP methods, so users won't have to constantly revalidate credentials after exiting and reentering the system.

The reason Crystal Enterprise supports more security models than its own is simple: If an IT organization has already implemented an existing security model, why re-create certain entities such as user accounts and passwords?

Fortunately, none of these options is mutually exclusive; they can all be used simultaneously. This can cause some management headaches, so proceed with caution. Every topic in this chapter up until this point has used native Crystal Enterprise security as an example.

This does not imply that if Windows NT authentication is used, for example, that administration is done exclusively from Windows NT. It simply implies that objects such as user accounts and passwords can be maintained within Windows NT, yet Crystal Enterprise will feed off of those existing accounts when users try to retrieve reports. The configuration of Crystal Enterprise groups and objects, as well as relevant restrictions to those objects, are still created and configured from the Crystal Management Console, in the same way that this chapter has shown. This is reviewed in greater detail later.

To configure system authentication settings, select Authorization from the drop-down menu in the Crystal Management Console.

CRYSTAL ENTERPRISE AUTHENTICATION Crystal Enterprise provides its own native security model. This means that Crystal Enterprise is not dependent on a foreign, third-party security database to configure and restrict access to any system function, object, or entity. The Crystal Enterprise authentication model is the default model. To leverage another security database, select either the Windows NT tab or the LDAP tab. In other words, if the Crystal Enterprise system administrator sets up users and groups and has not configured anything in the LDAP or Windows NT tabs, the native Crystal Enterprise security is being used. All user account information is stored in the APS system database.

Selecting the Enterprise tab, seen in Figure 10.50, enables the administrator to enforce password rules when using Crystal Enterprise authentication. The Crystal Enterprise administrator can use this tab to control the frequency that users are forced to change their passwords, as well as the length of the passwords and whether or not the password must contain mixed-case letters.

Figure 10.50

The administrator can set Crystal Enterprise password expiration rules on the Enterprise tab. This tab only applies to the Crystal Enterprise native authentication method, not LDAP or Windows NT.

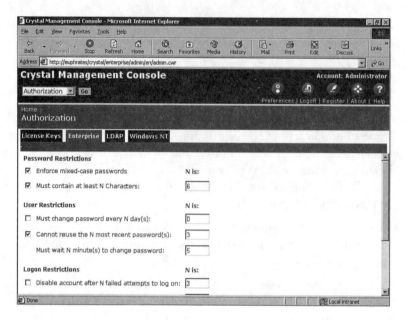

In general, the password options offered are similar to those provided by the Windows NT and Solaris operating systems.

DIRECTORY SERVER AUTHENTICATION THROUGH LDAP Selecting the LDAP tab allows a system administrator to configure LDAP connectivity to a directory server, as seen in Figure 10.51. LDAP (Lightweight Directory Access Protocol) enables a network administrator to maintain a central directory server for managing user access to a variety of applications and operating systems. Crystal Enterprise can be configured to work with a variety of directory servers via LDAP. Crystal Enterprise support for LDAP was designed and tested to the version 3 specification.

Crystal Enterprise can tie into an LDAP Server for User and Group information. Folder and Object permissions are still defined within Crystal Enterprise. When Crystal Enterprise is tied to an LDAP server, equivalent Crystal Enterprise accounts are either created, if they don't already exist, or aliased if they do exist. The Crystal Enterprise system must have references to users and groups inside the system such that report object restrictions can be configured. User passwords are not stored in Crystal Enterprise. When using LDAP, it's the job of the directory server to verify passwords. Any time a user attempts to access Crystal Enterprise resources, a password confirmation request is sent to the directory server. If the user authenticates properly, Crystal Enterprise will then compare the users' group membership and associated privileges assigned to those groups in Crystal Enterprise.

Any time a user attempts to use credentials that stem from a Directory server, Crystal Enterprise verifies this information through LDAP.

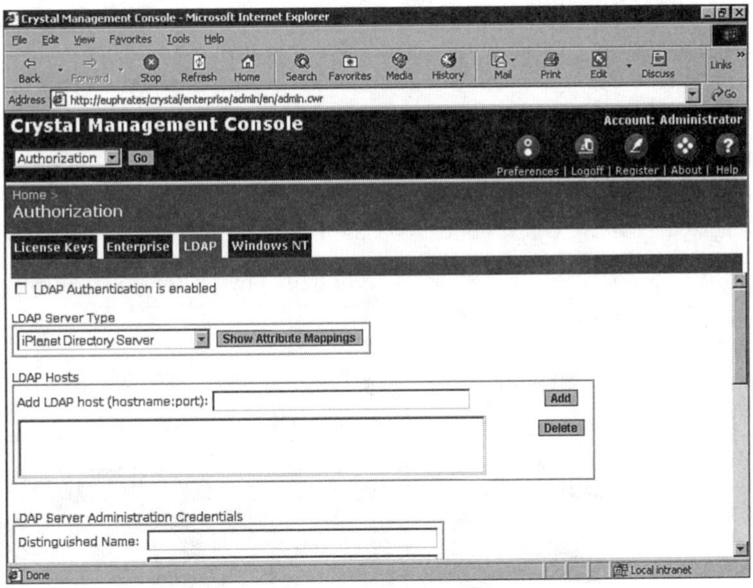

Figure 10.51
Configuring LDAP enables Crystal Enterprise to connect to a Directory server, such as Netscape iPlanet, and leverage existing usernames and passwords.

The current directory servers supported by Crystal Enterprise include

- iPlanet Directory Server
- Lotus Domino Directory Server
- IBM Secureway
- Novell Directory Services

Note

Version- and platform-specific information can be found in the supported platforms documentation that accompanies Crystal Enterprise.

To configure connectivity to a directory server such as iPlanet through LDAP, click the LDAP tab. Be sure the LDAP Authentication Is Enabled option is checked. Although the following instructions walk through configuring a connection to iPlanet through LDAP, all that's required to connect to iPlanet, assuming anonymous access is enabled, is the server name, port number, and base LDAP distinguished name. Entering just those values will enable access to users and groups to be authenticated by iPlanet for Crystal Enterprise.

It's also important to note that once user names and groups are added to Crystal Enterprise by clicking Add Group, no scheduled synchronization takes place between Crystal Enterprise and the directory server. If new users are added to the directory server and then the same users attempt to access a Crystal Enterprise resource, an update process between Crystal Enterprise and the directory server is kicked off.

That update process entails Crystal Enterprise referring to the directory server to authenticate the user. If the user is valid and belongs to groups that have access to Crystal Enterprise resources, the user account will be added to Crystal Enterprise. This process takes place on a user-by-user basis.

If, for example, a large number of users and groups were added to the directory server and the Crystal Enterprise administrator needed to configure Crystal Enterprise security settings, clicking the Update button on the LDAP page will force synchronization.

1. Select the type of LDAP server required. This example uses iPlanet 5.0, as seen in Figure 10.52.

Figure 10.52
Crystal Enterprise 8.5 supports iPlanet as a directory server.

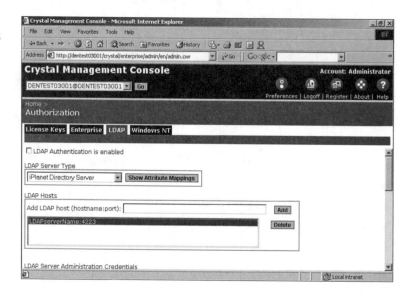

2. Enter the hostname and port. This should be entered as *Servername:portnumber*. In Figure 10.51, this was entered as Serverlucas:4225.

    Multiple LDAP servers can be added; however, they must be of the same type. The Show Attribute Mappings option displays the LDAP server attribute mappings and default search attributes. These settings can be modified if necessary.

3. In the LDAP Server Administration Credentials dialog box, enter the distinguished name and password that will enable binding to the directory tree. If anonymous access binding is allowed, no entry is required in this field.

4. The LDAP Referral Credentials section is used only under a certain set of conditions. Refer to the Crystal Enterprise admin guide for those conditions.

5. For the Maximum Referral Hops, enter a value to limit this to. In this example, it's set to zero because only one iPlanet server is being used and no referrals are being made.

6. In the Base LDAP Distinguished Name, enter a value such as `o=crystaldecisions`.

7. At the bottom of the LDAP page, click the Update button before proceeding.

8. In the Mapped LDAP Member Groups dialog box, seen in Figure 10.53, enter the group name by common name (cn=XYZgroup) or distinguished name (dn=XYZgroup). This example uses cn=Sales.

Figure 10.53
LDAP configuration settings for groups based on common names and distinguished names.

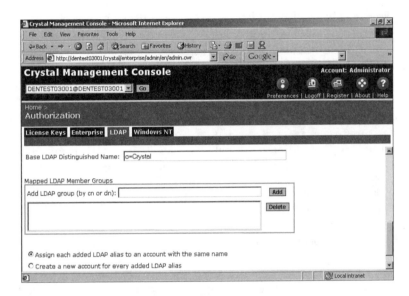

9. With the option Assign Each Added LDAP Alias to an Account with the Same Name, just as with Windows NT authentication, an LDAP account is aliased to an existing Crystal Enterprise account with the same username. If no Crystal Enterprise account that matches the LDAP account exists, one will be created.

10. Create a New Account for Every Added LDAP Alias creates a new account for every LDAP user. If a Crystal Enterprise account already exists, the user will have a separate LDAP and Crystal Enterprise account.

11. Click Update and select OK.

There's another option found in LDAP in addition to the four currently supported LDAP servers. Custom implies that a directory server schema has been modified. Custom enables mapping of various LDAP attributes to Crystal Enterprise functionality.

WINDOWS NT AUTHENTICATION   Crystal Enterprise provides the capability to tie in user authentication to the Windows NT security model. If the primary network operating system and application authentication method in an organization is Windows NT, this feature can be a useful timesaver.

> **Note**
>
> The Windows NT Authentication model also supports Windows 2000 because it's based on Windows NT.

Leveraging NT authentication ensures that usernames and passwords in Crystal Enterprise are consistent with those used on the actual network itself. Relying on NT to handle authentication also simplifies system administration from the perspective of user management. Instead of managing two separate user account databases (one in Crystal Enterprise and the other in Windows NT), the Crystal Enterprise administrator can standardize using the NT database and add or remove Crystal Enterprise users with User Manager for Domains. The implementation of Windows NT authentication is similar to that of LDAP, where usernames are created in Crystal Enterprise based on usernames in specific Windows NT groups. Crystal Enterprise still relies on Windows NT for authentication by validating a user's password as he enters the Crystal Enterprise system.

Windows NT authentication can be configured from the Windows NT tab, as seen in Figure 10.54. To enable NT authentication, select the NT Authentication Is Enabled option. Enter the name of the Default NT Domain. The default domain should be the same domain that contains the majority of the Windows NT users that will also be Crystal Enterprise end users.

Figure 10.54
Selecting the Windows NT tab enables the administrator to configure Crystal Enterprise to support NT authentication.

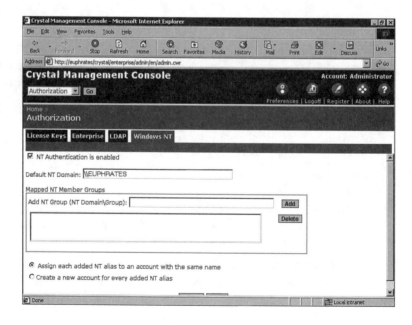

Users who do not have accounts in the specified default domain will need to specify their domain name each time they log in to Crystal Enterprise.

The Mapped NT Member Groups section enables specification of which NT user groups are permitted to access Crystal Enterprise. Any NT users who belong to mapped NT member groups will be able to log in to Crystal Enterprise using single sign on.

Users who are not a member of at least one mapped NT group will not be able to access Crystal Enterprise unless the administrator has specifically created a Crystal Enterprise user ID for them in the Crystal Management Console. To import a new NT group to Crystal Enterprise, type in the name of the NT group (preceded by the group's domain or machine name) and click the Add button. Remember to click the Update button when you're finished adding or removing NT groups.

The bottom of the Windows NT tab has two additional options for configuring NT integration. Assign Each Added NT Alias to an Account with the Same Name forces Crystal Enterprise to match imported NT usernames with existing Crystal Enterprise usernames. If Crystal Enterprise already has a username with the same name as an incoming Windows NT username, the two usernames will be mapped to each other so that a duplicate account name is not created. In other words, an alias will be created.

On the other hand, the Create a New Account for Every Added NT Alias option will cause Crystal Enterprise to add a new Crystal Enterprise username for each incoming NT username. If a duplicate username exists in Crystal Enterprise, an alias will not be created; instead, a new username will be created with a slightly different name. When the group is added, navigate to the Manage Groups section of the CMC. Note that \\DENTEST03001\TESTGROUP is now listed as a group within Crystal Enterprise. Selecting this user group allows access to the same options as a native Crystal Enterprise group.

THE CRYSTAL CONFIGURATION MANAGER

The Crystal Configuration Manager (CCM) is a Windows-based tool installed on the Crystal Enterprise server by default (see Figure 10.55). A Crystal Configuration Manager script is also available for the Solaris version of Crystal Enterprise. Refer to Appendix A, "Running Crystal Enterprise on Sun Solaris," for more information on this topic. The Crystal Enterprise administrator can use the Crystal Configuration to start and stop Crystal Services on the local machine or remote machines, as well as configure the Web Connector.

Tip

The administrator can use the Crystal Configuration Manager to remotely administer several Crystal Enterprise servers by changing the computer name.

To start the CCM, click Start, Programs, Crystal Enterprise, Crystal Configuration Manager. When the CCM loads, it will display a list of all Crystal Enterprise services running on the current machine, as well as the World Wide Web Publishing Service if the

PART
IV

CH
10

machine is also a Web server. The name of the current machine is indicated in the upper-right corner of the CCM. To administer another Crystal Enterprise server, type in a new server name and press Enter. The drop-down box of server names will maintain a list of each server visited. A Crystal Enterprise administrator can also click the Browse for Computer icon to select a different machine.

Figure 10.55
The Crystal Configuration Manager enables the Crystal Enterprise administrator to restart and configure Crystal services as well as configure the Web Connector.

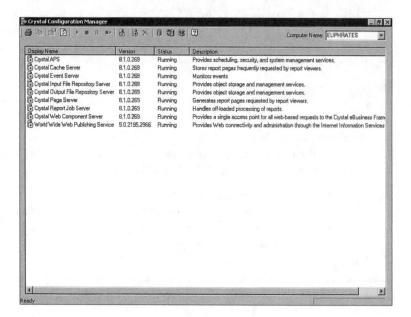

To start, stop, pause, or restart Crystal services, highlight a service name, and then click the appropriate icon at the top of the screen. Note that the Crystal Enterprise administrator can also select several Crystal services at once by using the Shift or Ctrl select methods. One interesting fact about the CCM is the use of command-line options to start various Crystal Enterprise servers. To view the command line used to startup a given server, such as the Web Component Server, right-click the service name and choose Properties. Notice that the dialog box title Command Line shows the server startup command as well as potential parameters supplied to the server service.

Starting up servers from a command line can be a useful approach to solving or troubleshooting problems that might arise. More will be discussed on server startup command lines later.

To view the properties of a service, right-click on the service and select Properties from the drop-down menu. Note that the Crystal Enterprise administrator must stop the service first to make changes to the service's properties. From the Properties dialog box, the Crystal Enterprise administrator can change the NT account used to run the service, and also view the service's dependencies. Depending on the service, the administrator might also be able to specify a communication port, although the default port is normally acceptable.

The Crystal Enterprise administrator can also use the Crystal Configuration Manager to add or remove instances of a service. To remove a service, highlight the service name, and then click the delete icon at the top of the screen. To add a new instance of a service, click the Add Server icon. A wizard will walk the administrator through the steps of adding the new service.

THE CRYSTAL CONFIGURATION MANAGER: CONFIGURING THE WEB CONNECTOR

The Web Connector resides on the Web server, intercepting .csp, .cwr, and .cwi requests and passing them on to the Web Component Server. To configure the Web Connector, start the Crystal Configuration Manager and be sure it's connected to the machine that has the Web Connector installed on it (this machine will always be a Web server). Click the Configure Web Connector icon to start the configuration process.

Figure 10.56
Each Web Component Server must be identified to the Web Connector. If a Web Component Server has not been identified to the Web Connector, it will not be used.

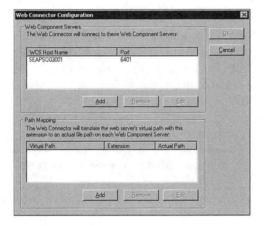

PART

IV

CH

10

A list of all configured WCS machines will appear in the Web Component Servers box. If there is more than one Web Component Server, the Crystal Enterprise administrator must be sure that each one is listed here. If a Web Component Server is not listed, the Web Connector will not be able to forward Crystal Enterprise requests to that server. To add a new WCS, click the Add button and type in the WCS Host Name. The WCS Host Name is the same as the machine name on which the WCS resides. The Crystal Enterprise administrator will also need to specify a port number; the default port is 6401. If a SOCKs server must be specified, click the Specify SOCKS button. After you have finished typing in the required WCS information, click OK to add the new WCS to the available Web Component Servers box.

CONFIGURING APS CLUSTERING FROM THE CONFIGURATION MANAGER

The Crystal Configuration Manager is also the location where the Crystal Enterprise APS can be clustered. Clustering in Crystal Enterprise does not require any special hardware; it's software based. The APS is the only server for which clustering is required because other servers, such as the Job Server, are managed from the APS.

Crystal Enterprise could have two or more physical Job Servers and the APS will actively load balance report processing tasks between those servers. If a Job Server fails, that APS no longer sends report processing requests to that physical server.

As for APS clustering, a few things are required for it to work:

- The APS System database must be in a supported format such as Microsoft SQL Server. MSDE is not sufficient.

- Multiple APS servers must be available, all using the same operating system.

- All APS servers must connect to the same APS database, and the connectivity options to the database must be identical.

- Multihomed APS servers are supported, but special consideration is required. Refer to the Crystal Enterprise admin guide for more information on multihomed server support.

After ensuring the system is properly configured and a backup of the APS system database is complete, open the CCM, right-click on the APS service, and choose Properties. Select the Configuration tab and check the Enable APS Clustering box. The Clustering Wizard will walk through the steps required to complete the APS cluster. Afterward, the cluster name can be changed.

Note

Crystal Enterprise refers to APS clusters with the server name of the first server in the cluster preceded by the @ symbol. For example, @Dentest03001 would be the APS cluster name.

STARTING CRYSTAL ENTERPRISE SERVERS FROM A COMMAND LINE

To understand how a server is started from the command line (DOS prompt), look no further than inside the properties of a server from the Crystal Configuration Manager. To view this, start the CCM and right-click on the Web Component Server. Select Properties. The Web Component Server properties dialog box launches.

Note that the Command option on the Properties tab lists something like the following:

```
"\\DENTEST03001\C$\Program Files\Crystal Decisions\WCS\
  WebCompServer.exe " -service -name DENTEST03001 -ns DENTEST03001  -restart
```

The important part of that command line is the following:

```
WebCompServer.exe -service -name DENTEST03001 -ns DENTEST03001  -restart
```

To break this statement down further, see Table 10.3.

TABLE 10.3 THE COMMAND-LINE EXECUTABLE FOR THE WEB COMPONENT SERVER, AND SEVERAL GENERIC SWITCHES

Component	Function
WebCompServer.exe	Launches the Web Component Server
-service	Specifies running the Web Component Server as a service
-name DENTEST03001	Registers the name of DENTEST03001 as the name for the Web Component Server service that just launched
-ns DENTEST03001	Specifies that the name server to register with is DENTEST03001
-restart	Indicates that the Web Component Server service should be restarted if an unusual exit code is thrown if the service shuts down

It's important to understand the different types of command-line arguments that can be passed to different Crystal Enterprise servers at startup. The example in Table 10.3 demonstrates some of the generic service arguments that can be passed to any Crystal Enterprise server. Individual Crystal Enterprise servers also have unique arguments that can be leveraged.

Some of the more useful commands for server startup include the defaultSessionTimeout argument for Web Component Server startup that sets end-user session length when using Crystal Enterprise.

A common task for most Crystal Enterprise administrators is to build up their own custom .bat file that starts up all the Crystal Enterprise services with certain parameters appropriate for a given scenario.

Refer to the Crystal Enterprise Admin guide for a complete listing of all the various server command-line arguments that can be leveraged at server startup.

OTHER SYSTEM TASKS: BACKING UP THE APS SYSTEM DATABASE

The APS system database stores information about users, groups, folders, and security. A corrupted or deleted APS database will cause the Crystal Enterprise system to malfunction. It's critical that the APS database be backed up frequently.

By default, Crystal Enterprise attempts to install the APS database on the local Crystal Enterprise server. If a SQL Server is not present on the Crystal Enterprise server, Crystal Enterprise will install the Microsoft Data Engine (MSDE), also known as Personal SQL Server. MSDE is generally not recommended for large, mission-critical deployments. It's better to store the APS system database on a true database server that's backed up nightly. Supported APS system database servers for the Windows platform include Microsoft SQL

Server, Oracle, DB2, and Informix. For the Solaris platform APS database support, refer to Appendix A.

SUMMARY

This chapter discussed the tools for administering Crystal Enterprise. The Crystal Management Console is a Web-based tool that's capable of performing almost every configuration task with the exception of setting up the Web Connector. The Web Connector is the plug-in to a Web server that routes certain traffic, such as report view requests or .csp processing requests to Crystal Enterprise.

Managing the different aspects of Crystal Enterprise can be as much an art as it is a science. Each individual component of the Crystal Enterprise system, from a standard Crystal Report object to the servers themselves, all are easily managed from the CMC.

The Crystal Configuration Manager, a Windows utility, is primarily used to configure the Web Connector, and it can also be used to add and manage Crystal Services.

Crystal Enterprise servers can also be stopped and started from a command line (DOS prompt) similar to other Windows NT–based services. Crystal Enterprise services can be passed special parameters at startup to affect certain behaviors, such as logging levels and verbosity.

CHAPTER 11

PLANNING CONSIDERATIONS WHEN DEPLOYING CRYSTAL ENTERPRISE

In this chapter

There is a direct relationship between the time spent planning a deployment of Crystal Enterprise and the success of that deployment. In other words, failing to plan is planning to fail. This year in North America, 75% of IT software deployment projects will fail due in part to inaccurate requirement gathering, inexperienced project team members, and insufficient executive interest and sponsorship.

All too often, the average scenario when deploying Crystal Enterprise consists of placing the Crystal Enterprise application CD into the CD tray, double-clicking setup.exe, crossing fingers, and hoping for the best. Whether the person in charge of deploying Crystal Enterprise is an experienced system administrator or a novice at deploying applications to a small or large group of users, certain steps can be taken to increase the deployment success and adoption of Crystal Enterprise.

With its system architecture and flexible SDK, Crystal Enterprise provides organizations with the capability to build uniquely customized information delivery environments scaling from a single-user or workgroup to enterprise-wide deployments with thousands of users. Because of this broad scope of functionality, project teams will find themselves planning to deploy an enterprise reporting environment as well as providing application development support to customize the user interface. This is, of course, assuming an organization chooses not to use ePortfolio (see Chapter 5, "Using the Crystal Enterprise Launchpad") or one of the out-of-the-box Crystal Enterprise end-user interfaces.

As a result of this, the first part of this chapter defines a project management *planning* approach that will enable a Crystal Enterprise system administrator or deployment manager to form a framework around which a Crystal Enterprise deployment project can be successfully built and delivered, thus increasing the rate of success.

The second portion of the chapter focuses on the specific topics related to actually *deploying* Crystal Enterprise, from organizational reporting requirements to server sizing and architecture.

APPROACHING THE PROJECT

Many organizations have standard application development practices and methodologies that are followed with every project that involves system deployment efforts and some level of programmatic customization. These methodologies can trace their ancestry to a simplistic methodology that was used with the invention of the wheel.

The "invention of the wheel" approach goes something like this: Ug is tired of carrying his mammoth tusks on his back all day (business pain); he needs something that will help reduce his effort and allow him to carry more, increasing his efficiency and keeping his boss happy (requirements). Once he finds and refines the solution (development) and tests it (pilot), Ug can show his colleagues and find out what they think (user acceptance testing). After this is completed, he can manufacture it and allow his colleagues to carry their tusks more efficiently (deployment). After his colleagues have their tusk carriers, Ug will monitor what they think of it and make changes where necessary (support and maintenance). Needless to say, Ug used this process to develop a cart with wheels, and the rest is history.

Things have changed somewhat since then, but the concept remains the same. The constituent parts of this process—identifying business pain, establishing project requirements, developing the application, completing user acceptance testing, deploying the technology, and supporting and maintaining the application—can help any person responsible for a Crystal Enterprise software project, or any project for that matter, increase his chances for success.

IDENTIFYING BUSINESS PAIN

Necessity is the mother of invention. As a result, most organizations implement new policies, systems, processes, and applications for good reasons: to improve efficiency; save money, time, and effort; and to improve work environments, for example.

Companies have their own processes for discovering business pain. Regardless of how it's discovered, business pain is the driving factor behind the success of the project. In the case of enterprise reporting, the business pain is often defined by existing user interface and application restrictions or datasource connectivity requirements and limitations. As previously discussed, Crystal Enterprise can be customized to suit most Web delivery GUI requirements and connect to virtually any ODBC-compliant, relational datasource, not to mention many native datasource connections—hence, the reason Crystal Enterprise and its associated report design tools (Crystal Reports) are looked to when solving these types of problems.

ESTABLISHING PROJECT REQUIREMENTS

Without question, the number one reason for a software project's downfall is the failure to gather requirements, and further to that point, gather them correctly. Anyone undertaking a project to deploy Crystal Enterprise must take the time to discover exactly what the tool is required to accomplish. This need is initially defined by the business problem. Remember, the business problem should be considered the starting point for a Crystal Enterprise solution, allowing the enterprise reporting technology to be embraced and extended to an entire organization.

Don't get caught in the trap that solving the immediate business problem defines the limits of the finished product. There might be additional functionality and technology that can be leveraged to fully maximize a solution. For example, initial requirements-gathering might produce a need for end users to export files to .PDF and Excel to view reports over the Web. With additional technology outside the scope of initial requirements, other users could be incorporated into the solution. For example, knowing that certain remote users take advantage of wireless devices, a project team might decide to export reports to XML so that data for the reports can be sent to these remote users.

With these points in mind, some of the key questions that need to be considered when defining the requirements for a deployment of Crystal Enterprise involve four concepts:

users, user interface, reports, and environments. The following bulleted lists show the important questions that should be considered:

Users

- How many users will you have?
- What are the skill sets of these users: business/end users; power users; administrators; developers?
- How many concurrent users will you have?
- Where will your users be located?
- How many users will be viewing reports only? (Clickers)
- How many users will design reports? (Designers)
- How many users will schedule reports? (Drillers)
- Will customers be using this application?
- What are the training requirements for administrators? Report designers? Users?

User Interface

- What look and feel is required for the user interface?
- Is this look and feel supposed to inherit the company's intranet appearance and functionality?
- Will users need to input data or will data extraction and delivery be sufficient?

  These questions will help determine whether an out-of-the-box Crystal Enterprise interface, such as ePortfolio, will meet end-user requirements, or if customization to ePortfolio will be necessary. Some organizations develop a completely custom front end to Crystal Enterprise based on end-user feedback to the previous questions. In the case of the latter scenario, some organizations integrate Crystal Enterprise information delivery as a portion of a larger application, which can involve data entry as well.

Reports

- Are legacy reports in use? If so, in which application environments were they created?

  Identifying any requirements for support of legacy reports will help identify the extent of the Crystal Enterprise solution. Use of the Crystal Enterprise SDK might be required to link new reports to legacy reports.
- What type of database(s) will be used with reports in Crystal Enterprise?
- What is the planned or preferred method of data connectivity, ODBC or native?
- Are any existing Crystal Reports connected to the target datasources?

  It's also important to consider the datasource connectivity methods provided with Crystal Enterprise. They might or might not match up with organizational requirements. Native drivers provide for many datasources, but some datasources can be connected to only through ODBC.

- Is a DBA available that is familiar with the required datasources?

- How many reports are required?

- Are enough human resources available with the skill set to develop all the initial reports required by end users?

   When setting out to develop reports, consider whether sufficient human resources are available to develop the reports to meet end-user requirements. If not, a third-party consulting organization might be leveraged here to complete report design. One of the biggest challenges organizations have when deploying Crystal Enterprise has nothing to do with Crystal Enterprise itself. It's with the datasource. Understanding the database schema and *where* the actual data is can be the most complex portion of the deployment.

- How frequently will reports be scheduled?

- How many total report instances will be maintained in the Crystal Enterprise system?

- What is an acceptable length of time for reports to process, from initial user request to completion?

   Also consider how many report objects Crystal Enterprise will store and manage. A report object in Crystal Enterprise doesn't hold any data. The report instances, reports that have been scheduled, actually contain the data. Chapter 10, "Administering and Configuring Crystal Enterprise," discusses this in more detail. Consider that each report instance occupies space in the File Repository Server. If an organization has 1,000 unique reports and allows 25 scheduled historical instances to be held in Crystal Enterprise for each report, that's 25,000 instances! If each instance held a large amount of data, the File Repository Server would clearly need an ample amount of disk space to manage those instances.

   Determining the target length of time for a report to run might not necessarily be achievable, but should be established nonetheless. If a report is based off of a database stored procedure that takes 12 hours to run in the database, it's unrealistic to blame Crystal Enterprise for the report taking a long time when, in fact, Crystal Enterprise has nothing to do with the long report runtime.

   Bear in mind that ODBC and native drivers affect report runtime; sometimes ODBC is faster and vice versa.

Environment

- What are the current software and hardware configurations on client workstations?

   Although Crystal Enterprise delivers information through a Web browser, there are many mechanisms by which this can be accomplished. For example, choosing to deploy the ActiveX viewer with Crystal Enterprise rather than the DHTML viewer can exclude Netscape viewers from using reports.

- Where will the database servers be physically located?

   The specialized roles of Crystal Enterprise servers, such as the Page and Job Servers, can be maximized through effective placement of physical servers. The Page and Job

PART

IV

CH

11

Servers should be placed close to the actual database servers to which reports connect. *Close* is a subjective word, in that it implies a substantial amount of bandwidth available between the Page and Job Server if reports contain a large amount of data. This reduces the impact to an organization's WAN traffic by isolating communication between the database and report processing servers.

- Will OLAP datasources be required?
- If so, which OLAP server types are required?

OLAP servers imply that another type of report object, Crystal Analysis Professional reports, will be stored in Crystal Enterprise. Although Crystal Reports connects to OLAP datasources, version 8.5 of Crystal Reports does not provide the same robust OLAP report and application creation that Crystal Analysis Professional does. Using Crystal Analysis Professional reports with Crystal Enterprise also implies that the Web Component Server will require OLAP server connectivity, because this is the hosting point for the Crystal Analysis Professional server side services.

If, for example, an organization were using Crystal Decisions' OLAP server, HOLOS, to stage data in OLAP cubes, Crystal Analysis Professional would be required, and the Web Component Server service would require some level of network access to the HOLOS server.

- What type of physical network is in place?

While most organizations use standard networking components and protocols, such as 10/100 Ethernet and TCP/IP, the speed of a physical network can affect where Crystal Enterprise server components are placed on the geographic network topology.

- What is the projected growth of the Crystal Enterprise system?
- What, if any, dedicated hardware resources are available for Crystal Enterprise?
- Will additional hardware be required?

Planning considerations must be made not only for an imminent Crystal Enterprise deployment, but how the system might look one year from now. Most deployments of Crystal Enterprise grow quickly because end users like to share the new source of information they have accessed.

- What are the security requirements for the reporting environment?

Determining a strategy for security can be a daunting one because many options are associated with Crystal Enterprise. Crystal Enterprise provides a native security model, where users, groups, and objects can be created and managed without the need for any third-party security components. Crystal Enterprise also supports Windows NT security integration, as well as support for a host of major directory servers through LDAP. As a final option, an organization could use the Crystal Enterprise SDK to link in or create a home-grown security model for Crystal Enterprise.

Crystal Enterprise also allows the creation of custom administration modules using the administrative portion of the SDK, which allows for certain users to be restricted to various portions of the product for system administration.

- What Crystal Enterprise licensing model is the best fit?

  Several licensing models are available for Crystal Enterprise, so understanding the current licensing program for Crystal Enterprise can save your organization some money when it comes time to purchase.

- On what operating system will Crystal Enterprise be deployed (Windows, Solaris or both)?

  Although Crystal Enterprise is available on both the Windows and Solaris platforms, many organizations will deploy a "mixed mode" environment, meaning some Crystal Enterprise components will be installed on different platforms. Windows was the first supported Crystal Enterprise platform, while Solaris was deployed in early 2002. The Solaris version has a few minor variations from the Windows version.

  These variations include support for Crystal Analysis Professional report objects, which are currently supported only on the Windows version of Crystal Enterprise. This means that if Crystal Reports are the only types of reports that will be used with Crystal Enterprise, then using the Solaris platform will prove to be a strong alternative to Crystal Enterprise. If Crystal Analysis Professional reports are to be deployed with Crystal Enterprise, then a Windows-based Web Component Server must be installed and linked to the Solaris Crystal Enterprise system.

- What bandwidth exists between LAN/WAN sites that will participate in the Crystal Enterprise deployment?

  As mentioned earlier, different server components of Crystal Enterprise benefit through close physical proximity to database servers. It's important to understand the various functions of the individual Crystal Enterprise servers and what data traffic is passed between them. Chapter 3, "Exploring the System Architecture," covers this in some detail. Understanding this will help the Crystal Enterprise system planner or administrator effectively place server components within a corporate LAN/WAN environment to maximize system performance.

- Will a firewall be incorporated in the solution?

  Crystal Enterprise was designed with a "DMZ" or firewall deployment in mind. This means that Crystal Enterprise can be effectively deployed in a multiple-firewall network environment with minimal impact to security, because all information and reports delivered by Crystal Enterprise can be DHTML. This means Port 80 delivery of data out to the Internet. For more information on deploying Crystal Enterprise in a complex network environment involving firewalls, refer to Chapter 12, "Deploying Crystal Enterprise in a Complex Network Environment."

- Will users require dial-up to access the Crystal Enterprise system?

  This might seem like a trivial consideration because Crystal Enterprise delivers reports that essentially amount to Web pages to an end user through a browser. If, for example, an organization chooses to deliver all reports from Crystal Enterprise as .PDF files rather than Crystal Reports as Web pages through the DHTML viewer, a significant feature is sacrificed: page on demand. Page on demand means that only one page of a

PART

IV

CH

11

report is delivered to an end user at a time. If a report contains 3MB worth of data, the user won't notice this because the server opens the report and delivers the requested page of the report to the viewer. This provides a responsive environment for end users, even in a dial-up session at less than 56Kbps.

- What is the current load and performance of existing Web servers that Crystal Enterprise will use?

  As pointed out in Chapter 3, Crystal Enterprise is not a Web server. It works with almost any existing Web server that is ISAPI-, NSAPI-, or CGI-compliant. Although Crystal Enterprise doesn't even place a significant load on a Web server, there is some load, nonetheless, especially if an organization decides to install Crystal Enterprise on the physical Web server itself. It's always preferable to have a dedicated server for Crystal Enterprise and leverage the Web connector for linking to an existing Web server.

- What is the current skill set of system or network administrators that might support Crystal Enterprise?

Crystal Enterprise is a complex, enterprise reporting and information delivery product that involves several systems, from databases to operating systems and development platforms. Troubleshooting issues with Crystal Enterprise might not have anything to do with Crystal Enterprise at all. More often than not, issues with reports often lie with database access, operating system permissions, and the like. It's of paramount importance that system administrators understand the spectrum of these issues.

This list is by no means complete. It is meant to be a solid foundation from which to formulate an implementation plan. Ideally, the temptation to install any software until after this stage is complete can be resisted.

Each answer should lead a Crystal Enterprise deployment manager to create an action item for delivery before, during, and after the project. For example, the answer to the question "What is the projected growth of the Crystal Enterprise system?" might be "Company A currently derives about $100M in annual revenue and has 200 employees. During the next two years we hope to double in size." This can lead to the deduction that, although current hardware availability will allow for an initial implementation of the project without further hardware and software purchase or budgeting, scalability planning should be performed or at least considered for future growth.

It might be useful to build these questions into a questionnaire format, breaking the organization down into management, users, and IT department members. Submitting a questionnaire to the end-user community is an exceptional way to get buy-in from all project stakeholders.

DEVELOPING THE APPLICATION (CUSTOMIZING CRYSTAL ENTERPRISE)

Although Crystal Enterprise comes with several out-of-the box client applications such as ePortfolio, this doesn't exclude the customization of one of those applications or development of a completely custom solution from the ground up. The good news is if an organization is deploying ePortfolio without any customizations, this section can be skipped entirely.

The approach to the development of a Crystal Enterprise application can be very personal. Whatever the approach, it should follow these guidelines:

1. **Pick the proper project manager**—Someone must be in command. This is not necessarily going to be a promotion for someone into the lofty ranks of a management position; instead, the person in this role must have the authority, knowledge, and character to implement command and control. The size of the project determines how many members are part of the team, but their actions should be controlled and they must have someone to refer to for information and direction. If possible, the project manager should be able to focus on the application without having to double hat on other jobs.

2. **Plan, plan, plan**—There are many project planning tools on the market. A company will probably have its own standard. Whether planning is done on a piece of paper, on a spreadsheet, or in an application, it is another cornerstone of a successful project. No plan survives the first shot of battle, so it is important to keep in mind that this will be a work in progress. Without a plan, coordination is impossible, chaos prevails, and the project stands a good chance of going off track. A project plan should involve the following:

   - Tasks
   - Delivery timelines
   - Specification as to who is responsible for delivering those tasks
   - A definition of task weightings

3. **Build the project team**—The project team's skill set must be put together very carefully. If internal team members cannot be found, outsourcing should be considered as a very cost-effective way to improve chances for success. In most cases, consultants with proven track records using the technologies surrounding Crystal Enterprise increase the chance of the project's success.

4. **Keep an eye on the prize**—Begin with the end in mind. After the project has started, the project manager and team members must be sure that they understand what the end goal is.

5. **Control change**—Change is inevitable, and the longer a project goes on and the more complex it becomes, the more likely change will occur. Change is a good thing. Without change you would be back where Ug started his tusk movement improvement project. The important thing to remember is that change must be controlled. Team members need to be encouraged to share their ideas and think outside the box.

   However, a process must be in place to manage this and be sure that any new changes are implemented with the support and knowledge of the project team, management, and end users. Another result of ignoring change management is the bane of any project, *scope creep*. Scope creep occurs when a project's deliverables, functionality, or look and feel extend past the project plan and definition. Scope creep can blow budgets away, extend project timelines by weeks, and can lead to bad morale on the project team.

One good example might be a specification to customize the look and feel of the DHTML viewer. A corporate logo is to be applied to the background of the viewer. After the addition of the logo, the end users ask whether each individual icon image in the viewer can be changed to match other images the company has, such as product images. Although this might seem trivial and seems to add little value to the overall solution, it could set the deployment timeline back at least half a day.

Table 11.1 is an example of a change control matrix.

TABLE 11.1 CHANGE CONTROL MATRIX

Change Ref.	Description	Requested By:	Assigned To:	Completed On:	Released To Test On:	Tested By:	Released To Live On:
1	Provide top 10 customer of user entry screen	10/10/01	John Doe	10/9/01	10/15/01	Test Team 1	10/22/01 parameter

6. **Control risk**—Risk mitigation is another cornerstone of success. The key to this mitigation is the ability to spot risk before it happens and plan ahead to be sure it does not happen. A useful way of doing this is to use the simple matrix shown in Table 11.2.

TABLE 11.2 RISK CONTROL MATRIX

Top Ten	Risk	Chances of It Happening (1–5)	Damage to Project If It Does Happen (1–5)	Risk Multiple	What to Do About It
1	Server hardware takes four weeks from order	4	5	20	Be sure server sizing is completed by week 2 and pass to procurement by week 3

7. **Get end user buy off ASAP**—User acceptance is the make or break point of a project. If they do not like what they are given to use on a daily basis, the project will not succeed. It will be relegated to the recycle bin very quickly. Involve users whenever possible from requirements gathering and development and training. Also give users the capability to provide feedback after the application is deployed.

8. **Set up environments**—Development of your application will be iterative and should go through a process to ensure that users get what they asked for. The standard formats for application development environments are

- **Sandbox (sometimes used)**—Initial proof of concept testing and development.

- **Development**—Phased development and testing. Strictly controlled, versioned environment.

- **Test**—Beta testing only. No development should occur here. Any faults and bugs should be referred back to the development team and tested again in development.

- **Production**—Application in everyday use.

9. **Documentation**—The application development process must be documented at all stages to ensure that if it needs improvement, if key project members leave, or if bugs need to be identified, people are not hunting around for the answers, wasting time unnecessarily. This documentation should be controlled by the project manager, and can also be used by training departments for the education of users and administrators.

COMPLETING USER ACCEPTANCE TESTING AND DEPLOYMENT

This phase should deliver the 99.9% finished application to a defined user base. End users should take the Crystal Enterprise application front end and follow a testing script that is given to them at the beginning of the phase. Users then should document and return their findings to the project team, and any last-minute changes will be made to the code.

This process could go through as many iterations as it takes for the users to finally put a check in the box that says, "We are satisfied." As mentioned previously, user acceptance ensures a successful project.

When the users are happy, the application can be deployed in a production environment.

SUPPORT AND MAINTENANCE

After the application is in production it is important that users understand who to call for support. This can be achieved through access to defined members of the project team, an organization's internal support desk, or an outsourced tech support organization. The Crystal Enterprise application manager should keep a log of issues, bugs, and any user feedback so that, where relevant, this information can implemented in the current application and any future releases.

UNDERSTANDING ORGANIZATIONAL REPORTING REQUIREMENTS

Designing reports is one of the initial steps in designing a Crystal Enterprise system, and easily is the most obvious consideration. An equally important consideration, and one that is most often left until much later in the implementation process, is how and when the reports will be run. Answering some of the questions asked earlier in the chapter will pay off when reports are actually published to Crystal Enterprise. Additional related questions include the following:

- Will reports be run on-demand or scheduled?
- Will reports be batch scheduled by an administrator while end users can only view these scheduled instances?
- Will end users be allowed to freely schedule their own reports?

Such questions are examples of key planning considerations that must be considered in conjunction with a report's design. Primarily, this needs to be analyzed from a business perspective. For example, perhaps end users need to run reports with impunity because the data is constantly changing and they always need an up-to-date view of the data. However, this perspective then must be tempered by a technological "sanity check" to determine whether such requirements are technologically feasible. For example, does it really make sense to run a 3,000-page report dynamically? Can parameters be added to the report so that less data is brought back to reduce the resultset of the database query?

The benefits of different reporting approaches will be explored through the next few sections of the chapter.

SCHEDULED REPORTING

As alluded to previously, Crystal Enterprise allows two modes of report execution: on-demand and scheduled. In the scheduled reporting case, a report template is scheduled to run either right now or at a future point in time and/or possibly on a recurring basis. When it is time for the report to run, the report template is accessed by the Crystal Report Job Server, the report is processed against the reporting database, and then the report is saved with data under a different file. This report with saved data is commonly referred to as a *report instance*. This instance is a snapshot of the data in a moment of time. End users can then view an instance to see the report's data from when it was run.

The advantages of scheduling reports and creating instances are numerous. The most important advantage of report instances is that when a user views an instance, the report loads almost instantaneously in the report viewer because the report does not need to execute the database query. In addition, because instances are a snapshot of data in time, you can leverage them as historical reports. For example, when reporting against a transactional information system, the database often contains volatile data. Consequently, running the report with the exact same parameters on different days might return different data because the database contains fewer records due to deletion and so on.

DETERMINING SCHEDULING PERMISSIONS AND REPORT RUNTIMES

If scheduled reports are the preferred method of reporting in Crystal Enterprise, it must be determined who will be allowed to schedule reports and when those reports can actually be scheduled. In a tightly controlled environment, either a system administrator individually schedules reports singly or on a recurring basis (for example, weekly, monthly). End users are not allowed to run reports; they can only view instances. Thus, by having a central scheduling authority, you can govern what and when database queries will be executed from your reporting application.

Additionally in this scenario, if scheduling is completed with regards to end-user viewing use, hardware use can be minimized. For example, if it is known that end users view reports only during the day, reports could be batch scheduled to run only at night or on the weekend. This means that report execution and report viewing are mutually exclusive, which they are. Report execution is processor-intensive and primarily the responsibility of the Crystal Enterprise Job Server component. Report viewing can be processor-intensive and a major responsibility of the Crystal Enterprise Page Server component.

In this scenario, common hardware can be shared between the Job and Page Servers because their functions will be used mutually exclusively. Otherwise, if report execution and report viewing occur at the same time, and the Job and Page Servers are on the same shared hardware, they might contend with one another for CPU resources. As a result, because the Page Server plays a key part in report viewing, report viewing responsiveness might be negatively affected during this period.

Although administrator-controlled scheduling makes for a tightly regulated system, it can be constrained by its potential inflexibility. For example, if the report has parameters, these parameters must be determined by the administrator. Thus, report instances might contain too much data or too little data for end users. In addition, if the database is updated and a user wants to see the latest data, because they cannot run the report manually they will have to wait until the next scheduled runtime. As a result, timely access to data can be an issue.

If these issues of data scope and timeliness of data can be acceptable or managed, controlled scheduling is an excellent solution for organizations with tight server access or hardware restrictions. For example, some data warehouses are updated at fixed intervals (weekly, for example), so the administrator can schedule the reports to run after the update process is complete. Thus, in this case, if data scope is also not an issue, it doesn't make much sense to allow end users to run reports because the data is unchanged between database update periods.

PART

IV

CH

11

> **Note**
>
> *Data scope* is the specific range or breadth of the data. For example, some reports are useful only if the user provides parameters. If you're checking frequent flyer points you're only interested in data related to you. Thus, a prescheduled report with all data for all customers in this case would not be relevant to you because you're only concerned with your personal data.

On the other end of the spectrum is the scenario where end users are allowed to schedule reports on their own, whenever they want. This allows for maximum flexibility for the end users because they can run reports at their leisure with the parameters they choose. However, if the parameters are unchecked, poor parameter selection (for example, due to user inexperience) can cause rogue database queries that tie up the DBMS if they become unnecessarily large or complex. This can lead to the scheduling queue backing up as other jobs waiting to execute are idling for a free spot on the Job Servers. If the Job Servers are configured to run too many concurrent jobs, this can overrun the DBMS with too many simultaneous queries. Thus, the Job Servers should be scaled back so that the number of concurrent jobs allowed is small enough that DBMS access is appropriately managed. If the Page Server and Job Server are on the same shared hardware, the issue might arise where these processes contend for server resources (CPU time, memory, file system, network bandwidth, and so on).

ON-DEMAND REPORTING

The second mode with which reports can be executed is called *on-demand* reporting. When used correctly, this can be a very powerful function in a Crystal Enterprise deployment. By simply writing a Web page that calls a URL, a parameterized report execution and report viewing request can be merged into one single step. The ease of Web development required to use this feature has caused numerous Web developers to abuse on-demand reports. More often than not, Web developers use on-demand reporting in a situation that is more suited for scheduled reporting. Thus, on-demand reporting is probably the most misused feature of Crystal Enterprise.

Still, in the right situation and when used correctly, on-demand reporting can be a very useful feature. This naturally begs the question, "What is the right situation in which on-demand reporting should be used?" The answer is quite simple—apply the eight-second rule as a guideline: "Users have eight seconds worth of patience while waiting for a Web page to load." To use this measurement, run the report in the Crystal Report designer and determine how long the report takes to execute. If it takes fewer than eight seconds, that report will be a good candidate for on-demand reporting in Crystal Enterprise.

Another consideration with on-demand reporting is whether the database driver and database client are *thread safe* (meaning that multiple threads can access the driver at the same time without unwanted interaction). If these components are not thread safe, database queries from the Page Servers will be serialized. Using the ODBC database drivers that ship with Crystal Enterprise will ensure this concurrency because they are thread safe and thoroughly tested.

COMPARING SCHEDULED VERSUS ON-DEMAND REPORTING

Even if reports are ideal candidates for on-demand reporting, scheduling reports still offers additional benefits. For example, scheduled reporting helps set the right expectations and context for a report. When end users schedule a report, even if it is scheduled to run right now, they will expect the report to take some time to process. Thus, they can better tolerate delays. For example, ePortfolio could easily be customized to display the amount of time it took the last report instance to complete, from schedule to finish. Users who are utilizing on-demand reporting typically don't understand that doing so actually requires the database query to execute. They expect the report to come up in the viewer instantly and are less tolerant of delays and might become frustrated as the only feedback they get is the spinning Web browser logo.

MANAGED VERSUS UNMANAGED REPORTING

Although this topic was explored in some detail in Chapter 7, "Publishing Content with Crystal Enterprise," it warrants discussion here as well. Crystal Enterprise supports two modes for hosting reports, *managed* and *unmanaged*. Crystal Enterprise can simultaneously support both modes of hosting. Managed reports are reports that are published to the Crystal Enterprise environment. This means that once a report template is added into Crystal Enterprise, access to the template is entirely controlled by Crystal Enterprise (as per Crystal Enterprise's security model). Unmanaged reports are simply report templates or reports with saved data placed in the virtual Web share of a Web server.

Unmanaged reports are accessed by a URL to the file (for example, `http://webserver/app/myreport.rpt`). If the report contains saved data, the report is simply presented in the browser. If the report contains no saved data, the report is processed on-demand against the database and then presented in the browser. As with managed reports, with unmanaged reports additional processing information can be specified using a URL line such as report parameters, viewer type, selection formula, database credentials, and so on.

Managed reports are the traditional method for hosting reports. The full potential of Crystal Enterprise is leveraged with managed reports. This provides the capabilities such as report scheduling, recurring schedules, report security, logical report organization, file management, default database credentials, default parameters, default selection formulas, and instance retention.

When designing a Web reporting application, consider whether managed or unmanaged reporting or a combination of the two will be used. Although unmanaged reporting is very simple to implement it is limited in security and flexibility. This might be better suited for smaller workgroup applications that have very simple and straightforward reporting requirements. Unmanaged reporting is also excellent for long-term hosting of reports with static saved data. For example, a public annual report that needs to be published to the Web indefinitely would make a great candidate for unmanaged reporting. In most instances though, managed reporting is the preferred route.

DETERMINING DATA ACCESS CONTROL METHODS

If the Crystal Enterprise reporting system is designed so that users can schedule reports or run reports on demand, a decision must be made about how access to the database is controlled. That is, what database user account is used to access the reporting database? With some implementations, individual users are given distinct database accounts that they would provide before running the report. In other implementations, a generic data reader account is used as the default database login for all reports. Having individual users with separate database accounts allows for better auditing from a DBMS perspective. You can easily track who is running what type of queries against your database. However, this comes with some costs.

First, more database administration is required because these user accounts must be managed. Second, users will potentially have to remember an additional set of usernames and passwords. Additionally, by providing individual users with database credentials, they do not necessarily need to use Crystal Enterprise to access the database. They could freely use any database access tool to communicate directly with the DBMS.

By using a generic database reader account, the shortcomings of individual accounts are eliminated. Database administration is simpler because only one account must be managed. The password for this account is abstracted from the end user, so they won't be able to use any other database tool to access the DBMS directly.

However, this data access model might not be able to leverage databases that have data level security invoked for users. For example, some databases have data-level security in that different users see different data from the same query based on who they are. This security often is based on which credentials were used to access the database. If an organization were using a generic database account for Crystal Enterprise, such a security model would not integrate well. As part of designing the Crystal Enterprise system, this determination of data access authentication should be agreed upon by all project stakeholders.

Note

> The deciding factor for using a generic database user account or individual user accounts typically is the data access level to be enforced.

PLANNING A CRYSTAL ENTERPRISE ARCHITECTURE

Crystal Enterprise is a system that can scale up on a single server by adding processors and memory. In addition, adding servers can scale Crystal Enterprise out. Scaling Crystal Enterprise provides benefits such as greater performance, high availability, fault tolerance, and redundancy. However, determining how to scale a system can be a bit of a challenge. Although there are no hard and fast rules in determining scaling, there are a few best practices and rules of thumb that can be followed. Ultimately, scaling will be determined by usage profile and behavior of the Crystal Enterprise system. One key point is for system administrators to not be fearful of experimenting and trying different configurations to achieve better performance. Different architectures have different benefits and considerations to judge. The idea is to choose those that have the best fit for the given Crystal Enterprise implementation.

DETERMINING PROCESSING REQUIREMENTS

The three key Crystal Enterprise server components that require some considerable thought in sizing are the Cache Server, Page Server, and Job Server. This section focuses on how many instances of these services, processors, and physical servers are required and what the settings for these system services should be. The first step in sizing a Crystal Enterprise environment is to answer a few important questions:

- How often will there be on-demand report and report instances viewing?
- When will scheduled reports be processed?
- Is there a report processing time window?
- Is redundancy required?

One key metric also needs to be determined: What is the number of concurrent users of Crystal Enterprise?

If you have an overall Web application into which Crystal Enterprise will integrate, it is important to remain concerned only with the number of concurrent users when sizing Crystal Enterprise. A concurrent user of Crystal Enterprise can be described as someone who is interacting with Crystal Enterprise. This includes logging into Crystal Enterprise, processing CSP pages, scheduling reports, querying the system, or viewing reports. If the number of concurrent users is unknown but the size of your total user base is known, a rule of thumb to estimate what the number of concurrent users might be is about 10% to 20% of the total application user base. For example, if your application has 1,000 total users, you can estimate the number of concurrent users for Crystal Enterprise to be between 100 and 200.

When reports are processed on-demand or report instances are viewed, a complex chain of processes takes place involving the Web browser, Web server, Web connector, WCS, Cache Server, and Page Server. When sizing the system for on-demand reporting and viewing, the last two components in the process are the most critical for consideration.

SIZING THE CACHE SERVER   The Cache Server is responsible for storing and forwarding epf cache pages created by the Page Servers. The Page Servers are primarily responsible for generating epf cache pages either from reports that are opened from report instances or opened and processed from report templates.

Consider one individual viewing request or on-demand reporting request to be equivalent to one thread being used by the Cache Server and one thread being used by the Page Server. This is an oversimplification of the viewing process but is a good starting point when making considerations and conservative considerations for sizing. Thus, if 200 concurrent users will be running on-demand reports or viewing report instances, then ideally 200 Cache Server threads and 200 Page Server threads should be available. Typically, 100 cache server threads per processor are recommended with up to a maximum of 400 threads per physical cache server service. Thus, on a quad processor server, a single cache server service could be set to 400 threads whereas with an eight-way server two cache server services would need to be installed, each set to 400 threads for a total thread count of 800 threads.

It is important to note that Crystal Enterprise allows a physical server to host multiple copies of the same logical server service for the same or different Crystal Enterprise system environments. This further increases the scalability of Crystal Enterprise. In the preceding example with the eight-way server, two cache server services were configured.

SIZING THE PAGE SERVER Whether viewing reports or running reports on-demand, Page Servers can optimally manage 50 threads per Page Server service per processor, so if a quad processor is available for the Page Server, a maximum of four Page Server services with 50 threads each for a total of 200 threads should be used. Also, keep the total number of cache server threads exactly equal to the total number of Page Server threads in the entire system for optimal performance.

Consider the following example.

A particular environment has a requirement for 300 concurrent users all running on-demand reports with some redundancy also built into the architecture. Because this is more than a single cache server can optimally handle, two cache server services will be needed. A good choice would be to have two cache server services set to 150 threads each. Because this requires two processors per service, at least a server with four processors will be needed. However, because a level of fault tolerance was required, the cache server services will be split over two dual processor servers. Therefore, the final architecture for the cache servers would have two dual processor servers each with a cache server service set to 150 threads each.

For the Page Servers, six Page Server services (300 threads/50 threads) will be required. This would also require six processors. Although you could use a single eight-way server to handle the Page Servers because you would like some fault tolerance, two quad processor servers will be used instead. Therefore, the final architecture for the Page Servers would be two quad processor servers with three Page Server services each set to 50 threads per service.

SIZING THE JOB SERVER If scheduled reporting is part of the Crystal Enterprise deployment, it will be necessary to determine how many Job Servers will be required to support the total Crystal Enterprise end user base.

Optimally, a Job Server service can process roughly five concurrent jobs per CPU. Given a quad processor server, no more than four Job Server services should be installed on a single server. Having too many Job Servers in the Crystal Enterprise system can overwhelm the DBMS as too many jobs try to process concurrently. Alternatively, having too few Job Servers could mean that users have to wait a long time as their job gets queued up waiting for other jobs to complete processing. If the Crystal Enterprise environment has a fixed reporting time window in which all reports can only be processed, the following formulas can be used as a rough guide to determine how many servers to dedicate as Job Servers:

Total Processing Time required = Average Process Time (per job) * number of jobs

Total Time to Process (per processor) = Total Processing Time Required / Number of Concurrent Jobs (per Job Server service)

Number of Job Servers Required = Total Time to Process / Time Window for Processing.

Here's an example applying these formulas:

A company needs to run 58 reports where each report takes on average 20 minutes to run. Because they will be reporting off a production database, they will be given a time window of only one hour nightly. How many Job Servers and processors will they need?

Total Processing Time required = 20 minutes/report * 58 reports = 1,160 minutes

Total Time to Process (per processor) = 1,160 minutes/5 concurrent jobs/Job Server service = 232 minutes

Number of Job Servers Required = 230 minutes/60 minutes = 3.87 Job Server services

Therefore, for Crystal Enterprise to process 58 20-minute reports in one hour, four Job Server services set to process five concurrent jobs each on four processors would be required.

Given the fact that four processors are required for the Job Server services, a single quad processor server, two dual processor servers, or four single processor servers could be used with the Crystal Enterprise system.

The option to use a single server does not provide any logical Job Server redundancy; that is, if a report processing job fails on one server it isn't picked up by another. Only physical hardware "high availability" is achieved. The four-server implementation also requires added administration and maintenance. In this situation, it would be advisable to use two dual processor servers because it provides a good balance between a level of physical fault tolerance, less resource contention/conflicts, and ease of maintainability. As mentioned before, if report processing of scheduled reports happens during office hours, it is advantageous if the Job Server services reside on dedicated physical servers. If report processing of scheduled reports occur off-hours, the Job Server services can potentially reside on the same physical servers as the Page Server services, given that the number of processors required is also satisfied.

Sample Crystal Enterprise Deployment Scenarios

This section describes several different classes of Crystal Enterprise configurations. The first is a centralized Crystal Enterprise architecture followed by a distributed architecture and then a fault-tolerant architecture.

A Centralized, Single-Server Deployment

A centralized architecture (see Figure 11.1) has all Crystal Enterprise system components installed on the same server. This is the simplest configuration and the easiest to manage because the entire system is self-contained.

This also is the easiest configuration to maintain; for example, it takes the guesswork out of performing backups because Web pages, report templates, and the system database all reside on this server. This is advantageous for smaller implementations and yet it still allows for outward scalability by adding additional servers when and if they are required. This setup is perfect for workgroup applications, small projects, or Web applications that have modest and light report processing and viewing needs. Such a configuration can be very CPU-intensive because all the Crystal Enterprise components, as well as the DBMS and Web server, are running concurrently.

Figure 11.1
Centralized architecture: single-server configuration.

Machine1:
Crystal APS (Automated Process Scheduler)
Crystal Web Component Server
Crystal Cache Server
Crystal Page Server
Crystal Report Job Server
Crystal Input File Repository
Crystal Output File Repository
Crystal Web Connector
Web Server (i.e. IIS)
CInfo System Database (i.e. SQL Server DBMS)

A system administrator must be proactive in identifying potential system bottlenecks and thus scale those components out onto other separate servers accordingly. Also, this configuration offers little in terms of fault tolerance because all components are centralized.

DISTRIBUTED COMPUTING: TWO-SERVER IMPLEMENTATION

The benefits of distributing components over multiple servers are numerous. By separating Crystal Enterprise components onto separate physical servers, contention for resources that would normally have to be shared in a single server configuration is reduced. For example, components on the same server usually contend with CPU time, context switching, memory substructure, and the disk subsystem sharing.

Admittedly, there are considerations involved with such a configuration. Although separate physical servers help resolve resource conflicts, components now must inter-communicate across the local area network. This adds network traffic and introduces network latency to the whole equation. Although this probably is a negligible issue when compared to the benefits, it is worthwhile to point out that there is always a trade-off. Additionally, adding more servers to the Crystal Enterprise architecture increases server operation and maintenance costs.

This two-server configuration (see Figure 11.2) is the most commonly used deployment by most organizations. The main feature of this configuration is the separation of the "middle tier" from the report processing tier. By separating these processes, user interaction processes have the highest priority and are not affected by CPU contention issues. Server 1 is responsible for user interaction such as logging in and out of the system, processing of Web scripts, and presentation of Web pages.

Figure 11.2
Distributed computing: two-server configuration.

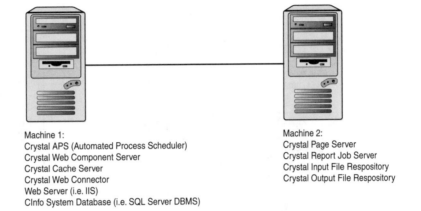

Machine 1:
Crystal APS (Automated Process Scheduler)
Crystal Web Component Server
Crystal Cache Server
Crystal Web Connector
Web Server (i.e. IIS)
CInfo System Database (i.e. SQL Server DBMS)

Machine 2:
Crystal Page Server
Crystal Report Job Server
Crystal Input File Respository
Crystal Output File Respository

Server 2 is tasked mainly with report processing duties. Report processing is a highly CPU-intensive activity. It's advisable to assign the best performing hardware for this server. As an example, most companies use a dual-processor server for Server 1 and have a quad-processor server for Server 2. With the distribution of components over two servers rather than just a single server, some fault tolerance is gained. The proverbial putting-all-your-eggs-in-one-basket scenario is avoided. If Server 2 ever becomes unavailable, Server 1 is still able to serve up Web pages, process scripts, log in users to the APS, serve APS queries, and display cached reports. End users just won't be able to process on-demand or scheduled reports or view noncached reports or answer file repository requests. However, if Server 1 becomes unavailable but Server 2 is still functioning, your entire system is effectively nonfunctioning.

In this simple example, Server 2 is processing on-demand reports, generating epf cache pages, and processing scheduled reports. Processing on-demand reports and cache page generation are also response time–sensitive tasks and should have high CPU-processor precedence. Thus, if these tasks are not mutually exclusive with the processing of scheduled jobs, it is advisable to separate Page Servers from Job Servers onto separate servers.

Notice that with this configuration, Server 1 houses both the Web server and the APS System Database. Often companies already have a Web server or APS supportable DBMS in place that they would like to leverage. In these cases, these Crystal Enterprise components can be offloaded from Server 1 (see Figure 11.3).

Note

The APS database, housed in an RDBMS, is commonly referred to as CInfo or the CInfo database. As mentioned in Chapter 3, the ASP database stores metadata about system objects, such as reports folders and user information. The default database name is CInfo.

Figure 11.3
Two-server configuration with offloaded system database and Web server.

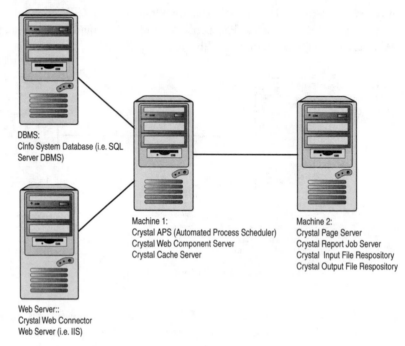

DBMS:
CInfo System Database (i.e. SQL Server DBMS)

Machine 1:
Crystal APS (Automated Process Scheduler)
Crystal Web Component Server
Crystal Cache Server

Machine 2:
Crystal Page Server
Crystal Report Job Server
Crystal Input File Respository
Crystal Output File Respository

Web Server::
Crystal Web Connector
Web Server (i.e. IIS)

Depending on hardware availability, this can have either a positive or negative effect on system performance (that is, network traffic, shared Web, and DBMS services). The APS database must be highly available to the APS. Thus, it is advisable not to put the APS database on the same DBMS as reporting databases (the databases that report access for end-user data). For those reasons it's also advisable not to place the APS database on the same server that houses either the Page or Job Servers because of their CPU-intensive activities. The Crystal Enterprise system administrator must examine issues such as leveraging of existing services, performance, and maintainability to determine which route to go.

A CRYSTAL ENTERPRISE DISTRIBUTED ARCHITECTURE: MULTIPLE REPORT PROCESSING SERVERS

Future growth commonly comes from more concurrent users and thus more report processing and viewing. In most Crystal Enterprise environments the report processing servers need to be "extended" first (see Figure 11.4). If this is the case, additional Page or Job Servers can be added to the architecture without impact or major change to the rest of the system. At the time of new report processing server addition, consider moving the File Repository Servers onto Server 1 so that all the report processing servers have equal access to the FRS service.

Figure 11.4
Configuration with multiple report processing servers.

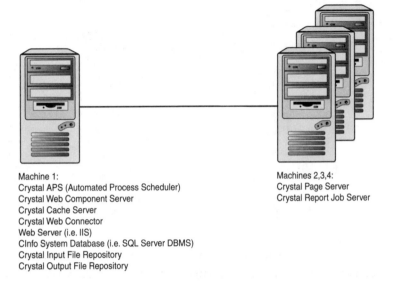

Machine 1:
Crystal APS (Automated Process Scheduler)
Crystal Web Component Server
Crystal Cache Server
Crystal Web Connector
Web Server (i.e. IIS)
CInfo System Database (i.e. SQL Server DBMS)
Crystal Input File Repository
Crystal Output File Repository

Machines 2,3,4:
Crystal Page Server
Crystal Report Job Server

Note

Page and Job Servers must access the Input File Repository to find the report template to process. The Job Server must access the Output File Repository to write out the completed processed reports.

When duplicating Crystal Enterprise components onto different physical servers, it is ideal if those servers have reasonable server affinity. That is, it is suggested that the servers with duplicated components should have similar hardware and run the same applications and services as their other counterparts. In addition, duplicated Crystal Enterprise components should all have the same configuration settings (number of threads, timeouts, and so on) to help ensure the correctness of the Crystal Enterprise load balancing algorithms.

The fault-tolerant configuration (see Figure 11.5) is for organizations that are looking for a highly available, reliable, and robust system architecture. This configuration can tolerate a higher level of server failures than previous configurations, thus eliminating single points of failure.

The key design feature of a fault-tolerant Crystal Enterprise architecture is that the APS, WCS, Cache Server, Page Server, and Job Server each have a minimum of two separate instances running each instance on a separate physical server. However, the price paid for this redundancy is the increase in number of servers and maintenance of those servers. A combination of either Server 2 or 3 and either Server 4 or 5 can fail at any time, and yet your overall system can still be functioning. Server 1 represents a logical server that houses the CInfo System Database and the File Repository Servers. The APS System Database is a shared resource between all APSs in a Crystal Enterprise system. The File Repository Servers (input and output) are also a shared service between other components in the system (Page and Job Servers). Both of these services must be made highly available.

Figure 11.5
Fault-tolerant
configuration.

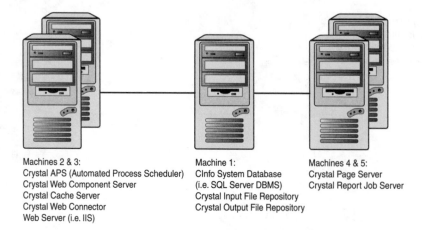

Machines 2 & 3:
Crystal APS (Automated Process Scheduler)
Crystal Web Component Server
Crystal Cache Server
Crystal Web Connector
Web Server (i.e. IIS)

Machine 1:
CInfo System Database
(i.e. SQL Server DBMS)
Crystal Input File Repository
Crystal Output File Repository

Machines 4 & 5:
Crystal Page Server
Crystal Report Job Server

The APS System Database can be made fault-tolerant depending on the functionality that the selected DBMS offers. For example, for Microsoft SQL Server, Microsoft Clustering services can be used on two servers for fail over. For the File Repository Servers, the input and output directories of their respective services can be actively mirrored onto another server. The File Repository Servers would also be installed onto this second server.

Note that this implementation also has redundancy at the Web server level; however, some method of redirecting Web requests to either Web server is required. This can be accomplished through the use of any Web farm load balancing mechanism (such as Hardware load balancer, DNS round robining, or Microsoft Network Load Balancing [NLB]).

A CRYSTAL ENTERPRISE DISTRIBUTED ARCHITECTURE: MULTIPLE WEB COMPONENT SERVERS

In the preceding sample configurations the Web Servers, Crystal Enterprise Web Connectors, and the Web Component Servers have one-to-one relationships.

Note

When this section refers to a "Web Server," this is not a Crystal Enterprise component. You might recall from Chapter 3 that the Web Connector is a component installed on a Web Server, be it Microsoft IIS, Netscape iPlanet, or otherwise, that redirects any Crystal Enterprise–related request to the Web component server for processing. The returned result to the Web server is essentially a Web page, which in turn is presented to the requesting end user.

However, Crystal Enterprise is not limited to such a configuration; it can support one-to-many, many-to-one, and many-to-many configurations between these server components. These additional configurations can help fine-tune scaling of a Crystal Enterprise system. As discussed in previous chapters, the Web Server/Web Connector in a Crystal Enterprise system is responsible strictly for serving up Web presentation. The Web component server is responsible for processing end-user requests via CSP script pages and serving up report pages for viewing. With traditional ASP, the presentation layer and script-processing layer are combined into IIS. However, by using CSP scripting, you can take advantage of this separation.

The following figures provide some examples of the possible configurations of the Web Server, Web Connector, and Web Component Server. Figure 11.6 scaled out the Web Component Servers because the Web application does heavy CSP script processing.

Figure 11.6
One Web Server with many Web Component Servers.

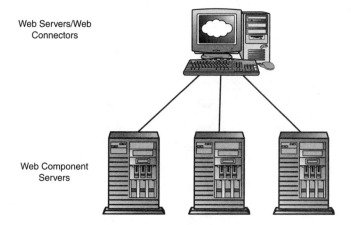

Web Servers/Web Connectors

Web Component Servers

Figure 11.7 is for an environment that has a very high user concurrency. Thus, a Web farm is required. However, most of the load is specific to HTML presentation versus CSP script processing.

Figure 11.8 has scaled both the Web Servers and the Web Component Servers as this environment requires heavy user concurrency and heavy script processing and report viewing.

Figure 11.7
A Web farm with a
single Web
Component Server.

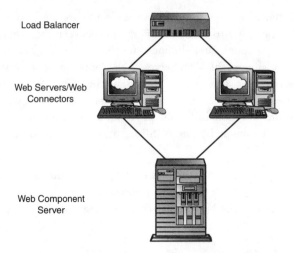

Figure 11.8
Many Web server
with many Web
Component Servers.

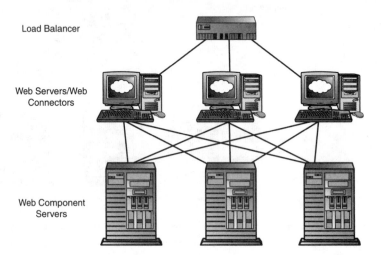

TROUBLESHOOTING

As with any form of troubleshooting, the main goals are first to be able to replicate the problem and second to be able to isolate the issue. Sometimes this sounds easier than it really is. However, keeping this philosophy in mind when troubleshooting will be very helpful. Because this chapter has dealt almost exclusively with process, methodology, and deployment scenarios, this troubleshooting section discusses solid troubleshooting techniques rather than specific troubleshooting issues.

Crystal Enterprise systems in a production environment can be quite complex. System components may be duplicated and spread across various servers, and these servers also can span firewalls and DMZs. Throw into the mix a custom-developed Crystal Enterprise Web application and it becomes obvious that the domain of the problem can initially appear quite large. By removing this "noise" from a Crystal Enterprise implementation, most issues can be condensed into a key issue. Many companies have separate development, QA, or test environments. If the problem also exhibits itself in these environments it would make troubleshooting much easier than having to tinker with a production system.

After reproducing the problem, preferably in a test environment, it is time to move on to problem isolation where the goal is to simplify the program. For example, if issues arise when viewing a report instance through a Web application, try to remove the Web application from the equation by verifying that the report instance can be viewed in ePortfolio or through the Crystal Management Console (CMC). Another tip in simplifying a problem is to remove duplicate services from Crystal Enterprise. For example, ensure that during troubleshooting only one APS, WCS, Cache, Page, and Job Server service are running.

When troubleshooting Crystal Enterprise one of the most valuable tools is to have Crystal Reports Designer installed onto the servers where the Page and Job Servers reside. Often, when a scheduled report fails in Crystal Enterprise, the properties of the instance display the infamous statement: `Cannot open SQL Server`. This is a very generic statement that can mean a multitude of error conditions.

With Crystal Reports installed on the Page and Job Servers, the report can be run interactively in Crystal Reports so a more meaningful error message can be supplied. If a report doesn't run correctly in Crystal Reports on the physical Job Server, there is certainly no chance of successfully scheduling the report in Crystal Enterprise.

An example of this is when a user designs and tests a report successfully on their local workstation and then publishes the report to their Crystal Enterprise system. They then test the published report by scheduling it, which in turn returns the `Cannot open SQL Server` message. If the system administrator were then to use Crystal Reports to open the published report from the Job Server he would quickly realize the error. In this case, the user's workstation was using an ODBC DSN that was different from that on the Job Server.

SUMMARY

Crystal Enterprise provides a company with a competitive advantage as a result of its Web-based, scalable, information delivery infrastructure. This highly customizable tool set means that careful planning and preparation must be undertaken to ensure that full use is made of every relevant facet and that the end user receives an application that meets and beats his requirements and expectations.

This chapter has outlined the steps that the person responsible for the deployment of Crystal Enterprise should go through to ensure success. From initial understanding, definition, and scoping surrounding the business problem through planning and delivery of the finished application, the steps have been defined to help you deploy Crystal Enterprise to your user community.

CHAPTER **12**

DEPLOYING CRYSTAL ENTERPRISE IN A COMPLEX NETWORK ENVIRONMENT

In this chapter

A key design consideration for Crystal Enterprise was for the delivery of information to be deployed as part of any Web-based delivery platform—intranet, extranet, or Internet. Increasingly, organizations are looking to standardize the access to corporate information within a Web-based infrastructure. Not only does this provide for a consistent development and integration platform but it also enables organizations to jump onto the information highway. Companies are now able to support a close relationship with their external constituents—be they customers or suppliers—through the delivery of information over the Web. Furthermore, considerable economies of scale can be realized by using the same architecture to deliver information internally.

Often, the means by which information can be rendered is through the display of a Crystal Report (or multiple Crystal Reports) as an integral part of a Web page executing on a client browser. Such integration with a company's Web-based information delivery system requires that the vehicle for providing that information (for example, a Crystal Report managed by Crystal Enterprise and integrated completely into a Web page) can also conform to the company's security requirements. In a nutshell, no matter what firewall standards a company chooses to adopt, Crystal Enterprise not only must be able to be configured within these standards, it also must do so without compromising the integrity (or performance) of information management and delivery.

This chapter concentrates on how the architecture of Crystal Enterprise allows for complete integration into complex networks with firewall systems to provide information delivery across intranets and the Internet without compromising network security. More often than not, providing examples of how Crystal Enterprise works with complex firewall scenarios produces enough information to relate this chapter to other network deployment scenarios.

To understand how Crystal Enterprise works in a complex network environment, a review of several server and system processes is provided in this chapter, extending discussions put forth from earlier chapters in this book.

Essentially, this chapter concentrates on firewalls and illustrating how Crystal Enterprise can be deployed within the various firewall architectures commonly available. First, however, we will start by defining what a firewall is and looking at the technology involved in supporting them.

A *firewall* is a set of related programs, located at a network gateway server (that is, the point of entry into a network), that protect the resources of a private network from users of other networks. It restricts people to entering and leaving your network at a carefully controlled point. A firewall is put in place to protect a company's intranet from being improperly accessed through the Internet. Additionally, firewalls can be used to enforce security policies and to log Internet activity.

UNDERSTANDING NETWORK PROTOCOLS

To have a clear understanding of how firewalls operate (and how Crystal Enterprise is configured within a firewall), it is necessary to review the protocols used within the Internet.

INTERNET SERVICES

A standard number of Internet services work in conjunction with firewalls. These services are the primary reason for firewalls because companies want to control who and what goes over these services to their internal network.

HYPERTEXT TRANSFER PROTOCOL

HTTP is the primary application protocol that underlies the Web: It provides users access to the files that make up the Web. These files can be in many different formats (text, graphics, audio, video, and so on), but the format used to provide the links between files on the Web is HTML.

SIMPLE MAIL TRANSFER PROTOCOL

SMTP is the Internet standard protocol for sending and receiving electronic mail. The most common SMTP server on Windows NT is Microsoft Exchange. Although SMTP is used to exchange electronic mail between servers, users who are reading electronic mail that has already been delivered to a mail server do not use SMTP. When they transfer that mail from the server to their desktop they use another protocol, POP (Post Office Protocol).

FILE TRANSFER PROTOCOL

FTP is the Internet standard protocol for file transfers. Most Web browsers support FTP, as well as HTTP, and automatically use FTP to access locations with names that begin "FTP:," so many people use FTP without ever being aware of it. FTP was the initial transfer protocol used for the Internet before the advent of the World Wide Web.

REMOTE TERMINAL ACCESS

Remote terminal access is most commonly known as *Telnet*. Telnet is the standard for remote terminal access on the Internet, and enables you to provide remote text access for your users.

HOSTNAME/ADDRESS LOOKUP

A naming service translates between the names that people use and the numerical addresses that machines use. The primary name lookup system on the Internet is Domain Name System, which converts between hostnames and IP addresses.

TCP/IP

TCP/IP (Transmission Control Protocol/Internet Protocol) is the communications protocol used on the Internet. TCP/IP uses what is termed a *data packet* to transfer information over the Internet from one computer to another. Packets contain the data that your browser shows when it is surfing the Net. Each packet is small, so many packets are needed to transmit the data contained on one HTML page. As more and more people access the Net and transmit data, more and more packets are being transferred. This increases the need to make sure all the packets that arrive at your door (Web server) are really supposed to come in.

THE TCP/IP PROTOCOL STACK

The TCP/IP protocol stack, or packet, is constructed of the following components:

- Application layer (FTP, Telnet, HTTP)
- Transport layer (TCP or UDP)
- Internet layer (IP)
- Network Access layer (Ethernet, ATM)

Packets are constructed in such a way that layers for each protocol used for a particular connection are wrapped around the packets, like the layers of skin on an onion.

At the Application layer the packet consists simply of the data to be transferred, such as an HTML page. As it moves down the layers, trying to reach the wire (network cable) that it needs to go out on, each layer adds a header to the packet; this preserves the data from the previous level. These headers are then used to determine where the packet is going and to make sure it all gets there in one piece. When the data packet reaches its destination the process is reversed. In the end, therefore, all that TCP/IP is responsible for is specifying how data can make its way from one computer to another. These computers may reside on the same network or in completely different locations. As far as firewalls are concerned, the main thing to remember is that it is not so much about how the packet physically gets to its destination but what is in that packet and whether it is supposed to be there.

TCP/IP "RULES"

TCP/IP is ideally suited to being the standard protocol for the delivery of information through both external and internal network architectures for the following reasons:

- TCP/IP is packet-based. There are no set limits to the size of a given message as long messages are broken down into multiple (and linked) packets.
- TCP/IP provides for decentralized control. After you own the domain name/number (crystaldecisions.com) you can assign anything in front of it to expand your domain. (support.crystaldecisions.com is an expansion to route traffic specifically to technical support within the Crystal Decisions organization.)
- Communicating devices are peers; every computer on the network is a peer. Each device can take on the role of either requester or server in the flow of information across multiple computers.
- TCP/IP is routable and easy to transmit between networks. The same rules apply whether communicating through an external or internal network.
- TCP/IP is an open free standard. A most important consideration because this, combined with the reasons detailed above, has led to widespread adoption.

NETWORK PORTS

A typical server sets up services to listen on ports. A *port* is a "logical connection place" and specifically, using the Internet's protocol, TCP/IP, the way a client program specifies a particular server program on a computer in a network. Higher-level applications that use TCP/IP, such as the Web protocol HTTP, have ports with preassigned numbers. These are known as *well-known ports* that have been assigned by the Internet Assigned Numbers Authority (IANA). Other application processes are given port numbers dynamically for each connection. When a service starts (or is initialized), it is said to bind to its designated port number. Any client program that wants to use that service must issue its request to the designated port number.

Port numbers range from 0 to 65536. Ports 0 to 1024 are reserved for use by certain privileged services. For example, for the HTTP service, port 80 is defined as a default. When a client makes a request, the server will assign that request to a port above 1024. Two pieces of information need to be passed in the TCP/IP header: the originating address of the source request, and the target address of the destination computer. This establishes the connection points for message exchange. Notice (in reference to our discussion of TCP/IP and ports) how the message itself will conform to the TCP/IP protocol while the transport of that message across the Internet will be defined as the ports that denote the origin and destination of the message (and where it needs to return to as well).

UNDERSTANDING FIREWALL TYPES

Firewalls primarily function using at least one of three methods: packet filtering, Network Address Translation (NAT), and proxy services. Crystal Enterprise works with each of these firewall types. Packet filtering rejects TCP/IP packets from unauthorized hosts and rejects connection attempts to unauthorized services. NAT translates the IP address of internal hosts to hide them from outside monitoring—NAT is often referred to as "IP masquerading." Proxy services make high-level application connections on behalf of internal hosts to completely break the network layer connection between internal and external hosts. Let's look at these different types in more detail.

PACKET FILTERING

Packet filtering deletes packets before they are delivered to the destination computer. Packet filtering can delete packets based on the following:

- The address from which the data is coming
- The address to which the data is going
- The session and application ports being used to transfer the data
- The data contained by the packet

Typically, there are two types of packet filtering: statefull and stateless. *Statefull* packet filters remember the state of connections at the network and session layers by recording the established session information that passes through the filter gateway. The filter then uses that information to discriminate valid return packets from invalid connection attempts. *Stateless* packet filters do not retain information about connections in use; they make determinations packet-by-packet based only on the information contained within the packet.

NETWORK ADDRESS TRANSLATION

Network Address Translation (NAT) converts private IP addresses in a private network to globally unique public IP addresses for use on the Internet. Its main purpose is internal host hiding. It makes it appear that all traffic from your site comes from a single IP address. NAT hides internal IP addresses by converting all internal host addresses to the address of the firewall as packets are routed through the firewall. The firewall then retransmits the data payload of the internal host from its own address using a translation table to keep track of which sockets on the exterior interface equate to which sockets on the interior interface. This is also a simple proxy.

There are several NAT types:

■ **Static translation (port forwarding)**—This is when a specific internal network resource has a fixed translation that never changes. If you're running an email server inside a firewall, a static route can be established through the firewall for that service.

■ **Dynamic translation (automatic, hide mode, or IP masquerade)**—This is where a large group of internal clients share a small group of internal IP addresses for the purpose of expanding the internal network address space. Because a translation entry does not exist until an interior client establishes a connection out through a firewall, external computers have no method to address an internal host that is protected using a dynamically translated IP address.

■ **Load Balance Translation**—In this configuration, a single IP address and port is translated to a pool of identically configured servers—a single IP address serves a group of servers. This allows you to spread the load of one very popular Web site across several different servers by using the firewall to choose which internal server each external client should connect to on either a round-robin or balanced load basis. This is somewhat similar to dynamic translation in reverse—the firewall chooses which server each connection attempt should be directed to from among a pool of clones.

■ **Network Redundancy Translation**—Multiple Internet connections are attached to a single NAT firewall. The firewall chooses and uses each Internet connection based on load and availability. The firewall is connected to multiple ISPs through multiple interfaces and has a public masquerade address for each ISP. Each time an internal host makes a connection through the firewall, that firewall decides, on a least-loaded basis, on which network to establish the translated connection. In this way, the firewall is able to spread the internal client load across multiple networks.

PROXY SERVERS

Proxy servers were originally developed to cache Web pages that were frequently accessed. As the Web went supernova the proxies became less effective as caching mechanisms, but another asset of proxy servers became evident. Proxy servers can hide all the real users of a network behind a single machine, and they can filter URLs and drop suspicious or illegal content. The primary purpose of the majority of proxy servers is now serving as a firewall rather than Web caching.

Proxy servers regenerate high-level service requests on an external network for their clients on a private network. This effectively hides the identity and number of clients on the internal network from examination by an external network user.

Proxies work by listening for service requests from internal clients and then sending those requests on the external network as if the proxy server itself was the originating client. When the proxy server receives a response from the public server, it returns that response to the original client as if it were the originating public server. You can even use the proxy server to load balance similar to the NAT load balancing. As far as the user is concerned, talking to the proxy server is just like talking directly to the real server. As far as the real server is concerned, it's talking to a user on the host that is running the proxy server; it doesn't know that the user is really somewhere else.

The use of proxies does not require any special hardware, but something somewhere has to be certain that the proxy server gets the connection. This might be done on the client end by telling it to connect to the proxy server (Socks), or it might be done by intercepting the connection without the client's knowledge and redirecting it to the proxy server.

Socks is a protocol that a proxy server can use to accept requests from client users in a company's network so that it can forward them across the Internet. Socks uses sockets, a method for communication between a client program and a server program in a network. A socket is an end-point in a connection. Sockets are created and used with a set of programming requests or function calls to represent and keep track of individual connections. A proxy must exist for each service. Protocols for which no proxy service is available cannot be connected through a proxy except by a generic TCP proxy service that would work similar to a NAT.

THE CRYSTAL ENTERPRISE ARCHITECTURE

Chapter 3, "Exploring the System Architecture," introduced the components that make up the Crystal Enterprise architecture. However, before looking at how Crystal Enterprise can be configured to support the implementation of the firewall types described previously, it is necessary to review the architecture of Crystal Enterprise, concentrating on how the components that make up the complete product architecture communicate with each other. In fact, the mechanism employed to support server communications has a significant bearing on how Crystal Enterprise can be deployed with one or multiple firewalls.

Additionally, more detail needs to be provided about the relationship between the Web Service Connector, the Web Server, and the Web Component Server. This will be done in a later section; first, let's look at the core of Crystal Enterprise server communication—the eBusiness Framework.

REVIEWING THE eBUSINESS FRAMEWORK

From our investigation of the Crystal Enterprise architecture in previous chapters, you know that at the core of Crystal Enterprise is a communication layer called the eBusiness Framework. The Crystal eBusiness Framework is made up of a collection of services, which provides a series of Business Intelligence–related functions implemented by one or more Crystal Enterprise servers. It is, effectively, a CORBA bus integrating enterprise information management facilities (Security, Deployment, Administration, and so on) with the CORBA 2 Open Standard services (Naming, Trading, Event, and so on). Common Object Request Broker Architecture (CORBA) is an architecture and specification for creating, distributing, and managing distributed program objects in a network. It allows programs in different locations to communicate in a network through an "interface broker."

It is certainly not the purpose of this chapter to provide a detailed review of CORBA architectures; however, a couple of important observations need to be made with reference to the deployment of Crystal Enterprise within a firewall. All the components that make up Crystal Enterprise are written on top of an Enterprise Transport Layer using an API that exposes all the functionality available from the core systems and services. This Enterprise Transport provides the basic messaging mechanism needed for Crystal Enterprise objects to communicate with one another across heterogeneous languages, tools, and networks. Essentially, it acts as an exchange broker providing a directory of services helping to establish connectivity between clients and those services available.

For example, using the Enterprise Transport, a client object can transparently (that is, without concern for implementation details such as programming language, host platform, and so on) request the services other objects stored locally or across the network. The Enterprise Transport intercepts the call and is responsible for finding a server object that can implement the request.

The implementation details of the Enterprise Transport are not important to administrators deploying the Enterprise system. (System developers will only need to be concerned with object interface details that can be found in the Crystal Enterprise SDK.) This form of information hiding will enhance the Crystal Enterprise system's maintainability—the ease with which the system can be modified to correct faults, improve performance, address other attributes, or adapt to a changed environment—because any component communication details will be hidden from users and isolated in the Enterprise Transport. From a firewall perspective, this communication handled by the Enterprise Transport layer sits on top of a TCP/IP communications protocol (through "exposed" ports) with requests/services essentially a two-way process such that configuration will require each side of the communication to be able to "see" the other.

Although CORBA is at the core of the Crystal eBusiness Framework, its use of CORBA is hidden from Crystal Enterprise administrators and developers (and, therefore, did not form part of the discussion of administration in Chapter 10, "Administering and Configuring Crystal Enterprise"). It is so seamlessly integrated that it is not a matter of great significance. This is because there is not any configuration to be done with CORBA that would be done differently from any other TCP/IP application. Some definition of port numbers is all that is required as far as eBusiness Framework Administration is concerned.

However, for the purpose of using firewalls, one concept about CORBA needs to be understood—the IOR (Interoperable Object Reference). The IOR is a unique identifier for an object and contains information about the CORBA object itself. An example of a CORBA object in the Crystal eBusiness Framework is a server that performs a specific task within the framework. For example, the Job Server appears to other CORBA clients using the eBusiness framework as an object that is available for those clients to use. Each time a server in the eBusiness Framework requires the use of another server object, it requests information about that object. This information comes in the form of an IOR. The information our servers contain in their IORs includes the IP address and port to be used for returning messages. This IP address and port information within the IOR is critical when working with firewalls.

To summarize, Crystal Enterprise uses CORBA for intra-server communication. Administrators and developers are not exposed to the technology, nor are they required to work with it.

CRYSTAL ENTERPRISE AND TCP/IP COMMUNICATION

With standard TCP/IP communications, two servers that communicate with each other do so over a single point-to-point connection—with each point defined as an IP address and a port (either as a defined well-known port or retrieved from the operating system) with the source and destination defined by the direction of the communication (which is the requester and which is the server). The use of CORBA in the eBusiness Framework, however, has a slightly different flavor. In an environment where many requests are to be served, traffic on a particular port can be overwhelming and slow the operations of the server—leading, obviously, to performance problems. The way that CORBA gets around this possible bottleneck is by listening on one port and communicating on others. Within the Crystal Enterprise environment, therefore, communication consists of the opening and closing of multiple ports for a single request/service interaction.

The basic scenario of communication begins just like a standard server TCP/IP communication. A client requests a TCP connection to the server on a given port. The server responds on a port that the client is waiting on. A TCP connection is established and data can be sent back and forth. In Crystal Enterprise server-to-server communication, a further step is involved—after the initial connection is complete, communication stops on this channel. Instead, another channel is established to send data back and forth, leaving the server that is listening on a given port free to service the next connection request quickly and efficiently.

UNDERSTANDING WEB CONNECTOR AND WEB COMPONENT SERVER COMMUNICATION

The gateway to the Crystal Enterprise information delivery environment is the Web Component Server (WCS) that is the interface between the Web Server and the Crystal Enterprise report processing servers—the components on the eBusiness Framework. It is responsible for processing requests from your browser, including those for Crystal Server Pages (CSP), which is a server-side script, Web-based technology that you can use to customize your access to Crystal Enterprise. The means by which the request for information from Crystal Enterprise (typing a URL at the browser that requests a Crystal Report to be viewed, for example) gets passed to the WCS (or, as we shall see later, gets passed to one of multiple WCSs) from the Web Server is via a Web Service Connector (WSC).

The connectors are Web server extension components that enable the Web server to respond to certain file types that are associated with the Crystal Enterprise system. For the purposes of this discussion, two particular file types are associated with Crystal Enterprise—Crystal Reports (a .rpt extension) and Crystal Server Pages (a .csp extension).

Note

For completeness, it should be added that the other extensions are .cri, .cwr, and .shtx—for the purposes of this discussion the .rpt and .csp extensions are the most significant.

With the installation of the Web Server Connector on the Web server, as soon as a URL is received by the Web server with the appropriate file extension, this loads the WSC, that, through a configuration performed either at installation or through subsequent administration, then directs the request to the Web Component Server. Because Crystal Enterprise supports multiple Web servers, there are several different Web connectors, each of which is appropriate for the Web server being used. The different Web connectors available with Crystal Enterprise are detailed in the following list:

- **WCSINSAPI.DLL**—Microsoft Internet Information Server native extension, Netscape, I-Planet Server native extension

Note

Installation procedures differ depending on which type of Web connector is being installed. The Crystal Enterprise Installation Guide details exactly which procedures are required for each connector type.

- **WCSDSAPI.DLL**—Lotus Domino native extension
- **WCSASAPI.DLL**—Apache native extension
- **WCSCGI.EXE**—CGI-based connector

- **WCSCGI.CGI**—CGI-based connector (Linux/Unix)
- **Mod_WCS.so**—Apache native extension (Linux/Unix)

The Web Server Connector can also be used to resolve a URL path to a physical directory for the Web Component Server. The Web Server Connector can be configured to direct the Web Component Server to the physical directory for specific files based on a URL request given to the Web server. This is a useful feature if you don't want to store files on the Web server.

For example, let's say it was necessary to provide users with the capability to browse directly to Crystal Report files (.rpt files). However, due to security reasons or network implementation, it is preferable not to store the files on the Web server. The users, however, still need to be able to browse to `http://servername/reports/reportname.rpt`. The Web Server Connector can be configured to recognize the URL directory `/reports` for .rpt files and have the Web Server Connector tell the WCS that the .rpt file should be loaded off the network share `\\DataFiles\reports`. That way, the user can browse to the Web server but the file doesn't need to be stored on the Web server. From a security perspective, this is important because it enables report files (which can contain sensitive data) to be further removed behind an additional layer of network security. Of course, it also makes the management of these files a more straightforward process.

<table>
<tr><td>**Note**</td><td>Because Unix does not have drive letter paths like Windows NT/2000, it is required to use a virtual path to the Web Component Server if the Web Server resides on a Unix platform.</td></tr>
</table>

The Web Server Connector can be configured to resolve many URLs that are file type–specific. This can be done in the Crystal Configuration Manager by selecting the Web connector configuration button and then adding the appropriate path and file type.

Click on the Configure Web Connector icon within the Crystal Configuration Manager. This will open the information shown in Figure 12.1.

Note how you can configure paths for each file type. Also note that with the .rpt file type, the indication here is that this is an unmanaged report (it does not reside as an object in the APS database).

THE WEB COMPONENT SERVER IN MORE DETAIL

Having clearly established the role of the Web Server Connector and described the means by which it communicates with the Web Component Sever, it is now necessary to look at the Web Component Server in more detail. If the Web Server Connector can be viewed as a trigger for the process by which Crystal Enterprise information delivery is invoked, the Web Component Server can be regarded as the gateway. In a sense, the Web Component

PART

IV

CH

12

Server also can be viewed as an application server where the preparation of the report for subsequent delivery to the Web page is performed. In this section, the specific functions for which the Web Component Server is responsible will be covered. We will illustrate this further by looking in some detail at what actions are performed, and how the Web Component Server interacts with both the Web server and the Web server connector during the process of rendering a report to a Web page. This is important because this communication is likely to occur within the context of a system architecture configured within a firewall.

Figure 12.1
Configuring virtual directories.

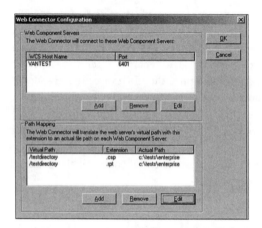

The Web Component Server is the gateway between the Web Server and the rest of the components on the Crystal eBusiness Framework. It is responsible for processing requests from your browser, including those for Crystal Server Pages (CSP). CSP is effectively the same as ASP (Active Server Pages); that is, a scripting language (both VBScript and JavaScript are supported) that is used to control the rendering of DHTML Web pages.

Each CSP page is a combination of HTML with the associated script actions embedded (it is possible to have a CSP contain only script—the breakdown of the content of each CSP is entirely a matter of application development). It is worth noting that because ASP is proprietary to Microsoft, this CSP abstraction allows for the same pages to be migrated onto a Unix platform (only, of course, VBScript cannot be the script language in this instance).

The Web Component Server uses plug-ins to translate the requests that have been forwarded from the Web server (via the Web Server Connector). Plug-ins help the Web Component Server process the request, and the WCS will use the appropriate plug-in depending on what type of file request has been made. As an example, if the request is to view a report, the request could be something like

```
http://Server Name/myreports/samplereport.rpt
```

This would use the Wcs_Xn_Reportviewer. dll plug-in. However, should the request be for a CSP with the request being something like the following, the Wcs_Xn_Csp.dll would be used:

```
http://Server Name/crystal/enterprise/ePortfolio/en/available.csp
```

The fact that the Web Component Server is responsible for processing the server-side scripting as well as generating the HTML is an extremely important facet of the Crystal Enterprise architecture. Placing this processing within the Crystal Enterprise framework—rather than leaving this burden on the Web server itself—is important for a number of reasons.

First, by implementing Crystal Enterprise, no additional processing burden is placed on the Web server itself—in a sense, the Web server merely acts as a "pass-through" mechanism (sending the request for Crystal processing—either viewing or executing a report—through to the Crystal Enterprise framework, and then receiving the resulting Web page back from the Web Component Server for display on the browser). The only "overhead" is loading the Web connector to identify the WCS to send the request to. Second, it removes any platform dependency between the Web server and Crystal Enterprise—thus, it is an easy configuration to have a Unix-based Web server with a Windows-based Crystal Enterprise deployment.

Also, with Crystal Enterprise 8.5 supporting a mixed deployment, it opens up the possibility of the Web Component Server being on a different OS platform from the rest of Crystal Enterprise—either as a temporary migration strategy or as a means of using available hardware resources. Finally, with the Web Component Server being a registered component on the Crystal eBusiness Framework, all of the scalability features that are available can now be used. For example, this allows the WCS to be scaled out to be multiple processes executing on a single machine, or, alternatively, scaled across multiple machines with one or many WCS processes being distributed across multiple machines. (How the Crystal Enterprise architecture supports comprehensive scaling and load-balancing approach will be covered later in this chapter.)

After obtaining a good understanding of the position of the Web connector and Web Component Server in the Crystal Enterprise architecture, it is time to look in some detail at how these interact within the context of how a browser request would be processed.

PART
IV

CH

12

INTERACTION BETWEEN THE WEB COMPONENT SERVER AND THE WEB CONNECTOR

To demonstrate the interaction between the Web connector and the Web Component Server, it's easiest to review the process of displaying a Crystal Report on a Crystal Viewer to examine exactly what traffic is being passed between the browser, Web server, Web connector, and the Crystal Enterprise report processing tier. Chapter 3 introduced this concept.

1. A request is made from the browser to the Web server for a specific report file. In this example, the user has clicked on a hyperlink (`http://<Server Name>/directory/myreport.rpt`), meaning that a request has been made to view a Crystal Report within the Crystal Viewer.

2. The connector on the Web server forwards the request to the Web Component Server.

3. The Web Component Server calls a plug-in; in this example it will call wcs_xn_reportviewer.dll. This plug-in tells the Web Component Server to send the appropriate HTML to the browser that will load a Crystal Report Viewer.

4. After the viewer has been loaded in the browser the viewer will request the same report file. To speed up the report delivery process the browser will be told by the WCS to load only the first page of the report. If the end user requires more pages of the report they will be served up on demand.

5. The viewer's request is received by the Web server and forwarded to the connector.

6. The connector forwards the request to the WCS. The plug-in parses the query string and tells the WCS to check with the APS.

7. The WCS asks the APS whether a guest account is available to access the report. This emulates a Crystal Reports .rpt request. One of the differences between Crystal Reports and Crystal Enterprise is that the APS keeps track of every Crystal Enterprise user, so a guest account is necessary. The concept is similar to the way anonymous authentication is used by Internet Information Server.

8. The APS returns the name of an available Cache Server. The WCS now checks with the connector to determine the location of the report file. (Remember that the connector can be configured to resolve the physical location of the report file through virtual directory mapping.)

9. The connector will check its configuration to see whether it resolves this URL to a specific directory for .rpt files. If not, the connector will ask the Web Server for the physical directory that this URL references.

10. The WCS goes to the specified Cache Server and asks for incomplete page 1 of the report (the viewer's URL request). The Cache Server checks for a cached copy of the page. If the page is not available, it forwards the request to a Page Server. The Cache Server knows which Page Server to pass the request to because the Page Server has broadcast its presence on the CORBA Bus.

11. The Page Server goes to the location (as specified either by the connector or the Web server) and retrieves a copy of the report. The Page Server processes the report.

12. The incomplete page is placed in cache and returned to the browser. Subsequent pages of the report may be requested by the user—in this case, the pages will be retrieved directly from the Cache Server.

In the previous discussion, you can see that the Web Component Server acts as the gateway from the Web Server to the APS. The Web Component Server receives requests from the Web Server, uses plug-ins to determine what to do with those requests, and processes the requests by calling the appropriate server (usually the APS). It is also worth noting that there are multiple communication points between the Web connector and Web Component Server: Servicing this request is not a single transfer of information. The advantage to this approach is that the user is not waiting for the complete report to be processed prior to any visible evidence that the request is actually being processed—first of all, the viewer is loaded immediately, and then, as soon as enough information is present to render a meaningful first page on the viewer, this is displayed on the browser. This represents the actual execution of two very important technologies employed by Crystal Enterprise: Page on Demand and Report Streaming. These are discussed in more detail in other chapters.

For the purposes of our discussion of firewall configuration there are essentially three discreet Crystal Enterprise entities that are likely to be deployed at different positions of a firewall architecture, seen in Figure 12.2. (The Web browser will be ignored because this is clearly outside the scope of the firewall!)

Figure 12.2
Three Crystal Enterprise security entities.

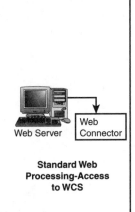

APS

Web Server   Web Connector   Web Component Server   Other Crystal Enterprise Servers

Standard Web Processing-Access to WCS   **Script Processing Access to Crystal Enterprise Resources (Potentially Others)**   **Report Processing Access to Internal Network Resources**

PART

IV

CH

12

Each of these entities is likely to require different levels of firewall protection determined by their closeness to the internal network. It is also worth noting that the Web Component Server interacts with different components within the report processing tier (the APS in step 7 and the Cache Server in Step 10, for example).

CRYSTAL ENTERPRISE LOAD BALANCING AND SCALABILITY—WEB FARM CONSIDERATIONS

So far, the only configuration considered in this chapter is a single Web connector communicating with a single Web Component Server, which is satisfactory for discussing their individual characteristics and responsibilities within the Crystal Enterprise architecture. However, this does not tell the full network story, because deployments of Crystal Enterprise can involve more than just two physical servers.

One of the key design objectives of Crystal Enterprise is to provide for information delivery to literally hundreds of thousands of users, with all users receiving an acceptable response time for their requests. Additionally, in a large enterprise it is quite unrealistic to assume that only a single server is going to be deployed; instead, a group of Web servers is going to be grouped together as a *farm* of servers (hence the term *Web farm*). This allows enterprises to satisfy load balancing and fault tolerance considerations within the same architecture. Crystal Enterprise fits in well with Web farm deployments because it supports multiple instances of both Web connectors and Web Component Servers—indeed, their deployment is so flexible that just about any realistic configuration is supported.

Take a look at the scenario in which multiple Web servers have been configured into a Web farm, seen in Figure 12.3. In this case, a Web connector will need to be installed on each Web server. A possible configuration could be multiple Web servers with a single Web Component Server. (In this instance, there could be a significant amount of Web traffic on the Web site but a limited amount of Crystal-based information delivery is required. Therefore, a single Web component is able to handle the volume of report processing required.) The Web connector installed on each Web server must be configured such that it points to the same Web Component Server machine and to the port on which the server will listen.

Figure 12.3
Multiple Web connectors configured to a single Web Component Server process on a single physical server.

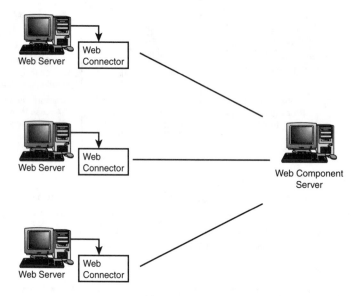

Furthermore, Crystal Enterprise supports the Web Component Server running as multiple processes on the same physical server. In this configuration, a small level of increased availability can be deployed such that if one of the processes fails (or is stopped in error), Crystal Enterprise processing can continue and the failed or stopped process can be restarted later.

Notice that another level of additional flexibility is illustrated in Figure 12.4. Because the Web connector is installed on each Web server it is also possible for one Web server to be able to see multiple Web connectors while another Web server can see only a single instance. (This would be configured with one Web server able to access a single port for the WCS—as defined using the Crystal Configuration Manager—while the other would have both ports defined in its Web connector configuration.) It is likely that this type of configuration in a product environment might be unusual but could easily be used as a variant if one was performing stress tests and was limited to a single machine.

Figure 12.4
Multiple Web connectors configured to multiple Web Component Server processes on a single machine.

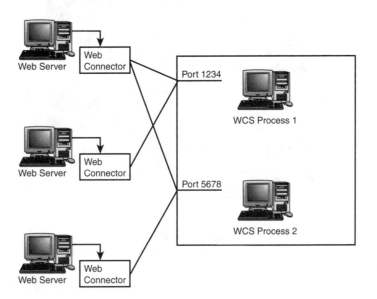

PART

IV

CH

12

For a more complete load balancing (and fault tolerant) architecture, the Web Component Server processes can be distributed across multiple servers, as seen in Figure 12.5. In this case, the fault tolerance increases significantly because the single point of failure is the server itself rather than just a single process running on a server. As before, the individual Web servers can be configured to "see" one or all the machines (in the same way that they could see the ports on an individual server in the previous example, they can also be configured to "see" or "not see" the physical servers).

Support for configurations involving multiple Web connectors, multiple Web Component Servers, or both, enables Crystal Enterprise to be readily deployed within a Web farm environment. One important note—the Crystal Enterprise configuration is not dependent upon the settings chosen in the load balancing setup. Typically, the Web farm would be installed and configured before installing Crystal Enterprise. For example, within a Windows-based Web farm deployment load balancing between IIS servers would be achieved through the use of Windows Load Balancing Software (WLBS).

Figure 12.5
Multiple Web connectors configured to multiple Web Component Servers running on multiple server machines.

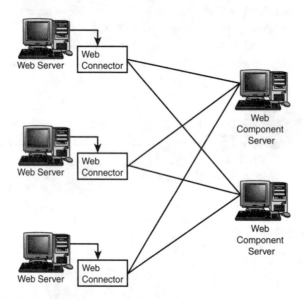

WLBS provides IP-based load balancing. When WLBS is installed, it is configured as a Virtual Network Interface card (NIC): The setup of the WLBS is provided through NIC properties. Here, at a node level, such attributes as a load-balancing setting (as a percentage of workload), affinity settings, and which ports will be load balanced would be defined.

The Crystal Enterprise environment effectively inherits whatever balancing has already been defined. It is only in a situation where there are multiple Web Component Servers where the request can be forwarded that any load balancing decision must be taken by the Web connector. In this case, the Web connector will forward requests on a round-robin basis—if one machine in unavailable, another will be chosen. Figure 12.6 illustrates the Crystal Enterprise environment within a Windows-based multiple Web server deployment.

Figure 12.6
Windows deployment
with multiple Web
servers.

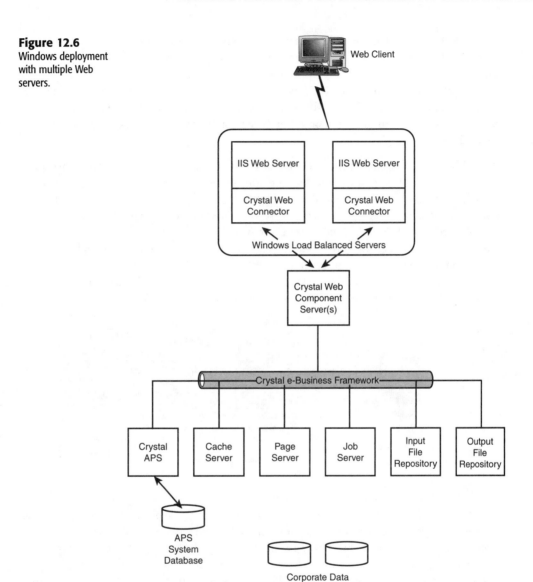

ADDITIONAL FIREWALL AND PORT CONSIDERATIONS FOR CRYSTAL ENTERPRISE

Now that some basic concepts around Crystal Enterprise system communication have been
reviewed, the actual implementation of Crystal Enterprise in a complex network environment can be explored.

PART

IV

CH

12

As previously mentioned, the barriers that a secure system provides are commonly broken down into distinct layers (with each layer defining a security measurement and effectively denoting an acceptable level of exposure). Each layer is identified by the communication from one network to another network via a firewall. Then, a detailed example involving Crystal Enterprise communication through a firewall will be provided as well as what the appropriate system settings should be and how the communication will be addressed at an IP/port level.

Figure 12.7 shows the most typical example of a firewall implementation. In this scenario, the browser-to-Web server communication is controlled through the standard firewall control, allowing only HTTP requests to be forwarded through to the Web server on port 80 (other services such as Telnet, mail, and so on will be permitted through other predefined ports as well). Clearly, Crystal Enterprise is not involved at this stage of the firewall. This does, however, represent the entry point into the resources managed by the target environment. From this point forward internal network resources will be used; this interim environment is normally called the DMZ (or Demilitarized Zone). The DMZ, therefore, is a network added between a protected network and an external network.

Figure 12.7
Crystal Enterprise tiers for firewall deployment.

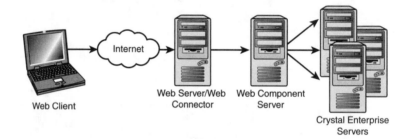

Web Client

Web Server/Web Connector

Web Component Server

Crystal Enterprise Servers

As shown in Figure 12.8, the architecture of Crystal Enterprise fits conveniently into this infrastructure. The separation of the Web connector from the Web Component Server enables the Web connector to remain within the DMZ along with the Web server. Consequently, an additional firewall can easily be deployed to protect the requests forwarded through the Web Component Server—this, after all, will be communicating directly to the other Crystal Enterprise servers and is a component on the Crystal eBusiness framework.

To look at the details of the communication of the Web connector to the Web Component Server through the second firewall, the discussion will be broken down into two distinct portions: the initialization of the communication (a request for service), and servicing of the request once the communication has been established. This two-stage nature of communication was detailed in the eBusiness Framework in an earlier section in this chapter.

Figure 12.8
Firewall configuration.

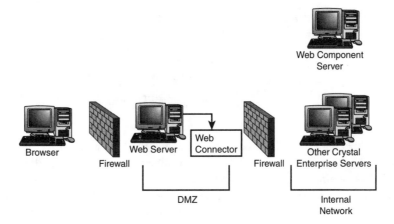

UNDERSTANDING INITIAL TCP/PORT PROCESSING

When the Web Server receives a Crystal Enterprise resource request from a Web browser, it forwards the request to the Web connector. For this example, assume that the Web server has an IP address of 10.55.222.241 (see Figure 12.9).

Figure 12.9
Browser to Web server request.

Web Server IP address: 10.55.222.241

The Web connector prepares to make a TCP connection to the WCS. A TCP connection request has four critical elements:

- Destination IP address (where it's going)
- Destination port (at which port/socket the request will be expected)
- Source IP (address of the sender, where to send return messages)
- Source port (port the sender will be listening on for a response)

The destination portion of this communication is determined by settings entered in the Web connector configuration dialog box in the Crystal Configuration Manager, shown in Figure 12.10.

Figure 12.10
Web connector port
configuration.

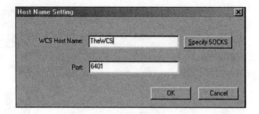

When making up the destination information, the Web connector reads this information from these settings. Because this is the machine name of the WCS, the IP address of the WCS is determined by network name resolution. The port destination takes less work—it's simply the number as entered in this dialog box. By default, this port is 6401. The only requirement is that this port number is the same as the WCS was set to use when the WCS started. The source portion of the requests are both determined by the Web Server's operating system.

The Source IP is the IP address of the machine sending the request—the Web server. This IP address is determined by a request to the operating system. The port is also chosen by an operating system request. The Web connector asks for an available socket (or port) that is not in use. The operating system randomly chooses an unused socket. The Web connector begins temporarily listening on this port for a response from the WCS as soon as the initialization request is sent. It will only accept a response from the IP address of the WCS—any other requests at this port will be dropped. At this point, the TCP connection request is ready to be sent with this information:

- **Source IP**—IP address of the Web Server machine as determined by a call to the operating system.
- **Source port**—Port deemed to be available by the operating system. This will be a port number higher than 1024.
- **Destination IP**—IP address of WCS as determined by network name resolution.
- **Destination port**—Port as entered into the Web connector configuration dialog box in Crystal Configuration Manager. This must match the configured port for the Web Component Server.

Assuming that the Web Component Server has an IP address of 10.55.222.242 and that the assigned port (retrieved by an operating system call) is 3333, for this example, the completed request will be as follows:

- **Destination IP**—10.55.222.242
- **Destination port**—6401
- **Source IP**—10.55.222.241
- **Source port**—3333

The Web Component Server is constantly listening on its defined port for service requests (the default 6401 in our example, though another port could be used for listening if configured to do so). When the Web Component Server receives the TCP Connection Request from the Web connector, it begins to form a response. The response will have the same four primary components that the request had—a source port and IP and a destination port and IP. Embedded in this response is the IOR of the WCS. The IOR of WCS contains the IP address of the WCS, as well as the port number specified in the `-requestport` option.

Note

> The `-requestport` option is available if the administrator wants to ensure that a fixed port is established for this communication—rather than an OS randomly generated port. More details in configuring this value are contained in the Crystal Enterprise Administrators Guide.

If the option is not specified, a free port is picked up at random by the CORBA library by asking the operating system for an available port. At this point, the WCS responds to the Web connector to complete the TCP connection. This TCP connection response will have this information:

- **Source IP**—IP address of the WCS as determined by a call to the operating system.
- **Source port**—A random port number, as determined by making a call to the operating system.
- **Destination IP**—The IP address as read from the Source IP address in the TCP Connection Request received from the Web connector.
- **Destination port**—The port as read from the source port in the TCP Connection Request received from the Web connector.

Assuming a randomly generated source port of 2345, we'll have the TCP connection confirmation of the following:

- **Destination IP**—10.55.222.241
- **Destination port**—3333
- **Source IP**—10.55.222.242
- **Source port**—2345

While the Web Component Server has been building its confirmation response, the Web Server machine has been listening for the response on the chosen port.

The Web Server/Connector will only accept packets from the IP to which it sent the request—this is for security. In our example, the operating system of the Web server machine has been listening on port 3333. When the TCP Connection Response/

PART

IV

CH

12

Confirmation is received, the OS of the Web server machine will determine whether it's from the correct location. If it is from the correct IP, it will accept the data and complete the TCP connection. The IOR is embedded inside this request, and the operating system passes it onto the Web connector for processing.

Now that all this work has been done to establish this connection, the Web connector immediately closes it. This was merely to establish that both client and server are up and running and accepting connections. The Web connector also received the IOR of the Web Component Server in this short connection. The listening port on the Web Component Server resumes listening to other clients, and the work of sending IP packets back and forth will be done on a second TCP connection.

UNDERSTANDING SECONDARY TCP/PORT PROCESSING

It is in the second TCP connection where CE works differently from most TCP/IP applications. The Web connector reads the IOR of the Web Component Server and acquires the IP address and port number from it. Using this port number and IP address a second connection is made—one that will be used for actually transferring the data. (A straight TCP/IP application doesn't have an IOR from which to read the IP and port of the server. It uses the source IP and port from the TCP connection confirmation to establish this second connection.) The Crystal Enterprise application will use the information in the IOR and discard the source IP and port from the TCP connection confirmation.

Continuing our example, upon reading the port and IP information from the IOR of the WCS, the Web connector initiates a second TCP connection. This request will use this information:

- **Destination IP**—The IP address of the WCS as reported in the IOR.
- **Destination port**—The port number to be used for communication as reported in the IOR. If the -requestport directive is used, it will be that port; otherwise, it will be a randomly generated port number (we will use this).
- **Source IP**—The IP address of the Web Server.
- **Source port**—The port on the Web Server to be used for this connection. This is determined by asking the operating system for an available port.

In our example, let's assume that the randomly generated destination port number is 2345 and the generated source port is 1061. We'll have the TCP connection confirmation of the following:

- **Destination IP**—10.55.222.242
- **Destination port**—4000
- **Source IP**—10.55.222.241
- **Source port**—1061

When the WCS receives this request, it will respond to the Web connector to complete the connection. The address to which it will send this connection is 10.55.222.241:1061. This destination and port was determined by reading the source information of the incoming TCP connection request. This is where the Web Component Server's connection response gets its destination. As demonstrated in the following list, this is really just the reversal of the information received from the Web connector. Completing our example, therefore, the WCS will communicate as follows:

- **Destination IP**—10.55.222.241
- **Destination port**—1061
- **Source IP**—10.55.222.242
- **Source port**—4000

After the Web Server/Connector machine receives the TCP connection response from the WCS, it is able to complete the TCP connection. Now that the TCP connection is made, IP packets will be sent back and forth on this channel. IP datagrams will be forwarded back and forth from the Web Server (10.55.222.241:1061) to the WCS (10.55.222.242:4000), and vice versa, on these ports. The secondary connection, therefore, is the one that does nearly all the data transference.

Now that we have seen exactly how the IP/port allocation is determined in the Crystal Enterprise environment, we can now look at a fully worked example applying a specific firewall technology. Initially, we will look at packet filtering and then apply NAT on top of this. We then will briefly consider how Crystal Enterprise would fit in with the application of a Proxy Server (Socks) firewall.

DEPLOYING CRYSTAL ENTERPRISE WITH AN IP PACKET FILTERING FIREWALL

Earlier in this chapter it was noted that IP Filter firewalls restrict network traffic based on IP address and port number. Crystal Enterprise works well with IP Filter firewalls with the proviso that the IP address and TCP port number used by the servers are predetermined. This section discusses a scenario where the Crystal Enterprise Web connector/Web Server and WCS has one IP Filter between the two of them and the WCS is separated from the rest of the CE servers by a second firewall. In other words, it's the common firewall scenario we looked at in the previous section. This is illustrated in Figure 12.11.

Let's look at two distinct parts of communication across the networks: first, the most external portion (that is, between Network C and Network B), and second, the communication between the Web Component Server and the other Crystal Enterprise servers (the internal portion—between Network B and Network A). Refer to Figure 12.12.

Figure 12.11
IP Filtering–firewall
definition.

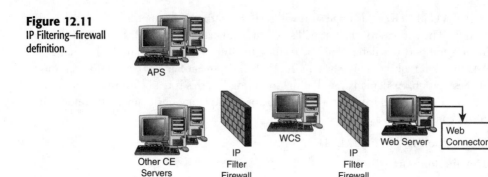

Figure 12.12
IP Filtering–external
firewall.

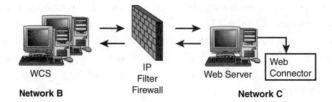

AN EXTERNAL PACKET FILTERING FIREWALL SCENARIO

Any requests of the Web connector machine would follow the same steps as described in the previous section. Initially, the Web connector would have to establish a TCP connection to the WCS. The Web connector would initiate this handshake communication. The IP Filter firewall would certainly stand to convolute this communication:

- **Destination IP**—The IP of the WCS as determined by network name resolution. The lookup would occur on the side of the Web Server—usually by a DNS server in this zone.

- **Destination port**—The port to use for this communication is taken from the Registry—it's the value as entered in the Web Connector Configuration dialog box in the Crystal Configuration Manager. By default, this is port 6401.

- **Source IP**—The IP of the Web Server/Web Connector machine as determined by a call to the operating system.

- **Source port**—The free port as returned by a request to the operating system.

The network rules of this side of the firewall will quickly determine that the destination IP of this request will have to go through the firewall. Therefore, the network forwards this TCP connection request to the firewall. The firewall then evaluates the information within the request—the destination port and IP address, as well as the source IP and source port. The firewall must have rules that allow this connection to go through—it must accept requests for the WCS's IP from the Web connector's IP and the request must be on the specified port. At this point in the request, the firewall will have to allow traffic through it that follows this configuration:

- **Source IP**—The IP of the Web connector/Web Server
- **Source port**—Any
- **Destination IP**—The IP of the WCS
- **Destination port**—6401 (or whichever is the WCS's listening port)
- **Action**—Accept

When the WCS receives this request, it must respond to it. It garners the information about where to respond from the information within the request. It takes the Source IP and Port and makes this the destination. Because this is a random port, the firewall must be configured to allow any ports to leave Network B and go to Network C. This is a generally accepted practice—strict port enforcement is done at the bastion host. Therefore, the firewall rules to complete this request should resemble the following:

- **Source IP**—Any IP from Network B
- **Source port**—Any
- **Destination IP**—Any IP outside the network
- **Destination port**—Any
- **Action**—Accept

When the connection request gets through the firewall, the network resolution will determine that the destination is in Network C. The request will hit the Web Server/Web connector. At this point, there is a TCP connection between the two machines, going through the firewall. The WCS will send the Web connector its IOR and the Web connector will close this TCP connection.

The IOR contains the IP and port on which the second connection will be made. The port number in the IOR will be one of many values depending on the existence or nonexistence of the `-requestport xxxx` directive on the Web Component Server's command line. If there is a `-requestport`, this is the value that will be in the IOR. If there isn't, it will be a random port as chosen by the WCS's operating system. Generally, a random port is not acceptable because administrators won't enable their firewall rules to accept any ports from a specific IP.

<table>
<tr><td>**Note**</td><td>The Crystal Enterprise Administrator's Guide suggests that the use of the `-requestport` option is required with IP Filter firewalls.</td></tr>
</table>

When this second connection is made, the `-requestport` directive should be set to a fixed port number and this port number should be accepted if the IP is from the Web Server/Connector machine. This second TCP connection information will look like this:

PART

IV

CH

12

- **Destination IP**—The IP of the WCS as read from the IOR.
- **Destination port**—The port as read from the IOR, the recommendation being to use the `-requestport` directive to define this value.
- **Source IP**—The IP of the Web Server/Web connector machine as determined by a call to the operating system.
- **Source port**—The free port as returned by a request to the operating system.

The firewall will evaluate this request and the port will have to be open. As an example, if the `-requestport` directive uses port 3333, the firewall rules will have to look like this:

- **Source IP**—The IP of the Web connector/Web server
- **Source port**—Any
- **Destination**—The IP of the WCS
- **Destination port**—3333 (or whichever is used with `-requestport` directive)
- **Action**—Accept

The WCS will respond to this request on whichever port the Web server/Web connector found to be available. This will be allowed through the firewall because any port is allowed from the internal network to the external. There will then be an established connection between the WCS and the Web connector, and IP packets will be sent on this channel. The configuration of the firewall rules for an IP Filter firewall between a WCS and Web connector are summarized in Table 12.1.

TABLE 12.1   FIREWALL CONFIGURATION RULES

Source	Destination	Port	Action
Network B	Any	Any	Accept
IP of Web connector	IP of WCS	6401, `-requestport`	Accept
Network C	Any	Any	Reject

> **Note**
>
> When the WCS is started with the `-requestport` switch, this port will have to be open going from Network B to Network C for the IP of the WCS.

AN INTERNAL PACKET FILTERING FIREWALL SCENARIO

There are several servers in the Crystal Enterprise environment with which the Web Component Server communicates. It must communicate with the APS as part of logon/security procedures, while the Cache Server will also be involved in a communication with the Web Component Server for report viewing requests. (Additionally, the WCS will communicate with the Input File Repository Server, where the report objects are maintained when the thumbnail of a report is displayed on the Web page.) Obviously, traffic to each of these servers from the Web Component Server will have to be allowed by the IP Filter firewall.

Figure 12.13
IP Filtering—internal firewall.

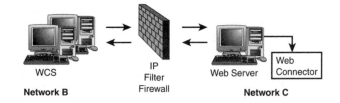

First and foremost, the WCS will have to communicate with the APS. The APS provides the Name Service in the Crystal Enterprise environment. Without this service, the Web Component Server will not be able to communicate with any of the servers. The APS listens for requests on the port designated, seen in Figure 12.14 under the configuration tab in the Crystal Configuration Manager (the default value for this port is 6400).

Figure 12.14
APS port configuration.

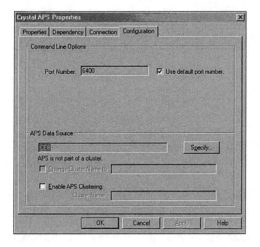

Whenever the WCS needs to communicate with the Name Service of the APS, it will do so on port 6400 by default. The first time the WCS has to communicate with the Name Service is when it starts. When the WCS starts, it must register itself with the Name Service as part of its initialization process. This communication will occur on port 6400. A TCP connection will occur between the WCS and APS for this to happen. The request will have the following information in it:

- **Destination IP**—The IP of the APS as determined by network name resolution.
- **Destination port**—The port number of the APS as defined in the SERVICES file.

PART

IV

CH

12

- **Source IP**—The IP of the WCS as determined by a call to the OS of the WCS.
- **Source port**—A random available port as determined by a call to the OS of the WCS.

After the APS receives this TCP connection request, it will respond back to the WCS to complete the initial connection. This connection response will contain this information:

- **Destination IP**—The IP of the WCS as determined by reading the Source IP from the TCP connection request.
- **Destination port**—The port the WCS is using as determined by reading the Source Port from the TCP connection request.
- **Source IP**—The IP of the APS as determined by a call to the OS of the APS.
- **Source port**—A random port as determined by a call to the OS of the APS.

After this initial connection is complete, the APS sends the WCS its IOR. The WCS then closes the initial connection and establishes a connection to the APS using the IP and port that is in the IOR. If the APS is using the -requestport directive, this is the port that the WCS will use to initiate communication with the APS. This second connection request will contain this information:

- **Source IP**—The IP of the WCS as determined by a call to the OS of the WCS.
- **Source port**—The port number of the WCS as determined by a call to the OS of the WCS.
- **Destination IP**—The IP of the APS as read from the IOR that the APS sent to the WCS in the initial connection.
- **Destination port**—The port the APS put in the IOR. If using the -requestport directive, this is the port the APS put in the IOR. Otherwise, it will be a port deemed available as per a request to the OS of the APS.

The APS will respond to this request to complete the connection. This response will contain this information:

- **Source IP**—The IP of the APS as determined by a call to the OS.
- **Source port**—A free port on the APS as determined by a call to the OS of the APS.
- **Destination IP**—The IP of the WCS as read from the Source IP of the connection request.
- **Destination port**—The port being used by the WCS as read from the Source Port of the connection request.

When this connection is complete, the WCS and APS will hold it open and use it whenever communication between the two is required. From a firewall configuration perspective, two ports are involved in the communication between the APS and the Web Component Server: first, the port the APS listens on—this is port 6400 by default—and second, the port that is established as the main communication channel between these two processes—this should be the value as defined by the `-requestport` directive. The "rules" for the firewall configuration can be defined as shown in Table 12.2.

TABLE 12.2 FIREWALL CONFIGURATIONS RULES (NETWORK A TO NETWORK B)

Source	Destination	Port	Action
Network A	Any	Any	Accept
WCS	APS	6400, `-requestport*`	Accept
Network B	Any	Any	Reject

Note

When the APS is started with the `-requestport` switch, this port will have to be open going from Network B to Network A for the IP of the WCS.

However, this is only one of three servers with which the WCS would need to communicate. Requests to the Input FRS and Cache Server would still need to be allowed through the firewall. The standard practice is when servers need to communicate with one another, they ask the Name Service for a copy of the IOR of the server they need to contact. To communicate with either the Input FRS or the Cache Server, therefore, the Web Component Server will need to ask the APS for information about the server to which it needs access.

When these servers start, they give the Name Service portion of the APS a copy of their IOR. As the other servers require access to it, they ask the APS for a copy of the IOR of the server they need information about. To determine the IOR of a given server, the WCS and APS collaborate. When the WCS has a copy of the IOR of the particular server, it will attempt to make a connection to the server using the information in the IOR. The information in the IOR will contain both the IP address and the port to be used for communication and security information. If the `-requestport` directive is used, the port will be that defined port; otherwise, it's a random port. When working with firewalls, the preferred method is to use `-requestport` so you can control on which port traffic will be allowed in. As a conclusion, therefore, the firewall rules between Network B and Network A would need be set up as shown in Table 12.3.

TABLE 12.3 FIREWALL CONFIGURATION RULES (NETWORK B TO NETWORK A)

Source	Destination	Port	Action
Network A	Any	Any	Accept
IP of WCS	IP of APS	6400, `-requestport` for each of the servers (APS, Input FRS, Cache Server)	Accept
Network B	Any	Any	Reject

The use of Network Address Translation within the IP Filtering firewall adds an additional level of complexity, something explored in the next section.

USING CRYSTAL ENTERPRISE WITH NETWORK ADDRESS TRANSLATION

Network Address Translation (NAT) takes IP Filtering one level further by masking the IP address of the internal server when its packet gets through the firewall. NAT makes it appear as if all traffic from inside the network comes from a different IP address. NAT hides internal IP addresses by converting all internal host addresses to the address of the firewall as packets are routed through the firewall. The firewall then retransmits the data payload of the internal host from its own address using a translation table to keep track of which ports/sockets on the exterior interface equate to which ports/sockets on the interior interface.

COMPARING NAT WITH STANDARD TCP/IP COMMUNICATION

To investigate how the NAT firewall configuration works in practice, let's first look at how a standard TCP/IP communication application would operate using a Telnet application as an example. Here, the communication is set up on a single pipe with all interaction passing through the same communication channel.

When the Telnet client needs to contact the Telnet server, it does so on a specific port—port 23 (the established default for Telnet applications). Also, in this example, assume that the Telnet client will be on machine 168.247.34.113 while the Telnet server will be on machine 172.18.10.202. When the request is received from the Telnet client, the network determines that the destination of 172.18.10.202:23 is not on the internal network and uses the default route to send the request outside the private network. The default route will be the internal IP address of the NAT firewall (let's assume that this value is 168.247.34.1). The NAT firewall takes the packet and alters the header information. Before hitting the firewall, therefore, the packet has this data:

- **Source IP**—168.247. 34.113
- **Source port**—1912 (randomly chosen by OS)
- **Destination IP**—172.18.10.202
- **Destination port**—23

When the NAT firewall receives the message, it checks to see that the destination port and IP are allowed by the firewall rules: This is just like what the IP filter does—determines whether the packet will or will not be allowed through. Generally, all destinations and all ports from the internal to external network will be configured so that they will be allowed. After the firewall determines that the packet will be allowed through, the NAT firewall alters the source information to make it look as if the packet was actually sent by the firewall.

In this example, a static NAT configuration will be used. With static NAT, each IP inside the firewall will have a corresponding IP in the outside network. For our example, the NAT firewall changes the packet (that is, masks it) so that the receiving server will receive a communication address as determined by the firewall. The source IP in the header is changed (with a predetermined value) as follows:

- **Source IP**—172.18.10.113 (the "NATted" IP)
- **Source port**—1912 (unchanged from before)
- **Destination IP**—172.18.10.202
- **Destination port**—23

After the source information is altered, the NAT firewall routes the packet and waits for a response. When the Telnet server at 172.18.10.202 gets the connection request (it will be listening on port 23), it will respond based on the data in the packet. Its response, therefore, will have this data:

- **Source IP**—172.18.10.202
- **Source port**—1242 (randomly chosen by OS)
- **Destination IP**—172.18.10.113 (the "NATted" address)
- **Destination port**—1912 (as read from source port)

The destination here is the NATted IP address, not the internal private IP address of 168.247.34.113. The internal address is hidden from the external server—this is the feature of NAT firewalls. When the packet gets back to the NAT firewall, it is expecting it. The firewall will evaluate the source and destination of the packet and determine whether the packet will be allowed through. At this point, the NAT firewall takes this packet and changes the destination back to the original IP address. The packet, therefore, will be altered to have this data:

- **Source IP**—172.18.10.202
- **Source port**—1242 (randomly chosen by OS)
- **Destination IP**—168.247.34.113 (the private IP)
- **Destination port**—1912

At this point, the NAT firewall forwards the packet and the Telnet client receives it. Both sides have received all the necessary confirmations and a connection is established between client and server. Each packet of data that is sent on this channel will be intercepted by the NAT firewall and will be altered on both the inward journey and on the outward journey.

EXPLORING THE NAT AND CRYSTAL ENTERPRISE RELATIONSHIP

It has been established that within Crystal Enterprise, server-to-server communication takes the single TCP connection approach one step further. A second TCP connection is made

PART
IV
CH
12

when servers communicate in Crystal Enterprise (listen on one, communicate on another). When it comes to firewalls, it is important to recognize that two ports need to be open.

However, with translated IP addresses in the NAT instance, there is an additional concern as it is the IOR that tells the servers which IP to use—this is not directly retrieved from the packets themselves. This section explains what is required to make Crystal Enterprise work with a NAT firewall—the Web connector and Web Component Server communication as an example.

When the Web connector communicates to the Web Server, it is on the outside of the firewall. This is how it will be in most configurations and the assumption made during this chapter. The Web connector/Web Server will reside in a DMZ and the rest of the servers inside the corporate network. As before, when the Web connector needs to communicate with the Web Component Server, it will send a TCP Connection request. To get there, it will need to resolve the name of the Web Component Server machine. Because the Web Component Server is inside the firewall, this can potentially create a problem with a NAT firewall. As was seen with the Telnet example in the previous section, generally the incoming rules for NAT firewalls only accept packets with destination IPs going to the firewall.

In the Telnet example, the client was inside the firewall and the outbound firewall rules allowed all IP destinations outside the wall, as well as any port (this is normal). The NAT firewall then altered the packet and sent it onto the Telnet server. The Telnet server responded back to the firewall. The firewall was expecting the response and allowed it through because it was expected. The NAT firewall altered the destination of this response back to the internal private IP of the Telnet client and routed it onto the Telnet client machine.

In Crystal Enterprise, the Web connector needs to send the initial TCP Connection request to the Web Component Server. This is somewhat different from the Telnet application because the machine in the external network (the Web connector) is initializing the communication instead of the machine inside the network. Because the request didn't originate inside the firewall, the firewall isn't expecting any communication. When the Web connector resolves the machine name of the Web Component Server to an IP address, this won't always be the IP as it exists on the internal network in a NAT environment. There are a number of options available where the features of NAT Firewalls could be configured to work in this situation:

- The NAT firewall could be configured to allow packets whose destination is the firewall
- The NAT firewall could be configured to allow packets whose destination is inside the firewall and have rules on which of these are allowed
- The NAT firewall could use a group of IP address in the external network that each represents one IP address in the internal network

There is still an outstanding question, however: To which IP address should the request be sent? Crystal Enterprise requires that the machine on the outside of the firewall be able to send packets to the private IP address of the Web Component Server. It might be possible to get away with not using the private IP address for the initial connection—if the initial connection request was sent to a statically mapped IP address or to the IP address of the firewall itself, the firewall could inspect its destination and forward it on without issue.

Remember that the data that is sent in the initial connection from the Web Component Server to the Web connector is the IOR of the WCS. The IOR contains the IP address and the port of the Web Component Server. Moreover, this is the internal IP address of the Web Component Server—it is not the address of the firewall or a static IP address of the firewall that is mapped to the internal IP address. To allow this traffic through, therefore, on a NAT firewall, the rule that needs to be in place for Web connector to Web Component Server communication is that the packets to the internal IP address must be allowed through the firewall. (This may, of course, require further rules to route these packets on the firewall.)

The ports that are allowed through can be narrowed, of course. The destination port on which the Web Component Server is listening and its request port need to be allowed through the firewall. In the end, the firewall rules with a NAT firewall are pretty much in line with what the firewall rules are on an IP filter firewall. For example, Table 12.4 assumes the Web Component Server is inside the network and the Web connector is external to the network.

TABLE 12.4   FIREWALL CONFIGURATION RULES (WCS INTERNAL AND WC EXTERNAL)

Source	Destination	Port	Action
Internal IP of WCS	External IP of WC	Any	Accept
External IP of WC	Internal IP of WCS	WCS listening port (6401 by default), `-requestport`	Accept
External Network	Internal Network	Any	Reject

If packets from the hosts on the external network sent to the internal IOP addresses are routed to the firewall and the firewall accepts the packets, the connection will be established successfully. Given that in many cases the external network is a DMZ and the firewall is a router on the LAN, this configuration is possible by adding static routes on the hosts in the DMZ to the firewall. Depending on network configuration, even static routes on the hosts won't be necessary if the firewall between the internal network and DMZ is the default route for all traffic.

CRYSTAL ENTERPRISE AND PROXY SERVERS

It is not the intention at this stage in the book to investigate how Crystal Enterprise can be configured to work with proxy servers in any great detail. This is covered in some depth in

PART
IV
CH
12

the Administrator's guide that accompanies Crystal Enterprise. However, some sample Socks configurations will be shown and there will be a brief discussion as to how Crystal Enterprise would operate effectively with each configuration.

Socks settings for each of the Crystal Enterprise servers are defined using the Crystal Configuration Manager (through the Connection tab).

SOCKS—THE WEB CONNECTOR AND WEB COMPONENT SERVER

Figure 12.15 illustrates the operation of socks between the Web connector and the Web Component Server.

Figure 12.15
Socks configuration–
Web connector to
Web Component
Server.

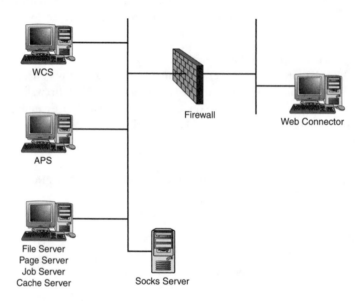

Given this scenario, the Socks setting through the Crystal Configuration Manager should be the following:

- On Web connector, specify the Socks server at the WCS Configuration tab.
- On APS, specify the Socks server at the Connection tab.

Access control rules on the Socks server should be set to something similar to that shown in Table 12.5.

TABLE 12.5 SOCKS CONFIGURATION (WEB CONNECTOR TO WCS)

Source	Destination	Port	Action
Web connector	Web Component Server	6401 `-requestport`	Accept
Otherwise			Reject

There are a couple of points worth noting:

- Although the Web connector connects to Web Component Server, the Socks server information is set up on APS rather than on Web Component Server. This is because the Web Component Server will obtain the Socks setting from APS.

- The initialization from Web connector to WCS port 6401 uses the host name for the WCS in the Socks request. Therefore, the Socks server must be able to resolve the host name for Web Component Server. For example, if the Web connector and WCS use NetBios names and the Socks server is a Unix box that doesn't support NetBios names, it is necessary to be sure the Socks server can resolve the same name as specified by the Web connector; that is, by using a local hosts file.

SOCKS–WEB COMPONENT SERVER AND APS

Figure 12.16 illustrates the operation of Socks between the Web Component Server and the APS.

Figure 12.16
Socks configuration–
Web Component
Server to APS.

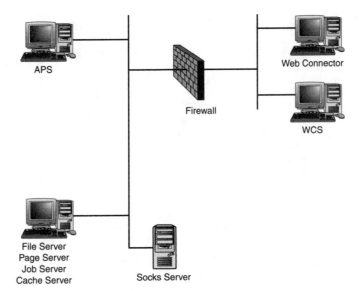

PART

IV

CH

12

In this instance the Socks setting at Crystal Configuration manager should be the following:

- On WCS, specify the Socks server at the APS Configuration tab.
- On APS, specify the Socks server at the Connection tab.

Access control rules on the Socks server should be set to something similar to that shown in Table 12.6.

TABLE 12.6   SOCKS CONFIGURATION (WCS TO APS)

Source	Destination	Port	Action
Web Component Server	APS	6400 -requestport	Accept
Web Component Server	Other Enterprise Servers	Default ports -requestports	Accept
Otherwise			Reject

Please note that when WCS makes the initial connection to APS on port 6400, it will pass the host name to the Socks server. Thus, the Socks server must resolve the APS hostname.

SOCKS—MULTIPLE CRYSTAL ENTERPRISE SERVERS

Figure 12.17 illustrates the operation of socks between multiple servers in the Crystal Enterprise environment.

Figure 12.17
Socks configuration–
multiple servers.

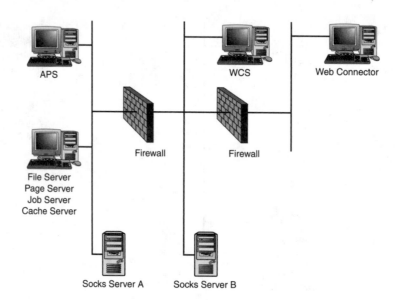

When multiple Socks servers are deployed in the network, the Crystal Enterprise Socks setup can facilitate the traversal of them. However, due care and attention should be taken in how the Socks servers are placed and traversed. In general, the Crystal Enterprise servers see these Socks servers as a chain, and the setup in the Crystal Console Manager should specify how to traverse them from the outermost to the innermost.

In this instance the Socks setting at Crystal Configuration Manager should be the following:

- On Web connector, specify the Socks server B at the WCS Configuration tab
- On WCS, specify the Socks server A at the APS Configuration tab

- On WCS, specify the Socks server B at the Connection tab
- On APS, specify the Socks servers B followed by A at the Connection tab

Access control rules on the Socks server should be set to something similar to that shown in Table 12.7.

TABLE 12.7   SOCKS CONFIGURATION (MULTIPLE SERVERS)

Source	Destination	Port	Action
Web connector	Web Component Server	6401 `-requestport`	Accept
Web Component Server	APS	6400	Accept
Web Component Server	Other Enterprise Servers	default ports `-requestports`	Accept
Otherwise			Reject

The point to note is that in the IOR for the APS, the Socks server chain B-A is embedded. However, because the WCS has been configured with a local Socks server B, the program will do a comparison of these two Socks server lists and deduce that WCS only needs to go through A to reach the APS.

SUMMARY

This chapter reviewed how Crystal Enterprise operates within a complex network that uses standard firewall deployments. Through the flexibility offered by the Crystal Enterprise architecture, the Crystal Enterprise system administrator should feel confident in the scalability of the server processes across the enterprise. The system as a whole can be deployed within the stringent security requirements that a Web-based delivery of information warrants, whether the deployment is on a small scale or part of a very large deployment to support hundreds of thousands of users.

Fundamentally, the wide variety of firewall-based security options supported by Crystal Enterprise represents the wisdom of an architecture design that was, from the ground up, designed strictly for the delivery of Web-based information.

Rather than the "front end" being a Web-based "bolt-on" to a standard client/server architecture, with all the overhead, inflexibility, and restriction that this brings to deployment options, all process communication between the servers contained in the Crystal Enterprise system are based upon TCP/IP and port protocol—the "currency" of the Web. With the opportunities offered by the Web (either as an external point of reference or as the standard interface to all systems if possible) the delivery of report-based information must be seen as indivisible from any other form of Web-based communication both inside and outside the "walls" of the organization.

PART

IV

CH

12

CUSTOMIZING CRYSTAL ENTERPRISE

EXTENDING CRYSTAL ENTERPRISE

In this chapter

Crystal Enterprise was intended from its inception to be completely customizable. Gone are the days when end users are required to take it or leave it when it comes to business intelligence application look, feel, and function.

Although Crystal Enterprise ships with many feature-rich applications and samples, such as ePortfolio, out of the box, a wealth of possibilities exists for custom applications and end-user portals to be developed using the extensive set of APIs available with Crystal Enterprise. Almost anything that Crystal Enterprise does is accessible through an open API.

The open API model of Crystal Enterprise allows application developers to create new Web applications that will satisfy exactly what end users or clients require to interact with the Crystal Enterprise system. Additionally, the SDK also allows Crystal Enterprise functionality to be integrated seamlessly into a wide variety of existing Web applications that an organization already has in place.

This chapter provides a review of how the Crystal Enterprise SDK APIs are used and work together. By the first section of this chapter, it will be evident that a good, well-rounded understanding of Web development technologies, such as HTML, JavaScript, server-side scripting, and so on, will come in handy for creating Web-based applications that use the Crystal Enterprise SDK.

Being familiar with these technologies will help those who are interested in designing new Crystal Enterprise Web applications to make better design decisions for their Web development projects. And for those who are new to Web development in general, not just Crystal Enterprise, it's strongly recommended this chapter be supplemented with a book on Microsoft's Active Server Pages (ASP), as well as reference books for HTML and client-side JavaScript.

UNDERSTANDING CRYSTAL SERVER PAGES

With Crystal Enterprise, Web applications such as ePortfolio are enabled on the Web Component Server (WCS) by using Crystal Server Pages (CSP), which work in a similar fashion to Microsoft's Active Server Pages (ASP) or Java Server Pages (JSP). In essence, CSP pages are HTML pages that contain embedded snippets of code or script.

In the same way that ASP pages work, CSP pages allow for COM objects to be used in the embedded code. The embedded code in a CSP page is dynamically processed server-side, on the WCS, with the results of the page being served back to the client as plain HTML content. The COM objects that are called within the script or code of a CSP page are the objects that comprise the Crystal Enterprise SDK. It's this power that enables an application developer to leverage any function of Crystal Enterprise in any way he chooses.

CSP is more than just a nifty name that Crystal Decisions gave to delineate between ASP and CSP. By providing CSP support in Crystal Enterprise, the generation of dynamic Web content is supported on a variety of Web server platforms. That is, because the server-side processing of CSP pages occurs on the WCS, which is connected to Web server(s) with a Crystal Web connector, Crystal Enterprise Web applications can be deployed with a wide variety of Web server platforms.

Note

Refer to Chapter 3, "Exploring the System Architecture," for more details on the role of the Web Component Server and the Web connector.

Similar to many other server-page technologies, such as ASP and JSP, the embedded server-side scripting code in a CSP page is enclosed between an opening <% tag and a closing %> tag. So, a very simple CSP page might look like this:

```
<%
strMessage = "Hello World"
%>
<html>
<p><%= strMessage %></p>
</html>
```

The variable strMessage is first assigned a value, and then the variable is embedded inline within the HTML code to display its value. Web application developers who are familiar with ASP will know that this code would also work in an ASP page. The only difference is that the code in the ASP page would be processed on a Web server, such as Microsoft Internet Information Server, while the code in the CSP page would be processed on the WCS. This delegation of processing is a fundamental advantage of CSP. Because the Web Component Server processes the server-side script, a minimal load is placed on a corporate Web server. Nor does the Web Component Server need to be installed on the same physical server as the Web server, such as Microsoft Internet Information Server.

In the Windows NT version of Crystal Enterprise, CSP supports two scripting languages, VBScript and Microsoft JScript. When using the Unix version of Crystal Enterprise, CSP supports the mozilla.org JavaScript engine. References for these scripting languages can be found at these Web sites:

- http://msdn.microsoft.com/scripting/
- http://www.mozilla.org/js/

CSP pages support several implicit objects that are commonly found in other similar server-pages technologies:

- **Server**—The Server object provides a series of utility methods, such as CreateObject. The CreateObject method allows new COM objects to be instantiated.
- **Request**—The Request object is used to retrieve data in an HTTP request from the client browser.
- **Response**—The Response object is used to send data in an HTTP response to the client browser.
- **Session**—The Session object provides a way of storing and accessing a user's current state and related session information.

Although these CSP-implicit objects behave very much like those in other server-pages technologies, keep in mind that they are native to the Crystal Enterprise environment, and hence, have the capability to retrieve information specific to the Crystal Enterprise system.

For example, the CSP Request object can retrieve server information, such as server name, server port, and so on, just as ASP and JSP request objects are able to do. However, in CSP, this object is processed on the WCS, which is connected to the Crystal Enterprise Framework, allowing it to retrieve Crystal Enterprise-specific information such as the APS name and the TCP/IP port to the Crystal Web connector.

For example:

```
'GET THE NAME OF THE APS TO WHICH THE WCS IS REGISTERED
apsname = Request.ServerVariables("WCS_NAME_SERVER")
```

USING THE CRYSTAL ENTERPRISE OBJECT MODEL

It's important to note that using the Crystal Enterprise object model is unavoidable. It's the only way to develop applications using Crystal Enterprise. All the applications provided with Crystal Enterprise, such as ePortfolio, use the SDK. This allows for some level of consistency between different applications using Crystal Enterprise.

There are three scenarios for which most developers will use the Crystal Enterprise SDK:

■ Customizing ePortfolio or one of the Developer Samples
■ Developing a Crystal Enterprise application from scratch
■ Integrating Crystal Enterprise functionality with another application or portal

In each of these scenarios, some basic steps are necessary to provide Crystal Enterprise services to end users. The first step is to determine which Crystal Enterprise services are to be provided to the end users and in what fashion.

For example, if a user wants to simply view a report, the following steps must be taken in the application code for Crystal Enterprise to make this happen:

1. Log on to Crystal Enterprise.
2. Query the APS for the location and ID of the report object and any parent objects it might have.
3. Write the location of the report in the Crystal Enterprise system as a hyperlink for the end user to select via a Web-based application, Web page, or portal.

Crystal Enterprise handles the rest. For the preceding scenario, after a hyperlink to a specific report object has been written for a user to click on, there isn't anything else that an application developer needs to worry about. Crystal Enterprise handles the confirmation of a user's rights to view that report, runs the report if necessary, and delivers the result as a Web page to the user's browser.

Of course, not every information delivery application is that simple. Users will want to leverage the capability of Crystal Enterprise to schedule reports, deliver reports to various destinations such as e-mail, and output reports to various formats such as .PDF.

This demand for the features of Crystal Enterprise fuels a Crystal Enterprise application's complexity, something that must be evaluated *before* application development begins. Hence, the reason ePortfolio is open source. Any code within ePortfolio can be leveraged for other applications.

LOGGING ON TO CRYSTAL ENTERPRISE

Any Crystal Enterprise application first must be able to log a user to the system before any interaction with reports can be accomplished. There are several methods by which this can be accomplished. The purpose of logging on to Crystal Enterprise is to establish a session, a method by which a user can interact with Crystal Enterprise seamlessly, retrieving any and all reports and objects to which they have access.

LOGGING ON TO CRYSTAL ENTERPRISE WITH A USERNAME AND PASSWORD

This is a fairly straightforward two-step procedure. First, a reference to the `SessionMgr` object is required. The `SessionMgr` (session manager) object is the top-level object in the Crystal Enterprise object model that manages all logons to the system.

The second step to logging on is to call the `SessionMgr` object's `Logon` method, passing it four parameters:

- Username
- Password
- APS name
- Authentication type

As reviewed in Chapter 10, "Administering and Configuring Crystal Enterprise," Crystal Enterprise has several different types of authentication models it supports, including the following:

- Crystal Enterprise authentication (`secEnterprise`)
- Windows NT authentication (`secWindowsNT`)
- LDAP authentication (`secLDAP`)

Naturally, whatever authentication model is in use with Crystal Enterprise will drive the username and password sent.

Put together, the sample code for these two steps looks like this:

```
'Create the session manager
Set sm = Server.CreateObject("CrystalEnterprise.SessionMgr")
'Logon to the system
Set es = sm.Logon("myUserName", "myPassword", "myAPSName", "secEnterprise")
```

Upon a successful logon, an `EnterpriseSession` object is returned.

PART

V

CH

13

LOGGING ON TO CRYSTAL ENTERPRISE WITH A LOGON TOKEN

Although the Crystal Enterprise Web Component Server (WCS) will automatically track an application user's current session, there will be situations when sessions will time out. For the application to seamlessly reaccess the system, it's possible to log the user on to the system with the use of a logon token.

CREATING A LOGON TOKEN

If there is one universal truth in application development, it's that end users do not like typing in usernames and passwords more than once, and sometimes that's too much! To avoid this, it's advisable to create a logon token at the beginning of a session; that is, when the user logs on to the system. After it's created, store the logon token as a cookie in the user's browser. This way, when the session expires, it's possible for the application to retrieve this "token" and relog the user on to the system.

Note

It's possible to control how long a session with Crystal Enterprise should last. Refer to a control of the `Session` object: `Session.Timeout`.

To create a logon token, enter the following code in a CSP page:

```
'Get the logon token manager
Set ltm = es.LogonTokenMgr
'Create a logon token for connection from any machine, valid for max. 1 day or
    100 uses
lt = ltm.CreateLogonToken("", 1, 100)
'Store the logon token as a cookie
Response.Cookies("myLogonToken").Value = lt
```

LOGGING ON WITH A LOGON TOKEN

Now that a logon token has been stored on the user's browser, when the user's session times out, the application may use the token to relog the user on to the system.

To reuse the token, include the following CSP script:

```
'Create the session manager
Set sm = Server.CreateObject("CrystalEnterprise.SessionMgr")
'Get the logon token from the browser's cookies
lt = Request.Cookies("myLogonToken")
'Logon with the token
Set es = sm.LogonWithToken(lt)
```

Listing 13.1 demonstrates the steps to log on to and off of the Crystal Enterprise system (see Figure 13.1).

Tip

When passing the APS token via a URL line for any given application, be sure to use the `URLEncode` command. This command is important because the APS token in Crystal Enterprise 8.5 includes nonalphanumeric characters. It's also important to update any existing Crystal Enterprise 8 applications to use the `URLEncode` command.

Figure 13.1

Logging on to Crystal Enterprise

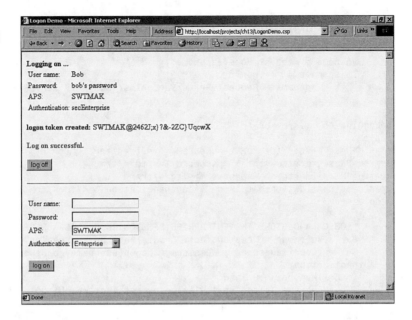

LISTING 13.1 LOGONDEMO.CSP

```
<%
'Written by Stephen Mak
'Name: LogonDemo.csp
'Description: Demonstrates how to log on and use logon tokens.

Option Explicit
On Error Resume Next

'PREVENT BROWSER FROM CACHING THE PAGE
Response.ExpiresAbsolute = Now() - 1
%>
<html>
<head>
<title>Logon Demo</title>
</head>
<body>
<%
Dim strAction
strAction = Request.Form("action")

Dim sessionmgr, enterprisesession, logontokenmgr, logontoken

If strAction = "logon" Then
        Dim username, password, apsname, authentication
        username = Request.Form("username")
        password = Request.Form("password")

        authentication = Request.Form("authentication")
```

LISTING 13.1 CONTINUED

```
            'GET APS NAME
            apsname = Request.Form("apsname")
            If apsname = "" Then
                    apsname = Request.ServerVariables("WCS_NAME_SERVER")
            End If
%>
<b>Logging on ...</b><br>
<table>
<tr><td>User name:</td><td><%= username %></td></tr>
<tr><td>Password:</td><td><%= password %></td></tr>
<tr><td>APS:</td><td><%= apsname %></td></tr>
<tr><td>Authentication:</td><td><%= authentication %></td></tr>
</table><br>
<%
        'LOG ON AND STORE THE ENTERPRISE SESSION OBJECT AS A SESSION VARIABLE
        Set sessionmgr = CreateObject("CrystalEnterprise.SessionMgr")
        Set enterprisesession = sessionmgr.Logon(username, password, apsname,
    authentication)
        If Err.Number <> 0 Then
                Response.Write "<p style='color:red;font-weight:bold'>Log on error
    ...<br>" & Err.Description & "</p>" & vbCrLf
        Else
                Set Session("enterprisesession") = enterprisesession
                Set logontokenmgr = enterprisesession.LogonTokenMgr
                logontoken = logontokenmgr.CreateLogonToken("", 1, 100)
                Response.Write "<b>logon token created:</b> "
    & Server.HTMLEncode(logontoken) & "<br>"
                Response.Cookies("logontoken") = logontoken
%>
<p style='color:green;font-weight:bold'>Log on successful.</p>
<form method="post" action="LogonDemo.csp">
<input type="hidden" name="action" value="logoff">
<input type="submit" value="log off">
</form>
<%
        End If
ElseIf strAction = "logoff" Then
        Response.Write "<b>Logging off ...</b><br><br>"
        logontoken = Request.Cookies("logontoken")
        If logontoken <> "" Then
                'GET THE LOGON TOKEN MANAGER AND RELEASE THE TOKEN
                Set enterprisesession = Session("enterprisesession")
                Set logontokenmgr = enterprisesession.LogonTokenMgr
                logontokenmgr.ReleaseToken(logontoken)
                Response.Write "<b>logon token released:</b> " &
    Server.HTMLEncode(logontoken) & "<br>"
        End If

        'RELEASE RESOURCES USED BY SESSION
        Session.Abandon
End If
%>

<hr><!-- Log on form-->
<form method="post" action="LogonDemo.csp">
```

LISTING 13.1   CONTINUED

```html
<input type="hidden" name="action" value="logon">
<table>
<tr>
    <td>User name:</td>
    <td><input type="text" name="username"></td>
</tr>
<tr>
    <td>Password:</td>
    <td><input type="password" name="password"></td>

</tr>
<tr>
    <td>APS:</td>
    <td><input type="text" name="apsname" value="<%=
    Request.ServerVariables("WCS_NAME_SERVER") %>"></td>
</tr>
<tr>
    <td>Authentication:</td>
    <td>
        <select name="authentication">
        <option value="secEnterprise">Enterprise</option>
        <option value="secWindowsNT">Windows NT</option>
    </td>
</tr>
<tr>
    <td><br><input type="submit" value="log on"></td>
    <td></td>
</tr>
</table>
</form>
</body>
</html>
```

ACCESSING THE INFOSTORE

After establishing a session with Crystal Enterprise via CSP code, the next step is to query the InfoStore, which is the Crystal Enterprise repository for objects, such as Crystal Reports.

The most important library in the Crystal Enterprise SDK, the one that allows an application to retrieve and modify information on the Crystal Enterprise system, is the InfoStore library. Within this library the key objects are the InfoStore itself, the InfoObjects collection, and the InfoObject. In the Crystal Enterprise 8.5 developer documentation, an object model diagram is available that clearly defines the relationship between these objects.

Starting at the most granular level, the InfoObject is an abstraction of an object that is persisted in the Crystal Enterprise system. An InfoObject contains information about itself, such as its name, description, type, and so on. Examples of the different types of InfoObjects that can exist on a Crystal Enterprise system are

- Reports (Crystal Report)
- Report instances
- Analytical reports (Crystal Analytical Report)
- Folders

An InfoObjects collection is, not surprisingly, a collection of InfoObject objects. After a reference to this collection is obtained, a developer can enumerate through it to get each InfoObject contained within.

The InfoStore object is the key object that allows retrieval, scheduling, and modification of reports as well as creation of new InfoObjects collections. To retrieve an InfoObjects collection from the Crystal Enterprise system, the Query method is called, passing in a SQL-like query statement.

> **Note**
>
> To get the InfoStore object, the user must be logged on first and the application must have reference to the EnterpriseSession object. The logged-on user's rights will determine what InfoObjects may be accessed by the InfoStore object.

To retrieve the top-level folder objects (which contain reports) in a Crystal Enterprise system, use the following CSP code:

```
'GET THE INFOSTORE OBJECT
Set infostore = es.Service("", "InfoStore")
'QUERY FOR THE TOP-LEVEL FOLDERS
Set infoobjects = infostore.Query("SELECT * FROM " & _
    "CI_INFOOBJECTS WHERE SI_PARENTID = 0 AND " & _
    "SI_PROGID = 'CrystalEnterprise.Folder'")
'ENUMERATE THROUGH THE COLLECTION AND DISPLAY THE NAME OF EACH OBJECT
For Each infoobject In infoobjects
    'Output the name of each infoobject
    Response.Write infoobjects.Properties("SI_NAME") & "<br>"
Next
```

After the InfoStore is queried for certain objects, the result is written via response.write back to the application end-user's browser as a hyperlink. The end user of an application would receive a simple hyperlink to a folder for instance, which could be clicked on to discover reports contained within the folder.

Querying the APS

It's apparent in the preceding section, "Accessing the InfoStore," that there is a requirement to query the InfoStore any time a user wants to view the contents of a folder, find a specific report, or view a scheduled instance of a report. To query the InfoStore is to submit a query directly to the APS, essentially the "keeper" of the InfoStore.

As previously mentioned, the APS is queried using a SQL-like syntax. The syntax is SQL-like because not all SQL keywords work when querying the APS as one would assume.

Regardless, understanding how to query the APS for objects in the InfoStore is the heart of Crystal Enterprise. If a user wants to view a specific folder's contents, a query must be submitted to the APS with the proper folder ID and user ID. The folder ID informs Crystal Enterprise that the user wants to view any report objects that are children of the folder. The user ID enables the APS to enforce security on the query result. The query result would only provide report IDs that were permitted for that particular user to view.

A very useful tool provided with Crystal Enterprise enables system administrators and developers to directly query the APS without writing CSP pages. The CSP Query Builder is available under the Developer Samples section of the Crystal Enterprise Launchpad.

For example, start the CSP Query Builder and enter the following query into the query window:

```
Select * From CI_INFOOBJECTS
```

After this is entered, click the Submit Query button. Notice that the logon information supplied to the CSP Query Builder application affects the returned resultset. Try using a specific user account with restrictions to a particular folder or object. Note that information for those objects is not returned in the query.

Effectively querying the APS is one of the most crucial pieces related to application performance when a large number of objects are present in the Crystal Enterprise system. Clearly, using `Select * from CI_INFOOBJECTS` is not an ideal query.

Just as with any other relational database, using efficient queries to retrieve data is a best practice and often can be the culprit when experiencing poor Crystal Enterprise application performance.

USING INFOOBJECTS, PLUG-INS, AND PluginInterfaces

As described in the previous section, an InfoObject is a representation of an object that is persisted on the APS. However, the interface exposed by the InfoObject is generic and does not expose any properties or methods that are specific to an object's type (report, folder, user, and so on). For example, a report's parameters are specific to and only applicable to a report InfoObject.

Each object type is represented by a supported plug-in installed on the Crystal Enterprise system, and each plug-in exposes an interface with properties and methods specific to it. To get this secondary interface from an InfoObject, use its `PluginInterface` property.

For example, to retrieve a specific report object's collection of parameters:

```
'GET A REPORT OBJECT
Set infoobjects = infostore.query("SELECT * FROM " & _
    "CI_INFOOBJECTS WHERE SI_INSTANCE = 0 AND " & _
    "SI_PROGID = 'CrystalEnterprise.Report'")
Set infoobject = infoobjects.Item(1)
'GET THE INFOOBJECT'S PLUG-IN INTERFACE
Set report = infoobject.PluginInterface("")
'GET THE REPORT OBJECT'S PARAMETERS COLLECTION
Set parameters = report.ReportParameters
```

PART
V

CH

13

After the parameters of an object are retrieved, they can be displayed to an end user or manipulated by adding application code to the developer's suiting.

UNDERSTANDING THE CI_INFOOBJECTS TABLE

The CI_INFOOBJECTS table was introduced in Crystal Enterprise 8.0 and was the only table exposed in that version. The CI_INFOOBJECTS table contains desktop objects, which are the objects that are commonly retrieved for end-user client applications. For example, all objects that appear in the ePortfolio application that ships with Crystal Enterprise are desktop objects that are retrieved from the CI_INFOOBJECTS table.

The CI_INFOOBJECTS table contains instances of Desktop objects, which include the following types of objects:

- Report
- Favorites Folder
- Folder
- Shortcut
- Excel
- PDF
- RTF
- Txt
- Word

THE CRYSTAL ENTERPRISE ADMINISTRATIVE API

In Crystal Enterprise 8.0, the InfoStore API and a small handful of plug-in interfaces were exposed to developers. For Crystal Enterprise 8.5, a new set of administrative APIs have been introduced. For the most part, this means that new types of InfoObjects (such as their plug-ins) are now accessible through the Crystal Enterprise SDK. Hence, it's now possible to do all the following when developing applications for Crystal Enterprise:

- Create new objects, such as users, user groups, server groups, and so on
- Delete users, user groups, server groups, and so on
- Assign users to user groups and vice versa
- Assign servers to server groups
- Manage servers; in other words, start, stop, and restart them
- Change the access roles on InfoObjects
- Assign granular rights on InfoObjects

In a nutshell, all functionality exposed in the Crystal Management Console is now exposed through the Crystal Enterprise 8.5 SDK. For more information on the CMC, refer to Chapters 5 and 10.

The potential of the Administrative functions is where the real power lies. A completely custom interface could be created for users who should only have access to certain administrative areas.

LEARNING THE NEW CI_SYSTEMOBJS TABLE AND NEW PLUG-INS

In Crystal Enterprise 8.5, a new table called CI_SYSTEMOBJS is introduced. The CI_SYSTEMOBJS table contains the administrative objects used in a Crystal Enterprise system. These objects are most commonly used for administrative tasks and for developing administrative applications. Although the Crystal Management Console (CMC) is not written using CSP pages, all its administrative functionality is based on objects retrieved from this table. Specifically, the CI_SYSTEMOBJS table contains the following:

- Instances of Desktop objects
  - Connection
  - Destination
  - Event
  - LicenseKey
  - Server
  - User
  - UserGroup
- Instances of Administration objects installed on the system:
  - APS Administration plug-in
  - Cache Page Server Admin plug-in
  - Event Server Admin plug-in
  - File Repository Admin plug-in
  - Job Server Admin plug-in
  - Web Component Server Admin plug-in
- Instances of plug-in objects installed on the system:
  - Desktop plug-ins
    - Excel plug-in
    - PDF plug-in
    - RTF plug-in
    - Txt plug-in
    - Word plug-in

- Authentication plug-ins
  - secEnterprise plug-in
  - secLDAPConfig plug-in
  - secWindowsNT plug-in
- Destination plug-in objects
  - DiskUnmanaged plug-in
  - FTP plug-in
  - SMTP plug-in

BASIC CRYSTAL ENTERPRISE FUNCTIONALITY

The rest of the chapter provides examples of how to use the Crystal Enterprise SDK for a variety of application purposes.

NAVIGATING FOLDER HIERARCHY AND RETRIEVING INFOOBJECTS

The desktop objects in the CI_INFOOBJECTS table are organized in a hierarchical fashion with the use of folders. The folder structure maintains a parent-child relationship between a folder and its content. Therefore, the key to navigating this hierarchical structure is the use of the properties SI_ID and SI_PARENTID.

At the top of the hierarchical structure are the top-level folders, which all have an SI_PARENTID property equal to 0. Note that only folder objects can reside at this level; that is, have SI_PARENTID = 0. Entering the following query in the CSP Query Builder will return all top-level folders:

```
SELECT SI_ID FROM CI_INFOOBJECTS WHERE SI_PARENTID = 0
```

Note

Refer to the section on Querying the APS for information on the CSP Query Builder. For reference, the CSP Query Builder is found in the Developer Samples section of the Crystal Launchpad.

To retrieve the objects that reside within a given folder, query for objects that have SI_PARENTID equal to the folder's ID. For example, if a folder has an ID of 123, the following query would return its contents:

```
SELECT SI_ID FROM CI_INFOOBJECTS WHERE SI_PARENTID = 123
```

The code in Listing 13.2 retrieves and displays the top-level folders and their contents.

PART

V

CH

13

LISTING 13.2   TOPLEVELFOLDERS.CSP

```
<%
'Written by Stephen Mak
'Name: TopLevelFolders.csp
'Description: Demonstrates how to navigate the folder hierarchy

Option Explicit

'PREVENT BROWSER FROM CACHING THE PAGE
Response.ExpiresAbsolute = Now() - 1

Dim username, password, apsname, authentication
username = ""
password = ""

'GET APS NAME
apsname = Request.ServerVariables("WCS_NAME_SERVER")
authentication = "secEnterprise"

Dim sm, es, infostore
'LOG ON AND INSTANTIATE INFOSTORE OBJECT
Set sm = CreateObject("CrystalEnterprise.SessionMgr")
Set es = sm.Logon(username, password, apsname, authentication)
Set infostore = es.Service("", "InfoStore")

Dim strQUery
Dim infoobjects, infoobject

'QUERY FOR THE TOP-LEVEL FOLDERS
strQUery = "SELECT SI_ID, SI_NAME FROM CI_INFOOBJECTS" & _
        " WHERE SI_PARENTID = 0"
Set infoobjects = infostore.Query(strQUery)

'WALK THROUGH THE LIST OF TOP-LEVEL FOLDERS
For Each infoobject In infoobjects
        Response.Write "Top-level folder: <b>" & _
                infoobject.Properties("SI_NAME") & "</b><br>" & vbCrLf

        'QUERY FOR THE CONTENTS OF THE FOLDER
        strQuery = "SELECT SI_ID, SI_NAME FROM " & _
                "CI_INFOOBJECTS WHERE SI_PARENTID = " & _
                infoobject.Properties("SI_ID")

        Response.Write "- contains:<br>" & vbCrLf
        Dim ios, io
        Set ios = infostore.Query(strQuery)

        'WALK THROUGH THE CONTENTS OF THE FOLDER
        For Each io In ios
                Response.Write "   <b>" & _
                        io.Properties("SI_NAME") & "</b><br>" & vbCrLf
        Next
Next
%>
```

RETRIEVING REPORT INSTANCES

Recall from Chapter 3 that when Crystal Enterprise has finished processing a report, the resulting report with its snapshot of data is stored as an instance in the Crystal Enterprise system. To retrieve these instances, it's necessary to query the APS.

Like a folder and its content, hierarchically, a report and its instances have a parent-child relationship. It's possible to retrieve the instances of a report by querying for objects with `SI_PARENTID` property equal to the report object's ID.

Given a report with ID of 234, entering the following query will retrieve its instances:

```
SELECT SI_ID FROM CI_INFOOBJECTS WHERE SI_PARENTID = 234
```

CREATING NEW FOLDERS

To create a new InfoObject:

1. Get the plug-in object for the type of InfoObject that you want to create.
2. Create a new `InfoObjects` collection.
3. Create a new InfoObject using the `Plugin` object.
4. Set some basic properties for the new InfoObject.
5. Commit the changes in the `InfoObjects` collection to the APS.

To create folders, it's necessary to get the folder plug-in (CrystalEnterprise.Folder) in step 1 and use it in creating the new InfoObject in step 3. Therefore, by applying different plug-ins, it's possible to create different types of InfoObjects, such as shortcuts, reports, and so on.

In Listing 13.3, a new folder called Example Folder is created as a top-level folder in Crystal Enterprise. If the CSP page runs successfully, the ID of the new folder will be displayed. To confirm that the folder is indeed created, run the Crystal Management Console (CMC). Note that if a folder by the same name already exists, the CSP page will return an error.

LISTING 13.3   CREATENEWFOLDER.CSP

```
<%
'Written by Stephen Mak
'Name: CreateNewFolders.csp
'Description: Demonstrates how to create new folders

Option Explicit

'PREVENT BROWSER FROM CACHING THE PAGE
Response.ExpiresAbsolute = Now() - 1

Dim username, password, apsname, authentication
'NOTE THAT USER NEEDS TO HAVE RIGHTS TO ADD FOLDER TO APS
username = "administrator"
password = ""
```

LISTING 13.3 CONTINUED

```
'GET APS NAME
apsname = Request.ServerVariables("WCS_NAME_SERVER")
authentication = "secEnterprise"

Dim sm, es, infostore
'LOGON AND INSTANTIATE INFOSTORE OBJECT
Set sm = CreateObject("CrystalEnterprise.SessionMgr")
Set es = sm.Logon(username, password, apsname, authentication)
Set infostore = es.Service("", "InfoStore")

'GET FOLDER PLUG-IN
Dim pluginmgr, folderplugin
Set pluginmgr = infostore.PluginManager
Set folderplugin = pluginmgr.PluginInfo("CrystalEnterprise.Folder")

Dim infoobjects, infoobject
'CREATE NEW (EMPTY) INFOOBJECTS COLLECTION
Set infoobjects = infostore.NewInfoObjectCollection()
'ADD A NEW FOLDER INFOOBJECT TO COLLECTION
Set infoobject = infoobjects.Add(folderplugin)

'SET NAME, DESCRIPTION AND PARENT ID FOR NEW INFOOBJECT
infoobject.Title = "Example Folder"
infoobject.Description = "Folder description"
infoobject.Properties("SI_PARENTID") = 0

'COMMIT THE NEW INFOOBJECTS TO THE APS
Call infostore.Commit(infoobjects)
%>
```

MOVING INFOOBJECTS

Each InfoObject has a ParentID property that determines where in the folder hierarchy it resides. Moving an InfoObject involves assigning a new value to its ParentID property, and then committing the changes to the system.

The following example moves the Example Folder folder (from the previous example) into the Report Samples folder:

```
'GET THE ID OF THE REPORT SAMPLES FOLDER
Set infoobjects = infostore.Query("SELECT SI_ID FROM CI_INFOOBJECTS WHERE
    SI_PARENTID = 0 AND SI_NAME = 'Report Samples'")
Set infoobject = infoobjects.Item(1)
id = infoobject.Properties("SI_ID")
GET THE EXAMPLE FOLDER OBJECT
Set infoobjects = infostore.Query("SELECT SI_PARENTID FROM CI_INFOOBJECTS WHERE
    SI_PARENTID = 0 AND SI_NAME = 'Example Folder'")
'SET EXAMPLE FOLDER'S PARENTID PROPERTY VALUE
Set infoobject = infoobjects.Item(1)
infoobject.Properties("SI_PARENTID") = id

'COMMIT THE CHANGES
Call infostore.Commit(infoobjects)
```

VIEWING REPORTS

Viewing reports in Crystal Enterprise is achieved by making requests to the Web Component Server (WCS). Actually viewing a report requires invoking the request, viewrpt.cwr. Viewrpt. cwr, like other Crystal extensions (such as .cwr and .csp) that are configured on the Web server, is forwarded to and handled by the WCS. All aspects of viewing the reports are subsequently controlled by additional parameters in the request. These additional parameters may be passed either in the query string of a GET request's URL or in the message body of a POST request.

For ease of demonstration, all examples in this section will pass parameters using the GET method. It should be noted, however, that often it is preferable to pass parameters to the Web Component Server using the POST method.

BASIC VIEWING OF A REPORT

To view a report, the minimum required information that needs to be passed to the WCS consists of a report ID and a valid logon token. So, the basic URL request to view a report will look like this:

```
http://myServerName/myCEApp/viewrpt.cwr?id=123&apstoken=
    MYAPS%401822J%5CTbKb%23%7D%3D%5FxnOy%2CY
```

where:

- The id parameter is the ID of the report object
- The apstoken parameter is the logon token for the session

Whenever possible, applications should use logon tokens when viewing a report to better control the use of the Crystal Enterprise licenses available on the system. However, if a logon token is not available or if an application does not use logon tokens, it's possible to pass a user's logon credentials in place of the apstoken parameter. These parameters are as follows:

- **apsuser**—username
- **apspassword**—password
- **apsauthtype**—authentication type

All parameters that are passed to the viewrpt.cwr Web request may be passed either as query string parameters in the URL or as part of the post data sent in the request header.

UNDERSTANDING REPORT VIEWERS

Recall from Chapters 1 through 5 that Crystal Enterprise provides several report viewers, such as DHTML, ActiveX, and Java, that enable interaction with a report through various technologies. To select a specific viewer for viewing a report, an additional init parameter is required to be passed in the request.

An example of a URL request to view a report using the ActiveX viewer would be

```
http://myServerName/myCEApp/viewrpt.cwr?id=123&apstoken=
    MYAPS%401822J%5CTbKb%23%7D%3D%5FxnOy%2CY&init=actx
```

Valid values for the `init` parameter are as follows:

- **actx**—ActiveX report viewer. An ActiveX control is embedded in an HTML page, and for obvious reasons, requires the client browser to support ActiveX controls.

- **nav_plugin**—Netscape Plug-in report viewer. This is similar to the ActiveX report viewer, except that it's implemented as a Netscape plug-in, allowing it to work in Netscape browsers.

- **java**—Java (using browser JVM) report viewer. A Java applet is embedded in an HTML page and requires a Java-enabled client browser. This applet uses the client browser's JVM.

- **java_plugin**—Java (using Sun Java Plug-in VM) report viewer. Also a Java applet that is embedded in an HTML page, but instead of using the client browser's JVM, uses the Sun Java Plug-in VM.

- **html_frame**—DHTML with frames. A true thin-client view of a report, requiring no downloads and only a client browser that supports W3C HTML 4.0 standards.

The `connect` parameter is used to reestablish a connection to the Page Server, allowing a user to reset the report's parameter values and, if necessary, reprocess the report. The syntax for using the `connect` parameter is as follows:

```
http://myServerName/myCEApp/viewrpt.cwr?id=123&apstoken=
    MYAPS%401822J%5CTbKb%23%7D%3D%5FxnOy%2CY&init=actx:connect
```

Notice that the `connect` parameter must be appended to the `init` parameter.

In Figure 13.2 and Listing 13.4, the provided server-side VBScript code logs on with the Administrator user account, creates a logon token, and gets the ID of the report InfoObject. Then the client-side JavaScript uses the ID and logon token to construct the URL request to view a report with the report viewer that the user selects.

LISTING 13.4   VIEWERDEMO.CSP

```
<%
'Written by Stephen Mak
'Name: ViewerDemo.csp
'Description: Demonstrates how to view a report using
'    different report viewers.

Option Explicit

'PREVENT BROWSER FROM CACHING THE PAGE
Response.ExpiresAbsolute = Now() - 1

Dim username, password, apsname, authentication
username = "administrator"
password = ""
'GET APS NAME
apsname = Request.ServerVariables("WCS_NAME_SERVER")
authentication = "secEnterprise"

Dim sm, es, infostore
'LOGON AND INSTANTIATE INFOSTORE OBJECT
```

LISTING 13.4 CONTINUED

```
Set sm = CreateObject("CrystalEnterprise.SessionMgr")
Set es = sm.Logon(username, password, apsname, authentication)
Set infostore = es.Service("", "InfoStore")

'CREATE A LOGON TOKEN
Dim tokenMgr, token
Set tokenMgr = es.LogonTokenMgr
token = tokenMgr.CreateLogonToken("", 1, 100)

Dim infoobjects, infoobject, id
'GET THE ID OF THE WORLD SALES REPORT
Set infoobjects = infostore.Query("SELECT SI_ID FROM " &_
        "CI_INFOOBJECTS WHERE " &_
        "SI_PROGID = 'CrystalEnterprise.Report' " &_
        "AND SI_NAME='World Sales Report'")
Set infoobject = infoobjects.Item(1)
id = infoobject.Properties("SI_ID")
%>
<html>
<head>
<title>Viewer Demo</title>
<script>
//JavaScript function that constructs the URL request
//to view the report using a selected viewer
function viewReport()
{
        var sel = document.forms["form"].elements["viewer"];
        var urlstring = "http://localhost/crystal/enterprise/";
        urlstring += "viewrpt.cwr?id=<%= id %>";
        urlstring += "&apstoken=<%= Server.HTMLEncode(token) %>";
        urlstring += "&init=" + sel.options[sel.selectedIndex].value;
        urlstring += escape(":connect");
        window.open(urlstring);
}
</script>
</head>
<body>

<form name="form">
Select viewer: <select name="viewer">
        <option value="actx" selected>ActiveX</option>
        <option value="nav_plugin">Netscape Plugin</option>
        <option value="java">Java</option>
        <option value="java_plugin">Java Plugin</option>
        <option value="html_frame">DHTML</option>
</select>
<input type='button' value='view' onclick='javascript:viewReport()'>
</form>

</body>
</html>
```

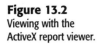

Figure 13.2
Viewing with the
ActiveX report viewer.

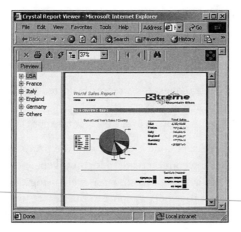

ENTERING PARAMETER FIELD VALUES

There are two ways to send report parameter field values to the server. The first method uses the report parameter name as part of the request's parameter name, and the second method uses the report's parameter index in the request's parameter name.

In the first method, simply append `promptex-` with the report parameter name. So then if a report has a parameter called `exampleparam`, the URL request to set its value would look like this:

```
http://myServerName/myCEApp/viewrpt.cwr?id=123&apstoken=
    MYAPS%401822J%5CTbKb%23%7D%3D%5FxnOy%2CY&promptex-exampleparam="example"
```

The second method identifies report parameters by their index number, appending the index number to the request parameter name `prompt`. The resulting URL request would look like this:

```
http://myServerName/myCEApp/viewrpt.cwr?id=123&apstoken=
    MYAPS%401822J%5CTbKb%23%7D%3D%5FxnOy%2CY&prompt0="example"
```

EXPORTING REPORTS

To export reports to a specific format, two parameters are required in addition to the basic report viewing parameters:

- **cmd**—This parameter's only valid value for exporting is `"export"`.
- **export_fmt**—Valid values for this parameter are:
  - `U2FPDF:0`—Adobe PDF
  - `U2FHTML:2`—HTML 3.2
  - `U2FHTML:3`—HTML 4.0
  - `U2FCR:0`—Crystal Reports (RPT)
  - `U2FXLS:3`—Excel 5.0 (XLS)

PART
V

CH

13

- `U2FXLS:4`—Excel 5.0 (XLS) Extended
- `U2FRTF:0`—Rich Text Format (RTF)
- `U2FWORDW:0`—Word Document (DOC)

For example, the following is a URL request for a report exported to PDF format:

```
http://myServerName/myCEApp/viewrpt.cwr?id=123&apstoken=
    MYAPS%401822J%5CTbKb%23%7D%3D%5FxnOy%2CY&cmd=export&export_fmt=U2FPDF:0
```

In Listing 13.5, the server-side VBScript code is identical to the previous example's code—it logs on with the Administrator user account, creates a logon token, and gets the ID of the report InfoObject. The client-side JavaScript is similar as well, using the ID and logon token to construct the URL request to export a report to the export format that the user selects. Figure 13.3 shows this code in action.

Figure 13.3
Exporting to Adobe PDF format.

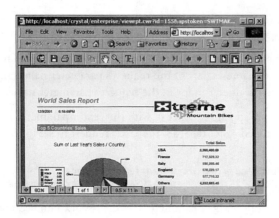

LISTING 13.5   EXPORTDEMO.CSP

```
<%
'Written by Stephen Mak
'Name: ExportDemo.csp
'Description: Demonstrates how to export a report.

Option Explicit

'PREVENT BROWSER FROM CACHING THE PAGE
Response.ExpiresAbsolute = Now() - 1

Dim username, password, apsname, authentication
username = "administrator"
password = ""

'GET APS NAME
apsname = Request.ServerVariables("WCS_NAME_SERVER")
authentication = "secEnterprise"
```

LISTING 13.5   CONTINUED

```
Dim sm, es, infostore
'LOGON AND INSTANTIATE INFOSTORE OBJECT
Set sm = CreateObject("CrystalEnterprise.SessionMgr")
Set es = sm.Logon(username, password, apsname, authentication)
Set infostore = es.Service("", "InfoStore")

'CREATE A LOGON TOKEN
Dim tokenMgr, token
Set tokenMgr = es.LogonTokenMgr
token = tokenMgr.CreateLogonToken("", 1, 100)

Dim infoobjects, infoobject, id
'GET THE ID OF THE WORLD SALES REPORT
Set infoobjects = infostore.Query("SELECT SI_ID FROM " &_
        "CI_INFOOBJECTS WHERE " &_
        "SI_PROGID = 'CrystalEnterprise.Report' " &_
        "AND SI_NAME='World Sales Report'")
Set infoobject = infoobjects.Item(1)
id = infoobject.Properties("SI_ID")
%>
<html>
<head>
<title>Export Demo</title>
<script>
//JavaScript function that constructs the URL request
//to export the report to a selected format
function exportReport()
{
        var sel = document.forms["form"].elements["export"];
        var urlstring = "http://localhost/crystal/enterprise/";
        urlstring += "viewrpt.cwr?id=<%= id %>";
        urlstring += "&apstoken=<%= Server.URLEncode(token) %>";
        urlstring += "&cmd=export";
        urlstring += "&export_fmt=";
urlstring += escape(sel.options[sel.selectedIndex].value);
        urlstring += "&" + escape("<%= Session.SessionID %>");
        window.open(urlstring);
}
</script>
</head>
<body>

<form name="form">
Select export format: <select name="export">
        <option value="U2FPDF:0">Adobe PDF</option>
        <option value="U2FHTML:2">HTML 3.2</option>
        <option value="U2FHTML:3">HTML 4.0</option>
        <option value="U2FCR:0">Crystal Report</option>
        <option value="U2FXLS:3">Microsoft Excel (XLS)</option>
        <option value="U2FXLS:4">Microsoft Excel (XLS)(extended)</option>
        <option value="U2FRTF:0">Rich Text Format (RTF)</option>
        <option value="U2FWORDW:0">Microsoft Word (DOC)</option>
</select>
<input type="button" value="export"
```

LISTING 13.5   CONTINUED

```
onclick="javascript:exportReport()">
</form>

</body>
</html>
```

SCHEDULING A REPORT

In the simplest of scenarios, scheduling a report results in the Job Server running the report and generating an instance of it. Report scheduling involves, at minimum, telling the system when and how often to run the report. However, report scheduling can be much more complicated depending on the complexity of the schedule, which may involve setting the following:

- **Events**—Creating and setting event dependents and dependencies.
- **Server Group**—Selecting which server group to process the report.
- **Output Destination**—By default, the output destination is the File Repository Server (FRS), but Crystal Enterprise 8.5 introduces four other destinations:

  FTP

  SMTP

  Unmanaged Disk

  Printer

For any scheduling task, the starting point is the SchedulingInfo interface, which may be retrieved as a property of an InfoObject. In Crystal Enterprise, the only InfoObjects that support scheduling are report objects. If an InfoObject does not support scheduling, the InfoObject's SchedulingInfo property will be null. Refer to the following example:

```
'GET A REPORT INFOOBJECT
Set infoobjects = infostore.Query("SELECT * FROM " &_
    "CI_INFOOBJECTS WHERE SI_INSTANCE = 0 " &_
    "AND SI_NAME = 'World Sales Report'")
Set infoobject = infoobjects.Item(1)
'GET THE SCHEDULINGINFO OBJECT
Set schedulinginfo = infoobject.SchedulingInfo
```

THE BASICS OF SCHEDULING

The simplest schedule to set is one that runs once and runs immediately; that is, it is put into the queue to run right away. To set this schedule, two properties in the SchedulingInfo interface need to be set:

- **Type**—This property should be set to 0 (ceScheduleTypeOnce), which will set the schedule to run only once. See "Enum CeScheduleType" in the Crystal Enterprise Web Developer's Guide for other possible values.

- **RightNow**—This is a Boolean property and should be set to 1, which indicates that the schedule should be run immediately.

```
'SET THE SCHEDULE TO RUN ONLY ONCE
schedulinginfo.Type = 0
'SET THE SCHEDULE TO RUN RIGHT NOW
'schedulinginfo.RightNow = 1
```

Finally, the `InfoStore` object's `Schedule` method is used to send the scheduling information to the system, as shown in the following example:

```
'SCHEDULE THE INFOOBJECTS COLLECTION
Call infostore.Schedule(infoobjects)
```

Listing 13.6 and Figure 13.4 demonstrate the simplest schedule that can be set up, which is to run a report once and have it run immediately.

Figure 13.4
Scheduling a report to run right now.

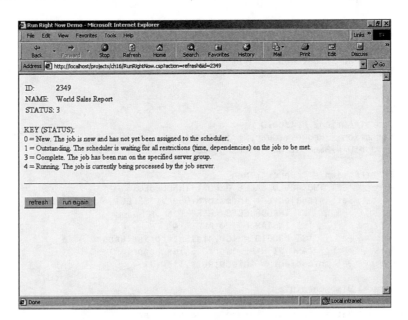

LISTING 13.6 RUNRIGHTNOW.CSP

```
<%
'Written by Stephen Mak
'Name: RunRightNow.csp
'Description: Demonstrates how to run a report right now.

Option Explicit

'PREVENT BROWSER FROM CACHING THE PAGE
Response.ExpiresAbsolute = Now() - 1
```

LISTING 13.6   CONTINUED

```
Dim username, password, apsname, authentication
username = "administrator"
password = ""

'GET APS NAME
apsname = Request.ServerVariables("WCS_NAME_SERVER")
authentication = "secEnterprise"

Dim sm, es, infostore
'LOGON AND INSTANTIATE INFOSTORE OBJECT
Set sm = CreateObject("CrystalEnterprise.SessionMgr")
Set es = sm.Logon(username, password, apsname, authentication)
Set infostore = es.Service("", "InfoStore")

Dim infoobjects, infoobject, id
%>

<html>
<head>
<title>Run Right Now Demo</title>
</head>
<body>

<%
Dim strAction, newJobID
strAction = Request.QueryString("action")
newJobID = Request.QueryString("id")

If strAction = "runnow" Then
        'GET THE WORLD SALES REPORT INFOOBJECT
        Set infoobjects = infostore.Query("SELECT * FROM " &_
                "CI_INFOOBJECTS WHERE " &_
                "SI_INSTANCE = 0 AND " &_
                "SI_PROGID = 'CrystalEnterprise.Report' " &_
                "AND SI_NAME='World Sales Report'")
        Set infoobject = infoobjects.Item(1)

        Dim schedinfo
        'GET THE SCHEDULINGINFO OBJECT
        Set schedinfo = infoobject.SchedulingInfo

        'SET THE SCHEDULE TO RUN ONLY ONCE
        schedinfo.Type = 0

        'SET THE SCHEDULE TO RUN NOW
        schedinfo.RightNow = 1

        'SCHEDULE THE REPORT
        Call infostore.Schedule(infoobjects)

        'GET THE NEW JOB ID
        newJobID = infoobject.Properties("SI_NEW_JOB_ID")
End If
```

LISTING 13.6 CONTINUED

```
If strAction = "runnow" Or strAction = "refresh" Then
        'GET THE NEWLY SCHEDULED JOB
        Set infoobjects = infostore.query("SELECT * FROM " &_
              "CI_INFOOBJECTS WHERE SI_ID = " & newJobID)
        Set infoobject = infoobjects.Item(1)
%>

<!--- TABLE OF ID, NAME AND DESCRIPTION -->
<table>
<tr>
        <td>ID:</td>
        <td><%= infoobject.Properties("SI_ID") %></td></tr>
<tr>
        <td>NAME:</td>
        <td><%= infoobject.Properties("SI_NAME") %></td></tr>
<tr>
        <td>STATUS:</td>
        <td><%= infoobject.SchedulingInfo.Status %></td></tr>
</table>

<p>
KEY (STATUS):<br>
0 = Running. The job is currently being processed by the job server.<br>
1 = Success. The job completed successfully.<br>
3 = Failure. The job failed. Use error message or outcome to get more
  ➥information.<br>
8 = Paused. The job is paused. Even if all dependencies are satisfied,
  ➥it will not run.<br>
9 = Pending. The job has not started because dependencies are not satisfied.
  ➥Dependencies include time constraints and events.<br></p>
<hr>

<%
End If
%>

<form action="RunRightNow.csp" method="get">
        <input type="hidden" name="action" value="runnow">
<% If strAction = "runnow" Or strAction = "refresh" Then %>
        <input type="button" value="refresh"
 onclick="javascript:location.replace('RunRightNow.csp?action=refresh&id=
    <%= newJobID %>')"> 
        <input type="submit" value="run again">
<% Else %>
        <input type="submit" value="run now">
<% End If %>
</form>
</body>
</html>
```

SETTING THE BeginDate AND EndDate PROPERTIES

The BeginDate and EndDate properties indicate when the schedule should run for the first time and when the schedule should be run for the last time. A BeginDate value is required for all schedules, except, of course, for schedules that are set to run `RightNow`. And, although a `BeginDate` value is mandatory, an `EndDate` value is optional.

These two properties will accept a date or a date/time string in the local date/time format defined for the server's default locale or in universal date/time format (yyyy-mm-dd hh:mm:ss).

For example, to set a schedule to run weekly starting on the first Monday of 2002, use the following code:

```
'GET THE SCHEDULINGINFO INTERFACE
Set schedulinginfo = infoobject.SchedulingInfo
'SET THE SCHEDULE TYPE TO WEEKLY
schedulinginfo.Type = 3 'ceScheduleTypeWeekly
'SET THE BEGINDATE
schedulinginfo.BeginDate = "2002-01-07 00:00:00"
```

SCHEDULING ON BEHALF OF ANOTHER USER

In some situations, it might be desirable to allow users who have rights to schedule reports on behalf of those who do not. When scheduling a report on behalf of another user, the owner ID property of the generated instance is different from the submitter ID of the scheduled job. Performing this task is fairly easy and involves retrieving the ID of the user object on behalf of whom you are scheduling. Use the following code:

```
'GET THE USER ID
Set infoobjects = infostore.Query("SELECT SI_ID FROM " &_
    "CI_SYSTEMOBJS WHERE SI_PROGID = 'CrystalEnterprise.User' " &_
    "AND SI_NAME = 'Bob'")
Set infoobject = infoobjects.Item(1)
id = infoobject.Properties("SI_ID")
'GET THE SCHEDULINGINFO INTERFACE
Set schedulinginfo = infoobject.SchedulingInfo
'SET THE SCHEDULEONBEHALFOF PROPERTY
schedulinginfo.ScheduleOnBehalfOf = id
```

CRYSTAL ENTERPRISE ADMINISTRATIVE FUNCTIONALITY

Although the Crystal Enterprise administrative SDK is technically part of the overall Crystal Enterprise object model, it's a significant addition and receives extra attention in this edition of the book.

CREATING NEW USERS AND USER GROUPS

The steps to create users and groups programmatically is no different than creating any other InfoObject, like a folder for example, on the Crystal Enterprise system. And the key to creating various types of InfoObject objects is the plug-in that is used.

In code, the steps to create a new user object looks like this:

```
'GET THE PLUG-IN MANAGER
Set pluginManager = infoStore.PluginManager
```

```
'GET THE PLUG-IN OBJECT
Set plugin = pluginManager.PluginInfo("CrystalEnterprise.User")
'CREATE A NEW INFOOBJECTS COLLECTION
Set newInfoObjectsCollection =
    infoStore.NewInfoObjectCollection()
'CREATE A NEW INFOOBJECT WITH THE PLUG-IN OBJECT
Set newInfoObject = newInfoObjectsCollection.Add(plugin)
'SET THE NAME AND DESCRIPTION OF THE NEW INFOOBJECT
newInfoObject.Title = "test name"
newInfoObject.Description = "test description"
'COMMIT THE CHANGES TO THE APS
Call infostore.Commit (newInfoObjectsCollection)
```

To create a new user group object, simply get the user group plug-in object instead of the user plug-in object. That is, change the line above that gets the plug-in object to the following:

```
'GET THE PLUG-IN OBJECT
Set plugin =
    pluginManager.PluginInfo("CrystalEnterprise.UserGroup")
```

When the InfoObject collection is committed, a new user group object will be created on the system.

In Listing 13.7 and Figure 13.5, a new user is created on the APS, based on the username and description submitted in form on the page.

Figure 13.5
Creating a new user.

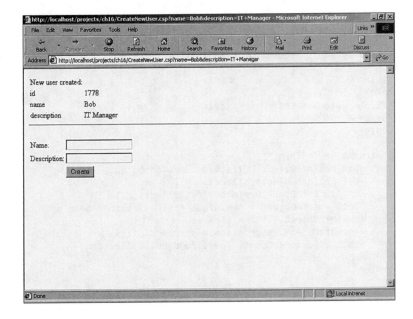

LISTING 13.7   CREATENEWUSER.CSP

```
<%
'Written by Stephen Mak
'Name: CreateNewUser.csp
'Description: Demonstrates how to create a new user.

Option Explicit

Dim username, password, apsname, authentication
username = "administrator"
password = ""

'GET APS NAME
apsname = Request.ServerVariables("WCS_NAME_SERVER")
authentication = "secEnterprise"

'LOGON AND GET AN INFOSTORE OBJECT
Dim sm, es, infostore
Set sm = CreateObject("CrystalEnterprise.SessionMgr")
Set es = sm.Logon(username, password, apsname, authentication)
Set infostore = es.Service ("", "InfoStore")

'GET THE USER PLUG-IN
Dim pmgr, plugin
Set pmgr = infoStore.PluginManager
Set plugin = pmgr.PluginInfo("CrystalEnterprise.User")

'GET NAME AND DESCRIPTION FROM THE REQUEST
Dim strName, strDescription
strName = Request.QueryString("name")
strDescription = Request.QueryString("description")
%>
<html>
<head>
<title>Create New User Demo</title>
</head>
<body>
<%
If strName <> "" Then
        Dim newInfoObjectsCollection, newInfoObject
        Set newInfoObjectsCollection = _
                infoStore.NewInfoObjectCollection()
        Set newInfoObject = newInfoObjectsCollection.Add(plugin)
        newInfoObject.Title = strName
        newInfoObject.Description = strDescription
        Call infostore.Commit (newInfoObjectsCollection)
%>
<table>
<tr>
        <td>New user created:</td>
        <td> </td>
        </tr>
<tr>
        <td>id</td>
        <td>
```

LISTING 13.7   CONTINUED

```
            <%= newInfoObjectsCollection.Item(1).Properties("SI_ID") %>
    </td></tr>
<tr>
    <td>name</td>
    <td>
            <%= newInfoObjectsCollection.Item(1).Properties("SI_NAME") %>
    </td></tr>
<tr>
    <td>description</td>
    <td>
        <%= newInfoObjectsCollection.Item(1).Properties("SI_DESCRIPTION") %>
    </td></tr>
</table>
<hr>
<%
End If
%>

<form method="get" action="CreateNewUser.csp">
<table>
<tr>
    <td>Name:</td>
    <td><input type="text" name="name"></td>
    </tr>
<tr>
    <td>Description:</td>
    <td><input type="text" name="description"></td>
    </tr>
<tr>
    <td> </td>
    <td><input type="submit" value="Create"></td>
    </tr>
</table>
</form>
</body>
</html>
```

As indicated previously, it's possible to modify this example to create new user groups instead, simply by replacing the user plug-in with the user group plug-in.

ASSIGNING USER GROUPS TO A USER

The User object exposes a Groups property in its interface that allows applications to add (and delete) the user object to (and from) user groups.

In general, to add a user to a user group, the following steps are required:

1. Get the ID of the user group object (InfoObject).
2. Get the user object (InfoObject).
3. Get the plug-in interface for the user object.
4. Get the Groups collection object from the plug-in interface.

PART
V

CH
13

5. Add the user group ID to the Groups object.

6. Commit changes to the InfoObjects collection that contains the user object.

For example, the code to add the Administrators user group to a user named Bob would be

```
'GET THE ID OF THE USER GROUP OBJECT
Set infoobjects = infostore.query("SELECT * FROM " &_
    "CI_INFOOBJECTS WHERE SI_PROGID = " &_
    "'CrystalEnterprise.UserGROUP' AND SI_NAME = 'Administators'")
Set infoobject = infoobjects.Item(1)
groupID = infoobject.Properties("SI_ID")
'GET THE USER OBJECT
Set infoobjects = infostore.query("SELECT * FROM " &_
    "CI_INFOOBJECTS WHERE SI_PROGID = 'CrystalEnterprise.User'" &_
    " AND SI_NAME = 'Bob'")
Set infoobject = infoobjects.Item(1)
'GET THE USER PLUG-IN INTERFACE
Set user = infoobject.PluginInterface("")
'GET THE GROUPS COLLECTION OBJECT FROM THE PLUG-IN INTERFACE
Set groups = user.Groups
'ADD THE USER GROUP ID TO THE GROUPS COLLECTION
groups.Add(groupID)
'COMMIT THE CHANGES TO THE APS
Call infostore.Commit(infoobjects)
```

ASSIGNING USERS TO A USER GROUP

Conversely, it's possible to associate users to a user group. The UserGroup object's plug-in interface exposes a Users property that is similar to the User object's Groups property discussed in the previous section. This Users property returns a collection object that contains the IDs of the users that belong to that user group, and this collection supports methods to add or delete user IDs to or from itself.

The code to add a user named Bob to the Administrators user group should look familiar and is similar to the example in the previous section:

```
'GET THE ID OF THE USER OBJECT
Set infoobjects = infostore.query("SELECT * FROM " &_
    "CI_INFOOBJECTS WHERE SI_PROGID = " &_
    "'CrystalEnterprise.User' AND SI_NAME = 'Bob'")
Set infoobject = infoobjects.Item(1)
userID = infoobject.Properties("SI_ID")
'GET THE USER GROUP OBJECT
Set infoobjects = infostore.query("SELECT * FROM " &_
    "CI_INFOOBJECTS WHERE " &_
        "SI_PROGID = 'CrystalEnterprise.UserGroup' AND " &_
        "SI_NAME = 'Administrator'")
Set infoobject = infoobjects.Item(1)
'GET THE USERGROUP PLUG-IN INTERFACE
Set usergroup = infoobject.PluginInterface("")
'GET THE USERS COLLECTION OBJECT FROM THE PLUG-IN INTERFACE
Set users = usergroup.Users
'ADD THE USER ID TO THE USERS COLLECTION
```

```
users.Add(userID)
'COMMIT THE CHANGES TO THE APS
Call infostore.Commit(infoobjects)
```

MANAGING SERVERS

With Crystal Enterprise 8.5, it's possible to programmatically start, stop, and restart the Crystal servers (Page Server, Job Server, Cache Server, Event Server, Input File Server, and Output File Server). The procedure to do this is fairly simple because it involves one simple call—ManageServer on the Server object. This Server object is a specific type of InfoObject that may be retrieved from the InfoStore, and should not be confused with the Server object that is available in the Crystal Enterprise Server Pages Library (CrystalServerPagesLib).

Given a generic InfoObject, it's necessary to apply the Server object's plug-in interface to it before calling ManageServer. ManageServer accepts integer values: 1 (start), 2 (stop), and 3 (restart). So, sample code to restart a server looks like this:

```
'GET THE SERVER OBJECT
Set serverObject = infoObject.PluginInterface("")
'CALL THE MANAGERSERVER METHOD, PASSING IN THE OPERATION ID
serverObject.ManageServer(3)
```

Note that because a Web application requires its connection to the Web Component Server and the APS, it's not possible to stop or restart these two servers while the application is connected to it. The Crystal Management Console (CMC) should be used to start, stop, or restart these servers.

Another common task to server management is to review the status of all servers. This task is very much like retrieving and displaying a list of reports. First, query for all servers, as follows:

```
Set infoObjects = infoStore.Query("SELECT * FROM " & _
    "CI_INFOOBJECTS WHERE SI_PROGID = 'CrystalEnterprise.Server'")
```

Next, loop through the collection of InfoObjects, and display their pertinent properties:

```
For Each infoObject In infoObjects
    Response.Write infoObject.Properties("SI_SERVER_NAME") & _
    ", " & infoObject.Properties("SI_SERVER_DESCRIPTION") & _
    ", " & infoObject.Properties("SI_SERVER_IS_ALIVE") & "<br>"
Next
```

One particularly useful server property is SI_SERVER_IS_ALIVE. This is a Boolean property that represents the current status of the server; that is, 0 if it is stopped and 1 if it is started. It's important for a server management application to have access to this property because an application cannot do the following:

- Start a service that has already been started.
- Stop a service that has already been stopped.
- Restart a service that has been stopped.

PART

V

CH

13

In Listing 13.8 and Figure 13.6, ManageServers.csp, the CSP page retrieves and displays the properties for all the servers on a Crystal Enterprise system. It also allows the user to start, stop, and restart the servers and refresh the list.

Figure 13.6
Starting, stopping, and restarting servers.

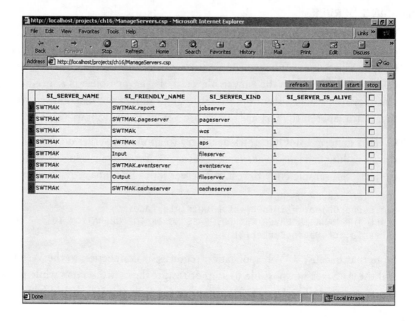

LISTING 13.8   MANAGESERVERS.CSP

```
<%
'Written by Stephen Mak
'Name: ManageServers.csp
'Description: Demonstrates how to start, stop & restart servers.

Option Explicit

'PREVENT BROWSER FROM CACHING THE PAGE
Response.ExpiresAbsolute = Now() - 1

Dim username, password, apsname, authentication
username = "administrator"
password = ""

'GET APS NAME
apsname = Request.ServerVariables("WCS_NAME_SERVER")
authentication = "secEnterprise"

Dim sm, es, istore
'LOGON AND INSTANTIATE INFOSTORE OBJECT
Set sm = CreateObject("CrystalEnterprise.SessionMgr")
Set es = sm.Logon(username, password, apsname, authentication)
Set istore = es.Service ("", "InfoStore")
%>
```

LISTING 13.8   CONTINUED

```html
<html>
<head>
<title>Managing Servers Demo</title>
<style>
body, input, tr, th, td {
    font-family:verdana;
    font-size:8pt;
}
</style>
<script>
//client-side javascript functions

//chkAll
//function to select/un-select all servers
function chkAll(cb)
{
        for(i = 0; i < document.forms["uiForm"].elements.length; i++)
                if(document.forms["uiForm"].elements[i].name.substr(0,3)
                == "cb_")
                {
                        document.forms["uiForm"].elements[i].checked =
                                cb.checked;
                }
}


//doAction
//function that sets the "ids" and "action" elements,
//then submits the form
function doAction(action)
{
        var ids = new Array();
        for(i = 0; i < document.forms["uiForm"].elements.length; i++)
                if(document.forms["uiForm"].elements[i].name.substr(0,3)
                == "cb_" && document.forms["uiForm"].elements[i].checked)
                {
                        ids.push(document.forms["uiForm"].elements[i].value);
                }

        document.forms["serversForm"].elements["ids"].value =
                ids.join(",");
        document.forms["serversForm"].elements["action"].value =
                action;
        document.forms["serversForm"].submit();
}
</script>
</head>
<body>
<%
Dim strIDs, strAction
strIDs = Request.QueryString("ids")
strAction = Request.QueryString("action")
If strAction <> "" And strIDs <> "" Then
        Response.Write DoAction(strAction, strIDs)
End If
%>
```

LISTING 13.8   CONTINUED

```
<!-- refresh / start / stop buttons -->
<form name="uiForm">
<table width="100%"><tr><td align="right">
        <input type="button" value="refresh"
                onclick="javascript:location.replace('ManageServers.csp')">
        <input type="button" value="restart"
                onclick="javascript:doAction('restart')">
        <input type="button" value="start"
                onclick="javascript:doAction('start')">
        <input type="button" value="stop"
                onclick="javascript:doAction('stop')">
        </td></tr></table>
<%
Response.Write DisplayServers()
%>
</form>
<form name="serversForm" method="get"
        action="ManageServers.csp">
        <input type="hidden" name="action" value="">
        <input type="hidden" name="ids" value="">
</form>
</body>
</html>


<%
'THE DisplayServers FUNCTION GENERATES AN HTML TABLE THAT
'LISTS ALL SERVERS AND SOME OF THEIR PROPERTIES
Function DisplayServers()
        Dim IObjs, IObj

        'QUERY FOR ALL SERVERS
        Set IObjs = istore.Query( _
                "SELECT " & _
                        "SI_ID, SI_SERVER_NAME, SI_FRIENDLY_NAME, " & _
                        "SI_SERVER_KIND, SI_SERVER_IS_ALIVE " & _
                "FROM CI_SYSTEMOBJS " & _
                "WHERE SI_PROGID = 'CrystalEnterprise.Server'")

        Dim strHTML, count
        strHTML = ""
        count = 1

        'START TABLE TO HOLD LIST OF SERVERS
        strHTML = strHTML & "<table border=1 cellspacing=0 " &_
                "width='100%'>" & vbCrLf
        strHTML = strHTML & "<tr><th> </th>" & vbCrLf
        strHTML = strHTML & "  <th>SI_SERVER_NAME</th>" & vbCrLf
        strHTML = strHTML & "  <th>SI_FRIENDLY_NAME</th>" & vbCrLf
        strHTML = strHTML & "  <th>SI_SERVER_KIND</th>" & vbCrLf
        strHTML = strHTML & "  <th>SI_SERVER_IS_ALIVE</th>" & vbCrLf
        strHTML = strHTML & "  <td><input type='checkbox' " &_
                "onclick='chkAll(this)'></td></tr>" & vbCrLf

        'LOOP THROUGH COLLECTION, AND DISPLAY LIST OF SERVERS
        'AND THEIR PROPERTIES IN THE TABLE
```

LISTING 13.8   CONTINUED

```
    For Each IObj In IObjs
            If IObj.Properties("SI_SERVER_IS_ALIVE") = 0 Then
                    strHTML = strHTML & "<tr><td bgcolor='red'>"
            Else
                    strHTML = strHTML & "<tr><td bgcolor='green'>"
            End If
            strHTML = strHTML & count & "</td>" & vbCrLf
            strHTML = strHTML & "  <td>" & _
                    IObj.Properties("SI_SERVER_NAME") & "</td>" & vbCrLf
            strHTML = strHTML & "  <td>" & _
                    IObj.Properties("SI_FRIENDLY_NAME") & "</td>" & vbCrLf
            strHTML = strHTML & "  <td>" & _
                    IObj.Properties("SI_SERVER_KIND") & "</td>" & vbCrLf
            strHTML = strHTML & "  <td>" & _
                    IObj.Properties("SI_SERVER_IS_ALIVE") & "</td>" & vbCrLf
            strHTML = strHTML & "  <td><input name='cb_" & count &_
                    "' type='checkbox' value='" & IObj.Properties("SI_ID") &_
                    "'></td></tr>" & vbCrLf
            count = count + 1
    Next
    strHTML = strHTML & "</table>" & vbCrLf

    DisplayServers = strHTML


End Function

'THE DoAction SUBROUTINE STARTS, STOPS, AND RESTARTS
'THE SELECTED SERVERS, AND ACCEPTS TWO STRING PARAMETERS:
'1) AN ACTION STRING: EITHER "start" OR "stop" OR "restart"
'2) AN ID'S STRING: A LIST OF OBJECT IDS DELIMITED BY COMMAS
'e.g., "123,234,345"
Function DoAction(strAction, strIDs)
    Dim IObjs, IObj, ServerObj
    Dim strHTML
    strHTML = ""

    'QUERY FOR SELECTED SERVERS
    Set IObjs = istore.Query( _
            "SELECT " & _
                    "SI_SERVER_NAME, SI_SERVER_KIND, SI_DESCRIPTION, " &_
                    "SI_SERVER_IS_ALIVE " & _
            "FROM CI_SYSTEMOBJS " & _
            "WHERE " & _
                    "SI_PROGID = 'CrystalEnterprise.Server' " &_
                    "AND SI_ID IN (" & strIDs & ")")

    'START SELECTED SERVERS
    If strAction = "start" Then
            For Each IObj In IObjs
                    If IObj.Properties("SI_SERVER_IS_ALIVE") = 0 Then
                            Set ServerObj = IObj.PluginInterface("")
                            ServerObj.ManageServer(1)
                    End If
            Next
```

LISTING 13.8 CONTINUED

```
'STOP OR RESTART SELECTED SERVERS
ElseIf strAction = "stop" Or strAction = "restart" Then
        For Each IObj In IObjs
                If IObj.Properties("SI_SERVER_KIND") <> "wcs" _
                AND IObj.Properties("SI_SERVER_KIND") <> "aps" Then
                        If IObj.Properties("SI_SERVER_IS_ALIVE") Then
                                Set ServerObj = IObj.PluginInterface("")
                                If strAction = "stop" Then
                                        ServerObj.ManageServer(2)
                                ElseIf strAction = "restart" Then
                                        ServerObj.ManageServer(3)
                                End If
                        End If
                Else
                        strHTML = strHTML & "<b>" & _
                                IObj.Properties("SI_SERVER_NAME")
                        strHTML = strHTML & " - " & _
                                IObj.Properties("SI_DESCRIPTION") & ":</b> "
                        strHTML = strHTML & "server cannot be " &_
                            "stopped/restarted while you are connected " &_
                            "to it.</br>"
                End If
        Next
End If

DoAction = strHTML

End Function
%>
```

TROUBLESHOOTING

For the application code samples provided in this chapter to work, be sure that the samples are located in a virtual directory on the Web server. Although this chapter focuses on developing code for Web applications using Crystal Enterprise, the code presented doesn't differ from what a developer would encounter when writing standard ASP pages.

That being said, it's best to use standard code debugging techniques or software when developing applications using the Crystal Enterprise SDK. More often than not, errors in application code lie with common issues such as syntactical errors. Some issues arise with improper referencing of other CSP pages, such as forgetting an #include reference to another page.

Once complete, publishing a CSP application to the Web might be troublesome if the Web Component Server or Web Connector is improperly configured. It's always good practice to have a test system with the Web Connector and the Web Component Server installed on the same physical server to quickly test for correct behavior.

Remember, a CSP application may call several different servers in a Crystal Enterprise system, so errors can come from several sources. Try to determine through methodical error checking whether an issue with a CSP application is being generated by the code or a problem with a particular Crystal Enterprise server.

SUMMARY

The InfoStore object is the key to accessing all InfoObjects stored in Crystal Enterprise system. To get the InfoStore object, it's necessary to log on first. The user's rights will determine what InfoObjects the InfoStore object can access.

InfoObjects are stored in a folder hierarchy in the system, and may be retrieved by querying the InfoStore with the use of SQL-like statements.

Viewing a report involves sending a URL request to viewrpt.cwr with the appropriate parameters to select the report, viewer type, parameter values, and export format.

The new administrative API is available in Crystal Enterprise 8.5 and allows for the creation and control of new types of objects, including users, groups, servers, and so on.

CHAPTER 14

INTEGRATING CRYSTAL ENTERPRISE WITH YOUR CORPORATE INTRANET

In this chapter

Undoubtedly, the most common application of Crystal Enterprise is to make Crystal Reports accessible via a corporate intranet or internet Web page. Chapter 13, "Extending Crystal Enterprise," reviewed the Crystal Enterprise object model and the concept of .csp pages, and provided some sample code for use in custom Crystal Enterprise development. Although Chapter 13 provides a thorough overview, the most challenging part of any custom development project can be the actual implementation of the code.

This chapter focuses on the actual integration of Crystal Enterprise into a corporate intranet site. Therefore, although some of the chapter is redundant with Chapter 13, this chapter was intended to provide a sample process to follow, not just sample code.

Using the examples in this chapter requires some experience with, or exposure to, Active Server Page development, including exposure to either VBScript or JavaScript. Any standard Web or text editor will suffice, such as Microsoft Visual InterDev or FrontPage. The tool used for editing this exercise is Microsoft Notepad.

THE COVERALL MANUFACTURING COMPANY PROJECT

A fictitious company, Coverall Manufacturing, will be used to demonstrate the examples within this chapter. To get access to the Coverall intranet site, a user needs to log on. The logon screen, as shown in Figure 14.1, captures the user information and grants or denies access to the intranet site.

Figure 14.1
Coverall Manufacturing's intranet logon page, without Crystal Enterprise.

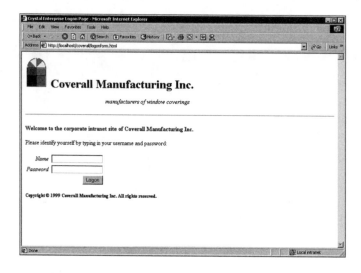

Coverall Manufacturing manufactures window coverings and has outlets throughout Canada and the United States. These two countries are divided into regions, with each region consisting of various branches. Figure 14.2 shows the default home page for Coverall Manufacturing.

Figure 14.2
Coverall
Manufacturing's
intranet Web site
before Crystal
Enterprise integration.

A need for sales tracking information has evolved whereby sales personnel, managers, and corporate executives need to track sales by representative, branch, and region as well as across the corporation.

Coverall has two specific requirements:

- Provide an easy way for end users to securely access a list of sales reports over the Web
- Distribute administrative tasks to certain "power users" within the organization

The first section of the chapter addresses the initial requirement through Crystal Enterprise integration with Coverall's corporate intranet. This includes accessing, listing, and viewing reports for an end user in Crystal Enterprise.

The second section of the chapter reviews the administrative tasks of adding and removing users, based on the role of the person adding these users (such as regional managers and branch managers).

Any integration must be seamless, whereby the user that logs in to the intranet site will automatically be logged in to the company's reporting back end and the user can only view reports and information pertinent to that user's position within the company.

For the second requirement, power users, such as branch managers, will only be allowed to add, schedule, and view reports in their folder, and the branch workers (sales representatives) can only view reports.

Reports are added to the system from the head office Crystal Enterprise administrator, who also is responsible for server administration. The task of user administration is to be done at the regional and branch level. All personnel will only be able to view reports. If there are no

PART
V

CH

14

prerun instances, the personnel will be able to view the reports on-demand, without scheduling the reports first. Ad-hoc report creation over the Web will not be enabled for this deployment.

PLANNING THE CRYSTAL ENTERPRISE INTEGRATION

The Coverall Manufacturing Web site, Coverall.htm, can be found on the Pearson Web site resource section, along with the source code used in this chapter.

To implement the desired solution of integrating Crystal Enterprise with the Coverall Web site, a planning meeting is held. It's determined that the following .csp, .asp, .css, and HTML pages will be created and integrated with Coverall.htm:

- **Default.asp**—Coverall intranet entry point.
- **Logon_form.csp**—Enables a user to log on to the Coverall Web site. This information then calls logon.csp.
- **Logonform.html**—Enables a user to log on to the Coverall Web site. This information then calls logon.csp.
- **Logon.csp**—Accepts the logon information from the Logonform.html page and validates the user within Crystal Enterprise. It then redirects to the welcome.csp page.
- **Welcome.csp**—Coverall intranet welcome page. This page has links to the reporting and administration screens. Validation is also done here for the "administration" link. A JavaScript error message is displayed if the user is not a member of the Regional Managers Group.
- **/css**—Style sheet directory.
- **/images**—Images directory.
- **admin.csp**—Administration frame set for the following:

  admin_header.csp—Administration header (top)

  admin_folders.csp—Administration folder tree (left)

  admin.html—Administration initial page (right)

  assign.csp—Administration user, folder assignment page (right)
- **reporting.csp**—Reporting frame set for the following:

  reporting_header.csp—Reporting header (top)

  folders.csp—Reporting folder tree (left)

  reporting.html—Reporting initial page (right)

  instances.csp—Report instance listing (right)

  view.csp—Report/instance viewer (right)

The planned flow of interaction for the user is as follows:

1. An end user accesses the Coverall site through a URL pointed to default.asp.

2. Default.asp redirects the user to logon_form.csp.

3. The user logs in.

4. If the login attempt is successful, the welcome page appears; otherwise, an error appears and the user is sent back to the logon form.

5. The end user selects Reporting, Administration, and so on from the welcome page.

6. The user can log off or change areas by selecting the appropriate link in the header.

The first portion of the Coverall Manufacturing project will be to complete the linking of reports to the Coverall Web site. This will satisfy the end-user's requirement of accessing reports in a list style from a Web page.

LINKING A CORPORATE INTRANET PAGE TO CRYSTAL ENTERPRISE

To provide a list of reports for the Coverall sales employees to access from a corporate intranet site, the following tasks must be accomplished:

- Obtaining a logon token to Crystal Enterprise
- Adding a list of folders and reports to a Web page

OBTAINING A LOGON TOKEN TO CRYSTAL ENTERPRISE

In this section, linking Crystal Enterprise to the Coverall existing corporate intranet site is the first task. Recall that this will meet the first requirement, which is to integrate reporting into the existing intranet site to track sales figures by corporation, region, branch, and finally, sales representative.

The first step is to analyze the business process for retrieving reports. In this case, a user will enter some Crystal Enterprise login information and receive a list of accessible reports in response. When the user is logged in to the Crystal Enterprise system, recall that they receive, in some shape, form, or fashion (typically a cookie) a Crystal Enterprise token. This token enables continued interaction with the Crystal Enterprise system without the need to relog on to the system.

The code example in Listing 14.1 describes how to create a function to log a user on to Crystal Enterprise and store the logon token and InfoStore. This example is similar to the code provided in Chapter 13.

PART

V

CH

14

LISTING 14.1   LISTING14-01.TXT—THIS ENABLES A USER TO LOG ON TO CRYSTAL ENTERPRISE

```
<%
Option Explicit
Response.Expires = 0

Dim SessionMgr      'Session Manager used to Log on to APS
Dim CeSession       'Crystal Enterprise Session
Dim LogonToken      'Logon Token used to pass to report viewer

Dim Username        'Stores user's logon ID
Dim Password        'Stores user's password
Dim ApsName         'Stores APS server name
Dim AuthMode        'Stores authentication mode

'* Retrieve fields from logon form *****

Username = Request.Form("username")
Password = Request.Form("password")

'* This app will use Enterprise Authentication *****

AuthMode = "secEnterprise"

'* Retrieve the APS Server Name *****

ApsName = Request.ServerVariables("WCS_NAME_SERVER")

'* Attempt Logon *****

Set SessionMgr = Server.CreateObject("CrystalEnterprise.SessionMgr")

On Error Resume Next    'Trap errors. Logon raises exception upon failure
  'Do the logon
  Set CeSession = SessionMgr.Logon(Username, Password, ApsName, AuthMode)

  'If error occurred, Err.Number will be non-zero
  If Err.Number<>0 Then
    'Use JavaScript alert to display error
    'and then redirect back to logon form.
    Response.Write "<script>"
    Response.Write "alert('" & Err.Description & "\nPlease try again.');"

    Response.Write "open('logon_form.csp','_top');"

    Response.Write "</script>"
    Response.End
  End If
On Error Goto 0         'End of error trapping

'* Save Session Information *****
Set Session("IStore") = CeSession.Service("","InfoStore")
Response.Cookies("LogonToken") = _
CeSession.LogonTokenMgr.CreateLogonToken("", 1, 100)

'* Redirect to Coverall Intranet Main Page *****
Response.Redirect "welcome.csp"
%>
```

After adding this code to Coverall's Web page, shown in Figure 14.3, an end user can log in to Crystal Enterprise; however, no reports have been returned to the end user for viewing. The hyperlink Reports will return the folder and APS information in the left hand frame.

Figure 14.3
Coverall
Manufacturing's Web
Site after adding the
Crystal Enterprise
logon integration.

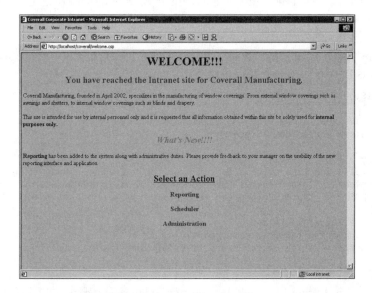

Tip

Inserting an ASP or CSP page into a Web page is often done via an IFRAME reference. The syntax is similar to

```
<IFRAME src="http://servername/cspPaGEname.csp" frameborder="0"
 allowtransparency="true" height="210" width="215"
scrolling="auto"></IFRAME>
```

Note

To test any of the code provided in this chapter, a virtual directory in Microsoft Internet Information Server should be created called Coverall, to which the default Web site for the Coverall application should be changed to covarall.htm. Refer to Chapter 7, "Publishing Content with Crystal Enterprise," for information about configuring a virtual Web in Microsoft Internet Information Server, or refer to the Microsoft Internet Information Server documentation.

ADDING A LIST OF REPORTS TO A WEB PAGE

The first step in populating a Web page with a list of reports from Crystal Enterprise is to query the InfoStore for folder information.

The beauty of querying Crystal Enterprise is that rather than listing all objects that exist in the CE system, the InfoStore only returns objects that the currently logged-in user has access to see. This means developers don't need to worry about filtering objects for certain users. Chapter 13 reviews how to query the InfoStore for a list of all the folders in the APS. The example in Listing 14.2 will return a list of folders from the APS.

LISTING 14.2   A LIST OF REPORTS FROM CRYSTAL ENTERPRISE FOR THE COVERALL USER TO VIEW IS RETURNED BASED ON THIS CODE

```
Dim IStore, Folders, Folder

'Retrieve the IStore from the session
Set IStore = Session("IStore")

'Query all of the folder names from APS
'The following line of code is concatenated but doesn't have to be "
Set Folders = IStore.Query("Select SI_NAME from CI_INFOOBJECTS where " +
"SI_PROGID = 'CrystalEnterprise.Folder'")

For Each Folder in Folders
    'Write the folder name property
    Response.Write Folder.Properties("SI_Name") & "<BR>"
next
```

The code in Listing 14.2 could be rewritten to improve the speed of folder retrieval.

Note

Effectively querying the APS can dramatically affect Crystal Enterprise system performance.

Simply query for the folder IDs (SI_ID) and use the `Title` property of the folder object shown in Listing 14.3.

LISTING 14.3   THE QUERY SEARCHES FOR FOLDERS BY TITLE

```
'Query all of the folder names from APS
'The following line of code is concatenated but doesn't have to be
Set Folders = IStore.Query("Select SI_ID from CI_INFOOBJECTS where " +
"SI_PROGID = 'CrystalEnterprise.Folder'")

For Each Folder in Folders
'Display the Folder title property(name) or other properties of the folder
    Response.Write Folder.Title & "<BR>"
Next
```

Note	A limited set of properties is available using this method. Please refer to Crystal Enterprise Web Developer's Guide under "InfoObject Object" for a list of available properties.

The folders that can be created within Crystal Enterprise are organized in a hierarchical fashion, with top-level folders containing an unlimited number of child folder elements. The assumption with the Coverall Manufacturing project is that end users will want to explore folders based on their intended hierarchy, because corporate reports might be stored in folders at any level within the hierarchy.

To provide this list of folders in a hierarchical format, a recursive function can be written. For the purpose of this application example and other applications that might be created, Listing 14.4 displays all the available folders in their hierarchy order.

LISTING 14.4   FOLDERS WITHIN CRYSTAL ENTERPRISE ARE DISPLAYED TO THE END USER IN THE INTENDED HIERARCHICAL FORMAT

```
Function GetFolders(sParentID, iStore, iLevel)

Dim sFolderQuery
Dim Folders
Dim Folder
Dim sWrite
Dim i


sFolderQuery = "Select SI_ID from CI_INFOOBJECTS where SI_PROGID =
     'CrystalEnterprise.Folder' AND SI_PARENT_FOLDER = '" & sParentID & "'
order by SI_NAME"

'Query all of the folder names from APS that have the same parent
set Folders = iStore.Query(sFolderQuery)

for each Folder in Folders
    sWrite = "<br>"
    'This loop indents the folder titles (for the hierarchy)
      for i = 0 to iLevel
        sWrite = sWrite & "  "
      next

'Displays the folder information
'Creates a URL with the folder id.  The folder ID can be used to retrieve a
 list of reports in that folder.
sWrite = sWrite & "<a href='report.csp?FolderID=" & Folder.ID & "'>"
& Folder.Title & "</a>"

      Response.Write sWrite
      'Recursive call to create the child folders
      GetFolders Folder.Properties("ID"), iStore, iLevel + 1
next
```

LISTING 14.4   CONTINUED

```
GetFolders = True

End Function

Usage:

Set IStore = Session("IStore")
GetFolders 0, IStore , 0
```

Figure 14.4 shows the code to this point, displayed on the Coverall Manufacturing Web site.

Figure 14.4
The Coverall
Manufacturing Web
site returns a list of
Crystal Enterprise
folders to an end
user.

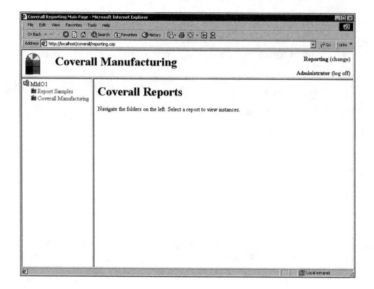

After the set of folders is returned and organized in a hierarchical order, it's necessary to retrieve the list of report objects available from the APS. To get the list of reports belonging to a folder, the folder ID must be referenced, as shown in Listing 14.5.

The desired result is that when a user clicks on a folder, he or she will see the list of reports in that folder, yet still have access to subfolders. From a business perspective, regional mangers and branch managers will be able to add, schedule, and view the reports, whereas the branch workers can only view the scheduled instances.

LISTING 14.5   REPORT OBJECTS WILL BE LISTED IN EACH FOLDER CONTAINER FOR END USERS TO SELECT

```
Function GetReports(sFolderID)

Dim sReportQuery
Dim Report
Dim Reports
```

LISTING 14.5   CONTINUED

```
Dim LogonToken
Dim iStore
Dim rv

Set IStore = Session("IStore")

'SI_INSTANCE is set to 0 in order to retrieve the report objects and
    not the instances
sReportQuery = "Select SI_NAME, SI_ID, SI_DESCRIPTION, SI_CHILDREN from
    CI_INFOOBJECTS where SI_PROGID='CrystalEnterprise.Report' AND SI_INSTANCE=0
    and SI_PARENT_FOLDER= '" & sFolderID & "' order by SI_NAME"

'Stores the report list from the IStore object
set Reports = iStore.Query(sReportQuery)

if Reports.Count > 0 then
    'Retrieve the logon token; it will be required for viewing reports
    LogonToken = Request.Cookies("LogonToken")
'Loop through all of the reports in the collection
for each Report in Reports
    'Create a hyperlink for reports for running then on demand
    Response.Write "<a href='viewrpt.cwr?init=actx:connect&promptOnRefresh=
    1&ID=" & ID & "&apstoken=" & LogonToken & "'>" & Report.Title & "</a><br>"
        'Check to see if the report has a history of instances
if Report.Properties("SI_Children") > 0 then
    'The following function retrieves the instances for this report
    GetInstances iStore, Report.Id
End If
    next
else
    Response.Write "No reports were found. "
end if
```

> **Note**
>
> For the purposes of this application, scheduling reports will not be covered. For information on scheduling reports refer to Chapter 13.

Upon returning the list of reports available to a folder, it's necessary to query the APS for a list of instances and history belonging to the reports. The APS is queried using the report ID associated with the report, as shown in Listing 14.6.

LISTING 14.6   THE APS IS QUERIED FOR A LIST OF REPORT INSTANCES

```
<%
Option Explicit
Response.Expires = 0

Dim IStore              'Connection to Crystal Enterprise
Dim ApsName             'APS server name
Dim ReportId            'Id of report
```

LISTING 14.6   CONTINUED

```
Dim List              'Stores InfoObjects Collection
Dim Item              'Stores InfoObject Object
Dim Prompts           'Store ReportParameters Collection
Dim Prompt            'Store ReportParameter Object
Dim PromptCount       'Stores Number of Prompts

Dim SplitArray        'Array used for parsing
Dim StartDate         'Store instance start date
Dim StartTime         'Store instance start time
Dim Duration          'Store time required for instance to process

'* Style Sheets ***

Response.Write "<link rel='stylesheet' type='text/css' href='css/common.css'>"
'The following line of code is concatenated but doesn't have to be
Response.Write "<link rel='stylesheet' " +
"type='text/css' href='css/instances.css'>"

'* Get report Id from QueryString ****

ReportId = CLng(Request.QueryString("reportid"))

'* Get InfoStore from Session ****

Set IStore = Session("IStore")

'* Print report information ****
'The following line of code is concatenated but doesn't have to be
Set List = IStore.Query("Select SI_DESCRIPTION, " +
"SI_PROCESSINFO.SI_PROMPTS From " &
 "CI_INFOOBJECTS Where SI_ID=" & ReportId)

Set Item = List(1)
Set Prompts = Item.PluginInterface("").ReportParameters
PromptCount = Prompts.Count

Response.Write "<h3><a href='view.csp?id=" & Item.Id & "'>"
Response.Write "<img src='images/tree_report.gif'> " & Item.Title
Response.Write "</a></h3>"

Response.Write Item("SI_DESCRIPTION") & "<p>"

'* Print instances ****

Response.Write "<table>"

Response.Write "<thead>"
Response.Write "<tr>"
Response.Write "  <th>View</th>"
Response.Write "  <th>Owner</th>"
Response.Write "  <th>Run Date</th>"
Response.Write "  <th>Time</th>"
Response.Write "  <th>Duration</th>"
```

LISTING 14.6   CONTINUED

```
'* Include instance parameter values ****

For Each Prompt in Prompts
    Response.Write "  <th>" & Prompt.ParameterName & "</th>"
Next

Response.Write "</tr>"
Response.Write "</thead>"

Response.Write "<tbody>"
'The following line of code is concatenated but doesn't have to be
Set List =
IStore.Query("Select SI_PROCESSINFO.SI_PROMPTS, SI_OWNER, SI_ENDTIME, " & _
  "SI_NEXTRUNTIME From CI_INFOOBJECTS Where SI_PARENTID=" & ReportId & _
  " And SI_PROGID='CrystalEnterprise.Report' And SI_INSTANCE=1")

For Each Item In List
    SplitArray = Split(FormatDateTime(Item("SI_NEXTRUNTIME"),0)," ")
    StartDate = SplitArray(0)
    StartTime = SplitArray(1)
    Duration = CLng((Item("SI_ENDTIME")-Item("SI_NEXTRUNTIME"))*86400)

    Response.Write "<tr>"
    Response.Write "<td><a href='view.csp?id=" & Item.Id & "'>"
    Response.Write "    <img src='images/tree_report.gif'></a></td>"
    Response.Write "<td>" & Item("SI_OWNER") & "</td>"
    Response.Write "<td>" & StartDate & "</td>"
    Response.Write "<td>" & StartTime & "</td>"
    Response.Write "<td>" & Duration & "s</td>"

    Set Prompts = Item.PluginInterface("").ReportParameters
    For Each Prompt in Prompts
        If Prompt.CurrentValues.Count>0 Then
'The following line of code is concatenated but doesn't have to be
            Response.Write "  <th>" &
                Prompt.CurrentValues(1).MakeDisplayString & "</th>"
        Else
            Response.Write "  <th>(not set)</th>"
        End If
    Next

    Response.Write "</tr>"
Next

Response.Write "</tbody>"

Response.Write "<tfoot>"
Response.Write "<tr>"
'The following line of code is concatenated but doesn't have to be
Response.Write "  <th colspan=" & 5+PromptCount & ">" &
List.Count & " Instance(s)</th>"
Response.Write "</tr>"
Response.Write "</tfoot>"

Response.Write "</table>"
%>
```

PART

V

CH

14

> **Note**
>
> For more information on report instances, refer to Chapter 3, "Exploring the System Architecture."

By making reference to each of these functions, a list of folders, reports, and instances is returned to a Crystal Enterprise end user. The user sees only the folders, objects, and instances pertinent to them, which is overseen by the security configured within the Crystal Management Console. Every query submitted to the APS is subject to the security configuration.

The entire code for the folder, report, and instance retrieval could be simplified by being more efficient in the query of the APS. Listing 14.7 has the code in a more simplified and condensed format.

LISTING 14.7   A SIMPLIFIED CODE BASE OF THE PRECEDING FEW EXAMPLES

```
<%
Option Explicit
Response.Expires = 0   'Prevent browser from caching this page

Dim IStore             'Connection to Crystal Enterprise
Dim ApsName            'APS server name
Dim FolderId           'Id of folder

Dim List               'Stores InfoObjects Collection
Dim Item               'Stores InfoObject Object

'* Style Sheets ****

Response.Write "<link rel='stylesheet' type='text/css' href='css/common.css'>"
Response.Write "<link rel='stylesheet' type='text/css' href='css/folders.css'>"

'* Get folder Id from QueryString ****

FolderId = CLng(Request.QueryString("folderid"))

'* Get InfoStore from Session ****

Set IStore = Session("IStore")

'* Print parent Folder - APS if top level ****

Response.Write "<nobr>"

If FolderId=0 Then
     ApsName = Request.ServerVariables("WCS_NAME_SERVER")
     Response.Write "<img src='images/tree_aps.gif'> " & ApsName
Else
        'The following line of code is concatenated but doesn't have to be
        Set List = IStore.Query("Select SI_ID From " +
        "CI_INFOOBJECTS Where SI_ID=" & FolderId)
```

LISTING 14.7   CONTINUED

```
    Set Item = List(1)
    Response.Write "<img src='images/tree_folder_open.gif'> " & Item.Title
End If

'* Print folder contents ****

Set List = IStore.Query("Select SI_PROGID From CI_INFOOBJECTS Where " & _
  "SI_ID!=18 And SI_PARENTID=" & FolderId & _
  "And SI_PROGID In ('CrystalEnterprise.Folder','CrystalEnterprise.Report')")

Response.Write "<blockquote>"

'* Show "Parent Folder" link if applicable ***

If FolderId<>0 Then
    Response.Write "<a href='folders.csp?folderid=" & Item.ParentId & "'>"
    Response.Write "<img src='images/tree_folder_up.gif'> "
    Response.Write "Parent Folder"
    Response.Write "</a><br>"
End If

'* Print folder/report links ***

For Each Item In List
    Select Case Item("SI_PROGID")

        Case "CrystalEnterprise.Folder"
            Response.Write "<a href='folders.csp?folderid=" & Item.Id & "'>"
            Response.Write "<img src='images/tree_folder_closed.gif'> "
            Response.Write Item.Title
            Response.Write "</a><br>"

        Case "CrystalEnterprise.Report"
'The following line of code is concatenated but doesn't have to be
            Response.Write "<a href='instances.csp?reportid=" &
            Item.Id & "' target=client>"
            Response.Write "<img src='images/tree_report.gif'> "
            Response.Write Item.Title
            Response.Write "</a><br>"
    End Select
Next

Response.Write "</blockquote>"
Response.Write "</nobr>"
Response.Write "</body>"
Response.Write "</html>"
%>
```

The completed codes for Logon.csp, folders.csp, and instances.csp appear in Listing 14.8.

PART

V

CH

14

LISTING 14.8   THE COMPLETE .CSP PAGE, INTEGRATED INTO THE COVERALL MANUFACTURING WEB SITE

```
'* Logon.csp gets information from logon_form.csp ****
<%
Option Explicit
Response.Expires = 0

Dim SessionMgr     'Session Manager used to Logon to APS
Dim CeSession      'Crystal Enterprise Session
Dim LogonToken     'Logon Token used to pass to report viewer

Dim Username       'Stores user's logon id
Dim Password       'Stores user's password
Dim ApsName        'Stores APS server name
Dim AuthMode       'Stores authentication mode

'* Retrieve fields from logon form *****

Username = Request.Form("username")
Password = Request.Form("password")

'* This app will use Enterprise Authentication *****

AuthMode = "secEnterprise"

'* Retrieve the APS Server Name *****

ApsName = Request.ServerVariables("WCS_NAME_SERVER")

'* Attempt Logon *****

Set SessionMgr = Server.CreateObject("CrystalEnterprise.SessionMgr")

On Error Resume Next    'Trap errors. Logon raises exception upon failure
  'Do the logon
  Set CeSession = SessionMgr.Logon(Username, Password, ApsName, AuthMode)

  'If error occurred, Err.Number will be non-zero
  If Err.Number<>0 Then
    'Use javascript alert to display error, then redirect back to logon form.
    Response.Write "<script>"
    Response.Write "alert('" & Err.Description & "\nPlease try again.');"
    Response.Write "open('logonform.html','_top');"
    Response.Write "</script>"
    Response.End
  End If
On Error Goto 0         'End of error trapping

'* Save Session Information *****
Set Session("IStore") = CeSession.Service("","InfoStore")
Response.Cookies("LogonToken") =
CeSession.LogonTokenMgr.CreateLogonToken("", 1, 100)

'* Redirect to Coverall Intranet Main Page *****
Response.Redirect "welcome.csp"
%>
```

LISTING 14.8   CONTINUED

```
'*Folders.csp ****
<%
Option Explicit
Response.Expires = 0   'Prevent browser from caching this page

Dim IStore              'Connection to Crystal Enterprise
Dim ApsName             'APS server name
Dim FolderId            'Id of folder

Dim List                'Stores InfoObjects Collection
Dim Item                'Stores InfoObject Object

'* Style Sheets ****

Response.Write "<link rel='stylesheet' " +
"type='text/css' href='css/common.css'>"
Response.Write "<link rel='stylesheet' type='text/css' href='css/folders.css'>"

'* Get folder Id from QueryString ****

FolderId = CLng(Request.QueryString("folderid"))

'* Get InfoStore from Session ****

Set IStore = Session("IStore")

'* Print parent Folder - APS if top level ****

Response.Write "<nobr>"

If FolderId=0 Then
    ApsName = Request.ServerVariables("WCS_NAME_SERVER")
    Response.Write "<img src='images/tree_aps.gif'> " & ApsName
Else
    Set List = IStore.Query("Select SI_ID From " +
"CI_INFOOBJECTS Where SI_ID=" & FolderId)
    Set Item = List(1)
    Response.Write "<img src='images/tree_folder_open.gif'> " & Item.Title
End If

'* Print folder contents ****

Set List = IStore.Query("Select SI_PROGID From CI_INFOOBJECTS Where " & _
  "SI_ID!=18 And SI_PARENTID=" & FolderId & _
  "And SI_PROGID In ('CrystalEnterprise.Folder','CrystalEnterprise.Report')")

Response.Write "<blockquote>"

'* Show "Parent Folder" link if applicable ***

If FolderId<>0 Then
    Response.Write "<a href='folders.csp?folderid=" & Item.ParentId & "'>"
    Response.Write "<img src='images/tree_folder_up.gif'> "
```

LISTING 14.8   CONTINUED

```
        Response.Write "Parent Folder"
        Response.Write "</a><br>"
End If

'* Print folder/report links ***

For Each Item In List
    Select Case Item("SI_PROGID")

        Case "CrystalEnterprise.Folder"
            Response.Write "<a href='folders.csp?folderid=" &
                    Item.Id & "'>"
            Response.Write "<img src=" +
                    "'images/tree_folder_closed.gif'> "
            Response.Write Item.Title
            Response.Write "</a><br>"

        Case "CrystalEnterprise.Report"
            Response.Write "<a href='instances.csp?reportid=" &
                    Item.Id & "' target=client>"
            Response.Write "<img src='images/tree_report.gif'> "
            Response.Write Item.Title
            Response.Write "</a><br>"
    End Select
Next

Response.Write "</blockquote>"
Response.Write "</nobr>"
Response.Write "</body>"
Response.Write "</html>"
%>

'* Instances.csp ****
<%
Option Explicit
Response.Expires = 0

Dim IStore              'Connection to Crystal Enterprise
Dim ApsName             'APS server name
Dim ReportId            'Id of report

Dim List                'Stores InfoObjects Collection
Dim Item                'Stores InfoObject Object
Dim Prompts             'Store ReportParameters Collection
Dim Prompt              'Store ReportParameter Object
Dim PromptCount         'Stores Number of Prompts

Dim SplitArray          'Array used for parsing
Dim StartDate           'Store instance start date
Dim StartTime           'Store instance start time
Dim Duration            'Store time required for instance to process

'* Style Sheets ***
```

LISTING 14.8   CONTINUED

```
Response.Write "<link rel='stylesheet' type='text/css' href='css/common.css'>"
Response.Write "<link rel='stylesheet' type='text/css' " +
"href='css/instances.css'>"

'* Get report Id from QueryString ****

ReportId = CLng(Request.QueryString("reportid"))

'* Get InfoStore from Session ****

Set IStore = Session("IStore")

'* Print report information ****

Set List = IStore.Query("Select SI_DESCRIPTION, " +
"SI_PROCESSINFO.SI_PROMPTS From " & _
  "CI_INFOOBJECTS Where SI_ID=" & ReportId)

Set Item = List(1)
Set Prompts = Item.PluginInterface("").ReportParameters
PromptCount = Prompts.Count

Response.Write "<h3><a href='view.csp?id=" & Item.Id & "'>"
Response.Write "<img src='images/tree_report.gif'> " & Item.Title
Response.Write "</a></h3>"

Response.Write Item("SI_DESCRIPTION") & "<p>"

'* Print instances ****

Response.Write "<table>"

Response.Write "<thead>"
Response.Write "<tr>"
Response.Write "   <th>View</th>"
Response.Write "   <th>Owner</th>"
Response.Write "   <th>Run Date</th>"
Response.Write "   <th>Time</th>"
Response.Write "   <th>Duration</th>"

'* Include instance parameter values ****

For Each Prompt in Prompts
    Response.Write "   <th>" & Prompt.ParameterName & "</th>"
Next

Response.Write "</tr>"
Response.Write "</thead>"

Response.Write "<tbody>"

Set List = IStore.Query("Select SI_PROCESSINFO.SI_PROMPTS, " +
"SI_OWNER, SI_ENDTIME, " & _
  "SI_NEXTRUNTIME From CI_INFOOBJECTS Where SI_PARENTID=" & ReportId & _
  " And SI_PROGID='CrystalEnterprise.Report' And SI_INSTANCE=1")
```

LISTING 14.8 CONTINUED

```
For Each Item In List
    SplitArray = Split(FormatDateTime(Item("SI_NEXTRUNTIME"),0)," ")
    StartDate = SplitArray(0)
    StartTime = SplitArray(1)
    Duration = CLng((Item("SI_ENDTIME")-Item("SI_NEXTRUNTIME"))*86400)

    Response.Write "<tr>"
    Response.Write "<td><a href='view.csp?id=" & Item.Id & "'>"
    Response.Write "    <img src='images/tree_report.gif'></a></td>"
    Response.Write "<td>" & Item("SI_OWNER") & "</td>"
    Response.Write "<td>" & StartDate & "</td>"
    Response.Write "<td>" & StartTime & "</td>"
    Response.Write "<td>" & Duration & "s</td>"

    Set Prompts = Item.PluginInterface("").ReportParameters
    For Each Prompt in Prompts
        If Prompt.CurrentValues.Count>0 Then
            Response.Write "  <th>" &
                        Prompt.CurrentValues(1).MakeDisplayString & "</th>"
        Else
            Response.Write "  <th>(not set)</th>"
        End If
    Next

    Response.Write "</tr>"
Next

Response.Write "</tbody>"

Response.Write "<tfoot>"
Response.Write "<tr>"
Response.Write "  <th colspan=" & 5+PromptCount & ">" & List.Count
 & " Instance(s)</th>"
Response.Write "</tr>"
Response.Write "</tfoot>"

Response.Write "</table>"
%>
```

Figure 14.5 shows the final version of the Coverall Manufacturing Web site with the sample code integrated to supply a reporting section from Crystal Enterprise.

Test the Coverall Web site to this point and confirm that report viewing requests are processed and delivered to a Web browser correctly.

After confirming that the logon to Crystal Enterprise and reports are listed correctly on the Coverall Web site, the second requirement for Coverall Manufacturing, a custom administrative Web site for power users and managers, can be completed.

Figure 14.5
The Coverall
Manufacturing Web
site with the integrated Crystal
Enterprise logon and
report listing.

DELEGATING ADMINISTRATIVE FUNCTIONS

This section reviews the concept of delegated administration tasks within Coverall Manufacturing. Recall that Coverall requires certain end users to take on traditional system admin tasks, such as creating new groups and folders or adding users to Crystal Enterprise. Although this task could be easily accomplished from the Crystal Management Console, the risk of accessing other administrative functions within the CMC is too high.

Coverall has determined that within the super or power user community, there will be a second level of administrators, which Coverall refers to as sheriffs and deputies. The Crystal Enterprise administrator will be the sheriff. This sheriff has control over the entire Crystal Enterprise environment through the Crystal Management Console. The sheriff is in charge of ensuring that correct security exists at the folder and object level, as well as to schedule reports. The sheriff also is responsible for adding the regional administrators, known as the deputies.

The deputy, on the other hand, is responsible for adding branches, folders, and users. The folders are added when a group is created. These folders match the group name.

Note

This sample application currently is not limiting the deputy user to creating subfolders just under their folder of control. These deputy users can create branches as deep as they want and add users to them.

PART

V

CH

14

The rest of this chapter focuses on the code required to create a custom administrative console for these deputies, through the use of the Crystal Enterprise Administrative SDK.

INITIAL CRYSTAL ENTERPRISE SYSTEM CONFIGURATION

To complete the following example, the Crystal Enterprise Administrator should create the following objects using the Crystal Management Console:

■ One Crystal Enterprise User: WestRegion—Leave the password blank

→ For information on using the Crystal Management Console, **see** Chapter 10, "Administering and Configuring Crystal Enterprise."

■ One Crystal Enterprise Group: Regional Managers—Group Description: Regional Managers Group

■ One Crystal Enterprise Folder: Coverall Manufacturing

The security on the preceding objects should be configured as follows:

■ Assign the Regional Managers group to be a member of the Administrators group.

■ Assign the user WestRegion to be a member of the Regional Managers group.

■ Set No Access to the Coverall Manufacturing folder for the Everyone group.

As far as the code for the regional manager (deputy in this scenario), which will enable the creation of new groups (*branches*) for their own region, see Listing 14.9.

> **Note**
>
> Creating branches involves creating both a branch group and a branch folder.

LISTING 14.9   THIS CODE ENABLES REGIONAL MANAGERS TO ADD NEW BRANCHES OR CRYSTAL ENTERPRISE GROUPS

```
Select Case LCase(Mode)
Case "add" ' Add Branch

'Add branch folder and group when user clicks 'OK

If Request.Form("action")="Add Branch" Then
 On Error Resume Next

'Create Folder
 Set Plugin = IStore.PluginManager.PluginInfo("CrystalEnterprise.Folder")
 Set FolderList = IStore.NewInfoObjectCollection
 Set Folder = FolderList.Add(Plugin)

'Set Folder Properties
 Folder.Title = Request.Form("Name")
 Folder.Description = Request.Form("Description")
 Folder("SI_PARENTID") = CLng(FolderId)

'Save Folder to APS
 IStore.Commit FolderList
 If Err.Number<>0 Then
```

LISTING 14.9   CONTINUED

```
'The following line of code is concatenated but doesn't have to be
Response.Write "<script>alert('An error occurred " +
"while adding branch.\nA branch"
 Response.Write " with same name may already exist.');history.back()</script>"
 Response.End
End If

'Create Group
Set Plugin = IStore.PluginManager.PluginInfo("CrystalEnterprise.UserGroup")
Set GroupList = IStore.NewInfoObjectCollection
Set Group = GroupList.Add(Plugin)

'Set Group Properties
Group.Title = Request.Form("Name")
Group.Description = Request.Form("Description")

'Save Group to APS
IStore.Commit GroupList
If Err.Number<>0 Then
'The following line of code is concatenated but doesn't have to be
Response.Write "<script>alert('An error occured " +
"while adding branch.\nA branch"
 Response.Write " with same name may already exist.');history.back()</script>"
 Response.End
End If

'Assign Group to Folder
Set SecurityInfo = Folder.SecurityInfo
Set Principal = SecurityInfo.ObjectPrincipals.Add(Group.Id)
Principal.Role = 4        'Assign 'View On Demand' access

'Save security assignment
IStore.Commit FolderList
If Err.Number<>0 Then
'The following line of code is concatenated but doesn't have to be
Response.Write "<script>alert('An error occured " +
"while adding branch.\nA branch"
 Response.Write " with same name may already exist.');history.back()</script>"
 Response.End
End If

'Redirect to Assignment Page
 Response.Redirect "assign.csp?folderid=" & FolderId
 Response.End
End If
'The following line of code is concatenated but doesn't have to be
Response.Write "<form method=post action='?"+
"folderid=" & FolderId & "&mode=add'>"
Response.Write "<table>"
Response.Write "<thead>"
Response.Write "<tr>"
Response.Write "<th colspan=2>Add Branch</td>"
Response.Write "</tr>"
Response.Write "<tfoot>"
Response.Write "<tr>"
```

PART

V

CH

14

LISTING 14.9 CONTINUED

```
Response.Write "<td>Branch Name</td>"
Response.Write "<td><input type=text name=Name></td>"
Response.Write "</tr>"
Response.Write "<tr>"
Response.Write "<td>Description</td>"
Response.Write "<td><input type=text name=Description></td>"
Response.Write "</tr>"

Response.Write "<tr>"
Response.Write "<th colspan=2>"
Response.Write "<input type=submit name='action' value='Add Branch'> "
Response.Write "<input type=button value='Cancel' onclick=""location.href="
Response.Write "'branch.csp?id=" & FolderId & "'"">"
Response.Write "</td>"
Response.Write "</tr>"
Response.Write "</tfoot>"
Response.Write "</form>"
```

In Figure 14.6 you can see how the code is displayed to add in a group. The folder is created in the background code so these folders will not show in the administration screen.

Figure 14.6
Adding in a Crystal Enterprise group to the application code.

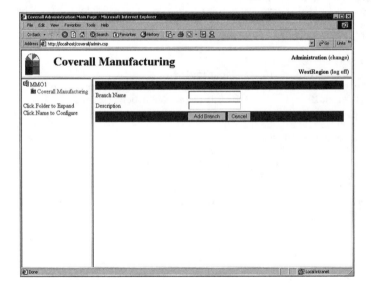

Listing 14.10 provides an example of how to add users to the Crystal Enterprise environment.

LISTING 14.10   THE REGIONAL MANAGERS WILL BE CAPABLE OF ADDING NEW USERS TO CRYSTAL ENTERPRISE

```
Case "New User"

If Request.Form("Username")<>"" Then

'Create User
  Set Plugin =IStore.PluginManager.PluginInfo("CrystalEnterprise.User")
  Set List = IStore.NewInfoObjectCollection
  Set User = List.Add(Plugin)

'Set Group Properties
  User.Title = Request.Form("Username")

'Save Group to APS
 On Error Resume Next
 IStore.Commit List
 If Err.Number<>0 Then
  Response.Write "<script>alert('An error occured while adding a user.\nA user"
  Response.Write " with same name may already exist.');history.back()</script>"
  Response.End
 End If
 On Error Goto 0

End If
```

In Figure 14.7 you can see how the code is displayed to add or delete users in a group.

Figure 14.7
The result of the code inserted to add or delete users.

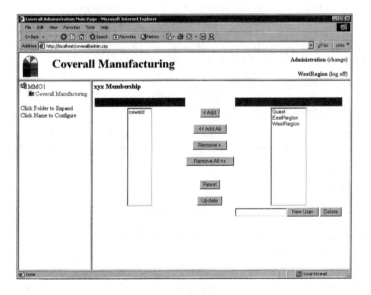

The custom code written for Coverall also provides the capability for regional managers to view all groups or branches and users within those branches.

The complete set of code to enable the custom administrative functions can be seen in Listing 14.11.

LISTING 14.11   THE COMPLETED ADMINISTRATIVE APPLICATION .CSP CODE SET

```
<%
Option Explicit
Response.Expires = 0   'Prevent browser from caching page

Dim IStore              'Connection to Crystal Enteprise

Dim FolderId            'Id of Folder to Adminstrate
Dim BranchName          'Name of folder to Administrate (Same as Group Name)
Dim Mode                'Page Mode
Dim Index               'Generic Loop index

Dim List                'Stores an InfoObjects Collection
Dim User                'Stores a User Object
Dim Users               'Stores a Users Collection
Dim Folder              'Folder InfoObject
Dim FolderList          'Folder collection to hold new folder InfoObject
Dim Group               'Group InfoObject
Dim GroupList           'Group collection to hold new group InfoObject
Dim Principal           'Principal object for assigning group to folder
Dim Principals          'Stores a ObjectPrincipals Collection
Dim Plugin              'Plugin Object for creating a folder and a user group
Dim SecurityInfo        'SecurityInfo Object

Dim MemberIds()         'Array of member user ids
Dim MembersString       'Comma delimited list of members
Dim Members             'InfoObjects Collection of members
Dim NonMembers          'InfoObjects Collection of non-members
Dim HtmlMembers         'Store members as an HTML string
Dim HtmlNonMembers      'Store non-members as an HTML string

Set IStore = Session("IStore")
FolderId = Request.QueryString("folderid")
Mode = LCase(Request.QueryString("mode"))

Response.Write "<link rel='stylesheet' type='text/css' href='css/common.css'>"
Response.Write "<link rel='stylesheet' type='text/css' href='css/assign.css'>"

Select Case LCase(Mode)
  Case "add" ' Add Branch

    'Add branch folder and group when user clicks 'OK

    If Request.Form("action")="Add Branch" Then
      On Error Resume Next

      'Create Folder
      Set Plugin = IStore.PluginManager.PluginInfo("CrystalEnterprise.Folder")
      Set FolderList = IStore.NewInfoObjectCollection
      Set Folder = FolderList.Add(Plugin)
```

LISTING 14.11   CONTINUED

```
      'Set Folder Properties
      Folder.Title = Request.Form("Name")
      Folder.Description = Request.Form("Description")
      Folder("SI_PARENTID") = CLng(FolderId)

      'Save Folder to APS
      IStore.Commit FolderList
      If Err.Number<>0 Then
'The following line of code is concatenated but doesn't have to be
         Response.Write "<script>alert('An error occurred " +
         "while adding branch.\nA branch"
         Response.Write " with same name may " +
         already exist.');history.back()</script>"
         Response.End
      End If

      'Create Group
'The following line of code is concatenated but doesn't have to be
      Set Plugin =
      IStore.PluginManager.PluginInfo("CrystalEnterprise.UserGroup")
      Set GroupList = IStore.NewInfoObjectCollection
      Set Group = GroupList.Add(Plugin)

      'Set Group Properties
      Group.Title = Request.Form("Name")
      Group.Description = Request.Form("Description")

      'Save Group to APS
      IStore.Commit GroupList
      If Err.Number<>0 Then
'The following line of code is concatenated but doesn't have to be
         Response.Write "<script>alert('An error occured " +
         "while adding branch.\nA branch"
         Response.Write " with same name may " +
         "already exist.');history.back()</script>"
         Response.End
      End If

      'Assign Group to Folder
      Set SecurityInfo = Folder.SecurityInfo
      Set Principal = SecurityInfo.ObjectPrincipals.Add(Group.Id)
      Principal.Role = 4        'Assign 'View On Demand' access

      'Save security assignment
      IStore.Commit FolderList
      If Err.Number<>0 Then
'The following line of code is concatenated but doesn't have to be
Response.Write "<script>alert('An error occurred " +
         "while adding branch.\nA branch"
         Response.Write " with same name may " +
         "already exist.');history.back()</script>"
         Response.End
      End If
```

LISTING 14.11   CONTINUED

```
        'Redirect to Assignment Page
        Response.Redirect "assign.csp?folderid=" & FolderId
        Response.End
      End If
'The following line of code is concatenated but doesn't have to be
      Response.Write "<form method=post action='?" +
      "folderid=" & FolderId & "&mode=add'>"
      Response.Write "<table>"
      Response.Write "<thead>"
      Response.Write "<tr>"
      Response.Write "<th colspan=2>Add Branch</td>"
      Response.Write "</tr>"

      Response.Write "<tfoot>"
      Response.Write "<tr>"
      Response.Write "<td>Branch Name</td>"
      Response.Write "<td><input type=text name=Name></td>"
      Response.Write "</tr>"
      Response.Write "<tr>"
      Response.Write "<td>Description</td>"
      Response.Write "<td><input type=text name=Description></td>"
      Response.Write "</tr>"

      Response.Write "<tr>"
      Response.Write "<th colspan=2>"
      Response.Write "<input type=submit name='action' value='Add Branch'> "
      Response.Write "<input type=button value='Cancel' onclick=""location.href="
      Response.Write "'branch.csp?id=" & FolderId & "'"">"
      Response.Write "</td>"
      Response.Write "</tr>"
      Response.Write "</tfoot>"
      Response.Write "</form>"

  Case "delete" ' Delete Branch

    '* Delete Folder ****
'The following line of code is concatenated but doesn't have to be
    Set List = IStore.Query("Select SI_ID From " +
    "CI_INFOOBJECTS Where SI_ID=" & FolderId)
    BranchName = List(1).Title
    List.Delete 1

    IStore.Commit List

    '* Delete User Group ****
'The following line of code is concatenated but doesn't have to be
    Set List = IStore.Query("Select SI_ID From " +
    "CI_SYSTEMOBJECTS Where SI_NAME='" & _
      BranchName & "' AND SI_PROGID='CrystalEnterprise.UserGroup'")
    List.Delete 1

    IStore.Commit List

    '* Go back to branch view ****
```

LISTING 14.11   CONTINUED

```
      Response.Redirect "assign.csp?folderid=" & Request.QueryString("p")

  Case "assign"

    '* Get branch name (ie., foldername) ***
'The following line of code is concatenated but doesn't have to be
    Set List = IStore.Query("Select SI_ID From " +
    "CI_INFOOBJECTS Where SI_ID=" & FolderId)
    BranchName = List(1).Title

    '* Perform action 'Update', 'Add' or , 'Delete' ***

    Select Case Request.Form("action")

      Case "Update"

        Users.Clear

        For Each User In Request.Form("members")
          Users.Add CLng(User)
        Next

        IStore.Commit List

      Case "New User"

        If Request.Form("Username")<>"" Then

          'Create User
'The following line of code spans two lines but doesn't have to be
          Set Plugin =
          IStore.PluginManager.PluginInfo("CrystalEnterprise.User")
          Set List = IStore.NewInfoObjectCollection
          Set User = List.Add(Plugin)

          'Set Group Properties
          User.Title = Request.Form("Username")

          'Save Group to APS
          On Error Resume Next
          IStore.Commit List
          If Err.Number<>0 Then
'The following lines of code are concatenated but doesn't have to be
            Response.Write "<script>alert('An error occured " +
            "while adding a user.\nA user"
            Response.Write " with same name may already " +
            "exist.');history.back()</script>"
            Response.End
          End If
          On Error Goto 0

        End If
```

LISTING 14.11   CONTINUED

```
        Case "Delete"
          For Each User In Request.Form("nonmembers")
'The following line of code is concatenated but doesn't have to be
            Set List = IStore.Query("Select SI_ID From " +
            "CI_SYSTEMOBJECTS WHERE SI_ID=" & _
              User)
            List.Delete 1
            IStore.Commit List
          Next
      End Select

      Redim Members(Users.Count-1)

      For Index = 0 to UBound(Members)
        Members(Index) = Users(Index+1)
      Next

      MembersString = Join(Members,",")
      If Len(MembersString)=0 Then MembersString = "0"

      '* Get collection of members (exclude admin) ***

      Set Members = IStore.Query("Select SI_ID From CI_SYSTEMOBJECTS Where " & _
        "SI_PROGID='CrystalEnterprise.User' And " & _
        "SI_ID In (" & MembersString & ") And SI_ID!=12")

      For Each User In Members
        HtmlMembers = HtmlMembers & "<option value=" & User.Id & ">" & User.Title
      Next

      '* Get collection non-members (exclude admin) ***
'The following line of code is concatenated but doesn't have to be
      Set NonMembers = IStore.Query("Select SI_ID From " +
      "CI_SYSTEMOBJECTS Where " & _
        "SI_PROGID='CrystalEnterprise.User' And " & _
        "SI_ID Not In (12," & MembersString & ")")
'The following line of code spans two lines but doesn't have to
      For Each User In NonMembers
        HtmlNonMembers = HtmlNonMembers & "<option value=" & User.Id & ">"
        & User.Title
      Next

      Response.Write "<script>"
      Response.Write "function shift(mode) {"
      Response.Write "  if(mode>0) {"
      Response.Write "    var src = document.all('nonmembers');"
      Response.Write "    var dest = document.all('members');"
      Response.Write "  } else {"
      Response.Write "    var src = document.all('members');"
      Response.Write "    var dest = document.all('nonmembers');"
      Response.Write "  }"

      Response.Write "  for(var i=src.length-1; i>=0; i--) {"
      Response.Write "    if(Math.abs(mode)>1||src[i].selected) {"
      Response.Write "      var o = document.createElement('OPTION');"
```

LISTING 14.11   CONTINUED

```
Response.Write "       o.text = src[i].text;"
Response.Write "       o.value = src[i].value;"
Response.Write "       dest.add(o);"
Response.Write "       src.remove(i);"
Response.Write "     }"
Response.Write "   }"
Response.Write "}"

Response.Write "function update() {"
Response.Write "  var l = document.all('members');"
Response.Write "  for(var i=0; i<l.length; i++)"
Response.Write "    l[i].selected = true;"
Response.Write "}"

Response.Write "function confirmDelete() {"
Response.Write "  if(!confirm('Delete the selected users?'))"
Response.Write "    return false;"
Response.Write "return true;"
Response.Write "}"
Response.Write "</script>"

Response.Write "<h3>" & BranchName & " Membership</h3>"

Response.Write "<form id=membersform method=post>"

Response.Write "<table>"

Response.Write "<thead>"
Response.Write "<tr>"
Response.Write "<th width='40%'>Members</th>"
Response.Write "<td></td>"
Response.Write "<th width='40%'>Non-members</th>"
Response.Write "</tr>"
Response.Write "</thead>"

Response.Write "<tbody>"
Response.Write "<tr>"
Response.Write "<td><select name=members size=16 multiple>" & HtmlMembers
Response.Write "</select></td>"
Response.Write "<td>"
Response.Write "<input type=button value='< Add' onclick='shift(1)'>"
Response.Write "<p><input type=" +
"button value='<< Add All' onclick='shift(2)'>"
Response.Write "<p><input type=" +
"button value='Remove >' onclick='shift(-1)'>"
Response.Write "<p><input type=" +
"button value='Remove All >>' onclick='shift(-2)'>"
Response.Write "<p><br><input type=" +
"reset onclick=""location.href='assign.csp?"
Response.Write "folderid=" & FolderId & "&mode=assign'"">"
Response.Write "<p><input type=submit name=action value='Update' "
Response.Write "onclick='return update()'>"
Response.Write "</td>"
Response.Write "<td><select name=" +
"nonmembers size=16 multiple>" & HtmlNonMembers
```

LISTING 14.11   CONTINUED

```
    Response.Write "</select></td>"
    Response.Write "</tr>"
    Response.Write "</tbody>"

    Response.Write "<tfoot>"
    Response.Write "<tr>"
    Response.Write "<td></td>"
    Response.Write "<td></td>"
    Response.Write "<td><nobr><input type=text name=Username>"
    Response.Write "<input type=submit name=action value='New User'> "
    Response.Write "<input type=submit name=action value='Delete' "
    Response.Write "onclick='return confirmDelete()'>"
    Response.Write "</nobr>"
    Response.Write "</td>"
    Response.Write "</tr>"
    Response.Write "</tfoot>"

    Response.Write "</table>"
    Response.Write "</form>"

Case Else ' Default Mode. View Branches

  '* Get branch name (ie., foldername) ***

  Set List = IStore.Query("Select SI_ID From " +
  "CI_INFOOBJECTS Where SI_ID=" & FolderId)
  BranchName = List(1).Title

  '* Print list of branchs (subfolders) ***

  Response.Write "<h3>Branches of " & BranchName & "</h3>"

  Response.Write "<table>"

  Response.Write "<thead>"
  Response.Write "<tr>"
  Response.Write "<td colspan=3 align=right>"
  Response.Write "<a href='assign.csp?folderid=" & FolderId & "&mode=add'> "
  Response.Write "Create New Branch</a>"
  Response.Write "</tr>"

  Response.Write "<tr>"
  Response.Write "<th>Name"
  Response.Write "<th>Description"
  Response.Write "<th>Action"
  Response.Write "</tr>"
  Response.Write "</thead>"

  Response.Write "<tbody>"

  Set List = IStore.Query("Select SI_DESCRIPTION From " +
  "CI_INFOOBJECTS Where " & _
    "SI_PARENTID=" & FolderId & " And SI_PROGID='CrystalEnterprise.Folder'")
```

LISTING 14.11   CONTINUED

```
    For Each Folder In List
      Response.Write "<tr>"
      Response.Write "<td>" & Folder.Title
      Response.Write "<td>" & Folder.Description
      Response.Write "<td><a href='assign.csp?folderid=" & Folder.Id
      Response.Write "&mode=assign'>Users</a> | "
      Response.Write "<a href='assign.csp?folderid=" &
      Folder.Id & "&p=" & FolderId
      Response.Write "&mode=delete'>Delete"
      Response.Write "</tr>"
    Next

    Response.Write "</tbody>"

    Response.Write "<tfoot>"
    Response.Write "<tr><th colspan=3>" & List.Count & " Branch(es)"

    Response.Write "</tfoot>"
    Response.Write "</table>"
    Response.Write "</form>"
End Select
%>
```

Linking the administrative code into the Coverall Manufacturing intranet site results in two accessible areas, shown in Figure 14.8. One is for the end user who wishes to view reports, and another area is for regional and branch managers who need to perform delegated administrative tasks.

Figure 14.8
The Coverall Web site with the report listing and administrative code linked together.

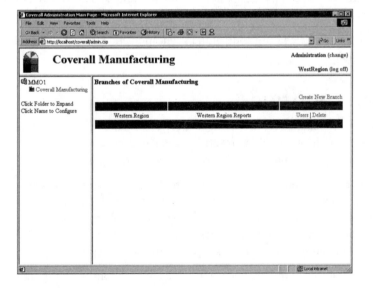

Looking at the code sample in more detail, when a branch is created by the regional manager (deputy), the following procedures take place:

- A folder is created for the branch under the corresponding region folder
- A user group is created for the branch
- The branch or group is assigned view rights to the branch folder
- General users or sales representatives, when assigned to a branch, will be added to the branch group and inherit the branch group rights

The branch users, or sales representatives, will be able to

- View reports

EXPLORING THE FINISHED COVERALL MANUFACTURING INTRANET SITE

Recall that the two requirements for Coverall Manufacturing were

- Provide an easy way for end users to securely access a list of sales reports over the Web
- Distribute administrative tasks to certain power users within the organization

As shown in Figure 14.4, the Coverall intranet site provides a simple portal that allows report viewers to log in and view reports, as well as an administrative portal for branch managers. To test the completed application, log in to the administrative portion of the application as the user Brad. Create a new folder (Branch) and call it Central Region.

Now log in to the end-user side of the application and verify that the folder Central Region was created.

TROUBLESHOOTING

To troubleshoot any custom coding, use error checking in your development application of choice. This chapter used Microsoft Notepad as the development tool for writing the custom .csp pages and modifying the welcome.csp intranet site.

If there are any problems logging on to the Crystal Enterprise system, scheduling reports, viewing reports, and so on, use the ePortfolio application (see Chapter 5, "Using the Crystal Enterprise Launchpad") to confirm whether the problem exists there as well. If it does, check the Crystal Management Console and Crystal Configuration Manager to confirm whether the problem is a server issue or a permissions setting that might cause problems.

As a general rule of thumb, if a report works in ePortfolio, step through the custom application code, using error checking, and diagnose the problem through applicable error messages.

SUMMARY

Using what was learned from Chapter 13, this chapter explored the topic of integrating Crystal Enterprise to an existing corporate intranet. The InfoStore and Administrative portions of the Crystal Enterprise SDK were used to write the code for this chapter.

A fictitious company, Coverall Manufacturing, had two requirements, which required integration with the Coverall corporate intranet site. To accomplish these tasks, the topics of logging into Crystal Enterprise, obtaining a token, and retrieving a list of reports were reviewed. The list of accessible reports was then written to the welcome.csp page as hyperlinks to reports within Crystal Enterprise.

To complete the second requirement, distributed administration via the concept of sheriffs and deputies, a custom application was written to allow limited administration for certain functions of Crystal Enterprise such as creating new groups and users.

CHAPTER 15

INTEGRATING CRYSTAL ENTERPRISE WITH THIRD-PARTY PORTALS

In this chapter

Many organizations have adopted a corporate standard interface, or *portal application*, into which other applications can snap. Such portal applications include Microsoft Digital Dashboard, Plumtree, Broadvision, and many more.

The portal application takes the place of an application's traditional front-end GUI (such as Crystal Enterprise). The idea is that a single interface for users to go to when they need information, or e-mail, or to check the weather or their company's stock price, reduces a user's learning curve, reduces support costs, and increases productivity. Of course, there's also the benefit the IT organization receives by always deploying application functionality to the same location.

To reemphasize a point made in many chapters previous to this one, Crystal Enterprise comes with its own opensource front-end applications, such as ePortfolio. You do not need a portal application to use Crystal Enterprise.

However, Crystal Enterprise was developed for integrating an application's end-user functionality with a front-end portal. Crystal Decisions clearly made a fundamental decision that it would focus on providing scalable information-delivery software and could easily integrate into enterprise portal software.

Whether the portal technology is Java-based, COM-based, or somewhere in between, Crystal Enterprise can service the reporting and information delivery requirements through the necessary front-end integration requirements. Credit the Crystal Enterprise open SDK with that capability.

It's also important to note that Crystal Enterprise can be programmatically integrated with almost any portal application available for the Web, but Crystal Decisions has gone the extra step by developing out-of-the-box portal components that can be readily integrated with portal applications without additional development efforts. These prebuilt Crystal Enterprise portal components include Microsoft Digital Dashboard Web Parts and Plumtree Gadgets.

There are two fundamental levels of portal integration this chapter will discuss:

- Portal integration through programmatic development. Understanding how Crystal Enterprise integrates with generic intranet Web sites will help the reader understand how Crystal Enterprise can programmatically integrate with portal applications. This chapter describes how to integrate Crystal Enterprise into any Web application.
- Portal integration using prebuilt report viewing and request components.

Whether using ePortfolio (see Chapter 6, "Customizing ePortfolio for Rapid Information Delivery") or a custom front-end Web interface as the preferred method of report and information delivery, it should be fairly clear that there is always a choice. This is due to the fact that the entire environment is content-aware, environment-aware, and is exposed via a robust SDK. See Chapter 14 for more details on using the Crystal Enterprise SDK.

UNDERSTANDING PORTALS

Before delving into the details of how Crystal Enterprise integrates with portal applications, it's helpful to know who the major portal vendors are, what functionality is offered, and, most importantly, on what application development technology the portal is based.

According to Leigh Gregg, a well-respected portal expert, "Today's most popular portals started as search engines, but they've extended their offerings to include e-mail, chat functions, instant messaging, and even personalized service." A few examples of the early portals (now termed consumer portals) were Yahoo!, Excite, and AOL. While providing relevant searching and categorized content, they also offered fingertip browsing, convenience, and a sense of continuity, which attracted tens of millions of technical and nontechnical users alike.

The corporate world caught on to this phenomenon and wanted to use the portal-like interface and function for their Web projects and internal intranets. This fueled much excitement and expanded project possibilities, as well as added one more technical build versus buy dilemma that CIOs, IT managers, and developers were now facing.

As always, software vendors were only too happy to comply with portal pitches and products to meet the new demand. Business intelligence vendors certainly weren't immune to this either. They touted and pushed newly formulated terms such as Corporate Portal, Knowledge Management Portal, Business Intelligence Portal, and Enterprise Information Portal (EIP), giving rise to an industry unto itself offering a broad depth and scope of services, applications, and architectures.

CATEGORIZING PORTALS

To understand portals in more detail, there is a spectacular resource available on the Internet. Refer to www.Traffick.com, The Guide to Portals and Search Engines, a site dedicated to the portal industry. It offers the following generic categories:

- Consumer portals, such as Yahoo!, Excite, and AOL
- Corporate portals or Executive Information Portals (EIP), such as Plumtree and Verity
- Vertical or niche portals, such as about.com and guru.com
- Industry or B2B portals, which are a fairly new phenomenon for information sharing and, most importantly, the completion of transactions

Traffick.com also offers various other categories and subcategories. This chapter examines one topic in particular—the corporate portals category—because this is where Crystal Enterprise is most often required to provide its services.

CORPORATE PORTALS

"The Enterprise Information Portal (EIP) is among the 'hottest' current information technology subjects," says Joseph M. Firestone, CEO and Chief Scientist of Executive Information Systems (EIS) Inc.

Note

EIPs are also known as corporate portals or Enterprise Resource Portals (ERPs).

With the advent of ERP systems and the general wide availability of corporate data (both structured and unstructured), organizations are coming to the realization that much of their valuable information has not been tapped. Many vendors are offering out-of-the-box solutions to unlock the heterogeneous information housed in organizational data warehouses and databases. This opportunity to leverage information and deliver it in an acute, focused, fashion via a portal offers a compelling solution for many organizations.

But what really is an EIP? In November 1998, when Shilakes and Tylman of Merrill Lynch Inc. published their report that predicted the Enterprise Information Portal, they defined Enterprise Information Portals as

> "Applications that enable companies to unlock internally and externally stored information, and provide users a single gateway to personalized information needed to make informed business decisions. They are: '…an amalgamation of software applications that consolidate, manage, analyze and distribute information across and outside of an enterprise (including Business Intelligence, Content Management, Data Warehouse & Mart and Data Management applications.)'

> This is a giant leap forward from simply providing some categorized searching or a simple doorway to the Internet. EIPs have the potential to be a knowledge workers' one stop shopping for the information they need to do their jobs, while at the same time providing this from any machine with a browser—An *Anytime Anywhere Knowledge Worker.*"

In the definition offered by Shilakes and Tylman, Business Intelligence is offered as a complementary service to the overall corporate portal infrastructure. This viewpoint is in concurrence with many of the demands placed upon Crystal Enterprise.

CRYSTAL ENTERPRISE AND PORTAL APPLICATIONS

When describing Crystal Enterprise, the terms *repository*, *personalized content*, and *Web delivery* are often mentioned. Some of these terms are also offered when describing EIPs. So, even though the introduction to this chapter explained that Crystal Enterprise is not a portal, this seems contradictory. Is it an Enterprise Information Portal?

Although it does appear that Crystal Enterprise possesses and manifests portal-like functions such as searching, Web delivery, content management, and personalization, it's important to understand that Crystal Enterprise is focused on providing rich information delivery capabilities. The goal of Crystal Enterprise is to be an open and flexible environment, providing a set of application services, file services, content services, and Web services for the consumption of a user brokered by a Web page, corporate Web site, or a portal.

Much as Yahoo! (see Figure 15.1) provides maps, weather, and people searching on behalf of the requestor, Crystal Enterprise is brokered by a portal or corporate intranet/extranet for its services and content: reports and analytic applications. As mentioned earlier in the chapter, these services are provided merely as a component of the overall portal solution. Each component of a portal must provide basic elements necessary for seamless (and relatively painless) application integration.

Figure 15.1
Yahoo!, one of the "early" portals.

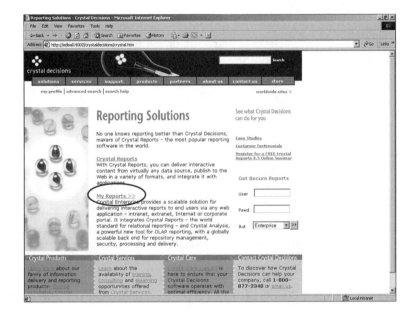

THE IMPLICATIONS OF CRYSTAL ENTERPRISE AS A PORTAL COMPONENT

Consider the following real-world scenarios:

- "I have a multitude of users in varying roles and departments that need to access reporting. The users need to be seamlessly transitioned from their portal desktop into reports or have the reports live within the desktop."

- "The application may call for users to be able to select report content without being required to render their credentials."

- "Users should have the capability to pick and choose which reports display within their personal home page as well as have access to supplemental content as needed. The ideal solution would work with my existing server farm and security model without requiring dual efforts to maintain."

When introducing any new component to a portal environment there are areas that must be considered for a seamless user experience. These include

- Component security
- Session management

COMPONENT SECURITY

Providing seamless integration capabilities to multiple applications is a fundamental requirement of any well-implemented portal solution. Crystal Enterprise, being part of the portal, complies with this by supporting multiple authentication strategies, which include the following:

- NT Authentication
- LDAP Authentication (based on the version 3 specification)

Note

Crystal Enterprise supports mapping into third-party authentication models. This means that, using the Crystal Management Console, users and groups would be mapped to the LDAP or NT server, *not* imported into Crystal Enterprise. The users would be, in essence, an alias within Crystal Enterprise, containing a pointer to the host authentication system. See Chapter 10 for more in-depth discussions about how Crystal Enterprise integrates with third-party authentication providers.

Currently, Crystal Enterprise supports NT Single Sign On and will continue to do so with future product releases.

Note

Single Sign On, or SSO, is the capability to have the user log in to the portal application once, without asking the user to provide authentication information for each portal component accessed.

LDAP AUTHENTICATION

By providing direct support within Crystal Enterprise for LDAP authentication it's straightforward for an organization to use a single LDAP server for both the Portal Server and Crystal Enterprise. Organizations can easily offer single sign-on capabilities using LDAP in conjunction with an authentication management system. There are several such systems on the market.

SESSION MANAGEMENT

After a user has been authenticated into Crystal Enterprise, the APS server generates and returns an APSToken. Typically this token is in the form of a browser cookie, but could also be a server-side token. Just keep your memory on the server in mind when managing tokens. This token is used in conjunction with the Crystal Enterprise session object, to track a user from the beginning until the session is terminated.

Crystal Enterprise handles all the business logic to allow and deny rights and actions to objects within the environment through its own permissions model. By passing the APS token back to Crystal Enterprise for a given report viewing request, only that user will gain access to the objects he is permitted to use.

When considering a portal implementation, this usually implies a high volume of users and transactions. This might require building a Web server farm to handle the capacity on the Web server. The important thing to note here is that Crystal Enterprise does not tie your user to a specific Web or application server within the farm; instead, it frees you to build a scalable environment.

This is the benefit of the token discussed previously, because it provides substantial flexibility when multiple physical Crystal Web Component Servers are used within a system. A user's request to view a report can enter the Crystal Enterprise system through one Web Component Server and fulfill the request. Depending on system load and deployment configuration, future requests by the same user could be fulfilled through an entirely different Web Component Server.

For a more in-depth look at sessions and token management, see Chapter 13, "Extending Crystal Enterprise."

CREATING A SEAMLESS USER EXPERIENCE

With integrated authentication in place, as well as Crystal Enterprise session and token management, combined with some good Web application practices, a portal as a front end to Crystal Enterprise will provide the end user with a seamless integrated Business Intelligence experience.

PROGRAMMATIC WEB SITE INTEGRATION

This portion of the chapter reviews the two most common scenarios within an organization when using Crystal Enterprise:

- How to deploy information reporting and analysis functionality on a dedicated reporting Web site
- How to hyperlink to reports and information off of an existing Web site

These topics are extremely relevant to programmatic integration with a portal, because the development efforts required to create these applications can be funneled into component creation for a portal.

SCENARIO 1: A DEDICATED REPORTING AND ANALYSIS WEB SITE

By itself, as is sometimes the case, Crystal Enterprise is required to deliver Crystal Reports or analytic reports (Crystal Analysis Professional) through a front-end Web application as a personalized Business Intelligence environment. This implies that the users require a Web application that would provide them with just Crystal Enterprise content. This type of front-end interface could be referred to as a dedicated reporting portal interface. This would include the delivery of Crystal Reports, Crystal Analysis Reports, and an ad hoc interface (smart reporting). This is the case with the first scenario.

A solution to these requirements entails a hyperlink from a central Web site advertising something to the effect of Reports or My Reports (see Figure 15.2). After the link is clicked, the user would be routed into the Business Intelligence interface (see Figure 15.3). While navigating within this environment, it's completely possible to provide content or hyperlinks to other areas within a corporate intranet, thereby providing some potential workflow. In other words, the interface is not fixed or rigid; it's open to other content as required. After all, the portal application in the solution is written in a scripting language such as JavaScript.

Figure 15.2
Web application with My Reports hyperlink to reporting.

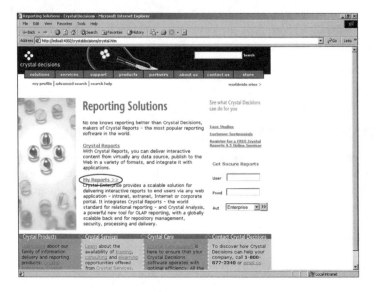

After a Web site with a list of relevant reports and data access has been created, it could easily be linked to an existing portal.

SCENARIO 2: INTEGRATING CRYSTAL ENTERPRISE WITH AN EXISTING WEB SITE

More often, business requirements call for Crystal Enterprise to bind to or become part of an existing Web application or Internet/intranet site, thereby relegating itself to streaming reporting or information content into the Web environment as requested (see Figure 15.4). Given these two scenarios, the latter is what most organizations desire and ultimately opt to pursue, for several reasons:

Figure 15.3
Business Intelligence content only: still having hyperlinks and some workflow possibilities.

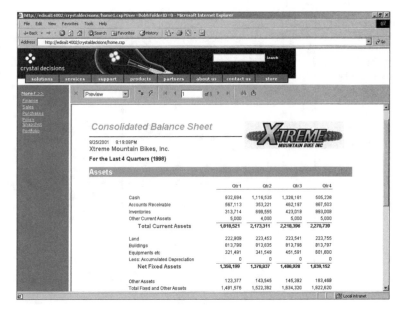

- Business Intelligence often is a subset of the larger goal of offering many forms of content and services via a central Web-based interface.

- It's not the intention of a Web site to disrupt or confuse the user by having him use an interface that is different from what he is accustomed to.

- The idea is to keep the workflow smooth and the learning curve minimized while providing necessary content in a seamless integrated manner.

- By offering one central access point, the distribution, maintenance, and security of the information or reports is substantially easier.

Together, this provides for a seamless transition and a professional, well-constructed site.

In a recent discussion with an IT professional using Crystal Enterprise, he commented that the less his users were aware that Crystal Enterprise was being used for their application, the better, but it was good that he knew that the product was there.

This comment refers to the fact that the application had some specifications for Business Intelligence. The first requirement was to use Crystal Enterprise and integrate the content seamlessly into the application so the user was not aware that that he was looking at vendor-provided Business Intelligence. In addition, they used the NT Single Sign On capabilities of Crystal Enterprise, which provided for a seamless experience for the end users. After the user entered the portal, he could request content from Crystal Enterprise without needing to provide additional authentication information.

Figure 15.4
Crystal Enterprise Content streamed into a Web site. The integration of Crystal Enterprise content within the Web site can be seen to the right of the Report viewer labeled Your Crystal Reports.

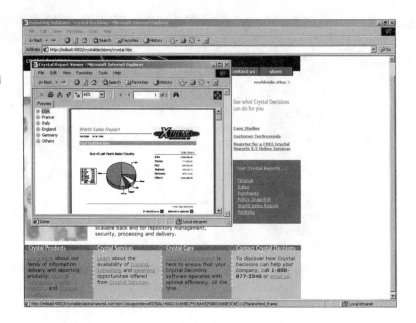

The second requirement was the need to support a growing user base, so the scalability of Crystal Enterprise's infrastructure offers him reassurance of scalability and high availability.

> **Note**
>
> Although the two previous scenarios describe either routing a user out to a separate reporting interface or streaming information from Crystal Enterprise inside an existing application, there was no mention of how security could be applied. This will be explored in more detail later in the chapter.

In either of the previous two scenarios, the development of the desired functionality takes place in a scripted development language such as JavaScript, using the Crystal Enterprise SDK.

A simple Web site with a static list of reports or a more complex site with intelligent actions and script could easily be inserted into a portal or linked to one using simple HTML.

LEVERAGING PREBUILT CRYSTAL ENTERPRISE PORTAL COMPONENTS

In this section, two portal integration scenarios will be explored:

- Microsoft's Digital Dashboard
- Plumtree

These two vendors and their associated portal applications represent some of the work and integration that Crystal Decisions has done from a portal component perspective. This means that Crystal Decisions has actually developed snap-in components or parts for these vendor's portal applications.

This does not preclude Crystal Enterprise from integrating with the other fine portals currently on the market; they are just not explored in this book. In fact, Crystal Decisions and SAP announced that they have signed a strategic agreement to integrate Crystal Decisions' formatted reporting and Web-based information delivery technologies within the data warehouse component (SAP Business Information Warehouse) of mySAP Business Intelligence (mySAP BI) and of the mySAP.com e-business platform (see Figure 15.5).

Note

For more information and updates on the Crystal Decisions SAP functionality and integration, refer to http://www.crystaldecisions.com/partners/ strategic/sap/.

Figure 15.5
Crystal Enterprise and SAP portals integration.

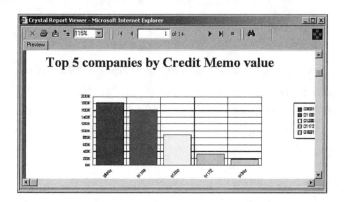

Note

The portal components discussed throughout this chapter, specifically the ones produced by Crystal Decisions, are meant to be sample components for developers to learn from and extend. They are not formal shipping components of Crystal Enterprise.

UNDERSTANDING MICROSOFT DIGITAL DASHBOARD

Microsoft's digital dashboard is a customizable portal framework that enables knowledge workers to view and collaborate on personal, team, corporate, and external information. Web-based content can be integrated into the portal via Web Parts (XML wrappers around existing Web-based code), which offer companies an effective way to integrate existing enterprise systems into their corporate portal. Web Parts shipping in the Digital Dashboard Resource Kit 3.0 can be used with SharePoint Portal Server, which was the first Microsoft product to be based on the Digital Dashboard framework, or SQL Server 2000 digital dashboards. The components that make up Microsoft Digital Dashboard include

- **Dashboard Store**—A metadata repository.
- **Dashboard Server**—A Web server that includes a dashboard factory and a store interface. The dashboard factory is a processing engine that assembles Web Parts into a dashboard by generating HTML pages that contain presentation information. The store interface is an API used to access the dashboard store, such as the SQL Server.
- **Dashboard Client**—A dashboard client runs a rendered dashboard. All components are rendered through the browser.
- **Content Services**—The source data consumed or manipulated by a Web Part. They may include a URL or embedded script (HTML—client side, JScript, VBScript, or XML—server side.) Microsoft clearly outlines these types of content in their documentation.

> **Note**
>
> Refer to the portal server vendor's documentation for detailed information regarding its architecture and recommended use.

USING CRYSTAL ENTERPRISE PREBUILT DIGITAL DASHBOARD WEB PARTS

Crystal Enterprise has provided five prebuilt server-side Web Parts that can be used to provide content for an application (see Figure 15.6). These include the following:

- **Logon**—Provides authentication, token/ticket, and session management into Crystal Enterprise. This part supports Crystal Enterprise authentication, NT, and LDAP (as described earlier in the chapter).
- **Thumbnail viewer**—Provides a picture of the Crystal Enterprise object as well as VCR button navigation. This allows picture navigation of content.
- **Object navigator**—Provides the customary folder navigation of Crystal Enterprise content. It enables the directory-style browsing of on-demand or scheduled content.
- **Content Viewer (Report Viewer)**—Provides the complete rendering of the content. Also, if needed, will interact with the prompting and the database.
- **Alerting**—Provides for the presentation of indicators or alerts from within Crystal Enterprise.

> **Note**
>
> These five Web Parts were created to provide for the basics of interacting with Crystal Enterprise, such as viewing and requesting reports, as well as to demonstrate possible programmatic integration points. Although they are prebuilt Web Parts, they are more of a starting point for developers, as undoubtedly organizations will want to enhance or modify their code to meet user requirements.

Figure 15.6
Crystal Enterprise
Web Parts.

Report alerts

Report instances

Report viewer

Logon

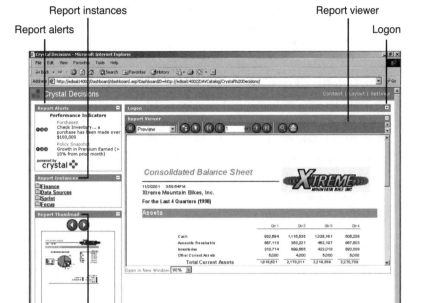

Thumbnail viewer

Note

Other Crystal Web Parts can be created and inserted into the Digital Dashboard environment depending on the application requirements. It is just as valid to add other prepackaged, external, or custom business Web Parts to a dashboard, thereby surrounding your Business Intelligence content with other pertinent information.

To use Microsoft Digital Dashboard and the Crystal Enterprise Web Parts, there are some requirements to be aware of:

■ Installation and administration requirements:

Microsoft Windows 2000 Professional, Windows 2000 Server, Windows 2000 Advanced Server, or Windows XP Professional

Microsoft Internet Explorer 5.5 installed on the server or administration client

Any edition of Microsoft SQL Server 2000

■ Viewing requirements:

Microsoft Internet Explorer 5.5 or compatible browser installed on the client

- Crystal Enterprise Web Part content requirements:

  Crystal Enterprise Professional

  Crystal Decisions Web Parts and Dashboard definition file—ddb

INSTALLING THE CRYSTAL ENTERPRISE WEB PARTS

After the Microsoft Digital Dashboard is installed, open the Administrator's Dashboard in a Web browser window. The Admin dashboard can be found at the following link, where *servername* is the server where you've installed the Dashboard:

```
http://servername/Dashboard/dashboard.asp?DashboardID=
➥http://<servername>/DAVCatalog/Dashboards/Welcome/Administration/
```

Under Dashboard View, select DAVCatalog, and then click Import. When the Import dialog box appears, select Files of Type Dashboard (*.ddb) (see Figure 15.7).

Figure 15.7
Digital Dashboard
Administration.

Select any of the Crystal .ddb files and click Open. A Crystal Decisions Dashboard under DAVCatalog will be available. (This might take a few seconds depending on the speed of your server.) Select Crystal Decisions and click Go (see Figure 15.8).

The Crystal Decisions Dashboard will load in the browser, as you have already seen in Figure 15.6.

To download Crystal Decisions Web Parts, or for more information, visit the Web site at www.crystaldecisions.com/digitaldashboard. Crystal Decisions Web Parts will also be available on the Microsoft Web Part Gallery, located at www.microsoft.com/digitaldashboard.

The Web Parts are relatively straightforward to use, so there isn't a real need to discuss the possible user scenarios in these chapters.

Figure 15.8
Choosing the Crystal
Enterprise
Dashboard.

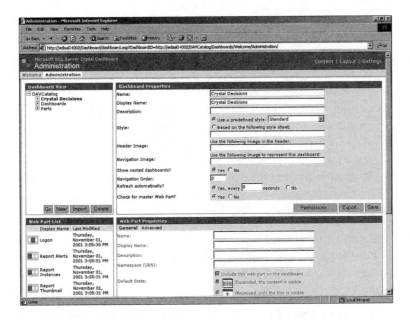

PART

V

CH

15

UNDERSTANDING PLUMTREE CORPORATE PORTAL

Similar to Microsoft Digital Dashboard, the Plumtree Corporate Portal is an open, scalable platform that allows organizations to apply portal concepts and integration to information and applications. This platform gives employees, partners, and customers a simple, personalized destination for the key information and services they need to do business with an organization.

The Plumtree Corporate Portal organizes access to documents in an enterprisewide Web directory, and integrates the most useful information and services from other systems as Plumtree Gadget Web Services. Similar in appearance to the sports scoreboards or stock portfolios of consumer portals, Gadget Web Services bring together the information and services most users really need every day, such as sales leads, inventory reports, e-mail, calendars, or industry news.

Built on Plumtree's Parallel Portal Engine, requests are sent in parallel to the Gadget Web Services operating on separate computers, using an architecture designed to provide a scalable, fault-tolerant solution.

The Plumtree Portal solution is comprised of the following:

- **Portal Server**—The Portal Server assembles personalized and community portal pages and processes user requests. To perform this task in a scalable, fault-tolerant way, Plumtree has developed the patent-pending Massively Parallel Portal Engine, which operates on the Portal Server to assemble services from Gadget Servers simultaneously.

■ **Job Server**—The Job Server indexes content in the portal's document directory, synchronizes user's security profiles with external user databases, and performs other periodic maintenance tasks. To index the content in various content repositories, Plumtree deploys a series of Crawlers. As the volume of content indexed in a deployment of the portal increases, customers can install more Job Servers to process new content.

■ **Gadget Server**—The Gadget Server interacts with applications and Internet sites to provide the information and services embedded in portal pages as Plumtree Gadget Web Services. Each Gadget Web Service communicates with an application or Internet service using an application programming interface, remote messaging interface, or the Internet-generating HTML or XML that can be transferred to the portal server.

USING CRYSTAL ENTERPRISE PREBUILT PLUMTREE GADGETS

Falling under the Gadget Services functionality within Plumtree, Crystal Enterprise has provided five server-side gadgets that can be used to provide content for an application. These gadgets are basically identical to the Microsoft Digital Dashboard Web Parts (refer to Figure 15.9). These include

■ **Logon Gadget**—Provides authentication, token/ticket, and session management into Crystal Enterprise. This gadget supports Crystal Enterprise authentication, NT, and LDAP (as described earlier in the chapter).

Figure 15.9
Crystal Enterprise
Plumtree Gadgets.

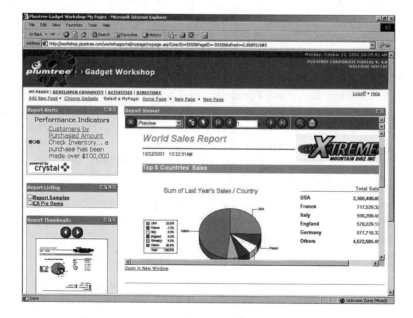

■ **Thumbnail Viewer Gadget**—Provides a picture of the Crystal Enterprise object as well as VCR button navigation. This allows "picture navigation" of content.

- **Object Navigator Gadget**—Provides the customary folder navigation of content. Enables the directory style browsing of on-demand or scheduled content.

- **Content Viewer (Report Viewer) Gadget**—Provides the complete rendering of the content. Also, if needed, the viewer gadget will provide interaction features for the user to enter report parameters or database logon information.

- **Alerting Gadget**—Provides for the presentation of indicators or alerts from within Crystal Enterprise.

Note

It's important to note the same points that are prevalent with the Microsoft Digital Dashboard Web Parts: These Gadgets were created to provide for the basics of interacting with Crystal Enterprise (viewing and requesting reports) as well as to demonstrate integration points. Additional Crystal Enterprise Gadgets could be created and inserted into the Plumtree Portal, depending on user and application requirements.

→ For more information on alerts in reports, **see** Chapter 8, "Creating Content with Crystal Reports."

Be sure Plumtree's corporate portal software is installed, specifically version 4.0, which is detailed here. At the time of writing this book, version 4.5 was the current release.

The Plumtree Corporate Portal is a distributed system whose components can be hosted on as many separate computers as necessary. The required configuration will depend on many details specific to each deployment.

Note

Refer to the portal vendor's installation manual for minimum hardware requirements and recommended deployment configurations.

Crystal Enterprise Gadget Installation requires two items:

- Crystal Enterprise Professional
- Crystal Decisions Gadgets—these currently are not available on the Crystal Decisions Web site; please contact your local Crystal Decisions sales representative

USING THE CRYSTAL ENTERPRISE GADGETS

After Plumtree version 4 or higher has been installed and administrative privileges have been granted within the Plumtree environment, the Crystal Enterprise Gadgets can be installed.

Note

This section assumes some knowledge of the Plumtree Corporate Portal environment.

Upon obtaining the Crystal Enterprise Gadgets, place the gadgets in the proper directory structure within Plumtree. In this sample the five gadgets were given their own directory: CrystalDecisions\viewer...CrystalDecisions\alerts, and so on. Then the individual gadgets were placed in their respective directories.

The following scenario describes how the Crystal Enterprise Logon Gadget will be installed:

1. Navigate to the Plumtree Portal site, `http://servername/portal40`.

2. Log in appropriately, choose Administration, and then select Add Native Gadget (see Figure 15.10).

Figure 15.10
Adding Native Gadgets.

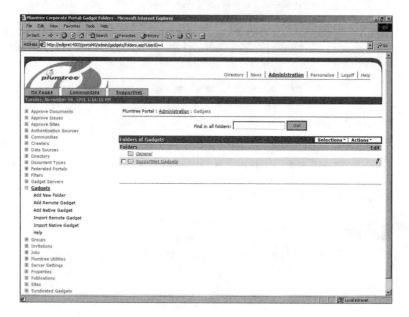

Note

For the sake of brevity, this chapter reviews adding Native Gadgets only. Plumtree's architecture allows for Remote Gadgets, which offload processing to other host servers for speed and scalability.

3. Follow the Gadget Wizard prompts and answer the series of questions about the Gadget, always selecting the defaults unless an experienced Plumtree administrator is available for assistance. Select Next (see Figure 15.11). Refer to the Plumtree Gadget documentation for additional Gadget installation specifications if necessary.

4. Continue through the wizard and when asked for Gadget folder/subfolder information, select the appropriate folder. In this sample, the Crystal_Decisions\logon folder was chosen (see Figure 15.12).

Figure 15.11
The Gadget Wizard.

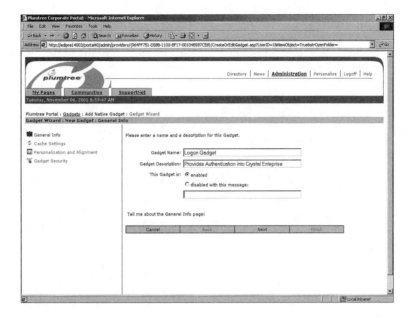

Figure 15.12
Choosing the
Crystal_Decisions\log
on folder.

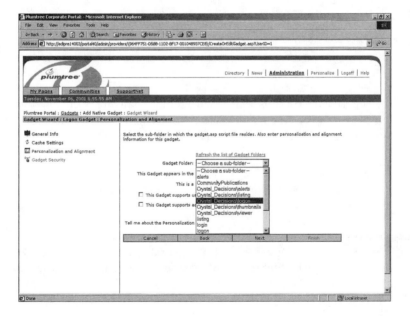

5. Select Next, and then apply the appropriate permissions to the Gadget object. For Microsoft Internet Information Server administrators, this is analogous to assigning a virtual directory for a hosted Web site.

6. Select Finished. The Logon Gadget will be added to the portal environment. Repeat this process for the remaining four Gadgets: Alerts, Viewing, Listing, and Thumbnails. When finished, all five gadgets should be available to the portal application (see Figure 15.13).

Figure 15.13
Five Crystal Decisions Gadgets.

7. To make the Gadgets available to a portal, configure the home page portion of a particular user's configuration. Select the Crystal Enterprise Gadgets desired for the user's page, and then select Finished (see Figure 15.14).

Then the user can interact with Business Intelligence information such as Crystal Reports and Crystal Analysis Professional applications from within Plumtree, as shown in Figure 15.9.

> **Note**
>
> Because of "real-estate" issues within the Web page, organizations may choose to limit the Gadgets to the Report Listing part within the Portal home page.

Figure 15.14
Administration of a
Plumtree user's home
page.

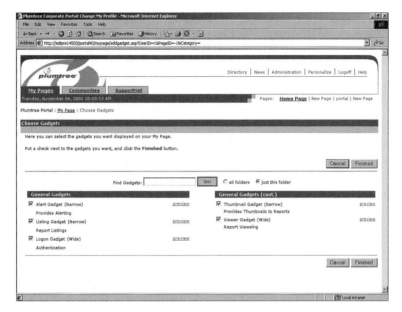

SUMMARY

Although Crystal Enterprise comes bundled with an out-of-the-box Web portal–like interface such as ePortfolio, it doesn't satisfy the custom front-end interface requirements of
many organizations that have adopted portal applications such as Microsoft Digital
Dashboard or Plumtree Corporate Portal.

By leveraging the prebuilt portal components provided by Crystal Decisions for various vendor portals and with a bit of customization to this interface, organizations can deliver
reports and information to users when they need it, from an integrated interface containing
other relevant business information.

It's important to note that, although Crystal Enterprise can integrate with a variety of portal
applications, a portal product isn't required to access reports and information.

Crystal Enterprise integrates with portal applications in two ways:

- Programmatic integration
- Prebuilt portal components

The first approach, programmatic integration, is similar to previously discussed efforts of application development with Crystal Enterprise, namely

- A hyperlink offering reporting content or Business Intelligence. This will route a user to a user interface with Crystal Enterprise reporting and information content only.
- Reports and information content streamed directly into the site.

From Crystal Enterprise's point of view, the user's front-end application interface, portal, Web site, or anything else doesn't make a difference because its goal is to provide Business Intelligence content, such as reports and analytic applications, in any form that the application requires. This flexibility comes from the powerful Crystal Enterprise SDK and being able to provide its services on demand. Crystal Enterprise also offers a flexible architecture that can grow with an organization and application requirements.

Portals themselves can be a very confusing topic because there are many kinds and concepts of what a portal really is. In its many variations, the main goal of a generic portal application is to provide users with secure, timely, and topical information through a central, convenient, and attractive interface. Two popular portals and their integration with Crystal Enterprise were discussed: Microsoft Digital Dashboard and Plumtree Corporate Portal.

Due to the number of portal categories and vendors, not all can be mentioned or discussed. Regardless of the portal application, the goal of Crystal Enterprise is to be an open and flexible environment providing a set of application services, file services, content services, and Web services for brokering by a Web page, corporate Web site, or a portal to a specified set of end users.

CRYSTAL ENTERPRISE SUPPLEMENTAL MATERIAL

RUNNING CRYSTAL ENTERPRISE ON SUN SOLARIS

In this chapter

Note

Recommended reading before this appendix includes, at a minimum, Chapters 1 through 3 and 5. Without first reading about the Crystal Enterprise system architecture and common system components this appendix will be difficult to understand. Chapters 13 and 14 are also good chapters to review because they explain the SDK (developer) portion of Crystal Enterprise.

A major milestone for Crystal Enterprise was reached with the release of version 8.5: 100% native support for Unix, which is native code, written from the ground up for Unix. The first Unix operating system supported by Crystal Decisions is Sun Solaris Version 2.7 and 2.8 with 700MB of disk space and 256MB of memory.

Note

Crystal Decisions has plans to support other Unix platforms in the future.

Crystal Decisions isn't new to Unix, as other Crystal Decisions products such as Crystal Holos have supported Unix systems from vendors such as Sun, IBM, and HP for many years. Just as with the Windows version, Crystal Enterprise also integrates with existing databases, such as Oracle, and Web servers, such as Apache.

Crystal Enterprise also comes with a set of valuable components for helping manage the Crystal Enterprise installation, when complete. These tools include

- **ccm.sh**—The script version of the Crystal Configuration Manager, which allows management of Crystal Enterprise servers.
- **apsdbsetup.sh**—Provides for the configuration of the APS database and APS clusters.
- **serverconfig.sh**—Delivers server status details as well as adds and removes server capability.
- **sockssetup.sh**—Allows advanced communication setup for the APS and Web Component Server when using SOCKS proxy server firewalls.
- **uninstall.sh**—This uninstalls Crystal Enterprise.

Some additional script templates are available for modification and customization by the Crystal Enterprise administrator.

The good news is that with few exceptions, the techniques and procedures in this book for managing Crystal Enterprise are the same on both the Windows and Solaris platforms.

CRYSTAL ENTERPRISE ON SOLARIS VERSUS CRYSTAL ENTERPRISE ON WINDOWS

To an end user, interacting with reports from Crystal Enterprise running on Solaris will look, feel, and function exactly the same as it would from the Windows NT version. This includes logging into ePortfolio and selecting and viewing reports.

For the most part, the same holds true for a system administrator when it comes to the Crystal Enterprise Sun Solaris version. The Crystal Management Console running on Solaris looks the same, acts the same, and allows the same administrative options, such as security and object management, that the Windows version provides. There are so many similarities between the Windows version and the Solaris version that it's easier to cover the differences.

If you're unfamiliar with Windows NT/2000 or the Windows version of Crystal Enterprise, this section might not be entirely relevant and certainly isn't required reading to be successful with the Sun Solaris version of Crystal Enterprise.

For Crystal Enterprise version 8.5, the current significant differences between the Windows and Solaris versions include the following:

- The system preparation process
- The Crystal Enterprise Installation procedure
- The Crystal Configuration Manager
- Geographic maps
- Crystal Analysis Professional functionality
- SmartReporting
- The Crystal Enterprise SDK implementation

Note

Please note that Crystal Decisions updates products quite frequently and might expand support for Unix after the printing of this book. It's always advisable to check the Crystal Decisions Web site at http://www.crystaldecisions.com for any updates to Crystal Enterprise, Unix, or Windows version.

THE SYSTEM PREPARATION PROCESS

Several system updates for Solaris need to be obtained for Crystal Enterprise to function smoothly. Before starting the installation process, the install script will post a notice of what components should be updated on the Solaris system. For reference, the release notes for Crystal Enterprise 8.5 specifies the following Solaris kernel revisions:

Solaris kernel revisions:

- Version 8: February 2000 and later
- Version 7: October 1998 and later

Runtime patches for all Solaris 8 systems:

- 108434-01 (shared library fix for C++ runtime SunOS 8)
- 108827-05 (libthread patch)

Solaris 7 patches:

- Install Solaris 7 Maintenance Update 4. Be sure this is installed before installing any other packages or patches.

Runtime patches for all Solaris 7 systems:

- 108367-16 (OpenWindows 3.6.1: XSun Patch)
- 106327-08 (shared library patch for C++)
- 106980-13 (libthread patch)
- 106541-14 (kernel update patch)

THE CRYSTAL ENTERPRISE INSTALLATION PROCEDURE

The Crystal Enterprise installation procedure is a single file, install.sh. Later sections in this chapter discuss the actual installation of Crystal Enterprise on Solaris.

With earlier versions of Crystal Enterprise, the APS database required an ODBC connection to a select number of databases, such as Microsoft SQL Server or Oracle. The Solaris version of Crystal Enterprise supports Oracle 8.0., 8.1, 9.0, and DB2. Some database preparation processes are required before installing Crystal Enterprise. Additional sections later in the chapter review this.

Note

As reviewed in Chapter 3, the APS (Automated Process Scheduler) relies on a relational database, such as Microsoft SQL Server or Oracle, to store data for objects stored in Crystal Enterprise such as usernames and passwords, report names, descriptions, and relationships with other objects in Crystal Enterprise. System security information is also stored in the APS database.

THE CRYSTAL CONFIGURATION MANAGER

Recall from earlier chapters that the Crystal Configuration Manager and the Crystal Management Console are different tools within Crystal Enterprise. Although the Windows version of the CCM can be used on a Windows desktop to detect and manage versions of the Crystal Enterprise servers, a dedicated CCM script is available for use on Solaris.

GEOGRAPHIC MAPS

Geographic maps are not available in the Solaris version of Crystal Enterprise. Because Crystal Decisions bundles MapInfo with Crystal Enterprise for Windows and the version of MapInfo that Crystal Decisions uses is a Windows-based technology, this makes geographic maps unavailable. This doesn't render the report useless; it just means the map won't show up in the report.

CRYSTAL ANALYSIS PROFESSIONAL FUNCTIONALITY

Crystal Analysis Professional applications and reports currently are not supported on a 100% Solaris Crystal Enterprise implementation. When Crystal Analysis Professional is installed, a plug-in is installed on the Web Component Server that's based on a set of COM components. There are currently plans at Crystal Decisions to make the Crystal Analysis Professional components available on Unix. In the interim, a Windows-based Web Component Server (see Chapters 3 and 4) would need to be installed alongside the Solaris Crystal Enterprise components for Crystal Analysis Professional Reports to function properly.

SMARTREPORTING

SmartReporting (or Report Application Server) is an add-in server for Crystal Enterprise that provides ad-hoc report creation and manipulation over the Web. Refer to Appendix B, "Using the Report Application Server," for a complete description of Report Application Server. A Unix version of the Report Application Server was not released at the time of publishing this book. A product update is planned to enable the Report Application Server to work with Crystal Enterprise on Solaris; however, the RAS server will be required to run on a Windows NT/2000 server. Check with Crystal Decisions for more information on the release of RAS on Solaris.

THE CRYSTAL ENTERPRISE SDK IMPLEMENTATION

As mentioned throughout the book, one of the major benefits of Crystal Enterprise is the front-end customizability via the SDK. The current implementation of the Crystal Enterprise SDK is COM-based, which means that custom development that uses the functions and capability of Crystal Enterprise can be done with virtually any COM-based scripting language.

The fact that the Crystal Enterprise SDK is COM-based raises an interesting question: What about Unix when it comes to custom development with Crystal Enterprise? Furthermore, what about customers who have developed Web-based applications for Crystal Enterprise on the Windows version who are considering moving to Unix?

The easiest solution to these questions would be to provide a Java version of the SDK for Unix. This is the proper solution and something that Crystal Decisions is providing in a beta form currently. There is a good chance that the Java version of the SDK will ship on or close to the release of Crystal Enterprise 8.5. However, if that were the end of the story, there wouldn't be a need for the rest of this section of the chapter. At the time of the writing of this book, the Java SDK was not released, so it's best to write this appendix in the context of what *can* be accomplished with custom development on Unix.

As covered in Chapters 1, 3, and 13, a Web-based application developed with Crystal Enterprise is a Web page with HTML and some inline script, referred to as a CSP page. A brief review of the Crystal Enterprise SDK is provided here. Similar in concept to an Active Server Page or a Java Server Page, the inline script in a CSP page is processed on the Crystal Enterprise Web Component Server and interpreted into end-user requests such as "I want to view a report," or "Show me what analytic applications I can view in this particular folder." Crystal Enterprise handles all the security, scheduling, management, delivery, and so on associated with fulfilling those requests. The fulfillment of such a request is nothing more than a DHTML page, which is returned to an end user via a Web browser.

The key to this discussion is that the inline script contained within a CSP page is processed *on* the Web Component Server, *not* on a Web server such as Apache or Netscape iPlanet. Recall from Chapter 3 that on Windows, the Web Component Server contains a built-in engine capable of processing VB Script and JavaScript.

Similarly, the Web Component Server for Solaris contains the Mozilla engine for inline script processing. This enables processing of CSP pages that were written in JavaScript, not VBScript on the Solaris version of Crystal Enterprise. The beauty of this implementation is that a CSP page that was developed in JavaScript on Windows will run without issue on the Solaris version of Crystal Enterprise. This is a significant benefit to organizations that have been using versions of Crystal Enterprise prior to the Unix release and have been waiting to migrate over to Solaris.

Note   Please refer to www.netscape.com for more information on the Mozilla engine.

It's important to note that when organizations typically develop applications on Windows against a COM SDK, they will use or address other common COM objects, such as a Calendar Control, that are not part of the Crystal Enterprise SDK. If this is the case, the Web Component Server will not provide that functionality on Unix because it won't be able to find such a "COM Control" on Unix.

To summarize this point, a CSP page, developed in JavaScript, will run on the Solaris version of Crystal Enterprise, provided the inline script addresses components of Crystal Enterprise only.

Knowing this begs the question: Is the Mozilla engine in the Web Component Server talking to ported COM objects? It is not, because Java provides a powerful and in many cases superior alternative to COM objects. Hence the reason Crystal Decisions is releasing a Java SDK.

In development of the Unix version of Crystal Enterprise, Crystal Decisions provided an equivalent set of lower-level C++ objects that provide identical functionality to the COM objects found in Windows. When the Java SDK is released it will essentially provide a wrapper to these C++ objects.

What enables all of this to function smoothly in the Solaris environment is a clever folder structure found when Crystal Enterprise is installed on Solaris. The folder structure on Solaris is identical to the Registry keys for each Crystal Enterprise object found in Windows: HKEY Local Machine\Software\ and so on.

This capability within Crystal Enterprise made for an easy port of the end-user application, ePortfolio, over to the Sun Solaris version because it's written entirely in JavaScript. The same holds true for the Crystal Management Console.

INSTALLING CRYSTAL ENTERPRISE ON SUN SOLARIS

It's recommended that the person installing Crystal Enterprise on Solaris have some experience with the Sun Solaris operating environment. The capability to create a new Group and User account will be required for this installation. The Crystal Enterprise installation process consists of five major procedures:

- Solaris system preparation
- Database configuration and account creation
- Installing Crystal Enterprise
- Starting the Crystal Enterprise servers
- Installing a Crystal Enterprise Web connector

Because there are several Web servers and database types/versions that could be used with Crystal Enterprise on Solaris, it would make for a book in and of itself, let alone a long chapter to cover each possible scenario. The Crystal Enterprise product documentation does contain references to most of these scenarios, so please check there if your exact scenario isn't covered here.

For this appendix, the most common installation scenario is covered, a single physical Solaris server, with Solaris version 2.7, Oracle Database Server version 8.1, and Apache Web Server 1.3.20 all installed and properly configured. Refer to the Oracle or Apache documentation for troubleshooting information.

SOLARIS SYSTEM PREPARATION

This installation procedure assumes that Crystal Enterprise is not being installed in a firewall environment. If this is the case, refer to the firewall section of this book for information about how to configure Crystal Enterprise with firewalls. Additional configuration of the Web Connector will be required.

Note

This chapter assumes connectivity between end users or clients who will use a Web browser to access Crystal Enterprise. If the installation plan involves installing certain Crystal Enterprise servers or components on multiple physical Unix servers, confirm that proper TCP/IP network connectivity exists between servers.

The first thing to confirm when installing Crystal Enterprise on Solaris is to be sure the Unix system has a fixed host name. To set this, refer to the Solaris system manual. Root privileges are required to do so.

Be sure to read the Release Notes on the Crystal Enterprise CD because additional updates for the Solaris operating system might be required. Refer to the Sun Web site for any Solaris updates.

CREATING A GROUP FOR CRYSTAL ENTERPRISE

To install Crystal Enterprise, a new group and a user account should be created on the Solaris system. For this exercise, both the group and user are assigned the name Crystal. The user does not need root privileges to run Crystal Enterprise, but root or appropriate privileges are required to create the group and user account.

Note

The group name Crystal is not required for the Crystal Enterprise system to work on Solaris. Any custom group name can be used. The username Crystal is used to affect the installation path of Crystal Enterprise.

1. To create a new group, log on to Solaris as Root or an equivalent account and select the Applications program menu shown in Figure A.1. Click on the Applications menu option.

2. From within the Applications group, select the System Admin program group. Within the System Admin Group, double-click on the Admintool shown in Figure A.2.

3. To create a new group, click on the Browse menu in the Admintool, as shown in Figure A.3. Select the Groups option from the menu. The Admin tool will display a list of groups currently installed on the system.

Figure A.1
Select the Application menu option in Solaris to access the Admintool.

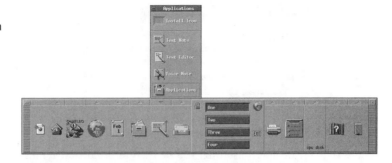

Figure A.2
The Solaris Admintool.

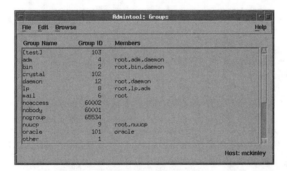

Figure A.3
The Admin tool displays installed groups on the Solaris operating system.

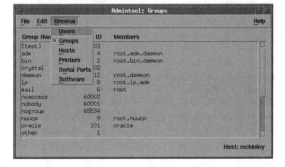

4. To create a new group, click on the Edit menu and select Add. The Add Group dialog box prompts for a new Group. As shown in Figure A.4, enter Crystal for the group name and an appropriate Group ID. If the Solaris system administrator has not provided an appropriate Group ID, enter an appropriate, unique ID not occupied by a current group. This example uses the Group ID 102.

5. After selecting OK, the new group will show up in the Group listing in the Admintool.

Figure A.4
The Solaris
Admintool: Add
Group dialog box.

CREATING A USER ACCOUNT FOR CRYSTAL ENTERPRISE

It's necessary to create a new user that will be used to install and administer the Crystal Enterprise system. Using the Solaris Admintool, click on the Browse menu and select Users, shown in Figure A.5.

Figure A.5
Select Users from the
Browse menu in the
Solaris Admintool.

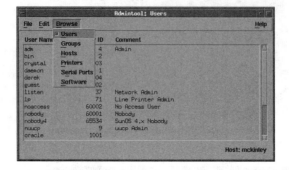

Select the Edit menu and choose Add. The Add User dialog box prompts for creation of a new user account. Assign a username of Crystal and a primary group ID equivalent to the Group ID previously created.

Based on the user account, Crystal, created earlier in the chapter, the installation script will use the default path of /usr/local/crystal unless specified otherwise during the installation process. If a specific installation directory is created on the system, be sure the user account's HOME directory is set to this location. This will enable a "user" installation type, which isolates installation files to the directory specified during the actual installation process. The Admintool dialog box in Figure A.5 provides for these settings.

Note

From a security standpoint, be sure that user Crystal is the owner and group owner of the specified installation directory.

After all the necessary Solaris updates have been applied and a group and user have been created, the Solaris system preparation is complete.

DATABASE CONFIGURATION AND ACCOUNT CREATION

As discussed earlier in the book, Crystal Enterprise requires the use of a relational database to store metadata about system objects such as reports and folders. This relational database can be either Oracle or DB2. For this exercise, Oracle version 8.1 is used. Refer to the Crystal Enterprise documentation for additional information.

First, an empty database or schema needs to be created in Oracle. It's advisable that an Oracle database administrator does this. This empty database shouldn't contain any tables because Crystal Enterprise will create the tables it needs during the installation. The fact that Crystal Enterprise will create the tables during the installation means that a user account must be created in Oracle that has the proper permissions to create and drop tables. Use the Create Database Oracle command to create a database called CEaps. The syntax should look something like:

CREATE DATABASE CEaps

The Create Database command initializes the control files and redoes log files and data files that comprise an Oracle database.

After the database has been created, be sure to create and grant a user account called Crystal the capability to create and drop tables within the CEaps database.

The syntax to create a user named Crystal in Oracle looks like this:

CREATE USER Crystal

Refer to the Oracle documentation for examples of how to use the Create User command. After the user has been created and the appropriate privileges have been granted, the installation of Crystal Enterprise can begin.

INSTALLING CRYSTAL ENTERPRISE

Installing Crystal Enterprise consists of running the installation script, install.sh, and providing installation configuration details during the installation process. Be sure the installation files are accessible by mounting the CD-ROM. It's advisable to copy all the installation scripts, files, and documentation to the local drive. The install.sh script contains all the required Crystal Enterprise binaries. If the install.sh script is transferred via FTP, perform a binary transfer.

Based on the user account, Crystal, created earlier in the chapter, the installation script will use the default path of /usr/local/crystal unless specified otherwise during the installation process. Refer to the section "Creating a User Account for Crystal Enterprise" for further information.

Before launching the installation script, it's important to note that a set of common commands should be available to the Crystal user account. Those commands are listed in the Crystal Enterprise product documentation. The commands are common enough that on most Solaris systems, there shouldn't be a problem.

The installation script will also access Oracle during the installation process to create the APS database, if it does not already exist.

1. To run the installation script, launch a Console and enter `./install.sh` as shown in Figure A.6.

Figure A.6
Install.sh launches the Crystal Enterprise installation process.

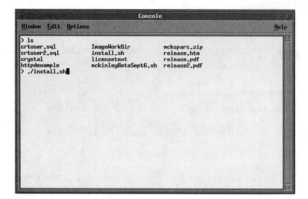

2. The first dialog box is the welcome screen, shown in Figure A.7. Press Enter to move to the license agreement dialog box.

Figure A.7
The Crystal Enterprise installation welcome screen.

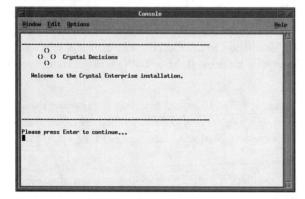

3. In Figure A.8, after reviewing the license agreement, scroll to the bottom of the screen, type **Yes**, and press Enter.

Figure A.8
Scroll to the bottom of the license agreement to proceed.

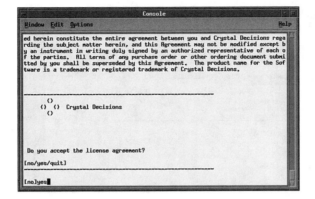

Figure A.9
Specify a user installation type for Crystal Enterprise.

4. The next dialog box, shown in Figure A.9, prompts for the type of installation: System or User. Selecting a User installation installs Crystal Enterprise into the location of the Crystal users' home directory or other path specified during the system preparation process. Refer to earlier sections of this chapter for details.

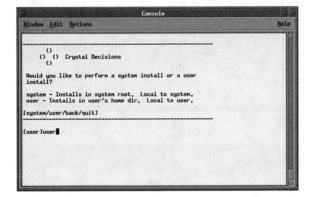

5. Type **user** and press Enter to continue.

6. The next dialog box prompts for an installation directory. The Crystal Users home directory was changed to /space/crystal in this example, as shown in Figure A.10. Press Enter to accept the default or specify a new directory. For this example, accept the default.

7. Figure A.11 prompts to confirm the start of the installation for all Crystal Enterprise files. Type **Begin** or press Enter to accept the default.

8. After the installation of all Crystal Enterprise files is complete, the install script prompts for the license key shown in Figure A.12. This can be obtained from Crystal Decisions and may be included on the installation CD.

Figure A.10
Specify the Crystal
Enterprise installation
directory.

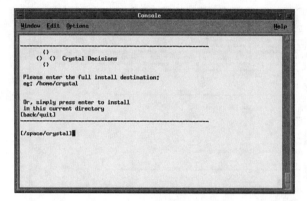

Figure A.11
The Crystal Enterprise
installation is ready to
begin.

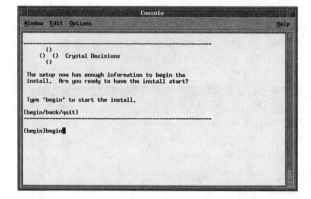

Figure A.12
Enter the license key
supplied with Crystal
Enterprise.

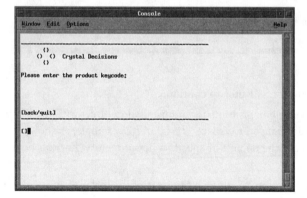

9. Figure A.13 shows the prompt for the type of setup for Crystal Enterprise. Type **new** and press Enter to continue.

Note

Refer to the Crystal Enterprise product documentation for information about advanced installation options.

Figure A.13
Type **new** to specify a new installation of Crystal Enterprise.

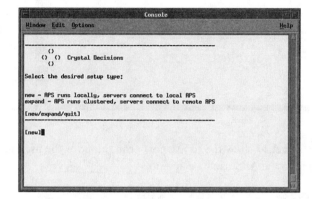

10. Recall from earlier in this chapter that the APS requires a database for object metadata storage. Figure A.14 shows the options for the supported APS database types. For this example, enter the database chosen to support the Crystal Enterprise. Figure A.14 shows Oracle 8.1 as the database type. This also is the point in the installation where the account, Crystal, must have create and delete privileges to the specified database. Confirm this with a database administrator.

Figure A.14
Enter the appropriate APS database type.

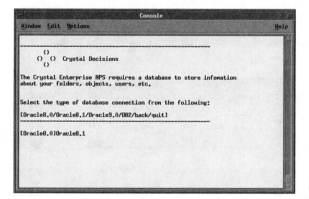

11. Specify the service name for connecting to the database. Figure A.15 shows the service name as ORCL. This will be different for every installation of Crystal Enterprise, so confirm this with a database system administrator. Press Enter to continue.

Figure A.15
Enter the service name for connecting to the specified database where the APS database will reside.

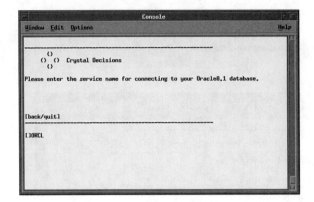

12. Figures A.16 and A.17 show the script, now prompting for the username and password for connecting to the APS database system.

Figure A.16
Enter a user account for Crystal Enterprise to connect to the database.

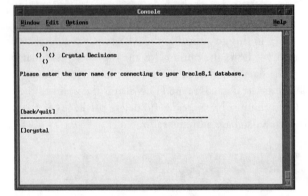

Figure A.17
Enter the user account password.

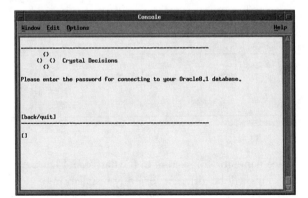

13. The script will prompt for a specific port by which the APS will communicate with other Crystal Enterprise servers, shown in Figure A.18. Confirm that this is an acceptable port for use on the corporate network. If all Crystal Enterprise components are installed on a single physical server, this should be of minimal concern. To accept the default port of 6400, press Enter.

Figure A.18
Select the default port for APS communication with other Crystal Enterprise servers.

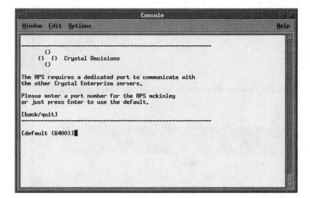

PART

VI

APP

A

14. Figure A.19 shows the next dialog box, which prompts for the default port on which the Web Component Server communicates with the Web connector. The default is 6401. Again, confirm that this port is acceptable for use on the corporate network. Little concern needs be given here if all Crystal Enterprise servers and components are installed on a single physical server.

> **Note**
>
> To learn more about the Web Component Server and the Web connector, refer to Chapters 3 and 10.

15. The next dialog box, shown in Figure A.20, prompts for the creation of a configuration template file, which contains an entry that must be added to the Web server configuration file. Adding this entry to the Web server configuration file will enable the Web server to properly route report requests to Crystal Enterprise. In the example used later in this chapter, the Apache configuration file, httpd.conf, will be edited and the entries found in this configuration template will be pasted into the httpd.conf file.

Type **yes** to allow the installation to create these scripts.

16. The installation will place these configuration template files in directories, nested in the HOME directory. The location will look something like the following (see Figure A.21):

/space/crystal/crystal/enterprise/solaris_sparc/Web Component Server/conf

Figure A.19
The Web Component
Server default port
dialog box.

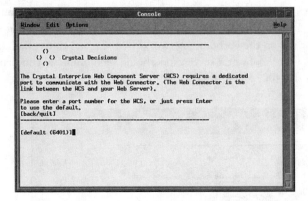

Figure A.20
Configuration tem-
plates files can be
created automatically
for use with a Web
server such as
Apache or Netscape
iPlanet.

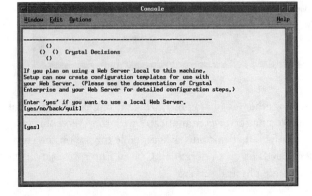

Figure A. 21
The installation script
places the configura-
tion templates in the
Crystal user's HOME
directory.

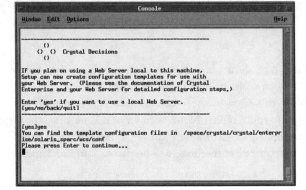

17. The install then prompts for any other Web Component Servers present in the Crystal Enterprise system, as shown in Figure A.22. Recall that the Web connector can be installed on a physically separate server from the Web Component Server. This is ideal in a DMZ (Demilitarized Zone) Web Server setup, where the Web connector could sit inside the DMZ and communicate with the Web Component Server through the firewall. The client side of the firewall scenario doesn't require any special ports to be open, as all information delivered out is DHTML, requiring only port 80. The fact that a single Web connector can communicate with multiple Web Component Servers provides the ability to design a fault-tolerant, load-balanced Crystal Enterprise system.

Figure A.22
The Web connector can communicate with more than one Web Component Server.

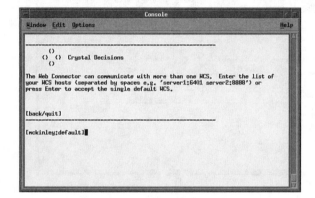

18. The next dialog box, shown in Figure A.23, prompts for a port number for the XVFB Daemon to use. XVFB stands for *X Virtual Frame Buffer* and allows the Crystal Enterprise report servers to generate and format report pages without an X server present.

Confirm that port 5222 is acceptable for use on the corporate network by the XVFB Daemon. If not, assign a custom port number. Press Enter to continue.

Figure A.23
The XVFB Daemon allows report generation without an X server.

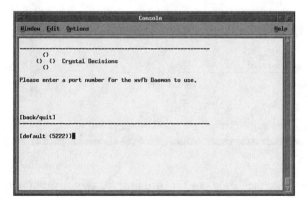

19. Figure A.24 shows the prompt for a display number for the XVFB Daemon to use. This is an important choice because a total of five frame buffer processes will be launched. The Crystal Enterprise system requires the use of all frame buffer processes; in turn, each frame buffer process requires a unique port for communication. If a value of 200 is given to the display value, ports 6200 though 6204 would be used for the five XVFB processes. The initial port, as indicated, can be selected by the system administrator. Consequently, be sure these ports are available on the corporate network before assigning them.

Figure A.24
The XVFB Daemon requires five frame buffer processes to be assigned to specific, sequential ports.

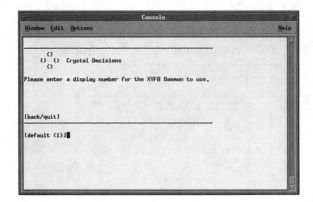

20. After entering the appropriate display for the XVFB Daemon, the install indicates that any existing system files can be overwritten, as shown in Figure A.25. Unless there is a particular reason to preserve existing Crystal Enterprise files, allow the installation process to overwrite all files by entering Yes.

Figure A.25
The installation can overwrite existing system files.

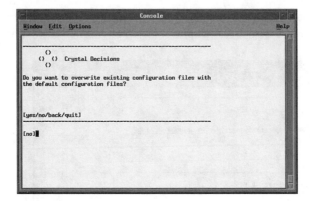

21. Figure A.26 shows the dialog box that prompts for re-initialization of the database. Essentially, if an existing Crystal Enterprise APS database is present and specified

earlier in the installation process, and then re-initialized here, all historical data will be lost. If there is no historical data to preserve in an old APS database, this issue is of no consequence. Continue by typing **yes**, and press Enter.

Figure A.26
Re-initializing an existing APS database will erase any existing system data.

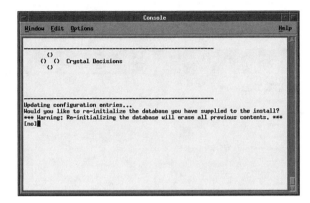

22. At this point, the installation is complete. The Crystal Enterprise servers have not yet been started because this is a function of the Crystal Configuration Manager.

STARTING THE CRYSTAL ENTERPRISE SERVERS

Note

Although the Crystal Enterprise servers can be launched automatically, doing so requires Root privileges. Refer to the Crystal Enterprise product documentation for details.

After installing Crystal Enterprise based on the earlier sections of this chapter, the Crystal Enterprise servers must be started and enabled, which are technically two separate procedures. Starting the servers will require the use of the Crystal Configuration Manager. The Windows version of the Crystal Configuration Manager (CCM) is discussed in some detail in this book. The Unix version provides equivalent functionality through the console.

1. To start the Crystal Enterprise servers as daemons, browse to the directory where ccm.sh is available. This is by default in the HOME directory specified when the Crystal user account was configured in an earlier section of this chapter. Recall that this directory for the example was /space/crystal.

2. Under this directory is a directory called Crystal. For the example used in the book, browse to the following directory:
/space/crystal/crystal/

or enter the following command:
```
Crystal Decisions $HOME/crystal
```

3. Using cd $HOME/crystal specifies that the crystal directory under the current user's home directory should be opened.

Under the crystal directory, the ccm.sh can be found, as shown in Figure A.27. To start all the Crystal Enterprise servers as daemons, enter the following command:

`./ccm.sh -start all`

Figure A.27
The Crystal Configuration Manager script can start all Crystal Enterprise servers.

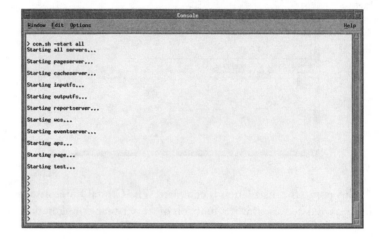

4. Now that the servers are started, they must be enabled. A server can be started as a daemon, but without enabling it, other Crystal Enterprise servers will not communicate with it. This can be advantageous for a number of reasons, including troubleshooting specific servers without always stopping and starting.

5. To enable the Crystal Enterprise servers, enter the following command, also shown in Figure A.28. Note that the installation of Crystal Enterprise enables servers by default.

`ccm.sh -enable all`

Note

Bear in mind that the ccm.sh script, and additional ones, might be in the Crystal subdirectory (for example, /space/crystal/crystal). If the current terminal session is in the /space/crystal directory, the appropriate command would be `./ccm.sh -enable all`. This holds true for all commands in the console.

6. The Crystal Configuration Manager enables a host of server management capabilities. To view all the options available for the CCM, use the following command:

`ccm.sh -help`

CONFIGURING THE CRYSTAL ENTERPRISE WEB CONNECTOR

Although a brief review of the Web connector is provided here, Chapter 3 provides a detailed review of the services provided therein.

Figure A.28

The Crystal Configuration Manager can enable all Crystal Enterprise servers.

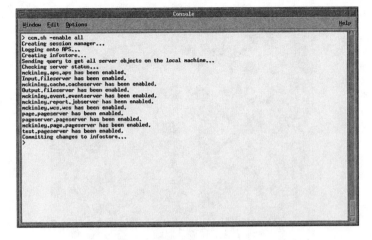

Now that the Crystal Enterprise server has been installed and enabled, the last step for Crystal Enterprise to start delivering reports to users over the Web is to make the Web server aware of Crystal Enterprise. To do this, Crystal Enterprise provides a Web connector. The Web connector is the only component of Crystal Enterprise that is required to be installed on a physical Web server, such as Apache.

The Web connector for Apache consists of an ASAPI module or CGI executable. For this example, the ASAPI module will be used; however, the CGI version is implemented in a similar fashion. The services the Web connector provides to the Web server and Crystal Enterprise might seem simple, but they're critical for system function and scalability.

The Web connector is aware of one or more Web Component Servers available within the Crystal Enterprise system. The installation section of this chapter discusses the Web connector configuration that takes place during the installation of Crystal Enterprise.

A single Web connector can connect to multiple Web Component Servers and provide a level of fault tolerance and load balancing.

For this example, Apache was installed, before installing Crystal Enterprise, on the same physical server on which Crystal Enterprise was installed. This certainly will not always be the case. The Web connector can be installed on a separate physical server from the rest of the Crystal Enterprise architecture by running the `webconn_install.sh` script on the intended server.

Apache contains a configuration file, httpd.conf, that contains the startup information for the Apache server and associated extensions. It is within this file that a pointer to the Crystal Enterprise Web connector must be made, such that any Web requests related to Crystal Enterprise will be routed directly to Crystal Enterprise through the Web connector.

1. If Apache was installed with the default configuration options, the httpd.conf file can be found in the /etc/apache directory, as shown in Figure A.29.

Figure A.29
The Apache httpd.conf file must be modified to contain the Crystal Enterprise Web connector location.

2. Open the httpd.conf file in any standard text editor, such as vi. If using the File Manager in Figure A.29, the file can be directly opened from there as well.

3. Scroll to the bottom of the file and add the following text, also shown in Figure A.30:

```
Include InstallPath/crystal/enterprise/solaris_sparc/wcs/conf/asapi.conf
```

Figure A.30
The Web connector must be referenced in the Apache httpd.conf file.

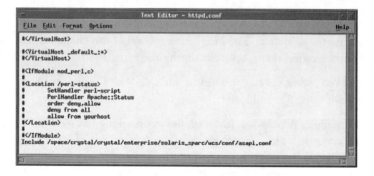

InstallPath is the path where Crystal Enterprise was installed. If the defaults were used, this would be inside the Crystal user's HOME directory.

4. Now restart the Apache Web server. Refer to the appropriate Apache version manual for how to do this.

Crystal Enterprise should now be fully running and ready for testing.

TESTING THE CRYSTAL ENTERPRISE INSTALLATION

To test the Crystal Enterprise installation, open a Web browser and enter the following URL:

```
http://WebServerName/crystal/enterprise
```

> **Note**
>
> This hyperlink is the same link used to access Crystal Enterprise on a windows platform.

This will open the Crystal Launchpad. For more information on the Launchpad, refer to Chapter 5.

To verify Crystal Enterprise is working, click on the ePortfolio link and open a sample report for viewing. Schedule a sample report. Refer to Chapter 5 as well for more information about using ePortfolio.

If ePortfolio functions without fail, chances are that all the Crystal Enterprise servers are functioning properly.

UNINSTALLING CRYSTAL ENTERPRISE ON SOLARIS

Uninstalling Crystal Enterprise is a simple process, enabled by an uninstallation script. First, remove any reference to Crystal Enterprise entered in the Apache configuration file if desired.

Next, enter the following command to open the directory where the Crystal Enterprise uninstallation script is located:

```
cd $HOME/crystal
```

Now enter the following command:

```
./uninstall.sh
```

Follow any prompts supplied to uninstall Crystal Enterprise.

PUBLISHING A REPORT TO CRYSTAL ENTERPRISE ON SOLARIS

Publishing a report to Crystal Enterprise on Solaris is no different than publishing a report to Crystal Enterprise on Windows NT/2000 via the Crystal Publishing Wizard or using the Crystal Reports Save As, Enterprise function. Refer to Chapter 7 for more information on publishing reports to Crystal Enterprise.

Although there aren't any functional differences in terms of publishing the report to Crystal Enterprise, there are a few extra considerations when Crystal Enterprise is running on Solaris, so a brief review of publishing content and some thing to look out for when doing so are provided in this section.

Chapter 7 reviews how to publish content to Crystal Enterprise in detail. This content is typically, but not restricted to, Crystal Reports and Crystal Analysis Professional applications.

> **Note**
>
> The Solaris version of Crystal Enterprise supports multiple report types; in other words, Crystal Reports and Crystal Analysis Professional reports. However, to deliver Crystal Analysis Professional reports to end users, a Windows-based Web Component Server is required. If an organization is not using Crystal Analysis Professional reports, this is not a consideration and should be disregarded.

Reports such as Crystal Reports can be connected to a variety of datasources such as flat files, relational databases, and OLAP cubes. Connecting to these types of datasources can be accomplished using a variety of mechanisms, including Native Driver and ODBC connections.

Refer to Chapter 7 to understand the benefits of individual connection types. For this chapter, it's sufficient to say that once published to Crystal Enterprise, a Crystal Report will be run by either the Page or Job Server for on-demand or scheduled reports, respectively.

Running a report consists of connecting to a database, executing the SQL statement contained within the report, receiving the query result from the server, and passing across the data again to apply any formatting, formulas, highlighting, and so on.

> **Note**
>
> Refer to Chapter 3 for more information on the roles and functions of the Page and Job Servers in the Crystal Enterprise architecture.

Recall that a Crystal Report contains a set of connection strings to a specific database, set at design time. This connection is referred to by a name or set of server and database connection information. This server and database connection information must be configured on the Page and Job Servers as well, if the Crystal Report is to process successfully in Crystal Enterprise.

> **Note**
>
> Crystal Reports database connection information can be changed programmatically by using the SmartReporting plug-in to Crystal Enterprise. Although SmartReporting is covered in Appendix B, it is not formally included in Crystal Enterprise and must be purchased separately from Crystal Decisions.

This connection to a database can be established through what is referred to as a Native connection and when a Native Driver is available, it's recommended to do so. For databases where Crystal Decisions doesn't provide or support a Native Connection, the next option is ODBC.

ODBC isn't a native Unix technology, so running Crystal Reports where ODBC is required is acceptable and supported with the Solaris version of Crystal Enterprise, but the ODBC configuration must be properly configured for Crystal Reports to run on Solaris. The good news is that Crystal Enterprise installs everything required to support Crystal Reports based off ODBC data sources on the Solaris system.

The most important factor involved in successful report publishing to Crystal Enterprise is consistency. This implies, as discussed in earlier chapters, that whatever the database configuration is set to on the Windows workstation when designing a Crystal Report, the exact same database information must be available on the Crystal Enterprise Page and Job Servers.

The analogy is simple. Suppose that when using Crystal Reports to design a report, an ODBC connection with the name of sales is used to connect to a particular database. When this report is published to Crystal Enterprise, how is Crystal Enterprise supposed to know that the ODBC connection for a given report isn't available on the server, or that an existing ODBC connection also called sales actually points to an entirely different database?

Naming consistency and configuration, above all else, is usually the culprit when reporting problems arise.

PUBLISHING A REPORT WITH A NATIVE DRIVER ON SOLARIS

Recall that when using a Native connection to a particular database, Crystal Enterprise is essentially piggybacking on top of the database's client software, such as Oracle client.

When a report is called in Crystal Enterprise to be updated, the Page or Job Server searches the library path environment variable (LD_LIBRARY_PATH) to locate the appropriate database client software. In the case of the example used in this chapter, Oracle, the ORACLE_HOME environment variable must define the top-level directory of the Oracle client installation.

Proper configuration of any Oracle environment variables and settings should be verified with the Oracle documentation. These commands would be added to the Crystal user's login script to support the Oracle implementation:

```
LD_LIBRARY_PATH=/opt/oracle/app/oracle/product/8.0.3/lib:opt/sybase/
lib:$LD_LIBRARY_PATH;export LD_LIBRARY_PATH
ORACLE_HOME=/opt/oracle/app/oracle/product/8.0.3;export ORACLE_HOME
```

After this has been added, reports can be published to Crystal Enterprise and run successfully. This assumes that the Oracle client software has been properly configured on Solaris. Refer to the Crystal Enterprise documentation for additional details.

PUBLISHING A REPORT WITH AN ODBC DRIVER ON SOLARIS

Crystal Enterprise installs all the necessary components on Solaris to support Crystal Reports that use an ODBC connection.

Note

Refer to Chapters 7 and 8 for more details on ODBC.

Those components include

- ODBC for Unix
- ODBC configuration files and templates
- Configured ODBC environment variables

If any Crystal Report will use DB2, refer to the Crystal Enterprise documentation for last-minute notes on special ODBC configuration details.

The Page and Job Servers on Solaris must have the proper ODBC connections configured. This is especially important to remember when considering a multiple physical server deployment where the Page and Job Servers are separated.

The main environment variables for ODBC on Unix consist of

- LD_LIBRARY_PATH
- ODBC_HOME
- ODBCINI

These are contained in a file called env.csh. This file should not be modified unless a custom ODBC configuration is required. To configure DSNs (Data Source Names) for ODBC, only one file needs to be manipulated: ODBC.ini. The ODBC.ini file can be found in the HOME directory of the Crystal user, which is the account used to install Crystal Enterprise.

Figure A.31
The ODBC.ini file should be configured to set up ODBC connections on Solaris.

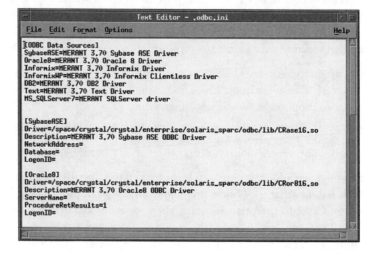

As an example, try publishing a report that connects to a SQL Server database to the Solaris version of Crystal Enterprise. The Northwind database sample on SQL server will suffice.

1. Set up an ODBC connection for Crystal Reports. For this report, set up a System DSN ODBC connection on the local Windows workstation where Crystal Reports is installed and name it TestSQL. The TestSQL connection should point to a SQL server that

   - Has the Northwind sample database installed
   - Can be accessed over the network from the Solaris server
   - Has Crystal Enterprise installed

2. Create a simple Crystal Report. Open Crystal Reports on a Windows workstation and create the report. Refer to Chapter 8 for more information on creating a Crystal Report. Select the Customers table. Select the CompanyName, City, and Phone fields from the Customers table. The report should look similar to Figure A.32.

Figure A.32
A sample Crystal Report, connected to the Northwind sample.

Save the report to a physical network resource such as a server share that the Solaris Server can access. For this example, save the report to the root of the C: drive on the local workstation where Crystal Reports is installed. Name the file Report1.rpt.

3. Set up an equivalent ODBC connection on the Solaris Server. From the Solaris Console, open the ODBC.ini file located in the HOME directory of the Crystal user, shown in Figure A.31. The ODBC.ini file contains configuration information for several database types, including Microsoft SQL server. The Microsoft SQL server section resembles the following:

```
[MS_SQLServer7]
Driver=/usr/local/crystal/enterprise/platform/odbc/lib/crmsss16.so
```

```
Description=MERANT 3.70 SQL Server ODBC Driver
Address=
Database=
QuotedId=Yes
LogonID=
```

Add the following information as a new entry to the bottom of the ODBC.ini connection:

```
[TestSQL]
Driver=/usr/local/crystal/enterprise/platform/odbc/lib/crmsss16.so
Description=MERANT 3.70 SQL Server ODBC Driver
Address= Database Server IP address
Database= Northwind
QuotedId=Yes
LogonID= sa
```

Notice that the connection information contains the ODBC DSN name of TestSQL and points to the server by IP address or name, depending on the driver. The `Database` tag should contain the name of the database; in this example, Northwind. Additional connection information might be required for drivers such as the text driver. Figure A.33 shows an updated ODBC.ini file.

Figure A.33
The ODBC.ini file updated with connection information to a Microsoft SQL server with the Northwind sample database.

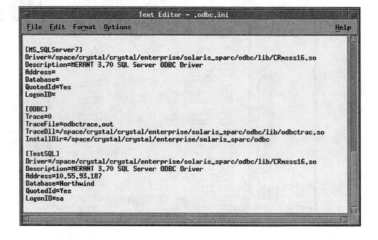

This connection string information must exist for any report that requires an ODBC connection, and be set up on any physical Page or Job Server that may process this report in the Crystal Enterprise system.

4. Publish the report to Crystal Enterprise on Solaris. After the ODBC.ini file has been updated, close and save the file. The report can be published into Crystal Enterprise and run against the ODBC data source.

There are a number of methods to publish the Crystal Report into Crystal Enterprise. The Save As feature in Crystal Reports, shown in Figure A.34, can be used, as well as the Publishing Wizard. Refer to Chapter 7 for more information on publishing content using the Publishing Wizard, or Chapter 8 for information on saving a Crystal Report to Crystal Enterprise.

Figure A.34
The Crystal Reports Save As feature allows reports to be published directly to Crystal Enterprise.

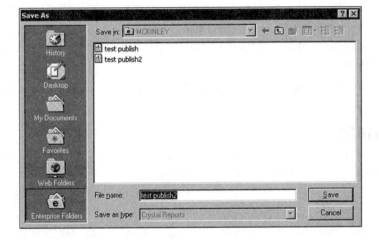

5. View the report from Crystal Enterprise. After publishing the report, launch ePortfolio from a Web browser by entering the following URL:

```
http://web_server_name/crystal/enterprise
```

Then select ePortfolio. Log on to ePortfolio as a user that can view the sample report. Browse to the folder location where the report was published, click on the report, and then select View.

The Page Server will connect via ODBC to the SQL Server database, execute the SQL query, and process the report. Try scheduling the report as well to confirm the Job Server is using the ODBC configuration information properly.

TROUBLESHOOTING

Troubleshooting techniques for Crystal Enterprise running on Solaris are similar to approaches for Windows. Chapter 10 contains many troubleshooting techniques for reports in general, as many issues are universal. The most common issues on Solaris are

- Servers not enabled
- Servers not started
- Connectivity issues to a database

The first two are easily solved by using the ccm.sh script to enable and start servers through commands such as ccm.sh -start all and ccm.sh -start all. To view the status of all servers, try ccm.sh -display.

The last issue, database connectivity, is best solved in the CMC. Open the Crystal Management Console, browse to the report object, and try to view the report from there, through the preview button. If the report fails there, a configuration issue with the ODBC.ini file is possible, or database authentication issues might be in play as well. Select the Database tab of the report object to confirm proper database connectivity configuration.

If the Page Server fails, try shutting it down and restarting the service. It's also helpful to investigate the behavior of the XVFB daemon in relation to the Page Server when troubleshooting.

Any other troubleshooting techniques discussed throughout the book are useful for Solaris.

SUMMARY

Crystal Decisions has reached a major milestone with the release of Crystal Enterprise version 8.5. A fully native version of Crystal Enterprise Solaris provides Enterprise customers a reliable, scalable platform upon which true Enterprise reporting solutions can be built.

Barring the obvious differences in the operating system platforms upon which Crystal Enterprise runs, namely Windows NT/2000 and Solaris, the function of Crystal Enterprise is largely the same. There are some exceptions to this, and it's important to become familiar with some of the configuration differences between the two environments.

All the Crystal Enterprise utilities discussed in Chapter 2 are provided as scripts for use on the Solaris platform; however, many of the Windows-based utilities, such as the Publishing Wizard and the Crystal Configuration Manager, also work with Unix.

Installing Crystal Enterprise on Solaris is a straightforward process once a number of system preparation tasks and updates have been performed.

After the installation of Crystal Enterprise, standard tasks such as administration of the system are identical to the Windows version. A majority of the chapters in this book are entirely applicable to Unix. Crystal Enterprise has a unique implementation of its SDK for Unix, as well as a soon-to-be-released Java version of the SDK.

Publishing reports to Crystal Enterprise on Solaris requires some additional considerations because the ODBC files that Crystal Enterprise installs must be configured to support Crystal Reports that require ODBC connectivity. Crystal Enterprise also supports Crystal Reports that use Native Drivers.

Leveraging the power and stability of Solaris to deliver Enterprise reporting solutions via Crystal Enterprise makes for a powerful and flexible solution that many organizations will undoubtedly adopt.

APPENDIX

USING THE REPORT APPLICATION SERVER

In this chapter

The Report Application Server (RAS), also known as *Smart Reporting*, is an add-on set of services for Crystal Enterprise that enables organizations to provide zero-client ad-hoc capabilities in their Web applications. These services provide the capability for end users, applications, and developers to create and modify Crystal Reports over the Web. With RAS, organizations can empower their end users by allowing them to modify or create objects such as tables, charts, and fields in their reports.

Report Application Server provides the ability to not only create and view reports within Web applications, but also to modify and interact with existing reports created with Crystal Reports. The report format, .rpt, is the same, regardless of where it has been created. By providing this level of portability with the report format, an organization does not need to decide ahead of time where the report is going to be created based on the user audience. It would be incredibly difficult to maintain an information infrastructure and delivery system if there was one report format for reports created in a thick client application and another for reports created in a Web application.

OVERVIEW OF RAS COMPONENTS

Like all other aspects of Crystal Enterprise, the Report Application Server provides a rich object model for Web application developers. As a result, the end user interface to the Report Application Server can be tailored to and organization's specific ad-hoc requirements.

The following list details the services and components added to the Crystal Enterprise Framework after installing Report Application Server:

- **Out-of-the-box components for zero client ad-hoc reporting**—When the Report Application Server is installed, end users are immediately able to gain access to report creation wizards and interactive viewers. This functionality is completely integrated with ePortfolio. This is important for organizations that want to add ad-hoc reporting and interactive viewing with little IT or application development involvement. This wizard is a self-contained application, so adding its functionality to any Web application is straightforward.

- **A rich reporting object model**—The Report Application Server provides an object model that the provides the ability to deliver as much or as little ad-hoc capabilities to applications using Crystal Enterprise services as necessary. By using the programming capabilities of the Report Application Server, organizations can customize the out-of-the-box sample applications or use the powerful data access capabilities of Crystal Enterprise, along with the object model, and build specific user interfaces that generate reports based on certain criteria.

   For example, rather than using the out-of-the-box Report Wizard found in ePortfolio, an organization could present end users with a Web form that asks the user about sales opportunity information she wants to see from a sales application. The interaction and connectivity with the data coming from the sales application is provided by the Report

Application Server. After an end user has chosen what information she wants to review for a sales opportunity, she could view that information as a Crystal Report using the zero client viewer.

- **Zero client viewer (DHTML)**—All reports, whether they were previously created by Crystal Reports or created using the Report Application Server, can be viewed using the zero client viewer. This viewer provides viewing and interaction with reports without the need to download any applets or controls.

  This is vital for organizations that are planning to provide access to reports outside a firewall. A good example might be a customer or partner extranet. The viewer itself has an object model that makes it possible for an organization to deeply embed Crystal Enterprise reporting technologies into any Web application. This integration can be done without the need to resort to using frames within the Web application because the viewer can be embedded into a section of a Web page, such as a DIV or a table.

- **A scalable Report Generation Server**—Providing users with ad-hoc report creation cannot be done with a rich object model alone. The object model requires the Report Application Server itself. The Report Application Server registers itself with the Crystal Enterprise Framework in the exact same manner as all other Crystal Enterprise servers. This server provides the applications created using the object model with access to the necessary databases that are required to populate the report.

→ For more information on the Crystal Enterprise Framework, **see** Chapter 3, "Exploring the System Architecture."

INSTALLING THE REPORT APPLICATION SERVER

As previously mentioned, the Report Application Server is an add-on component to Crystal Enterprise. Before it can be used in a Crystal Enterprise environment, the software must be installed. It's important to understand where each RAS component needs to be installed to ensure a successful deployment. The main components of the RAS install are the server itself, the SDK, and the associated applications. Because RAS operates in the same scalable, distributed manner as all other Crystal Enterprise servers, the install provides two options, custom install and expand install:

- **Custom install**—Custom install makes it possible to select certain components that will be installed. This install option is used if the sample RAS applications need to be installed on a particular machine. This install option is also used when initially configuring a Crystal Enterprise system with RAS. If Crystal Enterprise has been installed in a distributed configuration using multiple physical servers, the RAS installation should start with the server on which the APS is installed before installing RAS components on other servers.

  This will install the components necessary for the administrator to enable or disable the Report Application Server and set its properties via the Crystal Management Console. This installation option is also used when installing RAS client applications, such as the

Report Wizard. These applications must be installed on the Web Component Server. As part of the install, the RAS SDK gets installed as well.

- **Expand install**—The Expand install will install a new instance of a RAS Server and register it with the framework. This install option is used only if additional RAS Servers need to be added. It does not install any of the RAS applications.

When installing the Report Application Server the setup program prompts to confirm whether the RAS server should be enabled upon completion of installation. Answer Yes so that the RAS Server is available. The installation will communicate with the APS to enable the Report Application Server as part of the Crystal Enterprise framework.

THE RAS SERVER

The RAS server provides the services for building and customizing reports. This component uses the Crystal Report Engine (CRPE) to handle end-user requests, edit report properties, retrieve data from the back-end database, and save the results to a Crystal Enterprise folder. Another way to think of it is the RAS server is the back-end component that does the actual report manipulation.

Note

Just like all other Crystal Enterprise servers, it's possible to have multiple RAS servers registered with the framework—the report requests would be shared, or load-balanced, across different servers.

OVERVIEW OF RAS APPLICATIONS

As mentioned previously, RAS provides applications that can immediately be used to add value to an existing Web application. This section examines each of these applications and how they are integrated into the default Crystal Enterprise Web client, ePortfolio.

THE DHTML REPORT WIZARD

The DHTML Report Wizard, a functional addition to ePortfolio, is the report creation and modification tool that guides an end user through a series of report manipulation questions, such as which database fields should be placed on the report document. The end user can even select a destination Crystal Enterprise folder to save the customized report results.

THE DHTML WIZARD: MODIFYING AN EXISTING REPORT

Suppose an HR manager needs some employee information for an upcoming presentation. To get the information required, he decides to modify the existing Employee Profile report found in Crystal Enterprise. The actual report used in this example is the Employee Profile report found in Crystal Enterprise under the Report Samples folder.

New Report

Figure B.1
New Report on
ePortfolio is the link
to access the Report
Wizard tool.

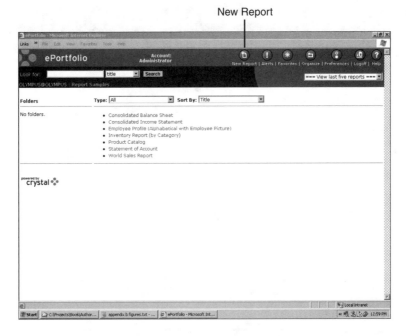

To customize the report, the following steps need to occur:

- **Remove the salary**—It's a violation of HR policy to show salary information to the whole company.

- **Change the grouping**—To provide a more meaningful report for the presentation the user should group the report data by city instead of by last name.

- **Add a summary field**—The HR user needs to be able to show how many employees are living in each city.

- **Change the sort order**—To quickly find information within the report, the HR user should sort the report by the city grouping defined earlier in descending order.

- **Add record filter criteria**—This step allows the user to remove data from the report and only display those employees not living in Canada.

- **Add a pie chart**—To easily visualize the information in the report, the HR user needs to add a pie chart to see employee distribution by city.

All these requests can be handled easily with RAS. To start the report modification, log on to ePortfolio and select the report Employee Profile. Now select Modify from the Action menu, as shown in Figure B.2.

Figure B.2
ePortfolio integration
of RAS with the
Modify Action item.

<table>
<tr><td>

</td></tr>
</table>

> **Note**
>
> The user modifying the report using RAS must have sufficient rights defined within Crystal Enterprise. If the user has the View on Demand access level set on the report, he will have enough rights to use the DHTML Wizard to modify the report.
>
> To save a report back to Crystal Enterprise, the user account must have the Full Control access level on the folder to which the report is being saved. It's common for users to save the report to their User or Favorites folder because of this requirement.

SELECTING FIELDS FOR DISPLAY   The first task previously outlined is to remove the salary field from the report. In Figure B.3, the database fields are split into two lists: The list on the left shows the database fields that are not on the report; the one on the right shows the database fields that are on the report.

Select a field from the available list and move it to the display list by clicking the select field button, denoted by a >. Similarly, select a field from the display list, and move it to the available list by clicking the deselect field button, denoted by a <.

It's possible to move all fields from the available list to the display list by clicking the select all fields button, denoted by a >>. Similarly, all fields can be moved from the display list to the available list by clicking the deselect all fields button (<<).

Select the Employee.Salary field and click the deselect field (<) button. Click the Next button to move on to grouping.

Figure B.3
Field selection in the
DHTML Report
Wizard.

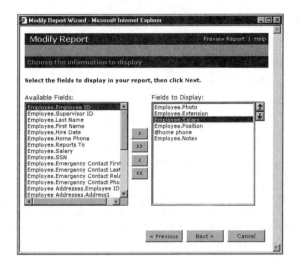

SETTING GROUPING OPTIONS HR wants to group the report by the city of the employee's address. To accomplish this requirement, the user must click the << button to clear all grouping, and then select the Employee Addresses.City field from the Available Fields list and click the > button, as seen in Figure B.4.

Figure B.4
Grouping selection in
the DHTML Report
Wizard.

Not all reports require grouping. This step is optional when designing a report.

Click the Next button to move on to summarization.

CONFIGURING SUMMARY FIELDS   Six summarization types are available in the DHTML Wizard:

- Sum
- Average
- Count
- Distinct Count
- Maximum
- Minimum

> **Note**
>
> Sum and Average types can only be applied to numeric fields. If a summary field isn't created here, a chart cannot be added without programmatic customization to the DHTML Wizard application.

To determine the number of employees in each city, set the Summary field to Employee.Employee ID, and then set the Summary Type to Count. This will count the number of employees in each grouping (see Figure B.5).

Figure B.5
Summarization in the DHTML Report Wizard.

Not all reports require summarization. This step is optional when customizing a report. Click Next to move on to the sorting option.

SORTING DATA   There are two levels for sorting: Group and Detail levels. Group level sorting can be set on the group name or on the summary of the group. Group name can be sorted in the following possible ways:

- All ascending
- All descending

Group summary can be sorted in the following possible ways:

- All ascending
- All descending
- Top 5
- Top 10
- Bottom 5
- Bottom 10

Detail level sorting can be set on multiple database fields, in ascending or descending order.

Detail level sorting will be noticeable when the end user clicks on a group within the report. By clicking on the group, the report will automatically show the next level of detail contained within it. This operation is known as a drill-down. An end user will first see the sorted groups based on their choices, and then see the detail level sorts when drilling down (moving to a lower detail level) to the base level of the report, where there are no more groups.

The HR user the requires the report to be sorted in reverse order by the name of the city. To accomplish this, select All Descending in the drop-down list box, as shown in Figure B.6.

Figure B.6
Sort order in the
DHTML Report
Wizard.

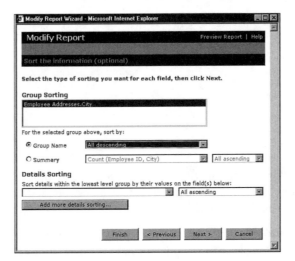

Not all reports require sorting. This step is optional if designing a report.

Click the Next button to move on.

FILTERING CRITERIA   The HR user needs the report to show only the employees who do not live in Canada. To accomplish this, set the filtering field to Employee Addresses.Country, set the filter type to "is not equal to," and then enter the value "Canada," as in Figure B.7.

Figure B.7
Record Filtering in the DHTML Report Wizard.

Not all reports require records filtering. This step is optional when designing a report. Filters can be a powerful capability for retrieving report data then allowing users to filter out certain data without sending a new query back to the database. Click Next to add a chart to the report.

ADDING A CHART TO THE REPORT   In the DHTML Wizard, charts can only be placed in the report header or footer section.

Choose between the following three chart types:

- Bar chart
- Line chart
- Pie chart

The numerical data for the chart is taken from the summarization of the group. Therefore, if the summarization were nonnumeric (for example, the maximum of Employee.Last Name field), there would be no value in the chart.

The HR user wants the pie chart to illustrate the proportion of employees in each city. To accomplish this, select the pie chart option, and enter the appropriate chart title, as in Figure B.8.

Not all reports will need to contain charts. This step is optional.

Click the Next button to choose a report style.

Figure B.8
Chart option in the
DHTML Report
Wizard.

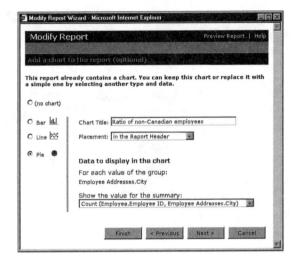

CHOOSE A REPORT STYLE   A report style, as discussed in other sections of the book, is a template that determines the default field placement, formats, on so on based on the style type. This minimizes the end-user's work in formatting the report to a presentation quality look and feel. There is a wide selection of report styles available with the Report Application Server:

- Standard
- Drop Table
- Shading
- Maroon/Teal Box
- Advanced/No Style Applied

Because the HR user didn't request a report style change, leave the radio box option at the default state: Advanced/No Style Applied. This style is also shown in the DHTML Wizard if a report previously created in Crystal Reports is being modified and is not using one of the other default styles.

PREVIEWING THE REPORT   At any point in the DHTML Report Wizard, it's possible to preview what the report would look like in its current state using the RAS Interactive Report Viewer. If the instructions have been followed up to this point, the report preview should look similar to the one Figure B.9.

> **Tip**
>
> At this stage, most end users will preview the completed report and export it using the Interactive Viewer into a format such as Excel or Adobe Acrobat.

After viewing the report, close the browser and return to the DHTML Report Wizard.

Figure B.9
Previewing the customized report with Interactive Viewer.

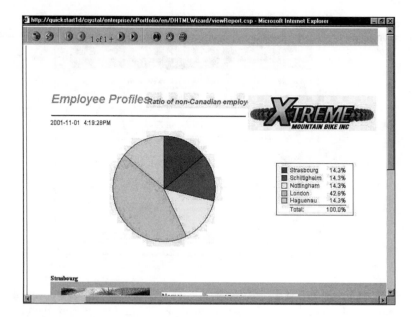

SAVING A MODIFIED NEW REPORT Saving the report is optional. Business analysts often use the DHTML Report Wizard to do an ad hoc report query, and then simply view the data with the Interactive HTML Viewer, which allows the report to be printed or exported to a different format. In fact, some organizations don't allow end users to save modified reports back to Crystal Enterprise at all. Others allow saving only to private folders.

Because the HR user wants the report to be modified permanently, save over the existing report, as shown in Figure B.10.

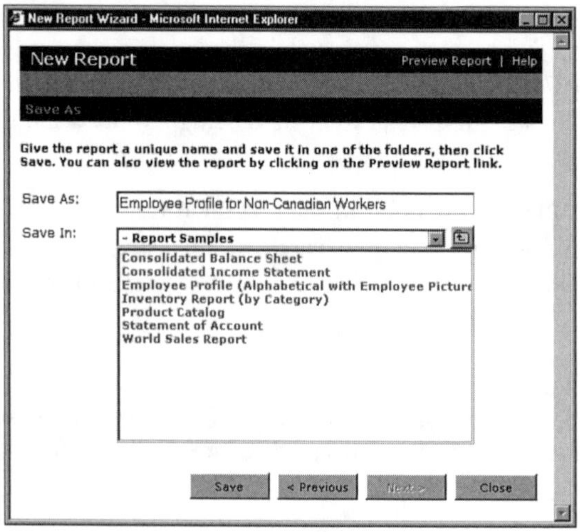

Figure B.10
Saving the report in the DHTML Report Wizard can be restricted to public or private folders within Crystal Enterprise.

CREATING A NEW REPORT

Creating a report with RAS is quite similar to modifying an existing report. The only major difference is how the process is started. Rather than reviewing all the options previously selected in the report, this scenario inherits the database settings from an existing report but defines the desired fields specific for this report.

CHOOSING A STARTING TEMPLATE

Creating a new report using the DHTML Wizard follows many of the same steps as modifying an existing report. The following describes how the two differ. Suppose a sales rep needs to quickly determine how many sales have been made so far in the quarter. The rep knows that someone else created a report with similar information. He browses Crystal Enterprise for the World Sales Report (found in the Report Samples folder by default) to be used as a starting template, as shown in Figure B.11. The DHTML Wizard uses existing reports as a starting point but RAS makes it possible for an application developer to provide a list of server-side ODBC datasources to end users as well. If the developer chooses to expose these datasources to the user, they must first be defined on the RAS Server itself.

PART

VI

CH

B

Figure B.11
Creating a new report from existing report templates with the DHTML Report Wizard.

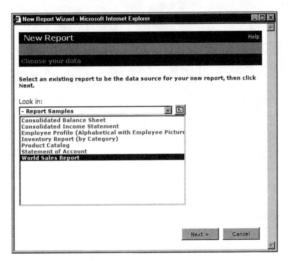

Now that the sales rep has chosen the World Sales Report to use as a starting template, he can follow the same steps outlined in the section that discussed modifying an existing report.

THE INTERACTIVE VIEWER

The Report Application Server introduces a new report viewer, the Interactive Viewer, that can provide functionality to end users beyond just viewing the report.

Note

The Interactive Viewer is a separate viewer from the default report viewers shipped with Crystal Enterprise. Recall those viewer types were ActiveX, Java, DHTML, and the Netscape Plug-In viewer.

The end user will have the ability to change fields visible on the report as well as other powerful capabilities, such as filtering the data down to what is most relevant. The Interactive Report Viewer is a RAS application based on the lightweight viewer component mentioned earlier as part of the RAS SDK that communicates with the back-end RAS server. After installing RAS and the Interactive Viewer option, this new viewer type can be found in the Report Wizard, as shown in Figure B.12. Chapter 5, "Using the Crystal Enterprise Launchpad," demonstrates how to select a specific report viewer for use with the ePortfolio application. The Interactive Viewer is a sample RAS application that can be found on the RAS CD. It is not installed through the main RAS installation.

Figure B.12
Preview Report is the link to access the Interactive Viewer.

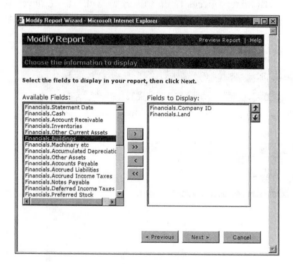

As another example of the flexibility the Interactive Viewer offers, consider the following: If and end user wanted to view a historical instance of a report with different sort directions and sort fields, the RAS Server could retrieve the report instance from the File Repository Server, modify the report properties, and then pass the result to the Interactive Viewer to display the report content (see Figure B.13).

INTEGRATING RAS APPLICATIONS INTO EPORTFOLIO

When Report Application Server is first installed on an existing Crystal Enterprise server, some basic modifications are made to ePortfolio:

■ A DHTML Report Wizard is added with the option to modify a report in addition to the options of View, Schedule, and History.

- The same DHTML Report Wizard, which can be used to create a new report, can be accessed from ePortfolio's heading, with the New Report button or text.
- The Interactive Viewer, which allows report viewing and customization from one interface, must be installed by running the self-extracting file found in the Tools directory on the RAS CD-ROM.

Figure B.13
The Interactive Viewer can display -modified report data without requerying the database.

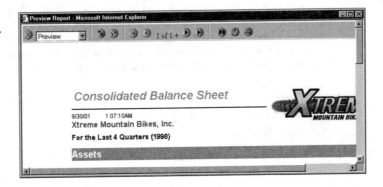

Like ePortfolio, the DHTML Report Wizard and Interactive Viewer are .CSP applications that use the SDK to communicate with the back-end Crystal Enterprise servers. A Web developer can edit the CSP files to customize the Report Wizards and Interactive Viewer to fit organizational needs, such as a specific look and feel of an intranet site.

THE REPORT APPLICATION SERVER SDK

The Report Application Server SDK consists of a set of COM libraries that provide the interface for application developers to develop Web applications. The RAS SDK communicates with the RAS server through the Crystal Enterprise Framework to perform numerous report manipulation and creation tasks.

UNDERSTANDING THE RAS SDK ARCHITECTURE

The architecture of the Report Application Server SDK is based on the concept of a model (or definition), controller, and view.

- The *model*, or definition, is used to describe the items on a report document—databases, tables, fields, charts, and many others.
- The *controller* is used to add, delete, or edit a collection or model.
- The *view* is used to create a snapshot of the data.

It's important to understand the relationship between the model and the controller. To find out how many tables are in a given database, the model can be used to find out the answer. To add another field to a report, the controller must be used to commit the changes to the back-end Report Application Server.

Tip

When editing the properties of a report, only the controller can add, delete, or edit the model.

Note

The notion of models and controllers can be applied to most RAS SDK objects. The view, however, refers to the fact that multiple sessions can work off the same report object, and each session has its own snapshot of the data in the report. It's like having multiple people opening a Microsoft Word document; each session is loaded in memory and is independent of what other sessions are doing to the data.

- **The Crystal Client Document Library**

  Model/Controller: Neither

  Overview: This library is the starting point for application development with RAS. It contains the report document object, which allows an application developer access to other model and controller libraries. With the report document object, an application developer can open the existing report, create a new report, or save the report in Crystal Enterprise folder.

  DLL Name: ClientDoc.dll

- **The Crystal Reports HTML Viewer Library**

  Model/Controller: Neither

  Overview: This library contains numerous object references that allow a developer to manipulate the properties of the Viewer. For example, an application developer can include or exclude the refresh button on the HTML toolbar. The viewer library is a new report viewer that is offered by the Report Application Server.

  The Viewer Library also has a powerful feature that makes it possible to provide a closed-loop reporting environment. This feature is an Event Model that will allow the application developer to capture the information contained in a report that the user clicks on so that they can use it in another part of their application.

  Events are actions that the program can respond to. For example, "after viewer state is changed" is an event. The program can respond to it by carrying out other tasks, such as launching another Web browser prepopulated with the information that the user clicked on. Another use of events is to link multiple viewers. If an end user clicks on a section of the report in one viewer, the events can be programmed to change the context of other viewers.

  DLL Name: HTMLViewer.dll

- **The Crystal Reports Controllers Library**

  Model/Controller: Controller

  Overview: This library contains numerous controller objects that an application developer can use to add, delete, or edit the models. For example, an application developer can use the `ResultFieldController` object to place more fields on the detail section of the report.

DLL Name: RptControllers.dll

- The Crystal Reports Report Definition Model Library

  Model/Controller: Model

  Overview: This library contains numerous definition objects that an application developer can use to manipulate the appearance of objects in the report. The "report appearance" objects that can be manipulated are charts, borders, and fonts. This library doesn't handle report data definition objects, such as databases, tables, fields, filters, and sort information. These objects are handled by another library, the Data Definition Model Library.

  DLL Name: RptDefModel.dll

- The Crystal Reports Data Definition Model Library

  Model/Controller: Model

  Overview: This library contains numerous objects and references for the report data definition, such as tables, database fields, formula fields, filters, grouping, sorting, parameters, and summary fields.

  DLL Name: DataDefModel.dll

By separating the control of the report's formatting from the data access, it's very easy for a developer to organize his logic based on what task needs to be carried out. Some developers might spend the majority of their application's time manipulating data objects. Other developers may focus more on manipulating formatting objects within the report, such as being able to change columns that already exist in the report into a chart for easier visualization of that data.

UNDERSTANDING THE RAS SDK OBJECT MODEL

The best way to understand the RAS SDK Object Model is to look at the object model diagram, as illustrated in Figure B.14. This diagram is like a road map; it shows where to start and how to get to the desired location.

This appendix serves as an introduction to RAS and the possibilities it offers for ad-hoc reporting in Web applications. For a full reference of RAS, including a listing of each object's properties and methods, refer to the RAS SDK Guide that's provided with the product. This guide can be found on the RAS Setup CD, under the DOC directory, with the filename RAS_SDK.CHM.

The object model diagram shows objects and collections of objects. An object is represented as a single rectangle. Collections are represented as multiple rectangles. For example, `Groups` is a collection of objects, which allows an application developer to access individual items, or `Group` objects.

Figure B.14
RAS SDK object
model diagram.

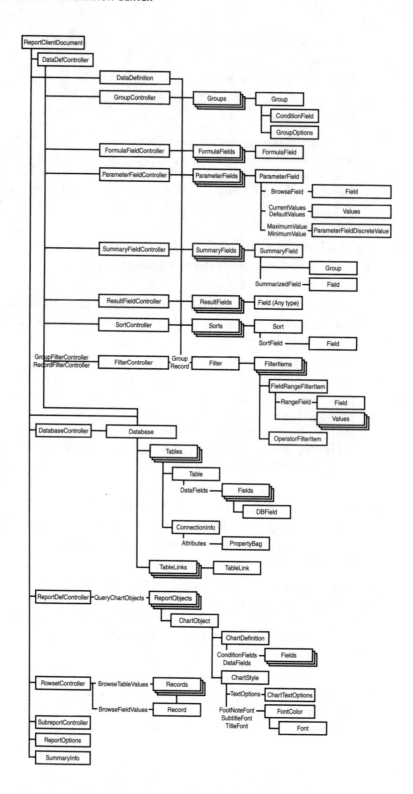

The starting point of the RAS SDK object model is on the upper-left corner of the diagram. This is the `ReportDocumentClient`.

The connecting lines between objects show the relationship between them. For example, the `ReportClientDocument` object gains access to other objects such as the `DataDefController` and `DataDefinition` objects.

In some cases there is more than one path to get to a specific object or objects. For example, the `Groups` collection can be accessed by either one of the following paths:

`ReportClientDocument, DataDefController, DataDefinition, Groups`

or

`ReportClientDocument, DataDefinition, Groups`

> **Note**
>
> The `ReportClientDocument` must be attached to a valid `EnterpriseSession` before this function can be used. For more examples on creating an `EnterpriseSession`, please refer to Chapter 13, "Extending Crystal Enterprise" and Chapter 14, "Integrating Crystal Enterprise with Your Corporate Intranet."

SAMPLE CODE

Now that you have seen the relationship of RAS SDK objects with object model diagram, let's look at some examples to help solidify the concepts discussed. Any remaining examples past the first one assume that the first sample code of opening a report has been executed.

Each example shows different report object manipulation tasks.

OPENING A REPORT USING THE RAS SDK

The first example shows how to connect to Crystal Enterprise and open a report using the RAS SDK. The code in this sample (or similar to it) must be used before any report manipulation tasks can be complete. In other words, the report object must be accessed first.

This example covers

- Providing logon credentials to the Crystal Enterprise system, and then querying Crystal Enterprise for the report object from the `InfoStore` object.

- Use the `ReportClientDocument` object from the RAS SDK to open the `InfoObject` from the previous query.

```
'Variables for CE Objects
Dim objSessionMgr
Dim objEnterpriseSession
Dim objInfoStore
Dim colInfoObjects
Dim objInfoObject
```

```
'Variables for RAS Objects, from the library CrystalClientDocLib
Dim objReportClientDocument

'Variables for RAS Objects, from the library CrystalReportsControllersLib
Dim objDataDefController
Dim objGroupController
Dim objResultFieldController

'Variables for RAS Objects, from the library CrystalReportsDataDefModelLib
Dim objDataDefinition
Dim colResultFields
Dim colTables
Dim objTable
Dim colDBFields
Dim objDBField

'Variable for the FOR...LOOP
Dim i

'Create an instance of SessionMgr object and assign it to the
➥variable objSessionMgr
Set objSessionMgr = CreateObject ("CrystalEnterprise.SessionMgr")


'Log in to the Crystal Enterprise
Set objEnterpriseSession = objSessionMgr.Logon
➥("UserID", "Password", "APSName", "AuthenticationType")
```

Note

The user ID, password, APS name, and authentication type must be modified to fit in the environment. For more information about the method Logon of SessionMgr object, refer to Chapter 13.

```
'Get an instance of InfoStore object
Set objInfoStore = objEnterpriseSession.Service ("", "InfoStore")

'Query the InfoStore to find
'the report Account Statement
Set colInfoObjects = objInfoStore.Query
➥("Select * from CI_INFOOBJECTS Where SI_PROGID=
➥'CrystalEnterprise.Report' AND SI_NAME='Statement of Account'")

'Only continue if we found
'the report in Crystal Enterprise
If colInfoObjects.Count > 0 Then
  'Assume the report we're looking for
  'is the first item on the InfoObjects
  'collection.  Please note that the
  'InfoObjects collection is 1-based.
  'So the first item has the index number of 1.
  Set objInfoObject = colInfoObjects.Item(1)
```

```
'************* RAS CODE START *************
Set objReportClientDocument = CreateObject
➥("CrystalClientDoc.ReportClientDocument")

'Before we can do anything else, the
'ReportClientDocument object needs to
'have a valid CE EnterpriseSession.
objReportClientDocument.EnterpriseSession = objEnterpriseSession
objReportClientDocument.Open objInfoObject
```

Tip

Remember, the `ReportClientDocument` object is the starting point of RAS programming. To learn RAS SDK quickly and effectively, cross-reference the CSP code with the RAS SDK Object Model diagram, as shown in Figure B.14.

ADDING AND REMOVING FIELDS

This example demonstrates how to remove the ordering date field from the report Statement of Account, and then add the shipping date field to the report.

Checking with the RAS SDK object model on Figure B.14, it's pretty easy to take a high-level guess at what needs to be done.

This example covers

- Retrieving the `ResultFieldController` object, because it must be used to add and remove fields from the report document.
- Obtaining the `ResultFields` collection and attempting to find the field {`Orders.Order Date`}. If found, delete it using `ResultFieldController` object.
- Obtaining the `Database` object, which provides access to the `Tables` collection, `Table` object, `Fields` collection, and the `Database Field` object.
- Looping through the `Fields` collection to find the field {`Order.Shipping Date`}. If found, add it using `ResultFieldController` object.
- Use the `ReportClientDocument` object to save the report.

```
<%
'This page will use CE and RAS SDK to remove
'{Orders.Order Date} column from the detail
'section.  In addition, the database field
'{Orders.Ship Date} will be added to the
'report.

Option Explicit
On Error Resume Next

'Declare variables

'Notation:
'All variable names will be in xxxYYYYYYY,
```

```
'where xxx is the type (for example, obj = object)
'and YYYYYYY is the object class (eg, SessionMgr)

  'After the EnterpriseSession has been
  'assigned to ReportClientDocument object,
  'we can go ahead and get instances to the
  'controller and model (or definition)
  'objects and collections.
  Set objDataDefController = objReportClientDocument.DataDefController

  'See how the property of objDataDefController
  'returns an instance of another object type?
  Set objResultFieldController = objDataDefController.ResultFieldController

  Set objDataDefinition = objReportClientDocument.DataDefinition

  Set colResultFields = objDataDefinition.ResultFields

  'Only continue if at least 1 field
  'were placed on the report
  If colResultFields.Count > 0 Then

    '************* Field Deletion START *************
    'Loop through each item in the collection
    'and exit the loop when we've found what we're
    'looking for.  In this case, we'll go through
    'each field object in the ResultFields
    'collection and see if we can find the field
    'with the long name "Orders.Order Date"
    For i = 0 To colResultFields.Count - 1
      If colResultFields.Item(i).LongName = "Orders.Order Date" Then
        Exit For
      End If
    Next
```

> **Tip**
>
> Sometimes it's easier working backward. In the preceding example, find out which controller has the method to delete a definition object, and then check to see what parameter that method requires. After this has been done, it's a matter of searching through the RAS SDK object model and finding the shortest path to get to the desired object or collection. In this case, we know that the ResultFieldController has the method called Remove to delete a field from the report document.

```
'Verify that we exited the loop because we have found the field object
'with matching name.
If i < colResultFields.Count Then
  'Remove the field, and we have accomplished
  'half of the assignment 1.
  objResultFieldController.Remove colResultFields.Item(i)
End If

'************* Field Insertion START *************
'Let's go through each table object the tables
'collection, and see if we can find the table
```

```
'with the long name "Orders"
Set colTables = objDataDefController.Database.Tables
For i = 0 To colTables.Count - 1
  If colTables.Item(i).Name = "Orders" Then
    Exit For
  End If
Next

'Verify that we exited the loop because we
'have found the field object with matching
'name.
If i < colTables.Count Then
  'So we found the table.
  Set objTable = colTables.Item(i)

  'Let's go through each fields on the table
  'object "Orders", and see if we can find
  'the field "Ship Date"
  Set colDBFields = objTable.DataFields
  For i = 0 To colDBFields.Count - 1
    If colDBFields.Item(i).LongName = "Orders.Ship Date" Then
      Exit For
    End If
  Next
```

Tip

If it's difficult to see why it's necessary to access the Database object, Tables collection, Table object, Fields collection, or Field object, look at this from the back side. The ResultFieldController object has an Add method that inserts a new field to the detail section of the report document. The Add method takes two parameters: the position in the ResultFields collection to insert the new Field object, and the Field object itself. Therefore, the Field object must be found from within the Database object so that the ResultFieldController object can insert the field into the report document.

```
  'Verify that we exited the loop because we
  'have found the field object with matching
  'name.
  If i < colDBFields.Count Then
    'Insert the field at first location, position 0.
    objResultFieldController.Add 0, colDBFields.Item(i)
  End If
End If
End If

'Check first to see if the report is read only.
If objReportClientDocument.IsReadOnly Then
  Response.Write "Sorry, the report is read only."
Else
  'Now we need to save the report
  objReportClientDocument.Save
```

> **Caution**
>
> The code `objReportClientDocument.Save` will overwrite the report template. Be sure to back up the original report template by creating copies using the Crystal Management Console, or use the Windows File Explorer and back up the source files.

```
    'Check for error.  Err.Number = 0 means no error.
    If Err.number <> 0 Then
      Response.Write "Something went wrong at the report saving stage.<BR>"
      Response.Write "Error Number = " & Err.Number & "<BR>"
      Response.Write "Error Description = " &
      ➥Err.Description & "<BR>"
    Else
      Response.Write "Report Successfully Saved"
    End If
  End If

End If

'Destroy all object created in this example
Set objDBField = Nothing
Set colDBFields = Nothing
Set objTable = Nothing
Set colTables = Nothing
Set colResultFields = Nothing
Set objDataDefinition = Nothing
Set objResultFieldController = Nothing
Set objGroupController = Nothing
Set objDataDefController = Nothing
Set objReportClientDocument = Nothing
Set colInfoObject = Nothing
Set colInfoObjects = Nothing
Set objInfoStore = Nothing
Set objReportClientDocument = Nothing
Set objEnterpriseSession = Nothing
Set objSessionMgr = Nothing

'Abandon the session to free up a user license
'in Crystal Enterprise
Session.Abandon

%>
```

Notice the difference between Figure B.15 and Figure B.16. These figures highlight the effects of the code that was just described.

CHANGING THE CHART TYPE IN A REPORT

This example modifies the World Sales Report by changing the chart type (from Pie to Doughnut), and then saves the resulting report back to Crystal Enterprise with a different filename. Try referring to the RAS SDK object model in Figure B.14 to get a general idea about what needs to be done to complete this task. The tasks are

- Get the `ReportDefinitionController` object, because you need to use it to apply a different chart style to the report document.

- Obtain the `Chart` object from the `ReportDefinitionController` object, because you need to modify the chart type value.

- Use the `ReportDefinitionController` object to commit the change.

- Use the `ReportClientDocument` object to save the report as a different filename.

Figure B.15
Statement of Account report, before running the script.

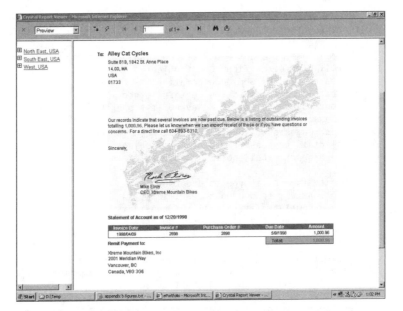

Figure B.16
Statement of Account report, after running the script.

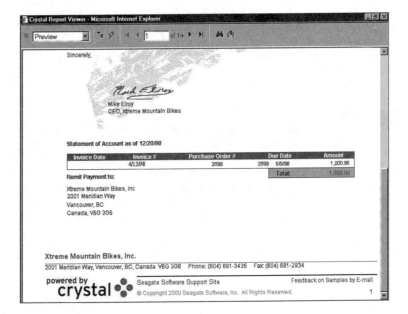

PART

VI

CH

B

```
<%
    'After the EnterpriseSession has been assigned to ReportClientDocument
    'object, we can go ahead and get instances to the controller and
    'model (or definition) objects and collections.
    Set objReportDefController = objReportClientDocument.ReportDefController

    'See how the method of objReportDefController
    'returns an instance of another object type?
    Set colReportObjects = objReportDefController.QueryChartObjects

    'Only continue if at least one chart were placed on the report
    If colReportObjects.Count > 0 Then

        '************* Chart Modification START *************
        'We'll modify the first Chart object.
        'Note the in the SDK documentation,
        'ReportObjects collection contains other
        'ReportObject objects.  However, it's possible
        'to assign object Chart as the element in the
        'ReportObjects collection because ReportObject
        'object is the base class of Chart object.
        Set objChart = colReportObjects.Item(0)

        'Modify the chart type to doughnut.
        'The constant to doughnut chart is 4.
        'For a complete list of all the constant,
        'please refer to the RAS SDK document.
        objChart.ChartStyle.Type = 4

        'Commit the change to object ReportDefController
        'The method ModifyChartObject accepts two parameters
        'The first one is the old chart object, and
        'the second one is the new chart object.
        objReportDefController.ModifyChartObject objChart, objChart

        '************* Report Saving START *************
        Set colInfoObjects = objInfoStore.Query
        ➥("Select * from CI_INFOOBJECTS Where SI_PROGID=
        ➥'CrystalEnterprise.Folder' AND SI_NAME='Report Samples'")
        objReportClientDocument.SaveAs "My Sales Report",
        ➥colInfoObjects.Item(1), 1
```

Note

Instead of using the Save method, which will write the change over the currently opened file, this example uses the SaveAs method to save into another report in Crystal Enterprise with a different name. The method SaveAs accepts three parameters: the report title, the folder path, and options. The folder path is actually the InfoObject object, which means a query to the InfoStore object must be submitted to access the InfoObjects collection. The option value of 1 specifies that the SaveAs method will overwrite the existing report object with the same report title, if any.

```
    'Check for error.  Err.Number = 0 means no error.
    If Err.number <> 0 Then
      Response.Write "Report was unable to be saved.<BR>"
      Response.Write "Error Number = " & Err.Number & "<BR>"
      Response.Write "Error Description = " & Err.Description & "<BR>"
    Else
      Response.Write "Sucessfully Saved Report"
    End If
  End If
End If

'Destroy all object created on this CSP page
Set objChart = Nothing
Set objReportClientDocument = Nothing
Set colInfoObject = Nothing
Set colInfoObjects = Nothing
Set objInfoStore = Nothing
Set objReportClientDocument = Nothing
Set objEnterpriseSession = Nothing
Set objSessionMgr = Nothing

'Abandon the session to free up a user license
'in Crystal Enterprise
Session.Abandon

%>
```

PART

VI

CH

B

The following figures show the effects of the preceding script. Note the difference between Figure B.17 and Figure B.18.

Figure B.17
World Sales Report, before running the script.

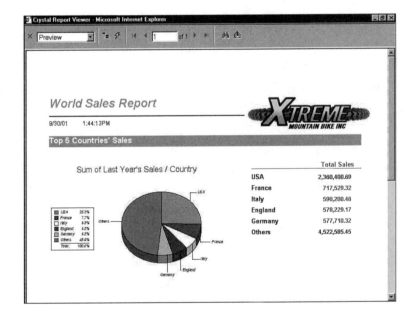

Figure B.18
My Sales Report, which is derived from World Sales Report by running the script.

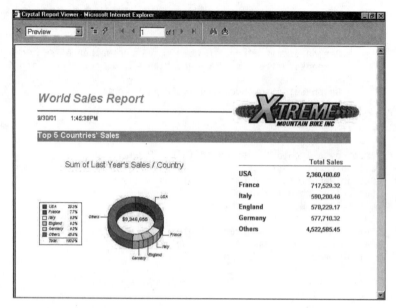

PROGRAMMATIC CREATION OF A NEW REPORT OVER THE WEB

This example demonstrates how to inherit database connection information from an existing report and then use this connection as the basis for a new report.

The scenario for this example has a user who wants to create a report that will be grouped by the employee's position. The details of the report will display the employee's first name, last name, and position. The Employee Profile report has the desired connection information and will be used in this example.

The RAS SDK object model in Figure B.14 provides a rough map of what needs to be done, and the following is a high-level overview of the process:

- Use the `DatabaseController` object to copy the database information from the existing Employee Profile report to a new report.

- Use `DataDefController` to gain access to the `GroupController` and the `ResultFieldController` objects.

- Use `GroupController` to add field position as the grouping field.

- Use `ResultFieldController` to add the `First Name` field, `Last Name` field, and `Position` field to the report.

- Use `ReportDefController` to apply a style to the report.

- Use the `ReportClientDocument` object to save the report as a different filename.

```
'Variables for RAS Objects, from the library
'CrystalClientDocLib
Dim objExistingReportClientDocument
Dim objNewReportClientDocument
```

PART

VI

CH

B

> **Note**
>
> Note that there are two variables of type `ReportClientDocument`. This is because we will be creating a new report based on the information from old existing reports. That means we need to have two `ReportClientDocument` objects open.

```
'************ RAS CODE START *************
Set objExistingReportClientDocument = CreateObject
➥ ("CrystalClientDoc.ReportClientDocument")
Set objNewReportClientDocument = CreateObject
➥("CrystalClientDoc.ReportClientDocument")

'Before we can do anything else, the
'ReportClientDocument object needs to
'have a valid CE EnterpriseSession.
objExistingReportClientDocument.EnterpriseSession = objEnterpriseSession
objExistingReportClientDocument.Open objInfoObject
objNewReportClientDocument.EnterpriseSession = objEnterpriseSession
objNewReportClientDocument.New

'************ Database Insertion START *************
'Before we can add the fields onto the report,
'we need to have database connection.
'Therefore, we need to use database controller
'to do this.
'
'In the worst case, we'll just loop through
'tables collection on the existing report,
'and copy each table to the new report
'Because we're not interested in the employee's address,
'we'll just add the table Employee
Set objNewDatabaseController = objNewReportClientDocument.DatabaseController
Set objExistingDatabase = objExistingReportClientDocument.Database
Set colExistingTables = objExistingDatabase.Tables
For Each objExistingTable in colExistingTables
  If objExistingTable.Alias = "Employee" Then
    objNewDatabaseController.AddTable objExistingTable
    Exit For
  End If
Next
```

> **Note**
>
> There is no need to get the `DatabaseController` object for the existing report because no tables are being added or removed from that report. Instead, use the `DatabaseController` object for the new report that is being created.

```
'************ Group Insertion START *************
'Now we'll get GroupController, and then add a new
'field to be the grouping criteria.
Set objNewGroupController = objNewReportClientDocument.DataDefController.
➥GroupController
```

```
'The method Add of objNewGroupController accepts 2
'parameters: the position of grouping to insert,
'and the Group object.  Because we haven't done
'anything yet with the Group object, we need to
'deal with it next.
Set objNewGroup = CreateObject("CrystalReports.Group")
```

Because the objExistingReportClientDocument object doesn't have the field grouping that's needed, it's necessary to create a new Group object, manipulate its properties, and use it as a part of the parameter for the GroupController's method: Add.

```
'The property ConditionField of Group object
'requires a database field.  We have to use
'objNewDatabase to get colNewTables, which
'leads to objNewTable, and then colNewFields,
'and finally objNewField.
'Because we know there's only one table, we
'could shorthand a few notations.
Set colNewFields = objNewDatabaseController.Database.
➥Tables.Item(0).DataFields
For Each objNewField in colNewFields
  If objNewField.Name = "Position" Then
    objNewGroup.ConditionField = objNewField
    Exit For
  End If
Next


'Finally, we had everything that
'we needed to add a new group.
objNewGroupController.Add -1, objNewGroup

'************* ResultField Insertion START *************
'Now we'll get ResultFieldController, and then add a new
'field to be the report.
Set objNewResultFieldController =
➥objNewReportClientDocument.DataDefController.
➥ResultFieldController

'The method Add of objNewResultFieldController accepts
'two parameters: the position of result fields on the
'report, and the Field object.  Again, we have to use
'objNewDatabase to get colNewTables, which
'leads to objNewTable, and then colNewFields,
'and finally objNewField.
Set colNewFields = objNewDatabaseController.
➥Database.Tables.Item(0).DataFields
For Each objNewField in colNewFields
  If objNewField.Name = "First Name" OR objNewField.Name = "Last Name" Then
    objNewResultFieldController.Add -1, objNewField
  End If
Next

'********* Applying Report Style START *********
'Now we'll get ReportDefController, and then apply
```

```
'report style to the report.
Set objNewReportDefController =
➥objNewReportClientDocument.ReportDefController
objNewReportDefController.ApplyReportStyle 8
```

> **Caution**
>
> There are 12 possible values for the report style. When the style is applied to the report, the report is physically reformatted. Be careful about applying the report format because there is no undo action. For more information about predefined report styles, refer to the Report Application Server SDK Guide.

```
'************* Report Saving START *************
Set colInfoObjects = objInfoStore.Query
➥("Select * from CI_INFOOBJECTS Where SI_PROGID=
➥'CrystalEnterprise.Folder' AND SI_NAME='Report Samples'")
objNewReportClientDocument.SaveAs "assignment3",
➥colInfoObjects.Item(1), 1

'Check for error.  Err.Number = 0 means no error.
If Err.number <> 0 Then
  Response.Write "Something went
  ➥wrong at the report saving stage.<BR>"
  Response.Write "Error Number = " & Err.Number & "<BR>"
  Response.Write "Error Description = " & Err.Description & "<BR>"
Else
    Response.Write "Successfully Saved the Report"
  End If
End If

'Destroy all object created on this CSP page
Set objNewGroup = Nothing
Set objNewField = Nothing
Set colNewFields = Nothing
Set objExistingTable = Nothing
Set colExistingTables = Nothing
Set objExistingDatabase = Nothing
Set objNewReportDefController = Nothing
Set objNewResultFieldController = Nothing
Set objNewGroupController = Nothing
Set objNewDatabaseController = Nothing
Set objNewReportClientDocument = Nothing
Set objExistingReportClientDocument = Nothing
Set objInfoObject = Nothing
Set colInfoObjects = Nothing
Set objInfoStore = Nothing
Set objEnterpriseSession = Nothing
Set objSessionMgr = Nothing

'Abandon the session to free up a user license
'in Crystal Enterprise
Session.Abandon

%>
```

Figure B.19 shows the results of the preceding script.

Figure B.19
Script results.

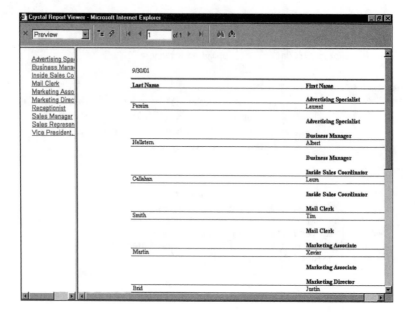

SUMMARY

Report Application Server (RAS) is an add-on to the Crystal Enterprise system that enables developers and end users alike to manipulate Crystal Report properties over the Web.

The Report Application Server is composed of a back-end server and a Software Developers Kit. With the Software Developers Kit, an application developer can create Web pages that allow end users to edit or create reports and add them to the Crystal Enterprise system.

The Software Developers Kit for RAS is based on the concept of a model, a controller, and a view. The model describes items on the report document, such as database, table, fields, and chart. The controller handles the requests to add, edit, and modify the models in the report. The view represents a snapshot of the data.

The RAS SDK is made up of five COM libraries. These libraries contain objects and collections that an application developer can use in application development, such as writing .CSP pages. The quickest way to learn application development with the RAS SDK is to look at the RAS SDK Object Model Diagram, and at the same time look over the Report Application Server SDK Guide for a detailed overview of each object as well as its related methods and properties.

As long as the APS, Web Server, Web Component Server, and RAS Server have the RAS components installed, RAS can be used in ePortfolio without additional programming. An end user can view reports with the Interactive Viewer, and also create or modify reports with the Report Wizard.

INDEX

Symbols

CI_INFOOBJECTS table, 462

.cub file, 278

.QRY files (Crystal Reports), 198-199

A

accessing
  CMC, 127
  corporate data (Crystal Reports), 193-194
  OLAP data, 276-277
  reports
    Crystal Reports, 223
    multiple users, 15-17

accounts
  CMC, 320-321
  Crystal Enterprise servers, troubleshooting, 108

actions
  Crystal Analysis Professional objects, 302-303
  Microsoft SQL Server Analysis Services, 302-305

Active Server Pages (ASP), 452

ActiveX, 468

ad hoc queries (Report Application Server), 67-68

ad-hoc data queries, 31

Add/Remove Subgroups button, 329-330

adding
  CMC users to groups, 325-328
  Crystal Dictionaries database fields, 201
  Crystal Dictionaries tables, 200
  Crystal Enterprise servers, 99-102
  Crystal Report Designer charts, 215
  ODBC connections (Crystal Reports), 196-197
  parameters (Crystal Reports), 223-225

Administrative functions, 463, 478
  CI_SYSTEMOBJECTS table, folder hierarchy, 464-465
  CI_SYSTEMOBJS table, 463
    instances, 463-464
  linking Crystal Enterprise to corporate intranet sites, 509

administrative interfaces (Crystal Enterprise), 126

administrative samples, 113-114

administrators
  Crystal Enterprise, CMC, 319-320
  Windows 2000, 81

Administrator account, 321
  usernames, 322

administrator default group (Crystal Enterprise), 128

Administrators group, 324

ADO connections
  initializing, 239-243

ADO library, 237

alerts
  Crystal Report, 230-231
  ePortfolio, 157-159

Alerts function, 157

analysis (Crystal Analysis Professional objects), 294

analysis buttons (Crystal Analysis Professional objects), 303-305

Analytical reports, 460

APIs, 462-463

application servers, 59

applications
  APS, querying, 460-461
  CI_INFOOBJECTS table, 462
  CSP, 61
  InfoObjects, 461-462
  InfoStore, 459-460
  logging on, 455
    logon token, 456-459
    Log on form, 458
    passwords, 455
    user names, 455
  plug-ins, 461-462
  portal, 528
    Crystal Enterprise, 530-536
    integration, 528